The Gigantic Book
of
Sailing Stories

The Gigantic Book
of
Sailing Stories

Edited by
Stephen Brennan

Skyhorse Publishing

Skyhorse Publishing books may be purchased in bulk at special discounts for sales promotion, corporate gifts, fund raising, or educational purposes. Special editions can also be created to specifications. For details, contact Special Sales Department, Skyhorse Publishing, 555 Eighth Avenue, Suite 903, New York, NY 10018 or info@skyhorsepublishing.com.

Library of Congress Cataloging-in-Publication Data

The gigantic book of sailing stories / edited by Stephen Brennan.
    p. cm.
ISBN 978-1-60239-209-0 (hardcover : alk. paper)
1. Sea stories, American. 2. Sea stories, English. 3. Seafaring life.
4. Voyages and travels. I. Brennan, Stephen Vincent.

PS648.S4G54 2008
823.008'032162—dc22   2007050819

10 9 8 7 6 5 4 3 2 1

Printed in the United States of America

Contents

Part III
Lea Shores, Wrecks, and other Catastrophes

Part IV
Shipboard Lore

Part V
Poetry

Introduction

"Some years ago—never mind how long precisely—having
little or no money in my purse, and nothing particular
to interest me on shore, I thought I would sail about a
little and see the watery part of the world."
—Herman Melville

Which one of us has not dreamed of that—to put away our troubles and run away to sea and lose ourselves in a life of daring and adventure? Without doubt, sailing is the *great escape*. We "turn our backs on the land," as the poet says, and all that that implies. When you take yourself to sea, you leave behind, at least for a time, all the mundane, humdrum imperatives of your day-to-day breathing in and out. You skip out on all your difficulties, shattered friendships, bad debts, and broken hearts. To sail away is to flee, certainly, but it must also be understood as a flight *to* something. Because the sailor aims to make a new start, to breath free air, to skin his eyes—or hers—afresh on impossible vistas, to test himself upon a hostile, or at any rate foreign element and match wits, skill, and luck with all the gods of the sea.

Of all tales ever written or told, sailing stories are among the best pedigreed. Just consider the authorial DNA here on offer: Mark Twain, Richard Henry Dana, Jr., Herman Melville, Daniel Defoe, Stephen Crane, Alfred Lord Tennyson, O. Henry, John Masefield, Arthur Conan Doyle, Gerard Manley Hopkins, Guy De Maupassant, Samuel Taylor Coleridge, Joseph Conrad, Jack London, Charles Dickens, Wilkie Collins—even Charles Dickens. Many of our founding epics also feature sailing stories. Homer's *Odyssey* may be said to be a tale of the wanderings of a sailing man. Even the Bible is shot through with sailing stories.

So, please find herein seventy stories. Even in a volume as large as this, we can only hope to scratch the surface—or, in this case, ruffle the waters—of the literature of sailing. Even so, this format easily permits a sampling of many of the best works of the genre. For no better reason than to bring a sort of rough order, I've divided this anthology in five: *Voyages, Tales, Lee Shores, Wrecks and Other Catastrophies*, and *Shipboard Lore and Poetry*. Now on the whole I wouldn't advise the reader to make too much a distinction between them, for the true tales each have elements of fiction in them, and the best of the invented stories are mostly true. Instead plunge in and read whatever story takes your fancy. Let yourself go, sail away.

As life upon the water, and under sail, can be said to be a metaphor for all of life, many of the best sailing stories appear to be largely about something else. And so you will find here collected stories of the sea that are also horror stories, mystery tales, sagas of exploration, allegories, coming of age stories, and all manner of stories of the heart. But my own guilty secret is that I love the stories best that are full of the *how-to's* of ship-handling and sailing. I like it well enough that Captain Riley stands to lose his life's work and all that he owns in "Shipwreck," but I like even more all the practical details; and should I ever find myself storm-tossed upon a jagged coast I will have some good idea as to how I can save the lives of my crew.

There are some people the sea does not suit—or so they claim—but even they dare not ignore it. Nobody turns his back on the sea; it's never a prudent thing to do. And anyway, our true inclinations are just the opposite. We are—always have been—drawn to the sea. We can't help but recognize our love, or at least our awful fascination with it. And though we admit this to be so, *why* it is so is not so clear.

There are many and various suggestions on offer. Some people claim that since all life came from the sea, it is in fact our natural element, and that this accounts for our attraction to it. Others remind us of our early great days afloat in the fluid of our mother's wombs. The anthropologist and archeologist both will tell you that water-craft developed as the most efficient technology for reaping the sea's harvest, for projecting expeditions of exploration and immigration, for the carrying of trade, and for the prosecuting of war. At the same time, Bible scholars assert that we'd do well to meditate on Jonah's attempted flight from God by sailing ship, and praise the Lord that Jesus walked on water.

In the end, any or all of this may be relevant so long as we also remember the awe-full majesty and mystery of the sea itself, its dead calms and vaulting storms, the infinite variety of its sea-life, its salt sting and bracing airs, its immense and somehow life-affirming emptiness, and its terrible unforgivingness. All of this, too, is fundamental to the sailing story.

No little wonder then that, to paraphrase Masefield, we feel as though we *gotta* go down to the sea in ships. But what are you to do if you have no sailboat handy? Suppose, unlike Ishmael in the quotation above, there is a *great* deal to occupy you on the land and you cannot simply sail away. What then? For that, dear reader, I offer you this gigantic book of sailing stories. It's all here: the history, romance, adventure, mystery, travel-log and ship-craft.

So read on. The wind blows fair. The taste is salt.

Stephen Brennan
Winter 2008

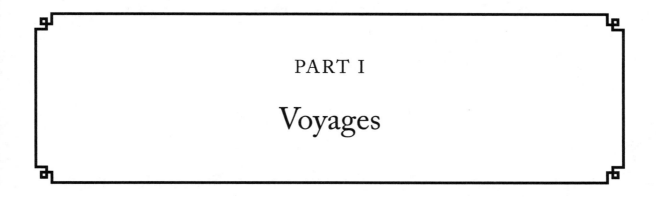

PART I

Voyages

Chronicle of the Voyages of Saint Brendan

STEPHEN BRENNAN

Remember Brendan, not as a graven saint, he was a man and suffered so; in no ways proud, he sought the will of the Lord God full meekly and contrite of heart. And I have seen his eyes start from his head at some marvel, and I have seen the cold gray oceans break over him for days, and I have seen him spit salt seas and tremble with the cold. But no thing overmanned him, because in every tempest he saw the hand of God, and in every trial he sought the will of God, and trusted so, and was not afraid, and thereby gave us heart and courage. And we brethren took example from him, and thereby saved our souls.

Remember Brendan, later called *Saint*, born in the land of Munster, hard by the loch Lein. A holy man of fierce abstinence, known for his great works and the father of almost three thousand monks, he lived at Clonfert then, where we knew him at the first and last.

Recall the night, just past compline it was, when the holy abbot Barrind, later called *Saint*, came out of the darkness into our circle to visit Brendan. And each of them was joyful of the other. And when Brendan began to tell Barrind of the many wonders he had seen voyaging in the sea and visiting in diverse lands, Barrind at once began to sigh and anon he threw himslf prostrate upon the ground and prayed hard and then began to weep. Now Brendan comforted him the best he could, and lifting him up said: *"Brother Abbot, have you not come to be joyful with us, to speak the word of God and to give us* heart? Therefore for God's love, do not be afraid, but tell us what marvels you have seen in the great ocean, that encompasses all the world."

So Barrind began to tell Brendan and all the gathered monks of a great wonder. These were his words:

"I have a son, his name is Meroc, who had a great desire to seek about by ship in diverse countries to find a solitary place wherein he might dwell secretly out of the business of the world, in order to better serve God quietly in devotion. I counseled him to sail to an island in the sea, nearby the mountain of stones, which everybody knows. So he made ready and sailed there with his monks. And when he came there, he liked the place full well, and there settled where he and his monks served our Lord devoutly. And then I saw in a vision that this monk Meroc was sailed right far westward into the sea more than three days sailing, and suddenly to those voyagers there came a dark cloud of fog that overcovered them, so that for a great part of the day they saw no light; then as our Lord willed, the fog passed away, and they saw a fair island, and thereward they drew. In that island was joy and mirth enough and all the earth of that island shone as brightly as the sun, and there were the fairest trees and herbs that ever any man saw, and here were many precious stones shining bright, and every herb was ripe, and every tree full of fruit; so that it was a glorious sight and a heavenly joy to abide there. Then there came to them a fair young man, and courteously he welcomed them all, and called every monk by his name, and said they were much bound to praise the name of our Lord Jesu, who would out of his grace show them that glorious place, where it is always day and never night, and that this place is called the garden of paradise. But by this island is another island whereon no man may come. And the fair young man said to them, 'You have been here half a year without meat or drink or sleep.' They supposed they had been there only half a day, so merry and joyful they were. The young man told them that this was the place where Adam and Eve lived first, and ever would have lived, if they had not broken the commandment of God. Then the fair young man brought them to their ship again and said they might no longer abide there, and when they were all shipped, suddenly the young man vanished away out of their sight. And then within a short time after, by the purveyance of the Lord Jesu, Meroc and the brothers returned to their own island where I and the other brothers received them goodly, and demanded where they had been so long. And they said that they had been in the Land of the Blest, before the Gates of Paradise. And they asked of us, 'Cannot you you tell from the sweetness of our clothes that we have been in Paradise?' And I and the other brothers said, 'We do believe you have been in God's Paradise, but we don't know where this Paradise is.'"

At hearing this we all lay prostrate and said, "The Lord God is just in all his works and merciful and loving to his servants, once again he has nourished our wonder with his holy spirit."

On the day following Barrind's visit, Brendan gathered twelve of the brothers and closed us up in the oratory saying, "If it is God's will, I will seek that holy land of which the brother Abbott spoke. Does this appeal to you? What do you say?"

We answered Brendan thus, *"Not our will, but God's. To know God's will, we leave our families, give away what we possess, put away the lives we led and follow you, if it is the will of God."*

To better know the will of God we fasted forty days, tho not oftener than for three days running as is the rule. And during this time we sought the blessing of the holy father Edna, later called *Saint*, in his western island. We stayed there three days and three nights only.

Old Edna's blessing got, we took ourselves to a lonely inlet place we called Brendan's Butt, for he had known this spot as a boy and there sat many hours, looking away out over the ocean to the west, his seat upon a butt of stone. Here we built a vessel sufficient for a voyage of seven years. With iron tools we ribbed and framed it of ash and oak, the stepping for the mast was oak, and covered it in ox hides, well tanned, stitched together and greased with lard. Therein we put provisions for a forty days journey and many spares of ox hide, and then we got ourselves aboard and here lived devoutly twelve days, afloat but well in sight of land.

On the day set for our departure we received the sacrament and got ourselves aboard, when just as Brendan blessed us all, there came another two of his monks who prayed him that they might come with us. And he said, *"You may sail with us, but one of you shall die and go to hell ere we return."* Even so, they would go with us.

And then Brendan bade the brethren raise the sail, and forth we voyaged in God's name, so that on the morrow we were out of sight of any land. For eleven days and nights we sailed plain, and then we saw an island afar from us. We sailed thitherward as fast as we could, and soon a great reach of stone appeared afar off above the waves, and for three days we worked our way around the island before we found an inlet fit for a landing. At last we found a little haven and there we beached our leather boat.

Suddenly, bounding up to us, there came a fair hound who laid down at Brendan's feet cheering him. So Brendan said to us, *"Be of good heart, for the Lord has sent his messenger to lead us into some good place."* And the hound brought us to a fair hall, where we found tables spread with good meat and drink. Then Brendan spoke the grace and then we brethren sat down and ate and drank. And there were beds made ready for us that we might sleep after our long labor. But Brendan did not sleep, but prayed the night away upon his knees.

On the morrow we returned again to our skin boat, pushed off and sailed a long time in the sea before we found any land. At last, by the purveyance of God, we saw a full fair island of green pasture, whereon were the whitest sheep that we had ever seen. And every sheep was as big as any ox. Just after dragging our ship ashore, we were welcomed by a goodly old man who said, *"This is the Isle of Sheep. Here it is never cold but ever summer. This is why the sheep are so huge, they feed all year on the best grasses and herbs anywhere."* When the old man took his leave he told us, *"Voyage on, and by God's grace, you soon will come upon a place like paradise, whereon you ought to spend your Eastertide."*

We sailed forth and soon came upon another island, but because of shallows and broken stone and the fury of the seas, we bore off and beached our skin ship instead upon a rock, where nothing grew, a small desolate island. Or so we thought, for when we lit the fire so that we might bake our grain and dress our meat, the island began to move under us. And all a panic then, amazed and full of fear, we threw ourselves into the boat, and pulled and twisted at the oars, swatting and thumping one another in our haste to be away. And lo, the island seemed to dip and we floated free and soon were well away. And all that night we spied the beacon of our fire leaping and dancing in the cold, dark ocean. Brendan must have smelled the terror on us, for he said, *"Do not be afraid. It is only a great fish, the biggest in the sea. He labors night and day to swallow his own tail, but he cannot because of his great size. He is called Jasconius."*

And then anon we oared three days and nights before we sighted any land and the weariness was heavy on us. But soon after, as God would, we saw a fair island, full of flowers, herbs, and trees, whereof we thanked God of his good grace, and then anon we found a little stream and followed it, walking our hide boat well in land. And then anon we found a full fair well, and thereby grew a mighty tree, full of boughs, and on every bough sat a white bird, and they so thick upon the tree, their number being so great, and their song being so merry that it was a heavenly noise to hear. Then Brendan fell to his knees and wept for joy, and made his prayers devoutly unto our Lord God that he might understand the meaning of the bird song. And then at once a white bird flew from the tree to Brendan. She flapped and fluttered, she hooked and danced and called, and made a merry noise full like a flute. It seemed to us no holy hymn ever was so joyful. And Brendan said, *"If you are the messengers of God, tell me why you sit so thick upon the tree and why you sing so merrily?"*

And the bird said, *"Once upon a time, we were angels in heaven, but when our master Lucifer fell down into hell for his high pride, we fell with him for our offenses, some higher, some lower, depending on the quality of their trespass; and because our trespass was but little, our Lord has sent us here, out of all pain to live in great joy and mirth, here to serve him on this tree in the best manner that we can. Today is Sunday, can you not guess why we are all white as snow?"*

And when we all remembered, we fell upon our knees and hymned praise to our good Lord Jesu Christ. And the white bird sang to Brendan, *"It is twelve month past that you departed from your abbey. In the seventh year you shall come unto the place of your desire. For each of those years you shall spend the Eastertide here with us, as you do today."*

Then all the birds began to sing evensong so merrily that it was truly a heavenly noise to hear. And after supper Brendan and all of us went to bed, and slept well, and on the morrow we rose early, to hear the birds sing matins, and later prime and all such services of the holy rule.

We all abided there with Brendan eight full weeks, til after Trinity Sunday when we again sailed for the Isle of Sheep, and there we victualed well and were blessed again by the goodly old man, and returned again to our leather boat, and waited for the wind to blow fair. And ere we put out, the bird of the tree came again to us, and danced upon our prow and flapped and fluttered and sang, *"I am come to tell you that you shall sail from here to an island whereon there is an abbey of twenty-four monks, and there you shall hold your Christmas, but Eastertide, do not forget, you spend with us."*

And then the bird flew off.

The wind with us now, we sailed forth into the ocean, but soon fell a great tempest on us, which we were greatly troubled by for a long time and sorely belabored. And we saw, by the purveyance of God, a little island afar off, and full meekly we prayed to our Lord to send us thither in safety. It took eleven days, and in this time we monks were so weary of the long pull and the mountain gray oceans that we set little price upon our lives, and cried continually to our Lord to show us mercy and bring us to that little island in safety. And by the purveyance of God we came at last into a little haven, but so narrow that only one ship might come in. And after we had come to anchor, the brethren went ashore, and when we had long walked about, at last we found two fair wells; one was of fair clear water, and the other was somewhat troubly and thick. At this we thanked our Lord full humbly that had brought us here, and made to drink the water, but Brendan charged us thus, "Take no water without license. If we abstain us a while longer, our Lord will purvey for us in the best wise."

And soon after came to us a good old hoar-haired man, who welcomed us full meekly and kissed Brendan, but did not speak, and by this we understood that he observed a rule of silence. And he led us past many a fair well til we came to an abbey, where we were received with much honor and solemn procession. And then the abbott welcomed Brendan and all our fellowship, and kissed him full meekly, but did not speak. And he drew Brendan by the hand, and led us into a fair hall, and sat us down in a row on benches; and the abbott of that place, in observance of the new commandment, washed all our feet with fair clear water. And afterward, in silence still, led us into the refractory, there to seat ourselves amoung the brothers of the abbey. And anon came one who served us well of meat and drink. For every monk had set before him a fair white loaf and white roots and herbs, which we found right delicious, tho none of us could name; and we drank of the water of the fair clear well that we had seen before when first we came ashore, that Brendan had forbade us. And then the abbott came, and breaking silence, prayed us eat and drink, *"For every day the Lord sends a good old man that covers this table with meat and drink for us. But we know not how it comes, for we do nothing to procure it, and yet our Lord feeds us. And we are twenty-four monks in number, yet every day of the week he sends us twelve loaves, and every Sunday and feast day, twenty-four loaves, and the bread we leave at dinner we eat at supper. And now at your coming our Lord has sent us forty-eight loaves, that all of us may be merry together as brethren. And we have lived twenty-nine years here in this abbey: tho we did first come out of the abbey of Saint Patrick in Ireland eighty years ago. And here in this land it is ever fair weather, and none of us is ever sick since we came here."*

And then Brendan and the abbott and all the company went into the church, and we said even-song together, and devoutly. And when we looked upward at the crucifix, we saw our Lord hanging on a cross made of fine crystal and curiously wrought; and in the choir were twenty-four seats for twenty-four monks, and seven unlit tapers, and the abbott's seat was made close upon the altar in the middle of the choir. And then Brendan asked the abbott, *"How long have you kept silence one with another?"*

And the abbott answered Brendan, *"For this twenty-nine years, no one has spoken to another."*

And Brendan wept for joy at this, and desired of the abbott, *"That we might all dwell here with you."*

And the abbott answered Brendan, *"That will not do, for our Lord has showed to you in what manner you will be guided til the seventh year is done, and after that term you will return with your monks to Ireland in safety; except that one of the two monks that came last to you will dwell in the island of anchorites, and the other will burn in hell."*

And as we knelt with Brendan in the church, we saw a bright shining angel fly in at the window that lighted all the tapers in the church and flew out again and then to heaven. And Brendan marveled greatly how fair the light burned but wasted not. And the abbott said to us that it is written how Moses saw a bush afire, yet it burned not, *"and therefore marvel not, for the might of our Lord is now as great as ever it was."*

And when we had dwelled there even til Christmas was gone twelve days and eight days more, we took leave of this holy abbott and his convent, and returned again to our skinned-ship. And then we sailed from thence toward the island of the abbey of Saint Hillary, but aching cold and furious tempests troubled us til just before the start of Lent, when we bespied an island, not far off; and then we pulled for it but weakly, our strength all spent, our stomachs empty, our bodies raw with thirst. And when at last we gained the island, and dragged our battered boat upon the beach, we found a well of clear water, and diverse roots that grew about it, and multitudes of sweet fleshed fish that swarmed in the river that flowed to the sea. And Brendan said, *"Let us gather up this bounty which the Lord makes a gift to us, and then let us renew our bodies with meat and drink, and our spirits in hymns devoutly sung."*

And we obeyed Brendan, and we dug many roots and put them in the fire to bake, likewise we netted many fish and cleaned and baked them also. But when we made to drink, our holy father Brendan said, *"Of this clear water drink only what is meet for your good health, lest this gift of God do you some harm."*

And after grace was said, we fell to meat and drink, and then when we had eaten and drunk, we began to sing the holy office and promptly, one by one, each man fell to sleep. Tho Brendan did not sleep, but prayed three days and nights upon his knees, and full devoutly for our awakening. And so at length we did awaken, and those of us who had drank three cups of that clear water slept three days and nights, and those who drank two cups slept two, and one cup only one day and night. And

Brendan gathered us about the fire and said, *"Brothers, we see here how a gift of God may do us harm. As Lent is nigh, let us now get ourselves to sea; take only meat and drink for one meal every three days, as is the rule, enough to last this holy season out."*

And then again we pulled our hide boat upon God's ocean, and for three full days the wind blew foul, and then a sudden all grew still. The wind blew not and the sea calmned and flattened and seemed to set into a thing solid. And Brendan said, *"Brothers, lay off your oars, let us drift; and in this show true submission to the will of God."*

And then we drifted twenty days. And this was a time of meditation and prayer, and of perfect observance of the rule, and of good fellowship among the brethren. Then at last by the purveyance of the Lord, the wind arose and blew fresh til Palm Sunday.

And then at last we came again unto the Isle of Sheep, and were received again by the goodly old man, who brought us again into the fair hall, and served us. And after soup on Holy Thursday, he washed our feet, and gave us each the kiss of peace, alike our Lord had done with his disciples. And on the Friday of the passion of our Lord we sacrificed the lamb of innocence, and on the Saturday we did all holy rite and prayed together full devoutly, that we might find ourselves prepared for the miracle of of the resurrection of our Lord Jesu. And at eventide we toiled our skin vessel into the sea, and as Brendan bid us, pulled our ashen oars against the seas that blow shorewards at eventide. And Brendan made his seat upon the oaken tiller and captained us unto a place in the sea that he did chose. And on that Easter vigil, just at the hour of lauds, when all the world is blue with first light, he bid us lay upon our oars, and Brendan asked unto us, *"Do you not know where it is you are?"*

And we did not know, but Brendan did know; and lo, we seemed to rise up heavenward, and the seas fell away from our frail craft, and we beheld ourselves again upon Jasconius' back. And we beheld the smear of char where twelve months past we laid a fire to bake our meat, and we were amazed, and Brendan seeing this said, *"Do not be afraid."*

And one by one we stepped out upon this living isle. And Brendan said, *"How splendid is the will of our good Lord, that even savage monsters do his bidding and make this place upon a fish's back to keep the holy service of the resurrection."*

And after Mass was said, and Brendan sacrificed the spotless lamb of innocence, we got ourselves again aboard our skin vessel, and lo Jasconius dove beneath the sea, and we sailed free. And on that same morning we gained the island where the tree of the birds was, and that same bird welcomed Brendan and sang full merrily. And there we dwelled from Easter til Trinity Sunday, as we had done the year before, in full great joy and mirth; and daily we heard the merry service of the birds sitting in the tree. And then the one bird told Brendan that he should return again at Christmas to the abbey of the monks, *"and Easterday, do not forget, you spend with us. But every other day of your journey, you labor in the full great peril of the ocean, from year to year til the seventh year has been accomplished when you shall find the Land of the Blest, before the gates of Paradise, and dwell there forty days in full great joy and mirth; and after you shall return home in safety to your own abbey and there end your life and be admitted to blessed heaven, which our Lord bought for you with his most precious blood."*

And then an angel of our Lord ordained all things needful to our voyage, in vitals and all other things necessary. And then we thanked our Lord for the great goodness that he had often shown us in our great need. And then we sailed forth in the great sea ocean, abiding in the mercy of our Lord through great troubles and tempests.

The Voyage of the Aquidneck

JOSHUA SLOCUM

I

To get underweigh, it was on the 28th of February, 1886, that the bark Aquidneck, laden with case-oil, sailed from New York for Montevideo, the capital of Uruguay, the strip of land bounding the River Platte on the east, and called by the natives "Banda Oriental." The Aquidneck was a trim and tidy craft of 326 tons' register, hailing from Baltimore, the port noted for clippers, and being herself high famed above them all for swift sailing, she had won admiration on many seas.

Her crew mustered ten, all told; twelve had been the complement, when freights were good. There were, beside the crew with regular stations, a little lad, aged about six years, and his mamma, (age immaterial), privileged above the rest, having "all nights in"—that is, not having to stand watch. The mate, Victor, who is to see many adventures before reaching New York again, was born and bred on shipboard. He was in perfect health, and as strong as a windlass. When he first saw the light and began to give orders, he was at San Francisco on the packet Constitution, the vessel lost in the tempest at Samoa, just before the great naval disaster at the same place in this year of 1889. Garfield, the little lad above mentioned, Victor's brother, in this family ship, was born in Hong Kong harbor, in the old bark Amethyst, a bona-fide American citizen, though first seeing the light in a foreign port, the stars and stripes standing sponsors for his nationality. This bark had braved the wind and waves for fifty-eight years, but had not, up to that date, so far as I know, experienced so lively a breeze as the one which sprung up about her old timbers on that eventful 3rd of March, 1881.

Our foremast hands on the Aquidneck, six in number, were from as many nations, strangers to me and strangers to each other; but the cook, a negro, was a native American—to the manner born. To have even so many Americans in one ship was considered exceptional.

Much or little as matters this family history and description of the crew: the day of our sailing was bitter-cold and stormy, boding no good for the coming voyage, which was to be, indeed, the most eventful of my life of more than five-and-thirty years at sea. Studying the morning weather report, before sailing, we saw predicted a gale from the nor'west, and one also approaching from the sou'west at the same time. "The prospect," said the New York *Tribune,* "is not encouraging." We were anxious, however, to commence the voyage, having a crew on board, and, being all ready, we boldly sailed, somewhat against our better judgment. The nor'wester blowing, at the time, at the rate of forty miles an hour, increased to eighty or ninety miles by March 2nd. This hurricane continued through March 3rd, and gave us serious concern for the ship and all on board.

At New York, on those days, the wind howled from the north, with the "storm centre somewhere on the Atlantic," so said the wise seamen of the weather bureau, to whom, by the way, the real old salt is indebted, at the present day, for information of approaching storms, sometimes days ahead. The prognostication was correct, as we can testify, for out on the Atlantic our bark could carry only a mere rag of a foresail, somewhat larger than a table-cloth, and with this storm-sail she went flying before the tempest, all those dark days, with a large "bone in her mouth," making great headway, even under the small sail. Mountains of seas swept clean over the bark in their mad race, filling her decks full to the top of the bulwarks, and shaking things generally.

Our men were lashed, each one to his station; and all spare spars not doubly lashed were washed away, along with other movables that were broken and torn from their fastenings by the wild storm.

The cook's galley came in for its share of the damage, the cook himself barely escaping serious injury from a sea that went thundering across the decks, taking with it doors, windows, galley stove, pots, kettles and all, together with the culinary artist; landing the whole wreck in the leescuppers, but, most fortunately, with the professor on top. A misfortune like this is always—felt. It dampens one's feelings, so to speak. It means cold hash for a time to come, if not even worse fare.

The day following our misfortune, however, was not so bad. In fact, the tremendous seas boarding the bark latterly were indications of the good change coming, for it meant that her speed had slackened through a lull of the gale, allowing the seas to reach her too full and heavy.

More sail was at once crowded on, and still more was set at every stage of the abatement of the gale, for the craft should not be lazy when big seas race after her. And so, on we flew, like a scud, sheeting home sail after sail, as required, till the 5th of March, when all of her white wings were spread, and she fairly "walked the waters like a thing of life." There was now wind enough for several days, but not too much, and our swift-sailing craft laughed at the seas trying to catch her.

Cheerily on we sailed for days and days, pressed by the favoring gale, meeting the sun each day one hour's span earlier, making daily four degrees of longitude. It was the time, on these bright days, to forearm with dry clothing against future stormy weather. Boxes and bags were brought on deck, and drying and patching went on by wholesale in the watch below, while the watch on deck bestirred themselves putting the ship in order. "Chips," the carpenter, mended the galley; the cook's broken shins were plastered up; and in a few days all was well again. And the sailors moving cheerfully about once more in their patched garments of varied hues, reminded me of the spotted cape pigeons, pecking for a living, the pigeons, I imagined, having the best life of the two. A panican of hot coffee or tea by sailors called "water bewitched," a "sea-biscuit" and "bit of salt-horse," had regaled the crew and restored their voices. Then "Reuben Ranzo" was heard on the breeze, and the main tack was boarded to the tune of "Johnny Boker." Other wondrous songs through the night-watch could be heard in keeping with the happy time. Then what they would do and what they wouldn't do in the next port was talked of, when song and yarn ran out.

Hold fast, shipmate, hold fast and belay! or the crimps of Montevideo will wear the new jacket you promise yourself, while you will be off Cape Horn, singing "Haul out to leeward," with a wet stocking on your neck, and with the same old "lamby" on, that long since was "lamby" only in name, the woolly part having given way to a cloth worn much in "Far Cathay;" in short, you will dress in dungaree, the same as now, while the crimps and landsharks divide your scanty earnings, unless you "take in the slack" of your feelings, and "make all fast and steady all."

Ten days out, and we were in the northeast "trades"—porpoises were playing under the bows as only porpoises can play; dolphins were racing alongside, and flying-fish were all about. This was, indeed, a happy change, and like being transported to another world. Our hardships were now all forgotten, for "the sea washes off all the woes of men."

One week more of pleasant sailing, all going orderly on board, and Cape Verde Islands came in sight. A grand and glorious sight they were! All hail, *terra firma!* It is good to look at you once again! By noon the islands were abeam, and the fresh trade-wind in the evening bore us out of sight before dark.

Most delightful sailing is this large, swinging motion of our bark over the waves, with the gale abaft the beam, driving her forward till she fairly skips from billow to billow, as if trying to rival her companions, the very flying-fish. When thwarted by a sea, at such times, she strikes it with her handsome bows, sending into the sunlight countless thousand sprays, that shine like a nimbus of glory. The tread on her deck-plank is lighter then, and the little world afloat is gladsome fore and aft.

Cape Frio (cold cape) was the next landfall. Upon reaching that point, we had crossed the Atlantic twice. The course toward Cape Verde Islands had been taken to avail ourselves of a leading wind through the southeast trades, the course from the islands to Frio being southwesterly. This latter stretch was spanned on an easy bow-line; with nothing eventful to record. Thence our course was through variable winds to the River Platte, where a "*pampeiro*" was experienced that blew "great guns," and whistled a hornpipe through the rigging.

These *pampeiros* (wind from the *pampas*), usually blow with great fury, but give ample warning of their approach: the first sign being a spell of unsurpassed fine weather, with small, fleecy clouds floating so gently in the sky that one scarcely perceives their movements, yet they do move, like an immense herd of sheep grazing undisturbed on the great azure field. All this we witnessed, and took into account. Then gradually, and without any apparent cause, the clouds began to huddle together behind the accumulating masses, then a distant rumbling noise. It was a note of warning, and one that no vessel should let pass unheeded. "Clew up, and furl!" was the order. To hand all sail when these fierce visitors are out on a frolic over the seas, and entertain them under bare poles, is the safest plan, unless, indeed, the best storm sails are bent; even then it is safest to goose-wing the tops'ls before the gale comes on. Not till the fury of the blast is spent does the ship require sail, for it is not till then that the sea begins to rise, necessitating sail to steady her.

The first onslaught of the storm, levelling all before it, and sending the would-be waves flying across in sheets—sailor sheets, so to speak—lends a wild and fearful aspect; but there is no dread of a lee-shore in the sailor's heart at these times, for the gale is off from the land, as indicated by the name it bears.

After the gale was a calm; following which came desirable winds, that carried us at last to the port we sought—Montevideo; where we cast anchor on the 5th of May, and made preparations, after the customs' visit, for discharging the cargo, which was finally taken into lighters from alongside to the piers, and thence to the warehouses, where ends the ship's responsibility to the owner of the goods. But not till then ceases the ship's liabilities, or the captain's care of the merchandise placed in his trust. Clearly the captain has cares on sea and on land.

II

Montevideo, sister city to Buenos Ayres, is the fairer of the two to look upon, from the sea, having a loftier situation, and, like Buenos Ayres, boasts of many fine mansions, comely women, liberal schools, and a cemetery of great splendor.

It is at Montevideo that the "beggar a-horse-back" becomes a verity (horses are cheap); galloping up to you the whining beggar will implore you, saying: "For the love of Christ, friend, give me a coin to buy bread with."

From "the Mont." we went to Antonina, in Brazil, for a cargo of mate, a sort of tea, which, prepared as a drink, is wholesome and refreshing. It is partaken of by the natives in a highly sociable manner, through a tube which is thrust into the steaming beverage in a silver urn or a calabash, whichever may happen to be at hand when "draughty neebors neebors meet;" then all sip and sip in bliss, from the same tube, which is passed from mouth to mouth. No matter how many mouths there may be, the *bombelia,* as it is called, must reach them all. It may have to be replenished to make the drink go around, and several times, too, when the company is large. This is done with but little loss of time. By thrusting into the urn or gourd a spoonful of the herb, and two spoonfuls of sugar to a pint of water, which is poured, boiling, over it, the drink is made. But to give it some fancied extra flavor, a live coal (*carbo vegetable*) is plunged into the potion to the bottom. Then it is again passed around, beginning where it left off. Happy is he, if a stranger, who gets the first sip at the tube, but the initiated have no prejudices. While in that country I frequently joined in the social rounds at *mate,* and finally rejoiced in a *bombelia* of my own.

The people at Antonina (in fact all the people we saw in Brazil), were kind, extremely hospitable, and polite; living in thrift generally, their wants were but few beyond their resources. The mountain scenery, viewed from the harbor of Antonina, is something to gloat over; I have seen no place in the world more truly grand and pleasing. The climate, too, is perfect and healthy. The only doctor of the place, when we were there, wore a coat out at the elbows, for lack of patronage. A desirable port is Antonina.

We had musical entertainments on board, at this place. To see the display of beautiful white teeth by these Brazilian sweet singers was good to the soul of a sea-tossed mariner. One nymph sang for the writer's benefit a song at which they all laughed very much. Being in native dialect, I did not understand it, but of course laughed with the rest, at which they were convulsed; from this, I supposed it to be at my expense. I enjoyed that, too, as much, or more, than I would have relished *areytos* in my favor.

With *mate* we came to Buenos Ayres, where the process of discharging the cargo was the same as at Montevideo—into lighters. But at Buenos Ayres we lay four times the distance from the shore, about four miles.

The herb, or *herva mate,* is packed into barrels, boxes, and into bullock-hide sacks, which are sewed up with stout hide thongs. The contents, pressed in tightly when the hide is green and elastic, becomes as hard as a cannon ball by the contraction which follows when it dries. The first load of the *soroes,* so-called, that came off to the bark at the port of loading, was espied on the way by little Garfield. Piled in the boat, high above the gunwhales, the hairy side out, they did look odd. "Oh, papa," said he, "here comes a load of cows! Stand by, all hands, and take them in."

III

From Buenos Ayres, we proceeded up the River Platte, near the confluence of the Parana and Paraguay, to salve a cargo of wine from the stranded brig Neovo San Pascual, from Marseilles.

The current of the great river at that point runs constantly seaward, becoming almost a sea of itself, and a dangerous one to navigate; hence the loss of the San Pascual, and many others before her.

If, like the "Ancient Mariner," we had, any of us, cried, "water, water all around, and not a drop to drink," we forgot it now, in this bountiful stream. Wine, too, we had without stint. The insurance agent, to leave no excuse for tampering with the cargo, rolled out a cask of the best, and, like a true Hans Briterman, "knocked out der bung." Then, too, cases were broken in the handling, the contents of which drenched their clothes from top to toe, as the sailors carried them away on their heads.

The diversity of a sailor's life—ah me! The experience of Dana and his shipmates, for instance, on a sunburnt coast, carrying dry hides on their heads, if not a worse one, may be in store for us, we cried, now fairly swimming in luxuries—water and wine alike free. Although our present good luck may be followed by times less cheerful, we preferred to count this, we said, as compensation for past misfortunes, marking well that "it never rains but it pours."

The cargo of wine in due course, was landed at Rosario, with but small loss, the crew, except in one case, remaining sober enough to help navigate even the difficult Parana. But one old sinner, the case I speak of, an old Labrador fisherman, became a useless, drunken swab, in spite of all we could do. I say "we" for most of the crew were on my side, in favor of a fair deal and "regular supplies."

The hold was barred and locked, and every place we could think of, for a time, was searched; still Dan kept terribly drunk. At last his mattress was turned out, and from it came—a dozen or more bottles of the best liquor. Then there was a row, but all on the part of Dan, who swore blue vengeance on the man, if he could but find him out, who had stowed that grog in his bunk, "trying to get" him "into trouble;" some of those "young fellows would rue it yet!"

The cargo of wine being discharged, I chartered to load alfalfa, packed in bales, for Rio. Many deaths had occurred about this time, with appalling suddenness; we soon learned that cholera was staring us all in the face, and that it was fast spreading through the country, filling towns and cities with sickness and death.

Approaching more frightfully near, it carried our pilot over the bar: his wife was a widow the day after he brought our bark to the loading berth. And the young man who commenced to deliver us the cargo was himself measured the day after. His ship had come in!

Many stout men, and many, many women and children succumbed to the scourge; yet it was our high privilege to come through the dark cloud without losing a loved one, while thousands were cast down with bereavements and grief. At one time it appeared that we were in the centre of the cloud which zig-zagged its ugly body, serpent-like, through districts, poisoning all that it touched, and leaving death in its wake. This was indeed cholera in its most terrible form!

One poor fellow sat at the Widow Lacinas' hotel, bewildered. "Forty-eight hours ago," said he, "I sat at my own hearth, with wife and three children by my side. Now I am alone in the world! Even my poor house, such as it was, is pulled down." This man, I say, had troubles; surely was his "house pulled down"!

There was no escaping the poison or keeping it off, except by disinfectants, and by keeping the system regular, for it soon spread over all the land and the air was full of it. Remedies sold so high that many must have perished without the test of medicinal aid to cure their disease. A cry went up against unprincipled druggists who were overcharging for their drugs, but nothing more was done to check their greed. Camphor sold as high as four dollars a pound, and the druggist with a few hundred drops of laudanum and as much chlorodyne could travel through Europe afterwards on the profits of his sales.

It was at Rosario, and at this time, that we buried our young friend, Captain Speck, well loved of young and old. His friends did not ask whether it was cholera or not that he died of, but performed the last act of friendship as became men of heart and feeling. The minister could not come that day, but Captain Speck's little friend, Garfield, said: "The flags were set for the angels to come and take the Captain to Heaven!" Need more be said?

And the flags blew out all day.

Then it became us to erect a memorial slab, and, hardest of all, to write to the widow and orphans. This was done in a homely way, but with sympathetic, aching hearts away off there in Santa Fe.

Our time at Rosario, after this, was spent in gloomy days that dragged into weeks and months, and our thoughts often wandered from there to a happy past. We preferred to dwell away from there and in other climes, if only in thought. There was, however, one happy soul among us—the child whose face was a sunbeam in all kinds of weather and at all times, happy in his ignorance of the evils that fall to the lot of man.

Our sailing-day from Rosario finally came; and, with a feeling as of casting off fetters, the lines were let go, and the bark hauled out into the stream, with a full cargo on board; but, instead of sailing for Rio, as per charter, she was ordered by the Brazilian consul to Ilha Grande [Great Island], the quarantine station of Brazil, some sixty-two miles west of Rio, there to be disinfected and to discharge her cargo in quarantine.

A new crew was shipped and put aboard, but while I was getting my papers, about noon, they stole one of the ship's boats and scurried off down the river as fast, no doubt, as they could go. I have not seen them or my boat since. They all deserted,—every mother's son of them! taking, beside the boat, a month's advance pay from a Mr. Dutch Harry, a sailor boarding master, who had stolen my inward crew that he might, as he boasted afterward, "ship new hands in their places." In view of the fact that this vilest of crimps was the loser of the money, I could almost forgive the "galoots" for the theft of my boat. (The ship is usually responsible for advance wages, twenty-four hours after she has sailed, providing, too, that the sailors proceed to sea in her.) Seeing, moreover, that they were of that stripe, unworthy the name of sailor, my vessel was the better without them, by at least what it cost to be rid of them, namely, the price of my boat.

However, I will take back what I said about Dutch Harry being the "vilest crimp." There came one to Rosario worse than he, one "Pete the Greek," who cut off the ears of a rival boarding-master at the Boca, threw them into the river, then, making his escape to Rosario, some 180 miles away, established himself in the business in opposition to the Dutchman, whom he "shanghaied" soon after, then "reigned peacefully in his stead."

A captain who, like myself, had suffered from the depredations of this noted gentry, told me, in great glee, that he saw Harry on a bone-laden Italian bark outward bound,—"even then nearly out of the river." The last seen of him by my friend, the captain, was "among the branches," with a rope around his neck—they hanged him, maybe—I don't know what else the rope was for, or who deserved more to be hanged. The captain screamed with delight:—"he'll get bone soup, at least, for a while, instead of Santa Fe good muttonchops at our expense."

My second crew was furnished by Mr. Pete, before referred to, and on the seventeenth of December we set sail from that country of revolutions. Things soon dropped into working order, and I found reason to be pleased with the change of crew. We glided smoothly along down the river, thence wishing never again to see Rosario under the distressing circumstances through which she had just passed.

On the following day, while slipping along before a light, rippling breeze, a dog was espied out in the current, struggling in the whirlpools, which were rather strong, apparently unable to extricate himself, and was greatly exhausted. Coming up with him our maintops'l was laid to the mast, and as we ranged by the poor thing, a sailor, plunging over the side in a bowline, bent a rope on to doggy, another one hauled him carefully on board, and the rescue was made. He proved to be a fine young retriever, and his intelligent signs of thankfulness for his escape from drowning were scarcely less eloquent of gratitude than human spoken language.

This pleasant incident happening on a Friday, suggested, of course, the name we should give him. His new master, to be sure, was Garfield, who at once said, "I guess they won't know me when I get home, with my new suit—and a dog!" The two romped the decks thenceforth, early and late. It was good to see them romp, while "Friday" "barkit wi' joy."

Our pets were becoming numerous now, and all seemed happy, till a stow-a-way cat, one day, killed poor little "Pete," our canary. For ten years or more we had listened to the notes of this wee bird, in many countries and climes. Sweetest of sweet singers, it was buried in the great Atlantic at last. A strange cat, a careless steward, and its tiny life was ended—and the tragedy told. This was indeed a great loss to us all, and was mourned over,—almost as the loss of a child.

A book that has been read at sea has a near claim on our friendship, and is a thing one is loth to part with, or change, even for a better book. But the well-tried friend of many voyages is, oh! so hard to part with at sea. A resting-place in the solemn sea of sameness—in the trackless ocean, marked only by imaginary lines and circles—is a cheerless spot to look to; yet how many have treasures there!

Returning to the voyage and journal: Our pilot proved incompetent, and we narrowly escaped shipwreck in consequence at Martin Garcia Bar, a bad spot in the River Platte. A small schooner captain, observing that we needlessly followed in his track, and being anything but a sailor in principle, wantonly meditated mischief to us. While I was confidently trusting to my pilot, and he (the pilot) trusting to the schooner, one that could go over banks where we would strike, what did the scamp do but shave close to a dangerous spot, my pilot following faithfully in his wake. Then, jumping upon the taffrail of his craft, as we came abreast the shoal, he yelled, like a Comanche, to my pilot to: "Port the helm!" and what does my mutton-headed jackass do but port hard over! The bark, of course, brought up immediately on the ground, as the other had planned, seeing which his whole pirate crew—they could have been little less than pirates—joined in roars of laughter, but sailed on, doing us no other harm.

By our utmost exertions the bark was gotten off, not a moment too soon, however, for by the time we kedged her into deep water a *pampeiro* was upon us. She rode out the gale safe at anchor, thanks to an active crew. Our water tanks and casks were then refilled, having been emptied to lighten the bark from her perilous position.

Next evening the storm went down, and by mutual consent our mud-pilot left, taking passage in a passing river craft, with his pay and our best advice, which was to ship in a dredging-machine, where his capabilities would be appreciated.

Then, "paddling our own canoe," without further accident we reached the light-ship, passing it on Christmas Day. Clearing thence, before night, English Bank and all other dangers of the land, we set our course for Ilha Grande, the wind being fair. Then a sigh of relief was breathed by all on board. If ever "old briny" was welcomed, it was on that Christmas Day.

Nothing further of interest occurred on the voyage to Brazil, except the death of the little bird already spoken of, which loss deeply affected us all.

We arrived at Ilha Grande, our destination, on the 7th day of January, 1887, and came to anchor in nine fathoms of water, at about noon, within musket-range of the guard-ship, and within speaking distance of several vessels riding quarantine, with more or less communication going on among them all, through flags. Several ships, chafing under the restraint of quarantine, were "firing signals" at the guard-ship. One Scandinavian, I remember, asked if he might be permitted to communicate by *cable* with his owners in Christiania. The guard gave him, as the Irishman said, "an evasive answer," so the cablegram, I suppose, laid over. Another wanted police assistance; a third wished to know if he could get fresh provisions—ten mil-reis' ($5) worth (he was a German)—naming a dozen or more articles that he wished for, "and *the balance in onions!*" Altogether, the young fellows on the guard-ship were having, one might say, a signal practice.

On the next day, Jan. 8th, the officers of the port came alongside in a steam launch, and ordered us to leave, saying the port had been closed that morning. "But we have made the voyage," I said. "No matter," said the guard, "leave at once you must, or the guard-ship will fire into you." This, I submit, was harsh and arbitrary treatment. A thunderbolt from a clear sky could not have surprised us more or worked us much greater harm—to be ruined in business or struck by lightning, being equally bad!

Then pointing something like a gun, Dom Pedro said, said he, *"Vaya Homem"* (hence, begone), "Or you'll give us cholera." So back we had to go, all the way to Rosario, with that load of hay—and trouble. But on our arrival there we found things better than they were when we sailed. The cholera had ceased—it was on the wane when we sailed from Rosario, and there was hardly a case of the dread disease in the whole country east of Cordova when we returned. That was, indeed, a comfort, but it left our hardship the same, and led, consequently, to the total loss of the vessel after dragging us through harrowing trials and losses, as will be seen by subsequent events.

IV

This Ilha Grande decree, really a political movement, brought great hardships on us, notwithstanding that it was merely intended by the Brazilians as retaliation for past offences by their Argentine neighbors; not only for quarantines against Rio fevers, but for a discriminating duty as well, on sugar from the empire; a combination of hardships on commerce—more than the sensitive Brazilians could stand—so chafing them, that a retaliation fever sprung up reaching more than the heat of *febre marello*, and they decided to teach their republican cousins a wholesome lesson. However, their wish was to retaliate without causing war, and it was done. In fact, closing ports as they did at the beginning of Argentine's most valuable season of exports to Brazil, and with the plausible excuse, namely, fear of pain in the stomach, so filled the Argentines with admiration of their equals in strategy that they on the earliest opportunity proclaimed two public holidays in honor of bright Brazil. So the matter of difference ended, to the delight of all—in firecrackers and champagne!

To the delight of all except the owner and crew of the Aquidneck. For our bark there was no way but to return where the cargo came from, at a ruinous loss, too, of time and money. We called at the first open port and wired to the owner of the cargo, but got no answer. Thence we sailed to Buenos Ayres, where I telegraphed again for instructions. The officers of the guard ship, upon receiving my report from Brazil, were convulsed with laughter, while I! I confess it—could not see the joke. After waiting two days, this diplomatic reply came from the owner of the cargo: "Act as the case may require." Upon this matter I had several opinions. One person suggested that the case required me to pitch the whole cargo into the sea! This friend, I may mention, was from Boston.

I have ever since regretted, however, that I did not take his advice. There seemed to be no protection for the vessel, the law that a ship must be allowed to live was unheeded, in fact this law was reversed and there were sharpers and beachcombers at every turn ready to take advantage of one's misfortunes or even drive one to despair. I concluded, finally, to shake the lot of them, and proceeding up the Parana, moored again at the berth where, a few weeks before, we had taken in the cargo. Spans and tackle were rigged, and all was made ready to discharge. It was now, "Come on, McCarthy, or McCarthy, come on!" I didn't care which, I had one *right* on my side, and I kept that always in view; namely, the right to discharge the cargo where I had first received it; but where the money to buy ballast and pay other charges was to come from I could not discover.

My merchant met me in great concern at my "misfortunes," but "carramba!" [zounds] said he, "my own losses are great." It required very little reasoning to show me that the least expensive course was the safest one for me to adopt, and my merchant offering enough to pay the marketing, I found it wisest not to disturb the cargo, but to lay up instead with it in the vessel and await the reopening of the Brazilian ports. This I did.

My merchant, Don Manuel, is said to be worth millions of *pesos*. The foundation of his wealth was laid by peddling charcoal, carrying it at first, to his credit be it said, on his back, and was then a good fellow. Many a hard bargain has he waged since, and is now a "Don," living in a $90,000 house. The Don doesn't peddle charcoal any more, but he's got a glass eye!

Moored at Rosario, waiting, waiting; but all of us well in body, and myself finally less agitated in mind. My old friend, Don Manuel, seems better also; he "may yet purge and live clean like a gentleman."

I found upon our return to Rosario that some of the old hands were missing; laid low by the scourge, to make room for others, and some were spared who would have been less lamented. Among all the ship brokers that I knew at Rosario, and I knew a great many, not one was taken away. They all escaped, being, it was thought, epidemic-proof. There was my broker, Don Christo Christiano—called by Don Manuel "El Sweaga" (the Swede)—whom nothing could strike with penetrative force, except a commission.

At last, April 9th, 1887, news came that the Brazilian ports were open. Cholera had long since disappeared in Santa Fe and Buenos Ayres. The Brazilians had established their own beef-drying factories, and could now afford to open their ports to competition. This made a great stir among the ships. Crews were picked up here and there, out of the few brothels that had not been pulled down during the cholera, and out of the street or from the fields. Some, too, came in from the bush. Mixed among them were many that had been let out of the prisons all over the country, so that the scourge should not be increased by over-crowded jails. Of six who shipped with me, four had been so released from prison, where they had been serving for murder or highway robbery; all this I learned when it was too late. I shall have occasion before long to speak of these again!

Well, we unmoored and dropped down the river a few miles the first day; with this crew, the hardest looking set that ever put foot on a ship of mine, and with a swarthy Greek pilot that would be taken for a pirate in any part of the world. The second mate, who shipped also at Rosario, was not less ill-visaged, and had, in addition to his natural ugly features, a deep scar across his face, suggestive of a heavy sabre stroke; a mark which, I thought upon further acquaintance, he had probably merited. I could not make myself easy upon the first acquaintance of my new and decidedly ill-featured crew. So, early the first evening I brought the bark to anchor, and made all snug before dark for prudent reasons. Next morning, the Greek, instead of getting the bark underweigh, as I expected him to do, came to me, demanding more pay for his services, and thinking, may-be that I could not do without him, demanded unless I chose to pay considerably in excess of his regular dues, to be put on shore. I took the fellow at his first bounce. He and his grip-sack were landed on the bank there and then, with but little "palaver" over it. It was then said, so I learned after, that "old S——" would drop into the wake of some ship, and save his pilotage; in fact, they didn't know "what else he could do," as the pilots were then all engaged for other vessels.

The money was taken care of all right, and so was the Aquidneck! By daylight of the following morning she was underweigh, and under full sail at the head of a fleet of piloted vessels, and, being the swiftest sailer, easily kept the lead, and was one of the vessels that did *not "rompe el banco,"* as was predicted by all the pilots, while they hunched their shoulders above their ears, exclaiming, "No *practico,* no *possebla!*" This was my second trip down the Parana, it is true, and I had been on other rivers as wonderful as this one, and, had moreover, read Mark Twain's "Life on the Mississippi," which gives no end of information on river currents, wind-reefs, sand-reefs, alligator-water, and all that is useful to know about rivers, so that I was confident of my ability; all that had been required was the stirring-up that I got from the impertinent pilot, or buccaneer, whichever is proper to call him—one thing certain, he was no true sailor!

A strong, fair wind on the river, together with the current, in our favor, carried us flying down the channel, while we kept the lead, with the Stars and Stripes waving where they ought always to be seen; namely, on the ship in the van! So the duffers followed us, instead of our following them, and on we came, all clear, with the good wishes of the officers and the crews. But the pilots drawing their shoulders up, and repeating the refrain, "No *practico*, no *possebla!*" cursed us bitterly, and were in a vile mood, I was told, cursing more than usual, and that is saying a great deal, for all will agree who have heard them, that the average "Dago" pilot is the most foul-mouthed thing afloat.

Down the river and past the light-ship we came once more, this time with no halt to make, no backing sails to let a pilot off, nothing at all to stop us; we spread all sail to a favorable breeze, and reached Ilha Grande eight days afterward, beating the whole fleet by two days. Garfield kept strict account of this. He was on deck when we made the land, a dark and foggy night it was! nothing could be seen but the dimmest outline of a headland through the haze. I knew the place, I thought, and Garfield said he could smell land, fog or coaltar. This, it will be admitted, was reassuring. A school of merry porpoises that gamboled under the bows while we stood confidently in for the land, diving and crossing the bark's course in every direction, also guarded her from danger. I knew that so long as deep-sea porpoises kept with us we had nothing to fear of the ground. When the lookout cried, "Porpoises gone," we turned the bark's head off shore, backed the main-tops'l, and sent out the "pigeon" (lead). A few grains of sand and one soft, delicate white shell were brought up out of fourteen fathoms of water. We had but to heed these warnings and guides, and our course would be tolerably clear, dense and all as the fog and darkness was.

The lead was kept constantly going as we sailed along in the intense darkness, till the headland of our port was visible through the haze of gray morning. What Garfield had smelled, I may mention, turned out to be coal-tar, a pot of which had been capsized on deck by the leadsman, in the night.

By daylight in the morning, April 29, we had found the inner entrance to Ilha Grande, and sailed into the harbor for the second time with this cargo of hay. It was still very foggy, and all day heavy gusts of wind came down through the gulches in the mountains, laden with fog and rain.

Two days later, the weather cleared up, and our friends began to come in. They found us there all right, anchored close under the highest mountain.

Eight days of sullen gloom and rain at this place; then brimstone smoke and fire turned on to us, and we were counted healthy enough to be admitted to *pratique* in Rio, where we arrived May 11th, putting one more day between ourselves and our friendly competitors, who finally arrived safe, all except one, the British bark "Dublin." She was destroyed by fire between the two ports. The crew was rescued by Captain Lunt, and brought safe into Rio next day.

At the fort entrance to the harbor of Rio we were again challenged and brought to, all standing, on the bar; the tide running like a mill race at the time brought the bark aback on her cables with a force, nearly cutting her down.

The Aquidneck it would seem had outsailed the telegram which should have preceded her; it was nevertheless, my imperative duty to obey the orders of the port authorities which, however, should have been tempered with reason. It was easy for them in the fort to say, "Come to, or we'll sink you," but we in the bark, between two evils, came near being sunk by obeying the order.

Formerly, when a vessel was challenged at this fort, one, two or three shots, if necessary to bring her to, were fired, at a cost to the ship, if she were not American, of fifteen shillings for the first shot, thirty for the second, and sixty for the the third; but, for American ships, the sixty shilling shot was fired first—Americans would always have the best!

After all the difficulties were cleared away, the tardy telegram received, and being again identified by the officers, we weighed anchor for the last time on this voyage, and went into our destined port, the spacious and charming harbor of Rio.

V

The cargo was at last delivered, and no one made ill over it. A change of rats also was made; at Rio those we brought in gave place to others from the Dom Pedro Docks were we moored. Fleas, too, skipped about in the hay as happy as larks, and nearly as big; and all the other live stock that we brought from Rosario—goodness knows of what kind and kith, arrived well and sound from over the water, notwithstanding the fumigations and fuss made at the quarantine.

Had the little microbes been with us indeed, the Brazilians would not have turned us away as they did, from the doors of an hospital! for they are neither a cruel or cowardly people. To turn sickness away would be cruel and stupid, to say the least! What we were expelled for I have already explained.

After being so long in gloomy circumstances we felt like making the most of pleasant Rio! Therefore on the first fine day after being docked, we sallied out in quest of city adventure, and brought up first in Ouvidor—the Broadway of Rio, where my wife bought a tall hat, which I saw nights looming up like a dreadful stack of hay, the innocent cause of much trouble to me, and I declared, by all the great islands—in my dreams—that go back with it I would not, but would pitch it, first, into the sea.

I get nervous on the question of quarantines. I visit the famous Botanical Gardens with my family, and I tremble with fear lest we are fumigated at some station on the way. However, our time at

Rio is pleasantly spent in the main, and on the first day of June, we set sail once more for Paranagua and Antonina of pleasant recollections; partly laden with flour, kerosene, pitch, tar, rosin and wine, three pianos, I remember, and one steam engine and boiler, all as ballast; "freight free," so the bill of lading read, and further, that the ship should "not be responsible for leakage, breakage, or rust." This clause was well for the ship, as one of those wild *pampeiros* overtook her, on the voyage, throwing her violently on her beam-ends, and shaking the motley cargo into a confused and mixed-up mess. The vessel remaining tight, however, no very serious damage was done, and she righted herself after awhile, but without her lofty topgallant-masts, which went with a crash at the first blast of the tempest.

This incident made a profound impression on Garfield. He happened to be on deck when the masts were carried away, but managed to scamper off without getting hurt. Whenever a vessel hove in sight after that having a broken spar or a torn sail, it was "a *pampeiroed* ship."

The storm, though short, was excessively severe, and swept over Paranagua and Antonina with unusual violence. The owner of the pianos, I was told, prayed for us, and regretted that his goods were not insured. But when they were landed, not much the worse for their tossing about, old Strichine, the owner (that was his name or near that, strychnine the boys called him, because his singing was worse than "rough on rats," they said, a bit of juvenile wit that the artist very sensibly let pass unheeded), declared that the ship was a good one, and that her captain was a good pilot; and, as neither freight nor insurance had been paid, he and his wife would feast us on music; having learned that I especially was fond of it. They had screeched operas for a lifetime in Italy, but I didn't care for that. As arranged, therefore, I was on deck at the appointed time and place, to stay at all hazards.

The pianos, as I had fully expected, were fearfully out of tune—suffering, I should say, from the effects of seasickness!

So much so that I shall always believe this opportunity was seized upon by the artist to avenge the damage to his instruments, which, indeed, I could not avert, in the storm that we passed through. The good Strichine and his charming wife were astonished at the number of opera airs I could name. And they tried to persuade me to sing Il Trovatore; but concluding that damage enough had already been done, I refrained, that is, I refracted my song.

And all parties finally seemed satisfied and happy.

VI

July 23rd, 1887, brings me to a sudden and shocking point in the history of the voyage that I fain would forget, but that will not be possible. Between the hours of 11 and 12 P.M. of this day I was called instantly to defend my life and all that is dear to a man.

The bark, anchored alone in the harbor of Antonina, was hid from the town in the darkness of a night that might well have covered the blackest of tragedies. My pirates thought their opportunity had surely come to capture the Aquidneck, and this they undertook to do. The ringleader of the gang was a burly scoundrel, whose boast was that he had "licked" both the mate and second mate of the last vessel he had sailed in, and had "busted the captain in the jaw" when they landed in Rio, where the vessel was bound, and where, of course, the captain had discharged him. It was there the villain shipped with me, in lieu of one of the Rosario gang who had been kindly taken in charge by the guard at Ilha Grande and brought to Rio to be tried before the American Consul for insubordination. Said he, one day when I urged him to make haste and help save the topsails in a squall, "Oh, I'm no soft-horn to be hurried!" It was the time the bark lost her topgallant-mast and was cast on her beam-ends on the voyage to Antonina, already told; it was, in fact, no time for loafing, and this braggart at a decisive word hurried aloft with the rest to do his duty. What I said to him was meant for earnest, and it cowed him. It is only natural to think that he held a grudge against me forever after, and waited only for his opportunity; knowing, too, that I was the owner of the bark, and supposed to have money. He was heard to say in a rum-mill a day or two before the attack that he would find the money and his life, too. His chum and bosom friend had come pretty straight from Palermo penitentiary at Buenos Ayres when he shipped with me at Rosario.

It was no secret on board the bark that he had served two years for robbing, and cutting a ranchman's throat from ear to ear. These records, which each seemed to glory in, were verified in both cases.

I met the captain afterwards who had been "busted in the jaw"—Captain Roberts, of Baltimore, a quiet gentleman, with no evil in his heart for any one, and a man, like myself, well along in years.

Two of the gang, old Rosario hands, had served for the lesser offence of robbery alone—they brought up in the rear! The other two of my foremast hands—one a very respectable Hollander, the other a little Japanese sailor, a bright, young chap—had been robbed and beaten by the four ruffians, and then threatened so that they deserted to the forest instead of bringing a complaint of the matter to me, for fear, as the Jap expressed it afterwards, when there was no longer any danger,—for fear the "la-la-long mans (thieves) would makee killo mi!"

The ringleader bully, had made unusual efforts to create a row when I came on board early in the evening; however, as he had evidently been drinking, I passed it off as best I could for the natural consequence of rum, and ordered him forward; instead of doing as he was bid, when I turned to hand my wife to the cabin he followed me threateningly to the break of the poop. What struck me most, however, was the conduct of his chum, who was sober, but in a very unusual high, gleeful mood. It was knock-off time when I came along to where he was seizing off the mizzen topgallant backstay, the last of the work of refitting the late *pampeiro* damage; and the mate being elsewhere engaged, I gave the usual order to quit work. "Knock off," I said to the man, "and put away your tools. The bark's rigging looks well," I added, "and if to-morrow turns out fine, all will be finished;" whereupon the fellow laughed impertinently in my face, repeating my words, "All will be finished!" under his breath, adding, "before to-morrow!" This was the first insult offered by the "Bloodthirsty Tommy," who had committed murder only a short time before; but I had been watched by the fellow, with a cat-like eye at every turn.

The full significance of his words on this occasion came up to me only next morning, when I saw him lying on the deck with a murderous weapon in his hand! I was not expecting a cowardly, night attack, nevertheless I kept my gun loaded. I went to sleep this night as usual, forgetting the unpleasant episode as soon as my head touched the pillow; but my wife, with finer instincts, kept awake. It was well for us all that she did so. Near midnight, my wife, who had heard the first footstep on the poop-deck, quietly wakened me, saying, "We must get up, and look out for ourselves! Something is going wrong on deck; the boat tackle has been let go with a great deal of noise, and—O! don't go that way on deck. I heard some one on the cabin steps, and heard whispering in the forward entry."

"You must have been dreaming," I said.

"No, indeed!" said she; "I have not been asleep yet; don't go on deck by the forward companion-way; they are waiting there; I am sure, for I heard the creaking of the loose step in the entry."

If my wife has not been dreaming, thought I, there can be no possible doubt of a plot.

Nothing justifies a visit on the poop deck after working hours, except a call to relieve sickness, or for some other emergency, and then secrecy or stealth is non-permissible.

It may be here explained to persons not familiar with ships, that the sailors' quarters are in the forward part of the ship where they (the sailors) are supposed to be found after working hours, in port, coming never abaft the mainmast; hence the term "before the mast."

My first impulse was to step on deck in the usual way, but the earnest entreaties of my wife awoke me, like, to a danger that should be investigated with caution. Arming myself, therefore, with a stout carbine repeater, with eight ball cartridges in the magazine, I stepped on deck abaft instead of forward, where evidently I had been expected. I stood rubbing my eyes for a moment, inuring them to the intense darkness, when a coarse voice roared down the forward companion-way to me to come on deck. "Why don't ye come on deck like a man, and order yer men forid?" was the salute that I got, and was the first that I heard with my own ears, and it was enough. To tell the whole story in a word, I knew that I had to face a mutiny.

I could do no less than say: "Go forward there!"

"Yer there, are ye?" said the spokesman, as with an oath, he bounded toward me, cursing as he came.

Again I ordered him forward, saying, "I am armed,—if you come here I will shoot!" But I forbore to do so instantly, thinking to club him to the deck instead, for my carbine was a heavy one. I dealt him a blow as he came near, sufficient I thought, to fell an ox; but it had, apparently, no effect, and instantly he was inside of my guard. Then grasping me by the throat, he tried to force me over the taffrail, and cried, exultingly, as he felt me give way under his brute strength, "Now, you damn fool, shoot!" at the same time drawing his knife to strike.

I could not speak, or even breathe, but my carbine spoke for me, and the ruffian fell with the knife in his hand which had been raised against me! Resolution had proved more than a match for brute force, for I then knew that not only my own life but also the lives of others depended on me at this moment. Nothing daunted, the rest came on, like hungry wolves. Again I cried, "Go forward!" But thinking, maybe, that my rifle was a single shooter, or that I could not load it so quick, the order was disregarded.

"What if I don't go forward?" was "Bloody Tommy's" threatening question, adding, as he sprang toward me, "I've got this for you!" but fell instantly as he, raised his hand; and there on the deck, was ended, his misadventure! and like the other he fell with deadly knife in his hand. I was now all right. The dread of cold steel had left me when I freed myself from the first would-be assassin, and I only wondered how many more would persist in trying to take my life. But recollecting there were only two mutineers left, and that I had still six shots in the magazine of my rifle, and one already in the chamber, I stood ready with the hammer raised, and my finger on the trigger, confident that I would not be put down.

There was no further need of extreme measures, however, for order was now restored, though two of the assailants had skulked away in the dark.

How it was that I regained my advantage, after once losing it, I hardly know; but this I am certain of, that being down I was not to be spared. Then desperation took the place of fear, and I felt more than a match for all that could come against me. I had no other than serene feelings, however, and had no wish to pursue the two pirates that fled.

Immediately after the second shot was fired, and I found myself once more master of my bark, the remaining two came aft again, at my bidding this time, and in an orderly manner, it may be believed.

It is idle to say what I would or would not have given to have the calamity averted, or, in other words, to have had a crew of sailors, instead of a gang of cut-throats.

However, when the climax came, I had but one course to pursue, this I resolutely followed. A man will defend himself and his family to the last, for life is sweet, after all.

It was significant, the court thought afterwards, that while my son had not had time to dress, they all had on their boots except the one who fell last, and he was in his socks, with no boots on. It was he who had waited for me as I have already said, on the cabin steps that I usually passed up and down on, but this time avoided. Circumstantial evidence came up in abundance to make the case perfectly clear to the authorities. There are few who will care to hear more about a subject so abhorrent to all, and I care less to write about it. I would not have said this much, but for the enterprise of a rising department clerk, who, seeing the importance of telling to the world what he knew, and seeing also some small emolument in the matter, was, I believe prompted to augment the consular dispatches, thus obliging me to fight the battle over. However, not to be severe on the poor clerk, I will only add that no indignities were offered me by the authorities through all the strict investigation that followed the tragedy.

The trial being for justice and not for my money the case was soon finished.

I sincerely hope that I may never again encounter such as those who came from the jails to bring harm and sorrow in their wake.

The work of loading was finished soon after the calamity to my bark, and a Spanish sailing-master was engaged to take her to Montevideo; my son Victor going as flag captain.

I piloted the Aquidneck out of the harbor, and left her clear of the buoy, looking as neat and trim as sailor could wish to see. All the damage done by the late *pampeiro* had been repaired, new top-gallant masts rigged, and all made ataunto. I saw my handsome bark well clear of the dangers of the harbor limits, then in sorrow I left her and paddled back to the town, for I was on parole to appear, as I have said, for trial! That was the word; I can find no other name for it—let it stand!

VII

As soon as the case was over I posted on for Montevideo by steamer, where the bark had arrived only a few days ahead of me. I found her already stripped to a gantline though, preparatory to a long stay in port. I had given Victor strict orders to interfere in no way with the Spaniard, but to let him have full charge in nearly everything. I could have trusted the lad with full command, young as he was; but there was a strange crew of foreigners which might, as often happens, require maturer judgment to manage than to sail the vessel. As it proved, however, even the *cook* was in many ways a better man than the sailing-master.

Victor met me with a long face, and the sailors wore a quizzical look as I came over the vessel's side. One of them, in particular, whom I shall always remember, gave me a good-humored greeting, along with his shake of the head, that told volumes; and next day was aloft, crossing yards, cheerfully enough. I found my Brazilian crew to be excellent sailors, and things on board the Aquidneck immediately began to assume a brighter appearance, aloft and alow.

Cargo was soon discharged, other cargo taken in, and the bark made ready for sea. My crew, I say, was a good one; but, poor fellows, they were doomed to trials—the worst within human experience, many of them giving up to grim death before the voyage was ended. Too often one bit of bad luck follows another. This rule brought us in contact with one of these small officials at Montevideo, better adapted to home life; one of those knowing, perhaps, more than need a cow-boy, but not enough for consul. This official, managing to get word to my crew that a change of master dissolved their contract, induced them to come on shore and claim pay for the whole voyage and passage home on a steamer besides, the same as though the bark had been sold.

What overwhelming troubles may come of having incompetent officials in places of trust, the sequel will show. This unwise, even stupid interference, was the indirect cause of the sufferings and deaths among the crew which followed.

I was able to show the consul and his clerk that sailors are always engaged for the ship, and never for the master, and that a change of master did not in any way affect their contract. However, I paid the crew off, and then left it to their option to re-ship or not, for they were all right, they had been led to do what they did, and I knew that they wanted to get home, and it was there that the bark was going, direct.

All signed the articles again, except one, a long-haired Andalusian, whom I would not have longer at any price. The wages remained the same as before, and all hands returned to their duty cheerful and contented—but pending the consul's decision, (which, by the way, I decided for him) they had slept in a contagioned house, where, alas, they contracted small-pox of the worst type.

We were now homeward bound. All the "runaway rum" that could be held out by the most subtle crimps of Montevideo could not induce these sober Brazilian sailors to desert their ship.

These "crimps" are land-sharks who get the sailors drunk when they can, and then rob them of their advance money. The sailors are all paid in advance; sometimes they receive in this way most of their wages for the voyage, which they make after the money is spent, or wasted, or stolen.

We all know what working for dead horse means—sailors know too well its significance.

As sailing day drew near, a half-day liberty to each watch was asked for by the men, who wanted to make purchases for their friends and relatives at Paranagua. Permission to go on shore was readily granted, and I was rewarded by seeing every one return to his ship at the time promised, and every one sober. On the morrow, which was sailing day, every man was at his post and all sang "Cheerily, ho!" and were happy: all except one, who complained of slight chills and a fever, but said that he had been subject to this, and that with a dose of quinine he would soon be all right again.

It appeared a small matter. Two days later though, his chills turned to something which I knew less about. The next day, three more men went down with rigor in the spine, and at the base of the brain. I knew by this that small-pox was among us!

We bore up at once, for Maldonado, which was the nearest port, the place spoken of in "Gulliver's Travels," though Gulliver, I think, is mistaken as to its identity and location, arriving there before a gathering storm that blew wet and cold from the east. Our signals of distress, asking for immediate medical aid were set and flew thirty-six hours before any one came to us; then a scared Yahoo, the country was still inhabited by Yahoos, in a boat rowed by two other animals, came aboard, and said, "Yes, your men have got small-pox." *"Vechega,"* he called it, but I understood the lingo of the Yahoo very well, I could even speak a few words of it and comprehend the meanings. *"Vechega!"* he bellowed to his mates alongside, and, turning to me, he said, in Yahoo: "You must leave the port at once," then jumping into his boat he hurried away, along with his scared companions.

To leave a port in our condition was hard lines, but my perishing crew could get no succor at Maldonado, so we could do nothing but leave, if at all able to do so. We were indeed short-handed, but desperation lending a hand, the anchor was weighed and sufficient sail set on the bark to clear the inhospitable port. The wind blowing fair out of the harbor carried us away from the port toward Flores Island, for which we now headed in sore distress. A gale, long to be remembered, sprung suddenly up, stripping off our sails like autumn leaves, before the bark was three leagues from the place. We hadn't strength to clew up, so her sails were blown away, and she went flying before the mad tempest under bare poles. A snow-white sea-bird came for shelter from the storm, and poised on the deck to rest. The incident filled my sailors with awe; to them it was a portentous omen, and in distress they dragged themselves together and prostrate before the bird, prayed the Holy Virgin to ask God to keep them from harm. The rain beat on us in torrents, as the bark tossed and reeled ahead, and day turned black as night. The gale was from E. S. E., and our course lay W. N. W. nearly, or nearly before it. I stood at the wheel with my shore clothes on, I remember, for I hadn't yet had time to change them for waterproofs; this of itself was small matter, but it reminds me now that I was busy with other concerns. I was always a good helmsman, and I took in hand now, the steering of the bark in the storm—and I gave directions to Victor and the carpenter how to mix disinfectants for themselves, and medicines for the sick men. The medicine chest was fairly supplied.

Flores, when seen, was but a few ship's lengths away. Flashes of lightning revealed the low cliffs, amazingly near to us, and as the bark swept by with great speed, the roar of the breakers on the shore, heard above the din of the storm, told us of a danger to beware. The helm was then put down, and she came to under the lee of the island like a true, obedient thing.

Both anchors were let go, and all the chain paid out to both, to the bitter end, for the gale was now a hurricane. She walked away with her anchors for all that we could do, till, hooking a marine cable, one was carried away, and the other brought her head to the wind, and held her there trembling in the storm.

Anxious fear lest the second cable should break was on our minds through the night; but a greater danger was within the ship, that filled us all with alarm.

Two barks not far from us that night, with pilots on board, were lost, in trying to come through where the Aquidneck, without a pilot and with but three hands on deck to work her, came in. Their crews, with great difficulty, were rescued and then carried to Montevideo. When all had been done that we three could do, a light was put in the rigging, that flickered in the gale and went out. Then wet, and lame and weary, we fell down in our drenched clothes, to rest as we might—to sleep, or to listen to groans of our dying shipmates.

When daylight came (after this, the most dismal of all my nights at sea), our signals went up telling of the sad condition of the crew, and begging for medical assistance. Toward night the gale went down; but, as no boat came off, a gloom darker than midnight settled over the crew of the pest-ridden bark, and in dismay they again prayed to be spared to meet the loved ones awaiting them at home.

Our repeated signals, next day, brought the reply, "Stand in." *Carramba!* Why, we could hardly stand at all; much less could we get the bark underway, and beat in against wind and current. No one knew this better than they on the island, for my signals had told the whole story, and as we were only a mile and a half from the shore, the flags were distinctly made out. There was no doubt in our minds about that!

Late in the day, however, a barge came out to us, ill-manned and ill-managed by as scared a set of "galoots" as ever capsized a boat, or trembled at a shadow! The coxswain had more to say than the doctor, and the Yahoo—I forgot to mention that we were still in Yahoodom, but one would see that without this explanation—the Yahoo in the bow said more than both; and they all took a stiff pull from a bottle of *cachazza,* the doctor having had the start, I should say, of at least one or two pulls before leaving the shore, insomuch as he appeared braver than the crew.

The doctor, having taken an extra horn or two, with Dutch courage came on board, and brought with him a pound of sulphur, a pint of carbolic acid, and some barley—enough to feed a robin a few times, for all of which we were thankful indeed, our disinfectants being by this time nearly exhausted; then, glancing at the prostrate men, he hurried away, as the other had done at Maldonado. I asked what I should do with the dead through the night—bury them where we lay? "Oh, no, no!" cried the Yahoo in the bow; but the doctor pointed significantly to the water alongside! I knew what he meant!

That night we buried José, the sailor whose honest smile had welcomed me to my bark at Montevideo. I had ordered stones brought on deck, before dark, ostensibly to ballast the boat. I knew they would soon be wanted! About midnight, the cook called me in sore distress, saying that José was dying without confession!

So poor José was buried that night in the great river Platte! I listened to the solemn splash that told of one life ended, and its work done; but gloomy, and sad, and melancholy as the case was, I had to smile when the cook, not having well-secured the ballast, threw it over after his friend, exclaiming, "Good-bye, José, good-bye!" I added, "Good-bye, good shipmate, good-bye! I doubt not that you rest well!"

Next day, the signal from the shore was the same as the day before, "Stand in," in answer to my repeated call for help. By this time my men were demoralized and panic-stricken, and the poor fellows begged me, if the doctor would not try to cure them, to get a priest to confess them all. I saw a padre pacing the beach, and set flags asking him to come on board. No notice was taken of the signal, and we were now left entirely to ourselves.

After burying one more of the crew, we decided to remain no longer at this terrible place. An English telegraph tender passing, outward-bound, caught up our signals at that point, and kindly reported to her consul at Maldonado, who wired it to Montevideo.

The wind blowing away from the shore, as may it always blow when friend of mine nears that coast, we determined to weigh anchor or slip cable without further loss of time, feeling assured that by the telegraph reports some one would be on the look-out for us, and that the Aquidneck would be towed into port if the worst should happen—if the rest of her crew went down. Three of us weighed one anchor, with its ninety fathoms of chain, the other had parted on the windlass in the gale. The bark's prow was now turned toward Montevideo, the place we had so recently sailed from, full of hope and pleasant anticipation; and here we were, dejected and filled with misery, some of our number already gone on that voyage which somehow seems so far away.

At Montevideo, things were better. They *did* take my remaining sick men out of the vessel, after two days' delay; my agent procuring a tug, which towed them in the ship's boat three hundred fathoms astern. In this way they were taken to Flores Island, where, days and days before, they had been refused admittance! They were accompanied this time by an order from the governor of Montevideo, and at last were taken in. Two of the cases were, by this time, in the favorable change. But the poor old cook, who stood faithfully by me, and would not desert his old shipmates, going with them to the Island to care for them to the last, took the dread disease, died of it, and was there buried, not far from where he himself had buried his friend José, a short time before. The death of this faithful man occurred on the day that the bark finally sailed seaward, by the Island. She was in sight from the hospital window when his phantom ship, that put out, carried him over the bar! His widow, at Paranagua, I was told, on learning the fate of her husband, died of grief.

The work of disinfecting the vessel, at Montevideo, after the sick were removed, was a source of speculation that was most elaborately carried on. Demijohns of carbolic acid were put on board, by the dozen, at $3.00 per demijohn, all diluted ready for use; and a *guardo* was put on board to use it up, which he did religiously over his own precious self, in my after-cabin, as far from the end of the ship where the danger was as he could get. Some one else disinfected *el proa*, not he! Abundant as the stuff was, I had to look sharp for enough to wash out forward, while aft it was knee-deep almost, at three dollars a jar! The harpy that alighted on deck at Maldonado sent in his bill for one hundred dollars—I paid eighty.

The cost to me of all this trouble in money paid out, irrelevantly to mention, was over a thousand dollars. What it cost me in health and mental anxiety cannot be estimated by such value. Still, I was not the greatest sufferer. My hardest task was to come, you will believe, at the gathering up of the trinkets and other purchases which the crew had made, thoughtful of wife and child at home. All had to be burned, or spoiled with carbolic acid! A hat for the little boy here, a pair of boots for his mamma there, and many things for the *familia* all around—all had to be destroyed!

VIII

After all this sad trouble was over, a new crew was shipped, and the Aquidneck's prow again turned seaward. Passing out by Flores, soon after, we observed the coast-guard searching, I learned, for a supposed sunken bark, which had appeared between squalls in the late gale with signals of distress set. I was satisfied from the account that it was our bark which they had seen in the gale, and the supposed flags were our tattered sails, what there was left of them, streaming in the storm. But we did not discourage the search, as it could do no harm, and I thought that they might perhaps find something else worth knowing about. This was the day, as I have said, on which my faithful cook died, while the bark was in sight from the window of his sick ward. It was a bright, fine day to us. We cannot say that it was otherwise than bright to him.

Breathing once more the fresh air of the sea, we set all sail for Paranagua, passing the lights on the coast to leave them flickering on the horizon, then soon out of sight. Fine weather prevailed, but with much head wind; still we progressed, and rarely a day passed but something of the distance toward our port was gained. One day, however, coming to an island, one that was inhabited only by birds, we came to a stand, as if it were impossible to go further on the voyage; a spell seemed to hang over us. I recognized the place as one that I knew well; a very dear friend had stood by me on deck, looking at this island, some years before. It was the last land that my friend ever saw. I would fain have sailed around it now, but a puff of fair wind coming sent us on our course for the time some leagues beyond. At sunset, though, this wind went down, and with the current we drifted back so much that by the next day we were farther off on the other side. However, fair wind coming again, we passed up inside, making thus the circuit of the island at last.

More or less favorable winds thenceforth filled our sails, till at last our destined port was gained.

The little town of Antonina, where my wife and Garfield had remained over during this voyage, twelve miles up the bay from Paranagua, soon after our arrival, was made alive with the noise of children marching to children's own music, my "Yawcob" heading the band with a brand-new ninety-cent organ, the most envied fellow of the whole crowd. Sorrows of the past took flight, or were locked in the closet at home, the fittest place for past misfortunes.

A truly hard voyage for us all was that to Montevideo! The survivors reached home after a while. Their features were terribly marked and disfigured; so much so that I did not know them till they accosted me when we met.

I look back with pleasure to the good character of my Brazilian sailors, regretting the more their hard luck and sad fate! We may meet again! *Quiem sabe!*

Getting over all this sad business as best we could, we entered on the next venture, which was to purchase and load a cargo of the famous Brazilian wood. The Aquidneck was shifted to an arm of the bay, where she was moored under the lee of a virgin forest, twenty minutes' canoe ride from the village of Guarakasava, where she soon began to load.

The timber of this country, generally very heavy, is nevertheless hauled by hand to the water, where, lashed to canoes, it is floated to the ship.

These canoes, formed sometimes from mammoth trees, skillfully shaped and dug out with care, are at once the carriage and *cariole* of the family to the *citio,* or the rice to mill. Roads are hardly known where the canoe is available; men, women and children are consequently alike, skilled in the art of canoeing to perfection, almost. There are no carriages to speak of in such places, even a saddle horse about the water-front is a *rara avis.* There was, indeed one horse at Guarakasava—the owner of it was very conspicuous.

The family canoe just spoken of, has the capacity, often, of several tons, is handsomely decorated with carvings along the topsides, and is painted, as the "Geordie" would say, "in none o' your gaudy colors, but in good plain red or blue"—sometimes, however, they are painted green.

The cost of these handsome canoes are, say, from $250 down in price and size, from the grand turnout to the one man craft which may be purchased for five mil reis ($2.50).

From the greatest to the smallest they are cared for, with almost an affectionate care, and are made to last many years.

One thing else which even the poorest Brazilian thinks much of is his affectionate wife who literally and figuratively is often in the same boat with her husband, pulling against the stream. Family ties are strong in Brazil and the sweet flower of friendship thrives in its sunny clime. The system of land and sea breezes prevail on the coast from Cape Frio to Saint Catherine with great regularity most of the year; the sail is therefore used to good advantage by the almost amphibious inhabitants along the coast who love the water and take to it like ducks and natural born sailors.

The wind falling light they propel their canoes by paddle or long pole with equal facility. The occupants standing, in the smaller ones, force them along at a great speed. The larger ones, when the wind does not serve, are pulled by banks of oars which are fastened to stout pegs in the gunwale with grummits, that fit loosely over the oars so as to allow them free play in the hand of the waterman.

Curling the water with fine, shapely prows as they dart over the smooth waters of the bays and rivers, these canoes present a picture of unrivalled skill and grace.

I find the following entry in my diary made near the close of transactions at Guarakasava which in the truthful word of an historian I am bound to record, if only to show my prevailing high opinion of the natives while I was among them:

"Guarakasava, Dec. 20th.

Heretofore I have doted on native Brazilian honesty as well as national seamanship and skill in canoes but my dream of a perfect paradise is now unsettled forever. I find, alas! that even here the fall of Adam is felt: Taking in some long poles to-day the negro tallyman persisted in counting twice the same pole. When the first end entered the port it was *"umo"* (one); when the last end disappeared into the ship he would sing out *"does"* (two).

I had no serious difficulty over the matter, but left Guarakasava with that hurt feeling which comes of being over persuaded that one and one make four.

We spent Christmas of 1887 at Guarakasava. The bark was loaded soon after, and when proceeding across the bay where currents and wind caught her foul, near a dangerous sand bar, she misstayed and went on the strand. The anchor was let go to club her. It wouldn't hold in the treacherous sands; so she dragged and stranded broadside on, where open to the sea, a strong swell came in that raked her fore and aft, for three days, the waves dashing over her groaning hull the while till at last her back was broke and—why not add "heart" as well! for she lay now undone. After twenty-five years of good service the Aquidneck here ended her days!

I had myself carried load on load, but alas! I could not carry a mountain; and was now at the end where my best skill and energy could not avail. What was to be done? What could be done? We had indeed the appearance of shipwrecked people, away, too, from home.

This was no time to weep, for the lives of all the crew were saved; neither was it a time to laugh, for our loss was great.

But the sea calmed down, and I sold the wreck, which floated off at the end of the storm. And after paying the crew their wages out of the proceeds had a moiety left for myself and family—a small sum.

Then I began to look about for the future, and for means of escape from exile. The crew (foreign) found shipping for Montevideo, where they had joined the Aquidneck, in lieu of the stricken Brazilian sailors. But for myself and family this outlet was hardly available, even if we had cared to go farther from home, which was the least of our thoughts; and there were no vessels coming our way.

IX

When all had been saved from the wreck that was worth saving, or that could be saved, we found ourselves still in the possession of some goods soon to become of great value to us, especially my compass and charts which, though much damaged, were yet serviceable and suggested practical usefulness; and the chronometer being found intact, my course was no longer undecided, my wife and sons agreeing with what I thought best.

The plan, in a word, was this: We could not beg our way, neither would we sit idle among the natives. We found that it would require more courage to remain in the far-off country than to return home in a boat, which then we concluded to build and for that purpose.

My son Victor, with much pride and sympathy, entered heartily into the plan, which promised a speedy return home. He bent his energies in a practical direction, working on the boat like an old builder.

Before entering on the project, however, all responsibilities were considered. Swift ocean currents around capes and coral reefs were taken into account; and above all else to be called dangerous we knew would be the fierce tropical storms which surely we would encounter.

But a boat should be built stout and strong, we all said, one in which we should not be afraid to trust our lives even in the storm.

And with the advantage of experience in ships and boats of various sizes and in many seas, I turned to the work of constructing, according to my judgment and means, a craft which would be best adapted to all weathers and all circumstances. My family with sympathetic strength pulling hard in the same direction.

Seaworthiness was to be the first and most prominent feature in our microscopic ship; next to this good quality she should sail well; at least before free winds, for we counted on favorable winds; and so they were experienced the greater part of the voyage that followed.

Long exposures and many and severe disappointments by this time, I found, had told on health and nerve, through long quarantines, expensive fumigations, and ruinous doctors' visits, which had swept my dollars into hands other than mine. However, with still a "shot in the locker," and with some feelings of our own in the matter of how we should get home, I say, we set to work with tools saved from the wreck—a meagre kit—and soon found ourselves in command of another ship, which I will describe the building of, also the dimensions and the model and rig, first naming the tools with which it was made.

To begin with, we had an axe, an adze and two saws, one 1/2 inch auger, one 6/8 and one 3/8 auger-bit; two large sail-needles, which we converted into nailing bits; one roper, that answered for a punch; and, most precious of all, a file that we found in an old sail-bag washed up on the beach. A square we readily made. Two splints of bamboo wood served as compasses. Charcoal, pounded as fine as flour and mixed in water, took the place of chalk for the line; the latter we had on hand. In cases where holes larger than the 6/8 bit were required, a piece of small jack-stay iron was heated, and with this we could burn a hole to any size required. So we had, after all, quite a kit to go on with. Clamps, such as are used by boat builders, we had not, but made substitutes from the crooked guava tree and from *massaranduba* wood.

Trees from the neighboring forest were felled when the timber from the wrecked cargo would not answer. Some of these woods that we sought for special purposes had queer sounding names, such as *arregebah, guanandee, batetenandinglastampai,* etc. This latter we did not use the saw upon at all, it being very hard, but hewed it with the axe, bearing in mind that we had but one file, whereas for the edged tools we had but to go down to a brook hard by to find stones in abundance suitable to sharpen them on.

The many hindrances encountered in the building of the boat will not be recounted here. Among the least was a jungle fever, from which we suffered considerably. But all that, and all other obstacles vanished at last, or became less, before a new energy which grew apace with the boat, and the building of the craft went rapidly forward. There was no short day system, but we rested on the Sabbath, or surveyed what we had done through the week, and made calculations of what and how to strike on the coming week.

The unskilled part of the labor, such as sawing the cedar planks, of which she was mostly made, was done by the natives, who saw in a rough fashion, always leaving much planing and straightening to be done, in order to adjust the timber to a suitable shape. The planks for the bottom were of iron wood, 1 1/4 × 10 inches. For the sides and top red cedar was used, each plank, with the exception of two, reaching the whole length of the boat. This arrangement of exceedingly heavy wood in the bottom, and the light on top, contributed much to the stability of the craft.

The iron wood was heavy as stone, while the cedar, being light and elastic, lent buoyancy and suppleness, all that we could wish for.

The fastenings we gathered up in various places, some from the bulwarks of the wreck, some from the hinges of doors and skylights, and some were made from the ship's metal sheathing, which the natives melted and cast into nails. Pure copper nails, also, were procured from the natives, some ten kilos, for which I paid in copper coins, at the rate of two *kilos* of coin for one *kilo* of nails. The same kind of coins, called *dumps,* cut into diamond-shaped pieces, with holes punched through them, entered into the fastenings as burrs for the nails. A number of small eyebolts from the spanker-boom of the wreck were turned to account for lashing bolts in the deck of the new vessel. The nails, when too long, were cut to the required length, taking care that the ends which were cut off should not be wasted, but remelted, along with the metal sheathing, into other nails.

Some carriage bolts, with nuts, which I found in the country, came in very handy; these I adjusted to the required length, when too long, by slipping on blocks of wood of the required thickness to take up the surplus length, putting the block, of course, on the inside, and counter-sinking the nut flush with the planks on the outside; then screwing from the inside outward, they were drawn together and there held as in a vise, the planks being put together "lap-streak" fashion, which without doubt is the strongest way to build a boat.

These screw-bolts, seventy in number, as well as the copper nails, cost us dearly, but wooden pegs, with which also she was fastened, cost only the labor of being made. The lashings, too, that we used here and there about the frame of the cabin, cost next to nothing, being made from the fibrous bark of trees, which could be had in abundance by the stripping of it off. So, taking it by and large, our materials were not expensive, the principal item being the timber, which cost about three cents per superficial foot, sawed or hewed. Rosewood, ironwood, cedar or mahogany, were all about the same price and very little in advance of common wood; so of course we selected always, the best, the labor of shaping being least, sometimes, where the best materials were used.

These various timbers and fastenings, put together as best we could shape and join them, made a craft sufficiently strong and seaworthy to withstand all the buffetings on the main upon which, in due course she was launched.

The hull being completed, by various other contrivances and makeshifts in which, sometimes, the "wooden blacksmith" was called in to assist, and the mother of invention also lending a hand, fixtures were made which served as well on the voyage as though made in a dockyard and at great cost.

My builders balked at nothing, and on the 13th day of May, the day on which the slaves of Brazil were set free, our craft was launched, and was named *Liberdade* (Liberty).

Her dimensions being—35 feet in length over all, 7 1/2 feet breadth of beam, and 3 feet depth of hold, who shall say that she was not large enough?

Her model I got from my recollections of Cape Ann dories and from a photo of a very elegant Japanese *sampan* which I had before me on the spot, so, as it might be expected, when finished, she resembled both types of vessel in some degree.

Her rig was the Chinese *sampan* style, which is, I consider, the most convenient boat rig in the whole world.

This was the boat, or canoe I prefer to call it, in which we purposed to sail for North America and home. Each one had been busy during the construction and past misfortunes had all been forgotten. Madam had made the sails—and very good sails they were, too!

Victor, the carpenter, ropemaker and general roustabout had performed his part. Our little man, Garfield, too, had found employment in holding the hammer to clinch the nails and giving much advice on the coming voyage. All were busy, I say, and no one had given a thought of what we were about to encounter from the port officials further up the coast; it was pretended by them that a passport could not be granted to so small a craft to go on so long a voyage as the contemplated one to North America.

Then fever returned to the writer, and the constructor of the little craft, and I was forced to go to bed, remaining there three days. Finally, it came to my mind that in part of a medicine chest, which had been saved from the wreck, was stored some *arsenicum,* I think it is called. Of this I took several doses (small ones at first, you may be sure), and the good effect of the deadly poison on the malaria in my system was soon felt trickling through my veins. Increasing the doses somewhat, I could perceive the beneficial effect hour by hour, and in a few days I had quite recovered from the malady. Absurd as it was to have the judgment of sailors set on by pollywog navigators, we had still to submit, the pollywogs being numerous.

About this time—as the astrologers say—a messenger came down from the *Alfandega* (Custom House), asking me to repair thither at midday on the morrow. This filled me with alarm. True, the messenger had delivered his message in the politest possible manner, but that signified nothing, since Brazilians are always polite. This thing, small as it seems now, came near sending me back to the fever.

What had I done?

I went up next day, after having nightmare badly all night, prepared to say that I wouldn't do it again! The kind administrator I found, upon presenting myself at his office, had no fault to charge me with; but had a good word, instead. "The little Liberdade," he observed, had attracted the notice of his people and his own curiosity, as being "a handsome and well-built craft." This and many other flattering expressions were vented, at which I affected surprise, but secretly said, "I think you are right, sir, and you have good taste, too, if you are a customs officer."

The drift of this flattery, to make a long story short, was to have me build a boat for the *Alfandega,* or, his government not allowing money to build new—pointing to one which certainly would require new keel, planks, ribs, stem and stern-post—"could I not repair one?"

To this proposition I begged time to consider. Flattering as the officer's words were, and backed by the offer of liberal pay, so long as the boat could be "repaired," I still had no mind to remain in the hot country, and risk getting the fever again. But there was the old hitch to be gotten over; namely, the passport, on which, we thought, depended our sailing.

However, to expedite matters, a fishing license was hit upon, and I wondered why I had not thought of that before, having been, once upon a time, a fisherman myself. Heading thence on a new diplomatic course, I commenced to fit ostensibly for a fishing voyage. To this end, a fishing net was made, which would be a good thing to have, any way. Then hooks and lines were rigged and a cable made. This cable, or rope, was formed from vines that grow very long on the sand-banks just above tide water, several of which twisted together make a very serviceable rope, then being light and elastic, it is especially adapted for a boat anchor rope, or for the storm drag. Ninety fathoms of this rope was made for us by the natives, for the sum of ten milreis ($5.00).

The anchor came of itself almost. I had made a wooden one from heavy sinking timber, but a stalwart ranchman coming along, one day, brought a boat anchor with him which, he said, had been used by his slaves as a pot-hook. "But now that they are free and away," said he, "I have no further use for the crooked thing." A sewing-machine, which had served to stitch the sails together, was coveted by him, and was of no further use to us; in exchange for this the prized anchor was readily secured, the owner of it leaving us some boot into the bargain. Things working thus in our favor, the wooden anchor was stowed away to be kept as a spare bower.

These arrangements completed, our craft took on the appearance of a fishing smack, and I began to feel somewhat in my old element, with no fear of the lack of ways and means when we should arrive on our own coast, where I knew of fishing banks. And a document which translated read: "A license to catch fish inside and outside of the bar," was readily granted by the port authorities.

"How far outside the bar may this carry us?" I asked.

"Queim sabe!" said the officer. (Literally translated, "Who knows?" but in Spanish or Portuguese used for, "Nobody knows, or I don't care.")

"Adieu, senor," said the polite official; "we will meet in heaven!"

This meant you can go since you insist upon it, but I must not officially know of it; and you will probably go to the bottom. In this he and many others were mistaken.

Having the necessary document now in our possession, we commenced to take in stores for the voyage, as follows: Sea-biscuits, 120 lbs.; flour, 25 lbs.; sugar, 30 lbs.; coffee, 9 lbs., which roasted black and pounded fine as wheaten flour, was equal to double the amount as prepared in North America, and afforded us a much more delicious cup.

Of tea we had 3 lbs.; pork, 20 lbs.; dried beef, 100 lbs.; *baccalao secca,* (dried codfish) 20 lbs.; 2 bottles of honey, 200 oranges, 6 bunches of bananas, 120 gallons of water; also a small basket of yams, and a dozen sticks of sugar-cane, by way of vegetables.

Our medicine chest contained Brazil nuts, pepper and cinnamon; no other medicines or condiments were required on the voyage, except table salt, which we also had.

One musket and a carbine—which had already stood us in good stead—together with ammunition and three cutlasses, were stowed away for last use, to be used, nevertheless, in case of necessity.

The light goods I stowed in the ends of the canoe, the heavier in the middle and along the bottom, thus economizing space and lending to the stability of the canoe. Over the top of the midship stores a floor was made, which, housed over by a tarpaulin roof reaching three feet above the deck of the canoe, gave us sitting space of four feet from the floor to roof, and twelve feet long amidships, supported by a frame of bamboo, made store-room and cabin. This arrangement of cabin in the centre gave my passengers a berth where the least motion would be felt; even this is saying but little, for best we could do to avoid it we had still to accept much tossing from the waves.

Precautionary measures were taken in everything, so far as our resources and skill could reach. The springy and buoyant bamboo was used wherever stick of any kind was required, such as the frame and braces for the cabin, yards for the sails, and, finally, for guard on her top sides, making the canoe altogether a self-righting one, in case of a capsize. Each joint in the bamboo was an air-chamber of several pounds buoyant capacity, and we had a thousand joints.

The most important of our stores, particularly the flour, bread and coffee, were hermetically sealed, so that if actually turned over at sea, our craft would not only right herself, but would bring her stores right side up, in good order, and it then would be only a question of baling her out, and of setting her again on her course, when we would come on as right as ever. As it turned out, however, no such trial or mishap awaited us.

While the possibility of many and strange occurrences was felt by all of us, the danger which loomed most in little Garfield's mind was that of the sharks.

A fine specimen was captured on the voyage, showing five rows of pearly teeth, as sharp as lances.

Some of these monsters, it is said, have nine rows of teeth; that they are always hungry is admitted by sailors of great experience.

How it is that sailors can go in bathing, as they often do, in the face of a danger so terrible, is past my comprehension. Their business is to face danger, to be sure, but this is a needless exposure, for which the penalty is sometimes a life. The second mate of a bark on the coast of Cuba, not long ago, was bitten in twain, and the portions swallowed whole by a monster shark that he had tempted in this way. The shark was captured soon after, and the poor fellow's remains taken out of the revolting maw.

Leaving the sharks where they are, I gladly return to the voyage of the Liberdade.

X

The efficiency of our canoe was soon discovered, for on the 24th of June, after having sailed about the bay some few days to temper our feelings to the new craft, and shake things into place, we crossed the bar and stood out to sea, while six vessels lay inside "bar-bound," that is to say by their pilots it was thought too rough to venture out, and they, the pilots, stood on the point as we put out to sea, crossing themselves in our behalf, and shouting that the bar was *crudo*. But the *Liberdade* stood on her course, the crew never regretting it.

The wind from the sou'west at the time was the moderating side of a *pampeiro* which had brought in a heavy swell from the ocean, that broke and thundered on the bar with deafening roar and grand display of majestic effort.

But our little ship bounded through the breakers like a fish—as natural to the elements, and as free!

Of all the seas that broke furiously about her that day, often standing her on end, not one swept over or even boarded her, and she finally came through the storm of breakers in triumph. Then squaring away before the wind she spread her willing sails, and flew onward like a bird.

It required confidence and some courage to face the first storm in so small a bark, after having been years in large ships; but it would have required more courage than was possessed by any of us to turn back, since thoughts of home had taken hold on our minds.

Then, too, the old boating trick came back fresh to me, the love of the thing itself gaining on me as the little ship stood out; and my crew with one voice said: "Go on." The heavy south Atlantic swell rolling in upon the coast, as we sped along, toppled over when it reached the ten fathom line, and broke into roaring combers, which forbade our nearer approach to the land.

Evidently, our safest course was away from the shore, and out where the swelling seas, though grand, were regular, and raced under our little craft that danced like a mite on the ocean as she drove forward. In twenty-four hours from the time Paranagua bar was crossed we were up with Santos Heads, a run of 150 miles.

A squall of wind burst on us through a gulch, as we swept round the Heads, tearing our sails into shreds, and sending us into Santos under bare poles.

Chancing then upon an old friend, the mail steamship Finance, Capt. Baker, about to sail for Rio, the end of a friendly line was extended to us, and we were towed by the stout steamer toward Rio, the next day, as fast as we could wish to go. My wife and youngest sailor took passage on the steamer, while Victor remained in the canoe with me, and stood by, with axe in hand, to cut the tow-line, if the case should require it—and I steered.

"Look out," said Baker, as the steamer began to move ahead, "look out that I don't snake that canoe out from under you."

"Go on with your mails, Baker," was all I could say, "don't blow up your ship with my wife and son on board, and I will look out for the packet on the other end of the rope."

Baker opened her up to thirteen knots, but the *Liberdade* held on!

The line that we towed with was 1 1/3 inches in diameter, by ninety fathoms long. This, at times when the steamer surged over seas, leaving the canoe on the opposite side of a wave astern, would become as taut as a harp-string. At other times it would slacken and sink limp in a bight, under the forefoot, but only for a moment, however, when the steamer's next great plunge ahead would snap it taut again, pulling us along with a heavy, trembling jerk. Under the circumstances, straight steering was imperative, for a sheer to port or starboard would have finished the career of the *Liberdade*, by sending her under the sea. Therefore, the trick of twenty hours fell to me—the oldest and most experienced helmsman. But I was all right and not over-fatigued until Baker cast oil upon the "troubled waters." I soon got tired of that.

Victor was under the canvas covering, with the axe still in hand, ready to cut the line which was so arranged that he could reach it from within, and cut instantly, if by mischance the canoe should take a sheer.

I was afraid that the lad would become sleepy, and putting his head "under his wing" for a nap, would forget his post, but my frequent cry, "Stand by there, Victor," found him always on hand, though complaining some of the dizzy motion.

Heavy sprays dashed over me at the helm, which, however, seeming to wash away the sulphur and brimstone smoke of many a quarantine, brought enjoyment to my mind.

Confused waves rose about us, high and dangerous—often high above the gunwale of the canoe—but her shapely curves balanced her well, and she rode over them all in safety.

This canoe ride was thrilling and satisfactory to us all. It proved beyond a doubt that we had in this little craft a most extraordinary sea-boat, for the tow was a thorough test of her seaworthiness.

The captain of the steamer ordered oil cast over from time to time, relieving us of much spray and sloppy motion, but adding to discomforts of taste to me at the helm, for much of the oil blew over me and in my face. Said the captain to one of his mates (an old whaler by the way, and whalers for some unaccountable reason have never too much regard for a poor merchantman) "Mr. Smith."

"Aye, aye, sir," answered old Smith.

"Mr. Smith, hoist out that oil."

"Aye, aye, sir," said the old "blubberhunter," in high glee, as he went about it with alacrity, and in less than five minutes from the time the order was given, I was smothering in grease and our boat was oiled from keel to truck.

"She's all right now," said Smith.

"That's all right," said Baker, but I thought it all wrong. The wind, meanwhile, was in our teeth and before we crossed Rio Bar I had swallowed enough oil to cure any amount of consumption.

Baker, I have heard, said he wouldn't care much if he should "drown Slocum." But I was all right so long as the canoe didn't sheer, and we arrived at Rio safe and sound after the most exciting boat-ride of my life. I was bound not to cut the line that towed us so well; and I knew that Baker wouldn't let it go, for it was his rope.

I found at Rio that my fishing license could be exchanged for a pass of greater import. This document had to be procured through the office of the Minister of Marine.

Many a smart linguist was ready to use his influence in my behalf with the above-named high official; but I found at the end of a month that I was making headway about as fast as a Dutch galliot in a head sea after the wind had subsided. Our worthy Consul, General H. Clay Armstrong, gave me a hint of what the difficulty was and how to obviate it. I then went about the business myself as I should have done at first, and I found those at the various departments who were willing to help me without the intervention of outside "influence."

Commander Marquis of the Brazilian navy, recommended me to His Excellency, the Minister of Marine, "out of regard," he said, "for American seamen," and when the new document came it was *"Passe Especial,"* and had on it *a seal as big as a soup plate.* A port naval officer then presented me to the good *Administradore,* who also gave me a *passe especial,* with the seal of the *Alfandega.*

I had now only to procure a bill of health, when I should have papers enough for a man o' war. Rio being considered a healthy place, this was readily granted, making our equipment complete.

I met here our minister whose office, with other duties, is to keep a weather eye lifting in the interest of that orphan, the American ship—alas, my poor relation! Said he, "Captain, if your *Liberdade* be as good as your papers" (documents given me by the Brazilian officials), "you may get there all right;" adding, "well, if the boat ever reaches home she will be a great curiosity," the meaning of which, I could readily infer, was, "and your chances for a snap in a dime museum* will be good." This, after many years of experience as an American shipmaster, and also ship owner, in a moderate way, was interesting encouragement. By our Brazilian friends, however, the voyage was looked upon as a success already achieved.

"The utmost confidence," said the *Journal Opiz*, of Rio, "is placed in the cool-headed, audacious American mariner, and we expect in a short time to hear proclaimed in all of the journals of the Old and New World the safe arrival of this wonderful little craft at her destination, ourselves taking part in the glory." "Temos confianca na pericia e sangue frio do audaciauso marinhero Americano por isso esperamos que dentro em pouco tempo veremos o seu nome proclamado por todos os jornaes do velho e novo mundo.

"A nos tambem cabera parte da gloria."

With these and like kind expressions from all of our *friends,* we took leave of Rio, sailing on the morning of July 23rd, 1888.

XI

July 23rd, 1888, was the day, as I have said, on which we sailed from Rio de Janeiro.

Meeting with head winds and light withal, through the day we made but little progress; and finally, when night came on we anchored twenty miles east of Rio Heads, near the shore. Long, rolling seas rocked us as they raced by, then, dashing their great bodies against defying rocks, made

---

*A place charging ten cents admission to an exhibit of freaks, monstrosities, hoaxes etc. W.T.

music by which we slept that night. But a trouble unthought of before came up in Garfield's mind before going to his bunk; "Mamma," cried he as our little bark rose and fell on the heavy waves, tumbling the young sailor about from side to side in the small quarters while he knelt seriously at his evening devotion, "mamma, this boat isn't big enough to pray in!" But this difficulty was gotten over in time, and Garfield learned to watch as well as to pray on the voyage, and full of faith that all would be well, laid him down nights and slept as restfully as any Christian on sea or land.

By daylight of the second day we were again underway, beating to the eastward against the old head wind and head sea. On the following night we kept her at it, and the next day made Cape Frio where we anchored near the entrance to a good harbor.

Time from Rio, two days; distance, 70 miles.

The wind and tide being adverse, compelled us to wait outside for a favorable change. While comfortably anchored at this place, a huge whale, nosing about, came up under the canoe, giving us a toss and a great scare. We were at dinner when it happened. The meal, it is needless to say, was finished without dessert. The great sea animal—fifty to sixty feet long—circling around our small craft, looked terribly big. He was so close to me twice, as he swam round and round the canoe, that I could have touched him either time with a paddle. His flukes stirring the water like a steamer propeller appeared alarmingly close and powerful!—and what an ugly mouth the monster had! Well, we expected instant annihilation. The fate of the stout whale-ship Essex* came vividly before me. The voyage of the *Liberdade*, I thought, was about ended, and I looked about for pieces of bamboo on which to land my wife and family. Just then, however, to the infinite relief of all of us, the leviathan moved off, without doing us much harm, having felt satisfied, perhaps, that we had no Jonah on board.

We lost an anchor through the incident, and received some small damage to the keel, but no other injury was done—even this, I believe, upon second thought, was unintentional—done in playfulness only! "A shark can take a joke," it is said, and crack one too, but for broad, rippling humor the whale has no equal.

"If this be a sample of our adventures in the beginning," thought I, "we shall have enough and to spare by the end of the voyage." A visit from this quarter had not been counted on; but Sancho Panza says, "when least aware starts the hare," which in our case, by the by, was a great whale!

When our breath came back and the hair on our heads settled to a normal level, we set sail, and dodged about under the lee of the cape till a cove, with a very enticing sand beach at the head of it, opened before us, some three miles northwest of where we lost the anchor in the remarkable

---

*The *Essex* was stove and sunk by a large sperm whale. W. T.

adventure with the whale. The "spare bower" was soon bent to the cable. Then we stood in and anchored near a cliff, over which was a goat-path leading in the direction of a small fishing village, about a mile away. Sheering the boat in to the rocky side of the cove which was steep to, we leaped out, warp in hand, and made fast to a boulder above the tidal flow, then, scrambling over the cliff, we repaired to the village, first improvising a spare anchor from three sticks and a stone which answered the purpose quite well.

Judging at once that we were strangers the villagers came out to meet us, and made a stir at home to entertain us in the most hospitable manner, after the custom of the country, and with the villagers was a gentleman from Canada, a Mr. Newkirk, who, as we learned, was engaged, when the sea was smooth, in recovering treasure that was lost near the cape in the British war ship Thetis, which was wrecked there, in 1830. The treasure, some millions in silver coins and gold in bars, from Peru for England, was dumped in the cove, which has since taken the name of the ship that bore it there, and as I have said, came to grief in that place which is on the west shore near the end of the cape.

Some of the coins were given to us to be treasured as souvenirs of the pleasant visit. We found in Mr. Newkirk a versatile, roving genius; he had been a schoolmaster at home, captain of a lake schooner once, had practiced medicine, and preached some, I think; and what else I do not know. He had tried many things for a living, but, like the proverbial moving stone had failed to accumulate. "Matters," said the Canadian, "were getting worse and worse even, till finally to keep my head above water I was forced to go under the the sea," and he had struck it rich, it would seem, if gold being brought in by the boat-load was any sign. This man of many adventures still spoke like a youngster; no one had told him that he was growing old. He talked of going home, as soon as the balance of the treasure was secured, "just to see his dear old mother," who, by the way, was seventy-four years old when he left home, some twenty years before. Since his last news from home, nearly two decades had gone by. He was "the youngest of a family of eighteen children, all living," he said, "though," added he, "our family came near being made one less yesterday, by a whale which I thought would eat my boat, diving-bell, crew, money and all, as he came toward us, with open mouth. By a back stroke of the oars, however, we managed to cheat him out of his dinner, if that was what he was after, and I think it was, but here I am!" he cried, "all right!" and might have added, "wealthy after all."

After hearing the diver's story, I related in Portuguese our own adventure of the same day, and probably with the same whale, the monster having gone in the direction of the diver's boat. The astonishment of the listeners was great; but when they learned of our intended voyage to *America do Norte*, they crossed themselves and asked God to lend us grace!

"Is North America near New York?" asked the village merchant, who owned all the boats and nets of the place.

"Why, America is *in* New York," answered the ex-schoolmaster.

"I thought so," said the self-satisfied merchant. And no doubt he thought some of us very stupid, or rude, or both, but in spite of manners I had to smile at the assuring air of the Canadian.

"Why did you not answer him correctly?" I asked of the ex-schoolmaster.

"I answered him," said Newkirk, "according to his folly. Had I corrected his rusty geography before these simple, impoverished fishermen, he would not soon forgive me; and as for the rest of the poor souls here, the knowledge would do them but little good."

I may mention that in this out-of-the-way place there were no schools, and except the little knowledge gained in their church, from the catechism, and from the fumbling of beads, they were the most innocent of this world's scheme, of any people I ever met. But they seemed to know all about heaven, and were, no doubt, happy.

After the brief, friendly chat that we had, coffee was passed around, the probabilities of the *Liberdade's* voyage discussed, and the crew cautioned against the dangers of the *balaena* (whale), which were numerous along the coast, and vicious at that season of the year, having their young to protect.

I realized very often the startling sensation alone of a night at the helm, of having a painful stillness broken by these leviathans bursting the surface of the water with a noise like the roar of a great sea, uncomfortably near, reminding me of the Cape Frio adventure; and my crew, I am sure, were not less sensitive to the same feeling of an awful danger, however imaginary. One night in particular, dark and foggy I remember, Victor called me excitedly, saying that something dreadful ahead and drawing rapidly near had frightened him.

It proved to be a whale, for some reason that I could only guess at, threshing the sea with its huge body, and surging about in all directions, so that it puzzled me to know which way to steer to go clear. I thought at first, from the rumpus made that a fight was going on, such as we had once witnessed from the deck of the Aquidneck, not far from this place. Our course was changed as soon as we could decide which way to avoid, if possible, all marine disturbers of the peace. We wished especially to keep away from infuriated swordfish, which I feared might be darting about, and be apt to give us a blind thrust. Knowing that they sometimes pierce stout ships through with their formidable weapons, I began to feel ticklish about the ribs myself, I confess, and the little watch below, too, got uneasy and sleepless; for one of these swords, they knew well, would reach through and through our little boat, from keel to deck. Large ships, have occasionally been sent into port leaky from the stab of a sword, but what I most dreaded was the possibility of one of us being ourselves pinned in the boat.

A swordfish once pierced a whale-ship through the planking, and through the solid frame timber and the thick ceiling, with his sword, leaving it there, a valuable plug indeed, with the point, it was found upon unshipping her cargo at New Bedford, even piercing through a cask in the hold.

XII

July 30th, early in the day, and after a pleasant visit at the cape, we sailed for the north, securing first a few sea shells to be cherished, with the Thetis relics, in remembrance of a most enjoyable visit to the hospitable shores of Cape Frio.

Having now doubled Cape Frio, a prominent point in our voyage, and having had the seaworthiness of our little ship thoroughly tested, as already told; and seeing, moreover, that we had nothing to fear from common small fry of the sea, (one of its greatest monsters having failed to capsize us), we stood on with greater confidence than ever, but watchful, nevertheless, for any strange event that might happen.

A fresh polar wind hurried us on, under shortened sail, toward the softer "trades" of the tropics, but, veering to the eastward by midnight, it brought us well in with the land. Then, "Larboard watch, ahoy! all hands on deck and turn out reefs," was the cry. To weather Cape St. Thome we must lug on all sail. And we go over the shoals with a boiling sea and current in our favor. In twenty-four hours from Cape Frio, we had lowered the Southern Cross three degrees—180 miles.

Sweeping by the cape, the canoe sometimes standing on end, and sometimes buried in the deep hollow of the sea, we sunk the light on St. Thome soon out of sight, and stood on with flowing sheet. The wind on the following day settled into regular south-east "trades," and our cedar canoe skipped briskly along, over friendly seas that were leaping toward home, doffing their crests onward and forward, but never back, and the splashing waves against her sides, then rippling along the thin cedar planks between the crew, and eternity, vibrated enchanting music to the ear, while confidence grew in the bark that was HOMEWARD BOUND.

But coming upon coral reefs, of a dark night, while we listened to the dismal tune of the seas breaking over them with an eternal roar, how intensely lonesome they were! no sign of any living thing in sight, except, perhaps, the phosphorescent streaks of a hungry shark, which told of bad company in our wake, and made the gloom of the place more dismal still.

One night we made shelter under the lee of the extensive reefs called the Paredes (walls), without seeing the breakers at all in the dark, although they were not far in the distance. At another time, dragging on sail to clear a lee shore, of a dark and stormy night, we came suddenly into smooth water, where we cast anchor and furled our sails, lying in a magic harbor till daylight the next morning, when we found ourselves among a maze of high reefs, with high seas breaking over them, as far as the eye could reach, on all sides, except at the small entrance to the place that we had stumbled into in the night. The position of this future harbor is South Lat. 16° 48', and West Long, from Greenwich 39° 30'. We named the place "PORT LIBERDADE."

The next places sighted were the treacherous Abrohles, and the village of Caravellas back of the reef where upon refitting, I found that a chicken cost a thousand reis, a bunch of bananas, four hundred reis; but where a dozen limes cost only twenty reis—one cent. Much whaling gear lay strewn about the place, and on the beach was the carcass of a whale about nine days slain. Also leaning against a smart-looking boat was a gray-haired fisherman, boat and man relics of New Bedford, employed at this station in their familiar industry. The old man was bare-footed and thinly clad, after the custom in this climate. Still, I recognized the fisherman and sailor in the set and rig of the few duds he had on, and the ample straw hat (donkey's breakfast) that he wore, and doffed in a seaman-like manner, upon our first salute. *"Filio do Mar do Nord Americano,"* said an affable native close by, pointing at the same time to that "son of the sea of North America," by way of introduction, as soon as it was learned that we, too, were of that country. I tried to learn from this ancient mariner the cause of his being stranded in this strange land. He may have been cast up there by the whale for aught I could learn to the contrary.

Choosing a berth well to windward of the dead whale—the one that landed "the old man of the sea" there, maybe!—we anchored for the night, put a light in the rigging and turned in. Next morning, the village was astir betimes; canoes were being put afloat, and the rattle of poles, paddles, bait boxes, and many more things for the daily trip that were being hastily put into each canoe, echoed back from the tall palm groves notes of busy life, telling us that it was time to weigh anchor and be sailing. To this cheerful tune we lent ear and hastening to be underweigh, were soon clear of the port. Then, skimming along near the beach in the early morning, our sails spread to a land breeze, laden with fragrance from the tropic forest and the music of many songsters, we sailed in great felicity, dreading no dangers from the sea, for there were none now to dread or fear.

Proceeding forward through this belt of moderate winds, fanned by alternating land and sea-breezes, we drew on toward a region of high trade winds that reach sometimes the dignity of a gale. It was no surprise, therefore, after days of fine-weather sailing, to be met by a storm, which so happened as to drive us into the indifferent anchorage of St. Paulo, thirty miles from Bahia, where we remained two days for shelter.

Time, three days from Caravellas; distance sailed, 270 miles.

A few fishermen lounged about the place, living, apparently, in wretched poverty, spending their time between waiting for the tide to go out, when it was in, and waiting for it to come in when it was out, to float a canoe or bring fish to their shiftless nets. This, indeed, seemed their only concern in life; while their ill-thatched houses, forsaken of the adobe that once clung to the wicker walls, stood grinning in rows, like emblems of our mortality.

We found at this St. Paulo anything but saints. The wretched place should be avoided by strangers, unless driven there for shelter, as we ourselves were, by stress of weather. We left the place on the first lull of the wind, having been threatened by an attack from a gang of rough, half-drunken fellows, who rudely came on board, jostling about, and jabbering in a dialect which, however, I happened to understand. I got rid of them by the use of my broken Portuguese, and once away I was resolved that they should stay away. I was not mistaken in my suspicions that they would return and try to come aboard, which shortly afterward they did, but my resolution to keep them off was not shaken. I let them know, in their own jargon this time, that I was well armed. They finally paddled back to the shore, and all visiting was then ended. We stood a good watch that night, and by daylight next morning, Aug. 12th, put to sea, standing out in a heavy swell, the character of which I knew better, and could trust to more confidently than a harbor among treacherous natives.

Early in the same day, we arrived at *Bahia do todos Santos* (All Saints' Bay), a charming port, with a rich surrounding country. It was from this port, by the way, that Robinson Crusoe sailed for Africa to procure slaves for his plantation, and that of his friend, so fiction relates.

At Bahia we met many friends and gentle folk. Not the least interesting at this port are the negro lasses of fine physique seen at the markets and in the streets, with burdens on their heads of baskets of fruit, or jars of water, which they balance with ease and grace, as they go sweeping by with that stately mien which the dusky maiden can call her own.

XIII

At Bahia we refitted, with many necessary provisions, and repaired the keel, which was found upon hauling out, had been damaged by the encounter with the whale at Frio. An iron shoe was now added for the benefit of all marine monsters wishing to scratch their backs on our canoe.

Among the many friends whom we met at Bahia was Capt. Boyd and his family of the Barque H. W. Palmer. We shall meet the Palmer and the Boyds again on the voyage. They were old traders to South America and had many friends at this port who combined to make our visit a pleasant one. And their little son Rupert was greatly taken with the "*Riber*dade," as he called her, coming often to see us. And the officials of the port taking great interest in our voyage, came often on board. No one could have treated us more kindly than they.

The venerable *Administradore* himself gave us special welcome to the port and a kind word upon our departure, accompanied by a present for my wife in the shape of a rare white flower, which we cherished greatly as coming from a true gentleman.

Some strong abolitionists at the port would have us dine in an epicurean way in commemoration of the name given our canoe, which was adopted because of her having been put afloat on the thirteenth day of May, the day on which every human being in Brazil could say, "I have no master but one." I declined the banquet tendered us, having work on hand, fortifying the canoe against the ravaging worms of the seas we were yet to sail through, bearing in mind the straits of of my great predecessor from this as well as other causes on his voyage over the Caribbean Seas. I was bound to be strengthened against the enemy.

The gout, it will be remembered, seized upon the good Columbus while his ship had worms, then both ship and admiral lay stranded among menacing savages; surrounded, too, by a lawless, threatening band of his own countrymen not less treacherous than the worst of cannibals. His state was critical, indeed! One calamity was from over high living—this I was bound to guard against—the other was from neglect on the part of his people to care for the ship in a seamanlike manner. Of the latter difficulty I had no risk to run.

Lazy and lawless, but through the pretext of religion the infected crew wrought on the pious feelings of the good Admiral, inducing him at every landing to hold mass instead of cleaning the foul ship. Thus through petty intrigue and grave neglects, they brought disaster and sorrow on their leader and confusion on their own heads. Their religion, never deep, could not be expected to keep *Terredo* from the ship's bottom, so her timbers were ravished, and ruin came to them all! Poor Columbus! had he but sailed with his son Diego and his noble brother Bartholomew, for his only crew and companions, not forgetting the help of a good woman, America would have been discovered without those harrowing tales of woe and indeed heartrending calamities which followed in the wake of his designing people. Nor would his ship have been less well manned than was the *Liberdade*, sailing, centuries after, over the same sea and among many of the islands visited by the great discoverer—sailing too, without serious accident of any kind, and without sickness or discontent. Our advantage over Columbus, I say, was very great, not more from the possession of data of the centuries which had passed than from having a willing crew sailing without dissent or murmur—sailing in the same boat, as it were.

A pensive mood comes over one voyaging among the scenes of the New World's early playground. To us while on this canoe voyage of pleasant recollection the fancied experience of navigators gone before was intensely thrilling.

Sailing among islands clothed in eternal green, the same that Columbus beheld with marvelous anticipations, and the venerable Las Casas had looked upon with pious wonder, brought us, in the mind's eye, near the old discoverers; and a feeling that we should come suddenly upon their ships around some near headland took deep hold upon our thoughts as we drew in with the shores. All was there to please the imagination and dream over in the same balmy, sleepy atmosphere, where Juan Ponce de Leon would fain have tarried young, but found death rapid, working side by side with ever springing life. To live long in this clime one must obey great Nature's laws. So stout Juan and millions since have found, and so always it will be.

All was there to testify as of yore, all except the first owners of the land; they alas! the poor Caribbees, together with their camp fires, had been extinguished long years before. And no one of human sympathy can read of the cruel tortures and final extermination of these islanders, savages though they were, without a pang of regret at the unpleasant page in a history of glory and civilization.

XIV

From Bahia to Pernambuco our course lay along that part of the Brazilian coast fanned by constant trade winds. Nothing unusual occurred to disturb our peace or daily course, and we pressed forward night and day, as was our wont from the first.

Victor and I stood watch and watch at sea, usually four hours each.

The most difficult of our experiences in fine weather was the intense drowsiness brought on by constantly watching the oscillating compass at night; even in the daytime this motion would make one sleepy.

We soon found it necessary to arrange a code of signals which would communicate between the "wheel" and the "man forward." This was done by means of a line or messenger extending from one to the other, which was understood by the number of pulls given by it; three pulls, for instance, meant "Turn out," one in response, "Aye, aye, I am awake, and what is it that is wanted?" one pull in return signified that it was "Eight bells" and so on. But three quick jerks meant "Tumble out and shorten sail."

Victor, it was understood, would tie the line to his arm or leg when he turned in, so that by pulling I would be sure to arouse him, or bring him somewhat unceremoniously out of his bunk. Once, however, the messenger failed to accomplish its purpose. A boot came out on the line in answer to my call, so easily, too, that I suspected a trick. It was evidently a preconceived plan by which to gain a moment more of sleep. It was a clear imposition on the man at the wheel!

We had also a sign in this system of telegraphing that told of flying-fish on board—manna of the sea—to be gathered up for the *cuisine* whenever they happened to alight or fall on deck, which was often, and as often they found a warm welcome.

The watch was never called to make sail. As for myself, I had never to be called, having thoughts of the voyage and its safe completion on my mind to keep me always on the alert. I can truly say that I never, on the voyage, slept so sound as to forget where I was, but whenever I fell into a dose at all it would be to dream of the boat and the voyage.

Press on! press on! was the watchword while at sea, but in port we enjoyed ourselves and gave up care for rest and pleasure, carrying a supply, as it were, to sea with us, where sail was again carried on.

Though a mast should break, it would be no matter of serious concern, for we would be at no loss to mend and rig up spars for this craft at short notice, most anywhere.

The third day out from Bahia was set fine weather. A few flying-fish made fruitless attempts to rise from the surface of the sea, attracting but little attention from the sea-gulls which sat looking wistfully across the unbroken deep with folded wings.

And the *Liberdade* doing her utmost to get along through the common quiet, made but little progress on her way. A dainty fish played in her light wake, till tempted by an evil appetite for flies, it landed in the cockpit upon a hook, thence into the the pan, where many a one had brought up before. Breakfast was cleared away at an early hour; then day of good things happened—"the meeting of the ships."

"When o'er the silent sea alone
For days and nights we've cheerless gone,
Oh they who've felt it know how sweet,
Some sunny morn a sail to meet.

"Sparkling at once is every eye,
'Ship ahoy! ship ahoy!' our joyful cry
While answering back the sound we hear,
'Ship ahoy! ship ahoy! what cheer, what cheer.'

"Then sails are backed, we nearer come,
Kind words are said of friends and home,
And soon, too soon, we part with pain,
To sail o'er silent seas again."

On the clear horizon could be seen a ship, which proved to be our staunch old friend, the Finance, on her way out to Brazil, heading nearly for us. Our course was at once changed, so as to cross her bows. She rose rapidly, hull up, showing her lines of unmistakable beauty, the stars and stripes waving over all. They on board the great ship, soon descried our little boat, and gave sign by a deep whistle that came rumbling over the sea, telling us that we were recognized. A few moments later and the engines stopped. Then came the hearty hail, "Do you want assistance?" Our answer "No" brought cheer on cheer from the steamer's deck, while the *Liberdade* bowed and courtesied to her old acquaintance, the superior ship. Captain Baker, meanwhile, not forgetting a sailor's most highly prized luxury, had ordered in the slings a barrel of potatoes—new from home! Then dump they came, in a jiffy, into the canoe, giving her a settle in the water of some inches. This was a valuable addition to our stores. Some other fresh provisions were handed us, also some books and late papers.

In return for all of these goods we gave sincere thanks, about the only thing we could spare— above the shadow of the canoe—which was secured through a camera by the Rev. Doctor Hodge, the worthy missionary, then on his way to a field of labor in Brazil.

One gentleman passed us a bottle of wine, on the label of which was written the name of an old acquaintance, a merchant of Rio. We pledged Mr. Gudgeon and all his fellow passengers in that wine, and had some left long after, to the health of the captain of the ship, and his crew. There was but little time for words, so the compliments passed were brief. The ample plates in the sides of the *Finance*, inspiring confidence in American thoroughness and build, we had hardly time to scan, when her shrill whistle said "good-bye," and moving proudly on, the great ship was soon out of sight, while the little boat filling away on the starboard tack, sailed on toward home, perfumed with the interchange of a friendly greeting, tinged though, with a palpable lonesomeness. Two days after this pleasant meeting, the Port of Pernambuco was reached.

Tumbling in before a fresh "trade" wind that in the evening had sprung up, accompanied with long, rolling seas, our canoe came nicely round the point between lighted reef and painted buoy.

Spray from the breakers on the reef opportunely wetting her sails gave them a flat surface to the wind as we came close haul.

The channel leading up the harbor was not strange to us, so we sailed confidently along the lee of the wonderful wall made by worms, to which alone Pernambuco is indebted for its excellent harbor; which extending also along a great stretch of the coast, protects Brazil from the encroachment of the sea.

At 8 P.M., we came to in a snug berth near the *Alfandega*, and early next morning received the official visit from the polite port officers.

Time from Bahia, seven days; distance sailed, 390 miles.

Pernambuco, the principal town of a large and wealthy province of the same name, is a thriving place, sending out valuable cargoes, principally of sugar and cotton. I had loaded costly cargoes here, times gone by. I met my old merchant again this time, but could not carry his goods on the *Liberdade*. However, fruits from his orchards and a run among the trees refreshed my crew, and prepared them for the coming voyage to Barbadoes, which was made with expedition.

From Pernambuco we experienced a strong current in our favor, with, sometimes, a confused cross sea that washed over us considerably. But the swift current sweeping along through it all made compensation for discomforts of motion, though our "ups and downs" were many. Along this part of the coast (from Pernambuco to the Amazon), if one day should be fine, three stormy ones would follow, but the gale was always fair, carrying us forward at a goodly rate.

Along about half way from Cape St. Roque to the Amazon, the wind which had been blowing hard for two days, from E. S. E., and raising lively waves all about, increased to a gale that knocked up seas, washing over the little craft more than ever. The thing was becoming monotonous and tiresome; for a change, therefore, I ran in toward the land, so as to avoid the ugly cross sea farther out in the current. This course was a mistaken one; we had not sailed far on it when a sudden rise of the canoe, followed by an unusually long run down on the slope of a roller, told us of a danger that we hardly dared to think of, then a mighty comber broke, but, as Providence willed, broke short of the canoe, which under shortened sail was then scudding very fast.

We were on a shoal, and the sea was breaking from the bottom! The second great roller came on, towering up, up, up, until nothing longer could support the mountain of water, and it seemed only to pause before its fall to take aim and surely gather us up in its sweeping fury.

I put the helm a-lee; there was nothing else to do but this, and say prayers. The helm hard down, brought the canoe round, bows to the danger, while in breathless anxiety we prepared to meet the result as best we could. Before we could say "Save us, or we perish," the sea broke over with terrific force and passed on, leaving us trembling in His hand, more palpably helpless than ever before. Other great waves came madly on, leaping toward destruction; how they bellowed over the shoal! I could smell the slimy bottom of the sea, when they broke! I could taste the salty sand!

In this perilous situation, buried sometimes in the foam of breakers, and at times tossed like a reed on the crest of the waves, we struggled with might and main at the helm and the sheets, easing her up or forcing her ahead with care, gaining little by little toward deep water, till at last she came out of the danger, shook her feathers like a sea bird, and rode on waves less perilous. Then we had time and courage to look back, but not till then.

And what a sight we beheld! The horizon was illumined with phosphorescent light from the breakers just passed through. The rainstorm which had obscured the coast was so cleared away now that we could see the whole field of danger behind us. One spot in particular, the place where the breakers dashed over a rock which appeared awash, in the glare flashed up a shaft of light that reached to the heavens.

This was the greatest danger we had yet encountered. The elasticity of our canoe, not its bulk, saved it from destruction. Her light, springy timbers and buoyant bamboo guards brought her upright again and again through the fierce breakers. We were astonished at the feats of wonder of our brave little craft.

Fatigued and worn with anxiety, when clear of the shoal we hauled to under close reefs, heading off shore, and all hands lay down to rest till daylight. Then, squaring away again, we set what sail the canoe could carry, scudding before it, for the wind was still in our favor, though blowing very hard. Nevertheless the weather seemed fine and pleasant at this stage of our own pleased feelings. Any weather that one's craft can live in, after escaping a lee shore, is pleasant weather—though some may be pleasanter than other.

What we most wished for, after this thrilling experience, was sea room, fair wind, and plenty of it. That these without stint would suit us best, was agreed on all hands. Accordingly then I shaped the course seaward, clearing well all the dangers of the land.

The fierce tropical storm of the last few days turned gradually into mild trade winds, and our cedar canoe skipped nimbly once more over tranquil seas. Our own agitation, too, had gone down and we sailed on unruffled by care. Gentle winds carried us on over kindly waves, and we were fain to count fair days ahead, leaving all thoughts of stormy ones behind. In this hopeful mood we sailed for many days, our spirits never lowering, but often rising higher out of the miserable condition which we had fallen into through misfortunes on the foreign shore. When a star came out, it came as a friend, and one that had been seen by friends of old. When all the stars shone out, the hour at sea was cheerful, bright, and joyous. Welby saw, or had in the mind's-eye, a day like many that we experienced in the soft, clear "trades" on this voyage, when writing the pretty lines:—

> "The twilight hours like birds flew by,
> As lightly and as free,
> Ten thousand stars were in the sky,
> Ten thousand on the sea.
>
> "For every rippling, dancing wave,
> That leaped upon the air,
> Had caught a star in its embrace,
> And held it trembling there."

"The days pass, and our ship flies fast upon her way."

For several days while sailing near the line we saw the constellations of both hemispheres, but heading north, we left those of the south at last, with the Southern Cross—most beautiful in all the heavens—to watch over a friend.

Leaving these familiar southern stars and sailing towards constellations in the north, we hoist all sail to the cheery breeze that carried us on.

In this pleasant state of sailing with our friends all about us, we stood on and on, never doubting once our pilot or our ship.

A phantom of the stately Aquidneck appeared one night, sweeping by with crowning skysails set, that fairly brushed the stars. No apparition could have affected us more than the sight of this floating beauty, so like the Aquidneck, gliding swiftly and quietly by, from her mission to some foreign land—she, too, was homeward bound!

This incident of the Aquidneck's ghost, as it appeared to us, passing at midnight on the sea, left a pang of lonesomeness for a while.

But a carrier dove came next day, and perched upon the mast, as if to tell that we had yet a friend! Welcome harbinger of good! you bring us thoughts of angels.

The lovely visitor remained with us two days, off and on, but left for good on the third, when we reached away from Avis Island, to which, maybe, it was bound. Coming as it did from the east, and flying west toward the island when it left, bore out the idea of the lay of sweet singer Kingsley's "Last Buccaneer."

> "If I might but be a sea dove, I'd fly across the main
> To the pleasant Isle of Avis, to look at it once again."

The old Buccaneer, it may have been, but we regarded it as the little bird, which most likely it was, that sits up aloft to look out for poor "Jack."

A moth blown to our boat on the ocean, found shelter and a welcome there. The dove! we secretly worshipped.

With utmost confidence in our little craft, inspired by many thrilling events, we now carried sail, blow high, blow low, till at times she reeled along with a bone in her mouth quite to the mind of her mariners. Thinking one day that she might carry more sail on the mast already bending hopefully forward, and acting upon the liberal thought of sail we made a wide mistake, for the mainmast went by the board, under the extra press and the foremast tripped over the bows. Then spars, booms and sails swung alongside like the broken wings of a bird but were grappled, however, and brought aboard without much loss of time. The broken mast was then secured and strengthened by "fishes" or splints after the manner in which doctors fish a broken limb.

Both of the masts were very soon refitted and again made to carry sail, all they could stand; and we were again bowling along as before. We made that day a hundred and seventy-five miles, one of our best days' work.

I protest here that my wife should not have cried "More sail! more sail!" when, as it has been seen the canoe had on all the sail that she could carry. Nothing further happened to change the usual daily events until we reached Barbadoes. Flying-fish on the wing striking our sails, at night, often fell on deck, affording us many a toothsome fry. This happened daily, while sailing throughout the trade-wind regions. To be hit by one of these fish on the wing, which sometimes occurs, is no light matter, especially if the blow be on the face, as it may cause a bad bruise or even a black eye. The head of the flying-fish being rather hard makes it in fact a night slugger to be dreaded. They never come aboard in the daylight. The swift darting bill-fish, too, is a danger to be avoided in the tropics at night. They are met with mostly in the Pacific Ocean. And the South Sea Islanders are loath to voyage during the "bill-fish season."

As to the flight of these fishes, I would estimate that of the flying-fish as not exceeding fifteen feet in height, or five hundred yards of distance, often not half so much.

Bill-fish darting like an arrow from a bow, has, fortunately for sailors, not the power or do not rise much above the level of the waves, and can not dart further, say, than two hundred and fifty feet, according to the day for jumping. Of the many swift fish in the sea, the dolphin perhaps, is the most marvelous. Its oft told beauty, too, is indeed remarkable. A few of these fleet racers were captured, on the voyage, but were found tough and rank; notwithstanding some eulogy on them by other epicures, we threw the mess away. Those hooked by my crew were perhaps the tyrrhena pirates "turned into dolphins" in the days of yore.

On the 19th day from Pernambuco, early in the morning, we made Barbadoes away in the West. First, the blue, fertile hills, then green fields came into view, studded with many white buildings between sentries of giant wind-mills as old nearly, as the hills. Barbadoes is the most pleasant island in the Antilles; to sail round its green fringe of coral sea is simply charming. We stood in to the coast, well to windward, sailing close in with the breakers so as to take in a view of the whole delightful panorama as we sailed along. By noon we rounded the south point of the island and shot into Carlysle Bay, completing the run from Pernambuco exactly in nineteen days. This was considerably more than an hundred miles a day. The true distance being augmented by the circuitous route we adopted made it 2,150 miles.

XV

Many old friends and acquaintances came down to see us upon our arrival at Barbadoes, all curious to inspect the strange craft. While there our old friend, the Palmer, that we left, at Bahia, came in to refit, having broken a mast "trying to beat us" so Garfield would have it. For all that we had beaten her time four days. Who then shall say that we anchored nights or spent much time hugging the shore? The Condor was also at Barbadoes in charge of an old friend, accompanied by a pleasant helpmeet and companion who had shared the perils of shipwreck with her husband the year before in a hurricane among the islands.

Meeting so many of this class of old friends of vast and varied experiences, gave contentment to our visit and we concluded to remain over at this port till the hurricane season should pass. Our old friend, the Finance too, came in, remaining but a few hours, however, she hurried away with her mails, homeward bound.

The pleasant days at Barbadoes with its enchantment flew lightly by; and on the 7th of October we sailed, giving the hurricane the benefit of eight days. The season is considered over on the 15th of that month.

Passing thence through the Antilles into the Caribbean Sea, a new period of our voyage was begun. Fair breezes filled the sails of the *Liberdade* as we glided along over tranquil seas, scanning eagerly the islands as they came into view, dwelling on each, in our thoughts, as hallowed ground of the illustrious discoverers—the same now as seen by them! The birds, too, of "rare plumage," were there, flying from island to island, the same as seen by the discoverers; and the sea with fishes teemed, of every gorgeous hue, lending enchantment to the picture, not less beautiful than the splendor on the land and in the air to thrill the voyager now, the same as then; we ourselves had only to look to see them.

Whether it was birds with fins or fishes with wings, or neither of these that the old voyagers saw, they discovered yet enough to make them wonder and rejoice.

"Mountains of sugar, and rivers of rum and flying-fish, is what I have seen, mother," said the son on his return home from a voyage to these islands. "John," said the enraptured mother, "you must be mistaken about the fish; now don't lie to me, John. Mountains of sugar, no doubt you saw, and even rivers of rum, my boy, but *flying-fish* could never be."

And yet the *fish* were there.

Among the islands of great interest which came in view, stretching along the Caribbean Sea, was that of Santa Cruz, the island famous for its brave, resolute women of days gone by, who, while their husbands were away, successfully defended home and happiness against Christian invaders, and for that reason were called fierce savages. I would fain have brought away some of the earth of the island in memory of those brave women. Small as our ship was, we could have afforded room in it for a memento thus consecrated; but the trades hauling somewhat to the northward so headed us off that we had to forego the pleasure of landing on its shores.

Pushing forward thence, we reached Porto Rico, the nearest land in our course from the island of Brave Women, standing well in with the southeast capes. Sailing thence along the whole extent of the south coast, in waters as smooth as any mill pond, and past island scenery worth the perils of ten voyages to see, we landed, on the 12th of October, at Mayaguez in the west of the island, and there shook the kinks out of our bones by pleasant walks in tropic shades.

Time, five days from Barbadoes; distance 570 miles.

This was to be our last run among the trees in the West Indies, and we made the most of it. "Such a port for mariners I'll never see again!" The port officials, kind and polite, extended all becoming courtesies to the quaint *"barco piquina."*

The American Consul, Mr. Christie, Danish Consul, Mr. Falby, and the good French Consul, vied in making our visit a pleasant one.

Photographers at Mayaguez desiring a picture of the canoe with the crew on deck at a time when we felt inclined to rest in the shade on shore, put a negro on board to take the place of captain.

The photographs taken then found their way to Paris and Madrid journals where, along with some flattering accounts, they were published, upon which it was remarked that the captain was a fine-looking fellow, but "awfully tanned!" The moke was rigged all ataunto for the occasion, and made a picture indicative of great physical strength, one not to be ashamed of, but he would have looked more like me, I must say, if they had turned him back to.

We enjoyed long carriage drives over rich estates at Mayaguez. We saw with pain, however, that the atmosphere of the soldier hung over all, pervading the whole air like a pestilence.

Musketed and sabred, and uniformed in their bed-ticking suits; hated by the residents and despised by themselves, they doggedly marched, countermarched and wheeled, knowing that they are loathsome in the island, and that their days in the New World are numbered. The sons of the colonies are too civil and Christianlike to be ruled always by sword and gun.

On the 15th of October, after three days' rest, we took in, as usual before sailing from ports, sufficient fresh supplies to carry us to the port steered for next, then set sail from pleasant Mayaguez, and bore away for the old Bahama Channel, passing east of Hayti, thence along the north coast to the west extremity of the island, from which we took departure for the headlands of Cuba, and followed that coast as far as Cardinas, where we took a final departure from the islands, regretting that we could not sail around them all.

The region on the north side of Cuba is often visited by gales of great violence, making this the lee shore; a weather eye was therefore kept lifting, especially in the direction of their source, which is from north to nor'west. However storms prevailed from other quarters, mostly from the east, bringing heavy squalls of wind, rain and thunder every afternoon, such as once heard will never be forgotten. Peal on peal of nature's artillery for a few hours, accompanied by vivid lightning, was on the cards for each day, then all would be serene again.

The nights following these severe storms were always bright and pleasant, and the heavens would be studded with constellations of familiar, guiding stars.

My crew had now no wish to bear up for port short of one on our own coast, but, impatient to see the North Star appear higher in the heavens, strung every nerve and trimmed every sail to hasten on.

Nassau, the place to which letters had been directed to us we forbore to visit. This departure from a programme which was made at the begining was the only change that we made in the "charter party" throughout the voyage. There was no hap-hazard sailing on this voyage. Daily observations for determining latitude and longitude were invariably made unless the sun was obscured. The result of these astronomical observations were more reliable than one might suppose, from their being taken on a tittlish canoe. After a few days' practising, a very fair off-hand contact could be made, when the canoe rose on the crest of a wave, where manifestly would be found the best result. The observer's station was simply on the top of the cabin, where astride, like riding horseback, Victor and I took the "sights," and indeed became expert "snap observers" before the voyage ended.

One night in the Bahama Channel, while booming along toward the Banks to the nor'west of us before stiff trades, I was called in the first watch by Victor, to come up quickly, for signs of the dread "norther" were in the sky. Our trusty barometer had been low, but was now on the cheerful side of change. This phenomenon disturbed me somewhat, till the discovery was made, as we came nearer, that it was but the reflection of the white banks on the sky that we saw, and no cause at all for alarm.

Soon after this phenomenon the faint glimmer of Labos Light was descried flickering on the horizon, two points on the weather bow. I changed the course three points to windward, having determined to touch at the small Cay where the lighthouse stands; one point being allowed for leeway, which I found was not too much.

Three hours later we fetched in under the lee of the reef, or Cay, as it is commonly called, and came to in one and a half fathoms of water in good shelter.

We beheld then overhead in wonderful beauty what had awed us from the distance in the early night—a chart of the illuminating banks marked visibly on the heavens.

We furled sails and, setting a light in the rigging, turned in; for it lacked three hours yet of daylight. And what an interesting experience ours had been in the one short night! By the break of day my crew were again astir, preparing to land and fill water at a good landing which we now perceived farther around the point to leeward, where the surf was moderate.

On the Cay is stored some hundred thousand gallons of rain water in cisterns at the base of the iron tower which carries the light; one that we saw from the canoe at a distance of fourteen miles.

The keeper of the light, a hardy native of Nassau, when he discovered the new arrival at his "island," hoisted the British Board of Trade flag on a pole in the centre of this, his little world, then he came forward to speak us, thinking at first, he said, that we were shipwrecked sailors, which indeed we were, but not in distress, as he had supposed when hoisting the flag, which signified assistance for distressed seamen. On learning our story, however, he regarded us with grave suspicions, and refused water to Victor, who had already landed with buckets, telling him that the captain would have to bring his papers ashore and report. The mate's report would not be taken. Thus in a moment was transformed the friend in need to *governor of an island*. This amused me greatly, and I sent back word to my veritable Sancho Panza that in my many voyages to islands my mate had attended to the customs reports; at which his Excellency chafed considerably, giving the gunwales of his trousers a fitful tug up now and then as he paced the beach, waiting my compliance with the rules of the island. The governor, I perceived, was suspicious of smugglers and wreckers, apparently understanding their ways, if, indeed, even he were not a reformed pirate himself.

However, to humor the punctiliousness of his Excellency, now that he was governor of an island, I placed my papers in my hat, and, leaping into the surf, waded ashore, where I was received as by a monarch.

The document I presented was the original *Passe Especial*, the one with the big seal on it, written in Portuguese; had it been in Choctaw the governor would have read it with the same facility that he did this, which he stared at knowingly and said, "all right, take all the water you want; it is free."

I lodged a careful report of the voyage with the governor and explained to his Excellency the whereabouts of the "Island of Rio," as his grace persistently called Rio de Janeiro, whence dated my papers.

Conversing on the subject of islands, which was all the world to him, the governor viewed with suspicion the absence of a word in my documents, referring even to an islet; this, in his mind, was a reprehensible omission; for surely New York to which the papers referred was built on an island. Upon this I offered to swear to the truth of my clearance, "as far as known to me," after the manner of cheap custom-house swearing with which shipmasters, in some parts of the world, are made familiar. "Not on the island!" quickly exclaimed the governor, " 'for thou shalt not disglorify God's name,' is written in the Bible."

I assured the governor of my appreciation of his pious sentiment of not over-swearing, which the Chinese adopt as a policy—laudable however, and one that I would speak of on my return home, to the end that we all emulate the laws of the island; whereupon the governor, greatly pleased, urged me to take some more water, minding me again that it was free.

In a very few minutes I got all the water I wished for; also some aurora shells from the governor's lady, who had arisen with the sun to grace the day and of all things most appropriate held in her generous lap beautiful aurora shells for which—to spoil the poem—I bartered cocoanuts and rusty gnarly yams.

The lady was on a visit only to her lord and master, the monarch of all he surveyed. Beside this was their three children also on a visit, from Nassau, and two assistant keepers of the light which made up the total of this little world in the ocean.

It was the smallest kingdom I had ever visited, peopled by happy human beings and the most isolated by far.

The few blades of grass which had struggled into existence, not enough to support a goat, was all there was to look at on the island except the lighthouse, and the sand and themselves.

Some small buildings and a flagstaff had once adorned the place, but together with a coop of chickens, the only stock of the islanders—except a dog—had been swept away by a hurricane which had passed over the island a short time before. The water for which we had called being now in the canoe, and my people on board waiting for me, I bade the worthy governor good-bye, and, saluting his charming island queen in a seamanlike manner, hastened back to my own little world; and bore away once more for the north. Sailing thence over the Great Bahama Banks, in a crystal sea, we observed on the white marl bottom many curious living things, among them the conch in its house of exquisite tints and polished surface, the star-fish with radiated dome of curious construction, and many more denizens of the place, the names of which I could not tell, resting on the soft white bed under the sea.

"They who go down to the sea in ships, they see the wonders of the Lord," I am reminded by a friend who writes me, on receipt of some of these curious things which I secured on the voyage, adding: "For all these curious and beautiful things are His handiwork. Who can look at such things without the heart being lifted up in adoration?"

For words like these what sailor is there who would not search the caves of the ocean? Words too, from a lady.

Two days of brisk sailing over the white Bahama Banks brought us to Bimini. Thence a mere push would send us to the coast of our own native America. The wind in the meantime hauling from regular nor'east trade to the sou'west, as we came up to Bimini, promising a smooth passage across, we launched out at once on the great Gulf Stream, and were swept along by its restless motion, making on the first day, before the wind and current, two hundred and twenty miles. This was great getting along for a small canoe. Going at the same high rate of speed on the second night in the stream, the canoe struck a spar and went over it with a bound. Her keel was shattered by the shock, but finally shaking the crippled timber clear of herself she came on quite well without it. No other damage was done to our craft, although at times her very ribs were threatened before clearing this lively ocean river. In the middle of the current, where the seas were yet mountainous but regular, we went along with a wide, swinging motion and fared well enough; but on nearing the edge of the stream a confused sea was met with, standing all on end, in every which way, beyond a sailor's comprehension. The motion of the *Liberdade* was then far from poetical or pleasant. The wind, in the meantime, had chopped round to the nor'east, dead ahead; being thus against the current, a higher and more confused sea than ever was heaped up, giving us some uneasiness. We had, indeed, several unwelcome visitor come tumbling aboard of our craft, one of which furiously crashing down on her made all of her timbers bend and creak. However, I could partially remedy this danger by changing the course.

"Seas like that can't break this boat," said our young boatswain; "she's built strong." It was well to find among the crew this feeling of assurance in the gallant little vessel. I, too, was confident in her seaworthiness. Nevertheless, I shortened sail and brought her to the wind, watching the lulls and easing her over the combers, as well as I could. But wrathful Neptune was not to let us so easily off, for the next moment a sea swept clean over the helmsman, wetting him through to the skin and, most unkind cut of all, it put out our fire, and capsized the hash and stove into the bottom of the canoe.

This left us with but a *damper* for breakfast! Matters mended, however, as the day advanced, and for supper we had a grand and glorious feast. Early in the afternoon we made the land and got into smooth water. This of itself was a feast, to our minds.

The land we now saw lying before us was hills of America, which we had sailed many thousands of miles to see. Drawing in with the coast, we made out, first the broad, rich forests, then open fields and villages, with many signs of comfort on every hand. We found it was the land about Bull's Bay on the coast of South Carolina, and night coming on, we could plainly see Cape Roman Light to the north of us. The wind falling light as we drew in with the coast, and finding a current against us, we anchored, about two miles from the shore, in four fathoms of water. It was now 8 P.M., October 28, 1888, thirteen days from Mayaguez, twenty-one days from Barbadoes, etc.

The following was the actual time at sea and distances in nautical miles from point to point on the courses steered, approximately:

	Days.	Distance.
From Paranagua to Santos	1	150
" Santos to Rio de Janeiro (towed by Finance)	3/4	200
" Rio to Cape Frio	2	70
" Cape Frio to Carvellas	4	370
" Carvellas to Saint Paulo	3	270
" Saint Paulo to Bahia	1/2	40
" Bahia to Pernambuco	7	390
" Pernambuco to Barbadoes	19	2,150
" Barbadoes to Mayaguez	3	570
" Mayaguez to Cape Roman	13	1,300
	33 1/4	5,510

Computing all the distances of the ins and outs that we made would considerably augment the sum. To say, therefore, that the *Liberdade* averaged roundly a hundred miles a day for fifty-five days would be considerably inside the truth.

This was the voyage made in the boat which cost less than a hundred dollars outside of our own labor of building. Journals the world over have spoken not unkindly of the feat; encomiums in seven languages reached us through the newspapers while we lay moored in Washington. Should the same good fortune that followed the *Liberdade* attend this little literary craft, when finished, it would go safe into many lands. Without looking, however, to this mark of good fortune, the journal of the voyage has been as carefully constructed as was the *Liberdade,* and I trust, as conscientiously, by a hand, alas! that has grasped the sextant more often than the plane or pen, and for the love of doing. This apology might have been more appropriately made in the beginning of the journal, maybe, but it comes to me now, and like many other things done, right or wrong, but done on the impulse of the moment, I put it down.

XVI

No one will be more surprised at the complete success of the voyage and the speedy progress made than were we ourselves who made it, with incidents and events among which is the most promiment of a life at sea.

A factor of the voyage, one that helped us forward greatly, and which is worthy of special mention, was the ocean current spoken of as we came along in its friendly sway.

Many are the theories among fresh water philosophists respecting these currents, but in practical sailing, where the subject is met with in its tangible form, one cause only is recognized; namely, the action of the wind on the surface of the water, pushing the waves along. Out on the broad ocean the effect at first is hardly perceptible, but the constant trades sending countless millions of waves in one direction, cause at last a mighty moving power, which the mariner meets sometimes as an enemy to retard and delay, sometimes as a friend, as in our case, to help him on his way. These are views from a practical experience with no theory to prove.

By daylight on the twenty-ninth, we weighed anchor and set sail again for the north. The wind and current was still adverse but we kept near the land making short boards off and on through the day where the current had least effect. And when night came on again came to once more close in with Cape Roman light. Next day we worked up under the lee of the Roman shoals and made harbor in South Santee, a small river to the north of Cape Roman, within range of the light, there to rest until the wind should change, it being still ahead.

Next morning, since the wind had not changed, we weighed anchor and stood farther into the river looking for inhabitants, that we might listen to voices other than our own. Our search was soon rewarded, for, coming around a point of woodland, a farmhouse stood before us on the river side. We came alongside the bank and jumped ashore, but had hardly landed when, as out of the earth a thousand dogs so it seemed, sprung up threatening to devour us all. However, a comely woman came out of the house and it was explained to the satisfaction of all, especially to a persistent cur, by a vigorous whack on the head with a cudgel, that our visit was a friendly one; then all was again peaceful and quiet. The good man was in the field close by, but soon came home accompanied by his two stalwart sons each "toting" a sack of corn. We found the Andersons—this was the family name—isolated in every sense of the word, and as primitive as heart could wish. The charming simplicity of these good people captivated my crew. We met others along the coast innocent of greed, but of all unselfish men, Anderson the elder was surely the prince.

In purchasing some truck from this good man, we found that change could not be made for the dollar which I tendered in payment. But I protested that I was more than content to let the few odd cents go, having received more garden stuff than I had ever seen offered for a dollar in any part of the world. And indeed I was satisfied. The farmer, however, nothing content, offered me a coon skin or two, but these I didn't want, and there being no other small change about the farm, the matter was dropped, I thought, for good, and I had quite forgotten it, when later in the evening I was electrified by his offering to carry a letter for us which we wished posted, some seven miles away, and call it "square," against the twenty cents of the morning's transaction. The letter went, and in due course of time we got an answer.

I do not say that we stuck strictly to the twenty-cent transaction, but I fear that not enough was paid to fair-dealing Anderson. However all were at last satisfied and warming into conversation, a log fire was improvised and social chat went round.

These good people could hardly understand how it was, as I explained, that the Brazilians had freed the slaves and had no war, Mr. Anderson often exclaiming, "Well, well, I d'clar. Freed the niggers, and had no wah. Mister," said he, turning to me after a long pause, "mister, d'ye know the South were foolish? They had a wah, and they had to free the niggers, too."

"Oh, yes, mister, I was thar! Over thar beyond them oaks was my house."

"Yes, mister, I fought, too, and fought hard, but it warn't no use."

Like many a hard fighter, Anderson, too, was a pious man, living in a state of resignation to be envied. His years of experience on the new island farm had been hard and trying in the extreme. My own misfortunes passed into shade as the harder luck of the Andersons came before my mind, and the resolution which I had made to buy a farm was now shaken and finally dissolved into doubts of the wisdom of such a course. On this farm they had first "started in to raise pork," but found that it "didn't pay, for the pigs got wild and had to be gathered with the dogs," and by the time they were "gathered and then toted, salt would hardly cure them, and they most generally tainted." The enterprise was therefore abandoned, for that of tilling the soil, and a crop was put in, but "the few pigs which the dogs had not gathered came in at night and rooted out all the taters." It then appeared that a fence should be built. "Accordingly," said he, "I and the boys made one which kept out the stock, but, sir, the rats could get in! They took every tater out of the ground! From all that I put in, and my principal work was thar, I didn't see a sprout." How it happened that the rats had left the crop the year before for their relations—the pigs—was what seemed most to bother the farmer's mind. Nevertheless, "there was corn in Egypt yet;" and at the family circle about the board that night a smile of hope played on the good farmer's face, as in deep sincerity he asked that for what they had they might be made truly thankful. We learned a lesson of patience from this family, and were glad that the wind had carried us thither.

Said the farmer, "And you came all the way from Brazil in that boat! Wife, she won't go to Georgetown in the batto that I built because it rares too much. And they freed the niggers and had no wah! Well, well, I d'clar!"

Better folks we may never see than the farmers of South Santee. Bidding them good-bye next morning at early dawn we sailed before a light land wind which, however, soon petered out.

The S. S. Planter then coming along took us in tow for Georgetown, where she was bound. We had not the pleasure, however, of visiting the beloved old city; for having some half dozen cocoanuts on board, the remainder of small stores of the voyage, a vigilant officer stopped us at the quarantine ground. Fruit not being admitted into South Carolina until after the first of November, and although it was now late in the afternoon of the first, we had to ride quarantine that night, with a promise, however, of *pratique* next morning. But there was no steamer going up the river the next day. The Planter coming down though supplied us with some small provisions, such as not procurable at the Santee farm. Then putting to sea we beat along slowly against wind and current.

We began now to experience, as might be expected, autumn gales of considerable violence, the heaviest of which overtaking us at Frying-pan Shoal, drove us back to leeward of Cape Fear for shelter. South Port and Wilmington being then so near we determined to visit both places. Two weeks at these ports refreshed the crew and made all hands willing for sea again.

Sailing thence through Corn-cake Inlet we cut off Cape Fear and the Frying-pan Shoals, being of mind to make for the inlets along the Carolina coast and to get into the inland waters as soon as practicable.

It was our good fortune to fall in with an old and able pilot at Corn-cake Inlet, one Capt. Bloodgood, who led the way through the channel in his schooner, the "Packet," a Carolina pitch and cotton droger of forty tons register, which was manned solely by the captain and his two sons, one twelve and the other ten years old. It was in the crew that I became most interested, and not the schooner. Bloodgood gave the order when the tide served for us to put to sea. "Come, children," said he, "let's try it." Then we all tried it together, the Packet leading the way. The shaky west wind that filled our sails as we skimmed along the beach with the breakers close aboard, carried us but a few leagues when it flew suddenly round to nor'east and began to pipe.

The gale increasing rapidly inclined me to bear up for New River Inlet, then close under our lee; with a treacherous bar lying in front, which to cross safely, would require great care.

But the gale was threatening, and the harbor inside, we could see, was smooth, then, too, cried my people: "Any port in a storm." I decided prompt: put the helm up and squared away. Flying thence, before it, the tempest-tossed canoe came sweeping in from sea over the rollers in a delightfully thrilling way. One breaker only coming over us, and even that did no harm more than to give us all the climax soaking of the voyage. This was the last sea that broke over the canoe on the memorable voyage.

The harbor inside the bar of New River was good. Adding much to our comfort too, was fish and game in abundance.

The "Packet," which had parted from us made her destined port some three leagues farther on. The last we saw of the children, they were at the main sheets hauling aft, and their father was at the helm, and all were flying through the mist like fearless sailors.

After meeting Carolina seamen, to say nothing of the few still in existence further north, I challenge the story of Greek supremacy.

The little town of South Port was made up almost entirely of pilots possessing, I am sure, every quality of the sailor and the gentleman.

Moored snug in the inlet, it was pleasant to listen to the roar of the breakers on the bar, but not so cheerful was the thought of facing the high waves seaward, therefore the plan suggested itself of sufficiently deepening a ditch that led through the marshes from New River to Bogue Sound; to let us through, thence we could sail inland the rest of the voyage without obstruction or hindrance of any kind. To this end we set about contrivances to heave the canoe over the shoals, and borrowed a shovel from a friendly schooner captain to deepen the ditch which we thought would be necessary to do in order to ford her along that way. However, the prevailing nor'east gales had so raised the water in the west end of the sound as to fill all the creeks and ditches to overflowing. I hesitated then no longer but heading for the ditch through the marshes on a high tide, before a brave west wind took the chances of getting through by hook or by crook or by shovel and spade if required.

The "Coast Pilot," in speaking of this place, says there is never more than a foot of water there, and even that much is rarely found. The *Liberdade* essayed the ditch, drawing two feet and four inches, thus showing the further good fortune or luck which followed perseverance, as it usually does, though sometimes, maybe, it is bad luck! Perhaps I am not lucid on this, which at best must remain a disputed point.

I was getting lost in the maze of sloughs and creeks, which as soon as I entered seemed to lead in every direction but the right one. Hailing a hunter near by, however, I was soon put straight and reassured of success. The most astonished man, though, in North Carolina, was this same hunter when asked if he knew the ditch that led through where I wished to go.

"Why, stranger," said he, "my gran'ther digged that ditch."

I jumped, I leaped! at thought of what a pilot this man would be.

"Well, stranger," said he, in reply to my query, "stranger, if any man kin take y' thro' that ditch, why, I kin;" adding doubtfully, however, "I have not hearn tell befo' of a vessel from Brazil sailing through these parts; but then you mout get through, and again ye moutent. Well, it's jist here; you mout and you moutent."

A bargain was quickly made, and my pilot came aboard, armed with a long gun, which as we sailed along proved a terror to ducks. The entrance to the ditch, then close by, was made with a flowing sheet, and I soon found that my pilot knew his business. Rushswamps and corn-fields we left to port and to starboard, and were at times out of sight among brakes that brushed crackling along the sides of the canoe, as she swept briskly through the narrows, passing them all, with many a close hug, though on all sides. At a point well on in the crooked channel my pilot threw up his hat, and shouted, with all his might:

"Yer trouble is over! Swan to gosh if it ain't! And ye come all the way from Brazil, and come through gran'ther's ditch! Well, I d'clar!"

From this I concluded that we had cleared all the doubtful places, and so it turned out. Before sundown my pilot was looking for the change of a five-dollar-piece; and we of the *Liberdade* sat before a pot-pie, at twilight, the like of which on the whole voyage had not been tasted, from sea fowl laid about by our pilot while sailing through the meadows and marshes. And the pilot himself, returning while the potpie was yet steaming hot, declared it "ahead of coon."

A pleasant sail was this through the ditch that gran'ther dug. At the camp fire that night, where we hauled up by a fishing station, thirty stalwart men talked over the adventures of their lives. My pilot, the best speaker, kept the camp in roars. As for myself, always fond of mirth, I got up from the fire sore from laughing. Their curious adventures with coons and 'gators recounted had been considerable.

Many startling stories were told. But frequently reverting to this voyage of the *Liberdade,* they declared with one voice that "it was the greatest thing since the wah." I took this as a kind of complimentary hospitality. "When she struck on a sand reef," said the pilot, "why, the captain he jumped right overboard and the son he jumped right over, too, to tote her over, and the captain's wife she holp."

By daylight next morning we sailed from this camp pleasant, and on the following day, November 28, at noon, arrived at Beaufort.

Mayor Bell of that city and many of his town folk met us at the wharf, and gave me as well as my sea-tossed crew a welcome to their shores, such as to make us feel that the country was partly ours.

"Welcome, welcome home," said the good mayor; "we have read of your adventures, and watched your progress as reported from time to time, with deep interest and sympathy."

So we began to learn now that prayers on shore had gone up for the little canoe at sea. This, was indeed America and home, for which we had longed while thousands of miles across the ocean.

From Beaufort to Norfolk and thence to Washington was pleasant inland sailing, with prevailing fair winds and smooth sea. Christmas was spent on the Chesapeake—a fine, enjoyable day it was! with not a white-cap ripple on the bay. Ducks swimming ahead of the canoe as she moved quietly along were loath to take wing in so light a breeze, but flapping away, half paddling, half swimming, as we came toward them, they managed to keep a long gun-shot off; but having laid in at the last port a turkey of no mean proportions, which we made shift to roast in the "caboose" aboard, we could look at a duck without wishing its destruction. With this turkey and a bountiful plum duff, we made out a dinner even on the *Liberdade.*

Of the many Christmas days that come crowding in my recollections now; days spent on the sea and in foreign lands, as falls to the lot of sailors—which was the merriest it would be hard to say. Of this, however, I am certain, that the one on board the *Liberdade* on the Chesapeake was not the least happy among them all.

The day following Christmas found us on the Potomac, enjoying the same fine weather and abundant good cheer of the day before. Fair winds carried us through all the reaches of the river, and the same prosperity which attended our little bark in the beginning of the voyage through tempestuous weather followed her to the end of the journey, which terminated in mild days and pleasant sunshine.

On the 27th of December, 1888, a south wind bore us into harbor at Washington, D.C., where we moored for the winter, furled our sails and coiled up the ropes, after a voyage of joys and sorrows; crowned with pleasures, however, which lessened the pain of past regrets.

Having moored the *Liberdade* and weather-bitted her cables, it remains only to be said that after bringing us safely through the dangers of a tropical voyage, clearing reefs, shoals, breakers, and all storms without a serious accident of any kind, we learned to love the little canoe as well as anything could be loved that is made by hands.

To say that we had not a moment of ill-health on the voyage would not tell the whole story.

My wife, brave enough to face the worst storms, as women are sometimes known, to do on sea and on land, enjoyed not only the best of health, but had gained a richer complexion.

Victor, at the end of the voyage, found that he had grown an inch and had not been frightened out of his boots.

Little Garfield—well he had grown some, too, and continued to be a pretty good boy and had managed to hold his grip through many ups and downs. He it was who stood by the bow line to make fast as quick as the *Liberdade* came to the pier at the end of the voyage.

And I, last, as it should be, lost a few pounds' weight, but like the rest landed in perfect health; taking it altogether, therefore, only pleasant recollections of the voyage remain with us who made it.

With all its vicissitudes I still love a life on the broad, free ocean, never regretting the choice of my profession.

However, the time has come to debark from the *Liberdade,* now breasted to the pier where I leave her for a time; for my people are landed safe in port.

Voyage in the Pilot-Boat Schooner Sea-Serpent

GEORGE COGGESHALL

After having settled the last voyage I made in the Volusia from New Orleans to Truxillo and Bonaco, and disposed of that vessel, I decided to make up a voyage to the Pacific. By recent accounts from Peru we learned that Lord Cochrane, with a Chilian fleet, was blockading Lima, aided by a strong land force under the command of General San Martin; that the Spaniards had concentrated their armies in Lima and its vicinity, and had strongly fortified themselves there and at the castles of Callao, and would probably hold out for at least six months longer. We also heard that the inhhabitants of Lima were in great want of every thing, especially provisions of almost every description. On the receipt of this information, Mr. H., a merchant of New-York, proposed to me in the month of October, 1821, to purchase a fast-sailing pilot-boat schooner and fit her out for Lima, with a view of evading the blockade, and profiting by the high prices which could be obtained for almost every thing sent to that place.

We soon made arrangements to purchase a suitable vessel, to be owned by Mr. H., Mr. B., an Italian gentleman and myself. I agreed to take one fifth interest in the schooner and cargo, and to command the vessel, and act as supercargo during the voyage. The enterprise was well planned, and had the cargo been laid in with good judgment, the voyage would have proved eminently successful. As it was managed by Mr. H. and Mr. B. it proved in the end rather a failure.

I had never been in Lima and knew nothing of its wants; Mr. B. had resided there several years, but as he was not a merchant, his information proved of little service. I relied entirely on the judgment of my two associates, and therefore took many articles not at all adapted to the market. Such articles as were wanted at Lima paid an enormous profit.

After searching about for a week or two, we at length found a sharp pilot-boat built schooner called the "Sea-Serpent." Her burthen was 139 tons. Though only three years old, she was soft and defective, and subsequently proved to be rotten, and, in bad weather, very leaky. The schooner had just returned from a voyage to Chagres, where she had lost her captain and officers and nearly all her crew by the yellow fever, and while in that hot climate she was not properly ventilated, and had thus suffered from dry rot.

The defect was not discovered by the carpenter who was sent to examine her before she was purchased by Mr. H. I think we gave seven thousand five hundred dollars for the schooner, and on or about the 20th of October we commenced loading. We first took in ten or twelve tons of English and Swedish iron and 100 flasks of quicksilver, which cost over $3,500. Six hogsheads containing 234 kegs of butter, about 2,500 pounds, and other articles of French, English and German goods, not at all adapted to the market, situated as the people of Lima were, in the midst of war and threatened with famine.

The whole cost of the vessel and cargo, including the insurance out, was $30,726.

Mr. B.'s interest amounted to $5,000, my own was one fifth of the adventure, and the remainder belonged to Mr. H. I subsequently, before sailing, sold to my friend Richard M. Lawrence, Esq., of New-York, half of my interest in both vessel and cargo, leaving for my account only about $3,000. Beside this amount, I had, however, for my own private adventure about $1,500 in jewelry and silk stockings. These articles, though valuable, occupied but a very small space in the stowage of the vessel. I took with me Mr. B. as passenger, my cousin Mr. Freegift Coggeshall as chief mate, my brother Francis Coggeshall as second mate, and a crew of nine men and boys, including the cook and steward.

Thus loaded and manned, we sailed from New-York, on the 15th of November, 1821, for Lima. For the first and second days out we had fine weather and fair winds from the westward. On the third day, November 17th, we met with strong gales from the eastward and a high head sea running, so that we were compelled to lay to ten or twelve hours. Our decks were filled with water and the schooner began to leak, which was a bad sign at the commencement of a long voyage. The next day the wind shifted to the westward, when we again made sail and stood on our course to the eastward. We continued to have strong gales from the westward and very bad weather until the 4th of December, when we made the Island of St. Mary's, bearing E. S. E. five leagues distant. This is one of the Azores or Western Islands, and lies in lat. 36° 59' North, long. 25° 10' West.

We lost here two days, by reason of strong gales from the S. S. W., with a high head sea, and very squally weather. After getting into lat. 24° N., we took the regular trade winds, and generally had pleasant weather; but whenever we encountered a strong breeze, we found the schooner leaked considerably, and being deeply laden, she was extremely wet and uncomfortable.

On the night of the 17th of December, 1821, when in lat. 16°, long. about 25° W., we caught fifty-eight flying-fish on deck. The schooner was so deep and low in the water, that large numbers of these fish came on board. The next day, December 18th, a great number of flying-fish were washed on board, and others flew on board in such numbers, that we had, during these two days, enough to serve all hands in abundance. The schooner continued to leak more and more, and we now kept one pump employed almost constantly.

From this time to the 25th, nothing remarkable occurred. Christmas being an idle day, we killed the only remaining pig, all the others, eight in number, having been drowned by the salt water, which almost always flooded the decks when there was a high sea.

On the 27th, saw a sail, standing to the northward; and this day we crossed the equinoctial line, in long. 26° W.; light winds and variable, with dark, rainy weather; thermometer stood at 84° at two P.M. We continued to experience light winds and variable, with dark, rainy weather, for forty-eight hours, when we struck the S. E. trades in lat. 4° S. We had for many days fine breezes from the S. E., and very pleasant weather. I have almost always found this region of the South Atlantic—say from 5° to 20° S. latitude—a delightful part of the ocean to navigate, the weather fine and mild, and the skies very beautiful, with a temperature generally not so hot as to be uncomfortable.

We sailed through these pleasant latitudes without any incident worth remarking until we reached lat. 22° 41' S., on the 6th of January, 1822, when we again had bad, rainy weather, with the wind from the westward. This continued for 24 hours, when we again had a return of the S. E. trades, and pleasant weather.

January 8th, lat. 24° 20' S.—Last night, the weather being very fine and clear, we saw for the first time what are called the Magellan clouds. They are three in number, and were not far above the horizon. They bore from us about S. S. E., and are evidently clusters of stars; two of them appeared white like the milky-way, the other was dark and indistinctly seen.

January 9th.—At 8 o'clock in the morning, the weather being hazy, with a light breeze from the S. E., the man on the lookout at the mast-head cried out "Land ho!" and told the officer of the deck that he saw something ahead that looked like a small island, and that there were thousands of birds on and around it. In a few minutes every eye was eagerly gazing at the supposed island.

I knew there was no land laid down on any of my charts near where we were, and therefore concluded that it must be the wreck of a ship. As the wind was very light we drew slowly up with the newly discovered object. It soon, however, became visible from the deck, when I took a spy-glass and examined it with close attention, but owing to the constant changes it assumed I was at loss to decide what it was, from its undulating appearance, alternately rising above the water and then again disappearing beneath, until within half a mile's distance, when all doubt was solved, and we found it to be an enormous dead whale floating on its back. It was very much swollen, and at times was apparently some six or eight feet above the water. There were innumerable flocks of wild fowl hovering over and alighting upon it. Many of them appeared to be devouring it, and making loud and wild screams, as if exulting over this grand but accidental feast.

In order to ascertain with more precision its length and size, I hove the schooner to, a short distance to windward, and went in my boat to examine it, which I did to my entire satisfaction.

When approaching near, it became so offensive that I was obliged to keep at a respectful distance to windward, and there watch the numerous flocks of sea-birds that were revelling upon it. In the midst of their din of discordant screams, it was strange to witness with what delight they tore off portions of the fish, and how at each moment their number seemed to augment.

After leaving this scene, I came to the conclusion that dead whales like this are one great cause of so many "dangers" and "small islands," being laid down on all the old charts, which dangers are found not to exist. Such objects as these were probably discovered in dark, windy weather, when it would have been dangerous to have approached near enough to the supposed islands to ascertain what they really were. Thus we have, even at the present time, laid down all over the Atlantic ocean, rocks, shoals, and dangers, the greater part of which do not in reality exist.

January 10th lat. 26° 10' S.—During the early part of the last two nights we have seen the four bright stars called the Southern Cross. They are very brilliant, and with a little help of the imagination form a pretty good representation of the Christian cross; and I have no doubt that many of the early Roman Catholic navigators believed they were placed in the heavens to substantiate the truth of the Christian religion.

January 15th.—This day, at noon, we fell in with and boarded the ship *Hannibal,* of Sag Harbor, seven months out on a whaling voyage. They informed me that they had on board 3000 barrels of oil.

At 9 o'clock, P.M., spoke the whaling ship *Fame,* of New London. We were now in lat. 37° 20' S., long. 49° W.

On the 17th Jan. we had clear, pleasant weather, with light and variable winds. At 10 o'clock A.M. our long., by a good lunar observation, was 50° 38' West, lat. at noon 41°1' South. At 6 o'clock of this day we fell in with the ships *Herald* and *Amazon.* They were cruising in company for whale, and both belonged to Fair Haven, Mass. The captain of the *Herald* came on board to ascertain his longitude;

he said they had seen no land for the last two months, and had been too busy to pay much attention to the course or position of the ship; that he knew nothing of lunar observations, and had no chronometer; he was therefore desirous to ascertain the present position of his ship. I had an excellent chronometer on board, and, as the lunar observation taken that day agreed with the chronometer, I told him there was no doubt that I could give him the exact latitude and longitude. He said he had only been eight months at sea, and had then on board 1400 barrels of oil; that the *Amazon* had taken 1100 barrels, and that he should soon steer to the northward on his way home.

When the whale-boat belonging to the *Herald* was alongside the *Sea-Serpent*, the boat was higher than the deep-loaded pilot-boat. The captain of the *Herald* said to me:—"Well, captain, you say you are from New-York, bound for Lima, but seriously, are you going round Cape Horn in this little whistle-diver?" "I shall certainly try it, captain," said I, "and hope I shall succeed." "Well, then, captain," he replied, "but tell me, did you get your life insured before you left home?" "No," said I, "but I left my family in comfortable circumstances, so that if I should be taken away they will have enough to live upon; besides, I am a good schooner sailor, and am accustomed to these whistle-divers, as you call them."—"Well, captain," said the whaler, "I must say you have good courage, and I hope you may succeed; but for my part, I had rather kill a hundred whales than go round the Horn in this little craft." After this dialogue we parted with mutual good wishes for future prosperity and happiness, and each resumed our course upon the great trackless deep. The next day, Jan. 18th, we had strong breezes from the S. E., and though the winds were fresh and strong, and considerable sea, we were able to steer on our S. W. course under reefed sails.

I must not omit to mention the singular fact, of a flock of seabirds which followed my schooner for the last ten days, namely from lat. 26° S., and were now still hovering near the vessel, sometimes a little ahead, and then again about thirty or forty yards astern. They were generally a little astern and frequently alighted on the water, and appeared to watch every small particle of food or grease that was thrown overboard. They were fifteen in number, and about the size of a common tame pigeon. They are called by seamen, cape pigeons.

From this time to the 22nd of January, nothing remarkable occurred until on that day, when we met with a severe gale from the southward, attended with a high head sea, so that at midnight we were obliged to lay to under a close reefed foresail. We were now in lat. 46° 50' S., long. 58° 26' W. At noon I caught three large albatross, with a hook and line buoyed up by several corks and baited with fat pork. One of the largest measured across his wings, from tip to tip, eight feet four inches. They were covered with white feathers three or four inches thick. They appear to be thus kindly protected by Providence from the cold in these inclement latitudes. In low latitudes, where the weather is hot and sultry, the birds are thinly covered with feathers, which are mostly of high and brilliant colors. The fish also, in hot climates, partake of the same gay and bright colors; such for instance as the parrot fish, the red snapper, and many others. After passing these hot regions and approaching the latitude of 50°, and so on to the latitude of Cape Horn, the birds are generally all white and clothed with an immense mat of down and feathers. Among the fish, likewise, I saw no gay-colored ones, in these cold regions; on the contrary, I frequently saw large schools of porpoises pied, and sometimes quite white.

While sailing and travelling about the world, I have often been struck with the wisdom and goodness of God, not only to man but to all His creatures, in adapting their condition to the different climates of the earth. We find the colored man adapted to the sultry, burning climates, and the white man constituted to endure the cold. So it is with beasts, birds, and fish.

I first began to notice the kindness of Providence, when only a boy trading to the islands in the West Indies. I observed that the sheep we used to take there from Connecticut, though thickly covered with wool, would shortly lose their fleeces, and eventually become hairy like goats. On the other hand, the higher the latitude, and where the cold is most intense, the thicker and finer is the fur on the animals, for example, where the bear, seal, and musk ox are found.

As we increased our latitude, the weather became daily more and more rough and boisterous; we encountered storm after storm, and the weather was more cloudy, cold and disagreeable, which kept us reefing and changing almost hourly. On the 26th of January, at 5 A.M., daylight, we made the Falkland Islands, bearing from S. to S. E., distant five leagues; the winds being light and the weather moderate, we stood in shore. The wind being at this time at W. S. W., we were unable to fetch to westward of the islands, and therefore commenced beating up along-shore to weather the westernmost island. These islands appear of a moderate height, and generally rocky and barren. Lat. by obs. this day 51° 18' S., long. about 61° 6' W. We continued to beat to the westward all this day and the day following; standing off and on the land with open, cloudy weather, and moderate gales from the S. W. Saw a high rock appearing like a lofty sail; marked on the charts Eddystone Rock.

On Monday, January 28th, the land still in sight; at meridian the wind shifted to the N. W., which enabled us to weather the land, and thus we passed to the westward of this group of islands and steered on our course to the southward, and westward towards Cape Horn; lat. by obs. at noon 50° 58' S., long. 61° 50' W. In the afternoon of this day the weather became thick and rainy; passed several tide rips, and saw a number of penguin. The little flock of cape pigeons before alluded to still followed the schooner, our constant companions by day and by night, in sunshine and in tempest. The variation of the compass here is from one and three-quarters to two points easterly. The weather was now cold and disagreeable, temperature by Fahrenheit's therm. 50° above zero.

Tuesday, January 29th.—Light winds and variable. This day the weather appeared to change every hour or two; at times the sun would shine out, and then suddenly disappear and become obscured by a thick fog. This would continue but for a short time, when a strong breeze from the northward would blow all the fog away and the sky remain pretty clear for a few hours, then the sun would again break out and shine for an hour or two, and perhaps another hour would bring a flight of snow. Sometimes, even when the sun was shining, the decks would be covered for a few minutes with snow, which would soon melt away and be followed by a violent shower of rain and hail. In fine, I find it very difficult to describe the weather in this dreary region; though we were in the midst of summer, we had all the seasons of the year in the course of a day. These continual changes kept us constantly making and taking in sail throughout these twenty-four hours. Lat. by obs. 53° 1' S., long. 64° 0' W.

Jan. 30th.—These twenty-four hours commenced with a strong gale from the westward, with a high head sea running. At 1 P.M., hove to under a two-reefed foresail; dark, cloudy, cold weather, with violent squalls of hail and rain. At midnight the gale moderated, when we again made sail, the schooner laboring violently and making much water. Lat., by observation, 53° 30' S., long. 64° W.

Jan. 31st.—This day commenced with strong gales from the westward, with a high head sea running; weather dark and gloomy. The wind throughout these twenty-four hours continued to blow strong from the westward, and being directly ahead, we found it impossible to gain to the westward, and were glad to hold our own without losing ground. During the day we had much thunder and lightning. Lat., by observation, 54° 1' S., long. 64° 00' W.

Feb. 1st.—Last night the sky was clear for a little while in the zenith, when we saw the Magellan clouds nearly over our heads. This day we had a continuation of strong gales from the westward, and very bad, stormy weather; we, however, continued to ply to the windward under close-reefed sails, but having a strong westerly gale and a lee current against us, we made but little progress. At 6 A.M. made Staten Land; this land, like the Falklands, appeared cold and dreary, and only a fit habitation for seal and wild fowl, which are here very abundant. The sea in this vicinity also abounds in whales of monstrous bulk. At noon the body of Staten Land bore N. by W., twelve leagues distant. At meridian the sun shone out, when we found our latitude to be 55° 31' S., long. 64° 8' W.

Feb. 2nd.—This day, like the last, was dark and gloomy, with a continuation of westerly winds, but not so strong as to prevent our plying to windward, under close-reefed sails. The thermometer fell down to 45° above zero. In consequence of contrary winds and a lee current we gained but little on our course during these twenty-four hours. Lat., by observation, 56° 20' S., long. 65° 27' W.

Feb. 3rd.—On this day, when within about 50 miles of Cape Horn, a terrible gale commenced blowing from the westward. It continued to increase until it blew a perfect hurricane, and soon created a mountainous sea. We got our foreyard on deck, and hove the schooner to, under the head of a new foresail. I then ordered all the bulwarks and waist-boards to be knocked away, that nothing might impede the water from passing over the decks without obstruction, otherwise so great a quantity would have lodged in the lee-waist that our little schooner would have been water-logged and swamped with the weight of it. With crowbars and axes the waist-boards were all demolished, and the sea broke over the decks and passed off without injury to our little bark, and she rose like a stormy petrel on the top of the sea, which threatened every moment to swallow us in its abyss. The ocean was lashed into a white foam by the fury of the tempest. The same weather continued with but little intermission for a space of five days. During a great part of this time it was almost impossible to look to windward, so violent were the hail and snow squalls. In the midst of this tempest, my officers and men behaved nobly: the most perfect order prevailed; not a whisper of fear or contention was heard during the whole of our perilous situation. To render the men more comfortable, I removed them all from the forecastle to the cabin, where they continued to live until we had fairly doubled the Cape and found better weather.

My Italian passenger was terribly alarmed during the tempest, and entreated me, in piteous tones, to put away for Rio Janeiro. He said if I would do so, he would instantly sign an agreement to give me all his interest in the vessel and cargo. I resolutely declined his offer, and told him that while we had masts and sails, and the vessel would float under us, I would never put back.

This Cape is rendered more dreadful from the fact of its inhospitable position, and being so far removed from any civilized port. It is a cold, cheerless, barbarous coast, where no provision, or supplies of any kind, can be had in case of shipwreck or disaster, so that the greatest vigilance and perseverance are necessary to bear the many obstacles that present themselves.

Feb. 8th.—The gale abated, and we were again enabled to make sail and ply to the westward. Our faithful little pigeons had hovered about us during the long tempest, and now resumed the journey with us. We got an observation of the sun this day at noon, and found ourselves in lat. 57° 33' S., long. 66° 12' W.

Feb. 9th.—We had, throughout these twenty-four hours, favorable gales from the N. E., and open, cloudy weather. Made all sail and steered to the westward, and gained 160 miles distance on a direct course, and every thing began to wear a better appearance. We made better progress this day than we had done since our arrival in these high southern latitudes. Lat., by observation at noon, 57° 16' S., long., by chronometer 71° 4' W.

Feb. 10th.—This day commenced with strong gales from the southward, with dark, squally weather; under reefed sails, standing to the northward and westward; made a distance of 155 miles per log. Towards noon the sun shone out, when we found ourselves, at meridian, in lat. 55° 44' S., long. 74° 48' W. We had now fairly doubled Cape Horn; and I hoped in a few days to descend to lower latitudes, and find warmer and better weather. It was how fifteen days since we made the Falkland Islands, so that we were from thirteen to fifteen days weathering Cape Horn, which is not an unusual length of time, and had our vessel been a good ship of three or four hundred tons, we should have suffered nothing in comparison with what we did undergo, in a deep loaded, pilot-boat schooner, of one hundred and forty tons, leaking badly. From the 10th of February to the 16th, we generally had light and variable winds from the northward and westward, so that we made but slow progress during the week, and nothing worth recording occurred.

Feb. 17th.—This day commenced with light breezes from the S. W., and fine weather. During the night, in a squall, a small fish was washed on board. It weighed before it was dressed about half a pound, and in appearance was not unlike a brook trout, except that it had a greenish color. I directed the cook to prepare it for my breakfast, and told him to fry it with a few slices of salt pork. At breakfast, I divided the fish between my passenger, the chief mate and myself. We all ate the fish with a good relish, and returned on deck; but very soon after, we were all taken sick: the mate was seized with violent vomiting, and became death-like pale and languid.—The passenger was also sick, but not so much so as the mate. I was not very ill, but felt a burning sensation in my mouth and throat for several hours afterwards. Upon examining the scales and intestines of the fish, and the knife with which it was cleaned, we found them all of a deep greenish color, indicating that the fish must have been very poisonous. What it was I know not. It is remarkable that one of so small a size could poison three persons.

During the remainder of this day we had light breezes from the W. and fine weather. We only made about 100 miles on our course through these twenty-four hours; at noon our lat. by obs. was 47° 56' S., long. 78° 17' W.

From the 17th of February, to the 22nd of the same month, we had light winds from the southward and westward, and generally good weather; we steered to the northward. We were daily getting the weather more mild and pleasant, as we approached the lower latitudes. We met with nothing worth remarking during the last five days. We were now in lat. 38° 45' S., long. 79° 29' W.

Feb. 23rd.—We had fresh breezes from the S. W. and fine weather throughout these twenty-four hours, and made 166 miles distance to the northward. Lat. by obs. at noon 36° 0' S., long. per chron. 79° 34' West.

Feb. 24th.—This day commenced with fine fresh breezes from the southward, and very pleasant weather, which we sensibly enjoyed after getting through those tempestuous regions into the bright and gentle Pacific Ocean, which daily became more and more mild and tranquil. At 8 o'clock in the morning we made the island of Mas Afuera bearing N. N. W., about eight leagues distant. At 11 o'clock A.M. it bore west, three leagues distant. This island lies in lat. 33°45' S., long. 80° 38' W. It is a high, abrupt, rugged looking place about fifteen or twenty miles long and perhaps five or six broad. The shores are very steep, and I believe it is only accessible on the N. W. side in a little bay, where boats can land in good weather. It has no harbor, notwithstanding it was formerly a famous island for taking seal. Some twenty-five or thirty years ago, several good voyages were made by ships from New England, which took seal skins from this island to Canton in China, where they disposed of them, and returned to the United States, richly laden with teas and other China goods.

One of these voyages was made by a ship called the *Neptune,* commanded by Captain Daniel T. Green (in which were two young men belonging to my native town, from whom I obtained this information). This ship was owned in New Haven, Connecticut, and took from this island fifty thousand seal skins and sold them in Canton for $2 each, and thence returned to New-York in the year 1799, with a cargo of teas silk goods, nankeens, &c. The owners and crew cleared by the voyage about $100,000.

This trade was carried on for several years very advantageously, until at length all the seal were killed or driven away from the island. The sealing ships were then compelled to search for a new field, in distant seas and on lonely desert islands, where the seal had never been disturbed by man. When they first commenced killing seal at Mas Afuero, the animals were so tame and gentle that thousands were killed with clubs. These poor animals, unconscious of the danger, made no attempt to escape; but in a few years after they became so knowing and shy, that it was difficult to kill them, except by stratagem. I have subsequently seen them in different places along the coast of Peru, and found them so extremely wild and timid that they would plunge into the water when approached, and at this time it is very difficult to kill them, even with spears and muskets.

This day we also saw and passed by Juan Fernandez. This island is not so high as Mas Afuero, but is more fertile and productive. It lies in latitude 33° 46' S., longitude 79° 6' W. It belongs to Chili, and is about 400 miles west of Valparaiso. It has a tolerable harbor on the south side, and has been used lately by the Chilian Government as a sort of Botany Bay for state prisoners. It has become a place of general interest to the world from its having been made the locality of Robinson Crusoe's adventures, by Defoe.

It was now one hundred days since we left New York, and we had still more than 1000 miles to sail before we could reach Lima, but as we expected to get into the S. E. trade winds in a day or two from this time, I anticipated the remainder of the passage with pleasure.

February 25th.—Throughout these twenty-four hours, we had fine breezes from the southward, and very pleasant weather. We were now sailing with a fair wind, with all our light sails set. Our little schooner was well adapted to these smooth seas and gentle breezes; we made 190 miles during the last twenty-four hours, and were at noon in latitude 30° 23' S., longitude 80° 28' W.

February 26th.—Fresh breezes from the S. E., and clear, pleasant weather throughout these twenty-four hours. We had now taken the regular S. E. trades. It was delightful to sail before the wind in this mild climate and smooth sea (which is so appropriately called the *Pacific* Ocean), after having been buffeted and tossed about off Cape Horn so long in so small a vessel. During the last twenty-four hours our little vessel made 200 miles with perfect ease, and almost without shifting a single sail. Lat. by obs. at noon 27° 4' S., long. 80° 28' W.

From the 26th of February to the 5th of March, we had a continuation of the S. E. trade winds, and fine pleasant weather, running constantly on our direct course, and daily making from 150 to 200 miles.

Our friendly birds, which had constantly followed us for the last fifty-six days, from the coast of Brazil and round Cape Horn, still kept about us. They were not so constantly near our vessel as before we came down into these mild latitudes, but they made little excursions and then returned. I sometimes missed them for an hour or two, and feared, in two or three instances, that they had entirely left us and would no more return to cheer us, but to my agreeable surprise they always came, and were at this time within a few yards of our stern, and appeared attached to our little bark and to the hands that occasionally fed them. They were indeed a great source of entertainment, and their fidelity was a constant theme of conversation and interest to us.

March 5th, 1822.—This day commenced with light winds from the S. E., and, as usual, fine, clear weather. At 4 o'clock in the afternoon we made the Island of Lorenzo, bearing about N. E., 25 miles distant. At 8 in the evening we got near the island. It being too late to run into port, I concluded to stand off and on under its lee, and wait until daylight to run in an anchor.

March 6th.—We came to anchor near the forts at Callao—the seaport of Lima—all well, after a passage of 110 days from New-York.

It was not until we came to anchor that our little guardian birds left us and flew out of the harbor.

We found Callao and Lima in the hands of the patriots (as the natives of the country were called), and that the Spanish army had retreated to the interior; of course, the blockade was raised, and the object of my voyage in a great measure defeated.

I have before stated, that we purchased this little, fast-sailing vessel, in order to evade the blockade by superior sailing, otherwise it would have been more advantageous to the owners to have bought a more burthensome vessel at a less cost, and far more comfortable for me to perform a voyage round Cape Horn in such an one, than it was in a small pilot-boat schooner.

After entering my vessel and going through the necessary forms at Callao, I forthwith proceeded up to Lima, and presented my letters of introduction to several gentlemen, who were merchants residing in that city, and was not long in making an arrangement with Don Francisco X. Iscue, a respectable merchant, to take charge of my business, and act as my general agent and consignee. Señor Iscue was a native of Old Spain, but was married to a lady born in Lima. He had an interesting family, and was an honest, worthy man, and a very correct merchant. Through this gentleman I disposed of most of that part of my cargo which was at all adapted to the market, such as provisions, and a part of my manufactured goods. All the butter sold at $1 per lb. Flour was at this time selling at $30 per barrel. Some articles of my cargo sold at an enormous profit, while many others would not bring prime cost.

Soon after my arrival at Callao, the ship *America,* Captain De Koven, of New-York, arrived with a full cargo of flour. I believe he brought about 3500 barrels, which were sold at a very great profit. To Capt. De Koven I sold my quicksilver at invoice price, which amounted to about $3500.

As all communication was cut off between Lima and the interior, I was unable to dispose of the quicksilver at any price, except to Capt. De Koven. He was bound to Canton, and took the article at invoice price to dispose of it in China. I subsequently lent him $11,500 in dollars (which, together with the quicksilver, amounted to $15,000), and took his bill on the owners of the *America,* in New York, for the amount at sixty days sight. The owners of the ship were Messrs. Hoyt and Tom, Elisha Tibbets, and Stephen Whitney.

I soon had all my cargo transported to Lima, and in about twenty days after my arrival sold the schooner *Sea-Serpent,* for ten thousand five hundred dollars. Such goods as I could not dispose of at private sale, I sold at public auction; and on the 6th of June, 1822, closed the accounts of the voyage, and I am sorry to add, made little or nothing for my owners. My own private adventure sold tolerably well; and what, with my wages, commissions, etc., I made for myself what is called a saving voyage.

I waited about a fortnight for a passage to Panama, but was unable to obtain one. On the 15th of June, I was offered the command of the fine Baltimore-built brig "*Dick,*" burthen 207 tons, and only two years old. This vessel belonged to the Italian gentleman who came out as a passenger with me in the *Sea-Serpent.* He was desirous of employing the *Dick* in the coasting trade, on the western coast of Chili and Peru. I was also glad of employment for a few months, until the sickly season had passed away in Panama and Chagrés, (having decided to return to the United States by the way of Panama and across the Isthmus of Darien to Chagrés). The Italian was an honest man, but, not having been bred a merchant, relied on me to manage the voyage of his brig.

After I had disposed of the *Sea-Serpent,* I paid off the mates and seamen, and allowed each of them two months' extra pay, according to law, and then procured nearly all of them situations on board of other vessels. Both mates, when I left Callao, were pleasantly situated as officers, on board of English vessels, coasting between Chili and Peru; and the seamen got good berths and generous wages; so that none of my crew were left in distress, or unprovided with employment.

As Mr. B. the owner of the brig had decided to proceed with her down the coast of Peru, to Truxillo and Pagusmayo, and there purchase a cargo of sugar, rice, and such other articles of provision as were then much wanted in Lima, I lost no time in shipping officers and seamen, and getting ready for the voyage, which under ordinary circumstances would require about two months to perform. On the 28th of July we were ready for sea.

Callao is the seaport of Lima, and lies in lat. 12° 2' S., long. 77° 4' W., seven or eight miles west of Lima. Callao is strongly protected by forts, castles and walls, with broad and wide exterior ditches. To a stranger the castles at first view appear like a small walled city. Outside of these vast and expensive fortifications, there is a considerable number of houses, magazines and shops, generally lying along the bay, and in some places extending back, perhaps, a short quarter of a mile.

This village is called Callao, and the fortifications are called the Castles of Callao. The road between Lima and the port is level and good. The port of Callao is formed by a bay which is sheltered by its own points and the Island of St. Lorenzo, which lies at the south entrance, about eight or ten miles distant from the Castles at Callao. As I have no map or book before me, and write entirely from memory, I may perhaps make some little error in the distance, but not in the main facts. Callao Bay is a fine, broad, clear expanse of water, and deep enough for a line-of-battle ship in almost any part of it, and on the whole, I should pronounce it a very safe and good harbor, particularly in this mild and gentle climate, where there are no violent gales or tempests. In this respect the inhabitants of this coast are favored beyond any part of the world I have ever visited. The oldest men in this country know nothing of a storm or a violent gale of wind; so uniform is the weather, that the Fahr. thermometer in Lima rarely varies more than six or eight degrees. It generally ranges between 75° and 80°. Although it is sometimes hot at noonday, the nights are cool and comfortable, owing to the snow and ice in the mountains not very far distant in the interior. When Peru was a colony of Spain, Lima was a populous and comparatively rich city; but in consequence of continued wars and revolutions it has become poor. For the last eight years there had been a constant demand for young men to join the armies, which has rendered the population less than it was previously. The city of Lima, the capital of Peru, lies about seven miles from the sea, and is pleasantly situated at the foot of the Cordilleras. The little river Rimac takes its rise in the mountains and runs through the city, and supplies the inhabitants with an abundance of excellent water. Over this stream there is a fine stone bridge with six arches. On this bridge and in recesses are placed seats for the citizens, which renders it a favorite resort for the *elite* of the city. It is said that before the revolution, Lima contained about eighty thousand inhabitants; at the time of which I write it numbers only about sixty thousand, exclusive of the military, who I should judge were about eight or ten thousand. There are several large churches and public buildings, which have rather an imposing appearance.

The Cathedral in the centre of the city, which forms the east side of the Plaza Maza, is the grand resort of all the better classes of people, and is a pleasant place. In consequence of the earthquakes to which Lima is subject, the houses are generally built low, not often more than one or two stories high, and of very slight materials, namely, dried clay and reeds, with a light coat of plaster, and then white-washed or painted. I believe that if it should blow and rain a few hours as it does sometimes in the Bay of Honduras, that the whole city would be washed away; but fortunately for the inhabitants, it never rains in the city. The high and long chain of Cordilleras in the interior, acts as a perfect conductor for the clouds and storms. There only the clouds break and the rain falls in torrents. It therefore becomes necessary, notwithstanding the heavy dews, to irrigate the fields and gardens in the neighborhood of Lima.

I think the city is about two miles long, and one and a half broad. Through the principal streets water is conducted from the Rimac. This tends very much to cool and cleanse the town, which, if blessed with peace and a good government, would be a very delightful city, bating an occasional alarm of earthquakes.

A few weeks before my arrival, the Castles at Callao and the city of Lima, were vacated by the Spanish army and taken possession of by General San Martin and Lord Cochrane; the former at the head of 8,000 or 10,000 Chilian and Peruvian troops, and the latter, the Admiral, command-ing the Chilian squadron of two or three frigates and several smaller vessels. I believe there was very little fighting but a kind of capitulation was agreed upon between the parties. The Spanish army marched out and retreated into the interior, when the patriot army took possession with little or no bloodshed. Still the inhabitants of Lima were, during the time I remained there, in constant dread of a return of the Spanish army. The city and its dependencies were daily agitated and unsettled, and the whole country was convulsed with war. The Government was almost daily making forced loans and contributions upon the inhabitants, which caused them to secrete their money for fear of its being taken from them. Every fine horse belonging to private individuals was seized for the use of the army; even the horses of foreigners were sometimes taken, but they were generally returned after a suitable remonstrance to the commanding officer.

This has been rather a long digression, and I will again return to my narrative.

The brig *Dick*, under my command, was ready for sea on the 28th of July. Before sailing, I wrote the particulars of the voyage to my owners, and also to my family up to this date, and the next day sailed for Truxillo, with the owner of the brig on board.

It was 6 o'clock in the evening when we got under way; we had light winds from the S. E., and foggy weather during the night, and ran to the leeward under easy sail until daylight.

July 30th.—During the first and middle part of these twenty-four hours we had a continuation of light winds and thick weather. After running about fifty-six miles log distance, it lighted up, when we found ourselves in mid channel between the Islands of Mazorque and Pelada, which are about two leagues asunder.

No observation of the sun, it being obscured by fog.

31st.—First and middle part of twenty-four hours light breezes from the S. E. with a continu-ation of cloudy weather. At 11 o'clock in the forenoon, we passed a schooner beating up the coast. We set our ensign, and indicated our wish to speak him, but the unsocial fellow would not shorten sail, and appeared to avoid us. At noon saw a ship running down to the westward. We continued to run along shore to the northward, and made about 100 miles by the log. At noon our lat. by obs. was 10° 29' S., long. about 77° 50' W.

Aug. 1st.—At 1 o'clock in the afternoon we saw the land, bearing E. S. E. eight or ten leagues distant. We had light breezes and calm weather all the twenty-four hours, and only made ninety-six miles, running down along the land, generally at a distance of ten leagues. Lat. by obs. at noon 9° 14' S.

Aug. 2nd.—First and middle part of these twenty-four hours, light airs from the S. E. and clear, pleasant weather. At 12, midnight, hove to and lay by until 3 A.M., daylight, when we made sail. At 5 in the morning, saw the island of Guanap, bearing S. E. about four miles distant. We then hauled in shore. Brisk breezes at S. E. and fine, clear, pleasant weather. At 10 o'clock in the forenoon, the city of Truxillo bore east, and in half an hour afterwards we came to anchor at Guanchaco, in seven fathoms water; the church at that place bearing E. by N. about a league distant. This is an Indian village situated on the beach of the sea, and is the seaport of Truxillo. It lies in lat. 8° 8' S., and long. about 79° 0' west of London.

I should perhaps rather have called Guanchaco the roadstead or anchoring ground of Truxillo, for it certainly cannot properly be called a harbor. It is open to the broad ocean, and has nothing to shelter ships that touch or trade on this part of the coast. The Indians who live in the village of Guanchaco are expert boatmen, and with their own boats transport all the goods and merchandise landed at that port for Truxillo, or exported therefrom. They are perhaps 500 to 800 in number, are governed by their own alcalde and under officers, and live almost entirely by boating and fishing. The ships that touch here cannot with any safety use their own boats, and always employ the boats or canoes of the Indians, the surf being too high to venture off and on without the aid of these men, who are almost amphibious. They are trained to swimming from their infancy, and commence with a small "Balsa," in the surf within the reefs, and by degrees, as they grow older and larger, venture through the surf, and out upon the broad ocean. These "Balsas," are made of reeds bound firmly together, with a hole near the after end, for one person; the forward end is tapered, and turned up like a skate or a Turkish shoe. Those for children are perhaps from five to eight feet long, and those used by the men are generally about ten or twelve feet long, and about as large in circumference as a small sized barrel. An Indian placed in one of these Balsas with a paddle bids defiance to the roaring billows and break-ing surf. I have seen the men go off through it in one of these reedy boats, when it seemed impossible that a human being could live in the surf, and have with, great anxiety observed them at times when a high rolling sea threatened to overwhelm them, watch the approaching roller and duck their heads down close to the reed boat, and let the billow pass over them, like a seal or a wild duck, and force their way with perfect confidence through the surf, where no white man would for a moment dare to venture. One of these men would, for half a dollar, convey a letter from the shore through the surf, to a ship laying at anchor in the Roads, when no boat dare attempt it. I was told that for a small sum of money, one of these Indians would take a valuable piece of silk goods (secured in oiled cloth and fastened round his body) on shore, and deliver it to the owner perfectly dry, even in a dark night. The moment they land they take up the Balsa and place it in an upright position in the sun to drain and dry, and thus it is kept ready at a moment's warning for any employment that may offer.

While here, I used sometimes to amuse myself with throwing small pieces of copper coin into the water, to see the Indian boys dive to the bottom and pick them up. I never could learn that any of these Indians were drowned, though the people of Truxillo told us of many accidents, when white men were drowned, in attempting to land in a high surf.

The morning we arrived at Guanchaco, there came in also an English ship from Lima, and anchored near our brig.—Very soon after, a large launch, manned with nine Indians, came alongside of us, to take the captains, supercargoes, and passengers of both vessels on shore. As there was considerable surf on, great anxiety was expressed by the supercargoes and passengers, respecting the safety of landing. I had a conversation with the patroon of the boat, on the subject of landing. He said that if we would commit ourselves entirely into his hands, there was no danger; and that he supposed the gentlemen would be willing to pay half a dollar each, if landed dry and in perfect safety. This we all readily agreed to, and soon started for the shore. I think we were five in number; and as we approached the shore, a few yards outside the surf, the sea was terrific, and breaking "feather white." Some of the gentlemen were in favor of returning, but were soon overruled by the majority. I attentively watched the eye of the patroon, who appeared cool and collected, and, by his manner, inspired me with confidence in his ability to perform what he had undertaken. He requested the gentlemen who feared the result, not to survey the scene, but to lie down in the stern-sheets of the boat, and thus give him room to manage the boat according to his own judgment. At this moment, I saw a man on the beach, on the watch for a favorable instant for us to pull for the shore. The man on the shore and our patroon made signals with a handkerchief on a cane. The boat's head was kept off shore until the signal was given and answered, to dash through the surf. In an instant the boat was wheeled round with her head towards the land, when every man pulled to the utmost of his strength, and in a few minutes we were safe within the breakers. These strong, brave fellows, then took each a passenger on his back, and carried him ashore in great triumph. We were all so sensibly touched with the conduct of these men, that many dollars were voluntarily thrown into their hats and caps; and a thrill of gratitude passed over my mind, that will remain with me till the hour of my death. We call these people savages, and say that they are incapable of great actions. I defy the white man to contend with them in the management of a boat in the surf, on the sea-shore.

The alcalde furnished us with horses, and we were soon on the road to the city of Truxillo, which is pleasantly situated on level ground, about eight or ten miles from the landing at Guanchaco. I think it contained, at this time, about eight or ten thousand inhabitants. There are two or three considerable churches; many of the houses are well built, and have a comfortable appearance. The ground and gardens around the city are well cultivated, and produce abundance of excellent fruit; and the whole aspect of the town and its vicinity is extremely pleasant. Although this place is located so near the equator, the climate is not uncomfortably warm. There is, however, a great drawback to a residence in this place, in the frequency of earthquakes. I was told by some of the most respectable citizens of Truxillo, that the town had been two or three times nearly destroyed by earthquakes, and that the great earthquakes were generally periodical,—say at intervals of forty years—that some thirty years had now passed away without a very destructive one, and that they had serious fears that they should experience another terrible convulsion before many years should elapse.

We found here no sugars or other produce to purchase, nor could we hear of any of consequence in the neighboring towns to leeward. Two vessels from Lima had lately been here, and to the adjacent towns, and bought up all the inhabitants had to dispose of.

After remaining here a few days, my owner and myself returned to Guanchaco, without making any purchases, except some poultry and fruit for sea-stores.

On our way back to the landing, we passed over very extensive ruins, which appeared at least two miles in length: they were the remains of clay walls, and various fragments of what had once been an extensive city of the Incas. We saw also a large mound near Guanchaco. It was 50 to 80 feet high, and, perhaps, from 150 to 200 feet long. These mounds were no doubt made by the ancient Peruvians, and are found all along this coast. Some of them are very high and large, others quite small. I have seen a great variety of Indian relics, that were dug out from this mound, such as earthen drinking vessels, made to resemble cats, dogs, monkeys, and other animals; others, again, were made exactly to resemble a fish, with a handle on its back, and its mouth open to drink from. These articles were well executed, and of very fine clay. The present race of Peruvians are altogether incapable of manufacturing any thing of the kind equal to these ancient Indian relics. I have no doubt, if these mounds were fairly excavated, that a great variety of valuable Indian relics could be found, which are now hidden from the world.

We arrived at the landing on Thursday, August 8th, in the afternoon, and found too much surf on the beach to attempt going on board until the next morning, and as there was no hotel or tavern in Guanchaco, we took up our abode for the night with the alcalde or chief magistrate of the village. This person was an intelligent Indian, who had in his early life made several voyages to Manilla, and appeared familiar with all parts of the western coast of Peru. He seemed to be a sensible, judicious person, and managed and governed the people of Guanchaco in a quiet, paternal manner. During the evening he entertained us with a narration of his voyages from Peru to the Philippine Islands, when Peru was a colony of Spain. He also related to us many anecdotes of his race, the ancient and rightful owners of this bloodstained soil.

The high mounds all along this part of the coast appear to be monuments of their wrongs and sufferings, and call to mind the days when Pizarro, with his band of merciless adventurers, sacrificed thousands and tens of thousands of these innocent worshippers of the sun, robbed them of their gold, and finally despoiled them of home and country. Even to the present day, these poor people are not exempt from severe persecutions in the way of taxation and oppression. They are now forcibly taken from their quiet homes to fill the ranks led by military chiefs, and thus compelled to mingle in the deadly strife of contending parties. Whether the one or the other governs, it is to them only a change of masters, for they cannot be supposed to feel any interest for, or sympathy with, either of them. And thus it has ever been in this wicked and unjust world, the strong triumph over and oppress the weak.

The good alcalde had supper prepared for us, and placed mattresses and blankets on the tables for Mr. B. and myself. Previous to retiring to rest I took a stroll round the house, and saw, beneath a shed or back piazza, three of the alcalde's children, little boys, I should judge between ten years old and three, lying asleep on a raw dry bullock's hide, covered only with another. The air was chilly, and it struck me at the moment as inhuman treatment to expose children thus to the open air without other covering than a raw hide. I immediately inquired of our friendly host why he thus exposed his children. His answer was, that it was their general custom to harden them and give them good constitutions; that he himself was brought up in the same manner; and being thus inured to the cold while young, they felt no inconvenience from it in after life.

In the morning the sea was smooth, and the surf not bad. After taking leave of the polite and friendly alcalde, we left Guanchaco in the Indian launch, got safe on board, and at 3 o'clock on the 9th of August, weighed anchor and made sail for Payta.

After getting our anchor on board, we found the stock broken in two pieces, and thus rendered unfit for use. We steered to the westward along shore with a good S. E. trade wind, and pleasant weather. Through the night we had moderate breezes and a continuation of fine weather. At 5 o'clock in the morning, daylight, saw the Islands of Lobos de Mer and Lobos de Terra, bearing S. W., three leagues distant. They are of moderate height, and without trees or cultivation. Towards noon the winds became light, inclining to a calm. Lat. by obs. 6° 32' S., long. about 81° W.

On the 10th of August, we had light winds and fine weather, and made but little progress on our course during the day, still steering down along shore with the land in sight.

Aug. 11th.—This day, like the last, commenced with light airs and calm, warm weather. At 8 P.M., Point de Ajuga bore E., two leagues distant. During the night, light airs and fine weather. At daylight, saw Point de Payta, bearing N. E., eight leagues distant; at 8, got near the Point, and steered up the Bay of Payta. At 11, a breeze sprung up from the S. E., when we ran up the bay and came to anchor at noon, in nine fathoms water, directly opposite the town. We had little or no cargo to dispose of, and there was no freight to be obtained, consequently we remained here only twenty-four hours, and got ready for sea.

Payta is situated on a fine bay of the same name, and is the principal seaport of Puira, a very considerable town in the interior, some ten or fifteen leagues distant from this place.

The town of Payta is located very near the beach, and the whole surrounding country for some miles distant is a barren, sandy desert, not even affording fresh water. The inhabitants are supplied with this article, brought from a little river running into the head of the bay, at a distance of six or eight miles. The town probably contains about 1,500 to 2,000 inhabitants of all colors; a great portion, however, are Indians, and a mixture of the Spanish and Indian races.

The houses are generally built of cane and straw, with thatched roofs. It is a very healthy place, and the people, who are generally poor, live to a great age. It lies in lat. 5° 3' S., long. 81° W. of London, and is one of the best harbors on the western coast of Peru. It is a great resort for American and English whale ships. The bay of Payta is large and clean, and I believe the whalers send their boats to the little river at its head, and soon get a bountiful supply of pure, wholesome water; at the same time the ships are safe and quiet while they remain in this capacious bay.

At 2 o'clock in the afternoon of the 12th, with a fine fresh S. E. trade wind, we sailed out of this bay, bound for Guayaquil. At 6 P.M., got abreast of Point de Parina, about a league off shore; at the same time saw Cape Blanco bearing N., half E., twenty-four miles distant. During the night we had fresh breezes, with a little rain. At 6 A.M. saw the land, bearing from S. W. to N. E., five or six leagues distant. Lat. by obs. at noon, 3° 37' S. At this time Point Los Picos bore S. E., distant about four leagues.

Aug. 13th.—This day commenced with light airs from the S., with very warm weather. At 4 P.M., passed near the American whale-ship *Rosalie*, of Warren, R.I., which was lying at anchor, near Tumbes. This ship had been thirteen months absent from the United States, and had only taken 200 barrels of oil.

At 8 P.M., we came to anchor in five fathoms' water, near the mouth of the Tumbes river, the small Island of Santa Clara bearing N. by W., distant about four leagues. Light wind at N. E. Here we lay at anchor all night.

Aug. 14th.—This day commenced with light breezes from the N. E., and fine weather. At 8 A.M., got under way with a light wind from the N. W. by N. The tide now commenced making up the river, which enabled us to gain ground, beating up with its assistance until noon, when the wind became more favorable, from the W. S. W. At 3 P.M., got abreast of the west end of the Island of Puna; pleasant breezes and fine weather.

At 7 P.M., we came to anchor in four and a half fathoms of water, the east end of Puna then bearing N. N. W., four leagues distant. It being dark, and having no pilot on board, I judged it imprudent to make sail, and therefore remained at anchor during the night.

Aug. 15th.—This day commenced with clear, pleasant weather, with light winds and variable. At 6 A.M., received a pilot on board, and at 8 got under way with the flood tide and stood up the river, which had now become more narrow, but was still deep and not difficult to ascend. The banks along the river on both sides are low, but the land rises as you recede from the river into the interior to immense mountains, many of which are volcanic. We continued to beat up the stream, and at 6 P.M., just before dark, came to anchor in the river opposite the city of Guayaquil in six fathoms of water, a short quarter of a mile off the town.

It is about forty miles from Guayaquil to the Island of Puna, where the river pilots reside, and it is at this place that the river fairly commences; for below Puna, it may more properly be called a wide bay or gulf opening into the sea.

We found lying at Guayaquil some fifteen or twenty sail of vessels of different nations, four or five of which were American ships and brigs, among them the ship *Canton*, of New-York, and the brig *Canton*, of Boston. The names of the others I do not now recollect.

After lying here a few days, undecided what to do with, or how to employ, the brig, my owner, on the 22d of August, sold his vessel for $14,000 to John O'Sullivan, Esq., captain and supercargo of the ship *Canton*. Captain O'Sullivan gave the command of the brig to Lieutenant Hudson, now Captain Hudson, of the U.S. Navy.

He loaded her in this port for a voyage to Upper Peru. At this time there were lying at Guayaquil two large Calcutta ships loaded with Indian goods. From these ships Captain O'Sullivan, purchased the greater part of a cargo for the *Dick*. The balance was made up of cocoa, and a few other articles. Myself, officers and crew were now paid off, and left the vessel in charge of the new owners.

I was anxious to return home to New-York, and of course did not regret being sold out of employment. I had long been acquainted with Capt. O'Sullivan, and was glad to meet him here. I also met with another acquaintance in the person of Francis Coffin, Esq., supercargo of the brig *Canton*.

Mr. Coffin got a fine freight of cocoa for Cadiz. I think it amounted to $17,500. I was glad to have good fortune attend him, as he was and is, if alive, an honorable gentlemanly man, of sterling worth and high integrity.

I was now living on shore, anxiously waiting a passage for Panama, to return home across the Isthmus. Capt. O'Sullivan had with him three or four young gentlemen, belonging to New-York.

These young men joined the ship *Canton,* in New-York, as ordinary seamen, but not liking a sea-life were anxious to return home. Capt. O'Sullivan gave two of them liberty to leave the ship, but would not supply them with money. He told me, however, that if I thought proper to take them along with me, that he had no doubt their friends in New-York would refund the money I should expend in paying their passages back to the U.S.; and as they were here destitute, I consented to take them, pay their passages and other necessary expenses to New-York, and rely upon the honor of their families to refund me the amount when we should arrive there.

After waiting a few days, we heard of a small coasting vessel which was to leave this place for Panama in a few days. She was a full-rigged brig, of about twenty-five tons burthen, with a captain, boatswain, and eight men before the mast. A vessel of the same size in the U.S. would have been sloop-rigged, and provided with a captain, one man, and a boy. In this vessel I agreed for a passage to Panama for myself and my two young American friends. This brig was called *"Los dos Hermanos."* There were two other (Guayaquil gentlemen) passengers, besides myself and the before-named young men, who agreed to sleep on deck; as I paid one hundred dollars for my passage, I was supplied with a berth in the cabin, if it deserved the name, for in fact it was more like a dog's kennel than a cabin. It had no windows or sky-light, and was nearly filled with bags and boxes, and had only two berths, and no table. The two passengers belonging to Guayaquil, occupied one of the berths, and I the other.

Guayaquil lies in lat. 2° 12' S., long. 79° 42' W., and is about 150 miles to the southward of Quito. The city of Guayaquil lies on the right bank of the river, and contains about 20,000 inhabitants, and although built of wood, a great portion of the houses are large and comfortable, and well adapted to the climate. Several of the public buildings are spacious and firmly built with tiled roofs, among which are the customhouse, college, and hospital. The city is located on low, level ground, and of course difficult to drain, which at certain seasons of the year renders it very unhealthy. The educated classes of society are polite and hospitable. The ladies dress in good taste, and are decidedly the handsomest women on the western coast of this continent; in fact, the beauty of the Guayaquil ladies is proverbial. The lower classes are a desperate looking race. They are a mixture of the Spaniard, Indian, and Negro, and appear ripe for any kind of villainy or disorder.

The principal wealth of Guayaquil proceeds from the cultivation of cocoa, which is their staple article. They also export timber, boards, hides, and some tobacco. The cocoa plantations lie on both sides of the river for several miles above the city. It is brought to Guayaquil upon floating rafts of light buoyant wood called, in this country, Balzas. These rafts are in general use for all kinds of transportation. Many of the poorer classes live upon them. They float up and down the river with perfect ease and safety. In them the cocoa is taken on board of the ships that load here. On these Balzas they erect tents and awnings, and thus protect themselves and their cargoes from the sun and rain. Along the river and thence down to the seacoast, the land is very flat, and in the rainy seasons a great portion of the low grounds are inundated; consequently the inhabitants in such places build their houses on large timbers, or posts, some eight or ten feet above the ground, and find it necessary to have ladders to get into them. When flooded in the rainy seasons, they pass from house to house in boats.

In this warm latitude, where the sun is nearly vertical, the weather is generally very hot, and the vegetation extremely luxuriant and rank; consequently none but those born and reared in this climate can reside in these low lands on the banks of the rivers and creeks, with any degree of safety.

To the eastward, some ten or fifteen leagues in the interior, I beheld lofty mountains rising one above another, until at last the eye rested on the majestic Chimborazo. There it stands, a mountain on the top of other mountains, terminating in a lofty sugar-loaf, snowcapped peak, alone, in its own grand and unrivalled sublimity; and although some seventy-five or eighty miles from Guayaquil, it appears as though it were within a very short distance. This grand sight, however, is not an every-day occurrence. On the contrary, one may remain at Guayaquil for several days, and even weeks, without getting a good view of the peak. When the clouds are dispelled, you behold the whole mountain from the base to the top in all its beauty and grandeur. The sight of this sublime object richly rewards the traveller for the expense and privation of coming to this country.

While I remained here the weather was extremely warm, and one can easily imagine that to be supplied with ice and ice-cream must have been a most acceptable luxury, and so we found it. As often as once or twice a week I saw a flag hoisted at a favorite cafe as a signal for ice and ice-cream for sale, announcing at the same time that some one had arrived from the mountains in the interior with a supply of this article, which was soon converted into excellent cream.

Guayaquil is supplied with great quantities of excellent fruit, common to tropical regions. Pineapples are very abundant and cheap, as are oranges, bananas and plantains. Water and musk melons are also cheap and plenty. The beef and mutton, as in most other hot climates, is indifferent, and the beef appears even worse than it otherwise would do, in consequence of the slovenly manner of cutting it up. They do not dress it as in other countries, but tear and cut the flesh from off the bone of the animal in strings, and sell it by the yard or "vara." As this is the first and only place in which I ever bought beef by the yard, I thought it worthy of notice in my narrative.

About noon, on the *31st of August*, the captain of the brig "*Los dos Hermanos*" sent me word that he was ready for sea, and wished all his passengers to repair on board forthwith. Not having much baggage to look after, I took leave of the few friends I had in Guayaquil, and hurried on board. On our way to the brig, we passed through the market and purchased a large quantity of fruit for sea-stores. Among other things, I purchased some twenty or thirty large water-melons, which I found preferable to every kind of fruit. I never shall forget how gratefully refreshing we found them on a hot, calm morning, under a vertical sun, with the ther. at 85° above zero.

We did not leave the town until 3 o'clock in the afternoon; and, as the wind was light and variable, we drifted slowly down the river with the ebb tide, until about 10 o'clock, when it became quite dark, and we anchored for the night. Here again I was pleased with what to me was a novel occurrence. Far away to the eastward, in the interior, I saw a great light and innumerable sparks of fire, which illuminated the sky, so as to render the scene vivid and beautiful. Upon inquiry, I found it was a burning volcano, at a great distance in the interior. It appeared to be some thirty or forty miles distant, while it was, in fact, perhaps fifty leagues off.

The next morning, at daylight, September 1st, we got under way, and made a short cut to the sea, through a passage to the northward of the island of Puna. Our brig drew very little water, and we were therefore able to pass through small rivers and creeks where larger vessels dare not venture.

I soon discovered that our captain was a vain, ignorant, superstitious man, and knew nothing of navigation. He had neither chart nor quadrant on board. Fortunately for us, however, our contramaéstre, or boatswain, was a good seaman and an excellent pilot. He was a native of Old Spain, and although deficient in education, was a discreet, respectable man. He disciplined and managed the crew, and left little or nothing for the captain to do, but eat, drink, smoke, and sleep. The man was only an apology for a captain, and was in the habit of following the land along shore on his voyages between Guayaquil and Panama; whereby, in lieu of making a straight course, he prolonged his passage to double the number of days necessary. I had with me a quadrant and many charts of the western coast, from Guayaquil to Panama, on a large scale, and politely pointed out to him the true and straight course. I say politely, for I have ever found, that with the ignorant and superstitious of all nations, the greatest possible caution and delicacy must be observed when advising them, otherwise their self-love and jealousy take fire, and they become your enemies.

This vulgar captain at first inclined to adhere to his own opinion,—said he had navigated this part of the coast for many years, and always with success, and was afraid of sudden changes. His countrymen, the two passengers, however, fell in with me and persuaded him to follow my advice, and endeavor to shorten the distance of the passage. The two passengers alluded to were merchants, or shopkeepers, who visited Panama occasionally to purchase and sell goods, and on their way up and down, used to touch at a small place called Monte Christi, to trade, and to this place we were now bound on our way to Panama.

There were five passengers,—making, with officers and crew, a total of fifteen souls on board the "*Dos Hermanos*"—all of whom lived on deck, night and day, except the two Guayaquil traders and myself. The contramaéstre had the entire management of the vessel, and appeared to be always on the watch, both by night and day. The sailors were not divided into watches, as is the custom on board of vessels of other nations, but all slept in the long-boat on deck, on a dry ox hide, with another spread over them. Whenever it was necessary to make or take in sail, they were all called; and when the work was done all lay down to sleep again. They appeared to work with alacrity, and were always ready to obey the boatswain without grumbling. We had been out but a few days before we encountered much hot, rainy weather. At these times our situation, in the little hole of a cabin, was deplorable. When it rained violently, a large tarpaulin was spread over the companion-way to keep the cabin dry.—On such occasions, particularly in the night, the captain and the deck passengers would crawl in for shelter, and I was often obliged to leave my berth, and struggle through the crowd to get a little air at the door to prevent suffocation.

We were provided with only two meals a day; the first, called breakfast, about 11 o'clock in the forenoon, was taken always on deck. This meal was either a fricassee or puchero, with bread and a little common, low Catalonia wine. The other meal we generally had at four or five o'clock in the afternoon, and it was composed of about the same in quality, served up in one large dish placed in the centre of the quarter-deck. Our polite captain always helped himself first, and then advised every body to do the like. The food of the sailors on the main-deck consisted of plantain and charque or dried beef. Thus situated, we passed some days, creeping along at a slow pace, and making but little progress on our course, with variable winds, and very hot, calm weather.

On Sunday morning, Sept. 5th, at daylight in the morning, we ran into the little bay of Monte Christi, and came to anchor very near the shore, in three fathoms of water.

This is a clean little bay, with a fine sand beach, and a few small houses, called ranchos and shops, at the landing. The town of Monte Christi is located three or four miles inland from the port, in an easterly direction. This lonely little harbor lies in lat. 1° 1' S., long. 80° 32' W. of London. It was quite destitute of shipping, there being no vessel there except our little brig. We procured horses from the rancheros at the landing, and soon galloped over a pleasant road, to the town. It being Sunday morning, the whole town, or as the French say, "tout le monde," were decked out in their holiday dresses. Our captain and the two Guayaquil traders had planned a great deal of business for the day, and were very impatient to attend mass, that they might proceed to its execution afterwards. Accordingly, we left our horses at a poor little posada, and then hurried to the church. I went with them near the door, and after having excused myself for leaving them, took a stroll about the town. Every body appeared to be on the move towards the church, arrayed in gaudy dresses, of bright red and yellow colors. These simple people seemed as fond of displaying their gay attire as children decked out in their holiday suits.

After a little survey of the town, I entered a house for some water, when the following dialogue occurred between the master of the house and myself. After presenting me with a chair and giving me a welcome reception, he said, "I suppose you landed this morning from the brigantine, on your way to Panama?" "Yes, I did so," I replied. "The captain and the passengers have all gone to mass, how is it that you did not go also—are you not a Christian?" I answered I was, but having a very imperfect knowledge of the Spanish language, I preferred walking about the town. I then took the same liberty with him, and inquired why he did not go. He replied that he attended early mass, and was always very attentive to his religious duties. He then questioned me on the religious faith and belief of my countrymen in England. I told him I was not from that country, but from North America. He then called me an Anglo-Americano, and seemed to have a confused idea that we were the descendants of the English, and lived in a distant region of which very little was known, and inquired whether our belief and faith was the same as that of the English; that he had always been told that the English were all heretics and unbelievers. I told him that the religion of the two countries was about the same, that neither of them were heretics or unbelievers. He expressed great surprise and then asked me if we believed in "el Padre et Hijo y el Espiritu Santo." On my answering him in the affirmative, he appeared still more astonished, and said, then he had always been greatly deceived, that he had from his childhood been told by the priests and friars that the English were all infidels, and did not believe in the Trinity, nor yet in the "Holy Mother of God, the pure and holy Virgin Mary." I then told him there was certainly a great difference between the belief of his countrymen and mine, on the subject of worship due to the Virgin Mary, and holy reverence to a great many saints, but that the greater part of the churches, both in England and North America, professed to believe in the Trinity. He appeared very well satisfied with my explanation,—and said he had no doubt we had been misrepresented and slandered; and that he would inquire further into the subject from the first intelligent Englishman he should meet.

While I am on this subject, I will relate an anecdote that occurred one evening at the lodging of Captain O'Sullivan, while I was at Guayaquil. Among other questions, the mistress of the house, a middle-aged, good looking lady, asked me whether there were any Jews in my country. I told her there were many. She then asked me what they looked like, and whether they had tails. I was for a moment surprised, and thought she was jesting, and hardly knew how to answer,—when she observed, that she had always been told that Jews were strange-looking creatures, and had long tails like cows hanging down behind them. She said she came to Guayaquil about two years before, from a village in the interior of Colombia; and that from her infancy she had been always told by the priests, that Jews had tails, and were odious, frightful-looking creatures. I was astonished at her simple ignorance, for she was not one of the lower order, but a woman of polite manners, and spoke the Spanish language with ease and grace.

I have related these two incidents from a thousand other similar ones, that have come under my observation while travelling about South America, not with a view of exposing the ignorance of these honest, simple-hearted people, as objects of ridicule, but to hold up to the world the wickedness of these vile priests and friars, who delude and darken the minds of unfortunate beings, who are the subjects of their cunning priestcraft. In the United States we abhor the military despot who enslaves and chains the body; but is not the man who darkens and enslaves the mind, ten times more guilty than the military despot? I can overlook with some degree of patience a great many defaults and superstitious prejudices in the uneducated and ignorant, but have very little patience or charity for these vile leaders of the blind, who know better than to prey upon the ignorance and credulity of their fellow-men, either in matters of church or state. The wicked policy of keeping mankind in ignorance, in order to profit by their want of knowledge, cannot but excite the indignation of him who loves his fellow-man.

Monte Christi is situated on an undulating surface, moderately high, with one considerable church located on rising ground, in the centre of the town, which probably contains about 1500 inhabitants. The houses are generally one story high, and are built of sun-dried brick; some, however, are two stories, and have tile roofs.

The weather here is so hot that the inhabitants keep within doors during the middle of the day. In the evening it becomes cool and pleasant. This town and its vicinity, like most other places near the equator, are subject to periodical wet and dry seasons. During the heavy rains, many of the people remove to the hills, taking their cattle and other domestic animals along with them; and at the commencement of the dry season, return to their former habitations. I understood that the dry seasons last from December to April, and the wet during the rest of the year.

My stay here was so short that I could collect little reliable information on the subject of the general state of this country. I found the people generally a mixed breed of Spaniard, Indian, and Mulatto.

Our captain and the two Guayaquil traders, after mass on the day of our arrival here, arranged their commercial affairs with the principal shop-keepers of the town, and when we had partaken of a tolerable dinner at the little posada, we all mounted our horses about 4 o'clock in the afternoon, and returned again to the port. Here we landed several bags of cocoa, and a quantity of boxes of merchandise; and took on board some dry hides, and eight or ten bags of dollars; and after renewing our sea-stores of plantain and live-stock, got under way just before dark, and steered out of the bay on our course for Panama.

I learned from the two Guayaquil traders, that they were in the habit of leaving goods with the shop-keepers at Monte Christi, to dispose of for their account, and always stopped on their way up and down from Panama to Guayaquil, to receive the amount of what they had sold, either in money or in the produce of the country. I was surprised at the amount of the cargo and money transported in this trifling little craft. I think one of these gentlemen told me there was about $30,000 on board of our little brig, besides other valuable articles, which we were now taking to Panama, with which to pay debts and purchase merchandise for Guayaquil and the western coast of Colombia.

I am thus minute on the subject of this small trading vessel, to show that although a craft of this description would not be considered capable or safe to make a sea voyage along the coast of the States, here the mild winds and smooth seas do not endanger almost any kind of vessel that will float, whilst trading along the coast between Guayaquil and Panama.

During the night there was a pleasant little breeze from off the land, and the next day, we had light and variable winds, with fine weather. At noon, I amused myself, while sailing along shore, by taking a meridian observation; and it so happened that the sun at noon was vertical, or directly over head, and I could therefore sweep his image with the quadrant all round the horizon, and fully realize that we were on the equator, and consequently in no latitude. Our longitude at this time was about 80° 00' W. from London.

We continued to have light and variable winds, with occasional showers, for several days after crossing the equator. The weather during the daytime was generally very warm, and we had little or nothing to screen us from the rays of the sun, in this small and very uncomfortable vessel. Our captain, as I have before said, was an ignorant, ill-bred man, and took no pains to secure the comfort or convenience of his passengers;—these evils rendered the time extremely tedious. We had, however, got about three degrees to the northward of the line, and were now making a pretty straight course for Panama. By the persuasion of the passengers and myself, our captain consented to steer boldly on our course to the northward, and not to follow the land along the whole length of Chuco bay, as he was inclined to do. He had neither chart nor quadrant on board,—and upon reflection, I was not surprised that he should not venture far out of sight of terra firma. The contramaéstre was a good seaman and an excellent fellow; and frankly acknowledged that he knew nothing of navigation, though he was well acquainted with the land, and could navigate up and down the coast almost by instinct. As we increased our latitude to the northward, the winds gradually freshened, and we got on without any material accident.

On the morning of the 16th of Sept., 1822, we made Point St. Francisco Solano, and the land to the eastward of the entrance of the bay of Panama. Point St. Francisco Solano is a prominent headland, and lies in lat. 6° 49' N., long. 77° 47' W. We steered up to the northward, keeping in sight of the land on the eastern side of the bay, and found the coast clear and easy to navigate. During the night the wind was light. The next day, Sept. 17th, we made several islands lying in this beautiful bay,—and as the weather was fine and the sea smooth, it was very pleasant sailing among the islands. We steered to the northward, and now had land on both sides of the bay. On passing the islands, we saw several men in boats employed in catching pearl oysters. The shells, I believe, are here not of much value, though considerable quantities are occasionally shipped from Panama to England.

The next day, Sept. 18th, we came to anchor off the town of Panama; and in a few minutes after went on shore, and forever bade adieu to our captain and the brig *Los Dos Hermanos.*

I was, of course, delighted to get on shore at Panama; but I was not a little disappointed to find the city so badly supplied with hotels. Although there were two or three tolerable cafés, where one could get something to eat and drink, still, I believe, there was not a good hotel in the place. I was told that the best way of living there, was to hire a room or two, and and then get a black woman to cook. I accordingly hired a few rooms for myself and my two young friends, and engaged a black woman to dress our food and keep the rooms in order. In this way we got along tolerably well, and without any great expense.

To my satisfaction, I met here Captain John Brown, of the schooner *Freemason,* of Baltimore. This schooner was lying at Chagres, and Captain Brown expected to sail for the Havana in about a fortnight. I engaged a passage with him for myself and the two young gentlemen who came with me from Guayaquil.

The *Freemason* was the only American vessel lying at Chagres; and we deemed ourselves fortunate in meeting with so good an opportunity to return to the United States, by way of the Havana.

Captain Brown soon introduced me to his consignee, J. B. Ferand, Esq., the American consul at this place. I found Mr. Ferand to be a polite, obliging, gentlemanly man, and he was to me always a kind friend.

As it was quite healthy at Panama, and very sickly at Chagres, I concluded to remain in the former city until the *Freemason* was ready for sea; and not having any business to do, I had sufficient leisure to walk about the town and its vicinity, and view the Key of the Isthmus, as Panama is sometimes called.

The city of Panama lies at the head of a fine broad bay, of the same name, sprinkled with islands sheltering the harbor, and beautifying the surrounding scenery. It lies in lat. 8° 59' N., and long. 79° 22' W.; and like most other towns built by the Spaniards, is strongly walled and tolerably well fortified. It belongs to the republic of Colombia, and contains about ten or twelve thousand inhabitants. The streets are generally regular—and many of the houses are commodious and well built. Some of the public buildings are large and substantial, particularly the cathedral and several convents, and also the college. The college of the Jesuits, however, is now but a ruin. The environs of the town are pleasant, and the grounds in the neighborhood tolerably well cultivated. It was once a great place for trade, but had, during the last twenty or thirty years, gradually declined in its commerce. There was, however, some little trade still carried on; and should a canal or a railroad be constructed across the Isthmus, Panama will revive again. The natural position of the city is excellent,—and it will, in my opinion, at some future day, become a place of considerable importance.

The tide rises here to a great height—(I do not recollect precisely how many feet)—at the full and change of the moon, but as near as I can remember, some eighteen or twenty feet. Large vessels anchor at a considerable distance from the town, and lie afloat at low water; the small coasting vessels anchor close in near the walls of the city, and consequently lie on the mud at low water. The inner harbor is quite dry; the sand and mud flats extend off to a great distance, which at low tide give to the harbor an unpleasant aspect; but at the flood, the tide rises rapidly; the mud and sand banks are soon covered, and the whole scene agreeably changed from dreary banks to a living sheet of healthful salt-water.

It often struck me while strolling about this town, how admirably it was situated for a great commercial city; with a wide and extensive coast,—one may even say, from Cape Horn to Behring's Straits—with innumerable islands in the vast Pacific Ocean—with an open and easy navigation to China, over a sea so mild and gentle, that it might almost be traversed in an open boat. All these facilities are open to this town on the Pacific; and when we add to these its capacities of a general commerce on the Atlantic Ocean to Europe, the United States, and the West Indies, its location surpasses every other on the face of the globe. And now, what is necessary to bring about this great result? I answer—a just and good government, with a few enterprising capitalists, and five hundred young men from New England to give the impetus. Whaling ships—merchant ships trading to China—coasting brigs, schooners, sloops, and steamboats, would spring up like mushrooms; and in a few years this place would become one of the greatest commercial emporiums in the world. A practical, intelligent merchant, acquainted with the commerce of the world, will see by a glance at the map, that I have stated nothing respecting it either unreal or extravagant.

A few days before we left Panama, Captain Brown made an arrangement with the municipal government of this place, or perhaps with an agent of the republic of Colombia, to take as passengers about eighty Spanish prisoners and their colonel, from Chagres to the Havana, and also a Colombian officer, by the name of Barientes (I think he was a major), to take charge of the business as commissioner.

These Spanish prisoners, I understood, capitulated at Quito, on the conditions that they should leave the country and be sent to the Havana in a neutral vessel, at the expense of the Spanish government. The Colombian government agreed to furnish them with provisions, and pay Captain Brown a certain sum to land them at the Havana; I think it was about $1800 or $2000. This money was paid in advance at Chagres.

Captain Brown had now so far accomplished his business, that I began to make my arrangements to leave Panama; and for that purpose, hired a guide and five mules to transport Messrs. B.C. and A.D., my two young American friends, myself and our baggage to Cruces. For the guide and the five mules,

I paid forty-two dollars;—and thus, after remaining at Panama fourteen days, on the 2nd of October, at 4 o'clock in the afternoon, we left the city for Cruces. We travelled slowly along—myself and the two young men mounted on the riding mules (the other two were loaded with our baggage), the guide generally walking, in order to pick the best of the road and take care of the mules. He, however, rode occasionally on one of the baggage mules. The road for three or four miles after leaving the city was tolerably good, or rather the different foot-paths, for I saw nothing like a road on the whole route from Panama to Cruces. From Panama to the foot of the hills—a distance of about five or six miles—there is a gradual elevation, and nothing to prevent making a good road at a small expense.

We passed over this part of the way rather pleasantly, and just before dark took up our abode for the night in a miserable posada, where neither a bed nor any thing eatable could be obtained. I got liberty to spread my mattress on the floor,—my young friends had each a blanket with them, and we all lay down in the same room; and though thus badly accommodated, were glad to get shelter for the night.

At daylight, our guide called us to mount the mules and make the best of our way. Our bedding was soon rolled up and packed on one of the animals; and we resumed our journey over one of the worst roads I ever travelled—up and down hill, through mud-holes, and over stony ground. Sometimes we met with large stones lying in the mud and sand, that had been washed out of the earth and not removed. Over these stones, many of which were the size of a barrel, we were obliged to pass. At other times the mules would mire above their knees, in passing through a deep slough. After getting through a low spot of mud and water, the next turn would bring us to a cut in the rocks, just wide enough for a loaded mule to pass. These passes are frequently made through the solid rocks; and as they have probably been used a century and a half, the mules' feet have worn large holes, and these are generally filled with water, so that the poor animals, whether going through the mud, slough, or rocky pass, have a difficult task to perform.

On the way, we frequently met with men carrying valuable goods on their backs, to and from Panama to Cruces. Almost all fragile and valuable goods are conveyed across the Isthmus by porters on their backs: such as China and glassware, clocks, and other merchandise. Coarser and heavier goods are transported by mules. During the day, we occasionally saw huts and small ranchos along the roadside, mostly inhabited by a miserable, sickly-looking set of creatures, a mixed breed of the Spaniard, Indian, and Negro.

There is very little cultivation of the soil. The hills and valleys are generally well wooded and watered, but in a wild, savage state; and the people that vegetate here, live by raising cattle, pigs and poultry, and are extremely filthy and ignorant. The porters that convey goods on their backs from Cruces to Panama, are paid, I was told, from five to six dollars each way. The labor, however, is extremely severe, and none but the most hardy can long endure the fatigue.

We could scarcely get any thing to eat on the road, and did not arrive at Cruces until late in the afternoon, and then very much worn down with fatigue. Although the distance from Panama to Cruces is only 21 miles, the journey is tedious from the badness of the roads.

Cruces is a small town,—consisting of some eighty or a hundred little houses, lying on the west bank of the river Chagres, about 50 miles above its mouth, at the head of navigation. The houses are one story high, and generally built of wood with thatched roofs. The ground on which the town is situated is pretty level, and about twenty feet above the river. We found here comfortable accommodations, and had a good night's rest, after the fatigue of a long day's ride.

The next morning, the weather being fine, I walked about the town. The inhabitants are generally shop-keepers and boatmen, with a small proportion of mechanics. As Captain Brown was still in Panama, I was in no hurry to push on, being told that this place was more healthy and pleasant than Chagres. His clerk, a young Spanish gentleman, whose name was Francisco, joined us here, and was a friendly, polite young man, and very companionable. During the day I hired a boat, or rather a large canoe, and four men to take us down to Chagres;—we were to furnish our own stores. The canoes on this river are very large and long. They are made by hollowing out a solid tree of Spanish cedar. Some of them carry over one hundred half barrels of flour. Whole barrels of flour are rarely brought to Chagres, owing to the difficulty of transporting them from Cruces to Panama. The canoe I hired for myself, and the three other passengers was of middle size, and the price agreed upon to take us down was thirteen dollars. After having purchased stores for the passage, we got a good dinner and remained at Cruces until near sunset, when we embarked.

The canoes have hoops of bamboo bent over the after part of the craft, which is covered with a water-tight awning, so that the passengers are sheltered from the sun by day, and the dews and rain by night. With our mattresses and blankets spread in the stern sheets, we managed to sleep pretty well during the night. The river is not very wide, but generally deep and extremely crooked, and runs down very rapidly. I should think it from a quarter to half a mile wide. Its banks are generally abrupt, and from thirty to fifty feet high. Near the river, the wood is frequently cleared off, with now and then a little village, or a few small plantations; but receding a mile or two from the river, it appears like a vast wild forest, and a suitable habitation for wild beasts. In these jungles one would imagine they could remain undisturbed by the slothful race of men who inhabit the Isthmus. The trees here grow to an enormous size, and vegetation is rank and green all the year round.

Our lazy boatmen knew that we were not in a hurry, and therefore let the canoe drift down the stream pretty much all night, without rowing. Early in the morning we stopped at a small village, and bought some eggs and milk for breakfast; after remaining here about an hour, we pulled slowly down with the current. Soon after mid-day we brought up again at a small landing place, purchased a few trifling articles, and took our dinner under the shade of a fine large old tree on the bank of the river. This was on the 5th of October, and at 2 o'clock in the afternoon we re-embarked and pulled down for our port of destination. At night-fall it became dark and foggy, and we did not reach Chagres until 9 o'clock in the evening. As there was no hotel on shore, we went directly to the vessel, and had scarcely got on board and taken out our baggage, before it commenced raining, and continued to pour in torrents during the whole night. From 10 o'clock till midnight we had loud peals of thunder, and vivid lightning. At daylight it ceased raining, but there was a dense vapor like fog until about nine o'clock in the morning, when the sun shone out, and as there was not a breath of wind, it was extremely hot and uncomfortable, and the exhalations were so dense and bad that we found it difficult to breathe the foul atmosphere. This was on the 6th of October. Chagres is a small insignificant village, lying on low wet ground, along the eastern bank of the river's mouth, in lat. 9° 21' N., long. 80° 4' W., of London. To the windward, or eastern entrance of the river, there is a point of land of moderate height, projecting somewhat into the sea, and forming a shelter for vessels lying at anchor in the mouth of the river, which here widens so as to form a sort of harbor; this, together with the bar at the entrance, renders it a safe port from all gales of wind. To the leeward, and along the western bank of the river, the land is low, and overgrown with rank grass, and high mangrove bushes.

At 10 o'clock, notwithstanding the sun was shining with intense heat, I went on shore to take a look at the village, or town. We soon brought up in a "pulperia" or grog-shop, which appeared to be the only resort for strangers, there being no hotel or tavern in this miserable place.

On the eastern point before mentioned, there is a small fort, at which, and about the town, there is a military garrison of perhaps thirty or forty sickly-looking soldiers. They are mostly mulattoes and negroes, badly clothed, and worse fed. The commanding officer of this little garrison, and the great man of the place, was a middle-sized mulatto, about thirty or thirty-five years old. Captain Brown's clerk, Mr. Francisco, told me we had better call on the commandant or captain of the garrison; that he no doubt expected all strangers to pay their respects to him on their arrival. This I was quite willing to do, and by all means to treat the public authorities with all proper respect and attention. We therefore forthwith repaired to the house of the commandant; we found him comfortably lodged in good quarters, and we were received with much ceremony. The commandant was dressed in full uniform, with two immense epaulettes, and assumed an air of consequential dignity; he offered us wine, and made a great flourish of male and female attendants. This visit of ceremony lasted about half an hour, when we took leave, the commandant politely bowing us out of his premises.

The Schooner *Freemason* was the only American vessel lying in port; there were two or three others, and these small coasting vessels which are employed trading up and down the coast.

Both of the mates and two of the seamen of our vessel were ill with the yellow fever, and hardly able to keep the deck; and here we were to remain for several days, to wait for our passengers and their stores, which were to be furnished by the Colombian government, and also to be brought from Panama. The stores for the eighty Spanish prisoners consisted of charque, plantain, and a small portion of hard biscuit. The colonel and commissioner were better provided, and were to mess with Captain Brown and myself in the cabin. Captain B. had agreed to furnish water, and the poor sick mates, who were hardly able to crawl about the deck, were endeavoring, with a few sailors, to get all the water casks filled up from the river before the captain should arrive.

Previous to leaving Guayaquil, I became acquainted with an elderly intelligent Spaniard, who had been for many years at Porto Bello and Chagres; he told me by all means to wear woollen stockings or socks during the time I remained at Chagres, and to bathe my feet two or three times a day with brandy or some other kind of alcohol, and by no means expose myself to the night air or noonday sun. I strictly followed the old man's advice while I remained here, and have to thank him, with God's blessing, that I escaped taking the fever. I enjoyed excellent health during my stay at Chagres, which is, perhaps, the most sickly place on the face of the globe.

During the day, I observed the clouds were driven by the N. E. trade-winds, and were collecting and hanging above and about the hills and mountains in the neighborhood, and I may also add all along the northern coast of the Isthmus; towards night they lay in immense masses, and appeared, as it were, to rest on the tops of the lofty forest trees, which crown these high hills and mountains. Soon after sunset we began to see the lightning, and hear the thunder above the mountains, and it was kept up with increasing fury until about 9 or 10 o'clock in the evening, when the rains began to fall in perfect sheets of water.

I have witnessed copious showers in other countries, but nothing to compare with the torrents that fell here during the night; I have also seen it lighten and heard it thunder in other parts of the world, but never saw or heard anything to equal what I nightly witnessed in this place. Peal after peal rends the air, and, to a stranger, throws an appalling gloom over this doomed portion of the earth. In the morning about ten o'clock the sun broke out as on the previous day, and I found it difficult and dangerous to go on shore without an umbrella to protect me from the rays of the burning sun.

As the history of one day is exactly that of another, I deem it unnecessary to say much more on the monotonous life I led. With respect to the weather, it continued about the same during my stay, a bright burning sun during the day, with torrents of rain during the night, accompanied with vivid lightning and thunder.

Although it is very easy to descend the river Chagres in a large canoe, well protected from the sun by day, and the dews and rain by night, it is not so easy to ascend it against a very rapid current running from three to six miles an hour, according to the high or low stage of the water. Loaded canoes are often a week getting from Chagres to Cruces; the men are obliged to track up the stream, and with boat-hooks haul up along shore by the trees and bushes.

To convey passengers, the light canoes are taken, and they generally make the passage in two days. If asked whether there is sufficient water in the river for a steamboat, I would answer that I believe there is, and no obstruction but want of sufficient employment to support the expense of a boat. At this time there were very few passengers crossing the Isthmus, and too little trade to give any encouragement to establishing a steamboat on the river.

On the 8th of October Captain Brown arrived, with the Spanish colonel and the commissioner, Major Barientes, with all the sea-stores, both for the Spanish soldiers and the officers, and now all was hurry and bustle getting ready for sea. The next day, Oct. 9th, I called with Captain Brown to pay our respects to the mulatto commandant, and to take a memorandum of this man in authority to purchase whatever he should please to order from Baltimore. Captain B. had already made two or three voyages from Baltimore to this place; and as he expected to return there again in a few months, he of course had a great many little commissions to execute for the élite of Panama and Chagres. On our arrival at the quarters of the commandant, we found him decked off in a new suit of gaudy uniform,—and here I witnessed a ludicrous farce between Captain Brown and the mulatto major. The latter was a vain and conceited coxcomb, evidently bent on showing off and playing the great man. Captain Brown was a plain, blunt Scotchman, and understood not a word of Spanish, but was endowed with a good understanding, and was by nature kind and benevolent. Independent of these qualities, it was his interest to keep smooth weather, and be upon good terms with the major;—he therefore waited with patience to receive the orders of the gallant commandant. I lament that I possess not the graphic powers of Dr. Smollett to describe the ludicrous.

Captain Brown's secretary, Mr. F., was seated at a table with pen, ink and paper, to note down the orders of the mulatto gentleman, who, to show his learning, endeavored to give his directions in phrases of bad French, interlarded with a few words of English. He would now and then walk about the room for a few moments, and admire himself, from head to foot, in a large mirror suspended at the head of the room. Mr. F. modestly requested him to give his orders in the Castilian language; but this plain dealing did not suit the taste of the major, who reproved him for his presumption, and then would reverse the order and direct him to commence anew, and strictly follow the orders given in his own way. The animated gesticulations and pomposity of the yellow major, and the unmoved indifference of the captain, formed so striking a contrast, that it was with the greatest difficulty I could command my risible faculties. This farce lasted about an hour, when we took our leave of "señor commandant," and left him to admire himself without interruption.

I can only imagine one reason why the Colombian government should place such a vain fool in the command of so important a post, and that is, that the place is so unhealthy that no white man could live there.

Oct. 11th.—At 9 o'clock in the morning we weighed anchor, and with the boat ahead to tow, and a light air off the land, sailed out of the harbor bound to the Havana. After getting a mile or two from the river's mouth, it became quite calm. There we lay exposed to the hot sun for two hours, waiting for the sea breeze, to beat up to windward far enough to stand to the northward, and thus clear the land to the westward, and make good our course out of the bay.

The schooner *Freemason* was a good vessel, of about 100 tons burthen, and a pretty fair sailer. In the cabin were the captain, the Spanish colonel, Major Barientes, and myself. In the steerage were the two sick mates, and the two young men that came with me from Guayaquil. The main-hold was left for the Spanish soldiers. Two of the crew in the forecastle were ill with the yellow fever, and the mates unfit for duty, and, notwithstanding all these evils, we were delighted to leave Chagres for the broad ocean, and once more to breathe the pure sea air, and thus fly from pestilence and death.

At 11 o'clock, after lying becalmed two hours, a breeze sprung up from the E. N. E., when we commenced beating up to windward; and just at sunset, after having made fifteen or twenty miles up along shore, we steered to the N. N. E. all night with a stiff trade-wind from the east, and the next day, Oct. 11th, at 4 P.M., made the island of St. Andrew. This island lies off the Mosquito shore, in lat. 12° 30' N., long. 81° W. After passing this island we kept the trade-wind, and as it was light, we made but little progress during the night. At 6 A.M., soon after daylight, we made the island of Providence. This island is of a moderate height, and lies in lat. 13° 27' N., long. 80° 39' W. of London; distant about sixty miles to the northward of St. Andrew. We ran within a mile or two of Providence, namely, to the westward, or in seamen's phrase, under the lee of the island. Thus we continued on our course to the northward, and passed to the windward of the numerous small islands, reefs, and shoals, lying off the coast of the Mosquito shore.

Just at night on this day, Oct. 13th (sea account), Captain Brown was taken very ill, and unable to come on deck; the second mate sick below, and the chief mate, poor fellow, so reduced from the effect of the fever contracted in Chagres that he was with difficulty able to keep the deck during the day. We were now in a dangerous and very difficult situation, surrounded with reefs and shoals, and no one to take the command of the vessel. The old Spanish colonel and Major Barientes saw our situation, and begged me for God's sake to take the command of the schooner. I was placed in a very delicate position; but under all the circumstances of the case, consented to do so. I mustered all the men in the forecastle, well enough to keep watch, and they numbered two. With these, and my two New-York friends, and the cook, I took command of the schooner; and as the weather was dark and squally, I kept the deck all night, beating about in the passage until daylight, when we again got a strong trade-wind from E. N. E., and fine, clear, pleasant weather. We were now clear of all the reefs and shoals, and made a fair wind for Cape Antonio, on the west end of Cuba. At 10 o'clock in the morning, Captain Brown was better, and able to come on deck and resume the command of the schooner.

The Spanish colonel was a gentlemanly man of about sixty. He had been in the armies in South America seven or eight years, and in many severe engagements, and always fought with honor to himself and to his country; but was beaten at last at the battle of Quito, where he and many of his countrymen laid down their arms and capitulated to be sent out of the country. He was indeed a war-worn soldier, and I fear had been poorly remunerated for his hard and severe sufferings. He was a kind, amiable man, with very modest and unassuming manners, and won the respect and esteem of all those about him.

Major Barientes, the commissioner, was a fine, healthy looking young man, about thirty or thirty-five years of age; he had been several years in the Colombian service, and I have no doubt was a gallant fellow, and was now on his way to a colony of Spain, to deliver the colonel and the Spanish soldiers up to the government of Cuba, and claim from it the money and the fulfilment of the capitulation made at the battle of Quito.

I was often amused with the conversation of these two gentlemen on the subject of the different battles fought in South America between their respective countrymen, each, of course, endeavoring to make his own countrymen superior and victorious. Generally, their conversations and recitals were carried on in a good spirit; sometimes, however, they would wax a little warm in these little disputes. I good-naturedly reminded them that here we were all friends together, and had no fighting to do; this always brought them to a just sense of their relative situations, when their arguments would take a gentle tone, and end in mutual good wishes that the war between Spain and her colonies might soon terminate. I found them both well-bred and agreeable fellow-passengers.

The mates and seamen were now convalescent, and every thing went on smoothly, and in a few days we made Cape St. Antonio, and proceeded on our course without any incident worth remarking, until off Mariel, the day before we arrived at Havana. Here we fell in with a Spanish sloop of war, ship-rigged, and mounting eighteen guns. She ranged up near us, and seeing so many men on our decks, either took us for a privateer or a pirate. Her guns were pointed, and every thing ready to give us a broadside, although so near that she could, no doubt, see we had no guns. Our captain expected every moment to receive her fire. We were lying to when she hailed and ordered us to send our boat on board instantly, or she would sink us. We had but one boat, and it was dried up with the sun, so that the moment it touched the water it leaked like a sieve. Still the order was imperative and must be obeyed. Captain B. requested the colonel and myself to go on board, and show him the schooner's papers. We got into the boat, and, with constant bailing, made out to get on board of the ship, though not in a very good condition, being wet up to our knees. We showed our papers to the captain, who was a very young man, and, after a little delay, we were requested to take seats on the quarterdeck.

The colonel explained the substance of the capitulation, his misfortunes, &c. &c. The captain appeared rather to upbraid than sympathize with the good colonel, who was old enough to be his father. I felt vexed with the upstart. Our visit was of short duration. The captain of the ship neither invited the veteran to take a glass of wine, nor any other refreshment, nor was he at all polite. I sincerely regret I do not recollect the name of this worthy old warrior, who bore such treatment with so much patience.

While in the boat, I observed to the colonel that his countryman, the captain of the ship, did not treat him with the consideration and courtesy due to his rank and misfortunes. He mildly replied that he was a very young man, and was probably promoted by family interest, and had little sympathy for the unfortunate.

The ship soon made sail, and we steered on our course, and the next day, Oct. 28th, came to anchor at Havana, eighteen days from Chagres. The health-boat soon came along-side, and we were allowed to go on shore.

Major Barientes went on shore in full Colombian uniform, and, I was told, was well received by the governor, but whether he ever recovered the money due to his government, I have never been able to learn. I took a kind farewell of these two worthy gentlemen, and we never again met.

I was very anxious to get home, and as there was no vessel to sail soon for New-York, engaged a passage to Philadelphia, on board the hermaphrodite brig *James Coulter*, to sail the next day. I advanced a small sum of money to my young protégés, taking their orders on their friends in New York for the money I had already paid for their passages and other expenses, and left them under the protection of the American Consul at this place.

The next day we got under way, and sailed out of the harbor, bound for Philadelphia. I regret I do not recollect the name of the young man who commanded the *J. C.*, he was an active, capable ship-master, and a worthy man. I had the good fortune to meet on board the *James Coulter*, an old friend, Captain Frazer, of Baltimore, and as we were the only passengers on board, we were very happy to meet each other, and renew our former acquaintance. We had formerly met in Europe, and now, after many years separation, it was delightful to make a passage together. I do not recollect any thing remarkable during our passage home. Every thing went on in perfect good order, and we had a very pleasant passage of only fifteen days to the city of Philadelphia.

I think I paid $50 for my passage, and was well satisfied with both the vessel and the captain. We landed in the afternoon of the 14th of November, 1822, and the next day I took the steamboat for New-York, and arrived in that city at noon, the next day following, after an absence of just twelve months.

I had not received a syllable from home during my long and tedious absence, and was extremely anxious to hear from my family and friends, and therefore with precipitation I hurried to the counting-office of my friend. I met my friend B., and not a word was spoken, but I saw in his face that I was doomed to be a miserable man, and that I was bereft of the dearest object for me that earth contained. I conjured him to speak out and let me know the worst. I told him I was a man, and could bear grief. He then told me that my wife died in Brooklyn, on the 3rd of October, and was interred on the 5th, and that she had left me a fine little daughter, about seven months old.

I forthwith proceeded to my melancholy abode, and although I was stricken and cut to the soul, and bereft of her my soul held the dearest of earth's treasures, still, what could I say, but repeat the words of a man more afflicted than myself, "The Lord gave, and the Lord hath taken away, and for ever blessed be his holy name."

A few weeks after my return home, my worthy friend Richard M. Lawrence, Esq., who at this period was President of the Union Marine Insurance Company in New-York, called at my house, and generously offered me a situation as inspector of ships in that company. The situation had lately been vacated, and was now offered to me with a very handsome salary. I, however, declined the kind offer of my excellent friend, with many thanks; not wishing at this time to remain long on shore.

Had my wife been spared me, I should have thankfully accepted the offer, but being bereft and disappointed in my anticipations in life, I was again cast adrift and almost alone in this world of change and disappointment.

Adventures of John Nicol

MARINER

Having reached the age of sixty-seven years, when I can no longer sail upon discovery, and weak and stiff, can only send my prayers with the tight ship and her merry hearts, at the earnest solicitation of friends I have here set down some account of my life at sea. Twice I circumnavigated the globe; three times I was in China; twice in Egypt; and more than once sailed along the whole land-board of America, from Nootka Sound to Cape Horn and twice I doubled it.

I was born in the small village of Currie, about six miles from Edinburgh, in the year 1755. The first wish I ever formed was to wander, and many a search I gave my parents in gratifying my youthful passion.

My father, a cooper, was a man of talent and information, and made it his study to give his children a good education; but my unsteady propensities did not allow me to make the most of the schooling I got. I had read Robinson Crusoe many times over, and longed to be at sea. Every moment I could spare was spent in the boats or about the shore.

When I was about fourteen years of age, my father was engaged to go to London. Even now, I recollect the transports my young mind felt, when he informed me that I was to accompany him. I counted the hours and minutes to the moment we sailed on board the Glasgow packet. It was in the month of December we sailed, and the weather was very bad; all the passengers were seasick; I never was. This was in the year 1769, when the dreadful loss was sustained on the coast of Yorkshire—above thirty sail of merchantmen were wrecked. We were taken in the same gale, but rode it out. Next morning, we could hardly proceed for wreck; and the whole beach was covered. The country people were collecting and driving away the dead bodies in wagons.

My father embraced this opportunity to prejudice me against being a sailor; he was a kind but strict parent, and we dared not disobey him. The storm had made no impression upon my mind sufficient to alter my determination; my youthful mind could not separate the life of a sailor from dangers and storms, and I looked upon them as an interesting part of the adventures I panted after. I enjoyed the voyage much, was anxious to learn every thing, and was a great favorite with the captain and crew.

After my arrival in London, as I was going on an errand, in passing near the Tower, I saw a dead monkey floating in the river. I had not seen above two or three in my life; I thought it of great value; I stripped at once, and swam in for it. An English boy, who wished it likewise, but who either would or could not swim, seized it when I landed, saying he would fight me for it. We were much of a size; had he been larger than myself, I was not of a temper to be easily wronged; so I gave him battle. A crowd gathered, and formed a ring; stranger as I was, I got fair play. After a severe contest, I came off victor. The English boy shook hands, and said, "Scotchman, you have won it." I had fought naked as I came out of the water; so I put on my clothes, and carried off the prize in triumph; came home, and got a beating from my father for fighting, and staying my errand; but the monkey's skin repaid me for all vexations.

I remained in London scarcely twelve months, when my father sent me to Scotland to learn my trade. I chose the profession of a cooper, to please my father; but my heart was never with the business. While I was hooping barrels, my mind was at sea, and my imagination in foreign climes.

After my apprenticeship had expired, I entered the navy, and sailed for America in the *Proteus*, 20 gun ship, with ordnance stores, and one hundred men, to man the floating batteries upon Lake Champlain. After convoying the fleet to Quebec, and another from St. John's, Newfoundland, to the West Indies and back, I remained on shore in the Canadas for eighteen months, when I was ordered by Admiral Montague on board the *Surprise*, 28 gun frigate, commanded by Captain Reeves. Her cooper had been killed, a few days before, in a severe action with an American vessel. We kept cruising about, taking numbers of the American privateers. After a severe action, we took the *Jason*, of Boston, commanded by the famous Captain Manly, who had been commodore in the American service, had been taken prisoner, and broke his parole. When Captain Reeves hailed, and ordered him to strike, he returned for answer, "Fire away! I have as many guns as you." He had heavier metal, but fewer men, than the *Surprise*. He fought us for a long time. I was serving powder as busy as I could, the shot and splinters flying in all directions, when I heard the men call from one of the guns, "Halloo, Bungs, where are you?" I looked to their gun, and saw the two horns of my anvil across its mouth; the next moment it was through the *Jason's* side. The rogues thus disposed of my anvil, which I had been using just before the action commenced, and had placed in a secure place, as I thought, out of their reach. "Bungs forever!" they shouted, when they saw the dreadful hole it had made in the *Jason's* side. Bungs was the name they always gave the cooper. When Captain Manly came on board the *Surprise*, to deliver his sword to Captain Reeves, the half of the rim of his hat was shot off. Our captain returned his sword to him again, saying, "You have had a narrow escape, Manly."—"I wish to God it had been my head," he replied.

When we boarded the *Jason*, we found thirty-one cavalry, who had served under General Burgoyne, acting now as marines on board the *Jason*. During the remainder of the American war, our duty was the same, taking convoy and capturing American privateers. We crossed the Atlantic several times. I became quite weary of the monotonous convoy duty, and, having seen all I could see, I often sighed for the verdant banks of the Forth. At length, my wishes were gratified by the return of peace. We were paid off in March, 1783. When Captain Reeves came ashore, he completely loaded the long-boat with flags he had taken from the enemy. When one of the officers inquired what he would do with them, he said, laughing, "I will hang one upon every tree in my father's garden."

I no sooner had the money that was due me in my hat, than I set off for London direct, and, after a few days of enjoyment, put my bedding and chest on board a vessel bound for Leith: every halfpenny I had saved was in it but nine guineas, which I kept upon my person to provide for squalls. The trader fell down the river, but, there being no wind, and the tide failing, the captain told us we might sleep in London, only to be sure to be on board before eight o'clock in the morning. I embraced the opportunity, and lost my passage.

As all my savings were in my chest, and a number of passengers on board whom I did not like, I immediately took the diligence to Newcastle. There were no mails running direct for Edinburgh every day, as now; it was the month of March, yet there was a great deal of snow on the ground; the weather was severe, but not so cold as at St. John's. When the diligence set off, there were four passengers—two ladies, another sailor, and myself. Our lady companions, for the first few stages, were proud and distant, scarcely taking any notice of us. I was restrained by their manner; my companion was quite at home, chatting to them, unmindful of their monosyllabic answers. He had a good voice, and sung snatches of sea-songs, and was unceasing in his endeavors to please. By degrees their reserve wore off, and the conversation became general. I now learned they were sisters, who had been on a visit to a relation in London, and were now returning to their father, who was a wealthy farmer. Before it grew dark, we were all as intimate as if we had sailed for years in the same ship. The oldest, who appeared to be about twenty, attached herself to me, and listened to my accounts of the different places I had been in, with great interest. The youngest was as much interested by the conversation of my volatile companion.

I felt a something uncommon arise in my breast as we sat side by side; I could think of nothing but my pretty companion; my attentions were not disagreeable to her, and I began to think of settling, and how happy I might be with such a wife. After a number of efforts, I summoned resolution to take her hand in mine; I pressed it gently; she drew it faintly back. I sighed; she laid her hand upon my arm, and, in a whisper, inquired if I was unwell. I was upon the point of telling her what I felt, and my wishes, when the diligence stopped at the inn. I wished we had been sailing in the middle of the Atlantic; for a covered cart drove up, and a stout, hearty old man welcomed them by their names, bestowing a hearty kiss upon each. I felt quite disappointed. He was their father. My pretty Mary did not seem to be so rejoiced at her father's kind salutation as might have been expected.

My companion, who was an Englishman, told me he would proceed no farther, but endeavor to win the hand of his pretty partner. I told him my present situation, that my chest and all I had was on board the Leith trader, and no direction upon it; on this account, I was forced to proceed as fast as possible, or I would have remained and shared his fortunes with all my heart. I took leave of them with a heavy heart, resolving to return. I could perceive Mary turn pale, as I bade her farewell, while her sister looked joy itself when Williams told them he was to proceed no farther. Before the coach set off, I made him promise to write me an account of his success, and that I would return as soon as I had secured my chest and seen my father. He promised to do this faithfully. I whispered Mary a promise to see her soon, and pressed her hand as we parted; she returned the pressure. I did not feel without hope. When the farmer drove off, Williams accompanying them, I only wished myself in his place.

When the coach reached Newcastle, I soon procured another conveyance to Edinburgh, and was at Leith before the vessel. When she arrived, I went on board, and found all safe. I then went to Borrowstownness, but found my father had been dead for some time. This was a great disappointment and grief to me. I wished I had been at home to have received his last blessing and advice; but there was no help. He died full of years; and that I may be as well prepared when I shall be called hence, is my earnest wish. After visiting his grave, and spending a few days with my friends, I became uneasy at not hearing from Williams. I waited for three weeks; then, losing all patience, I set off myself to see how the land lay. I took leave of home once more, with a good deal of money in my pocket, as I had been almost a miser at home, keeping all for the marriage, should I succeed.

The spring was now advancing apace, when I took my passage in a Newcastle trader, and arrived safe at the inn where I had last parted from Mary. It was night when I arrived, and, being weary, soon went to bed. I was up betimes in the morning; when I met Williams, he was looking very dull. I shook hands, and asked, "What cheer?" He shook his head, and said, "Why, Jack, we are on the wrong tack, and, I fear, will never make port. I had no good news to send, so it was of no use to write. I was at the farmer's last night; he swears, if ever I come near his house again, he will have me before the justice as an idle vagrant. My fair jilt is not much concerned, and I can scarce get a sight of her; she seems to shun me." I felt a chillness come over me at this information, and asked him what he meant to do. "Why, set sail this day; go to my mother, give her what I can spare, and then to sea again. My store is getting low here. But what do you intend to do, Jack?" "Truth, Williams, I scarce know. I will make one trip to the farm; and if Mary is not as kind as I hope to find her, I will be off too."

Soon after breakfast, I set off for the farmer's, with an anxious heart. On my arrival, I met Mary in the yard. She seemed fluttered at sight of me; but, summoning up courage as I approached, she made a distant bow, and coldly asked me how I did. I now saw there was no hope, and had not recovered myself, when her father came out, and, in a rough manner, demanded what I wanted, and who I was. This in a moment brought me to myself; and, raising my head, which had been bent towards the ground, I looked at him. Mary shrunk from my gaze; but the old man came close up to me, and again demanded what I wanted. "It is of no consequence," I answered; then, looking at Mary, "I believe I am an unwelcome visitor—it is what I did not expect—so I will not obtrude myself upon you any longer." I then walked off, as indifferent, to appearance, as I could make myself; but was tempted to look over my shoulder more than once. I saw Mary in tears, and her father in earnest conversation with her.

I made up my mind to remain at the inn the rest of that day and all night, in hopes of receiving an appointment to meet Mary. I was loath to think I was indifferent to her; and, the feeling of being slighted is so bitter, I could have quarrelled with myself and all the world. I sat with Williams at the window all day; no message came; in the morning we bade adieu to the fair jilts, with heavy hearts—Williams for his mother's, and I for London.

After working a few weeks in London, at my own business, my wandering propensities came as strong upon me as ever, and I resolved to embrace the first opportunity to gratify it—no matter whither, only let me wander. I had been many times on the different wharves, looking for a vessel; but, the seamen were so plenty, there was great difficulty in getting a berth.

I met, by accident, Captain Bond, who hailed me, and inquired if I wished a berth. He had been captain of a transport in the American war. I had favored him at St. John's. I answered him, "It was what I was looking after." "Then, if you will come and be cooper of the *Leviathan*, Greenland ship,—I am captain,—you may go to 'Squire Mellish, and say I recommend you for cooper." I thanked him for his good-will, went, and was engaged, and on board at work next day.

We sailed in a short time for the coast of Greenland, and touched at Lerwick, where we took on board what men we wanted. In the first of the season, we were very unsuccessful, having very stormy weather. I at one time thought our doom was fixed; it blew a dreadful gale, and we were for ten days completely fast in the ice. As far as we could see, all was ice, and the ship was so pressed by it, every one thought we must either be crushed to pieces, or forced out upon the top of the ice, there ever to remain. At length, the wind changed, and the weather moderated; and, where nothing could be seen but ice, in a short time after, all, as far as the eye could reach, was open sea. What were our feelings at this change, it were vain to attempt a description of; it was a reprieve from death. The horrors of our situation were far worse than any storm I ever was in. In a storm, upon a lee shore, there, even in all its horrors, there is exertion to keep the mind up, and a hope to weather it. Locked up in ice, all exertion is useless; the power you have to contend with is far too tremendous and unyielding; it, like a powerful magician, binds you in its icy circle, and there you must behold, in all its horrors, your approaching fate, without the power of exertion, while the crashing of the ice, and the less loud, but more alarming cracking of the vessel, serve all to increase the horrors of this dreadful sea-mare.

When the weather moderated, we were very successful, and filled our ship with four fish. I did not like the whale fishing; there is no sight for the eye of the inquisitive, after the first glance, and no variety to charm the mind. Desolation reigns around—nothing but snow, or bare rocks and ice. The cold is so intense, and the weather often so thick, I felt so cheerless, that I resolved to bid adieu to the coast of Greenland forever, and seek to gratify my curiosity in more genial climes.

We arrived safe in the river, and proceeded up to our situation; but how strange are the freaks of fate! In the very port of London, as we were hurrying to our station, the tide was ebbing fast, when the ship missed stays, and yawed round, came right upon the Isle of Dogs, broke her back, and filled with water. There was none of us hurt, and we lost nothing, as she was insured. I was one of those placed upon her to estimate the loss sustained amongst the casks, and was kept constantly on board for a long time.

My next voyage was on board the *Cotton Planter*, commanded by Captain Young, bound for the Island of Granada, W. I. Under Captain Young, I was very happy. We sailed in the month of October, and arrived safe at St. George's, Granada.

I worked a great deal on shore, and had a number of blacks under me. They are a thoughtless, merry race; in vain their cruel situation and sufferings act upon their buoyant minds. They have snatches of joy that their pale and sickly oppressors never know. On the evenings of Saturday and Sunday, the sound of the benji and rattle, intermixed with song, alone is heard. I have lain upon deck, of an evening, faint and exhausted from the heat of the day, to enjoy the cool breeze of the evening; and their wild music and song, the shout of mirth, and dancing, resounded along the beach, and from the valleys. There the negroes bounded in all the spirit of health and happiness.

Captain Young did not keep his crew upon allowance; we had "cut and come again" always. I often took a piece of lean beef and a few biscuits with me when I went to the plantation, as a present to the blacks. This the poor creatures would divide among themselves, to a single fibre. There were two or three slaves upon the estate, who, having once run away, had iron collars round their necks, with long hooks, that projected from them to catch the bushes, should they run away again; these they wore night and day. There was a black slave, a cooper, with a wooden leg, who had run away more than once; he was now chained to the block at which he wrought.

They are much given to talking and story-telling; the Scripture characters of the Old Testament are quite familiar to them; they talk with astonishment of Samson, Goliah, David, &c. I have seen them hold up their hands in astonishment at the strength of the white Buccaras. I have laughed at their personifications. Hurricane—they cannot conceive what it is. There are planters of the name of Kane on the island. "Hurricane," they will say, "he a strong white Buccara, he come from London."

There was a black upon the estate, who had been on the Island of St. Kitt's when Rodney defeated the French fleet. He had seen the action, and was never tired of speaking of it, nor his auditors of listening. He always concluded with this remark—"The French 'tand 'tiff, but the English 'tand far 'tiffer. De all de same as game cock; de die on de 'pot."

They are apt to steal, but are so very credulous, they are easily detected. Captain Young gave a black butcher, by the name of Coffee, a hog to kill. When the captain went to see it, Coffee said,—

"This very fine hog, massa, but I never see a hog like him in all my life; he have no liver, no light."

"That is strange, Coffee," said Captain Young, "let me see in the book." He took a memorandum-book out of his pocket, turned over a few leaves, and looked very earnest.

"I see,—Coffee go to hell bottom,—hog have liver and lights." Coffee shook like an aspen leaf, and said,—

"O massa, Coffee no go to hell bottom,—hog have liver and lights." He restored them and, trembling, awaited his punishment. Captain Young only laughed, and made him a present of them.

I one time went with Captain Young to a planter's, where he was to dine that I might accompany him back to the ship in the evening, as he was weakly. Upon our arrival, I was handed over to a black, who was butler and house-steward. He had been in England, and, as he said, seen London and King George. He was by this become a greater man than by his situation, among the other slaves; and was as vain in showing the little he knew, as if he had been bred at college; and was perpetually astonishing the other slaves, whom he looked down upon with the depth of his knowledge, and his accounts of London and King George. No professor could have delivered his opinions and observations with more pomp and dogmatism. One of the blacks inquired of me what kind of people the Welsh were. To enjoy the sport, as one of the crew, William Jones, a Welshman, was in company with me at the time, I referred him to the black oracle, who, after considering a moment or two, replied, with a smile of satisfaction upon his sooty features, "The English have ships, the Irish have ships, and the

Scotch have ships, but Welshmen have no ships; they are like the negro man; they live in the bush." The Welshman started to his feet, and would have knocked him down, had I not prevented. He poured out a volley of oaths upon him; he heard him with indifference, and his assertion was not the least shaken, in the opinion of his hearers, by the Welshman's violence. It, like many others of equal truth, was quoted and received as gospel. It was long a byword in the ship—"Welshman live in the bush like negro man."

We brought to England, as passenger from the island, a planter, who was very rich, and had a number of slaves. He had been a common seaman on board of a man-of-war, had deserted, and lived on shore concealed until his ship sailed. He afterwards married a free black woman, who kept a punch house, who died and left him above three thousand pounds. With this he had bought a plantation and slaves, and was making money fast. He brought as much fresh provisions and preserves on board as would have served ten men out and out, and was very kind to the men, in giving them liquor and fresh provisions.

Upon our arrival in London, I learned that my old officer, Lieutenant Portlock, now captain, was going out in the *King George*, as commander, in company with the *Queen Charlotte*, Captain Dixon, upon a voyage of discovery and trade round the world. This was the very cruise I had long wished for; at once I made myself clean, and waited upon Captain Portlock. He was happy to see me, as I was an excellent brewer of spruce beer, and the very man he wished, but knew not where to have sent for me. I was at once engaged, on the most liberal terms, as cooper, and went away rejoicing in my good fortune. We had a charter from the South Sea Company, and one from the India House, as it was to be a trading voyage for furs, as well as discovery. This was in the year 1785.

With a joyful heart I entered on this voyage. The first land we made was Santa Cruz, in the Island of Teneriffe, where we staid ten days, getting fruit and provisions; then made the Island of St. Jago,—it belongs to the Portuguese,—where we watered, and took in fresh provisions. While here, we caught a number of fish called bass, very like salmon, which we ate fresh. The island is badly cultivated, but abounds in cattle. We exchanged old clothes for sheep, or any thing the men wanted. The Portuguese here are great rogues. I bought two fat sheep from one of them. The bargain was made, and I was going to lead away my purchase, when he gave a whistle, and my sheep scampered off to the fields. The fellow laughed at my surprise. I had a great mind to give him a beating for his trick, and take my clothes from him; but we had strict orders not to quarrel with the people upon any account. At length, he made a sign that I might have them again by giving a few more articles. I had no alternative but to lose what I had given, or submit to his roguery. I gave a sign I would; he gave another whistle, and the sheep returned to his side. I secured them before I gave the second price. With all their roguery, they are very careless of their money, more so than any people I ever saw. In walking through the town, I have seen kegs full of dollars, without heads, standing in the houses, and the door open, without a person in the house to look after them.

Having watered, we run for the Falkland Islands. When we arrived, we found two American vessels, the *Anchor* and *Hope*, busy whaling. We hoisted our colors and the Americans took us for Spaniards, and set off in all haste. When we landed, we found a great number of geese ready plucked, and a large fire burning; so we set to work, and roasted as many as served us all, and enjoyed them much.

Next morning, the Americans came near in their boats, and found out their mistake. Captain Portlock thanked them for their treat. We then had a busy time killing geese. There are two kinds, the water and upland. The water ones are very pretty, speckled, like a partridge. The penguins were so plenty, we were forced to knock them out of our way as we walked along the beach. The pelicans are plenty, and build their nests of clay; they are near each other, like a honey-comb. I was astonished how each bird knew its own nest. They appear to hatch in the same nest, until they are forced to change, by the accumulation of dung. They are so tame, I have stood close by when they arrived with their pouch distended with fish, and fed their young, without being in the least disturbed. We killed a number of hogs. Our doctor broke his double-bar-celled gun in despatching one, and sold it afterwards, in China, for £42. What was of more value to us was, a great many iron hoops, and bees-wax, the remains of some wreck. We picked up some of the wax, but took every inch of the hoops; they were more valuable than gold to us, for trading with the natives.

When off Cape Horn, we perceived an object floating at a small distance from the ship. Not one of us could make out what it was. All our boats being fast, two then went down into the water, and swam to it, and made it fast in the slings. When it came on board, it was a cask, but so overgrown with weeds and barnacles, the bung-hole could not be discovered. I was set to work to cut into it. To our agreeable surprise, it was full of excellent port wine. All the crew got a little of it, and Captain Portlock gave us brandy in place of the rest.

We next made Staten's Land; the weather was fine, but very cold. We stood away for latitude 23°, where we cruised about for some time in quest of islands laid down in our charts. We could find none, but turtle in great abundance. They were a welcome supply, but we soon tired of them, cook them as we would, in every variety. Not finding the islands, we bore away for the Sandwich Islands. The first land we made was Owhyee, the island where Captain Cook was killed. The *King George* and *Queen Charlotte* were the first ships which had touched there since that melancholy event. The natives came on board in crowds, and were happy to see us; they recognized Portlock and others, who had been on the island before, along with Cook. Our decks were soon crowded with hogs, bread-fruit, yams, and potatoes. Our deck soon resembled shambles; our butcher had fourteen assistants. I was as busy and fatigued as I could be, cutting iron hoops into lengths of eight and nine inches, which the carpenter ground sharp. These were our most valuable commodity, in the eyes of the natives. I was stationed down in the hold of the vessel, and the ladders were removed to prevent the natives from coming down to the treasury. The king of Owhyee looked to my occupation with a wistful eye; he thought me the happieset man on board, to be among such vast heaps of treasure. Captain Portlock called to me to place the ladder, and allow the king to come down, and give him a good long piece. When the king descended, he held up his hands, and looked astonishment personified. When I gave him the piece of hoop of twenty inches long, he retired a little from below the hatch into the shade, undid his girdle, bent the iron to his body, and, adjusting his belt in the greatest haste, concealed it. I suppose he thought I had stolen it. I could not but laugh to see the king concealing what he took to be stolen goods.

We were much in want of oil for our lamps. The sharks abounding, we baited a hook with a piece of salt pork, and caught the largest I ever saw in any sea; it was a female, nineteen feet long; it took all hands to hoist her on board; her weight made the vessel heel. When she was cut up, we took forty-eight young ones out of her belly, eighteen inches long; we saw them go into her mouth after she was hooked. The hook was fixed to a chain attached to our main-brace, or we never could have kept her. It was evening when she snapped the bait; we hauled the head just above the surface, the swell washing over it. We let her remain thus all night, and she was quite dead in the morning. There were in her stomach four hogs, four full-grown turtle, besides the young ones. Her liver, the only part we wanted, filled a tierce.

Almost every man on board took a native woman for a wife while the vessel remained, the men thinking it an honor or for their gain, as they got many presents of iron, beads, or buttons. The women came on board at night, and went on shore in the morning. In the evening, they would call for their husbands by name. They often brought their friends to see their husbands, who were well pleased, as they were never allowed to go away empty. The fattest woman I ever saw in my life our gunner chose for a wife. We were forced to hoist her on board; her thighs were as thick as my waist; no hammock in the ship would hold her; many jokes were cracked upon the pair.

We had a merry, facetious fellow on board, called Dickson. He sung pretty well. He squinted, and the natives mimicked him. Abenoue, king of Atooi, could cock his eye like Dickson better than any of his subjects. Abenoue called him Billicany, from his often singing "Rule Britannia." Abenoue learned the air, and the words, as near as he could pronounce them. It was an amusing thing to hear the king and Dickson sing. Abenoue loved him better than any man in the ship, and always embraced him every time they met on shore, or in the ship, and began to sing, "Tule Billicany, Billicany tule," &c.

We had the chief on board who killed Captain Cook, for more than three weeks. He was in bad health, and had a smelling-bottle, with a few drops in it, which he used to smell at; we filled it for him. There were a good many bayonets in possession of the natives, which they had obtained at the murder of Cook.

We left Owhyee, and stood down to Atooi, where we watered, and had a feast from Abenoue, the king. We took our allowance of brandy on shore, and spent a most delightful afternoon, the natives doing all in their power to amuse us; the girls danced, the men made a sham fight, throwing their spears; the women, standing behind, handed the spears to the men, the same as in battle, thus keeping up a continued shower of spears. No words can convey an adequate idea of their dexterity and agility. They thought we were bad with the rheumatism, our movements were so slow compared with their own. The women would sometimes lay us down, and chafe and rub us, making moan, and saying, "O rume! O rume!" They wrestled, but the stoutest man in our ship could not stand a single throw with the least chance of success.

As the summer now advanced apace, we stood over to Cook's River, on the Northwest Coast of America, where we arrived in 1786, eleven months after we left England.

At the entrance of Cook's River is an immense volcanic mountain, which was in action at the time, and continued burning all the time we lay there, pouring down its side a torrent of lava as broad as the Thames. At night, the sight was grand, but fearful. The natives here had their spears headed with copper; but, having no one on board who could speak their language, we had no means of learning where they obtained the copper. While we lay here, it was the heat of summer; yet the ice never melted, and the snow was lying very deep on the heights. What a contrast from the delightful islands we had so lately left!

Our long boat, decked and schooner-rigged, proceeded up the river, in hopes of finding an outlet, or inland sea. After proceeding with great difficulty and perseverance, until all hopes of success vanished, they returned. We then bore to the southward, to Prince William's Sound, to pursue our trade with the Indians. They are quite different from the Sandwich Islanders in appearance and habits; they are not cruel, but great thieves.

I was employed on shore brewing spruce all day, and slept on board at night. One night, the Indians, after starting the beer, carried off all the casks; they were iron-hooped. All our search was vain; no traces of them were to be discovered. To quarrel with the Indians would have defeated the object of our voyage. At length, they were discovered by accident, in the most unlikely place, in the following manner: One of our boats had been, on a trading excursion, detained so long, we became alarmed for its safety. Captain Portlock sent some of our men, armed, to the top of a high hill, to look out for the boat. To the surprise of the men, they found the staves and ends of the barrels, and some large stones they had used in breaking them to pieces. How great must their labor have been in rolling up the barrels, and then in dashing them to pieces! yet I have no doubt they thought themselves richly rewarded in obtaining the iron hoops. The men brought back a stave or two with the ship's name branded on them, to evidence the truth of their discovery. We then moved the brewing-place to the other side of the island, within sight of the ship. I was much annoyed by the natives for some time, while working; they would handle the hoops, and every now and then a piece would vanish. There was only a quarter-master and boy with me. While the natives swarmed around, I felt rather uncomfortable. They became more and more bold. The captain, seeing, from the deck, my disagreeable situation, hailed me to set Neptune, our great Newfoundland dog, upon them, saying they would fear him more than fifty men. I obeyed with alacrity, and hounded Neptune, who enjoyed the sport as much as I, to see the great fellows run, screaming like girls, in all directions. I was soon left to pursue my labor unmolested; and, whenever they grew troublesome, Neptune, without orders, put them to running and screaming. When one approached, if Neptune was near, he would stretch out his arms, and cry, "Lally, Neptune;" that is, *friend,* in their language.

One Sabbath day, all the ship's company, except the captain, two boys, and the cook, were on shore, amusing themselves. During our absence, an immense number of the natives came alongside, and took complete possession of the vessel, and helped themselves to whatever took their fancy. The captain, boys, and cook, barricadoed themselves in the cabin, and loaded all the muskets and pistols within their reach. Their situation was one of great danger. The surgeon and myself were the first that arrived upon the beach; the captain hailed us from the cabin window, and let us know his disagreeable situation, telling us to force the Indians to put us on board. We having our muskets, they complied at once. Thus, by adding strength to the captain, we gained new assurance; and the others, doing as we did, were all put on board as they came to the beach. The Indians offered no violence to the ship; and, when the crew were nearly all on board, they began to leave the vessel, shipping off their booty. Captain Portlock ordered us to take no notice of the transaction in way of hurting the Indians, but to purchase back the articles they had taken away that were of use to us; but they had only taken what pieces of iron they found loose about the ship. After having hid the things they had stolen, they began to trade, as if nothing had happened; and we bought back what few bolts they had taken. They had plundered the smith's tent in the same manner, although they looked upon him as a greater man than the captain. He was a smart young fellow, and kept the Indians in great awe and wonder. They thought the coals were made into powder. I have seen them steal small pieces, and bruise them, then come back. When he saw this, he would spit upon the anvil while working the hot iron, and give a blow upon it; they would run away in fear and astonishment when they heard the crack.

One or other of our boats, often both, were absent for some time upon trading voyages. In one of these trips, our boat was nearly cut off, and would, in all probability, had it not been for the presence of mind of an American, one of the crew, Joseph Laurence. I never was more alarmed for my safety, in the whole voyage. We were rowing through a lagoon, to get a near cut to the ship; the tide was ebbing fast; the boat took the ground, and, before we could do any thing to get her off, the whole bay was dry. The natives surrounded the boat in great numbers, and looked very mischievous. We knew not what to do. In this dilemma, Laurence, who knew their ways, took a small keg of molasses, and went to the beach; at the same time, he sat down by it, and began to sing and lick, inviting them to follow his example. They licked, and listened to him for a good while, and even joined him in singing; but the molasses wore down, and they were weary of his songs. We looked about in great anxiety, and discovered a small height that commanded the boat. To this we ran, but dared not to fire, even while they were plundering the boat; they could have killed us all with spears and stones, had we even shot one hundred of them, and wasted all our ammunition. We stood like bears at the stake, expecting them every moment to commence the attack, resolved to sell our lives as dear as we could. At length, the wished return of tide came, and we got to the boat, and she floated soon after. Then we cared not one penny for them. We began to trade, and bought back the articles they had stolen. Even our compass we were forced to buy back. We set sail for the *King George,* resolved to be more circumspect in future, and happy we had escaped so well.

The party who had taken possession of the vessel on the Sabbath day, the next time they came back, had their faces blacked, and their heads powdered with the down of birds. They had done this as a disguise, which showed they had a consciousness of right and wrong. Thinking we knew them not, as we took no notice of them, they were as merry and funny as any of the rest.

While the boats were absent on a trading voyage, the canoe was sent to haul the seine for salmon. There were fourteen men and boys in it. About half-way between the vessel and the shore, she filled with water; those who could swim made for the beach; the boys, and those who could not, clung to the canoe. Captain Portlock saw from the deck the danger they were in, and requested the boatswain, who was an excellent swimmer, to go to their assistance; he refused. The sail-maker and myself leaped into the water. I had a line fixed round my waist, as I swam first, which he supported at a short distance behind, to ease its weight. When I came up to the canoe, they were nearly spent. I fixed the line to the canoe, and we made a signal to the ship, when those on board drew her to the vessel, John Butler and I attending to assist and encourage them. There was a son of Sir John Dick's, and a son of Captain Gore's, among the boys. Captain Portlock never could bear the boatswain afterwards. Before this, he was a great favorite.

While in Prince William's Sound, the boat went on an excursion to Snug Corner Cove, at the top of the sound. She discovered the *Nootka,* Captain Meares, in a most distressing situation from the scurvy. There were only the captain and two men free from disease. Two-and-twenty Lascars had died through the course of the winter; they had caused their own distress, by their inordinate use of spirits on Christmas eve. They could not bury their own dead; they were only dragged a short distance from the ship, and left upon the ice. They had muskets fixed upon the capstan, and manropes that went down to the cabin, that, when any of the natives attempted to come on board, they might fire them off to scare them. They had a large Newfoundland dog, whose name was Towser, who alone kept the ship clear of the Indians. He lay day and night upon the ice before the cabin-window, and would not allow the Indians to go into the ship. When the natives came to barter, they would cry, "Lally, Towser," and make him a present of a skin, before they began to trade with Captain Meares, who lowered from the window his barter, and in the same way received their furs. The *Beaver,* the *Nootka's* consort, had been cut off in the beginning of the winter, and none of her people were ever heard of. We gave him every assistance in our power, in spruce and molasses, and two of our crew to assist in working the vessel, Dickson and George Willis, who stopped at Canton until we arrived; then, wishing him well, took our leave of him. Captain Portlock could have made a fair prize of him, as he had no charter, and was trading in our limits; but he was satisfied with his bond not to trade on our coast; but the bond was forfeit as soon as we sailed, and he was in China before us.

We now stood for Nootka Sound, but encountered a dreadful gale, and were blown off the coast, and suffered much in our sails and rigging, which caused us to stand for the Sandwich Islands to refit, which gave us great joy. The American coast is a hostile region, compared with the Sandwich Islands. The American Indians are very jealous; and if any of our men were found with their women, using the least freedom, they would take his life, if it was in their power; but their women are far from being objects of desire, they are so much disfigured by slitting their lips, and placing large pieces of wood in them, shaped like a saucer. I have seen them place berries upon it, and shake them into their mouth, as a horse would corn out of a mouth-bag, or lick them in with their tongue. The men have a bone, eight inches long, polished, and stuck through the gristle of their nose; we called it their spritsail-yard. We had suffered a good deal of hardship on this coast, and bade it adieu with joy.

Soon as we arrived at Owhyee, our old acquaintance flocked on board to welcome us, each with a present. Then such a touching of noses and shaking of hands took place! "Honi, honi,"—that is, touch nose,—and "How are you?" were the only words to be heard. Our deck was one continued scene of joy.

Having refitted, and taken in provisions, we again set sail for Cook's River, Prince William's and Nootka Sound, to obtain more fur-skins. We were pretty successful. While on shore in Prince William's Sound, brewing spruce beer, I and the quarter master made an excursion up the river, and discovered a large space covered with snakeroot, which is of great value in China. My comrade, who had been in China, informed me of its value. It is the sweetest smelling plant I ever was near, when it is growing. We set to work, and dug up as much as we chose, and dried it, letting no one know, for lessening the value of what we got. It was got safe on board the day before we sailed, and we sold it well at Wampoa.

We parted company from the *Queen Charlotte.* She had been absent for a long time, when a party of Indians came to the *King George,* having in their possession a pair of buckles that belonged to one of the people on board our consort; we became alarmed for her, thinking she had been cut off. We immediately set sail for Nootka Sound, leaving a large quantity of salmon, half dried. After waiting in Nootka Sound, our place of rendezvous, for some time, and she not appearing, we immediately set sail for Owhyee, but got no word of our consort until we came to Atooi, when we perceived Abenoue in his single canoe, making her scud through the water, crying, "Tattoo for Potipoti," as he jumped upon deck with a letter from Captain Dixon, which removed our fears, and informed us he had discovered an island, and got a very great number of skins, and had sailed for China. We watered, and laid in our provisions as quick as we could, to follow her.

After taking on board as much provisions as we could stow, we sailed for China. At the Ladrones, or Mariana Islands, a number of pilots came on board. The captain agreed with one. The bargain was made in the following manner: He showed the captain the number of dollars he wished by the number of cass—a small brass coin—the captain taking from the number what he thought too much, the pilot adding when he thought it too little. He was to pilot the *King George* to the Island of Macao. From thence we sailed up the Bocca Tigris to Wampoa, where we sold our cargo of skins. We were engaged to take home a cargo of tea for the East India Company.

I was as happy as any person ever was to see any thing. I scarcely believed I was so fortunate as really to be in China. As we sailed up the river, I would cast my eyes from side to side: the thoughts and ideas I had pictured to my mind of it were not lessened in brilliancy, rather increased: the immense number of buildings, that extended as far as the eye could reach; their fantastic shapes and gaudy colors; their trees and flowers, so like their paintings, and the myriads of floating vessels; and, above all, the fanciful dresses and gaudy colors of their clothes,—all serve to fix the mind of a stranger, upon his first arrival.

Soon as we cast anchor, the vessel was surrounded with sampans; every one had some request to make. Tartar girls requested our clothes to wash, barbers to shave the crews, others with fowls to sell—indeed, every necessary we could want. The first we made bargain with was a barber, Tommy Linn. He agreed to shave the crew, for the six months we were to be there, for half a dollar from each man, and he would shave every morning, if we chose, on board the ship, coming off in his sampan. The Tartar girls washed our clothes for the broken meat, or what rice we left at mess. They came every day in their sampans, and took away the men's shirts, bringing them back the next, and never mixed the clothes. They all spoke less or more English, and would jaw with the crew as fast as any women of their rank in England.

I was on shore for a good while at Wampoa, making candles, for our voyage home. I had a number of Chinese under me. My greatest difficulty was to prevent them from stealing the wax. They are greater and more dexterous thieves than the Indians; a bambooing for theft, I really believe, confers no disgrace upon them. They will allow no stranger to enter the city of Canton. I was different times at the gate, but all my ingenuity could not enable me to cross the bar, although I was eight days in the suburbs.

The Chinese, I really believe, eat any thing there is life in. Neptune was constantly on shore with me at the tent; every night he caught less or more rats. He never ate them, but laid them down, when dead, at the tent door. In the morning, the Chinese gave vegetables for them, and were as well pleased as I was at the exchange.

After the candles were made, I removed to Banks Hall, to repair the cooper work, and screen sand and dry it, to pack the tea-boxes for our voyage home. One day, a boy was meddling rather freely with the articles belonging to me. Neptune bit him. I was extremely sorry for it, and, after beating him, dressed the boy's hurt, which was not severe. I gave the boy a few cass who went away quite pleased. In a short time after, I saw him coming back, and his father leading him. I looked for squalls; but the father only asked a few hairs out from under Neptune's fore leg, close to the body; he would take them from no other part, and stuck them all over the wound. He went away content. I had often heard, when a person had been tipsy the evening before, people tell him to take a hair of the dog that bit him, but never saw it in the literal sense before.

A short time before we sailed, all the crew got two months' pay advance, for private trade, and purchased what articles they chose. The dollars are all stamped by the captain, as the Chinese are such cheats, they will dexterously return you a bad dollar, and assert, if not marked, it was the one you gave.

With all their roguery, they are not ungrateful. One day, two Chinese boys were playing in our boat; one of them fell overboard. The current was strong, and the boy was carried down with rapidity. I leaped into the river, and saved him with great difficulty, as the current bore us both along until my strength was almost spent. By an effort I got into the smooth water, and soon had the pleasure of delivering him to his father, who stood upon the beach wringing his hands. I wished to go on board, but the Chinese would have me to his house, where I was most kindly received, and got my dinner in great style. I like their manner of setting out the table at dinner. All that is to be eaten is placed upon the table at once, and all the liquors at the same time. You have all before you, and you may make your choice. I dined in different houses, and the same fashion was used in them all. The Chinese never thought he could show me kindness enough.

Having completed our cargo, we set sail for St. Helena, where we made a present to the governor of a number of empty bottles; he, in return, gave us a present of potatoes,—a valuable gift to us. While here, I and a number of the crew were nearly poisoned by eating albicores and bonettos. We split and hung them in the rigging to dry; the moon's rays have the effect of making them poisonous. My face turned red and swelled; but the others were far worse; their heads were swelled twice their ordinary size; but we all recovered. In a few days, we set sail for England, where I arrived without any remarkable occurrence, after an absence of three years, having, in that time, circumnavigated the globe. We came into the River Thames in the month of September, 1788.

I now returned to Scotland with a sensation of joy only to be felt by those who have been absent for some time. Every remembrance was rendered more dear, every scene was increased in beauty. A piece of oaten cake tasted far sweeter in my mouth than the luxuries of Eastern climes. I was for a time reconciled to remain; the love of country overcame my wandering habits. I had some thought of settling for life, as I had saved a good deal of my pay. In the middle of these musings, and before I had made up my mind, a letter I received from Captain Portlock upset all my future plans, and rekindled my wandering propensities with as great vigor as ever.

The letter requested me to come to London without delay, as there were two ships lying in the river, bound for New South Wales, the *Guardian* and *Lady Julian,* in either of which I might have a berth. The *Guardian* was loaded with stores and necessaries for the settlement. There was a vine-dresser, and a person to superintend the cultivation of hemp, on board. She sailed long before us. The *Lady Julian* was to take out female convicts.

I would have chosen the *Guardian,* only she was a man-of-war; and, as I meant to settle in Scotland upon our return, I could not have left her when I chose. My only object was to see the country, not to remain at sea; I therefore chose the *Lady Julian,* as she was a transport, although I did not, by any means, like her cargo; yet, to see the country, I was resolved to submit to a great deal.

We lay six months in the river, before we sailed, during which time, all the jails in England were emptied to complete the cargo of the *Lady Julian.* When we sailed, there were on board 245 female convicts. There were not a great many very bad characters; the greater number were for petty crimes, and a great proportion for only being disorderly, that is, street-walkers; the colony, at the time, being in great want of women.

One, a Scottish girl, broke her heart, and died, in the river; she was buried at Dartford. Four were pardoned on account of his majesty's recovery. The poor young Scottish girl I have never yet got out of my mind; she was young and beautiful, even in the convict dress, but pale as death, and her eyes red with weeping. She never spoke to any of the other women, or came on deck. She was constantly seen sitting in the same corner from morning to night; even the time of meals roused her not. My heart bled for her; she was a countrywoman in misfortune. I offered her consolation, but her hopes and heart had sunk. When I spoke, she heeded me not, or only answered with sighs and tears; if I spoke of Scotland, she would wring her hands, and sob, until I thought her heart would burst. I endeavored to get her sad story from her lips, but she was silent as the grave to which she hastened. I lent her my Bible to comfort her, but she read it not; she laid it on her lap, after kissing it, and only bedewed it with her tears. At length, she sunk into the grave, of no disease but a broken heart.

I went every day to the town to buy fresh provisions and other necessaries for them. As their friends were allowed to come on board to see them, they brought money, and numbers had it of their own; particularly a Mrs. Barnsley, a noted sharper and shoplifter. She herself told me her family, for one hundred years back, had been swindlers and highwaymen. She had a brother, a highwayman, who often came to see her, as well dressed and genteel in his appearance as any gentleman. She petitioned the government agent and captain to be allowed to wear her own clothes in the river, and not the convict dress. This could on no account be allowed; but they told her she might wear what she chose when once they were at sea. The agent, Lieutenant Edgar, had been with Captain Cook, was a kind, humane man, and very good to them. He had it in his power to throw all their clothes overboard when he gave them the convict dress; but he gave them to me to stow in the after-hold, saying they would be of use to the poor creatures when they arrived at Port Jackson.

Those from the country came all on board in irons; and I was paid half a crown a head by the country jailers, in many cases, for striking them off upon my anvil, as they were not locked, but riveted. One day, I had the painful task to inform the father and mother of one of the convicts, that their daughter, Sarah Dorset, was on board; they were decent-looking people, and had come to London to inquire after her. When I met them, they were at Newgate; the jailer referred them to me. With tears in her eyes, the mother implored me to tell her if such a one was on board. I told them there was one of that name; the father's heart seemed too full to allow him to speak, but the mother, with streaming eyes, blessed God that they had found their poor, lost child, undone as she was. I called a coach, drove to the river, and had them put on board. The father, with a trembling step, mounted the ship's side; but we were forced to lift the mother on board. I took them down to my berth, and went for Sarah Dorset; when I brought her, the father said, in a choking voice, "My lost child!" and turned his back, covering his face with his hands; the mother, sobbing, threw her hands around her. Poor Sarah fainted, and fell at their feet. I knew not what to do. At length, she recovered, and, in the most heart-rending accents, implored their pardon. She was young and pretty, and had not been two years from her father's house at this present time; so short had been her course of folly and sin. She had not been protected by the villain that ruined her above six weeks; then she was forced by want upon the streets, and taken up as a disorderly girl; then sent on board to be transported. This was her short but eventful history. One of our men, William Power, went out to the colony when her time was expired, brought her home, and married her.

Mrs. Nelly Kerwin, a female of daring habits, banished for life for forging seamen's powers of attorney, and personating their relations, when on our passage down the river, wrote to London for cash, to some of her friends. She got a letter, informing her it was waiting for her at Dartmouth. We were in Colson Bay when she got this letter. With great address she persuaded the agent that there was an express for him and money belonging to her lying at Dartmouth. A man was sent, who brought on board Nell's money, but no express for the agent. When she got it, she laughed in his face, and told him he was in her debt for a lesson. He was very angry, as the captain often told him Kerwin was too many for him.

We had on board a girl, pretty well behaved, who was called, by her acquaintance, a daughter of Pitt's. She herself never contradicted it. She bore a most striking likeness to him in every feature, and could scarce be known from him as to looks. We left her at Port Jackson.

When we were fairly out at sea, every man on board took a wife from among the convicts, they nothing loath. The girl with whom I lived—for I was as bad in this point as the others—was named Sarah White-lam. She was a native of Lincoln, a girl of a modest, reserved turn, as kind and true a creature as ever lived. I courted her for a week and upwards, and would have married her upon the spot, had there been a clergyman on board. She had been banished for a mantle she had borrowed from an acquaintance. Her friend prosecuted her for stealing it, and she was transported for seven years. I had fixed my fancy upon her from the moment I knocked the rivet out of her irons upon my anvil, and as firmly resolved to bring her back to England, when her time was out, my lawful wife, as ever I did intend any thing in my life. She bore me a son in our voyage out. What is become of her, whether she is dead or alive, I know not. That I do not is no fault of mine, as my narrative will show. But to proceed. We soon found that we had a troublesome cargo, yet not dangerous or very mischievous,—as I may say, more noise than danger.

When any of them—such as Nance Ferrel, who was ever making disturbance—became very troublesome, we confined them down in the hold, and put on the hatch. This, we were soon convinced, had no effect, as they became, in turns, outrageous, on purpose to be confined. Our agent and the captain wondered at the change in their behavior. I, as steward, found it out by accident. As I was overhauling the stores in the hold, I came upon a hogshead of bottled porter, with a hole in the side of it, and, in place of full, there was nothing but empty, bottles in it. Another was begun, and more than a box of candles had been carried off. I immediately told the captain, who now found out the cause of the late insubordination and desire of confinement. We were forced to change the manner of punishing them. I was desired by the agent, Lieutenant Edgar, who was an old lieutenant of Cook's, to take a flour barrel, and cut a hole in the top for their head, and one on each side for their arms. This we called a wooden jacket. Next morning, Nance Farrel, as usual, came to the door of the cabin, and began to abuse the agent and captain. They desired her to go away between decks, and be quiet. She became worse in her abuse, wishing to be confined, and sent to the hold; but, to her mortification, the jacket was produced, and two men brought her upon deck, and put it on. She laughed, and capered about for a while, and made light of it. One of her comrades lighted a pipe and gave it to her. She walked about, strutting and smoking the tobacco, and making the others laugh at the droll figure she made; she walked a minuet, her head moving from side to side, like a turtle. The agent was resolved she should be heartily tired, and feel, in all its force, the disagreeableness of her present situation. She could only walk or stand; to sit, or lie down, was out of her power. She began to get weary, and begged to be released. The agent would not, until she asked his pardon, and promised amendment in future. This she did, in humble terms, before evening, but, in a few days, was as bad as ever; there was no taming her by gentle means. We were forced to tie her up, like a man, and give her one dozen, with the cat-o'-nine-tails, and assure her of a clawing every offence; this alone reduced her to any kind of order.

The first place we stopped at was Santa Cruz, in the Island of Teneriffe, for water. As we used a great quantity, the agent, at the captain's request, had laid in tea and sugar in place of beef or pork allowed by government. We boiled a large kettle of water, that served the whole convicts and crew, every night and morning. We allowed them water for washing their clothes, any quantity they chose, while in port. Many times they would use four and five boat-loads in one day.

We then stood for Rio Janeiro, where we lay eight weeks, taking in coffee and sugar, our old stock being now reduced very low.

In crossing the line, we had the best sport I ever witnessed upon the same occasion. We had caught a porpoise the day before the ceremony, which we skinned to make a dress for Neptune, with the tail stuffed. When he came on deck, he looked the best representation of a merman I ever saw painted, with a large swab upon his head for a wig. Not a man in the ship could have known him. One of the convicts fainted, she was so much alarmed at his appearance, and had a miscarriage after. From Rio Janeiro we sailed for the Cape of Good Hope, where we took on board seventy-three ewes and a ram, for the settlement.

At length, we sailed for Port Jackson. We made one of the convicts shepherdess, who was so fortunate in her charge of the flock as not to lose one. While we lay at the Cape, we had a narrow escape from destruction by fire. The carpenter allowed the pitch pot to boil over upon the deck, and the flames rose in an alarming manner. The shrieks of the women were dreadful, and the confusion they made running about drove every one stupid. I ran to my berth, seized a pair of blankets to keep it down until the others drowned it with water. Captain Aitken made me a handsome present for my exertions.

At length, almost to our sorrow, we made the land upon the 3rd of June, 1790, just one year, all but one day, from our leaving the river. We landed all our convicts safe. My charge, as steward, did not expire for six weeks after our arrival, as the captain, by agreement, was bound to victual them during that time.

The days flew on eagles' wings; for we dreaded the hour of separation, which at length arrived. It was not without the aid of the military we were brought on board.

They have an herb in the colony they call sweet tea. It is infused and drank like the China tea. I liked it much; it requires no sugar, and is both a bitter and a sweet. There was an old female convict, her hair quite gray with age, her face shriveled, who was suckling a child she had borne in the colony. Every one went to see her, and I among the rest. It was a strange sight; her hair was quite white. Her fecundity was ascribed to the sweet tea. I brought away with me two bags of it, as presents to my friends; but two of our men became very ill of the scurvy, and I allowed them the use of it, which soon cured them, but reduced my store. When we came to China, I showed it to my Chinese friends, and they bought it with avidity, and importuned me for it, and a quantity of the seed I had likewise preserved. I let them have the seed, and only brought a small quantity of the herb to England.

Upon our arrival at Wampoa, I renewed my acquaintance with my Chinese friends, and was as happy as I could be, with the thoughts of Sarah's situation upon my mind; but this was the dullest voyage I ever made. We touched at St. Helena on our way to England. When we arrived, I was paid off, and immediately made every inquiry for a ship for New Holland; but there was none, nor any likely to be soon.

There was a vessel called the *Amelia,* Captain Shiels, fitting out as a South Sea whaler. She belonged to 'Squire Enderborough, Paul's Wharf, London. I got myself engaged as cooper of her. The whole crew were on shares. I, as cooper, had a larger share than a seaman; but this was not my present aim, neither did I think of gain. I had all my money secured about my person, sewed into my clothes, ready for a start, and with it to pay the passage of Sarah and my son to England.

In two months after my leaving the *Lady Julian,* I was again at sea, in hopes of reaching Port Jackson by some means or other. In our first offset, we were stranded upon the Red Sand, near the Nore. While we lay in distress, the Deal men came out, and wished to make a wreck of us, by cutting away our masts. I, with alacrity, aided the captain, and stood guard, with a brace of pistols, and threatened to blow out the brains of the first man of them that offered to set his foot upon our deck. The weather, fortunately, was moderate. We, having no long boat, carried out our anchor between two boats, into deep water; and, as the tide flowed, we got her off. To my great disappointment, we were forced to put back into dock to have her examined, by removing the copper sheathing. All the crew left her, except myself, as the engagement was broken by our return to dock, and the men would not continue in her, as they thought no good would come of the voyage; her stranding was an omen of her bad luck.

There was no ship in the river for New South Wales; and the Indiamen would not sail until about the month of March; the *Amelia* would still be the first vessel. I had no inducement, therefore, to leave her. We were soon again ready for sea, and set sail with an entire new crew. The first land we made was the Island of Bona Vista, which belongs to the Portuguese, where we took in live stock, and salt to salt down our sealskins, then stood for St. Jago and took in more live stock; from thence to the Falkland Islands for geese and swine. We next made Staten Land, and passed the Straits of Magellan and Straits le Mair, but did not go through either of them. We doubled the Cape, then stood down to our fishing-ground, which was between latitude 18° and the line. We had nothing to do but commence, as we had been busy all the voyage, preparing and fitting our tackle.

Our boilers were fitted up before we left England, as, in the South Seas, the spermaceti is all boiled upon the deck. The boiler is built up with fire brick, and a space left between the lower tier and the deck, about nine inches high, quite water-tight. When once the fire is kindled,—which is never after allowed to go out until the ship is fully fished,—the space between the bricks and the deck is kept full of water. There are two plugholes, one on each side; so that, when the water heats, and would melt the pitch, upon whatever tack the ship may be, the plug is drawn from the under side, and the space immediately filled with cold water from the higher side. Great attention is required to watch the boilers. We do not require to carry out fuel to boil our oil, as the refuse of the oil is used ever after the first fire is kindled. The ashes of the fire is better than any soap. Let our clothes be ever so black and greasy, as they must be from our employment, one shovel full of ashes in a tub of water, will make them as clean as when we bought them.

I pursued my labors with all the ardor of a seaman. After taking a sufficient quantity of spermaceti, we stood as far down as latitude 3°, to the Island of Lopes, where we killed thirty thousand seals. We had a busy time chasing and killing them. When we had a sufficient number, we began to kill sea-lions, to get their skins for the ship's use. One of their skins was a sufficient load for two men. We used to stand in a gap of the rocks in the morning, and knock them down with our clubs as they approached the sea, then stab them with our long knives.

George Parker, our mate, made a blow at one, and missed him; he made a snap at George, and sent his tusk right through his arm, a little above the wrist, and walked away at his leisure with him into the sea, Parker roaring like a bull, from the pain and terror. Robert Wyld, perceiving his danger, rushed into the water to rescue him, and was up to the arm-pits before he succeeded in despatching the unwieldly monster. He then dragged them both on shore, where, with difficulty, the tusk was drawn from between the bones, it was so firmly jammed.

After visiting Payta and Lima, on the western coast of South America, we returned into the Atlantic, and put into Rio Janeiro for refreshments.

The governor's linguist came on board the *Amelia,* and requested, as a personal favor, that Captain Shiels would allow four of his men to go on board the commodore, to assist in the voyage home, as it would be a winter's passage. I immediately volunteered. I hoped by this means to reach England sooner, and obtain more money for Sarah, as I would receive a full share of the *Amelia* in England, the same as if I had continued in her. Had I known the delays, the fatigue and vexations,

I was to endure from these execrably superstitious Portuguese sailors, I never would have left the *Amelia* for any reward the commodore could have given me; and he was very kind to us. He knew our value, and his whole reliance was upon us. We were to work the ship, and fight the ship, should an enemy lay us alongside. He had been forty years trading between Lisbon and Rio Janeiro, and, in all that time, never had made a winter's voyage. The Portuguese are the worst sailors in the world, in rough or cold weather, and we had plenty of both; but, worse than all, we had a black fellow of a priest on board, to whom the crew paid more attention than to the captain. He was forever ringing his bell for mass, and sprinkling holy water upon the men. Whenever it blew harder than ordinary, they were sure to run to the quarter-deck, to the black priest. We were almost foundered, at one time, by this unseamanlike conduct. The whole crew ran to the quarter-deck, kneeling down, resigned to their fate, the priest sprinkling holy water most profusely upon them, while we four Englishmen were left to steer the vessel and hand the sails. It required two of the four to steer, so that there were only two to hand the sails. The consequence was, she broached to. William Mercer and I ran and cut the fore-gears, and allowed the yard to swing; at the same time, the captain, mate, and boatswain, hauled in the fore-brace, and she righted in a moment. Had her commons not been very high, she must have filled while she lay upon her beam ends. The sea was all over her deck, round the hatch; but so soon as she righted, and we were going to make sail, the Portuguese left their priest, and lent us a hand.

We were wrought almost to death, and never could have made out the voyage had we not been well fed, and the captain given us plenty of liquor. The black priest rung his bell at his stated time, whatever we were doing; and the Portuguese would run to their berths for their crosses. Often, the main tack was left half hauled aboard, at the sound of his bell, and the vessel left to drift to leeward until prayers were over. As two men could do nothing to the sail, when the wind was fresh, after prayers they would return, and begin bawling and hauling, calling upon their saints, as if they would come to assist. We were thus almost driven to distraction by them, and could scarce keep off our hands from boxing their ears. Many a hearty curse they and their saints got. Then they would run to the captain or priest, and make complaint that the Englishmen had cursed St. Antonio, or some other of their saints. I often wondered the captain did not confine the priest to his cabin in foul weather, as he was sure to be busiest then. When they complained, the captain took our part, and overawed the Portuguese, or I really believe they would have thrown us overboard.

At length, after a tedious voyage of three months, I got out of this vile crew. When we reached the Tagus, the Portuguese began to quarrel, and knock us about. We stood our ground the best way we could, until the captain got five of them sent on shore under a guard of soldiers. We remained at the captain's house until we got our wages. The owners gave us a doubloon a-piece, over and above our agreement, for saving the ship, as the captain did us every justice to the owners at the time, saying,

"If the English were as careful of their souls as they are of their bodies, they would be the best people in the world."

We assisted at a religious ceremony before we came away, at the special request of our kind friend, the captain. The foresail, that was set when she broached to, was given, as an offering, to the church, as the black priest told them it was through it they were saved. Although the worst sailor in the ship knew it was the sail that would have sunk us, they dared not contradict the priest. The whole ship's crew carried it through the streets of Lisbon upon handkerchiefs to the church, where it was placed upon the altar with much mummery. We came away and left them; but the owners of the vessel bought back the sail again, after the priests had blessed it to their minds, as the church had more use for money than foresails.

With a joyful heart, I set sail for London, to look out for an Indiaman, that I might get to Bombay, and inquire for Sarah; for she was still the idol of all my affections. At this time, I was all anxiety to reach England. I often hoped she had reached her father's house, and was there pining at my absence. I used, for days, to flatter myself with these dreams.

When we arrived at Gravesend, a man-of-war's boat came on board to press any Englishman there might be on board. William and I did not choose to trust to our protections, now that we were in the river. So we stowed ourselves away among some bags of cotton, where we were almost smothered, but could hear every word that was said. The captain told the lieutenant he had no more hands than he saw, and they were all Portuguese. The lieutenant was not very particular, and left the brig without making much search. When the boat left the vessel, we crept from our hiding-hole; and, not long after, a custom-house officer came on board. When we cast anchor, as I had a suit of long clothes in my chest, that I had provided, should I have been so fortunate as to have found Sarah at Port Jackson, to dash away with her a bit on shore, I put them on immediately, and gave the custom-house officer half a guinea for the loan of his cocked hat and powdered wig; the long gilt-headed cane was included in the bargain. I got a waterman to put me on shore. I am confident my own father, had he been alive, could not have known me, with my cane in my hand, cocked hat, and bushy wig. I inquired of the waterman the way to the inn where the coach set out from, for London; I, at the same time, knew as well as he. I passed for a passenger. At the inn, I called for a pint of wine, pens and ink, and was busy writing any nonsense that came in my head, until the coach set off. All these precautions were necessary. Had the waterman suspected me to be a sailor, he would have informed the press gang in one minute. The waiters at the inn would have done the same. By these precautions, I arrived safe in London, but did not go down to Wapping until next day, where I took up my old lodgings, still in my disguise. My landlord went on board, and brought on shore my bedding and chest. I left them under his charge while I went to Lincoln, to Sarah's parents, where I made every inquiry; but they knew not so much of her as I did myself. The last information they had obtained was from the letter I had put in the post-office for them, before I sailed in the *Amelia*. I immediately returned to London, where, to my disappointment, I found there was not a berth to be got in any of the Indiamen who were for Bombay direct. They were all full. I then, as my next best, went to be engaged as cooper on board the *Nottingham*, for China direct, depending on Providence, if we were ever to meet again. To find some way to effect my purpose, my landlord took me to be impressed. He got the six guineas allowed the bringer, which he returned to me. He was from Inverness,—as honest a man as ever lived. I had always boarded in his house when in London. A curious scene happened at my entry. There were a few more impressed on the same day, one an old tar. When asked by Captain Rogers, in his examination, how they hauled the main tack aboard, he replied, "I can't tell, your honor, but I can show." He clapped his foot into Captain Roger's pocket, at the same instant leaped on his shoulders, tore his coat to the skirts, saying, "Thus we haul it aboard." Captain Barefoot, of the *Nottingham*, and the other captains, laughed heartily, as well as Rogers, who said, rather peevishly, "You might have shown without tearing my coat." "How could I, your honor?" was the reply.

I thus again set off as cooper of the *Nottingham*, in 1793. Nothing worthy of notice happened. I did not get any intelligence from Sarah, nor did I ever hear from her again. As I have gone over the same voyage before, I will not detain the reader; but one circumstance, that I witnessed off the Cape of Good Hope, I cannot avoid mentioning, as a dreadful example of what man will dare, and the perils he will encounter, to free himself from a situation he dislikes. A man-of-war had been washing her gratings, when the India fleet hove in sight. They are washed by being lowered overboard, and allowed to float astern. Four or five men had slipped down upon them, cut them adrift, and were thus voluntarily committed to the vast Atlantic, without a bit of biscuit, or a drop of water, or any means of guiding the gratings they were floating upon, in the hope of being picked up by some vessel. They held out their arms to us, and supplicated, in the wildest manner, to be taken on board. The captain would not. The *Nottingham* was a fast-sailing ship, and the first in the fleet. He said, "I will not; some of the stern ships will pick them up." While he spoke, these unfortunate and desponding fellow-creatures lessened to our view, while their cries rung in our ears. I hope some of the stern ships picked them up. Few things I have seen are more strongly impressed upon my memory, than the despairing looks and frantic gestures of these victims in quest of liberty. Next morning, the frigate they had left came alongside of us, and inquired if we had seen them. The captain gave an indirect answer to their inquiries, as well he might.

On my return home from China, nothing uncommon happened, until we reached the Downs. I had allowed my beard to grow long, and myself to be very dirty, to be as unlikely as possible, when the man-of-war boats came on board to press the crew. As we expected, they came. I was in the hold, sorting among the water-casks, and escaped. They took every hand that would answer. I rejoiced in my escape, but my joy was of short duration. One of the men they had taken had a sore leg; the boat brought him back, and I had the bad luck to be taken, and he was left. Thus were all my schemes blown into the air. I found myself in a situation I could not leave, a bondage that had been imposed upon me against my will, and no hopes of relief until the end of the war—not that I disliked it, but I had now become weary of wandering, for a time, and longed to see Scotland again. My heart always pointed to my native land. Remonstrance and complaint were equally vain.

I therefore made up my mind to it, and was as happy as a man in blasted prospects can be. I was taken on board the *Venerable*, Admiral Duncan. She was the flag-ship, and commanded by Captain Hope, now Admiral Hope. The *Venerable's* boats had made a clean ship of the *Nottingham*. She was forced to be brought up the river by ticket-porters and old Greenwich men. Next morning, sixty of us, who had belonged to the *Nottingham*, were turned over to the *Edgar*, 74, Captain Sir Charles Henry Knowles. This was on the 11th June, 1794. I was stationed in the gunner's crew.

We shortly after sailed on a cruise in the North Seas, and encountered a dreadful gale on the 17th October. I never was in such danger in all my life. The *Edgar* was only newly put in commission, and her rigging was new, and not properly seasoned. We in a few hours carried away our bowsprit and foremast in this dreadful night; then our mizzen and maintopmast. With great difficulty we cut them clear. Soon after, our mainmast loosened in the step, and we every moment expected it to go through the bottom. Then no exertion could have saved us from destruction. The carpenter, by good fortune, got it secured. We lost all our anchors and cables in our attempts to bring her to, save one. At length, it moderated a little, when we rigged jury masts, and made for the Humber, where we brought to with our only remaining anchor, when the *Inflexible*, Captain Savage, hove in sight, and took us in tow. When in this situation, the coasters, as they passed, called to the *Inflexible*, "What prize have you got in tow?" A fresh gale sprung up, and the *Inflexible* was forced to cast us off. The weather moderated again, and we proceeded up the Swain the best way we could, into Blackstakes, Chatham. My berth, during the storm, as one of the gunner's crew, was in charge of the powder on deck we used in firing our guns of distress. The ship rolled so much, we were often upon our beam-ends, and rolled a number of our guns overboard. We were forced to start all our beer and water, to lighten the ship; but we rode it out, contrary to our expectation, and were shortly after turned over, captain and all, to the *Goliah*, 74 guns, and sailed to join Sir John Jervis in the blockade of Toulon. We boarded a Spanish ship, and found on board thirty Austrian prisoners. They every man entered with us as marines.

We next sailed for St. Forensa Bay, in the Island of Corsica, to water, but found the French in possession of the watering-place, and could get none. I belonged to the launch, and had charge of the powder and match. I was constantly on shore, when any service was to be done in destroying stores, spiking guns, blowing up batteries, and enjoyed it much. We carried off all the brass guns, and those metal ones that were near the edge of the rocks we threw into the sea. This was excellent sport to us; but we were forced to leave it, and sail to Gibraltar for water and provisions, but could obtain no supplies, and sailed for Lisbon, where we got plenty, having been on short allowance for some time before.

While we lay at Lisbon, we got private intelligence, overland, that the Spanish fleet was at sea. We, with all despatch, set sail in pursuit of them. We were so fortunate as to come in sight of them by break of day, on the 14th of February, off Cape St. Vincent. They consisted of twenty-five sail, mostly three-deckers. We were only eighteen; but we were English, and we gave them their Valentines in style. Soon as we came in sight, a bustle commenced not to be conceived or described. To do it justice, while every man was as busy as he could be, the greatest order prevailed. A serious cast was to be perceived on every face, but not a shade of doubt or fear. We rejoiced in a general action; not that we loved fighting, but we all wished to be free to return to our homes, and follow our own pursuits. We knew there was no other way of obtaining this than by defeating the enemy. "The hotter war, the sooner peace," was a saying with us. When every thing was cleared, the ports open, the matches lighted, and guns run out, then we gave them three such cheers as are only to be heard in a British man-of-war. This intimidates the enemy more than a broadside, as they have often declared to me. It shows them all is right, and the men, in the true spirit, baying to be at them. During the action, my situation was not one of danger, but most wounding to my feelings, and trying to my patience. I was stationed in the after-magazine, serving powder from the screen, and could see nothing; but I could feel every shot that struck the *Goliah;* and the cries and groans of the wounded were most distressing, as there was only the thickness of the blankets of the screen between me and them. Busy as I was, the time hung upon me with a dreary weight. Not a soul spoke to me but the master-at-arms, as he went his rounds to inquire if all was safe. No sick person ever longed more for his physician than I for the voice of the master-at-arms. The surgeon's mate, at the commencement of the action, spoke a little; but his hands were soon too full of his own affairs. Those who were carrying, ran like wild creatures, and scarce opened their lips. I would far rather have been on the decks, amid the bustle, for there the time flew on eagle's wings. The *Goliah* was sore beset; for some time, she had two three-deckers upon her. The men stood to their guns as cool as if they had been exercising. The admiral ordered the *Britannia* to our assistance. Iron-sides, with her forty-twos, soon made them sheer off. Towards the close of the action, the men were very weary. One lad put his head out of the porthole, saying, "Damn them, are they not going to strike yet?" For us to strike was out of the question.

At length, the roar of the guns ceased, and I came on deck to see the effects of a great sea engagement; but such a scene of blood and desolation I want words to express. I had been in a great number of actions with single ships, in the *Proteus* and *Surprise,* during the seven years I was in them. This was my first action in a fleet; and I had only a small share in it. We had destroyed a great number, and secured four three-deckers. One they had the impiety to call the Holy Ghost, we wished much to get; but they towed her off. The fleet was in such a shattered situation, we lay twenty-four hours in sight of them, repairing our rigging. It is after the action the disagreeable part commences; the crews are wrought to the utmost of their strength; for days they have no remission of their toil, repairing the rigging, and other parts injured in the action; their spirits are broke by fatigue; they have no leisure to talk of the battle; and when the usual round of duty returns, we do not choose to revert to a disagreeable subject. Who can speak of what he did, where all did their utmost? One of my messmates had the heel of his shoe shot off; the skin was not broken, yet his leg swelled, and became black. He was lame for a long time. On our return to Lisbon, we lost one of the fleet, the *Bombay Castle*. She was stranded, and completely lost. All her crew were saved. We were in great danger in the *Goliah;* Captain Sir C. H. Knowles was tried for not lending assistance, when he needed it himself. The court-martial honorably acquitted him. Collis, our first lieutenant, told us not to cheer when he came on board; but we loved our captain too well to be restrained. We had agreed upon a signal with the coxswain, if he was, as he ought to be, honorably acquitted. The signal was given, and in vain Collis forbade. We manned the yards, and gave three hearty cheers. Not a man on board but would have bled for Sir C. H. Knowles. To our regret, we lost him to our ship at this very time. He was as good a captain as I ever sailed with. He was made admiral, and went home in the *Britannia.*

Captain Foley took command of the *Goliah,* and we joined the blockade of Cadiz, where we remained, sending our boat to assist at the bombardments, and covering them until Admiral Nelson came out again, and picked out thirteen seventy-fours from the fleet; the *Goliah* was one. She was the fastest sailing ship in the fleet. We did not stay to water, but got a supply from the ships that were to remain, and away we set, under a press of sail, not knowing where. We came to an anchor in the Straits of Messina. There was an American man-of-war at anchor; Captain Foley ordered him to unmoor, that the *Goliah* might get her station, as it was a good one, near the shore; but Jonathan would not budge, but made answer, "I will let you know I belong to the United States of America, and will not give way to any nation under the sun, but in a good cause." So we came to an anchor where we could. We remained here but a short time, when we got intelligence that the French fleet were up the Straits. We then made sail for Egypt, but missed them, and came back to Syracuse, and watered in twenty-four hours. I was up all night filling water. The day after we left Syracuse, we fell in with a French brig, who had just left the fleet. Admiral Nelson took her in tow, and she conducted us to where they lay at anchor in Aboukir Bay.

We had our anchors out at our stern port with a spring upon them, and the cable carried along the ship's side, so that the anchors were at our bows, as if there was no change in the arrangement. This was to prevent the ships from swinging round, as every ship was to be brought to by her stern. We ran in between the French fleet and the shore, to prevent any communication between the enemy and the shore. Soon as they were in sight, a signal was made from the admiral's ship for every vessel, as she came up, to make the best of her way, firing upon the French ships as she passed, and "every man to take his bird," as we, joking, called it. The *Goliah* led the van. There was a French frigate right in our way. Captain Foley cried, "Sink that brute; what does he there?" In a moment, she went to the bottom, and her crew were seen running into her rigging. The sun was just setting as we went into the bay, and a red and fiery sun it was. I would, had I had my choice, been on the deck; there I should have seen what was passing, and the time would not have hung so heavy; but every man does his duty with spirit, whether his station be in the slaughter-house or the magazine.

I saw as little of this action as I did of the one on the 14th February, off Cape St. Vincent. My station was in the powder magazine, with the gunner. As we entered the bay, we stripped to our trousers, opened our ports, cleared, and, every ship we passed, gave them a broadside and three cheers. Any information we got was from the boys and women who carried the powder. The women behaved as well as the men, and got a present for their bravery from the Grand Seignior. When the French admiral's ship blew up, the *Goliah* got such a shake, we thought the after-part of her had blown up, until the boys told us what it was. They brought us, every now and then, the cheering news of another French ship having struck, and we answered the cheers on deck with heartfelt joy. In the heat of the action, a shot come right into the magazine, but did no harm, as the carpenters plugged it up, and stopped the water that was rushing in. I was much indebted to the gunner's wife, who gave her husband and me a drink of wine every now and then, which lessened our fatigue much. There were some of the women wounded; and one woman, belonging to Leith, died of her wounds, and was buried on a small island in the bay. One woman bore a son in the heat of the action; she belonged to Edinburgh. When we ceased firing, I went on deck to view the state of the fleets, and an awful sight it was. The whole bay was covered with dead bodies, mangled, wounded, and scorched, not a bit of clothes on them except their trousers. There were a number of French, belonging to the French admiral's ship, the *L'Orient*, who had swam to the *Goliah*, and were cowering under her forecastle. Poor fellows! they were brought on board, and Captain Foley ordered them down to the steward's room, to get provisions and clothing. One thing I observed in these Frenchmen, quite different from any thing I had ever before observed. In the American war, when we took a French ship,—the *Duke de Chartres*,—the prisoners were as merry as if they had taken us, only saying, "Fortune de guerre,—you take me to-day, I take you to-morrow." Those we now had on board were thankful for our kindness, but were sullen, and as downcast as if each had lost a ship of his own. The only incidents I heard of are two. One lad, who was stationed by a salt-box, on which he sat to give out cartridges and keep the lid close,—it is a trying berth,—when asked for a cartridge, he gave none, yet he sat upright; his eyes were open. One of the men gave him a push; he fell all his length on the deck. There was not a blemish on his body, yet he was quite dead, and was thrown overboard. The other, a lad who had the match in his hand to fire his gun. In the act of applying it, a shot took off his arm; it hung by a small piece of skin. The match fell to the deck. He looked to his arm, and, seeing what had happened, seized the match in his left hand, and fired off the gun, before he went to the cockpit to have it dressed. They were in our mess, or I might never have heard of it. Two of the mess were killed, and I knew not of it until the day after. Thus terminated the glorious first of August, the busiest night in my life.

Soon after the action, the whole fleet set sail with the prizes, and left the *Goliah* as guard-ship. We remained here until we were relieved by the *Tigre,* 74, when we sailed for Naples, to refit. After refitting, we sailed for Malta, to join in the blockade, where we remained eight months, without any occurrence worthy of notice. At length, the *Goliah* became so leaky, we were forced to leave our station and sail for Gibraltar, where after watering, we sailed for England. We got some marines from the Rock, to reënforce the *Goliah's* complement,—one of them a tall, stout Englishman, who had been cock of the Rock. He was very overbearing. There are often quarrels at the ship's fires, when the men are boiling their kettles. We had a stout little fellow of an Irishman, who had been long in the *Goliah;* the marine pushed his kettle aside. Paddy demanded why he did so. "Because I choose to do it." "I won't allow you while the life is in me," was the reply. "Do you wish to fight?" said the Englishman. "Yes, and I do," said Paddy; "I will take the Gibraltar rust out of you, or you shall beat the life out of my body before we are done." A fight was made up in a minute; and they went well forward on the deck, to be out of sight of the officers. To it they went, and fought it out, we forming a ring, and screening them from observation. Paddy was as good as his word; for he took the rust off the marine so well, he was forced to give in; and we were all happy to see the lobster-back's pride taken out of him. On our arrival, she was put out of commission, and the crew turned over to the *Royal William,* the guard-ship, and had two or three days' liberty on shore, by the admiral's order.

I was next draughted on board the *Ramillies,* and sailed for Belleisle, but remained only a short time in her, when I was turned over to the *Ajax,* Captain Alexander F. Cochrane, upon preferment. We sailed for Ferrol, and attempted to cut out some vessels, but did not succeed; then stood for Algiers to water, having a fleet of transports with troops on board under convoy. The troops were commanded by Sir Ralph Abercrombie. Having watered, we sailed with the army to Mamarice Bay, and the troops were encamped upon a fine piece of ground, with a rivulet running through the centre. The French had just left the place, having first done all the mischief in their power. While we lay here, an engineer, named William Balcarras, went, in a frigate to reconnoitre the French works. He landed, and, having attained his object, was coming off in his boat, when he was followed by another from the shore, and shot dead before he reached the frigate. We left Mamarice Bay, and sailed to Rhodes, where we took in forage for the cavalry. We then sailed for Alexandria, and landed the troops.

I belonged to one of the boats. Captain A. F. Cochrane was beach master, and had the ordering of the troops in the landing. We began to leave the ships about twelve o'clock, and reached the shore about sunrise in the morning. We rowed very slow, with our oars muffled. It was a pleasant night; the water was very still; and all was silent as death. No one spoke; but each cast an anxious look to the shore, then at each other, impatient to land. Each boat carried about one hundred men, and did not draw nine inches of water. The French cavalry were ready to receive us; but we soon forced them back, and landed eight thousand men the first morning. We had good sport at landing the troops, as the Frenchmen made a stout resistance. We brought back the wounded men to the ships.

For some time, we supplied the troops on shore with provisions and water. After the advance of the troops into the country, I was with the seamen on shore, assisting at the siege of Alexandria, and working like a laborer in cutting off the branch of the Nile that supplied the city with water. One of the *Ajax's* boats, at Sir Ralph Abercrombie's request, carried him, after receiving his wound, on board the hospital ship.

Of all the countries I was ever in, in all my wanderings, I could not remain in Egypt, the air is so dry, and I felt so disagreeable. It is, on the whole, sandy and barren; yet what I saw of it that was cultivated is very agreeable. For some days before the town surrendered, I had been so bad with the flux, I was forced to go on board. After the town surrendered, and the operations of the army ceased, we sailed for Malta. At this time, I was blind with the ophthalmia, and continued thus for six weeks. My sufferings were most acute. I could not lie down for a moment, for the scalding water, that continually flowed from my eyes, filled them, and put me to exquisite torture. I sat constantly on my chest, with a vessel of cold water, bathing them. If I slept, I awoke in an agony of pain. All the time, the flux was most severe upon me, and the surgeon would not dry it up, as it, he said, relieved my eyes. When we came to Malta, a French surgeon cured me by touching the balls of my eyes with tincture of opium; but the pain of the application was very severe. Thank God, however, I soon after recovered my health and spirits. From Malta, we sailed to Gibraltar, where we watered, then sailed for England, where, to my joy, I found that peace was concluded. We were all paid off shortly after our arrival. I was ship's corporal when I was discharged.

I was once more my own master, and felt so happy, I was like one bewildered. Did those on shore only experience half the sensations of a sailor at perfect liberty, after being seven years on board ship without a will of his own, they would not blame his eccentricities, but wonder he was not more foolish. After a few days, my cooler reason began to resume its power, and I began to think what should be my after pursuits. It was now seven years since I had been pressed from the *Nottingham*. In that time, the thoughts of Sarah had faded into a distant, pleasing dream. The violent desire I at one time felt to repossess her was now softened into a curiosity to know what had become of her.

I could not settle to work, but wandered up and down. At length I fell in with a cousin of my own. We had been playfellows, and a friendly intimacy had continued until I went to sea. I fixed my affections on her, and we were married. I gave her my solemn promise never again to go to sea, during her life. I then thought sincerely of settling, and following my trade. I bought a house in the Castle

Hill, and furnished it well; then laid in a stock of wood and tools. I had as much work as I could do for a soapwork at the Queen's Ferry. For one year, my prospects were as good as I could have wished, and I was as happy as ever I had been in my life. But, in a few months after, the war broke out again, and the press-gang came in quest of me. I could no longer remain in Edinburgh and avoid them. My wife was like a distracted woman, and gave me no rest until I sold off my stock in trade and the greater part of my furniture, and retired to the country. Even, until I got this accomplished, I dared not to sleep in my own house, as I had more than one call from the gang.

For eleven years I lived at Cousland. Year followed year, but still no views of peace. I grew old apace, and the work became too heavy for me. I was now fifty-eight years of age, and they would not have taken me, had I wished to enter the service. I therefore removed to Edinburgh, and again began to work for myself. My first employers had failed in business long before. The times were completely changed; I could not get constant employment for myself. I therefore wrought for any of the other masters who were throng; but the cooper business is so very poor, I have been oftener out of employment than at work. Few of them keep journeymen. They, like myself, did all their work with their own hands.

I never had any children by my cousin during the seventeen years we lived together. Margaret, during all that time, never gave me a bad word, or made any strife by her temper; but all have their faults. I will not complain; but more money going out than I by my industry could bring in, has now reduced me to want in my old age.

At her death, which happened four years ago, I was forced to sell all my property, except a small room, in which I live, and a cellar where I do any little work I am so fortunate as to obtain. This I did to pay the expenses of her funeral, and a number of debts that had been contracted unknown to me. As my poverty will not allow me to pay for a seat in a church, I go in the evenings to the Little Church; but my house is in the Tolbooth parish.

I eke out my subsistence in the best manner I can. Coffee, made from the raspings of bread, (which I obtain from the bakers,) twice a day, is my chief diet. A few potatoes, or any thing I can obtain with a few pence, constitute my dinner. My only luxury is tobacco, which I have used these forty-five years. To beg I never will submit. Could I have obtained a small pension for my past services, I should then have reached my utmost earthly wish, and the approach of utter helplessness would not haunt me, as it at present does, in my solitary home. Should I be forced to sell it, all I could obtain could not keep me and pay for lodgings for one year; then I must go to the poor's house, which God, in his mercy, forbid. I can look to my death-bed with resignation; but to the poor's house I cannot look with composure.

I have been a wanderer, and the child of chance, all my days; and now only look for the time when I shall enter my last ship, and be anchored with a green turf upon my breast; and I care not how soon the command is given.

Voyages to Canton and North America

JOHN BARTLETT

On March 19th, 1790, I shipped on board the ship *Massachusetts,* Capt. Job Prince, commander, bound on a voyage to Canton in China. She had been built at Quincy, by Daniel Briggs, for the firm of Shaw & Randall, and when brought to Boston, under jury masts, she excited a considerable sensation for she was the largest merchant vessel built at that time in the United States and nearly eight hundred tons burthen. As the voyage to China was almost new to Americans at that time hundreds of persons made application for a station on board.

The *Massachusetts* was acknowledged by all to be a fine ship and as she lay at her wharf, the officers from several French men-of-war, then in the harbor, frequently came aboard to gratify their curiosity and express their admiration. On her arrival at Batavia and also at Canton, the commanders of various foreign vessels came aboard to examine her and admire her model. She undoubtedly was the handsomest vessel in the two ports. But when her lower hold was opened at Canton, for the first time since she left Boston, she was rotten. She was loaded principally with green masts and spars, taken on board in winter, directly out of the water, with ice and mud on them. The lower deck hatches were caulked down in Boston and when opened at Canton the air was so foul that a lighted candle was put out by it almost as soon as by water. We had four or five hundred barrels of beef in the lower hold placed in the broken stowage and when the fresh air was admitted so that men could live under the hatches, the beef was found almost boiled; the hoops were rotted and fallen off and the inside of the ship was covered with blue mould an inch thick.

It is of interest to remark that the ship had three full crews shipped before she sailed, due to a prediction made by an old woman fortune teller, Moll Pitcher of Lynn, that the ship would be lost on the voyage and every man on her.

We set sail from off Hancock's wharf on Sunday, the 28th of March, 1790, at 4 o'clock, P.M. When the anchor was hauled to the cathead and the block was brought up suddenly against the under side of it, the hook of the cat-block snapped short and the anchor ran to the bottom stopping the ship's way. This occurred before the eyes of a great crowd of spectators thronging the wharves, houses and stores. We fired a salute after getting under way a second time. We then proceeded down the harbor and came to anchor at Congress Road where we remained until the next day when we slipped our cable, leaving the pinnace to take it up, and with a fair breeze ran outside of the light house and hove to for the boat.

We sailed eastward, making some southing, until April 24th, and then set a course south by west along the coast of Barbary and Guinea in water that was discolored much of the time.

On June 25th, we ran in for Cape Agulhas with steering sails below and aloft. Saw a large flock of birds. At 5 P.M. got soundings in eighty fathoms of water with soft, muddy bottom. Nothing of consequence took place during our passage across the Indian Ocean.

On July 21st, while scraping the ship's sides in order to paint and varnish, one of the stage ropes accidentally gave way and three men were thrown overboard. One other man caught hold of something alongside the ship but the others went astern. The second mate, with four hands, went to their assistance in the jolly boat. Two of the lads swam to the stage and were saved but Samuel Tripe of Portsmouth, N. H. was drowned, not being able to swim. This happened off Java Head.

Made the Island of Java on August 22nd, being 140 days from Boston. Five days later spoke the ship *Laurient*, of London, bound for Canton. We gave her a salute of seven guns which she returned. The captain and merchant went on board of her at four P.M. On the 30th we saw Pigeon Island and ran in for it and anchored. Just as we let go our anchor, Thomas French, midshipman, while handling our mainsail, lost his hold on a gasket that was slack and fell from the mainyard across the barracade or rail and was instantly killed. He was a fine young man and was much lamented by the ship's company.

On August the 31st we got under way at 8 A.M. and ran in for an island called "the henroost," which lays before Batavia town, and at one P.M. came to anchor in seven fathoms of water and saluted the fort with nine guns. We buried Mr. French on Pigeon Island. When the captain and merchant went ashore they found that American trade was stopped in Batavia and so after wooding and watering we bought stock enough to last for our passage to China, and on September 8th got under way bound for Canton.

Batavia is built much after the manner of Amsterdam in Holland, with canals running through every street with a large one let in from the sea. The morning after sailing from Batavia, two strange men came on deck. They were called aft and examined and it was found by their discourse that they had run away from the hospital. One was named John Armstrong, an Irishman, and the other was John Vannable, an Englishman. September 11th saw a sail standing to the northward and westward which we supposed to be a Chinese junk.

We made the Grand Ladrone Island on October 7th and kept beating to windward all night. The next day we steered to the northward and eastward trying to find a passage through the islands as we could not get a pilot out of any of the China junks, of which there were two or three hundred in sight. Saw a ship standing towards us from the northward and hove our main and mizzen topsails to the mast to speak to her. She proved to be Captain Le Gray bound to Canton. We followed him through the islands towards Macao and came to anchor in Macao Roads on the 9th, where we found the *Washington* of Providence, Captain Donnison. The captain and merchant went ashore to get a pilot for Wampoo and at 12 meridian, he came in a lare boat called the *Venger,* belonging to Captain Kendrick of the sloop *Lady Washington,* of Boston. Got under way that night with several East India ships (the *Sir Edward Huse, Royal Admiral, Belvidere* and *Abergavanna*) and the *Washington* of Rhode Island, all bound up to Wampoo. The next day we went through the Bocca or Tiger's Mouth, where there is a small fort kept up by the mandarins to board ships that go up the river to Wampoo.

Before we reached a landing the wind died away and some two hundred China boats that they called sampans, with many men, women and children in them, towed us up the river and at 6 P.M. we moored above all the rest of the shipping finding three American vessels there,—the *Nancy* of New York, the *Brothers* of Philadelphia, and the *Washington* of Rhode Island.

On October 25th, the captain representing the Danish Company, with an English Commodore and several other gentlemen came on board with the intention to buy our ship and our merchant went up to Canton with them to agree upon a price. While here our people began to grow sick daily. The ship was attended by a hopoo boat that found us in vegetables. About this time the servants of the captain and the merchant died; one a black man named Charlestown and the other a mulatto called Isaac. Our ship was sold for $65,000 and all the men paid off. Some expected to be sent home; the English sailors went on board of English ships; and I and eight others shipped on board the snow *Gustavus,* Thomas Barnet, commander, bound to the Northwest Coast of North America. The other men were: Thomas Williamson, John Wall, John Harris, Thomas Lunt, Charles Treadwell, Joseph Grounard, Benjamin Head, and Malachi Foot. We preferred this to going home in an old Danish ship that had lost her masts and bowsprit in a gale of wind and was eleven months from Denmark to Wampoo. She had been bought by Captain Metcalf to be sent to New York.

On November 5th I received my wages amounting to forty-nine dollars, and spent about thirty dollars for various articles to be sent home by Captain Prince who was returning in the ship *Washington.* At this time fifteen or sixteen of our old hands lay sick at the Bank's Hall. Those of us who belonged to the *Gustavus* went up to Canton, the next day, to the factory of our new owner, 'Squire Cox, and received two months' advance pay, ten dollars of which went for our stores for the voyage. Most of us were sick at the time including myself. On the 11th, we went down to Wampoo and carried our chests and bedding on board the *Carnetic,* a country ship bound for Bombay, she having our stores on board, as our vessel lay at Lark's Bay, one of the Ladrone Islands, about twelve miles below Macao.

Two days later we went on board the *Gustavus* and for some days were employed in fitting our vessel for sea. We were allowed salt beef and fresh pork which was hardly eatable on account of its fatness which is the fault of all Chinese pork. The animals generally weigh from one hundred and fifty to two hundred pounds and it is remarkable that they can live upon so little. A Chinese hog doesn't eat more than half as much as an American hog of the same weight and their fat is very disagreeable being more like hog lard than American pork. Their bellies hang down to the ground when they are on their feet. We had plenty of bread aboard that had been in China for more than eighteen months and was hardly fit for hogs to eat. This was the beginning of our voyage and only God knew how it would end.

November 14th, 1790, we got under way from Lark's Bay bound for the Northwest Coast of North America with thirty-one men on board, all in good health.

On December 19th we made the Island of Sanquin and came to anchor in Troner Bay close in shore in twenty-five fathoms of water and sent the long boat ashore for wood and water. The natives of this island are Malays and are governed by the Dutch. We found here one black Dutch sergeant who told us that our vessel was the first one that had been in the bay for three years. The natives were very shy and kept themselves armed during the entire time that we were in the bay. They behaved very civil to us but more from fear than for any other cause. They are a very deceitful people and when they laugh and play round you that is the time to be on guard against attack. The captain gave the sergeant a long coat and other small articles to buy some stock for the ship and he went ashore and did not return. After we were done watering, the third mate and four hands went ashore well armed to make trade with the natives who turned out to be well armed themselves and in less than two hours' time they loaded our boat as deep as she could swim with cocoa nuts, plantains, fowls, etc.

December 30th, we saw a small, low island not shown on our charts and about that time the native of O-why-hee died of scurvey. A week later we sighted a lot of driftwood and rock weeds and other signs of land to the windward, the wind to the E. S. E. Probably undiscovered land as the charts make no mention of land in that direction. Sounded several times but could get no bottom.

We made the Northwest Coast of America on March 5th, 1791, after a tedious passage of seventy days attended with gales and dirty weather most of the time, and ran into Bartlett's Sound, coming to anchor with great difficulty as we could not find less than thirty fathoms of water a cable's length from the shore. The next day we came to anchor with a kedge under the lee of a small island where the canoes came off to us to trade with fish and furs. We soon parted from the kedge and not being able to find a good anchorage in this Sound we plied along shore in search of a safe harbor in which to overhaul and repair our rigging. This Sound takes it name from Captain Bartlett of the ship *Lourden* of Ostend, and lays in Latitude 48° 56' North.

After sailing along shore for several days we at last found the harbor of Wickannish which was pointed out to us by an Indian named Captain Hannah who came on board not long before. Near the entrance was an island that had three trees on it that appear like a ship in stays and is called Ship Island. At four P.M. we saw the smoke at Wickannish. Captain Hannah had been in this harbor but once before but we steered according to his best judgement. Before long the natives on shore began to make signs to us to steer more to the northward which were not regarded by our captain and soon we ran on a ledge of rocks and came near losing our vessel. We hove all sails back and fortunately she fell off the ledge into twelve fathoms of water. A boat sent to sound for the channel soon discovered the entrance between two islands and at five P.M. we came abreast of Wickannish town or village which contained about two hundred houses or long huts of square form built about twenty yards from the water. We were soon honoured by a visit from their chief whose name was Wickannish. He was a tall, raw boned fellow who came attended by thirty or forty canoes with fish and furs to sell. Several of them were bound out a whaling with gear in the canoes. Their lances and harpoons were very curious being made of bone neatly polished. Their lines were made of animals' hides and their drags were made of skins blown full of wind in the form of a winter squash.

Early the next morning we weighed anchor and ran up to Cox's Harbour with the boat sounding ahead of us. The tide was running very strong at the entrance of the harbour and we were swept in alongside of some rocks and so near the shore as to rack the limbs of the trees with our yards and very near being cast away a second time. In this harbour we lay moored for several days as it was land-locked and a safe place in which to overhaul our rigging. One day the boat went ashore to kill geese which were very plentiful.

On Saturday, March 15th, the boat was sent with the carpenter and Charles Treadwell to cut wood at a point about a mile from the vessel and out of sight of her. Late in the afternoon the boat went to get the man and just as she went ashore three canoes put out from where our men had been cutting wood. They had stolen a large iron maul and threatened to pick out the carpenter's eyes with their arrows when our boat coming just at that time saved their lives. The next day, at 10 o'clock, our second mate died of the scurvey having been sick for some time. He was born in Cork and was twenty-eight years old. We did not bury him until the sun was down and it was so dark when our captain was reading prayers that he began to damn his eyes because he could not see the print plainly.

We remained at this village until the 26th when we got under way at four P.M. bound to the north on our trading voyage. In all we bought forty skins at this place. A week later we made Douglass Island at the entrance of Queen Charlotte's Sound and saw Cape St. James.

On Thursday, April the 3rd, we ran into a small bay and a great number of canoes came off with men, women and children in them. The dress of the men was made of three or four skins sewed together which covered them from their shoulders down to their knees. They were ornamented with bird's feathers all over their heads and besmeared with grease and paint. On their heads there were a great number of tails or locks of hair which were full of lice and grease and made them look very frightful. We learned that whenever they kill a man in battle, they cut off his hair and mat it up in tails and tie it on their own heads. The women, when young, bore a hole in their under lips and run a piece of copper through it and as the girls grow up they put in bigger and bigger pieces of wire so that at the age of twelve or thirteen they can put in a small piece of wood of oval form, about the size of a half-crown piece. At the age of thirty, they can put in a piece as big as the palm of your hand. It hangs down below their chins. The morning when we first came into the bay they clapped their hands over their mouths to hide their teeth when they laughed, for they seemed to know themselves to be frightful to all strangers. When they are better acquainted they put aside all modesty. The young women were well featured. We had them on board at from ten to twenty years of age. Their fathers would instruct them how to behave while our men had to do with them. We bought some dried halibut of these natives. They cure it without salt. They had no furs but wanted us to go into the bay to anchor. It had the appearance of being a fine harbour but our captain would not agree to it and stood off and on all night while the natives made fires as a sign for us to come in. Their chief's name was Huegur.

While running alongshore, the next day, we fired one of our three pounders and five canoes came off with about seventy natives. Their chief was a young man who came on board and behaved very civil and made it his business to trade for the rest of the company. We bought eighty skins which brought up our total in the hold to about one hundred and twenty. At eight o'clock this morning (April 4th), Louis Anthony died of the scurvey. He was born at Lisbon and was about thirty-one years old. As there was an appearance of bad weather we stood offshore and made a good offing.

For the next three weeks we had dirty weather and spent most of the time laying to under a Bellamy trisail and Dungarvin reef in the fore-topmast staysail. Our people began to grow sickly on account of the short allowance of one pound of beef and a pint of rice every twenty-four hours. One day, six pounds of sugar was served for a mess of six men and once a week, a pound of pork and a pint of peas. On April 24th, the weather became more moderate and we stood for land and the next day saw land and ran close in and came to anchor in twelve fathoms of water with a hawser run out on each quarter and made fast to the limbs of trees ashore. The place was called Cloak Bay and their chief's name was Connehow. The natives came off with plenty of large halibut and other fish. The carpenter's mate, Charles Treadwell and I went ashore to cut wood and the natives behaved very civil while we were at work. There were thirty to forty there at a time, the most of whom were women who kept up a continual singing. The ship while here was surrounded by two or three hundred canoes at a time with a plenty of furs. The chief trade was iron, buttons and old clothes.

The next day, April the 26th, while trading with the natives on the quarter deck, a large canoe came alongside having on board a great number of spears and bows and arrows. The men began to flock on board in great numbers and at the same time we noticed that they were sending their women ashore which seemed to show a bad design. They also were seen to put on their shields and hand up their targets and pass their knives from one to the other on the quarter deck there being about one hundred and fifty of the natives there at the time. Seeing this we manned our tops with blunderbusses and the remainder of our men with small arms. Charles and I were on shore at the time of the fray with the natives on board. The women surrounded us on shore singing their war song. We both took up our pistols, resolved to sell our lives as dearly as possible if they molested us. Soon the noise on board began to abate and the natives would not trade any more unless we would disarm our men. We did so as all was quiet. Their armed canoes went away and trade went on brisker than ever.

The next day the natives began to come in large numbers from all parts of the islands and the captain began to grow dubious of the appearance of things and at ten o'clock cast off at the stern and hove up the anchor to go out but we were prevented by a variable wind in the passage. Trade went on faster than ever when the natives saw that we intended to go out. There were about six hundred canoes alongside at the time. We bought about four hundred skins in this bay. The next morning we got under way bound southward with a great many canoes following us.

For several days we ran down the shore, part of the time bad weather holding us off. Our people who had been sick for the past month were now getting better daily. A few greens that we had picked up on shore had been a great service. Thank God! I was not sick at any time though sometimes eight or nine were sick at a time.

On Monday, May 4th, we hauled in shore in Queen Charlotte's Sound, with a light wind and a great swell but being a considerable distance from the land no canoes came off and we proceeded on our course to double Cape St. James. At this time the people began to grow uneasy on account of the food, as we had nothing but rice and fish to live upon and since the 24th of March all the fish had been purchased by the ship's company with their own clothes except the 3rd of May, when the captain served out two strings of beads to a mess to buy fish. But the beads were of little service to us and of little value to the natives so that it was fair to say that three-quarters of the fish was bought by the ship's company with no other allowance but rice and salt. When there was any beef allowed at 12 o'clock, the boatswain was always damning and swearing for his share of the slush for the rigging and the captain's servant was bottling off the remainder to fry fish to save the captain's butter of which he had four firkins aboard at that time.

At six A.M., on May 5th, we saw a breaker a point off the lee bow and with difficulty got clear of it for there was little wind and a strong current and heavy swell setting us directly upon it, but fortunately a light breeze sprung up and we wore ship and soon left the breaker astern. We then stood into Queen Charlotte's Sound and at four o'clock a canoe came alongside with sixteen natives in her of whom we bought forty skins. Five prime skins could be bought here for a sheet of copper; one skin for about two feet of bar iron or for ten spikes. 180 beads were served out here to each six men. Cape St. James may be well known by the five islands that lay to the southward of it. The next day no natives came off notwithstanding we fired a gun.

No pork was allowed this day and the slush barrel being empty the captain passed word forward for us to buy train oil with which to fry our fish, which was miserable, indeed, there being on board at that time sixteen tierces of beef, four of pork and two of flour and two of split peas; four hogsheads of bread; five bags of sago; fifteen bags of rice and one cask of raisins.

On the morning of May 8th, we discovered an island in this Sound that the charts gave no account of. It bore N. E. from us in Latitude 52° 33' N. Saw a great number of whales—two or three hundred at a time. At 2 P.M. two canoes came off to us and soon there were a hundred canoes alongside. Their chief's name was Clutiver. We bought a hundred skins here. At sunset the canoes went away. We lay offshore all night and the next morning four canoes came off having nothing but fish to sell. Continued steering alongshore to the northward and at 11 o'clock saw a smoke inshore. Four canoes came off with their chief whose name was Comeeshier. Bought seventy skins here bringing the whole number up to 775 now in the hold. The chief and his son remained on board all night. The next morning the tribe came off to the number of two hundred and fifty men, women and children and we bought 210 skins. The natives of this place were a very quiet set of people. At 2 P.M. made sail alongshore, sounding all the way, in from thirty-five to five fathoms of water.

Continued steering to the northward and at 10 A.M. on Monday, May 11th, saw a smoke in shore in Latitude 53° 4' N. and at 3 P.M. came abreast of a bay. Two canoes came off and said that their chief would come off the next morning. The captain bought a few salmon and served out two to each mess. The next morning we beat in shore with all sail set and at 2 P.M. brought up with the small bower in five fathoms of water. Several canoes came alongside and we bought one hundred and fifty skins. Their chief's name was Skoitscut. Got under way at 4 P.M. and stood off shore. From here may be seen at one view the main continent of America; the island on the west, the continent on the east, which forms Queen Charlotte's Sound. At 2 P.M. the water growing shoal we brought up with the small bower and soon several canoes came alongside. Bought one hundred and fifty skins here. At 4 P.M. got under way and stood offshore. One canoe lay astern all night and early the next morning we began trading.

Several more canoes came off and we bought about fifty more skins which were cheaper here than at any other place that we had visited. A prime skin was bought for about ten inches of iron.

For several days we continued beating down the Sound and near Cape St. James. Several canoes came off and we bought a few skins and some dried fish. Our allowance between the sixth and the nineteenth of May was four small salmon, weighing about four pounds each, with rice and salt as usual. We expected to leave the coast about the first of August.

On May 26th we ran in close to the land and sent the boat ashore twice for wood having little left on board. The boat's crew discovered two or three fine harbours that could not be seen at a mile's distance from the land. The coast was so bold that a ship of five hundred tons could come within twice her length of the rocks. They saw many wild berries—raspberries, mulberries and blackberries, and a great number of sea otters. The land had a very remarkable appearance. The mountains were nearly perpendicular and appeared to be an entire rock. We supposed them to be three-quarters of a mile high. That day we were cut short four pints of rice and issued only sixteen pints for twenty men and had had nothing but fish for six days past. The next day began with dirty weather. Several canoes came off from which we bought a few fish. At 7 P.M. bore away from the shore and proceeded on our course to the northward for the latitude 59° under close-reefed topsails.

On June 1st, 1791, in the latitude of 63° 6' we saw a remarkable high land to the northward and westward, which was supposed to be about 160 miles off. Saw several smokes on shore and fired a gun but no natives came off. We supposed that they were not much acquainted with Europeans. The day ended with thick weather. Still running along to the southward. The next day at six A.M. came abreast of a sound that our drafts gave no account of but the weather continuing thick we kept beating off the entrance and the next day continued our course southward. The land appeared to be very high all along the coast. The tops of the mountains appeared high up in the clouds.

We had several days of dirty weather and the supply of wood and water began to be short. On June 6th several canoes came off to us, the first we had seen in that part of the coast. The men wore whiskers and the females ornamented themselves with fish bones and wore one run through the division of their nostrils in their noses. I bought a fresh seal and had it fryed for breakfast. It proved to be a delicate meat and was the first fresh meat we had had for nearly six months. The next day a canoe came off with a chief from whom we bought two beaver skins and some fish.

Nothing remarkable happened for several days but on the 10th four canoes came off with seventy natives. These were the stoutest men that we had seen on any part of the coast. They had no women with them and by their actions they seemed to have in mind an attempt on the vessel. At 11 o'clock they went away singing their war song and throwing their arms about them in a very savage manner. Bought nineteen skins of them which brought the total up to 1,218. They made signs for us to go into their harbour but our captain didn't think proper to go in and so we proceeded alongshore to the eastward. At 4 p.m., Samuel Gray died of the scurvey, aged about 32 years. He was born in the West of England. This was the fourth man that we had lost. Our ship was very crank owing to the greater part of the water being out.

June the 12th, we stood in for land and saw Mount Fairweather. This mountain was the highest land that we had seen on the Northwest Coast of America. The top of it appeared a vast height up in the clouds. Filled seventeen casks with salt water for the hold. Two days later we saw a sail astern. She soon came up with us and fired one of her lee guns and proved to be the brig *Grace,* of New York, Captain Douglass, from Canton, six weeks out. She gave us our first intelligence of the Spanish War and of five sail of English men-of-war going round Cape Horn.

On the 19th of June we finished wooding and watering in a very convenient harbour in Latitude 57° N. Here we tarred the rigging, blacked the masts and yards and painted and caulked the ship round. The natives were the most quiet and civil of any that we had seen. The chief trade was in old clothes of any kind. We lay here until the 23rd and then dropped down the Sound followed by the natives who pitched their huts on shore abreast of the vessel. The next day we got under way and directed our course for Queen Charlotte's Islands, bound for Cloak Bay, and two days later came to in 19 fathoms of water and ran a hawser ashore from each quarter and made fast to the limbs of trees to steady the ship. There were few natives here in comparison with the number here when we left it before. Most of them wore red jackets and we knew by this that Captain Douglass had been here. We did not get a single skin here.

Connehaw, their chief, came on board and informed us that most of his tribe had left their winter quarters and distributed themselves among the islands for the summer. They return to their winter houses about the end of August. The natives at this place use no bread nor do they at any other part of the coast. The most of their living is fish which they cook in baskets by first digging holes in the sand and making the sand hot; then setting the basket in it and feeding it with hot stones until the fish is boiled enough. We went ashore where one of their winter houses stood. The entrance was cut out of a large tree and carved all the way up and down. The door was made like a man's head and the passage into the house was between his teeth and was built before they knew the use of iron. Our people were very uneasy and wished to proceed homewards on account of provisions being very short; bread in particular. Captain Douglass' assistance was inadvisedly refused as we were in need of bread and he of liquor of which we had a great plenty aboard. On the 3rd of July, all hands went on the quarterdeck and told the captain that we could not live on our allowance of bread, it being three days between allowances. The captain said that it wouldn't do to eat up all at once and would not give us any more bread but allowed us caravansers one more meal per week and took away the allowance of flour—a fine exchange indeed, the flour being better than all the caravansers aboard. We told the captain that it wouldn't do for him and his officers, eleven in number with their servants, to have as much provisions as they could eat and keep fifteen hands before the mast upon a very short allowance and he had much to do to get the men to their duty again.

July 4th, the glorious day of America's independence, but our circumstances allowed us nothing to celebrate equal to our wishes. Unexpectedly the captain gave us an allowance of grog, extra, and the mates gave half a gallon of rack which was sufficient to last until night. In the morning we saw a brig bearing W. N. W. Several canoes came alongside and we bought twenty skins which brought up the number to about 1,683 in all. At 10 A.M. made all sail to speak the brig but could not come up with her. Supposed her to be Captain Kendrick from Lark's Bay.

July 6th, we ran in close with the cape and a canoe came off with three natives who told us that their chief with all their tribe had gone to war with Skeitcutes who appeared to be the greatest chief in the Queen Charlotte Islands. Bought some halibut of them and continued on our course up the Sound.

Nothing very remarkable happened for several days after this. We bought more skins bringing the number in the hold up to 1869 and on the 16th had a narrow escape from running on a reef in Norfolk Sound. Two days later we ran into Civility Harbour where we formerly were and moored the ship and began to paint her and tar the rigging. Here we lay for several days, the weather being dirty most of the time. On the 23rd we unmoored and dropped down to the reef and the next morning sailed for Queen Charlotte's Island, which we saw on the 27th and here we left with pleasure the Northwest Coast of America, bound for the Island of O-why-hee where Captain Cook was killed. On the passage we ran into a gale that lasted for thirty-six hours the wind blowing all round the compass. It was called a "tuffune." We were upon a short allowance of three pounds of bread per week and no beef, having nothing but our own salmon that we had bought with our clothes before we left the coast. At the Sandwich Islands we had expectations of getting a good supply of yams. The boatswain piped to dinner and turned the hands out as usual whether we had anything to eat or not. Our vessel also began to leak in her upper works.

On the 22nd of August we began to see a great number of birds and much seaweed and early the next morning sighted land on the bow. It proved to be O-why-hee. At 10 A.M. several canoes came off with potatoes and hogs to trade. They craved nothing but iron in return. We bought their hogs at the rate of two spikes apiece. At 4 P.M. we came abreast of Kelacokoo Bay where Captain Cook was killed. Here we had upwards of three hundred double and single canoes alongside at a time with men, women and children aboard. Their chief's name was Tianner. He would not come on board on account of his taking and killing Captain Metcalf's son in a schooner and only left one man alive in her. This was done while young Metcalf's father lay in another bay only six leagues away. Captain Metcalf commanded the brig *Eleanore*, mounting 16 guns. About the same time that his son was killed he had his boat moored astern with one man in her to keep the natives from stealing her but they swam off in the night and killed the man and took the boat ashore. The next day they brought out some of the man's bones to sell.

They had been scraped. This unfortunate man was a Portuguese. His name was Anthony. Seeing this man's bones put Captain Metcalf into such a rage that he ordered all his guns loaded with grape shot and the hinges of the ports greased and after he got his vessel all clear for action he got one of the chiefs to taboo one side of her so that he might have a good chance to fulfill his desire. Tabooing is an authority that the chiefs use over the lower sort of the people and is death if anyone of his class break it. The taboo on one side of Captain Metcalf's brig brought all the natives over on the opposite side. The captain then ordered all hands to heave beads overboard to draw the natives as near as possible to the vessel and when he had collected upwards of three hundred canoes alongside he called out "Anthony," the name of the man who was killed, as a signal for his men to fire. They did so and killed upwards of three hundred men, women and children. At the time he knew nothing of the death of his son.

All the next day we lay with the main-topsail to the mast and the courses held up, trading with the natives off Kelacokoo Bay. We bought a great number of hogs, potatoes, bread fruit, grass lines and tapper which they make from the bark of trees and use for their clothing. It looks very much like calico but will not stand the water. We had upwards of one hundred girls on board at a time but not a man excepting one at a time. One of their chiefs came alongside with one of young Metcalf's muskets. He was one of the stoutest men that I ever saw. Our captain compared his hind quarters to that of a bullock and would not suffer him to come aboard. Afterwards the captain asked him for his musket and made signs for him to stand on the quarter bridge of our vessel and when he did so the captain gave him his musket and at the same time fired a musket over his head with made him jump overboard and swim ashore. At night every man took his girl and the rest jumped overboard to swim upwards of three miles for the shore.

Early on the morning of the 25th of August, we took our departure from the island of O-why-hee which is a very fine island with level land as far as we could see to the windward and with mountains on the lee shore with snow on them all the year round. At 10 A.M. saw the island of Moue. A great number of natives followed us from the island of O-why-hee. At six o'clock the next morning we saw the island of Worhoo and at 10 A.M. came to in twenty fathoms of water. A great many natives came alongside with plenty of hogs, potatoes, yams, bread fruit, grass lines, spears, mats, mother of pearl beads and a great number of curiosities. All hands were employed the next day in buying hogs and vegetables for a sea stock. During the morning the natives stole the buoy from our anchor and kept stealing and cutting all the hooks and thimbles they could get at.

The next day, Sunday, August 28th, the king, his brother and son, came on board and made the captain a present of three red feather caps and some tapper cloth. Our captain gave them a musket and some powder. This day they sent all the handsomest girls they had on board and gave every one their charge how to behave that night. When they gave a signal every one of them was to cling fast to the Europeans and to divert them while they cut our cable. At night every man in the ship took a girl and sent the remainder ashore. At 12 o'clock at night the watch perceived the ship adrift and at the same time every girl in the ship clung fast to her man in a very loving manner. All hands were called immediately. I had much to do to get clear of my loving mistress. The girls all tried to make their escape but were prevented by driving them all into the cabin. We found the cable cut about two fathoms from the hawse hole and made sail and stood off and on in the bay all night and the next morning ran in and came to with the best bower. Saw a number of canoes trying to weigh our anchor. Three of the girls jumped overboard and two canoes came and picked them up. We fired a musket at one of them and a native turned up his backsides at us. We fired three or four more times so they were glad to leave off and make for the shore.

The following morning a double war canoe came off with the men singing their war song. They paddled round our vessel and when abreast of the lee bow, seeing no anchor, they gave a shout and went on shore again. At eight o'clock forty or fifty canoes came off to trade but seemed shy of us. We bought some hogs and potatoes and sent several messages on shore to the king but could not get our anchor from him. At 12 meridian, the king sent a man off to dive for the anchor pretending they had not stolen it. The boat was manned and two bars put in her as a reward for the native if he found the anchor. He dived several times but did not go to the bottom. He would stay under water longer than any man we ever saw. We could see him lay with his back against the bottom of the canoe for some minutes and then let himself sink down and come up again about three or four yards from the canoe, pretending that he had been to the bottom. Seeing this we were fully convinced that they had our anchor ashore and meant to keep it so we sent another message to the king and told him if he didn't send the anchor aboard that we should be obliged to fire on his town and lay it in ashes.

The next day we could not get a canoe to come alongside and could see natives running in from all parts of the island to assist the king if we attempted to land, which our mate was for doing but our captain didn't approve of it and so at 11 o'clock we got under way and fired four or five broadsides into the village. We could see thousands of the natives running, one on top of the other. On the beach were a number of canoes off the lee bow so we made for them and fired a broadside that stove a great many of them and sent the natives a swimming and diving under water. We ran by two men swimming and shot one of them through the shoulder and killed him. We also ran alongside of a canoe with a man in her. We stood by with ropes to heave to him to get him on board at the same time pointing six muskets at him if he refused to take hold of the rope. He laved hold of it and hauled himself aboard and let his canoe go adrift. We then hove about and came abreast of the village a second time when the natives on the beach fired a musket and kept running along with white flags flying in defiance for us to land. Seeing no possibility of our getting our anchor we bore away and ran out to about two miles from the shore where we gave the native on board six spikes and let him go to swim ashore. The seven girls on board we gave a number of beads and let them go likewise.

From here we set a course for the island of Otehy where we were in expectation of getting a new supply of yams. At 6 A.M. saw the island bearing E. by N. and ran down the lee side. A great number of natives came alongside with articles to barter for iron. Several of their chiefs came aboard when we came abreast the watering place. One brought a letter to the captain the contents of which gave us warning of the bad intentions of the natives. It was written by Captain Ingraham of the brig *Hope* of Boston. He said the natives of that island were treacherous and deceitful and required good looking after. They informed us of an anchor lying in Anahoo Road. Whether it was cut away from some vessel or parted while trying to heave it we were not certain. We took this to be a deceitful story to decoy us into the bay. Their intentions were happily prevented by our taking our farewell of the Sandwich Islands at 3 P.M., September 1st, when we bore away for Canton with one of the natives on board. After all our trouble at these islands our captain bought but only three hundred weight of yams to last us on our passage. Of bread, we had but fifty pounds on board.

For the next three weeks nothing of importance happened. We were attended with clear and pleasant weather. But on the 23rd the weather began to look black and stern. The next morning the topsails were sent down and the top-gallant yards and mast and we scudded under the foresail. The vessel began to make water fast so that it was necessary to keep one pump going all the time. The pump that was made in China, out of two pieces of wood, began to blow and would not work. At 12 o'clock at night we shipped a very heavy sea which broke in the main grating and the water kept pouring down the main hatchways until it was up to the lower deck. In this miserable condition our ship was so waterlogged that she would not steer. In about half an hour she broached to. The foresail being handed would not wear and we were under the disagreeable necessity of cutting away our mainmast. After the mast went she wore round before the wind and all hands were called to clear the wreck for the mast kept beating under the counter so that we had much ado to get clear of it. All hands then turned to the pump and sucked her in about four hours' time, to our great joy, as we were expecting every minute to go to the bottom. At 8 o'clock the next morning, a sea pooped and stove in all the dead-lights which kept the pump going continually. All hands then went to work and took the lower deck-hatches for dead-lights to keep the tops of the seas from beating in at the cabin windows and stove up the chest to nail over the main hatchways.

The next day at 4 P.M. the gale died away to a calm but the weather still looked black all round the compass and we went to work and stove up the long boat that lay in the lee scuppers and hove her overboard and lashed the small boat, bottom upwards, to the ring bolts. It was well that we did so for at 10 P.M. another gale sprang up which blew harder than the first. At one o'clock a sea pooped us which stove in all the hatches that we had for dead-lights and set us a bailing out of the after hatchway which wet one half of our cargo.

At eight o'clock in the evening of the next day, September 27th, we shipped a sea that struck us on the larboard quarter and stove the small boat into a thousand pieces. It also washed overboard three men and we could not give them any assistance. They were John Wall, Antony Frair and Jose Antony. At the same time all the spars broke adrift and broke two men's legs. The next morning the topmast was hanging over the bows and the wind blew to that degree that there was not a man on the ship that heard the topmast when it broke. The fore-yard also got loose and blew twenty or thirty yards from the vessel. All hands were obliged to lash themselves to the pumps and could but just keep her free by pumping and bailing all the time. All hands were beat out for want of victuals having had nothing to eat but half a biscuit and about an ounce of cheese since the 24th of the month. God only knows what kept us alive for the wind would take the tops of the seas and blow them continually over us. If our vessel had not had a high quarter deck we should all have perished from the top of the seas that blew over us so that we could not tell whether it rained or not. At 4 o'clock that afternoon, a sea pooped us that filled our cabin half-full of water, wet all the bread and upset the cogs of the wheel and broke it in two pieces and cut in two pieces the man's lip who was steering. In this pitiful condition our ship would not steer but lay in the trough of the seas. At the same time the pump got choked and all hands became discouraged expecting every minute to be the last. After much ado, however, we got the pump working and she sucked again in about five hours' time. At 10 P.M. the gale died away and one man was set to watch and the rest of the hands went to sleep.

The next day the wind abated and the water began to grow smooth and at 12 meridian, all hands were called to get up a jury mast and set the fore-topmast gallant sail upon the foremast to keep her steady. We cut a mortise in the stump of the mainmast to step the jurymast and at night the mast was all ready to get up in the morning. We also overhauled the hold and found all the water spoiled except two hogsheads and the liquor also spoiled as well as was all the bread on board, so there was nothing left but Sandwich Island pork and sago to last us the passage to China.

It was October 22nd when we made the island of Formosa and ran alongshore, the natives making smokes as a sign for us to come in but none would venture off. Four days later we saw about a hundred Chinese fishing boats but they all seemed very shy of us. After a great deal of trouble we got a pilot out of one of them who agreed to pilot us to Macao for nineteen dollars, and at four o'clock that afternoon we saw the Grand Ladrone Island, and at six came to anchor at Macao Roads and heard the news of the death of our owner, 'Squire Cox. The next morning the boats came alongside with plenty of bread and eggs and fruit but the captain bought for himself and none for the ship's company. This day, the last of the water was used and as the captain would not get any in during the time we lay in the Road the ship's company bought their own water of the Chinese at the rate of two dollars for five gallons.

The Northwest men having been stopped from trading at Canton, at 9 A.M. on the 28th, we got under way and ran down to Lark's Bay, intending to smuggle our skins. After mooring at 4 P.M. the captain called all hands aft and gave them notes to receive their wages at Macao from Mr. McIntire and as we received our notes he sent us into the boat and would not suffer any to come aboard again for fear we should take skins out of the vessel. He also took care to search our chests before they went over the side for he well knew that we all had skins in the vessel and for that reason he took every advantage of us to try to wrong us out of our wages. The fear of losing them made us put up with more than we otherwise would have done. At 6 P.M. we put off for Macao leaving William Emery, my partner aboard, for the boat was overloaded and could not carry him. We landed at Macao at nine o'clock that night and the mandarins or custom house officers overhauled our chests to see if we had any skins with us, for their laws were very strict so that if they found any skins in our possession the Governor could send us as slaves to Goa. If a Chinese was found with any it meant present death for him. We all went to lodgings at a Portuguese house where we paid at the rate of ten dollars per month.

October the 30th, I received my wages from Mr. McIntire, amounting to ninety dollars, and then hired a China boat and went down to Lark's Bay and went on board the *Gustavus* to see if there was any possibility of getting my skins. When I went aboard I told them I had turned a fisherman and hoped to carry passengers with my boat up and down from Lark's Bay to Macao. The captain commended me for it and said that I was an industrious man and would live where one half of the ship's company would die. I then went to my partner to see how we could manage to get our skins out of the vessel, for I was resolved to lose my life or to gain what I had so dearly earned. He told me there was a strict watch kept every night, with pistols and cutlasses, to keep boats from coming alongside and he believed that the captain mistrusted that I was coming aboard that night, knowing that I had skins in the vessel, for he had ordered all the arms to be loaded in case I should come on board. My partner and myself then laid the plan out so that I was to anchor my boat so that I might hear his signals and not be seen. I did so by anchoring my boat under the land. He was to have the twelve o'clock watch that night and they were all Portuguese in his watch. Their custom was to strike the bell before they rang her and he said he would bribe them with a skin and would strike the bell himself. The signal was to strike one bell over the number and I was then to come under the bows and take the skins from him. At twelve the signal was given and I went under the bows and got the skins safe in the boat. Just then one of the Chinese went and told the second mate that I was on board but the mate proved to be my friend and held the Chinese fast until I got clear with my skins—seventeen in number—which I sold the next day for six hundred dollars. So there was an end to my Northwest voyage.

On November 12th, 1791, I shipped on board the Portuguese ship *St. Cruiz*, Capt. Jose Francisco, commander, bound for Lisbon, at six dollars and a half per month wages. With me went Robert Lovis of Marblehead in Massachusetts. The captain gave us a note to the boatswain for he had command of the ship while she lay in the harbour. The captain told us if we wanted liberty to go on shore for a day, the boatswain would grant it, but if for a longer time, to come to him and we should have three or four days liberty if we desired it. The Portuguese were a very kind people to strangers and used both of us very well for they would call their own men out to work at four o'clock in the morning and let us lay in our hammocks until we pleased to turn out ourselves.

In a few days we were obliged, for some time, to keep ourselves armed on account of a Manilla man who had killed three Chinese. It appeared that this man and the Chinese were gambling together when the Manilla man found that the Chinese were cheating him. He immediately drew his knife and killed two of them on the spot and with the bloody knife in his hand he ran through the streets crying for all Christians to keep out of the way, and made his way to the waterside. To get across, he got into a boat but the man refused to put him over the water and he stuck his knife into the poor man's body and killed him. His knife broke of in the man's body which prevented him from killing any more. He then made off and was away three days before they caught him. The Chinese wanted three Christians in place of the three Chinese who were killed.

On December 25th, 1791, I shipped myself on board the *Lady Washington*, Captain Kendrick, commander, bound for the Northwest Coast of America, then laying at Lark's Bay. This brig had been taken by the natives on the Northwest Coast on a previous voyage. They were lying at Coyours on the coast and the captain was in liquor one day and trusted more to the natives than did his own people and would suffer great numbers of them to come on board. His gunner went to the quarter deck and told him the natives would take the vessel and that it was dangerous to let so many come on board. The captain struck the gunner and pushed him off the quarter deck so that he had no time to take the keys out of the arm chest. When the natives saw this they took possession of the arm chest immediately and began to flock on board from the shore in great numbers and made a terrible noise with their war songs. They took the men's hats off their heads and laid their knives across their throats and threatened to kill them if they made the least resistance and then drove them all into the hold. They then went to work and divided the copper that lay upon the deck and kept running out on the bowsprit and yelling to their women on shore to come aboard and assist them for it seems that the women are more courageous than the men. All this time Captain Kendrick was on the quarter deck with a piece of bar iron in his hand treating with them. Twelve of the savages stood with knives pointing at the captain's body to prevent him from going below. All this time he was conversing with his men below, telling them to muster up all the arms that they could find, which was only two pistols, one musket and two cutlasses, and be in readiness to make a sally up on deck when he should give the watch word, which was—*Follow me*. Coyour, the chief, knowing that he had sufficient command of the deck, made a spring below to see what force was below and Captain Kendrick at once jumped down the hatch upon the chief's back and at the same time called out *Follow me*. At that, all the men made a sally and the chief seeing this, was for making off with all his tribe. In less than five minutes the ship's company had possession of the deck and had broken open the arm chest and killed forty of the natives on the spot without losing a man.

On January 16th, 1792, I shipped myself as gunner on board the snow *Eleanore*, Capt. Simon Metcalf, commander, bound for the Isle of France. We sailed the next day and on February 26th ran into Bantam Roads, at the island of Java, and came to in twelve fathoms of water. We were about three miles distant from the fort and soon sent a boat ashore to buy a few hogs and vegetables for our sea stock. At the landing we were met by a Dutchman who conducted us to the gates of the castle and in about a half an hour a sergeant came out with a halbert and walked before us up to the Governor's house. He received our officers kindly and gave us liberty to buy anything we pleased. Here I fell in with an Irishman, one Robertson, that I formerly knew at Amsterdam, and he showed me all about the place except where the monument was erected over the people killed at the massacre of Bantam.

We arrived at Port Louis, on the Isle of France, on March 12th and discharged our cargo of 2,500 chests of tea and then began to repair our vessel; got in new beams, fore and abaft and bought copper and iron and other trade for a Northwest voyage. On May 9th, our captain bought a small French brig, about 90 tons burthen, for $4,000. She was full of water at the time which was the reason they sold her so cheap. She had struck coming in and they thought she was bilged. We hove her down and found her to be a good vessel. We mounted ten guns on her and got her in readiness to go with us on our Northwest voyage. I was sent on board as gunner and had my wages raised. Young Robert Metcalf, the captain's son, was appointed captain of the brig which was named the *I no*. Here I found Captain Low, an old shipmate of mine, lying sick in the hospital. He had been there and at Bourbon for three years and had sent his vessel home. The American captains made a contribution and collected upwards of four hundred dollars to pay his passage in the ship *Sally*, Captain Kenneday. The ship sailed and left him behind. When Captain Low heard of it he took opium and put an end to his life.

By the middle of July we had taken in our copper and iron for the trading voyage and also a great quantity of cordage and canvas for China, on our return there from the Northwest coast; but buying all this trade and also the brig *I no*, and repairing the *Eleanore*, brought down our captain's purse so low that he was obliged to sell off all the trade that he had on board for the Coast and alter his voyage from the Northwest coast to that of an oil, and sealskin voyage to the island of Desolation or Munsair, Kerguelen, in the southern Indian Ocean. He had just enough money left to pay his men their advance and get his vessels out of port.

I received my wages on the *Eleanore*, to the amount of sixty dollars in paper, on September 9th, and ten days later we cast off our head fast and hung to stern moorings and at 12, meridian, the pilot came aboard and at 4 P.M. we dropped down to the buoys and came to anchor. At 12 o'clock at night we got under way with the *Eleanore* in company, bound for the island of Madagascar, to wood our vessels and buy rice and other things for a sea stock to last us the passage to Kurguelen. The first day we were out the *Eleanore* began to make water on account of her striking on an old rock when coming out of the Isle of France.

On September 23rd, at 12, meridian, we came to anchor at Port Dauphin, Madagascar, in 12 fathoms of water with a rocky bottom, it being a very bad roadstead. Later we weighed anchor and beat up under the fort which was called the one-gun battery. The natives came down with white flags flying to direct us to the best anchorage and would have had us haul our stern close in to the landing place and make fast to a gun that the French had laid down for that use, but our captain paid but little attention to their signs and came to anchor in twenty-five fathoms, about half a musket-shot from the battery. Sent a boat ashore and found one white man here, a German, a renegade from the Isle of France, who had but little command over the natives. They met us at the landing armed with muskets, spears and knives and conducted us to the fort where the white man was who informed us that the king lived at a town four miles in the country and would be down the next day. He told us that we must make the king a present or we should not be able to get any rice. The next day the king came down with a large train of armed men and we sent him two muskets, a barrel of powder and a kittysol as a present and desired him to come on board; but he thought the present was not sufficient and would not come that night.

Early on the morning of the 25th, the king made his appearance again on the bank and the boat was sent ashore for him to come on board but he would not except that we left an officer on shore in his room. Mr. Cartright, the second mate of the *Eleanore,* agreed to stay on shore and accordingly the king came off with his queen. She had lived at the Isle of France for two years and understood the French tongue very well and served as an interpreter for the king. With them was an Arabian, a stout, savage-looking fellow who wanted as many presents from us as though we had come to slave instead of to wood and water. The king asked for a great number of things that took his fancy, particularly our muskets that he saw laying in the cabin. When he found that our captain would not give him any more presents he began to grit his teeth in a very savage manner, being about half drunk at the time, and soon went ashore grumbling, and knocked down two of our wood cutters. Seeing this our people all took to the boat and came aboard bringing Mr. Cartright with them. At the time, the *Eleanore* had five girls and three men aboard and wouldn't let them go on shore.

In the afternoon they began to fetch down the wood that we had cut and piled it up on the beach and made signals to us to come and fetch it. Accordingly we sent a boat ashore for it but by the time we got our boat half laden the king made a signal with his spear, from a hill near by, for his people to close upon our boat's crew and they flew upon our men and took two of them on their shoulders, viz., John Bradley and Francis de Mace, a Frenchman, and ran away like a parcel of deer. The rest of our men took to the boat and defended themselves with billets of wood for the natives ran into the surf and tried to drag the boat on shore. It was upwards of half an hour before they could get clear of them and the boat was no sooner out of the surf than they began to fire with muskets. One musket ball went through the stern of the boat and wounded the boatswain in the arm. By this time both vessels began to fire at them. Our vessel had a brass four pounder which I loaded with nearly half a nine pound cartridge, but the captain insisted upon having more powder put in and so I loaded her almost up to the muzzle and after elevating the gun for the shore, I took a long stick of fire, for with the common britchens the gun would fly round against the capstan, and for the same reason I went behind the capstan to fire her, to prevent her breaking my legs. But our cook, being about half drunk, ran with a brand of fire and fired her before I could do it myself and the gun burst and wounded the captain on his lip and the cook in his arm and knocked all the victuals out of the caboose. At the same time two men were killed on shore which soon put an end to their firing for before that they were firing from behind every bush on shore.

The next morning, at daylight, we saw the natives busily employed in digging a hole in the wall of the fort and at 8 A.M. they pointed a gun at us, but at 12, meridian, they sent a flag of truce down to the shore for our boat to come on shore and make an exchange of prisoners. We did so and got our two men on board but kept two of the natives still on board. The next day it blew a very heavy gale, right upon shore, so that we expected every minute to break adrift and drive ashore to be left to the mercy of the savages; but fortunately at four o'clock the wind died away and we got up the yards and topmasts.

The morning after began with clear and pleasant weather with light airs off land. At 6 A.M. both vessels got under way and ran out of the harbour and hove to while our boats went in and tried to find the anchor of the *Eleanore* which she lost while trying to weigh. They went in close under the fort and kept sweeping for the anchor and all the time the natives kept pointing their gun at us and threatening to fire if we did not send their two men ashore. Our captain told them if they fired at us he would hang them both at the yard arm and that prevented them from doing any mischief. At 4 P.M. we gave up looking for the anchor and ran alongshore to find another harbour, called Port Louis.

On the morning of September 28th, we came to anchor at Port Louis and their king came off and gave us liberty to wood and water. The captain gave him a small swivel and some liquor and he promised to supply us with rice. He seemed to be fully acquainted with what had happened at Fort Dauphin. We also bought a bullock. They behaved very civil to us but told a great many deceitful stories about the rice for in a day or two we found that they hadn't got any for themselves to eat, much less to trade to us.

October 1st, 1792, began with clear weather and all hands employed in getting everything clear for sea and at 10 A.M., seeing no prospect of getting any rice, we weighed anchor and got under sail eastbound for the islands of Kerguelen. Until the 25th, nothing remarkable happened save that the *Eleanore* continued making water so as to keep one pump going continually. That day she hoisted a signal for our boat to come on board and when coming away, Captain Metcalf gave to his son a small copper speaking trumpet to take on board with him, but Mr. Porter, the chief mate on the *Eleanore,* claimed the trumpet and said that it was his and refused to give it up. The captain then asked the armourer and found that his two mates had cut the top of the copper stove without orders, which put him into such a rage that he broke his two mates and made Mr. Williamson, the mate of the *I no,* the mate of the *Eleanore,* in place of Mr. Porter, and made me mate of the *I no,* in the place of Mr. Williamson.

November 29th began with clear and pleasant weather it being the first fair day that we had had for the past ten days. Early in the morning we saw a great number of penguins, divers, and rock weeds and other signs of land. At 5 P.M. saw Mr. Blith's Cape, distant about four leagues, and several other barren rocks covered all over with birds, after a tedious passage of fifty days attended with dirty, rainy and blowing weather with our decks covered with water most of the passage. At 7 P.M. we ran by Cape Francisco, which is a high, barren rock standing nearly perpendicular with penguins covering it nearly one third of the way up. It makes one side of Christmas Harbour. When we doubled the cape we saw the *Eleanore* laying at anchor in Christmas Harbour and ran in and came to in twenty-five fathoms of water about half a mile from the arch that Captain Cook gives an account of in his voyage to this place. We sent the boat on shore at the arch and found it covered over with penguins. The boat's crew brought off a great number of their eggs.

The next morning it blew very fresh out of the harbour and both vessels broke adrift and drifted out a considerable ways and hove to in our cables and found that each vessel had lost one fluke from its anchor. Later in the morning we beat up into the harbour and sent a boat ashore and went by the directions that Captain Cook gave and found the bottle laying in a pile of stones with a lead cap over it. Broke it open and found the English two-penny piece and *Mons'r Kurguelen's* and Captain Cook's letters and also a letter of Captain Durgin of the brig *Phœnix*, from Macao. Saw a great number of sea elephants, sea lions, bears and seals but very few of the seals were furred ones.

Seeing no prospect of getting any skins for China on account of their being the wrong sort for that market, the next morning we weighed anchor bound southward in quest of a good harbour in which to load our vessels with oil for the Isle of France and to overhaul and repair our rigging and also to heave the *Eleanore* down to stop her leaks. Saw a great amount of kelp and rockweed with sunken rocks, their tops about two feet below the surface and very dangerous to shipping, for alongside these rocks will be found twenty-seven fathoms of water. At 4 P.M. came to anchor in a very fine bay and sent a boat ashore and found plenty of sea elephants, lions and seals. Moored both of vessels' sterns inshore and made fast to the rocks.

All hands went ashore the next morning to erect a couple of tents in which to boil our oil and at 6 P.M. all was completed and we killed eighteen or twenty lions and elephants and took the blubber from them and got our pots at work the evening. All hands were then put upon an allowance of flour—four pints for four men and no bread—so that our chief living was penguins and their eggs and a sort of wild cabbage that we picked up on the shore. It had a kind of peppery taste and was the only vegetable that grew on that barren land. During the next two weeks we were employed in making oil and fetching blubber from other parts of the island. On the 16th, we hove the *Eleanore* down to try to stop her leaks.

On January 1st, 1793, Captain Metcalf made or marked out the thirteen stripes and "U. S. A." on a sheet of copper and stuck it in a rock with an iron standard with braces of the same to prevent the wind from blowing it down and left a bottle with a letter in it and named the place *Port I no.*

Twelve days later we finished getting on board the oil—six hundred barrels in all—and at 10 A.M. got under way bound for the Isle of France. Hove to off Christmas Harbour to send on shore the bottle with Captain Cook's letter, but the wind blew so fresh that it was impossible for a boat to land and we proceeded on our course. Made the islands of St. Paul and Amsterdam and ran close in towards Amsterdam which we could see was on fire in several places.

I sailed from the Isle of France on March 17th, 1793, in the ship *Pen,* a South Seaman belonging to Dunkirk, Capt. Obed Fitch, commander. This ship belonged to Mr. Rotch, an American merchant living at Dunkirk. At 6 P.M. ran by the island of Bourbon, bound into Mosambique Channel to cruise for spermaceti whales and thence to Delegoa Bay to load our ship with right whale oil for Dunkirk.

Saw large schools of spermaceti whales on April 5th and the first and second mates' boats put off and gave chase to them while the captain, with his boat's crew, stayed on board to follow the boats with the ship until they got fast to some of the whales. They rowed for upwards of an hour when all the whales went down and they lay on their oars and kept a good outlook for their rising again. In about half an hour's time, a whale came up and the chief mate got fast to her which soon raised the rest of the school round her, for if you strike a whale, and the rest of the school are at the bottom, they will rise immediately and lay like so many logs of wood on the water for some time. Then they will draw up in straight lines and run to windward, side by side, as if they were so many soldiers. When the captain saw that the chief mate had got fast, he put off with his boat. We met a whale coming with head towards the head of our boat so that we struck her head which hove the line out of the chocks of the boat and nearly swept every man out of her. The whale sounded and took the line abaft to the loggerhead of the boat and brought her stern down to the water.

Four days later we saw a school of whales and killed six of them and got four on board. They made sixty-two barrels of oil. On the 14th, while still cruising in the Mosambique Channel, early in the morning we saw a large school of spermaceties and loaded away all three boats. Our boat killed three, the chief mate two, and the second mate two. Got them all cabled safe alongside when the wind sprung up and blew very fresh and two of the ropes, that we had fast, broke and we lost two whales but saved the other five which made us forty-two barrels of oil.

On May 8th we killed two more whales and saw twelve or thirteen waterspouts which were broken up by a heavy clap of thunder. The next day, sent the mate's boat after a humpback, but it came back without her. On the 12th, saw a large school of spermaceties, killed seven and saved four. Began to cut in at 6 P.M. and finished cutting and got the try works under way at 6 o'clock the next morning. The body made us eighty barrels of oil and the head matter, ten barrels. We then had 255 barrels in the hold. During the rest of the month we killed five whales. On the 31st spoke the ship *Leveret,* Obed Bunker, commander, from Dunkirk bound into Delegoa Bay after a load of right whale oil. We agreed to mate our ships and to go as partners and at 6 P.M. we shaped our course for Delegoa Bay.

At 4 P.M. the next day we made Cape St. Mary's, which makes on side of Delegoa Bay, and ran into five fathoms of water and lay to that night with our heads off shore, about two leagues from the land. Two days later we sighted three ships laying in a small bay. One of them was trying out. On June 4th saw a right whale but could not make fast. Lost the fishhook overboard at 10 A.M. At meridian, Capts. Hess and Gardiner came on board and informed that the Portuguese governor had ordered the ship *Dolphin* out of the bay and not to kill any more whales. He said that he would send for a frigate to drive all the ships out of the bay. At 2 P P.M. came to anchor in nine fathoms of water off Red Head. Found here three whaling ships, viz. the *Dolphin*, Capt. Aaron Gardiner, the *Niger*, Capt. Hess, belonging to Laurient, and the *Edward*, Capt. Cager Gardiner, from Dunkirk. Hove up the small bower and found it stranded about two fathoms from the clinch. Cut it off and shifted it end for end.

June 5th began clear and pleasant. At 4 P.M. called all hands out to get their breakfast before daylight to be in readiness to go in the boat, which is the rule of whalers. At 6 A.M. saw a whale and all the boats put off in chase. The second mate got fast to her and Mr. Hammond, Captain Bunker's chief mate, got fast to the calf. There were six boats on her. Hove three irons into her which made her spout blood. Gave her three lances and killed her. The killing place of a right whale is between the eye and the fin. At 12, meridian, the ship *Planter*, Capt. George Hale, arrived from London, and the ship *America*, Capt. *Thuten* Gardiner, commander, from Dunkirk, both whaling ships. The whale that we killed, Captain Bunker took; the next is for our ship. At 3 A.M. the next morning our ship broke adrift. We let go the small bower and brought her up again. At 9 A.M., hove short and our captain, being unacquainted in taking up anchors, would heave in both cables at once which brought the sheet cable across the small bower and put us to a great deal of trouble. We hove up the small bower, hooked the cat and brought the anchor to the opposite cat head, unbent the cable and cleared it of the other cable and then bent it again. At 4 P.M. we saw a cow whale with her calf and two boats went after her. She got galled and ran out of the bay, which put them to a great deal of trouble. At 6 P.M. they came aboard.

Mr. Whippey killed a porpoise on July 9th and that morning we saw the tarpaulin hoisted on board Captain Bunker's ship, for all captains to come on board and dine on roast pork. This afternoon our chief mate took a hand to moor the ship but made as bad a hand of it as the captain did. The next morning all the captains went on shore to the Portuguese fort to see if they could make any trade with the governor and also to buy some refreshment for their men. At the landing we were met by a great number of the natives, more civil than we expected. The governor gave us liberty to buy anything from the natives except ivory and we bought one bullock, a calf, a goat and some fowls, sweet potatoes and plantains. The governor set the natives to kill the bullock for us and they drove spears into him. When the beast found himself wounded he began to run at a great rate, with thirty or forty natives after him, until they had twenty-two or three spears in him which at last brought the beast to his knees. They then came up and soon killed him. The man that skinned him was to have his guts which made a great disturbance amongst them. In fighting for the guts one man cut another man's hand almost off. The natives took the guts as they came out of the bullock and ate them without cleaning and the dung would cling to each side of their mouths while they were eating. What spare guts were left they hung down their breasts to eat some other time. We were told the natives were descendants from the Hottentots who inhabit about the Cape of Good Hope. At 12 o'clock at night we got all safe on board.

The next day was Tuesday and at 6 A.M. all the mates from the ships went down to Cow Bay to look out for whales and all the captains went on board of Captain Bunker to divide the stock that had been bought at the fort. The mates came back at 4 P.M., not having sighted any whales. As they came down the river they cut some mangroves for iron poles. Saw a troup of sea horses and a man on shore fishing who made off as fast as possible as soon as he saw the boats. This day our people invited Captain Bunker's people on board to partake of a sea pie. We entertained them with a fiddle and had plenty of grog. At 7 P.M. they went on board. The most of them, and also our own people, were drunk as a result of the frolic.

June 12th, the mates put off in search of whales and late in the morning we saw a whale coming with eight or nine boats following close after her. She was coming with her head towards the head of our boat. When she was within twice the length of our boat we laid upon our oars by which means we lost our chance of her and the boats of the ship *America* killed her. This day the *Planter* killed one and the *Edward* one. The next morning three vessels arrived from Dunkirk, viz., the ship *Benjamin*, Capt. Isaac Hussey, the ship *Corjue*, Captain Swain, and the brig ————, Capt. James Whippey.

The next Saturday Mr. Whippey got fast to a whale which ran him a great way off and the sun going down and we being about seven leagues from our ship, with the wind and tide against us, we made a signal with a jacket upon an oar for Mr. Whippey to cut from the whale and to go aboard. We got on board at 12 o'clock at night after rowing nineteen hours against wind and tide the most of the time that day.

Tuesday, June 18th, 1793, at 6 A.M. our boat and one other went out to look for whales and found one drifted on the shore. It burst and made a report as loud as a three pounder. We cut the irons out. The *America* killed one today and the *Planter* one. The next day our captain went up the river to go on board of Captain Whippey's brig, to bury Christian Johnson in the earth for the scurvey in his legs. Also went to make trade with John Eney, one of the head chiefs belonging to King Copall country but could not make any trade for bullocks. The next day we went on shore to the King Copall country and at the landing saw John Eney standing at high water mark, dressed in an old surtout coat and a small cocked hat. He made it his business to place all the natives on the grass as they came down to trade with us. When the captains advanced up the beach he came down to meet them and saluted them with a low bow.

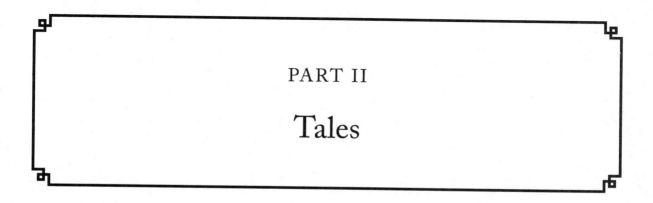

PART II

Tales

The Saloon Passenger

E. W. HORNUNG

As the cable was hauled in, and the usual cheering passed between tug and ship, Skrimshire unclenched his teeth and gave tongue with a gusto as cynical as it was sincere. It had just come home to him that this was the last link with land, and he beheld it broken with ineffable relief. Tuskar Rock was already a little thing astern; the Australian coast lay the width of the world away; the captain did not expect even to sight any other, and had assured Skrimshire that the average passage was not less than ninety days. So, whatever was to happen in the end, he had three months more of life, and of such liberty as a sailing-ship affords.

He descended to his cabin, locked himself in, and lay down to read what the newspapers had to say about the murder. It seemed strange to Skrimshire that this was the first opportunity he had had of reading up his own crime; but the peculiar circumstances of his departure had forbidden him many a last pleasure ashore, and he was only too glad to have the papers to read now and a stateroom to himself in which to read them. There was a heavy sea running, and Skrimshire was no sailor. But he would not have been without the motion, or even its effects upon himself. Both were an incessant reminder that his cabin was not a prison cell, and could not turn into one for three months at all events. Besides, he was not the man to surrender to a malady which is largely nervous. So he lay occupied in his berth; medium-sized, dark-skinned, neither young nor middle-aged; only respectably dressed, and with salient jaw unshaven since the thing of which he read without a flicker of the heavy eyelids or a tremor of the hairy hands.

He had five papers of that morning's date; the crime was worthily reported in them all; one or two had leaders on its peculiar atrocity. Skrimshire sighed when he came to the end; it was hard that he could see no more papers for three months. The egotism of the criminal was excited within him. It was lucky he was no longer on land; he would have run any risk for the evening papers. His very anonymity as author of the tragedy—the thing to which he owed his temporary security—was a certain irritation to him. He was not ashamed of what he had done. It read wonderfully, and was already admitted to have shown that diabolical cleverness and audacity for which Skrimshire alone deserved the credit; yet it looked as though he would never get it. Thus far, at least, it was plain that there was not a shred of evidence against him, or against any person upon earth. He sighed again; smiled at himself for sighing; and, closing his eyes for the first time since the murder, slept like a baby for several hours.

Skrimshire was the only passenger in the saloon, of which he presently became the life and soul. At the first meal he yielded to the temptation of a casual allusion to the murder on the Caledonian Railway; but though they had heard of it, neither captain nor officers showed much interest in the subject, which Skrimshire dropped with a show of equal indifference. And this was his last weakness of the kind. He threw his newspapers overboard, and conquered the morbid vanity they had inspired by a superb effort of the will. Remorse he had none, and for three months certain he was absolutely safe. So he determined to enjoy himself meanwhile, and, in doing so, being a dominant personality, he managed to diffuse considerable enjoyment throughout the ship.

This man was not a gentleman in either the widest or the narrowest sense of that invidious term. He wore cheap jewellery, cheap tweeds as yellow as his boots, paper collars, and shirts of a brilliant blue. He spoke with a Cockney intonation which, in a Scottish vessel, grated more or less upon every ear. But he had funds of information and of anecdote as inexhaustible as his energy and as entertaining as his rough good-humour. He took a lively interest in every incident of the voyage, and was as ready to go aloft in a gale of wind as to make up a rubber in any part of the ship. Within a month he was equally popular in the forecastle, the steerage, and the captain's cabin. Then one morning Skrimshire awoke with a sense that something unusual was happening, followed by an instantaneous premonition of impending peril to himself.

There were too many boots and voices over his head; the ship was bowling sedately before the north-east trades, and otherwise as still as a ship could be. Skrimshire sat up and looked through his port-hole. A liner was passing them, also outward-bound, and some three or four miles to port. There was nothing alarming in that. Yet Skrimshire went straight on deck in his pyjamas; and, on the top rung of the poop-ladder, paused an instant, his now bearded jaw more salient than it had been for weeks.

Four little flags fluttered one above the other from the peak halliards, and at the weather-rail stood the captain, a powerful figure of a man, with his long legs planted well apart, and a marine binocular glued to his eyes. Near him was the second mate, a simple young fellow, who greeted Skrimshire with a nod.

"What's up, M'Kendrick? What is she?"

"A Castle liner; one o' Donal' Currie's Cape boats."

"Why did you signal her?" whispered Skrimshire.

" 'Twas she signalled us."

"Do you know what it's all about?"

"No, but the captain does."

The captain turned round as they were speaking, and Skrimshire read his secret at a glance. It was his own, discovered since his flight and flashed across the sea by the liner's pennons. Meanwhile the captain was looking him up and down, his hitherto friendly face convulsed with hatred and horror; and Skrimshire realised the instant necessity of appearing absolutely unsuspicious of suspicion.

" 'Mornin', captain," said he, with all the cheerful familiarity which already existed between them; "and what's all this bloomin' signallin' about?"

"Want to know?" thundered the captain, now looking him through and through.

"You bet I do."

And Skrimshire held his breath upon an insinuating grin, parrying plain abhorrence with seeming unconcern, until the other merely stared.

"Then you can mind your own business," roared the captain at last, "and get off my poop—and speak to my officer of the watch again at your peril!"

"Well—I'm—hanged!" drawled Skrimshire, and turned on his heel with the raised eyebrows of bewildered innocence; but the drops stood thick upon his forehead when he saw himself next minute in his stateroom mirror.

So he was found out; and the captain had been informed he had a murderer aboard; and detectives would meet the ship in Hobson's Bay, and the murderer would be escorted back through the Suez Canal and duly hanged, after nothing better than a run round the world for his money! The thing had happened before: it had been the fate of the first train murderer; but he had taken the wrong hat in his panic. What on earth had Skrimshire left behind him that was going to hang him after all?

He could not think, nor was that the thing to think about. The immediate necessity he had seen at once, with extraordinary quickness of perception, and he had already acted upon it with a nerve more extraordinary still. He must preserve such a front as should betray not the shadow of a dream that he could by any possibility be suspected by any soul on board; absolute ease must be his watchword, absolute security his pose; then they might like to save themselves the inconvenience of keeping him in irons, knowing that detectives would be waiting to do all the dirty work at the other end. And in two months' thinking a man should hit upon something, or he deserved to swing.

The opening day was not the worst. The captain's rudeness was enough to account for a change in any man's manner; and Skrimshire did both well and naturally to sulk for the remainder of that day. His unusual silence gave him unusual opportunities for secret observation, and he was thankful indeed that for the time being there was no necessity to live up to his popular reputation. The scene of the morning was all over the ship; yet, so far as the saloon passenger could see, the captain had not told anybody as yet. The chief mate invited him into his cabin for a smoke, spread the usual newspaper for a spittoon, and spun the inevitable yarns; but then the chief was a hard-bitten old dog with nerves of iron and a face of brass; he might know everything, or nothing at all; it was for Skrimshire to adapt his manner to the first hypothesis, and to impress the mate with the exuberance of his spirits and the utter lightness of his heart. Later in the morning he had some conversation with the second officer. It was but a word, and yet it confirmed the culprit in his conviction about the signals.

"What have I done," he asked M'Kendrick, "to make the old man jump down my throat like that?"

"It wasna you," replied the second; "it was the signals. But ye might have known not to bother him wi' questions just then."

"But what the deuce were the signals about?"

"That's more than I ken, Bennett."

This was Skrimshire's *alias* on board.

"Can't you find out?"

"Mebbee I might—after a bit."

"Why not now?"

"The old man's got the book in his cabin—the deectionary-book about the signalling, ye ken. It's my place to keep yon, but the old man's carried it off, and there's no' another in the ship."

"Aha!"

"Oh, ay, it was somethin' for hissel', nae doot; but none of us kens what; an' noo we never wull, for he's as close as tar, is the old man."

The "old man" was in point of fact no older than Skrimshire, but he had worked his way aft from ship's boy, and a cruel boyhood followed by an early command had aged and hardened him. A fine seaman, and a firm, though fiery, commander, Captain Neilson had also as kind a heart as one could wish to win, and a mind as simple as it was fair. It was on these qualities that Skrimshire determined to play, as he sulked in his deckchair on the poop of the four-masted barque *Lochwinnoch*, while the captain thumped up and down in his rubber soles, his face black with thought, and a baleful eye upon the picture of offended oblivion behind the novel in the chair.

It was an interesting contest that was beginning between this pair, both of whom were strong, determined, wilful men; but one was as cunning as the other was kind, and he not only read his better like a book, but supplied in his turn a very legible and entirely plausible reading of himself. He never dreamt of impressing the captain as an innocent man; that would entail an alteration of pose inconsistent with the attitude of one who entertained no tittle of suspicion that the morning's signalling had been about himself. On the contrary, what he had really been, and what he must now doubly appear, was the guilty man who had very little fear of ever being detected, and not the fleeting shadow of a notion that such detection had already taken place.

This was the obvious and the only rôle; he had played it instinctively thus far, and need only go on as he had begun. The reward was at best precarious. It depended entirely upon the character and temperament of Captain Neilson. Skrimshire credited him with sufficient strength and sufficient humanity to do nothing and to tell nobody until the Australian detectives came aboard. But that remained to be proved. Neilson might leave him a free man all the voyage, and yet put him in irons before the very end; it would be kinder to do so at once. However, he should not do so at all if Skrimshire could help it; and he was not long in letting fall an oblique and delicate, though an excessively audacious hint upon the responsibility of such a course in his own particular case.

It was at the midday meal, while the smoke of the accursed liner was still a dirty cloud on the horizon. Neilson remained morose and silent, while the offended passenger would not give him word or look, but, on the other hand, talked more than ever, and with invidious gaiety, to the first and second officers. The captain glowered at his plate, searching his transparent soul for the ideal course and catching very little of the conversation; how the topic of suicide arose he never knew.

"An' I call it th' act of a coward," young M'Kendrick was declaring; "you can say what you like, but a man's no' a man that does the like o' that."

"Well, you think about it next time you're havin' a shave, old man," retorted Skrimshire pleasantly. "Think o' buryin' a razor in your neck, and the pain, and the blood comin' over your fingers like as though you'd turned on the hot tap; and if you think long enough you'll know whether it's the act of a coward or whether it ain't."

"I'd blow my blessed head in," said the chief officer. "It'd be quicker."

"Oh, if it comes to that," said Skrimshire, "I'd take prussic acid for choice. It would take a lot to make me, I admit; but I'd do it like a shot to escape a worse death. I've often thought, for instance, what a rum thing it is, in these days, that a man of any sense or education whatever should let himself live to be hung!"

The captain looked up at this; so far he had merely listened. But Skrimshire was addressing himself to the chief mate at the other end of the table; neither look nor tone was intended to include Captain Neilson, the one being averted, and the other lowered, to a nice degree of insolent disregard. On the other hand, the manner of this theoretical suicide was all audacity and nonchalance, combined with a certain underlying sincerity which gave it a peculiar value in the mind of one listener. In a word, it was the manner of a man so convinced of his own security as to afford the luxury of telling the truth about himself in jest.

"They don't give you a chance," said the mate. "They watch you night and day. You'd be a good man, once you'd got to dance the hornpipe on nothing, if you went out any other way."

"Nevertheless, I'd do it," said Skrimshire, with cheery confidence. "I'd back myself to do it, and before their eyes."

"Poison?"

"Yes."

"In a ring, eh?"

"A ring! Do you suppose they'd leave you your rings? No; it might be in a hollow tooth, and it might not. All I say is that I'd back myself to cheat the hangman." Skrimshire said it through his black moustache. "And I'd do it, too," he added after a pause.

Then at last the captain put in his word. "You would do well," said he quietly. "I once saw a man swing, and I never want to see another. Ugh!"

His eyes met Skrimshire's, which fell deliberately; and the talkative tongue wagged no more that meal.

Thereafter Neilson was civility itself, only observant civility. He had made up his mind in the knotty matter of the suspected murderer, and the latter read his determination as he had read the difficulty which it solved, if only for the present.

"So he means to let me go loose, only keeping an eye on me; so far, so good. But how long—how long? If I thought he was going to put me in irons as soon as he sights the land———"

He looked over the side, and a slight shudder shook even his frame. It was very blue water now, the depth unfathomable. A shark had been seen that morning. And, shark or no sharks, Skrimshire could not swim. But he had two months of steady thought before him.

Meanwhile the captain showed some cunning in his turn. He evidently wished to convince himself that Skrimshire had not suspected the signalling. One day, at anyrate, the passenger was invited into the captain's cabin, in quite the old friendly fashion, for a pipe and a chat; in the middle of which Neilson left him for five minutes to speak to the officer of the watch. As the north-east trades blew as strong and true as ever, as the yards had not been touched for days, and as no sail was in sight, Skrimshire scented a trap, and presently beheld one set under his nose in the shape of the signalling book. Skrimshire smiled. The captain found him buried in a magazine, and his little trap untouched. And the obvious deduction was also final to the sailor's mind.

Six weeks produced no change in the outward situation, but brought the voyage so near its end that every soul but one waxed merry with the thought of shore—and that one seemed the merriest of them all. They had come from the longitude of the Cape to that of Kangaroo Island in twenty days, and in all probability would enter Port Philip Heads in two days more. In one week the *Lochwinnoch* had logged close upon two thousand miles; boy and man, her commander had never made such an "easting" in his sea-going life. His pleasure and his pride were alike enormous, and Skrimshire conceived that his general goodwill towards men could scarcely have suffered by the experience. He determined, at all events, to feel his way to such compassion as an honest man could be expected to extend towards an unhung murderer; and he felt it with that mixture of cautious craft and sheer impudence which made him the formidable criminal he was.

It was the night that might prove the last of the voyage, and the last night of freedom for the unhappy Skrimshire. Unhappy he undoubtedly was, for the strain of continuing as he had begun, "the life and soul of the ship," had told upon even his nerves in the end, though to the end it had been splendidly borne. Tonight, however, as he paced the poop by the captain's side, he exhibited for the first time a despondency which exactly fitted in with Neilson's conception of his case.

"I shall never forget this voyage," said Skrimshire, sighing. "You may not believe me, captain, but I'm sorry it's over. I am, indeed; no doubt I'm the only man in the ship who is."

"And why are you?" asked Neilson, eyeing his passenger for once with the curiosity which had so long consumed him, as also with the sympathy which had grown upon him, despite, or en account of, those sinister signals from the Castle liner.

Skrimshire shrugged.

"Oh, that's a long story. I've had a rum life of it, and not what you would call the life of a saint. This voyage will stand out as one of its happiest chapters, that's all; and it may be one of the last."

"Why do you say that?"

"Oh, one can never tell."

"But what did you think of doing out there?"

"God knows!"

Neilson was miserable. There was a ring in the hoarse voice that went straight to his heart. He longed to tell this man what was in store for him—what he himself knew—but he conquered the longing as he had conquered it before. Time enough when the detectives came on board; dirty work and all responsibility would very well keep for them.

So the good captain thought to himself, as the pair took turns in silence; so the dominant brain at his side willed and intended that he should think.

"Whatever you hear of me," resumed Skrimshire at last, "and however great a beast I may some day turn out, remember that I wasn't one aboard your ship. Will you, captain? Remember the best of me and I'll be grateful, whatever I am, and whatever happens."

"I will," said Neilson, hoarse in his turn; and he grasped the guilty hand. Skrimshire had some ado to keep from smiling, but there was another point upon which he required an assurance, and he sought it after a decent pause.

"So you expect to pass the *Otway* some time to-morrow?"

"By dinner-time, if we're lucky."

"And there you signal?"

"Yes, they should hear of us in Melbourne early to-morrow afternoon."

"And what about the pilot?"

"Oh, he'll come aboard later—certainly not before evening. It's easy as mid-ocean till you come to the Heads, and we can't be there before nightfall, even if the wind holds fair."

"Well, let's hope it may. So long, captain, and a thousand thanks for all your kindness. Dark night, by the way!"

"Yes, let's hope to-morrow won't be like it."

But the next night was darker still; there was neither moon nor star, and Skrimshire was thankful to have had speech with the captain while he could, for now he would speak to nobody, and to-morrow———

There was no to-morrow in Skrimshire's mind, there was only to-night. There was the hour he had been living for these six long weeks. There was the plan that had come to him with the south-east trades, and rolled in his mind through the Southern Ocean, only to reach perfection within the last few hours. But it was perfect now. And all beyond lay dark.

"Isn't that their boat, sir?"

It was the chief steward who wanted to know; he was dallying on the poop in the excitement of the occasion. The captain stood farther aft; an anxious face, a red cigar-end, and a blue Tam-o'-Shanter were all of him that showed in the intense darkness. The main-yard had just been backed, and the chief officer was now on the quarter-deck, seeing the rope ladder over the side. It was through his glasses that Skrimshire was watching the pilot's cutter, or rather her lights, and as well as he could, by their meagre rays, the little boat that now bobbed against the cutter's side.

"It is the boat, ain't it, sir?" persisted the steward.

"Yes, I think so," said Skrimshire. "How many men come with the pilot as a rule?"

"Only himself and a chap to row him."

"Ah! You might give these to the chief officer, steward. I'm going to my cabin for a minute. Don't forget to thank the mate for lending me his glasses; they've been exceedingly useful to me."

And Skrimshire disappeared down the ladder; his tone had been strange, but the steward only remembered this afterwards; at the time he was too excited himself, and too glad of a glass to level at the boat, to note any such nicety as a mere tone.

"Four of them, by Jingo!" mused the steward. "I wonder what that's for?"

But he did not wonder long: in a very few minutes the four were on board, and ascending the same ladder by which Skrimshire had gone below, the pilot at their head. Neilson received them at the break of the poop.

"I congratulate you, captain," was the pilot's greeting; "we didn't expect you before next week. Now, first allow me," and he lowered his voice, "to introduce Inspector Robins, of the Melbourne police; this gentleman is an officer he has brought with him; and my man has come aboard for a message for the shore. Mr. Robins would like a word with you before we let him go. There is no hurry, for I'm very much afraid I can't take you in till daylight."

Neilson took the inspector to the weather-rail.

"I know what's coming," he said. "The *Garth Castle* signalled——"

"I know, I know. Have you got him? Have you got him?" rapped out Robins.

"Safe and sound," whispered the captain; "and thinks himself as right as the bank, poor devil!"

"Then you didn't put him in irons?"

"No; I thought it better not to. He'd have committed suicide. I spotted that; sounded him without his knowing," said the crafty captain. "I happened to read the signals myself, and I never let on to a soul in the ship."

The good fellow looked delighted with himself behind his red cigar, but the acute face of the detective scarcely reflected his satisfaction.

"Well, that's all right if *he's* all right," said Robins. "If you don't mind, captain, I'd like to be introduced to him. One or both of us will spend the night with him, by your leave."

"As you like," said Neilson; "but I can't help feeling sorry for him. He's no more idea of this than the man in the moon. That you, steward? Where's Mr. Bennett? He was here a minute ago."

"Yes, sir; only just gone below, sir."

"Well, go and ask him to come up and drink with the pilot. I'll introduce him to the pilot, and you can do what you like," continued the captain, only wishing he could shirk a detestable duty altogether. "But I give you fair warning, this is a desperate man or I'm much mistaken in him."

"Desperate!" chuckled the inspector; "don't we know it? It seems to have been as bad a murder as you've had in the old country for a long time. In a train. All planned. Victim in one carriage, our friend in the next; got along footboard in tunnel, shot him dead through window, and got back. Case of revenge, and other fellow no beauty, but this one's got to swing. On his way to join your ship, too; passage booked beforehand. The most cold-blooded plant——"

It was the chief steward, breathless and panic-stricken.

"His door's locked——"

"He always does lock it," exclaimed the captain, as Robins darted to the ladder with an oath.

"But now he won't answer!" cried the steward.

And even with his words the answer came, in the terrific report of a revolver fired in a confined space. Next instant the inspector had hurled himself into the little saloon, the others at his heels, and half the ship's company at theirs. There was no need to point out the culprit's cabin. White smoke was streaming through the ventilated panels; all stood watching it, but for a time none spoke. Then Robins turned upon the captain.

"We have you to thank for this, Captain Neilson," said he. "It is you who will have to answer for it."

Neilson turned white, but it was white heat with him.

"And so I will," he thundered, "but not to you! I don't answer to any confounded Colonial policeman, and I don't take cheek from one either. By heaven, sir, I'm master of this ship, and for two pins I'll have you over the side again, detective or no detective. Do your business and break in that door, and you leave me to mind mine at the proper time and in the proper place."

He was furious with the fury of a masterful mariner, whose word is law aboard his own vessel, and yet beneath this virile passion there lurked a certain secret satisfaction in the thought that the companion of so many weeks was at all events not to hang. But the tragedy which had occurred was a greater unpleasantness for himself; indeed, it might well lead to something more, and Neilson stood in the grip of grim considerations in his own doorway, while Robins sent for the carpenter without addressing another syllable to the captain.

The saloon had been invaded by steerage passengers, and even by members of the crew, but discipline was for once a secondary matter in the eyes of Captain Neilson, and their fire was all for the insolent intruder who had dared to blame him aboard his own ship. The carpenter had to fight his way through a small, but exceedingly dense, crowd, beginning on the quarterdeck outside, and at its thickest in the narrow passage terminating in the saloon. On his arrival, however, the lock was soon forced, and the door swung inwards in a sudden silence, broken as suddenly by the detective's voice.

"Empty, by heaven!" he shrieked. "Hunt him—he's given us the slip!"

And the saloon emptied only less rapidly than it had filled, till Neilson had it to himself; he stepped over to the passenger's cabin, half expecting to find him hiding in some corner after all. There he was wrong; nor did he at once grasp the full significance of what he did find.

A revolver was dangling from a peg on one side of the cabin—dangling by a yard of twine secured to the trigger. A few more inches of the twine, tied to the butt, had been severed by burning, as had another yard dangling from another peg at the opposite side of the cabin. An inch of candle lay upon the floor. The twine had been passed through it; there was its mark in the wax. The whole had been strung across the cabin and the candle lighted before Skrimshire left; the revolver, hung by the trigger as a man is hanged by the neck, had been given a three-foot drop, and gone off duly as the flame burnt down to the string. Such was the plan which an ingenious (if perverted) mind had taken several weeks to perfect.

Neilson rushed on deck, to find all hands at the rail, and a fresh sensation in the air. The pilot met him on the poop.

"My boat's gone!" he cried. "And the night like pitch!"

Neilson stood thunderstruck.

"Did you leave a man aboard?"

"No, he came up for a telegram for the police in town."

"Then you can't blame me there."

And the captain leapt upon the rail at the break of the poop.

"Silence!" he roared. "Silence—every man of you! If we can't see we must listen . . . that's it . . . not a whisper . . . now. . . ."

At first there was nothing to be heard but the quick-drawn breath from half a hundred throats; then, out of the impenetrable darkness, came the thud, thud, thud of an oar in a rowlock, already some distance away; but in which direction it was impossible to tell on such a night.

The Lady, of the Barge

W. W. JACOBS

The master of the barge *Arabella* sat in the stern of his craft with his right arm leaning on the tiller. A desultory conversation with the mate of a schooner, who was hanging over the side of his craft a few yards off, had come to a conclusion owing to a difference of opinion on the subject of religion. The skipper had argued so warmly that he almost fancied he must have inherited the tenets of the Seventh-day Baptists from his mother while the mate had surprised himself by the warmth of his advocacy of a form of Wesleyanism which would have made the members of that sect open their eyes with horror. He had, moreover, confirmed the skipper in the error of his ways by calling him a bargee, the ranks of the Baptists receiving a defender if not a recruit from that hour.

With the influence of the religious argument still upon him, the skipper, as the long summer's day gave place to night, fell to wondering where his own mate, who was also his brother-in-law, had got to. Lights which had been struggling with the twilight now burnt bright and strong, and the skipper, moving from the shadow to where a band of light fell across the deck, took out a worn silver watch and saw that it was ten o'clock.

Almost at the same moment a dark figure appeared on the jetty above and began to descend the ladder, and a strongly built young man of twenty-two sprang nimbly to the deck.

"Ten o'clock, Ted," said the skipper, slowly.

"It'll be eleven in an hour's time," said the mate, calmly.

"That'll do," said the skipper, in a somewhat loud voice, as he noticed that his late adversary still occupied his favourite strained position, and a fortuitous expression of his mother's occurred to him: "Don't talk to me; I've been arguing with a son of Belial for the last half-hour."

"Bargee," said the son of Belial, in a dispassionate voice.

"Don't take no notice of him, Ted," said the skipper, pityingly.

"He wasn't talking to me," said Ted. "But never mind about him; I want to speak to you in private."

"Fire away, my lad," said the other, in a patronising voice.

"Speak up," said the voice from the schooner, encouragingly. "I'm listening."

There was no reply from the bargee. The master led the way to the cabin, and lighting a lamp, which appealed to more senses than one, took a seat on a locker, and again requested the other to fire away.

"Well, you see, it's this way," began the mate, with a preliminary wriggle: "there's a certain young woman———"

"A certain young what?" shouted the master of the *Arabella*.

"Woman," repeated the mate, snappishly; "you've heard of a woman afore, haven't you? Well, there's a certain young woman I'm walking out with I———"

"Walking out?" gasped the skipper. "Why, I never 'eard o' such a thing."

"You would ha' done if you'd been better looking, p'raps," retorted the other. "Well, I've offered this young woman to come for a trip with us."

"Oh, you have, 'ave you!" said the skipper, sharply. "And what do you think Louisa will say to it?"

"That's your look out," said Louisa's brother, cheerfully. "I'll make her up a bed for'ard, and we'll all be as happy as you please."

He started suddenly. The mate of the schooner was indulging in a series of whistles of the most amatory description.

"There she is," he said. "I told her to wait outside."

He ran upon deck, and his perturbed brother-in-law, following at his leisure, was just in time to see him descending the ladder with a young woman and a small handbag.

"This is my brother-in-law, Cap'n Gibbs," said Ted, introducing the new arrival; "smartest man at a barge on the river."

The girl extended a neatly gloved hand, shook the skipper's affably, and looked wonderingly about her.

"It's, very close to the water, Ted," she said, dubiously.

The skipper coughed. "We don't take passengers as a rule," he said, awkwardly; "we 'ain't got much convenience for them."

"Never mind," said the girl, kindly; "I sha'nt expect too much."

She turned away, and following the mate down to the cabin, went into ecstasies over the space-saving contrivances she found there. The drawers fitted in the skipper's bunk were a source of particular interest, and the owner watched with strong disapprobation through the skylight her efforts to make him an apple-pie bed with the limited means at her disposal. He went down below at once as a wet blanket.

"I was just shaking your bed up a bit," said Miss Harris, reddening.

"I see you was," said the skipper, briefly.

He tried to pluck up courage to tell her that he couldn't take her, but only succeeded in giving vent to an inhospitable cough.

"I'll get the supper," said the mate, suddenly; "you sit down, old man, and talk to Lucy."

In honour of the visitor he spread a small cloth, and then proceeded to produce cold beef, pickles, and accessories in a manner which reminded Miss Harris of white rabbits from a conjurer's hat. Captain Gibbs, accepting the inevitable, ate his supper in silence and left them to their glances.

"We must make you up a bed, for'ard, Lucy," said the mate, when they had finished.

Miss Harris started. "Where's that?" she inquired.

"Other end o' the boat," replied the mate, gathering up some bedding under his arm. "You might bring a lantern, John."

The skipper, who was feeling more sociable after a couple of glasses of beer, complied, and accompanied the couple to the tiny forecastle. A smell compounded of bilge, tar, paint, and other healthy disinfectants emerged as the scuttle was pushed back. The skipper dangled the lantern down and almost smiled.

"I can't sleep there," said the girl, with decision. "I shall die o' fright."

"You'll get used to it," said Ted, encouragingly, as he helped her down; "it's quite dry and comfortable."

He put his arm round her waist and squeezed her hand, and aided by this moral support, Miss Harris not only consented to remain, but found various advantages in the forecastle over the cabin, which had escaped the notice of previous voyagers.

"I'll leave you the lantern," said the mate, making it fast, "and we shall be on deck most o' the night. We get under way at two."

He quitted the forecastle, followed by the skipper, after a polite but futile attempt to give him precedence, and made his way to the cabin for two or three hours' sleep.

"There'll be a row at the other end, Ted," said the skipper, nervously, as he got into his bunk. "Louisa's sure to blame me for letting you keep company with a gal like this. We was talking about you only the other day, and she said if you was married five years from now, it 'ud be quite soon enough."

"Let Loo mind her own business," said the mate, sharply; "she's not going to nag me. She's not *my* wife, thank goodness!"

He turned over and fell fast asleep, waking up fresh and bright three hours later, to commence what he fondly thought would be the pleasantest voyage of his life.

The *Arabella* dropped slowly down with the tide, the wind being so light that she was becalmed by every tall warehouse on the way. Off Greenwich, however, the breeze freshened somewhat, and a little later Miss Harris, looking somewhat pale as to complexion and untidy as to hair, came slowly on deck.

"Where's the looking-glass?" she asked, as Ted hastened to greet her. "How does my hair look?"

"All wavy," said the infatuated young man; "all little curls and squiggles. Come down in the cabin; there's a glass there."

Miss Harris, with a light nod to the skipper as he sat at the tiller, followed the mate below, and giving vent to a little cry of indignation as she saw herself in the glass, waved the amorous Ted on deck, and started work on her disarranged hair.

At breakfast-time a little friction was caused by what the mate bitterly termed the narrow-minded, old-fashioned ways of the skipper. He had arranged that the skipper should steer while he and Miss Harris breakfasted, but the coffee was no sooner on the table than the skipper called him, and relinquishing the helm in his favour, went below to do the honours. The mate protested.

"It's not proper," said the skipper. "Me and 'er will 'ave our meals together, and then you must have yours. She's under my care."

Miss Harris assented blithely, and talk and laughter greeted the ears of the indignant mate as he steered. He went down at last to cold coffee and lukewarm herrings, returning to the deck after a hurried meal to find the skipper narrating some of his choicest experiences to an audience which hung on his lightest word.

The disregard they showed for his feelings was maddening, and for the first time in his life he became a prey to jealousy in its worst form. It was quite clear to him that the girl had become desperately enamoured of the skipper, and he racked his brain in a wild effort to discover the reason.

With an idea of reminding his brother-in-law of his position, he alluded two or three times in a casual fashion to his wife. The skipper hardly listened to him, and patting Miss Harris's cheek in a fatherly manner, regaled her with an anecdote of the mate's boyhood which the latter had spent a goodly portion of his life in denying. He denied it again, hotly, and Miss Harris, conquering for a time her laughter, reprimanded him severely for contradicting.

By the time dinner was ready he was in a state of sullen apathy, and when the meal was over and the couple came on deck again, so far forgot himself as to compliment Miss Harris upon her appetite.

"I'm ashamed of you, Ted," said the skipper, with severity.

"I'm glad you know what shame is," retorted the mate.

"If you can't be'ave yourself, you'd better keep a bit for'ard till you get in a better temper," continued the skipper.

"I'll be pleased to," said the smarting mate. "I wish the barge was longer."

"It couldn't be too long for me," said Miss Harris, tossing her head.

"Be'aving like a schoolboy," murmured the skipper.

"I know how to behave *my*self," said the mate, as he disappeared below. His head suddenly appeared again over the companion. "If some people don't," he added, and disappeared again.

He was pleased to notice as he ate his dinner that the giddy prattle above had ceased, and with his back turned towards the couple when he appeared on deck again, he lounged slowly forward until the skipper called him back again.

"Wot was them words you said just now, Ted?" he inquired.

The mate repeated them with gusto.

"Very good," said the skipper, sharply; "very good."

"Don't you ever speak to me again," said Miss Harris, with a stately air, "because I won't answer you if you do."

The mate displayed more of his schoolboy nature. "Wait till you're spoken to," he said, rudely. "This is your gratefulness, I suppose?"

"Gratefulness?" said Miss Harris, with her chin in the air. "What for?"

"For bringing you for a trip," replied the mate, sternly.

"*You* bringing me for a trip!" said Miss Harris, scornfully.

"Captain Gibbs is the master here, I suppose. He is giving me the trip. You're only the mate."

"Just so," said the mate, with a grin at his brother-in-law, which made that worthy shift uneasily. "I wonder what Loo will say when she sees you with a lady aboard?"

"She came to please you," said Captain Gibbs, with haste.

"Ho! she did, did she?" jeered the mate. "Prove it; only don't look to me to back you, that's all."

The other eyed him in consternation, and his manner changed.

"Don't play the fool, Ted," he said, not unkindly; "you know what Loo is."

"Well, I'm reckoning on that," said the mate, deliberately. "I'm going for'ard; don't let me interrupt you two. So long."

He went slowly forward, and lighting his pipe, sprawled carelessly on the deck, and renounced the entire sex forthwith. At tea-time the skipper attempted to reverse the procedure at the other meals; but as Miss Harris steadfastly declined to sit at the same table as the mate, his good intentions came to naught.

He made an appeal to what he termed the mate's better nature, after Miss Harris had retired to the seclusion of her bed-chamber, but in vain.

"She's nothing to do with me," declared the mate, majestically. I wash my hands of her. She's a flirt. I'm like Louisa, I can't bear flirts."

The skipper said no more, but his face was so worn that Miss Harris, when she came on deck in the early morning and found the barge gliding gently between the grassy banks of a river, attributed it to the difficulty of navigating so large a craft on so small and winding a stream.

"We shall be alongside in 'arf an hour," said the skipper, eyeing her.

Miss Harris expressed her gratification.

"P'raps you wouldn't mind going down the fo'c'sle and staying there till we've made fast," said the other. I'd take it as a favour. My owners don't like me to carry passengers."

Miss Harris, who understood perfectly, said, "Certainly," and with a cold stare at the mate, who was at no pains to conceal his amusement, went below at once, thoughtfully closing the scuttle after her.

"There's no call to make mischief, Ted," said the skipper, somewhat anxiously, as they swept round the last bend and came into view of Coalsham.

The mate said nothing, but stood by to take in sail as they ran swiftly towards the little quay. The pace slackened, and the *Arabella*, as though conscious of the contraband in her forecastle, crept slowly to where a stout, middle-aged woman, who bore a strong likeness to the mate, stood upon the quay.

"There's poor Loo," said the mate, with a sigh.

The skipper made no reply to this infernal insinuation. The barge ran alongside the quay and made fast.

"I thought you'd be up," said Mrs. Gibbs to her husband. "Now come along to breakfast; Ted'll follow on."

Captain Gibbs dived down below for his coat, and slipping ashore, thankfully prepared to move off with his wife.

"Come on as soon as you can, Ted," said the latter. "Why, what on earth is he making that face for?"

She turned in amazement as her brother, making a pretence of catching her husband's eye, screwed his face up into a note of interrogation and gave a slight jerk with his thumb.

"Come along," said Captain Gibbs, taking her arm with much affection.

"But what's Ted looking like that for?" demanded his wife, as she easily intercepted another choice fatal expression of the mate's.

"Oh, it's his fun," replied her husband, walking on.

"*Fun?*" repeated Mrs. Gibbs, sharply. "What's the matter, Ted?"

"Nothing," replied the mate.

"Touch o' toothache," said the skipper. "Come along, Loo; I can just do with one o' your breakfasts."

Mrs. Gibbs suffered herself to be led on, and had got at least five yards on the way home, when she turned and looked back. The mate had still got the toothache, and was at that moment in all the agonies of a phenomenal twinge.

"There's something wrong here," said Mrs. Gibbs as she retraced her steps. "Ted, what are you making that face for?"

"It's my own face," said the mate, evasively.

Mrs. Gibbs conceded the point, and added bitterly that it couldn't be helped. All the same she wanted to know what he meant by it.

"Ask John," said the vindictive mate.

Mrs. Gibbs asked. Her husband said he didn't know, and added that Ted had been like it before, but he had not told her for fear of frightening her. Then he tried to induce her to go with him to the chemist's to get something for it.

Mrs. Gibbs shook her head firmly, and boarding the barge, took a seat on the hatch and proceeded to catechise her brother as to his symptoms. He denied that there was anything the matter with him, while his eyes openly sought those of Captain Gibbs as though asking for instruction.

"You come home, Ted," she said at length.

"I can't," said the mate. "I can't leave the ship."

"Why not?" demanded his sister.

"Ask John," said the mate again.

At this Mrs. Gibb's temper, which had been rising, gave way altogether, and she stamped fiercely upon the deck. A stamp of the foot has been for all time a rough-and-ready means of signalling; the fore-scuttle was drawn back, and the face of a pretty girl appeared framed in the opening. The mate raised his eyebrows with a helpless gesture, and as for the unfortunate skipper, any jury would have found him guilty without leaving the box. The wife of his bosom, with a flaming visage, turned and regarded him.

"You villain!" she said, in a choking voice.

Captain Gibbs caught his breath and looked appealingly at the mate.

"It's a little surprise for you, my dear," he faltered; "it's Ted's young lady."

"Nothing of the kind," said the mate, sharply.

"It's not? How dare you say such a thing?" demanded Miss Harris, stepping on to the deck.

"Well, you brought her aboard, Ted, you know you did," pleaded the unhappy skipper.

The mate did not deny it, but his face was so full of grief and surprise that the other's heart sank within him.

"All right," said the mate at last; "have it your own way."

"Hold your tongue, Ted," shouted Mrs. Gibbs; "you're trying to shield him."

"I tell you Ted brought her aboard, and they had a lover's quarrel," said her unhappy spouse. "It's nothing to do with me at all."

"And that's why you told me Ted had got the toothache, and tried to get me off to the chemist's, I s'pose," retorted his wife, with virulence. "Do you think I'm a fool? How dare you ask a young woman on this barge? How dare you?"

"I didn't ask her," said her husband.

"I s'pose she came without being asked," sneered his wife, turning her regards to the passenger; "she looks the sort that might. You brazen-faced girl!"

"Here, go easy, Loo," interrupted the mate, flushing as he saw the girl's pale face.

"Mind your own business," said his sister, violently.

"It is my business," said the repentant mate. "I brought her aboard, and then we quarrelled."

"I've no doubt," said his sister, bitterly; "it's very pretty, but it won't do."

"I swear it's the truth," said the mate.

"Why did John keep it so quiet and hide her for, then?" demanded his sister.

"I came down for the trip," said Miss Harris; "that is all about it. There is nothing to make a fuss about. How much is it, Captain Gibbs?"

She produced a little purse from her pocket, but before the embarrassed skipper could reply, his infuriated wife struck it out of her hand. The mate sprang instinctively forward, but too late, and the purse fell with a splash into the water. The girl gave a faint cry and clasped her hands.

"How am I to get back?" she gasped.

"I'll see to that, Lucy," said the mate. "I'm very sorry—I've been a brute."

"*You?*" said the indignant girl. "I would sooner drown myself than be beholden to you."

"I'm very sorry," repeated the mate, humbly.

"There's enough of this play-acting," interposed Mrs. Gibbs. "Get off this barge."

"You stay where you are," said the mate, authoritatively.

"Send that girl off this barge," screamed Mrs. Gibbs to her husband.

Captain Gibbs smiled in a silly fashion and scratched his head. "Where is she to go?" he asked feebly.

"What does it matter to you where she goes?" cried his wife, fiercely. "Send her off."

The girl eyed her haughtily, and repulsing the mate as he strove to detain her, stepped to the side. Then she paused as he suddenly threw off his coat, and sitting down on the hatch, hastily removed his boots. The skipper, divining his intentions, seized him by the arm.

"Don't be a fool, Ted," he gasped; "you'll get under the barge."

The mate shook him off, and went in with a splash which half-drowned his adviser. Miss Harris, clasping her hands, ran to the side and gazed fearfully at the spot where he had disappeared, while his sister in a terrible voice seized the opportunity to point out to her husband the probably fatal results of his ill-doing. There was an anxious interval, and then the mate's head appeared above the water and after a breathing space disappeared again. The skipper, watching uneasily, stood by with a lifebelt.

"Come out, Ted," screamed his sister as he came up for breath again.

The mate disappeared once more, but coming up for the third time, hung on to the side of the barge to recover a bit. A clothed man in the water savours of disaster and looks alarming. Miss Harris began to cry.

"You'll be drowned," she whimpered.

"Come out," said Mrs. Gibbs, in a raspy voice. She knelt on the deck and twined her fingers in his hair. The mate addressed her in terms rendered brotherly by pain.

"Never mind about the purse," sobbed Miss Harris; "it doesn't matter."

"Will you make it up if I come out, then," demanded the diver.

"No; I'll never speak to you again as long as I live," said the girl, passionately.

The mate disappeared again. This time he was out of sight longer than usual, and when he came up merely tossed his arms weakly and went down again. There was a scream from the women, and a mighty splash as the skipper went overboard with a lifebelt. The mate's head, black and shining, showed for a moment; the skipper grabbed him by the hair and towed him to the barge's side, and in the midst of a considerable hubbub both men were drawn from the water.

The skipper shook himself like a dog, but the mate lay on the deck inert in a puddle of water. Mrs. Gibbs frantically slapped his hands; and Miss Harris, bending over him, rendered first aid by kissing him wildly.

Captain Gibbs pushed her away. "He won't come round while you're a-kissing of him," he cried, roughly.

To his indignant surprise the drowned man opened one eye and winked acquiescence. The skipper dropped his arms by his side and stared at him stupidly.

"I saw his eyelid twitch," cried Mrs. Gibbs, joyfully.

"He's all right." said her indignant husband; " 'e ain't born to be drowned, 'e ain't. I've spoilt a good suit of clothes for nothing."

To his wife's amazement, he actually walked away from the insensible man, and with a boat-hook reached for his hat, which was floating by. Mrs. Gibbs, still gazing in blank astonishment, caught a seraphic smile on the face of her brother as Miss Harris continued her ministrations, and in a pardonable fit of temper the overwrought woman gave him a box on the ear, which brought him round at once.

"Where am I?" he inquired, artlessly.

Mrs. Gibbs told him. She also told him her opinion of him, and without plagiarising her husband's words, came to the same conclusion as to his ultimate fate.

"You come along home with me," she said, turning in a friendly fashion to the bewildered girl. "They deserve what they've got—both of 'em. I only hope that they'll both get such awful colds that they won't find their voices for a twelvemonth."

She took the girl by the arm and helped her ashore. They turned their heads once in the direction of the barge, and saw the justly incensed skipper keeping the mate's explanations and apologies at bay with a boat-hook. Then they went in to breakfast.

Dead Reckoning

RALPH STOCK

I have killed a man because he disagreed with me. Anything more futile it is hard to imagine in cold blood, for by killing him I have proved nothing. He still holds his view. I know it because I have spoken to him *since*, and he still laughs at me, though softly, compassionately, not as he laughed on that night when the absurdity happened.

Perhaps I am mad, but you shall judge. In any case, that is of no great importance, for by the time you read this, my confession—if, indeed, it is ever read—I shall have ceased to encumber the earth.

He was young and strong, and filled with that terrible self-assurance of youth that sets an older man's teeth on edge. During his short term of tuition in the schools of the South there was nothing that he had not learned to do better (in theory) than a man of fifty years' experience; and obstinate—But I must not let myself go. It is my duty to set down here precisely what happened, without prejudice, without feeling even, if that were possible. Yet as I write, my pulse quickens—I will wait a little. It is unfair to him to continue at present.

Here on this reef off the Queensland coast there are unbelievable quantities of fish. Even I have never seen so many, nor of such brilliant colouring. It is possible to wade into the tepid water and catch them with the hand. I have caught hundreds to-day, for lack of something better to do—and set them free; for I will have no more blood on my hands, even that of a fish. Besides, what is the use? There is no drinking water here, nothing but blinding sunlight, a ridge of discoloured coral cleaving the blue mirror of the sea like a razor edge, and myself—a criminal perched upon it as upon a premature scaffold.

But I have overlooked the pickle bottle. It came to me floating, not quite empty, and corked against the flies, just as he and I had left it after the last meal. When the wreck sank, it must have risen from the fo'c'sle table and up through the hatch—it is curious that nothing else should rise—and it occurred to me that by its aid, and that of the little notebook with pencil attached which I always carry, it would be possible to set my case before the world. I must continue, or there may not be time to say all.

I am what they call an old man on Thursday Island, for none but blacks live to any age in the neighbourhood of this sun-baked tile on the roof of Australia. But I come of Old Country stock, and blood will tell.

I have mixed little with others, preferring the society of my only child, a daughter, to the prattlers and drinkers of a small equatorial community. Perhaps I have been too circumscribed, too isolated, from my fellow-creatures. I only know that until *he* came I was content. My small weather-board house ashore, the ketch in which I brought sandalwood from the mainland coast, were my twin worlds. In each all things were conducted according to my wishes—according, rather, to the methods I had evolved from long experience, and that their merits were borne out by results none could deny.

The house, with its small, well-tended garden, was the best on Thursday Island. My daughter, dutiful and intelligent, managed it according to my wishes, so that it ran like a well-oiled mechanism. And the ketch—that was my inviolable domain. Above and below decks, although only a twenty-ton cargo-carrier, she would have put many a yacht to shame. There was nothing superfluous, nothing lacking. Everything aboard had its place and uses; that is how I contrived to work her single-handed for nearly ten years.

They called me a curmudgeon and a skinflint, but I could afford to smile. My cargoes were not so large as theirs, and took longer to gather, but while they were eating into their profits by paying wages and shares to lazy crews, mine came solely to myself, and never in all those years did I have a mishap. Trust an owner to look after his craft, say I, and trust none other.

Then, as I have said, *he* came. How he gained entrance I have never known, but he had a way with him, that boy, and when one evening I returned from a trip, he was sitting on the verandah with Doris. She was evidently embarrassed.

"This is Mr. Thorpe, father," she said, and went in to prepare supper, which was late for the first time that I could remember.

"Indeed?" said I, and remained standing, a fact that Thorpe appeared to overlook, for he reseated himself with all the assurance in life.

"Yes," he said in a manner that I believe is called "breezy," "that is my name, Captain Brent, and I'm pleased to make your acquaintance. Have you had a good trip?"

"Passable," said I. "And now, if you'll excuse me, I must go in and change."

"Oh, don't mind me," returned Thorpe, spreading himself in the cane chair and lighting a cigarette; "I'm quite comfortable."

For a moment I stood speechless, then went into the house.

Doris was preparing the meal, but turned as I entered. Never before had I seen the look that I saw in her face at that moment—fear battling with resolve.

"Who is that boy?" I asked her.

"I have already told you, father," she answered; "he is a young man named Thorpe—Edward Thorpe."

"Ah," said I, momentarily at a loss, "a young man—named Thorpe. And why does he come here?"

"To see me," returned Doris in her quiet, even voice, but I saw that she trembled.

I took her by the arm.

"Girl," said I, "tell me all."

"We love one another," she told me, looking full into my eyes with no hint of timidity; "we are engaged to be married."

I could not speak. I could not even protest when, at no invitation of mine, this youth had the effrontery to come in to supper. The world—my twin worlds—rocked under my feet.

It was a terrible meal. I, speechless, at one end of the table, my daughter, pale, but courteous, at the other, and this clown sat between us, regaling us, as he no doubt thought, with anecdotes of life down South.

And this was not enough, but he must come into the kitchen afterwards and help to wash up. He said it made him feel more at home. Now, it has been my custom, ever since leaving a civilisation that I abhor and finding comfort in this far corner of the earth, to help wash up when I am at home. The thing is part of the routine of life, and as such demands proper management. A nice adjustment of the water's temperature is necessary, for if too hot it may crack glass and china and ruin knife-handles; and if too cold, in spite of a certain amount of soda, it fails to remove grease. Then, too, it is my invariable habit at the end to turn the washbowl upside down to drain, and spread the dishcloth upon it to dry. It occurs to me that these may appear small matters to some, but is not life composed of such, and do they not often turn out to be the greater? And our uninvited guest disorganised the entire routine by pathetic efforts at buffoonery such as tying one of Doris's aprons about his waist, making a napkin-ring climb his finger by a circular motion of the hand, and laughing openly at what he evidently regarded as our fads.

The spreading of the dishcloth on the wash-bowl appeared to amuse him most of all.

"I suppose you always do that," he said.

"It is the custom in this house," said I.

"And when you come to think of it, why not?" he reflected, with his handsome head at an angle.

"There are many things one has to come to think of before one knows anything," said I.

And at that he laughed good-naturedly. He always laughed.

At length he went. From my easy-chair in the living-room I heard the last "Good-night" and his assured footfall on the verandah steps. Doris came straight to me. I knew she would. Perching herself on the arm of my chair, as she used to when a child, she encircled my shoulder with her arm.

"Do you hate him, father?" she asked me.

I answered her question with another.

"Do you fear me, Doris?" For the look in her face that evening had shocked me.

"I used to sometimes," she said, "but not now."

"And what has worked the transformation?"

She leaned over and whispered in my ear.

I held her from me and studied her as though for the first time. She was young, beautiful, fragile, yet she was stronger than I. I am no fool. I knew that nothing I could do or say would have one particle of weight with her now. She loved, and was loved. So it is with women; and such is this miracle of a day, an hour, a fraction of time, that shatters lifelong fealty like glass.

"Then I have nothing to say," said I.

"Nothing?" she questioned me, and again presently, "nothing?"

And at last I heard myself muttering the absurd formula of wishes for their happiness.

It was bound to come some time. It had come, that was all, and I made the best of it. Of an evening that boy would sit with us and make suggestions for the betterment of the business—my business. He pointed out that new blood was needed—his blood. By heavens, how he talked! And there is an insidious power in words. Utter them often enough, with youthful enthusiasm behind them, and they resolve themselves into deeds.

I cannot explain even to myself how it came about, but this was the plan—to take my ketch to Sydney, where she would apparently realise an enormous sum as a converted yacht, and buy another, installing an auxiliary motor-engine with some of the profits. With an engine, and this new blood, it seemed, we were to make a fortune out of sandalwood in three years.

I wanted neither engine, new blood, nor fortune, yet in the end I gave way.

So it was that, rather late in the season, we let go moorings, he and I, and set sail for the South. For the first time in my life I had a crew. My inviolable domain was invaded. What with the thought of this, and the unworthy mission we were engaged upon, it was all I could do to look my ketch in the face. Those with the love of ships in their bones will understand.

More than once I caught Thorpe smiling at one or another of my own small inventions for the easier handling of the boat, or the saving of labour or space below; but he said nothing beyond called them "gadgets," a word that was new to me.

"Not a bad little packet," he said, after the first hour of his trick at the tiller.

"I am glad to hear you say so," said I, with an irony entirely lost on one of his calibre.

"But she ought to sail nearer the wind than this," he added, staring up at the quivering top-sail. "Six points won't do. Under-canvased, that's what she is. By the way, when we get through the reef pass, what's the course?"

"Sou'-sou'-east," said I.

"And where's your deviation card?"

"Never had to bother with one," I told him.

He seemed thunderstruck.

"Of course, she's wooden," he began; "but surely—"

"The course is sou'-sou'-east," I repeated, and went below.

From then onwards he took to reeling me off parrot-like dissertations on devioscopes, new pattern compasses, and whatnot, until the sound of his voice sickened me. Amongst his other accomplishments, he had sat for a yachting master's ticket, and passed, though every one knew, it appeared, how much stiffer were the examinations nowadays than in the past, when half the men called ship's masters had no right to the title, nor even knew the uses of a chronometer.

"Yet they managed to circumnavigate the globe," I pointed out.

"By running down their latitude!" he scoffed.

"Perhaps," said I, whereat he burst into a gale of laughter, and expressed the devout hope that I would never expect him to employ such methods.

"I expect you to do nothing but what you are told," said I, exasperated beyond endurance. "At the present moment you are not getting the best out of her. Give her another point, and make a note of time and distance in the scrap log hanging on yonder rail."

"Dead reckoning," he muttered contemptuously.

"Just that," said I, and left him.

Why did I "leave him"? Why did I "go below"? At all costs I must be fair. I did both these things because I knew that he could argue me off my feet if I remained, that he knew more about deep-sea navigation than I, that I was one of those he had mentioned who are called ship's masters and have no right to the title, nor even knew the uses of a chronometer.

Such a confession is like drawing a tooth to me, but it is made. And as vindication I would point to my record—ten years, single-handed and by dead reckoning without mishap. Can an extra master show better?

As day succeeded day, the tension grew. Often I would sit on a locker gazing on my familiar and beloved surroundings and ask myself how long I could suffer them to be sneered at and despised. Trust small craft for discovering one man to another. Before three days and three nights had passed, we stood before each other, he and I, stripped to our souls. His every movement was an aggravation to me, especially when he played with the bespangled sextant and toy chronometer he had brought, and when each day, on plotting out my position on the chart according to dead reckoning, I found his, by observation, already there. I rubbed it out. I prayed that there would come such a fog as would obscure the sun and stars for ever.

And it was as though my prayer were answered, for that night we ran into a gale that necessitated heaving to. Luckily it was off the shore, and for forty-eight hours we rode it out in comparative comfort, until it died as suddenly as it had been born, and was succeeded by a driving mist that stilled the sea as though with a giant white hand.

"You see," said Thorpe, "dead reckoning is all right up to a point, as a check, but how do you know where you are now?"

"Can you tell me?" said I.

"Not until the mist clears," he admitted.

"Well, then—" said I.

He flung away from me with an impatient movement.

"These are the methods of Methuselah," he muttered.

"Nevertheless," I returned, the blood throbbing at my temples, "I know our position at this moment better than any upstart yachtsman."

He turned and looked at me strangely, then of a sudden his mouth relaxed into a smile. At that moment I could have struck him.

"There is no call for us to quarrel," he said gently, "but how—how can you possibly know where we have drifted to in the last forty-eight hours?"

"I have my senses," said I, "and to prove them we will carry on."

"In this mist?"

"In this mist," I thundered. "The wind is fair, the course is now south-half-east, and you'll oblige me by taking the tiller."

He seemed about to speak, but evidently changed his mind, and turned abruptly on his heel.

In silence we shook out the reef and got under way. In silence we remained until the end of his watch, when the mist was dispersed by a brazen sun. Thorpe at once took a sight, and again at noon, and when I had plotted our position on the chart, he was still poring over volumes of nautical tables.

Towards dusk he came to me at the tiller.

"Are you holding this course after dark?" he asked.

"That is as may be," said I.

"Because if you are," he went on, as though I had not spoken, "you'll be on the Barrier Reef inside of five hours."

"I thank you for the information," said I, and he went below.

He knew ship's discipline; I'll say that for him. He might consider myself and my methods archaic, but he recognised my authority and carried out instructions. I am aware that up to the present my case appears a poor one, but I can convey no idea of the pitch to which I was brought by these eternal bickerings, by the innovation of another will than my own, and the constant knowledge that he was laughing at me up his sleeve.

But it was a little thing that brought matters to a climax. It is always the little things.

With a fair wind, and in these unfrequented waters, it has always been my habit to lash the tiller and eat in comfort. We were washing up after supper, or, rather, he was washing and I was drying, for the dryer puts away the utensils, and I knew better the proper place for each. At the end he tossed the dishcloth in a sodden mass upon the table and turned to go.

"The dishcloth, if you remember," said I, "is spread on the washbowl to dry."

He turned and looked at me, and in his eyes I saw a sudden, unaccustomed flame leap to life.

"It'll do it good to have a change," he said.

"I do not think so," said I.

"Naturally," he returned; "but I do."

"And who is the master of this ship?" I asked him.

"As for that, you are," he admitted, "but a dishcloth is another matter." Suddenly he dropped on to a locker and laughed, though there was a nervous catch in it. "Heavens!" he giggled, "we're arguing over a dishcloth now!"

"And why not," said I, "if you don't know how to use one? Will you be so good as to put it in its proper place?"

He did not answer, but sat looking down at his naked feet.

"This is impossible," he muttered.

"As you will," said I.

"It can't go on; I can't stand it."

"Do you imagine it is any pleasanter for me?" I asked him.

"And who's fault is it?"

"That is a matter of opinion," said I; "but in the meantime things are to be done as I wish. Kindly put the dishcloth in its proper place."

Again he did not answer, but when he looked up it was with compressed lips.

"You are a frightful old man," he said. Those were his words. I remember every one, and they came from him in deliberate, staccato sentences. "You are that, though no one has dared to tell you so until this minute. You have lived in a rut of your own making so deep and so long that you don't know you're in it. That is your affair, but when you drag others in with you, it is time to speak. I rescued Doris—bless her!—just in time. Why, man, can't you see? There's no light down there; you can never take a look at yourself and laugh. You have no more sense of humour than a fish. If you had, this absurd quibble could never have come to a head. We should have been sitting here laughing instead. Think of it—a dishcloth! You are my senior; I ought not to be talking like this to you, but I am; it's just been dragged out of me, and you can take it or leave it. Why not open up a bit—do something different just because it is different, admit there may be something others know that you don't, fling the dishcloth in a corner . . ."

Those were some of the things he said to me, and I stood there listening to them from a—from my future son-in-law on my own ship. It seemed incredible to me now, but I was dazed with the unexpectedness of this attack. All that remained clearly before me was the issue of the dishcloth. In the midst of his endless discourse I repeated my command, whereat he burst into another of his inane fits of laughter.

"You find it amusing," said I in a voice I scarce recognised as my own.

"Amusing!" he chuckled. "Think—try and think—a dishcloth!"

"And one that you will put in its proper place," I told him.

"What makes you think that?" he said, sobering a little.

"Because I say so."

"And if I refuse?" His face was quite grave now. He leant forward, as though interested in my reply. Somehow the sight of it—this handsome, impertinent face of his—caused a red mist to swim before my eyes.

"You will be made to," I said.

"Ah!" was all he answered at the moment, and resumed the study of his feet. If he had remained so, all might have been well. I cannot tell. I only know that at that moment one word stood for him between life and death, and he chose to utter it.

"How?"

I tried to show him, that was all. I swear that was my sole intention. But he was obstinate, that boy. I had not thought it possible for a man to be as obstinate as he.

I rushed on deck to be caught by a roller.

My weight carried him to the floor; besides, I am strong, and the accumulated fury of days and nights were behind me. He was like a doll in my hands, yet a doll that refused to squeak when pressed. There is a sail-rack in the fo'c's'le, and we were under it, my back against it, my knee at his chest; and I asked him, lying there laughing up at me, if he intended to do as I had ordered. He rolled his head in a negative. It was all he could do, and the pressure was increased. I must have asked him many times, and the answer was invariably the same. At the last something gave beneath my knee, and his jaw dropped, and no movement came from him, even from the heart.

The ripple of water past the ketch's sides brought me back to the present. I rose and stood looking down on him. As I live, it seemed that there was a smile still upon his face!

Of the rest I have no clear recollection. At one moment I was standing there trying—trying to realise what I had done; the next I was flung against the bulkhead as the ketch struck and rose—I can describe it in no other way—struck and rose. Even as I rushed on deck to be caught by a roller and hurled headlong, it seemed to me that a mocking voice called after me: "Dead Reckoning!"

It was the Barrier Reef.

And for me it is the Barrier Reef to the end, which is not far off. When I came to, the ketch had sunk, and I tried again to think. I have been trying ever since, and I can get no further than that I have killed him—for a dishcloth; that if by some miracle I am rescued, such is the message I shall have for Doris. . . . Is it comedy or tragedy? I am not so sure now. *He* seemed to find it amusing to the very end, and he was right in some things. Perhaps he is right in this.

I never laugh? Did I not catch myself laughing aloud just now? Perhaps I am developing, somewhat late in life, to be sure, the "sense of humour" he tells me I lack. . . . I have finished. It is for you to read and judge.

The foregoing, with such editing as was necessary to render it intelligible, is the message I found in a pickle bottle firmly wedged amongst the mangrove roots of a creek in the Gulf of Carpentaria. It must have been there for years.

I was duck-shooting at the time, but somehow, after happening on to this quaint document besmeared with pickle juice, my interest in the sport flagged. I wanted to know more, and there is only one way to do that on Thursday Island—ask Evans. Consequently, that evening found me, not for the first time, on his wide verandah, discussing whisky and soda, and the impossible state of the shell market.

"By the way," I ventured presently, "did you ever know a Captain Brent?"

"Still know him, for the matter of that," said Evans. "Why?"

"Then he—I mean he still lives on T.I.," I stammered like a fool.

"Certainly. I used to buy his sandalwood. Buy his son-in-law's now."

"His son-in-law's?"

Evans rolled over in his chair and grinned at me.

"What's the game?" he questioned good-naturedly. "I never saw such a fellow." He rolled back again. "But, come to think of it, there might be something in him for you. The old man's ketch is the first thing I ever heard of to jump the Barrier Reef. I thought that'd make you sit up. But it's the truth. Ask Thorpe—he was aboard when she did it. He and the old man were going South for something—I forget what—and they took the Great Barrier bow on at night. It's been done before, you know, but never quite like that. Must have struck it in a narrow place or something. Anyway, Thorpe says that ketch jumped like a two-year-old, slithered through rotten coral for a bit, and plumped into deep water beyond, carried by the surf, I expect, and nothing more to show for it than a scored bilge—oh, and a couple of broken ribs—Thorpe's not the ketch's. He was beaten up pretty considerably when we took him ashore. Is there anything else I can serve you with to-day, sir?"

Evans is a good fellow, but provokingly incomplete.

"Yes," said I. "What happened to the old man?"

"Oh, he rushed on deck at the first shock, it seems, and was promptly bowled over the side by a breaker. But there's no killing him. He just sat on the reef, thinking his ketch sunk and Thorpe dead, until some one came and took him off. Shook him up, though. He's never been quite the same since. Which is all to the good, most of us think."

The next evening I took occasion to wander down T.I.'s grass-grown main street, through its herds of cavorting goats, and up the galvanised hillside to where a neat little weather-board house stood well back from the road.

In the garden, enjoying the cool of the evening, were four people—a white-bearded man seated in a cane-chair, a bronzed giant, prone and smoking, on the grass, and a woman beside him, sitting as only a woman can. Curiously enough, their eyes were all turned in the same direction—to where, in short, the fourth member of the party was engaged in the solemn procession of learning to "walk alone." His progress towards his mother's outstretched arms was as erratic as such things usually are—a few ungainly steps, a tottering pause, and an abrupt but apparently painless collapse.

"Seven!" exclaimed the white-bearded man, with an air of personal accomplishment.

"I made it five," grinned the giant.

"I said seven," boomed the other, and I left them at it.

They were Captain Brent and his son-in-law, and somehow I wanted to preserve that picture of them intact.

That, too, was partly why at the summit of the hill I tore my quaint, pickle-stained document into minute fragments and scattered them to the four winds of Torres Straits.

Hollis's Debt

LOUIS BECKE

One day a small Sydney-owned brigantine named the *Maid of Judah*, loaded with coconut oil and sandalwood and bound for China, appeared off the little island of Pingelap, in the Caroline Group. In those wild days—from 1820 to the end of the "fifties"—the sandalwood trade was carried on by ships whose crews were assemblages of the most utter ruffians in the Pacific Ocean, and the hands that manned this brigantine were no exception. There may have been grades of villainy among them; perhaps if any one of them was more blood-stained and criminal than the others, it was her captain.

There being no anchorage at Pingelap, the captain sailed in as close as he dared, and then hove-to under the lee of the land, waiting for the natives to come aboard with some turtle. Presently a canoe put off from the long curve of yellow beach. She was manned by some eight or ten natives. As she pulled up alongside, the captain glanced at the white man who was steering and his face paled. He turned quickly away and went below.

The mate of the sandalwooder shook hands with the white man and looked curiously at him. Only by his speech could he be recognised as an Englishman. His hair, long, rough and dull brown, fell on his naked shoulders like that of a native. A broad-brimmed hat, made from the plaited leaf of the pandanus palm, was his only article of European clothing; round his lions was a native girdle of beaten coconut leaves. And his skin was as dark as that of his savage native crew; he looked, and was, a true Micronesian beachcomber.

"You're under mighty short canvas, my friend," said the mate of the vessel by way of pleasantry.

The man with the brown skin turned on him savagely.

"What the hell is that to you? I don't dress to please a pack of convicts and cut-throats! Do you want to buy any turtle? that's the question. And where's the captain?"

"Captain Matson has gone below sick, sir," said the steward, coming up and speaking to the mate. "He says not to wait for the turtle but to fill away again."

"Can't," said the mate sharply. "Tell him there isn't enough wind. Didn't he see that for himself ten minutes ago? What's the matter with him?"

"Don't know, sir. Only said he was took bad sudden."

With an oath expressive of disgust the mate turned to the beachcomber. "You've had your trouble for nothing, you see. The old man don't want any turtle it seems— Why, what the hell is wrong with *you*?"

The bearded, savage-looking beachcomber was leaning against a backstay, his hands tightly clenched, and his eyes fixed in a wild, insane stare.

He straightened himself up and spoke with an effort.

"Nothing: I'm all right now. 'Tis a fearful hot day, and the sun has giddied me a bit. I dare say your skipper has got a touch of the same thing. But gettin' the turtle won't delay you. I want tobacco badly. You can have as many turtle as you want for a couple of pounds o' tobacco."

"Right," said the mate—"that's dirt-cheap. Get 'em aboard as quick as you can. Let's have twenty."

The beachcomber laughed. "You don't know much about Pingelap turtle if you think a canoe would hold more than two together. We've got 'em here five hundredweight. You'll have to send a boat if you want that many. They're too heavy to bring off in canoes. But I'll go on ahead and tell the people to get 'em ready for you."

He got over the side into the canoe, and was paddled quickly ashore.

The mate went below to tell the skipper. He found him sitting at the cabin table with white face and shaking limbs, drinking Sydney rum.

"That beachcombing cove has gone ashore; but he says if you send a boat he'll give us twenty turtle for some tobacco. We want some fresh meat badly. Shall I lower the boat?"

An instantaneous change came over the skipper's features, and he sighed as if a heavy load was off his mind.

"Has he gone, Willis? . . . Oh, yes, we must have the turtle. Put a small twelve-pound case of tobacco in the whaleboat, and send half a dozen Sandwich Island natives with the second mate. Tell Barton to hurry back. We're in too close, and I must tow out a bit when the boat comes back—and I say, Willis, keep that beachcombing fellow on the main-deck if he comes aboard again. I don't like his looks, and don't want him down in the cabin on any account."

The second mate and his crew followed the white man and a crowd of natives to the pond where the turtle were kept. It was merely a huge pool in the reef, with a rough wall of coral slabs built round it to prevent the turtle escaping when the tides rose higher than usual.

"A real good idea—" began the second mate, when there was a lightning rush of the brown-skinned men upon him and his crew. At knocking a man down and tying him up securely your Caroline Islander is unmatched, he does it so artistically. I know this from experience.

"This is rather sudden, isn't it, Barton?" The beachcomber was speaking to him, looking into his eyes as he lay upon the ground. "You don't remember my face, do you? Perhaps my back would improve your memory. Ah, you brute, I can pay both you and that murderous dog of a Matson back now. I knew I should meet you both again some day."

Across the sullen features of the seaman there flashed a quick light—the gleam of a memory. But his time was brief. The beachcomber whispered to a native. A heavy stone was lashed to the second mate's chest. Then they dropped him over the wall into the pond. The native sailors they left where they lay.

And now ensued a hurried, whispered colloquy. The story of that day's work is not yet forgotten among the old hands of Ponape and Yap. Suffice it to say that by a cunningly contrived device the captain was led to believe that the second mate and his men had deserted, and sent the chief mate and six more of his crew to aid the natives in recapturing them. The presence of numbers of women and children walking unconcernedly about the beach made him assured that no treachery was intended. The mate and his men were captured in one of the houses, where they had been taken by the beachcomber for a drink. They were seized from behind and at once bound, but without any unnecessary rough usage.

"What's all this for?" said the mate unconcernedly to the white man. He was an old hand, and thought it meant a heavy ransom—or death.

The beachcomber was standing outside in the blazing sun, looking at the ship. There were a number of natives on board selling fish and young coconuts. The women and children still sauntered to and fro on the beach. He entered the house and answered the query.

"It means this; no harm to you and these six men here if you lie quiet and wait till I send for you to come aboard again. The other six Sandwich Islanders are alive but tied up. Barton is dead, I have settled my score with *him*."

"Ah," said the mate, after a brief outburst of blasphemy, "I see, you mean to cut off the ship."

"No, I don't. But I have an old debt to settle with the skipper. Keep quiet, or you'll follow Mr. Barton. And I don't want to kill you. I've got nothing against *you*."

Then the beachcomber, with some twenty natives, went to where the first six men were lying, and carried them down into the mate's boat.

"Here's the second mate's chaps, sir," said the carpenter to Matson; "the natives has 'em tied hand and foot, like pigs. But I don't see Barton among 'em."

"No," said the captain, "they wouldn't tie up a white man. He'll come off with Willis and the turtle. I never thought Barton would bolt."

The *ruse* succeeded admirably. The boatload of natives had hardly been ten seconds on deck ere the brigantine was captured. Matson, lashed in a sitting position to the quarter railing, saw the last man of the cutting-out party step on board, and a deadly fear seized him. For that last man was the beachcomber.

He walked aft and stood over him. "Come on board, Captain Thomas Matson," he said, mockingly saluting him. Then he stepped back and surveyed his prisoner.

"You look well, Matson. You know me now, don't you?"

The red, bloated face of the skipper patched and mottled, and his breath came in quick, short gasps of rage and terror.

"Ah, of course you do! It's only three years ago since that Sunday at Vaté in the New Hebrides, when you had me triced up and Barton peeled the hide off me in strips. You said I'd never forget it—*and I've come to tell you that you were right*. I haven't. It's been meat and drink to me to think that we might meet again."

He stopped. His white teeth glistened beneath the black-bearded lips in a low laugh—a laugh that chilled the soul of his listener.

A light air rippled the water and filled the sails, and the brigantine moved. The man went to the wheel and gave it a turn to port.

"Yes," he resumed, casting his eye aloft, "I'm delighted to have a talk with you, Matson. You will see that your crew are working the ship for me. You don't mind, do you, eh? And we can talk a bit, can't we?"

No answer came.

"None of the old hands left, I see, Matson—except Barton. Do you know where he is now? No? He's dead. I hadn't any particular grudge against him. He was only your flogger. But I killed him, and I'm going to kill you." He crossed his bare, sinewy arms on the wheel, and smiled again at the bound and terrified wretch.

"You've had new bulwarks and spars since, I see. Making money fast now, I suppose. I hope your mate is a good navigator, Matson. *He's* going to take this ship to Honolulu."

Then the fear-stricken man found his tongue, and a wild, gasping appeal for mercy broke from him.

"Don't murder me, Hollis. I've been a bad man all my life. For God's sake, let me off! I was a brute to you. I've got a wife and children. For Christ's sake—!"

The man sprang from the wheel and kicked him savagely in the mouth with his bare foot.

"Ha! you've done it now. 'For Christ's sake. For Christ's sake!' Don't you remember when *I* used those words: 'For Christ's sake, sir, hear me! I did not run away. I got lost coming from the place where we were cutting the sandalwood.'" A flicker of foam fell on his tawny hand. "You dog, you bloody-minded fiend! For three years I have waited . . . and I have you now."

A choking groan of terror came from Matson.

"Hollis! Spare me! . . . my children."

The man had gone back to the wheel, calm again. A brisk puff was rippling over the water from the westward. His seaman's eye glanced aloft, and the wheel again spun round. "Ready, about!" he called. The brigantine went and stood in again—to meet the mate's boat.

"Come this way, Mr. Willis. Captain Matson and I have been having a chat about old times. You don't know me, do you? Captain Matson is a little upset just now, so I'll tell you who I am. My name is Hollis. I was one of the hands of this ship. I am owner now. Funny, isn't it? Now, now; don't get excited, Mr. Willis, and look about you in that way. There isn't a ghost of a chance; I can tell you that. If you make one step towards me, you and every man Jack will get his throat cut. And as soon as I have finished my business with our friend here you'll be captain—and owner, too, if you like. By the by, what's the cargo worth?"

The mate told him.

"Ah, quite a nice little sum—two thousand pounds. Now, Mr. Willis, that will be practically yours. With only one other white man on board, you can take the vessel to Honolulu and sell both her and the cargo, and no questions asked. Hard on our friend here, though; isn't it?"

"Good God, man, what are you going to do to the captain—murder him?"

"For God's sake, Willis, help me!" The mute agony in the skipper's face, more than the spoken words, moved even the rough and brutal nature of the mate, and he opened his lips to speak.

"No!" said the man at the wheel; "you shall not help him. Look at this!"

He tossed aside the mantle of tangled hair that fell down his shoulders, and presented his scarred and hideous back to the mate.

"Now, listen to me, Mr. Willis. Go below and pass up as much tobacco and trade as will fill the small boat. I don't want plunder. But these natives of mine do."

In a few minutes the goods were hoisted up and lowered into the boat. Then the two six-pounders on the main-deck were run overboard, and all the small arms taken from the cabin by the natives.

"Call your men aft," the white man said to Willis. They came along the deck and stood behind him.

"Carry that man on to the main hatch."

He seized the fated man by the hair

Two of the strongest of the native sailors picked up the burly figure of the captain and laid him on the spot the beach-comber indicated and cut his bonds.

A dead silence. The tall, sun-baked figure of the muscular beachcomber, naked save for his grass girdle, seemed, as he stood at the wheel, the only animate thing on board. He raised his finger and beckoned to a sailor to come and steer. Then with quick strides he reached the hatch and stood in front of his prey.

"Captain Tom Matson. Look at, me well; and see what you have made me. Your time . . . and *mine* . . . at last."

He extended his hand. A native placed in it the hilt of a knife, short, broad-bladed, heavy and keen-edged.

"Ha! Can't you speak? Can't *you* say 'for Christ's sake'? Don't the words stick in your throat?"

The sinewy left hand darted out and seized the fated man by the hair, and then with a savage backward jerk bent back his head, and drew taut the skin of the coarse, thick throat. Then he raised the knife. . . .

He wiped the knife on his girdle, and looked in silence at the bubbling arterial stream that poured down over the hatch-coamings.

"You won't forget my name, will you?" he said to the mate. "Hollis; Hollis, of Sydney; they know me there; the man that was flogged at Vaté by him, *there*—and left ashore to die at Santo."

He glanced down at the limp, huddled-up mass at his feet, got into the boat, and with his naked associates, paddled ashore.

The breeze had freshened up, and as the brigantine slowly sailed past the crowded huts of the native village a hundred yards distant, the mate saw the beachcomber standing by his thatched house. He was watching the ship.

A young native girl came up to him with a wooden water-bowl, and stood waiting. With his eyes still fixed on the ship he thrust his reddened hands into the water, moved them slowly to and fro, then dried them on his girdle of grass.

Smith *Versus* Lichtensteiger

WESTON MARTYR

Smith stood five feet five inches in his boots, weighed nearly ten stone in his winter clothes and an overcoat, and he had a flat chest and a round stomach. Smith was a clerk in a small branch bank in East Anglia; he was not an athlete or a fighting man, although he followed the fortunes of a professional football team in the newspapers with great interest, and he had fought for a year in France without ever seeing his enemy or achieving a closer proximity to him than one hundred and twenty yards. When a piece of shrapnel reduced his fighting efficiency by abolishing the biceps of one arm, Smith departed from the field of battle and (as he himself would certainly have put it) "in due course" returned to his branch bank.

For forty-nine weeks each year Smith laboured faithfully at his desk. In his free hours during the winter he read Joseph Conrad, Stevenson, and E. F. Knight; he did hardly anything else. But every year in early April, Smith suddenly came to life. For he was a yachtsman, and he owned a tiny yacht which he called the *Kate* and loved with a great love. The spring evenings he spent fitting out, painting and fussing over his boat. Thereafter, as early as possible every Saturday afternoon, he set sail and cruised alone amongst the tides and sandbanks of the Thames Estuary, returning again as late as possible on Sunday night. And every summer, when his three weeks' holiday came round, Smith and his *Kate* would sail away from East Anglia together and voyage afar. One year Smith cruised to Falmouth in the West Countree, and he likes to boast about that cruise still. Once he set out for Cherbourg, which is a port in foreign parts; but that time, thanks to a westerly gale, he got no farther than Dover. The year Smith encountered Lichtensteiger he had sailed as far east as Flushing, and he was on his way back when a spell of bad weather and head winds drove him into Ostend and detained him there three days.

Lichtensteiger was also detained at Ostend; but not by the weather. Lichtensteiger had come from Alexandria, with a rubber tube stuffed full of morphine wound round his waist next to his skin, and he was anxious to get to London as quickly as he could. He had already been as far as Dover, but there a Customs official (who had suspicions but no proof) whispered to a friend in the Immigration Department, and Lichtensteiger found himself debarred as an "undesirable alien" from entering the United Kingdom. He had therefore returned to Ostend in the steamer in which he had left that place.

Lichtensteiger stood six feet one inch in his socks, weighed fourteen stone stripped, and he had a round chest and a flat stomach. He was as strong as a gorilla, as quick in action as a mongoose, and he had never done an honest day's work in his life. There is reason to believe that Lichtensteiger was a Swiss, as he spoke Switzer-Deutsch, which is something only a German-Swiss can do. His nationality, however, is by no means certain, because he looked like a Lombard, carried Rumanian and Austrian passports, and in addition to the various dialects used in those two countries, he spoke French like a Marseillais, German like a Würtemberger, and English like a native of the lower West-side of New York.

When Smith and Lichtensteiger first set eyes on each other, Smith was sitting in the *Kate's* tiny cockpit, smoking his pipe and worrying about the weather. For Smith's holiday was nearly over; he was due at his bank again in three days, and he knew he could not hope to sail back while the strong northwesterly wind continued to blow straight from East Anglia towards Belgium. Said Smith to himself, "Hang it! I've got to sail to-morrow or get into a nasty fix. And if only I had two sound arms I *would* sail to-morrow and chance it; but a hundred-mile beat to wind'ard all by myself is going to be no joke. What I need is another man to help me; but there isn't an earthly hope of getting hold of any one in this filthy hole."

Lichtensteiger was walking along the quay. He glanced at the *Kate* and her owner with a disdainful eye and passed on, because neither the boat nor the man held any interest for him. But in Lichtensteiger's card-index-like mind, in which he filed without conscious effort most of the things he heard and saw, there were registered three impressions and one deduction: "A yacht. The British flag. An Englishman. A fool." Having filed these particulars, Lichtensteiger's mind was about to pass on to the problem of how to get Lichtensteiger to London, when an idea flashed like a blaze of light into his consciousness. To translate Lichtensteiger's multi-lingual thoughts is difficult; a free rendering of them must suffice. Said Lichtensteiger to himself, "Thunder and lightning. Species of a goose. You poor fish. Of course. It is *that*! If *you* had a yacht—if *you* were a sailor—*there* is the obvious solution. Then there no more need would be to risk placing oneself in the talons of the sacred bureaucrats of Customs or within the despicable jurisdiction of blood-sucking immigration officials. Why, say! If I had a little boat I guess I wouldn't worry myself about smuggling my dope through no Dovers and suchlike places. With a boat of my own then veritably would I be a smuggler classical and complete. But what's the use! I ain't got no boat and I ain't no sailor. But hold! Attention! The English yacht. That fool Englishman. There are possibilities in that direction there. Yes. I guess I go back and take another look at that guy."

Lichtensteiger's second survey of Smith was detailed and thorough, and it confirmed his previous judgment. "Easy meat," said Lichtensteiger to himself, and then, aloud, "Evening, stranger. Pardon me, but I see you're British, and I guess it'll sound good to me to hear some one talk like a Christian for a change. I'm from New York, and Otis T. Merritt's my name. I'm over this side on vacation; but I'll tell you the truth, I don't cotton to these darned Dagoes and Squareheads here, not at all. So I reckon to catch the next boat across to your good country, mister, and spend the balance of my trip there with white men. That's a peach of a little yacht you got. I'll say she certainly is. She's a pippin, and I guess you have a number one first-class time sailing around in her. It's just the kind of game I've always had in mind to try for myself. It 'd suit me down to the ground, I reckon. If you've no objections, I'll step aboard. I'd sure like to look her over. Where are you sailing to next after here?"

"Harwich," answered Smith. "Come aboard and look round if you like, by all means; but I'm afraid you won't find very much to see here."

"Why, she's the finest little ship I ever set eyes on," cried Lichtensteiger a few minutes later, settling himself on the cabin settee. "And to think you run her all alone. My gracious! Have a cigar?"

"Thanks," said Smith. "I do sail her by myself usually, but this time I'm afraid I've bitten off more than I can chew. You see, I've got to get back to Harwich within three days. If I had another man to help me I'd do it easily, but with this wind blowing it's a bit more than I care to tackle alone."

After that, of course, it was easy for Lichtensteiger. He did not ask Smith if he could sail with him; he led Smith on to make that suggestion himself. Then he hesitated awhile at the unexpectedness of the proposal, and when he finally yielded to persuasion, he left Smith with the impression that he was doing him a favour. It was very beautifully done.

That night Lichtensteiger transferred himself and two suitcases from his hotel and slept aboard the *Kate*. At daybreak next morning they sailed. Once outside the harbour entrance Smith found the wind had fallen to a moderate breeze, but it still blew out of the north-west, making the shaping of a direct course to Harwich impossible. Smith, therefore, did the best he could. He put the *Kate* on the starboard tack and sailed her to the westward along the Belgian coast.

It did not take Smith long to discover that Lichtensteiger was no sailor. He could not steer or even make fast a rope securely. In half an hour it became clear to Smith that Lichtensteiger literally did not know one end of the boat from the other, and within an hour he realised that his passenger, instead of helping him, was going to be a hindrance and an infernal nuisance as well. Lichtensteiger did all those things which must on no account be done if life is to be made livable in the confined space aboard a small boat. In addition to other crimes, Lichtensteiger grumbled at the motion, the hardness of the bunks and the lack of head-room in the cabin. He left his clothes scattered all over the yacht, he used the deck as a spittoon, and he sprawled at ease in the cockpit, so that every time Smith had to move in a hurry he tripped over Lichtensteiger's legs. By midday Smith had had as much of Lichtensteiger's company as he felt he could stand. Now that the weather was fine and looked like remaining so, he knew he could easily sail the *Kate* home by himself. He said, "Look here, Merrit; I'm afraid you don't find yachting in such a small boat is as much fun as you thought it was going to be. See those buildings sticking up on the shore there? Well, that's Dunkerque, and I'll sail in and land you, and then you can catch the night boat over to Tilbury nice and comfortably. I'll run you in there in half an hour."

Smith's suggestion astounded Lichtensteiger, and produced in him so profound an alarm that he forgot for a moment that he was Merritt. His eyes blazed, the colour vanished from his face, and tiny beads of sweat hopped out upon it. Then Lichtensteiger emitted some most extraordinary sounds which, had Smith but known it, were Switzer-Deutsch curses of a horrid and disgusting kind, coupled with an emphatic and blasphemous assertion that nothing, not even ten thousand flaming blue devils, could force him to set foot upon the suppurating soil of France. In fairness to Lichtensteiger it must be stated that he very rarely forgot himself, or any part he might happen to be playing, and it was also always difficult to frighten him. But the toughest ruffian may be, perhaps, excused if he shrinks from venturing into a country which he has betrayed in time of war. And this is what Lichtensteiger had done to France, or, more precisely, he had twice double-crossed the French Army Intelligence Department; Section Counter-Espionage, and Sub-section N.C.D. And the penalty for doing this, as Lichtensteiger well knew, is death. Since 1916, when Lichtensteiger succeeded in escaping from that country by the skin of his teeth, France was a place which he had taken the most sedulous pains to avoid, and at the sudden prospect of being landed there he lost his grip of himself for fifteen seconds. Then he pulled himself together and grinned at Smith and said, "Dunkerque nix! Nothing doing. I guess not. And don't you make any mistake, brother; I think this yachting stuff's just great. I'm getting a whale of a kick out of it. So we'll keep on a-going for Harwich. Sure, we will. You bet. And no Dunkerque. No, sir. No Dunkerque for mine. Forget it."

Smith said, "Oh! All right," and that was all he said. But he was thinking hard. He thought, "By God! That was queer. That was *damned* queer. The fellow was scared to death. Yes—to *death*! For I'll swear nothing else could make a man look like that so suddenly. He turned absolutely green. And he sweated. And his eyes. . . he was terrified. He yammered, panicked, and babbled—in German, too, by the sound of it. By gosh! I wonder who he is? *And what it is he's been up to?* Something damnable, by the look of it. And whatever it was, he did it in Dunkerque—or in France, anyway. That's plain. To look like that at the mere thought of landing in France! My God, he might be a murderer, or anything. Cleared out into Belgium and hanging about, waiting his chance to get away probably. And here I am, helping him to escape. Oh Lord, what a fool I was to let him come. I actually *asked* him to come. Or did I? Yes, I did; but it seems to me now, with *this* to open my eyes, that he meant to come all the time. He did! He led me on to ask him. I can see it all now. He's a clever crafty devil—and he's twice my size! Oh, hang it all. This is *nasty*."

Smith was so absorbed by his thoughts that he did not notice the change of wind coming. The *Kate* heeled suddenly to the puff, her sheets strained and creaked, and she began to string a wake of bubbles and foam behind her. "Hallo," said Smith, "wind's shifted and come more out of the north. We'll be able to lay our course a little better now; she's heading up as high as nor'-west. I'll just see where that course takes us to if you'll bring up the chart."

Lichtensteiger brought the chart from the cabin table, and Smith spread it out upon the deck. "Not so good," said he, after gazing at it for a while. "We can't fetch within forty miles of Harwich on this tack. A nor'-west course only just clears the Goodwins and the North Foreland. Look."

"Then why don't you point the boat straight for Harwich," said Lichtensteiger, "instead of going way off to the left like that?"

"Because this isn't a steamer, and we can't sail against the wind. But we'll get to Harwich all right, although if this wind holds we won't be there before to-morrow night."

"To-morrow night," said Lichtensteiger. "Well, that suits me. What sort of a kind of a place is this Harwich, anyway? Walk ashore there, I suppose, as soon as we get in, without any messing about?"

"Oh, yes. But we'll have to wait till the morning probably, for the Customs to come off and pass us."

"Customs!" said Lichtensteiger. "Customs! I thought—you'd think, in a one-hole dorp like Harwich, there wouldn't be no Customs and all that stuff. And anyways, you don't mean to tell me the Customs'll worry about a little bit of a boat like this?"

"Oh, yes, they will," Smith answered. "Harwich isn't the hole you seem to think it is. It's a big port. We're arriving from foreign, and if we went ashore before the Customs and harbour-master and so on passed us there'd be the very devil of a row."

"Well, crying out loud!" said Lichtensteiger. "What a hell of a country. Not that the blamed Customs worry me any; but—well, what about all this Free Trade racket you Britishers blow about? Seems to me, with your damned Customs and immigration sharps and passports an' God knows what all, you've got Great Britain tied up a blame sight tighter than the United States." Saying which, Lichtensteiger spat viciously upon the deck and went below to think things over.

Before Lichtensteiger finished his thinking the sun had set, and when he came on deck again, with his plan of action decided upon, it was night. Said he, "Gee! It's black. Say, how d'you know where you're going to when you can't see? And where the hell are we now, anyway?"

"A mile or so nor'-west of the Sandettie Bank."

"That don't mean nothing to me. Where is this Sandettie place?"

"It's about twenty miles from Ramsgate one way and eighteen from Calais the other."

"Twenty miles from Ramsgate?" said Lichtensteiger. "Well, listen here, brother. I guess I've kind of weakened on this Harwich idea. It's too far, and it's going to take too long getting there. And I find this yachting game ain't all it's cracked up to be by a long sight. To tell you the truth, without any more flim-flam, I'm fed right up to the gills with this, and the sooner you get me ashore and out of it the better. See? Twenty miles ain't far, and I reckon Ramsgate, or anywhere around that way, will do me fine. Get me? Now you point her for Ramsgate right away and let's get a move on."

"But, I say—look here!" protested Smith. "I don't want to go to Ramsgate. I mean, I've got to get back to Harwich by to-morrow night, and if we put into Ramsgate I'll lose hours and hours. We can't get there till after midnight, and you won't be able to land before daylight at the very earliest, because the Customs won't pass us till then. And. . . ."

"Oh, hell!" broke in Lichtensteiger. "Customs at Ramsgate, too, are there? Well, say, that's all right. I'll tell you what we'll do. We won't trouble no flaming Customs—and save time that way. You land me on the beach, somewheres outside the town, where it's quiet and there's no one likely to be around. I'll be all right then. I'll hump my suitcases into this Ramsgate place and catch the first train to London in the morning. That'll suit me down to the ground."

"But, look here! I can't do that," said Smith.

"What d'you mean, you can't? You can. What's stopping you?"

"Well, if you will have it, Merritt," answered Smith, "I'll tell you straight, I don't like being a party to landing a man—any man—in the way you want me to. It's illegal. I might get into trouble over it, and I can't afford to get into trouble. If they heard in the bank I'd lose my job. I'd be ruined. I'm sorry, but I can't risk it. Why, if we got caught they might put us in prison!"

"Caught! You poor fish," said Lichtensteiger. "How can you get caught! All you've got to do is to put me ashore in the dark in that little boat we're pulling behind us, and then you vamoose and go to Harwich—or hell if you like. I'll be damned if I care. And you can take it from me, now, brother, you've got to put me ashore whether you like it or not. And if you don't like it, I'm going to turn to right here and make you. See? All this darned shinanyking makes me tired. I'm through with it and it's time you tumbled to who's boss here—you one-armed, mutt-faced, sawn-off little son of a b. . . you. You steer this boat for Ramsgate, *now*, pronto, and land me like I said, or by Gor, I'll scrape that fool face off the front of your silly head and smear the rest of you all over the boat. So—jump to it! Let's see some action, quick!"

If Smith had not been born and bred in the midst of a habitually peaceful and law-abiding community, he might perhaps have understood that Lichtensteiger meant to do what he said. But

Smith had never encountered a really *bad* and utterly unscrupulous human being in all his life before. In spite of the feeble imitations of the breed which he had seen inside the cinemas, Smith did not believe in such things as human wolves. It is even doubtful if Smith had ever envisaged himself as being involved in fight by the Marquis of Queensberry's rules. It is a fact that Smith would never have dreamed of kicking a man when he was down or of hitting any one below the belt, and he made, the mistake of believing that Lichtensteiger must, after all, be more or less like himself. Smith believed that Lichtensteiger's threats, though alarming, were not to be taken seriously. He therefore said, "Here! I say! You can't say things like that, you know. This is my boat and I won't. . . "

But Smith did not get any further. Lichtensteiger interrupted him. He drove his heel with all his might into Smith's stomach, and Smith doubled up with a grunt and dropped on the cockpit floor. Lichtensteiger then kicked him in the back and the mouth, spat in his face and stamped on him. When Smith came to he heard Lichtensteiger saying, "You'll be wise, my buck, to get on to the fact that I took pains, that time, not to hurt you. Next time, though, I reckon to beat you up good. So—cut out the grunting and all that sob-stuff and let's hear if you're going to do what I say. Let's hear from you. Or do you want another little dose? Pipe up, you. . . "

Smith vomited. When he could speak, he said, "I can't. . . Ah, God! Don't kick me again. I'll do it. I'll do what you want. But—I can't—get up. Wait—and I'll do it—if I can. I think my back's—broken."

Smith lay still and gasped, until his breath and his wits returned to him. He explored his hurts with his fingers gingerly, and then he sat up and nursed his battered face in his hands. He was thinking. He was shocked and amazed at Lichtensteiger's strength and brutal ferocity, and he knew that, for the moment, he dare do nothing which might tempt Lichtensteiger to attack him again. Smith was sorely hurt and frightened, but he was not daunted. And deep down in the soul of that under-sized bank clerk there smouldered a resolute and desperate determination to have his revenge. Presently he said, "Better now. But it hurts me to move. Bring up the chart from the cabin. I'll find out a quiet place to land you and see what course to steer."

Lichtensteiger laughed. "That's right, my son," said he. "Pity you didn't see a light a bit sooner, and you'd have saved yourself a whole heap of grief." He brought the chart and Smith studied it carefully for some minutes. Then he put his finger on the coastline between Deal and Ramsgate and said, "There, that looks the best place. It's a stretch of open beach, with no houses shown anywhere near. It looks quiet and deserted enough on the chart. Look for yourself. Will that spot suit you?"

Lichtensteiger looked and grunted. He was no sailor, and that small-scale chart of the southern half of the North Sea did not convey very much to him. He said, "Huh! Guess that'll do. Nothing much doing around that way by the look of it. What's this black line running along here?"

"That's a road. I'll put you on the beach here, and you walk inland till you get to the road and then turn left. It's only two miles to Deal that way."

"Let her go then," said Lichtensteiger. "The sooner you get me ashore the sooner you'll get quit of me, which ought to please you some, I guess. And watch your step! I reckon you know enough now not to try and put anything over on me; but if you feel like playing any tricks—*look out*. If I have to start in on you again, my bucko, I'll tear you up in little bits."

"I'll play no tricks," replied Smith. "How can I? For my own sake, I can't risk you being caught. You're making me do this against my will, but nobody will believe that if they catch me doing it. I promise to do my best to land you where no one will see you. It shouldn't be hard. In four or five hours we'll be close to the land, and you'll see the lights of Ramsgate on one side and Deal on the other. In between there oughtn't to be many lights showing, and we'll run close inshore where it's darkest and anchor. Then I'll row you ashore in the dinghy, and after that it'll be up to you."

"Get on with it, then," said Lichtensteiger, and Smith trimmed the *Kate's* sails to the northerly wind and settled down to steer the compass course he had decided on. The yacht slipped through the darkness with scarcely a sound. Smith steered and said nothing, while Lichtensteiger looked at the scattered lights of the shipping which dotted the blackness around him and was silent too.

At the end of an hour Lichtensteiger yawned and stretched himself. "Beats me," he said, "how in hell you can tell where you're going to." And Smith said, "It's easy enough, when you know how."

At the end of the second hour Lichtensteiger said, "Gee, this is slow. Deader'n mud. How long now before we get there?" And Smith replied, "About three hours. Why don't you sleep. I'll wake you in time."

Lichtensteiger said, "Nothing doing. Don't you kid yourself. I'm keeping both eyes wide open, constant and regular. I've got 'em on you. Don't forget it either!"

Another hour went by before Lichtensteiger spoke again. He said, "What's that light in front there? The bright one that keeps on going in and out."

"Lighthouse," said Smith. "That's the South Foreland light. I'm steering for it. The lights of Deal will show up to the right of it presently, and then we'll pick out a dark patch of coast somewhere to the right of that again and I'll steer in for it."

By 2 A.M. the land was close ahead, a low black line looming against the lesser blackness of the sky. "Looks quiet enough here," said Lichtensteiger. "Just about right for our little job, I reckon. How about it?"

"Right," said Smith, sounding overside with the lead-line. "Four fathoms. We'll anchor here." He ran the *Kate* into the wind, lowered the jib and let go his anchor with a rattle and a splash.

"Cut out that flaming racket," hissed Lichtensteiger. "Trying to give the show away, are you, or what? You watch your step, damn you."

"You watch yours," said Smith, drawing the dinghy alongside. "Get in carefully or you'll upset."

"You get in first," replied Lichtensteiger. "Take hold of my two bags and then I'll get in after. And you want to take pains we don't upset. If we do, there'll be a nasty accident—to your neck! I guess I can wring it for you as quick under water as I can here. You watch out now and go slow. You haven't done with me yet, don't you kid yourself."

"No, not yet," said Smith. "I'll put you on shore all right. I'll promise that. It's all I can do under the circumstances; but, considering everything, I think it ought to be enough. I hope so, anyhow. Get in now and we'll go."

Smith rowed the dinghy towards the shore. Presently the boat grounded on the sand and Lichtensteiger jumped out. He looked around him for a while and listened intently; but, except for the sound of the little waves breaking and the distant lights of the town, there was nothing to be heard or seen. Then, "All right," said Lichtensteiger. And Smith said nothing. He pushed off from the beach and rowed away silently into the darkness.

Lichtensteiger laughed. He turned and walked inland with a suitcase in each hand. He felt the sand under his feet give way to shingle, the shingle to turf, and the turf to a hard road surface. Lichtensteiger laughed again. It amused him to think that the business of getting himself unnoticed into England should prove, after all, to be so ridiculously easy. He turned to the left and walked rapidly for half a mile before he came to a fork in the road and a signpost. It was too dark for him to see the sign; but he stacked his suitcases against the post and climbing on them struck a match. He read: "Calais—1 1/2."

A Cigar Cat

W. L. ALDEN

About forty years ago, said Captain Foster, settling himself comfortably in his arm-chair and taking a long pull at his pipe, I came across one of the curiousest chaps that ever I was shipmates with. I was before the mast in the old *Hendrick Hudson,* of the Black X line, and she was about the leakiest old tub sailing the Western ocean. This man I am speaking of came aboard about half an hour before we warped out of London Dock, clean and sober, which was an unusual thing in those days. He was a tall, lean, wiry fellow, with a shifty sort of look in his eye. He carried a big canvas bag of dunnage on his shoulder, and in one hand he had another bag that must have had some sort of frame inside of it, for it was pretty near square in shape. I was in the fo'c's'le when he came down and hove his bags into an empty bunk and sat down on my chest to rest a bit.

"What might you have in that there bag?" says I, in a friendly sort of way.

"I've got my best friend there," says the chap.

"Then," says I, "suppose we have the cork out of him before the other chaps notice it. I'm everlastingly thirsty this morning."

"My friend ain't no bloomin' bottle," says the fellow, "and he ain't no sort of use to a thirsty man. But if you want to see him, here goes."

With that he opened the bag and hauled out a tremendous big black cat, who licked his face, and then curled up in the bunk and went to sleep as sudden as if he had just come below after twenty-four hours on deck.

"That," says the man, "is an old shipmate of mine, and I never goes to sea without him. He's a cigar cat, that's what he is; and you'll see what he can do to make a man comfortable, if you keep dark about his being aboard, so that the old man and the mates don't get a sight of him."

"Well!" said I. "Having been to sea, man and boy, for twenty years, I've seen some queer things; but this is the first time I ever knew a sailorman to carry a cat with him, and the first time I ever heard of a cigar cat."

"Live and learn," says the chap. "That's what Elexander the Great here has done. There was a time when he didn't know no more about tobacco than a baby, and now he knows where to find cigars, and how to bring 'em to me on the quiet. You keep mum about Elexander, and if the old man or either of the mates smokes cigars you'll have one of them now and again, and then you'll understand what a cigar cat is."

Well, we went on deck, leaving Elexander in the bunk, and as there was a lot of work to do, I didn't see any more of him till we knocked off for supper. We'd chose watches by that time, and the fellow with the cat, whose name was Harry, was with me in the starboard watch. The men naturally noticed that there was a cat in Harry's bunk, but they didn't take any interest in him. Harry brought out a bottle and invited all hands to have a tot, and then asked them not to say anything about there being a cat in the fo'c's'le. He had a pleasant kind of way with him, and the bottle was pretty near full, so we all promised not to let it be known aft that we had a cat for'ard.

For the next three or four days Elexander kept himself below all day, and didn't show up on deck until dark, or pretty near it. Then he'd come up for a little fresh air, and would generally sit on the lee cathead and meditate for an hour or two. I reckoned that he chose the cathead on account of the name of it, and fancied that it was meant for his convenience. Later on in, the night he would take exercise by climbing up the forestay and having a little game with his tail in the foretop. He knew just as well as anybody that he wasn't to be seen by the officers, and he took such good precautions that not a soul outside of the fo'c's'le knew of his existence.

One evening, just after eight bells, when our side had gone below, Harry says to Elexander, "Now, old man, go and fetch me a cigar." The cat looked at him for a minute and then darted up the ladder out of the fo'c's'le and we didn't see him for the next ten minutes. I would have turned in before that time, but Harry whispered to me to wait and see what Elexander would do. Pretty soon back comes the cat, and, if you'll believe it, he carried a big cigar in his mouth—just such a one as the old man smoked. Harry took it, and patted the cat, and lighted the cigar. He took three or four pulls, and then passed it on to me, and so we smoked it turn and turn about, and it was prime.

"How on earth," says I, "did you ever learn that cat to steal cigars?"

"Never you mind," says Harry; "I done it, and that's all about it. Elexander has got a nose for cigars that no regular tobacconist ever dreamed of having. Put him aboard a ship where cigars are smoked, and he'll find out where they are kept, and he'll steal 'em, provided, of course, they ain't locked up or kept in a chest with a lid too heavy for him to lift. He's found out where the old man's cigars are, and unless he has the bad luck to get caught, he'll bring me a cigar every night till we sight Sandy Hook. I wouldn't go to sea without Elexander, not if you was to offer me double wages and all night below. The only fault with him is that his mouth ain't big enough to hold more than one cigar at a time. If he only had a mouth like the second mate, he'd bring me a dozen cigars a day—so long as the supply lasted."

Now, I'm telling you the cold truth when I tell you that Elexander brought Harry a cigar every night regular from that time on—that is to say, for the next three weeks or so. Nobody ever caught him on the quarter-deck during that time, and the officers never dreamed that there was a cat aboard. But one night, when we were coming up with the Banks, the old man caught a sight of Elexander bolting out of his room with a cigar in his mouth, and he called the steward and says to him: "Steward! What do you let the cat into my room for?"

"Cat, sah!" says the steward. "There ain't no sort nor description of cat aboard this vessel. Our cat fell overboard and was drownded just before we sailed, and I didn't have time to go ashore and get another."

"What do you mean by telling me that," says the old man, "when I see with my own eyes a black cat coming out of my room with a mouse, or something else, in his mouth?"

"Beggin' your pahdon, sah, all I can say is that there ain't no suspicion nor insinuation of a cat aboard here."

The steward was a nigger that was fond of using big words, but he always told the truth, except, of course, to passengers, and the captain couldn't very well help believing him. So he said no more about the cat, but went into his room, feeling considerable worried, as any man naturally would at seeing a black cat where he was sure that there wasn't any real cat. But he was a cool-headed man, was old Captain Barbour, and the next morning he made up his mind that he had seen a shadow and mistook it for a cat.

The next night Harry was sitting on the windlass, smoking one of the old man's cigars, which was a risky thing to do, for it wasn't dark yet, and there was always a chance that the old man might happen to come for'ard and catch him. Elexander was sitting alongside of Harry, rubbing his head against the man's leg and purring like a steam winch. All of a sudden Harry catches sight of the old man about amidships, coming for'ard with his usual quick step. Now, Harry didn't want to waste that cigar by heaving it overboard, for he had only smoked about half an inch of it. So he shoves it athwartship into Elexander's mouth and tells him to go below. But Elexander either didn't understand exactly what Harry said, or else he preferred to stop on deck; so he runs out on the cathead, and sits there as usual with the smoke curling up from the lighted end of the cigar.

"Where did that cat come from?" says the old man, as soon as he caught sight of Elexander.

"Cat, sir!" says Harry. "I haven't seen no cat aboard this ship."

"Do you mean to tell me," says the captain, "that there ain't a cat sitting at this identical minute on the port cathead?"

"Very sorry, sir," says Harry, who could be particular polite when he wanted to be, "I can't see no cat nowhere."

Just then the captain caught sight of the smoke curling up from Elexander's cigar, and that knocked him silly.

Harry said that the old man turned as white as a cotton skysail. He said to himself in a curious sort of way, as if he was talking in his sleep: "A cat, sitting up and smoking a cigar!—a cat smoking a cigar!—smoking a cigar!" And then he turned and went aft, walking as if his knees were sprung, and catching hold of the rail to steady himself. If ever a man was scared it was Captain Barbour, and it was probably the first time in his life that he really knew what it was to be scared all the way through.

The captain went up to the mate, who was on the quarter-deck, and says he, "Mr. Jones! If I don't live till we get into port, I want you to see my wife and break it to her easy."

"Why, what's the matter, sir?" says Jones. "You're all right, ain't you?"

"I've had an awful warning," says the old man. "What would you say if you'd been seeing cats when there wasn't a cat within a thousand miles?"

"I should say," says Jones, "that it was time for me to knock off rum, and go slow in future. But then you ain't much of a drinking man, and you can't have been seeing things."

"Mr. Jones," says the captain, solemnly, "I've seen a black cat twice since we sailed from London, and the last time that cat was sitting up and smoking a cigar—a cigar as big as the ones I smoke myself. Now, there ain't no cat aboard this ship; and there never was a cat since cats were first invented that smoked cigars. And what's more, as you say yourself, I ain't a man as drinks more than is good for him, especially when I'm at sea. That cat didn't mean drink. It meant something a sight worse; and I know, just as well as I stand here, that I'm not long for this world."

"You go below, sir, and try to sleep," said the mate. "And if I was you I'd overhaul the medicine chest, and take a good stiff dose of something."

"There's medicine for a lot of things in that chest," says the captain; "but there ain't no sort of medicine for black cats that sits up and smokes cigars. Salts and laudanum, and porous plasters wouldn't do me any good, not if I was to take them all at once. No, sir! I'm a doomed man, and that's all there is about it."

After the old man had gone aft Harry jumped up, and, being pretty mad at Elexander for stopping on deck after he had been told to go below, he lays hold of him by the tail and yanks him off the cathead and tosses him down the fo'c's'le ladder, giving him a few heavy cuffs over the head at the same time. Now, sir, I don't know if you are well acquainted with cats, but if you're not, I can tell you one curious thing about them. You can hit a cat, and hit him hard, and you can kick him clean across a room, and you can heave cold water on him, and if he judges that it's good policy for him to keep friends with you, he'll overlook it. But a cat always draws the line at his tail; he won't allow you to take the least liberty with his tail, and if you do he'll never forgive you. It hurts a cat's self-respect to have his tail meddled with, and a cat has a heap of self-respect.

Now, when Harry hauled Elexander off that cathead by his tail he made the biggest mistake of his life. Elexander couldn't have overlooked it with justice to himself, even if he had wanted to. When Harry went below there wasn't any Elexander in his bunk, and he couldn't find him nowhere. The next day he found him, but he found at the same time that Elexander wouldn't have anything to do with him. The cat had selected the boy Jim, who was in the port watch, for his new master, and he was snuggled up against him in his bunk, and letting on to be everlastingly fond of him. Harry tried to pick the cat up and take him over to his side of the fo'c's'le, but Elexander swore at him in a way that any second mate would have envied, and when Harry put a hand on him, he bit him clean to the bone. It was all over between Harry and Elexander, and after a while Harry gave up all hope of ever making up the quarrel.

Of course, Harry and me didn't have any more cigars. Elexander wouldn't have brought one to Harry not if there had been hundreds of cigars lying about the deck. Jim said that Elexander didn't bring him any, and he pretended to be astonished that Harry should think such a thing possible as that a cat should sneak cigars; but then Jim was an able liar, and what he said didn't convince either Harry or me. We watched Jim pretty close, but we couldn't catch him smoking anything but his pipe, and we watched Elexander, but we never saw him bringing any cigars for' ard. All the same, he brought them, and Jim, of course, had the benefit of them.

I noticed after a while that Jim got into a way of being missing some time in the course of the dog-watches, and Elexander was generally missing at the same time. Neither of them could be found in the fo'c's'le, and when I spoke of the matter to Harry he calculated that Jim had been sent for by the mate to clean out his room, the mate having a way of putting Jim at that job at all odd times.

But one day I saw a little whiff of smoke sailing up from the foretop, and I naturally thought that I had caught Jim out. So I went aloft, and when I got into the top there I found Jim, sure enough, with Elexander sleeping by the side of him. But Jim had his pipe in his hand, and there wasn't any sign of a cigar to be seen. He let on that he had come up there so as to have a quiet half-hour while he read over an old letter from his mother, and that was all I could get out of him.

One of the men—a chap from Nova Scotia, and a pretty mean one even at that—said one day that he had found Elexander alone in the foretop with the ashes of a cigar sprinkled around the place where he was lying. The chap said that he believed the cat smoked cigars, and another chap—an Irishman—who told the truth every now and then when he was feeling good and fit, said that he had seen Elexander more than once with a cigar in his mouth, though he had always calculated that it was the quality of the rum that he drank at his boarding-house in the Highway that made him see such a curious sight. Gradually it got round among the crew that the cat was a smoker, and they used to try him with pipes. Of course, Elexander wasn't going to come down to a pipe. He was a sight too aristocratic for that, but the men stuck to their theory that Elexander smoked cigars, and the wonder was where he got hold of them.

Captain Barbour had been feeling very low ever since he saw Elexander sitting on the cathead. He hardly ever swore at the men, and when he did it didn't seem to do him any real good. Once on a Sunday, when I was at the wheel, I saw him overhauling a prayer-book, and when a skipper comes to doing that it looks pretty bad for him. The captain had made up his mind that he had had a warning, and that he wouldn't live to see New York, and, of course, he didn't feel very cheerful at the prospect, partly because he wanted to see New York and his wife and the other captains of the Black X. line again, and partly because he hadn't the least idea where he would bring up if he slipped his cable.

One afternoon, in the first dog-watch, the old man, who had been walking the quarterdeck with the mate, suddenly stopped, and catching the mate by the arm said, "There's that cat again! He's sitting up in the foretop and smoking, just as he was doing the last time I saw him. This is the end of me, Mr. Jones."

The mate looked aloft and there he saw Elexander, sitting on the edge of the top and looking down around as if he was looking for a sail on the horizon. He didn't have any cigar in his mouth, but there wasn't the least doubt that smoke was drifting gently out of the top, there being just a breath of wind from the southward.

"I see him, sir," said the mate. "He's a sure enough cat, and if he's smoking I'll learn him what the regulations of this ship are." So saying the mate jumps into the rigging and runs up to the foretop in next to no time, he being an active man and a first-class sailor. The next thing was a yell from the foretop, and then we could see the mate holding Jim by the scruff of the neck and lecturing to him on the evils of smoking, there happening to be a rope's end in the top that was just the thing for lecturing purposes.

You never saw a happier man than Captain Barbour when the mate came down from aloft with Jim and introduced him to the old man as the real smoker. The captain cussed Jim as cheerful as ever he had cussed in his best days, and before he had got through he made the boy confess that the cat had been stealing cigars and bringing them for'ard. Jim swore that the cat never brought any to him and that they all went to Harry, who owned the cat and had trained him to sneak cigars, and he pretended that he had accidentally found one under a bunk in the fo'c's'le, and had gone into the top to smoke it on the quiet, thinking that it wouldn't be right to hand it over to Harry for fear of encouraging him and the cat in stealing cigars. Naturally nobody believed what Jim said, but, having already had his licking from the mate, the old man let him off with a cuff or two, and passed the word for Harry to come aft.

But he couldn't get anything out of Harry either. Harry swore that he had never laid eyes on the cat until four or five nights before, and that he never dreamed that Elexander stole cigars. "The cat belongs to that there boy Jim," said Harry, "and you can see for yourself, sir, that he won't have anything to say to me, if you call him aft."

The old man sent for Jim again and ordered him to bring the cat on to the quarter-deck, which Jim accordingly did, holding the cat in his arms and petting it while Elexander licked the boy's face. Harry went up to the cat and spoke to him fair and polite, but Elexander only swore at him and tried to hit him in the eye.

"You see, sir," said Harry, "how it is. Ain't it plain enough whose cat that is? As for me, I wouldn't allow no cat of no kind to come within a mile of me if I could help it. They're nasty, treacherous beasts, and I never see a cat yet who wasn't a thief."

Well, the upshot of it was that Jim got a first-class licking for lying about his cat, and another for training the cat to steal the old man's cigars, and he got thirty shillings stopped from his wages to pay for the cigars that Elexander had stole, and he was ordered to heave the cat overboard. He'd have done so then and there, but the mate being a sensible man, and as good a sailorman as ever trod a deck, sort of interceded for the cat, arguing that there was nothing in the world half so unlucky as drowning a cat. So the old man finally agreed that the cat should be put down in the run, with a pannikin of water, and told that unless he worked his passage by catching rats he might starve. And starve he did—not because there weren't plenty of rats in the run, but because Elexander was that aristocratic and high-toned that he made up his mind to starve sooner than turn to and work his passage. When we got to New York I saw the steward come on deck with the remains of a cat in his hand, and then I knew that Elexander wouldn't never steal anybody's cigars no more.

The Haven of Dead Ships

SYLVESTER BAXTER

The great brown patch of gulfweed had a strange look in the midst of the deep blue water. There was a certain effect of beauty in the golden tone that varied the dark mass, spreading in the sunlight. There was also something weird in its appearance. In the distance the illusion of solidity was complete.

I stood at the rail of *Fulda,* eastward bound, making the Mediterranean trip. All day we had been passing these brown patches with extraordinary frequency. I had often seen the stuff floating abundantly in the Gulf Stream, and had even picked it up on the beach at home. But I had never seen it spreading by the acre before. The ocean was dotted with it; off ahead, on the horizon, it had the effect of a long reach of very low coast.

One of the passengers came to the rail and stood near me, looking out pensively over the water. It was Mr. Hubert Manson, my neighbor at table, a youngish-looking man of middle age, pleasant-spoken, well informed, an agreeable member of the smoking-room company, responsive in conversation, though not talkative. He had the air of prosperous circumstances, and in voice and bearing there was the indescribable something that told of seafaring associations.

"We must be near the Sargasso Sea," I remarked.

"Nearer than I ever thought to be again," replied Mr. Manson. "We are on the verge of it. Something has brought it unusually far north."

"Some fluctuation in the ocean currents, I presume. I am glad to see something of it. This perpetual movement and accumulation of the gulfweed is strangely interesting. What a great crop of it there must be growing somewhere on the bed of the sea! Growing through the ages and harvested by the Gulf Stream; carried by the whirl of the currents and woven into a vast mid-Atlantic blanket for the ocean."

"And I was its prisoner once!"

My companion spoke earnestly; his voice had a shade of intensity, and his face looked very grave as he gazed on the sea.

I looked inquiringly, and he continued: "But I am indebted to it also, in a way. Very much indebted, in fact. The Sargasso Sea is a strange place to go for one's fortune, is it not? I did not seek it there. But I found it."

"May I ask you to tell me how?"

"Do you care for strange stories?"

"The stranger the better."

"Then you will care for this. Let us seat ourselves."

We brought our steamer-chairs together, and my companion proceeded: "At the time of which I speak, I was the master of the bark 'Carib,' bound from Mobile to Bordeaux with a load of Southern pine. It was in the winter, but we had nothing worse than the customary rough weather of the season until we were considerably beyond the Western islands—say about two hundred miles to the north-eastward of Flores. Then came one of those terrific North Atlantic northeasters. Early in the storm our rudder was carried away, and we were dismasted. Luckily the 'Carib' was a stanch, Mystic-built craft, still classing 'A No. 1,' and so long as she kept away from a lee shore we were safe, for with a load of lumber she could not sink. We were tossed to and fro, the wind shifting all round the compass and blowing great guns most of the time. At last, when it did clear, the storm had handed us over to the care of the trade-wind, and we found ourselves in latitude 36° north, longitude 28° 47' west. All the time we had not sighted a sail. We were drifting like a log, stripped of everything; not so much as a spare spar left for a jury-mast, nothing bigger than an oar or a boat-hook. Three boats were left—two long-boats and the gig. Three of the crew had been washed overboard.

"The storm over, the question was, what to do. The whole ship's company, myself excepted, were for taking to the boats and making for the Western islands. I favored staying aboard, for we were safer than in an open boat, and there was a chance we might be picked off, sooner or later. But the others objected to getting farther out of the track of navigation. I agreed to their going, but I determined to stand by the ship. Her hull was sound as a nut, she would float indefinitely, and I believed that some steamer would come across us. I wanted to save the ship for her owners, if there was any possibility. We had one passenger, a boy of seventeen, the son of the chief owner. He had overstudied and had been sent on a sea-voyage for his health. Walter Lawson was his name. He was a companionable youth, and though I made no effort to influence his choice, in my heart I was glad when he elected to remain with me.

"Alone on a craft that was practically a derelict, we drifted at the mercy of winds and currents. The days passed and the weeks passed. Not a sail appeared, though we took turns in watching, with anxious eyes, from dawn to dusk. Meanwhile the sluggish mid-ocean currents were carrying us to the more unfrequented parts of the Atlantic, and the chances for salvation, on which I had been counting, were growing remote. The changing winds had been urging us hither and yon, but the wide current that the Gulf Stream becomes in its deflection to the right, had been taking us steadily southward to trade-wind latitudes. So we found ourselves on the confines of the Sargasso Sea, the gulfweed daily floating more and more thickly about us. When the far-spreading patches appeared, Walter ran to me crying, in joyful excitement, 'Land! land!'

"But what he saw was the doom of our hopes. Day by day the gulfweed grew thicker and thicker; the floating fields closed together like ice-floes in the Arctic; the blue water shrank to devious channels like creeks meshing a salt marsh, and the brown expanses grew from acres into miles. The mocking semblance of terra firma closed us in; a tawny crust, spreading illimitably, had formed upon the free, liquid Atlantic. To the eye it seemed as if the time had come when there was no more sea—it had been replaced by an interminable prairie of mud flats; one might have fancied that the tropic sun had sucked the ocean dry, down to the primal ooze of the Atlantic's floor.

"Still we did not despair, though rescue seemed out of the question. With the buoyancy of boyhood, Walter looked for favoring fortune. In the long hours of those days together, not a little of his talk was given to castle-building; he would tell about his plans for the future, and he still seemed to count upon their realization as confidently as in the remote life at home—a life that to me began to seem dreamlike, as that of a former existence. Somehow I, too, was sanguine at heart. I felt very vividly the force of the proverb, 'While there's life there's hope.' The optimism of youth was mine, as well, for I was only twenty-four years old then. Therefore, though seafaring had matured me, in our unbroken companionship Walter and I were boys together.

" 'We are going to get out of this somehow, I am sure,' " said Walter. 'Perhaps we shall go drifting on and on to the westward until we strike the Windward islands.'

"I explained to him that the action of the currents in that part of the ocean was like that of water swirling round in a tub, and I illustrated it by throwing a lot of chips in a tub of water on the deck and keeping the water moving round in one direction, urging it at the edge with a flat stick. The chips gathered in a mass at the center. 'That is what causes the Sargasso Sea,' I said. 'The Gulf Stream carries the weed with it to the northward; then it sweeps it round in a southerly direction and swirls it toward the center, where it collects in great masses. Naturally the derelicts take a course similar to that of the gulfweed.'

"Walter's face fell, but it brightened as his curiosity was aroused. My description kindled his imagination. 'Then perhaps we shall see other derelicts making the same round as ourselves,' he exclaimed. 'And when we get to the center there ought to be a big fleet of them—like the fishermen on the Grand Banks!'

"Hardly so sociable as that, though,' I replied. 'The Atlantic is a big place, and even the center of the Sargasso must be reasonably spacious.'

"The spectacle conjured up by the boy's fancy struck me as a bit gruesome—a fleet of derelicts would look as uncanny as a company of specters in a midnight graveyard.

"Walter clung to the idea, and would often dwell on the looks of the various craft that he expected to find when we got to the center. Old water-logged schooners would probably be the most common, he said, and they would be lumber-laden, like ourselves; there would be some whalers, the oil in them keeping them afloat; and we should see ships of all sorts, abandoned steamers with broken shafts, and perhaps even some very old craft, like slavers and pirates—'long, low, black and rakish.' We little dreamed what in reality we should see.

"Physically we were comfortable. There was an abundance of provisions for the two of us. The water-casks were well filled, and we took care to spread a canvas on the deck when it rained, to maintain the supply. We were, moreover, not entirely dependent upon the stores for food; the gulfweed was a little world of animal life, for upon it and within it were myriads of diminutive crabs, and it also sheltered enormous numbers of small fish. Both crabs and fish were excellent—the former particularly delicate.

"Months and months went by. Alone it would have been intolerable; madness might have come with solitude so complete. But it seems remarkable how the two of us managed to make the best of the situation: we longed for relief with intensest longing, and still we were not unhappy any of that time. We busied ourselves in all possible ways; we made much of our meals, taking pains in their preparation and observing a certain formality at table; we kept our clothing in order and on Sundays we dressed with special care, observing the day with a simple little service. How strange it seemed, we two singing together under the great sky! Our vast isolation led us to discuss the great problems of existence, and Walter, naturally a thoughtful boy, matured in mind uncommonly fast.

"We did see some derelicts. We spied the first one at a considerable distance; we would have seen her long before but for her color, so much like that of the weed-strewn waste. The glass brought her near; she was all barnacles and rockweed, like a sea-washed ledge, and was a dismal sight with her three mast-stumps, her bulwarks gone, no sign of a name, and so soggy that her deck was but a foot or so above the water. She stayed in sight some days, the distance between us getting gradually greater, till one morning she was gone. We were not sorry.

"Another was a craft that had 'turned turtle,' the coppered bottom showing a smooth green; she was evidently a rather small schooner—probably a fisherman.

"There was not much variety in the appearance of the derelicts that we sighted; some were fresher-looking, and we made out the names of a few, recognizing three reported in the Hydrographic Office bulletins as seen at intervals in various parts of the Atlantic. It was usually many weeks from derelict to derelict. Had we been going at ordinary speed, instead of merely drifting, we should have encountered them fully as often as sails are seen on the great lanes of navigation in the North Atlantic.

"One morning Walter was first on deck, I following a moment later. Walter suddenly stood petrified. He pointed to the distance and gasped, 'What is that?' And his lips blanched, a mottled pallor underspreading the healthy brown of his cheeks.

"It was, indeed, an object so strange that I could scarcely credit my eyes, and I ran for the glass to see if it could actually be what it seemed. I gazed long, Walter standing eager for my report. Finally I handed him the glass. 'The most unearthly sight I ever saw,' I said.

" 'Can it be this sea is haunted?' asked the boy.

" 'The *Flying Dutchman* gone to seed, it looks like,' I exclaimed.

"Outside of a picture I had never seen a craft like that. This vessel was much like the *Santa Maria*, only far bigger; she had the same high poop and the same sort of rich carved work about her stern, though there were no traces of paint or gilding. She showed gray and phantom-like in the early morning sunshine—the same kind of soft, weather-beaten gray you see on the old carved woodwork of temples in Japan. She was dismasted, and the hull loomed so, with the clumsy big stern and queer high house, as to give her the effect of enormous size. An extraordinary circumstance was that there was no sign of barnacle or rockweed about her.

"All day our eyes were fixed upon her, and all the next day, and the next, for she remained in sight and kept getting gradually nearer. We marveled and speculated, but the fourth day found her so near that we determined to solve the riddle. We got the gig into the water and set out toward the mysterious stranger. Our enterprise was favored by the peculiar circumstance that when the wind is blowing in the Sargasso Sea it has the effect of dividing the great fields of gulfweed as by furrows, with long lanes of water at frequent intervals. The antique craft lay to windward, and was drifting toward us very slowly, standing so high out of the water that the wind carried her along at a faster rate than it impelled the *Carib*. The distance between us was therefore gradually lessening. We rowed along one of these water lanes for about a mile, coming abreast of the curious vessel hardly a stone's-throw away. She was drifting stern foremost, of course, with that high poop catching the wind; and we saw that she was rudderless like ourselves. As we came nearer, we made out the name, carved on her stern, *Reyna del Cielo.* She was a Spanish galleon!

"When we clambered to her deck we looked about us with a feeling of awe, half expecting to encounter a ghostly crew in ancient garb. All was silent between the high bulwarks. The hue of everything was the same weather-beaten gray as without. There was no trace of rigging or ropes, and the three mast-stumps were weather-worn and rounded where they had been broken. There was not a sign of decay; the deck was singularly sound and well preserved, and the timbers everywhere had the look of healthy wood. I could have believed that some magic spell had been wrought upon the ship.

"The cabin opened directly upon the deck, and the closed door easily swung inward at our touch. The room was large and stately, wainscoting and ceiling were beautifully carved, and the wood was black with age, like old oak. At the end of the cabin was a shrine with an image of the Virgin. A handsome table stood in the center. Here, in a drawer, I found a large book, with entries in a graceful Castilian hand filling its pages. It proved to be the ship's log. I had been in the South American trade and had made a study of Spanish, and so I had little trouble in making out the record that had been entered nearly two hundred years before. For it appeared that the *Reyna del Cielo*—the 'Queen of Heaven'—had been one of a fleet that had sailed from Vera Cruz, bound for Cadiz, on December 17, 1690, with a strong convoy of warships. She was commanded by Capt. Antonio de Guerras y Sandival, and carried a cargo of Mexican products, together with spices, gums, silks and other Oriental goods, brought from the Philippines across the Pacific to Acapulco, thence by pack-mules overland by way of Cuernavaca, Mexico City and Puebla to Vera Cruz. She also carried an exceptionally valuable treasure—gold from Honduras, silver from the mines of Mexico. The *Reyna del Cielo* having been the largest and fastest of the fleet, the greater part of the bullion had been intrusted to her. The good captain had set forth this fact with considerable circumstance and with evident pride.

"They had taken sixteen passengers from Vera Cruz—among them five friars and an abbot returning from the Philippines. Stopping at Havana, they had added a considerable consignment of tobacco to their cargo, and eleven more passengers had joined them. The second day out from Havana the fleet was attacked by a squadron of buccaneers; there was a sharp battle; two of the attacking craft were destroyed by the warships and one was captured; the buccaneers got away with two of the galleons. For three weeks there was no further mishap, no occurrence to warrant more than monotonous recordings of daily happenings. Then a great storm arose; the fleet was scattered; when the wind fell the *Reyna del Cielo* was lying dismasted. For ten days they drifted. Then the record stopped in the midst of an entry—an uncompleted sentence, an unfinished word.

"What could have happened? That will always remain one of many mysteries of the deep. Possibly a cry of 'Sail ho!' may have startled the captain from his log and sent him in haste to the deck. The ship must have been suddenly abandoned, it would seem. But, in case of a rescue, why was the treasure left?

"Was it left? The thought occurred to us simultaneously. I had translated to Walter as I read. When I stopped at the broken word marking the un-ended end, I looked questioningly in the boy's face. His eyes were sparkling. He spoke the words he read in mine: 'The treasure!'

"'What use is it?' I asked.

"'What was the use of our boarding this craft?' he retorted. 'It would be curious to see.'

"In truth, I was as eager to look for it as he. I knew that in the galleons the treasure-hold was beneath the cabin. A glance showed us that the hatch was underneath the table, strongly barred and padlocked, both bar and padlock made of bronze. In the drawer where we found the log was a large key, also of bronze. This proved to be what we wanted.

"When we raised the hatch, the hold was not empty. The space was half filled with orderly stacks of metallic bars that glimmered dull and whitish in the dim light that streamed into the cabin from the open door. We leaped down and groped about us. The weight of a bar, as I lifted it, left no doubt of the metal's nature.

"'Here are some smaller bars!' called Walter from the darkness of a far corner. 'Gracious! Aren't they heavy!' he added, as he reached one out to me. I held it toward the light and recognized the yellowness that gladdens greedy eyes.

"When we came out into the bright sunshine of the galleon's deck, I said: 'There is no doubt of the fortune we have in there. But what good can it do us?'

"'As much good as their fortunes do to many men that own them,' the boy answered. 'It is ours. We can say that now. And we are still alive.'

"But to me the worthlessness of possession never appeared so complete as at that moment, and I felt a sinking at my heart. 'We might as well be in heaven for all the worth it has for us,' I said, and I laughed in bitter fashion.

"The next moment the gate of heaven itself seemed to open before me. I saw Walter give a casual glance to the westward over the tawny expanse; suddenly his eyes dilated, amazement in their gaze, and a wave of joy unutterable came over his face. 'Look! look! look!' he cried.

"We had seen a smoke-pennant, faint and far, but black against the silvered blue of the horizon!

"Then a great fear came into Walter's face. 'We can see only the smoke, faint in the distance,' he said. 'The steamer is still hull down. So they cannot sight us yet. They may never see us. Perhaps there is clear water off there; indeed, there must be, for how could she make headway through all this stuff?'

"'Clear water or not, somehow she is coming this way,' I said. I had grown hopeful, for I had seen that the dark smoke-pennant was growing larger and plainer. 'Rescue is sure,' I added.

"We watched long and long, unmoving, and heeded not the hours that passed. The steamer drew nearer and nearer; we made out the masts and yards, the smokestack, and at last the white hull, gleaming on the brown level like a very star to our eyes. 'If we only had the glass here,' I said, looking toward the *Carib*.

"'We might row over and get it,' suggested Walter.

"'No; let us make sure we are found here. There is a reason, you know.'

"'I understand,' he responded.

"The steamer came up, not swiftly, but at a fairish pace, and I marveled how it was that she could be making her way through the weed. It was soon evident that they had sighted the *Reyna del Cielo;* we could see the black speck of the lookout at the masthead, and then we noted that the shrouds were swarming with men, manifestly staring with all their eyes at the ancient ship before them. As the steamer got near, I could see that her sharp bow was cutting through the gulfweed like a razor, and next I noted that there was no kicking of the water astern. She was a sizable steamer; her build yacht-like. *Penetrator* was the name on her quarter.

"At last she was close at hand. Obedient to our pantomime, she drew slowly alongside. A rope was thrown us, and the oldest ship afloat was soon made fast to the newest sort of steamer.

"There was a chorus of ejaculation from marveling mouths, but we kept silent until addressed by a man who proved to be the owner of the yacht—for such she turned out to be. He was a young man with an alert look that contrasted with the somewhat indolent quality of his voice. 'We shall be exceedingly happy to have you come aboard,' I said, most courteously, but with a very eager and indescribably joyous tone.

"'I'm relieved to find that it is English you speak,' he replied. 'When I saw there was life aboard, I began to brush the cobwebs off my Spanish; I was expecting to find the Almirante of the Sargasso squadron; some Castilian Barbarossa, or Rip Van Winkle of the sea.' Glancing about him as he stepped on the galleon's deck, he continued: 'But what is the meaning of this most extraordinary encounter? Are you sure you are not adrift on a piece of shipwrecked grand-opera scenery?'

"We related our adventures while sitting at the well-spread table of the *Penetrator*. In return we learned how and why it was that that remarkable craft—for the *Penetrator* was unique among steamers—had come into that desert sea. It appeared that her owner, Mr. Rupert Legage, was a wealthy New Yorker whose passion for geographical knowledge and theoretical taste for exploration were restrained by an exceptional regard for his personal comfort.

"'If it weren't for that, I'd make my mark as a discoverer,' he said, one day, to his old college chum, Dr. Felix Casterman, who had ransacked a goodly part of North America in his botanical quests and now was of the company about us, making the voyage with his friend for the sake of studying the marine flora of the Sargasso Sea. It was the doctor who told us this.

"'But it's so deuced uncomfortable, you know,' Legage had said to him. 'I've been everywhere that a Pullman can go, and in every port where a good steam yacht can take me. Polar expeditions are altogether too common, even if I didn't have a most decided objection to cold weather. Central Africa, or Central South America, would suit me better; but there again are the insects, the snakes, and other undesirable manifestations of a superabundant fauna.'

"His friend told him he had just the idea for him—a voyage of discovery, that he might undertake in perfect comfort, to a vast and unexplored portion of the earth's surface that yet awaited its Columbus, although Columbus himself had seen its borders. In short, it was the Sargasso Sea. The notion struck Legage's fancy. But both sailing vessels and steamers had always shunned that part of the ocean, practically impenetrable as it was. How could they penetrate its midst when either paddle wheels or screw would be hopelessly clogged by the tangle of gulfweed?

"The ingenious doctor had thought it all out, and he described a new form of steamer that he had in mind. It would be impelled by a pair of 'pushers,' as he called them—two huge cylindrical pistons, or plungers, thrust with great power out behind, under the stern, and working in rapid alternation. The ends, several feet in diameter, disk-like and slightly concaved, would strike the water with such an impact as to send the craft ahead with corresponding force. By no possibility could any entangling substance check the action of a propeller like that.

"This talk resulted in the building of the *Penetrator*. The novel scheme was a complete success. Not only was there no interference with the pushing of the propellers, but her passage through the gulfweed was still further facilitated by the peculiar construction of her stem with a sharpened knife-edge of tempered bronze. Thus did the *Penetrator* cut her way so smoothly into the Sargasso, as we had seen. Legage spared no expense in fitting out his expedition in the most complete style. His well-organized scientific staff had been rewarded by many interesting discoveries, and he himself had made out a descriptive list of an amazing number of derelicts that they had encountered. Some of these unfortunate craft had extraordinary histories. However, the crowning achievement in this line, and, indeed, of the whole expedition, was the finding of the *Reyna del Cielo*.

"What puzzled everybody was the existence of the ancient galleon in mid-ocean for nearly two centuries. There were, to be sure, some vessels that had been afloat for over a hundred years and were still in service. But they had been repaired and reconstructed; a ship abandoned to the elements would naturally long since have rotted away or been devoured by the worms. The chemist of the expedition, Professor Ilmenholtz, surmised that there must have been some element in the cargo that had exerted a preservative effect on the galleon's hull. This was corroborated by the examination instituted the next morning. The hatches were found to be tightly sealed. When they were opened, a rich odor, powerful almost to suffocation, came pouring up. Bales and boxes in admirable preservation filled the hold. These contained splendid silks, superb brocades, beautiful porcelains, quantities of spices—and that evening we all smoked some of the oldest Havana tobacco that ever was known.

"There were also in the cargo many bags filled with a curious sort of powder, yellowish, resinous and strangely fragrant. Dr. Ilmenholtz pronounced this to be a residuum of a peculiar sort of gum that in those days was extensively imported from the islands of the Pacific. Time had gradually volatilized the essential oils from this gum, he said; and analyses of pieces of the wood taken from all parts of the vessel confirmed his inference that the subtile vapors had gradually penetrated the wood, and had produced the same results as the modern creosoting process, acting as a perfect preservative.

"The treasure was removed to the *Penetrator* the first thing. Mr. Legage insisted on waiving all claim to salvage, but he permitted us to remember officers and crew, and likewise his corps of scientists, with what amounted to a very handsome equivalent for prize-money; and, after thus disposing of half the treasure, Walter and I had over half a million dollars apiece left to our own account.

"How much the rest of the cargo carried by the *Reyna del Cielo* was worth, not to speak of the ancient craft herself, we never had the opportunity of learning. The *Penetrator* took the galleon in tow and we headed for St. Thomas, regretfully leaving the *Carib* in the haven of dead ships.

"It was the third night. We sat on the afterdeck under the stars, the strange relic of Spain's imperial commerce looming mystically astern. Suddenly a bright flash gleamed from the galleon's deck. Then a column of pitchy flame went roaring up—and in an instant the *Reyna del Cielo* was hopelessly ablaze.

"The two men who had been left to look after the galleon were rescued with considerable difficulty. It appeared that a bag of the resinous powder, opened for examination, had been left standing near the forecastle. One of the men, lighting his pipe, had thrown down the match and it had dropped into the open bag.

"You wonder, of course, why this strange story has never been made public. Scientific reputations were at stake. Out of all the men that have seen the sea-serpent, how many do you suppose have ventured to tell of it?"

The Floating Beacon

ANONYMOUS

One night we were on a voyage from Bergen to Christiansand in a small sloop. Our captain suspected that he had approached too near the Norwegian coast, though he could not discern any land, and the wind blew with such violence that we were in momentary alread of being driven upon a lee-shore.

We had endeavored, for more than an hour, to keep the vessel away; but our efforts proved unavailing, and we soon found that we could scarcely hold our own. A clouded sky, a hazy atmosphere, and irregular showers of sleety rain, combined to deepen the obscurity of night, and nothing whatever was visible, except the sparkling of the distant waves, when their tops happened to break into a wreath of foam. The sea ran very high, and sometimes broke over the deck so furiously that the men were obliged to hold by the logging, lest they should be carried away.

Our captain was a person of timid and irresolute character, and the dangers that environed us made him gradually lose confidence in himself. He often gave orders and countermanded them in the same moment, all the while taking small quantities of ardent spirits at intervals. Fear and intoxication soon stupefied him completely, and the crew ceased to consult him, or to pay any respect to his authority, in so far as regarded the management of the vessel.

About midnight our mainsail was split, and shortly after we found that the sloop had sprung a leak. We had before shipped a good deal of water through the hatches, and the quantity that now entered from below was so great that we thought she would go down every moment. Our only chance of escape lay in our boat, which was immediately lowered. After we had all got on board of her, except the captain, who stood leaning against the mast, we called to him, requesting that he would follow us without delay.

"How dare you quit the sloop without my permission?" cried he, staggering forwards. "This is not fit weather to go a-fishing. Come back—back with you all!"

"No, no," returned one of the crew; "we don't want to be sent to the bottom for your obstinacy. Bear a hand there, or we'll leave you behind."

"Captain, you are drunk," said another; "you cannot take care of yourself. You must obey *us* now."

"Silence! mutinous villain!" answered the captain. "What are you afraid of? This is a fine breeze—Up mainsail and steer her right in the wind's eye."

The sea knocked the boat so violently and constantly against the side of the sloop, that we feared the former would be injured or upset if we did not immediately row away; but, anxious as we were to preserve our lives, we could not reconcile ourselves to the idea of abandoning the captain, who grew more obstinate the more we attempted to persuade him to accompany us.

At length one of the crew leaped on board the sloop, and having seized hold of him, tried to drag him along by force; but he struggled resolutely, and soon freed himself from the grasp of the seaman, who immediately resumed his place among us, and urged that we should not any longer risk our lives for the sake of a drunkard and a madman. Most of the party declared they were of the same opinion, and began to push off the boat; but I entreated them to make one effort more to induce their infatuated commander to accompany us.

At that moment he came up from the cabin, to which he had descended a little time before, and we immediately perceived that he was more under the influence of ardent spirits than ever. He abused us all in the grossest terms, and threatened his crew with severe punishment, if they did not come on board, and return to their duty. His manner was so violent that no one seemed willing to attempt to constrain him to come on board the boat; and after vainly representing the absurdity of his conduct, and the danger of his situation, we bade him farewell, and rowed away.

The sea ran so high, and had such a terrific appearance, that I almost wished myself in the sloop again. The crew plied the oars in silence, and we heard nothing but the hissing of the enormous billows as they gently rose up, and slowly subsided again, without breaking. At intervals our boat was elevated far above the surface of the ocean, and remained for a few moments trembling upon the pinnacle of a surge, from which it would quietly descend into a gulf so deep and awful that we often thought the dense black mass of waters which formed its sides were on the point of overarching us, and bursting upon our heads. We glided with regular undulations from one billow to another; but every time we sank into the trough of the sea my heart died within me, for I felt as if we were going lower down than we had ever done before, and clung instinctively to the board on which I sat.

Notwithstanding my terrors, I frequently looked towards the sloop. The fragments of her mainsail, which remained attached to the yard, and fluttered in the wind, enabled us to discern exactly where she lay, and showed, by their motion, that she pitched about in a terrible manner. We occasionally heard the voice of her unfortunate commander, calling to us in tones of frantic derision, and by turns vociferating curses and blasphemous oaths, and singing sea-songs with a wild and frightful energy. I sometimes almost wished that the crew would make another effort to save him, but next moment the principle of self-preservation repressed all feelings of humanity, and I endeavored, by closing my ears, to banish the idea of his sufferings from my mind.

After a little while the shivering canvas disappeared, and we heard a tumultuous roaring and bursting of billows, and saw an unusual sparkling of the sea about a quarter of a mile from us. One of the sailors cried out that the sloop was new on her beam ends, and that the noise to which we listened was that of the waves breaking over her.

We could sometimes perceive a large black mass heaving itself up irregularly among the flashing surges, and then disappearing for a few moments, and knew but too well that it was the hull of the vessel. At intervals a shrill and agonized voice uttered some exclamations, but we could not distinguish what they were, and then a long-drawn shriek came across the ocean, which suddenly grew more furiously agitated near the spot where the sloop lay, and in a few moments she sank down, and a black wave formed itself out of the waters that had engulfed her, and swelled gloomily into a magnitude greater than that of the surrounding billows.

The seamen dropped their oars, as if by one impulse, and looked expressively at each other, without speaking a word. Awful forebodings of a fate similar to that of the captain appeared to chill every heart, and to repress the energy that had hitherto excited us to make unremitting exertions for our common safety. While we were in this state of hopeless inaction, the man at the helm called out that he saw a light ahead. We all strained our eyes to discern it, but at the moment the boat was sinking down between two immense waves, one of which closed the prospect, and we remained in breathless anxiety till a rising surge elevated us above the level of the surrounding ocean. A light like a dazzling star then suddenly flashed upon our view, and joyful exclamations burst from every mouth.

"That," cried one of the crew, "must be the floating beacon which our captain was looking out for this afternoon. If we can but gain it, we'll be safe enough yet." This intelligence cheered us all, and the men began to ply the oars with redoubled vigor, while I employed myself in baling out the water that sometimes rushed over the gunnel of the boat when a sea happened to strike her.

An hour's hard rowing brought us so near the lighthouse that we almost ceased to apprehend any further danger; but it was suddenly obscured from our view, and at the same time a confused roaring and dashing commenced at a little distance, and rapidly increased in loudness. We soon perceived a tremendous billow rolling towards us. Its top, part of which had already broke, overhung the base, as if unwilling to burst until we were within the reach of its violence. The man who steered the boat brought her head to the sea, but all to no purpose, for the water rushed furiously over us, and we were completely immersed. I felt the boat swept from under me, and was left struggling and groping about in hopeless desperation for something to catch hold of.

When nearly exhausted, I received a severe blow on the side from a small cask of water which the sea had forced against me. I immediately twined my arms round it, and after recovering myself a little, began to look for the boat, and to call to my companions; but I could not discover any vestige of them, or of the vessel. However, I still had a faint hope that they were in existence, and that the intervention of the billows concealed them from my view. I continued to shout as loud as possible, for the sound of my own voice in some measure relieved me from the feeling of awful and heart-chilling loneliness which my situation inspired; but not even an echo responded to my cries, and, convinced that my comrades had all perished, I ceased looking for them, and pushed towards the beacon in the best manner I could.

A long series of fatiguing exertions brought me close to the side of the vessel which contained it, and I called out loudly, in hopes that those on board might hear me and come to my assistance; but no one appearing, I waited patiently till a wave raised me on a level with the chains, and then caught hold of them, and succeeded in getting on board.

As I did not see any person on deck, I went forwards to the skylight and looked down. Two men were seated below at a table; and a lamp, which was suspended above them, being swung backwards and forwards by the rolling of the vessel, threw its light upon their faces alternately. One seemed agitated with passion, and the other surveyed him with a scornful look. They both talked very loudly, and used threatening gestures, but the sea made so much noise that I could not distinguish what was said. After a little time they started up, and seemed to be on the point of closing and wrestling together, when a woman rushed through a small door and prevented them.

I beat upon deck with my feet at the same time, and the attention of the whole party was soon transferred to the noise. One of the men immediately came up the cabin stairs, but stopped short on seeing me, as if irresolute whether to advance or hasten below again. I approached him, and told my story in a few words, but instead of making any reply, he went down to the cabin, and began to relate to the others what he had seen. I soon followed him, and easily found my way into the apartment where they all were. They appeared to feel mingled sensations of fear and astonishment at my presence, and it was some time before any of them entered into conversation with me, or afforded those comforts which I stood so much in need of.

After I had refreshed myself with food, and been provided with a Change of clothing, I went upon deck, and surveyed the singular asylum in which Providence had enabled me to take refuge from the fury of the storm. It did not exceed thirty feet long, and was very strongly built, and completely decked over, except at the entrance to the cabin. It had a thick mast at midships, with a large lantern, containing several burners and reflectors, on the top of it; and this could be lowered and hoisted up again as often as required, by means of ropes and pulleys.

The vessel was firmly moored upon an extensive sand-bank, the beacon being intended to warn seamen to avoid a part of the ocean where many lives and vessels had been lost in consequence of the latter running aground. The accommodations below decks were narrow, and of an inferior description; however, I gladly retired to the berth that was allotted me by my entertainers, and fatigue and the rocking of billows combined to lull me into a quiet and dreamless sleep.

Next morning, one of the men, whose name was Angerstoff, came to my bedside, and called me to breakfast in a surly and imperious manner. The others looked coldly and distrustfully when I joined them, and I saw that they regarded me as an intruder and an unwelcome guest. The meal passed without almost any conversation, and I went upon deck whenever it was over. The tempest of the preceding night had in a great measure abated, but the sea still ran very high, and a black mist hovered over it, through which the Norwegian coast, lying at eleven miles distance, could be dimly seen.

I looked in vain for some remains of the sloop or boat. Not a bird enlivened the heaving expanse of waters, and I turned shuddering from the dreary scene, and asked Morvalden, the youngest of the men, when he thought I had any chance of getting ashore. "Not very soon, I'm afraid," returned he. "We are visited once a month by people from yonder land, who are appointed to bring us supply of provisions and other necessaries. They were here only six days ago, so you may count how long it will be before they return. Fishing boats sometimes pass us during fine weather, but we won't have much of that this moon at least."

No intelligence could have been more depressing to me than this. The idea of spending perhaps three weeks in such a place was almost insupportable, and the more so as I could not hasten my deliverance by any exertions of my own, but would be obliged to remain, in a state of inactive suspense, till good fortune, or the regular course of events, afforded me the means of getting ashore. Neither Angerstoff nor Morvalden seemed to sympathize with my distress, or even to care that I should have it in my power to leave the vessel, except in so far as my departure would free them from the expense of supporting me.

They returned indistinct and repulsive answers to all the questions I asked, and appeared anxious to avoid having the least communication with me. During the greater part of the forenoon, they employed themselves in trimming the lamps and cleaning the reflectors, but never conversed any. I easily perceived that a mutual animosity existed between them, but was unable to discover the cause of it. Morvalden seemed to fear Angerstoff, and at the same time to feel a deep resentment towards him, which he did not dare to express. Angerstoff apparently was aware of this, for he behaved to his companion with the undisguised fierceness of determined hate, and openly thwarted him in everything.

Marietta, the female on board, was the wife of Morvalden. She remained chiefly below decks, and attended to the domestic concerns of the vessel. She was rather good-looking, but so reserved and forbidding in her manners that she formed no desirable acquisition to our party, already so heartless and unsociable in its character.

When night approached, after the lapse of a wearisome and monotonous day, I went on deck to see the beacon lighted, and continued walking backwards and forwards till a late hour. I watched the lantern, as it swung from side to side, and flashed upon different portions of the sea alternately, and sometimes fancied I saw men struggling among the billows that tumbled around, and at other times imagined I could discern the white sail of an approaching vessel. Human voices seemed to mingle with the noise of the bursting waves, and I often listened intently, almost in the expectation of hearing articulate sounds.

My mind grew somber as the scene itself, and strange and fearful ideas obtruded themselves in rapid succession. It was dreadful to be chained in the middle of the deep—to be the continual sport of the quiet-less billows—to be shunned as a fatal thing by those who traversed the solitary ocean. Though within sight of the shore, our situation was more dreary than if we had been sailing a thousand miles from it. We felt not the pleasure of moving forwards, nor the hope of reaching port, nor the delights arising from favorable breezes and genial weather. When a billow drove us to one side, we were tossed back again by another; our imprisonment had no variety or definite termination; and the calm and the tempest were alike uninteresting to us.

I felt as if my fate had already become linked with that of those who were on board the vessel. My hopes of being again permitted to mingle with mankind died away, and I anticipated long years of gloom and despair in the company of these repulsive persons into whose hands fate had unexpectedly consigned me.

Angerstoff and Morvalden tended the beacon alternately during the night. The latter had the watch while I remained upon deck. His appearance and manner indicated much perturbation of mind, and he paced hurriedly from side to side, sometimes muttering to himself, and sometimes stopping suddenly to look through the skylight, as if anxious to discover what was going on below. He would then gaze intently upon the heavens, and next moment take out his watch and contemplate the motions of its hands. I did not offer to disturb these reveries, and thought myself altogether unobserved by him, till he suddenly advanced to the spot where I stood, and said, in a loud whisper:

"There's a villain below—a desperate villain—this is true—he is capable of anything—and the woman is as bad as him."

I asked what proof he had of all this.

"Oh, I know it," returned he; "that wretch Angerstoff, whom I once thought my friend, has gained my wife's affections. She has been faithless to me—yes, she has. They both wish I were out of the way. Perhaps they are now planning my destruction. What can I do? It is very terrible to be shut up in such narrow limits with those who hate me, and to have no means of escaping or defending myself from their infernal machinations."

"Why do you not leave the beacon," inquired I, "and abandon your companion and guilty wife?"

"Ah, that is impossible," answered Morvalden; "if I went on shore I would forfeit my liberty. I live here that I may escape the vengeance of the law, which I once outraged for the sake of her who has now withdrawn her love from me. What ingratitude! Mine is indeed a terrible fate, but I must bear it. And shall I never again wander through the green fields, and climb the rocks that encircle my native place? Are the weary dashings of the sea, and the moanings of the wind, to fill my ears continually, all the while telling me that I am an exile?—a hopeless, despairing exile. But it won't last long," cried he, catching hold of my arm; "they will murder me!—I am sure of it—I never go to sleep without dreaming that Angerstoff has pushed me overboard."

"Your lonely situation and inactive life dispose you to give way to these chimeras," said I; "you must endeavor to resist them. Perhaps things aren't so bad as you suppose."

"This is not a lonely situation," replied Morvalden, in a solemn tone. "Perhaps you will have proof of what I say before you leave us. Many vessels used to be lost here, and a few are wrecked still; and the skeletons and corpses of those who have perished lie all over the sand-bank. Sometimes, at midnight, I have seen crowds of human figures moving backwards and forwards upon the surface of the ocean, almost as far as the eye could reach. I neither knew who they were, nor what they did there. When watching the lantern alone, I often hear a number of voices talking together, as it were, under the waves; and I twice caught the very words they uttered, but I cannot repeat them—they dwell incessantly in my memory, but my tongue refuses to pronounce them, or to explain to others what they meant."

"Do not let your senses be imposed upon by a distempered imagination," said I; "there is no reality in the things you have told me."

"Perhaps my mind occasionally wanders a little, for it has a heavy burden upon it," returned Morvalden. "I have been guilty of a dreadful crime. Many that now lie in the deep below us might start up and accuse me of what I am just going to reveal to you. One stormy night, shortly after I began to take charge of this beacon, while watching on deck, I fell into a profound sleep. I know not how long it continued, but I was awakened by horrible shouts and cries. I started up, and instantly perceived that all the lamps in the lantern were extinguished.

"It was very dark, and the sea raged furiously; but notwithstanding all this, I observed a ship aground on the bank, a little way from me, her sails fluttering in the wind, and the waves breaking over her with violence. Half frantic with horror, I ran down to the cabin for a taper, and lighted the lamps as fast as possible. The lantern, when hoisted to the top of the mast, threw a vivid glare on the surrounding ocean, and showed me the vessel disappearing among the billows. Hundreds of people lay gasping in the water near her. Men, women, and children writhed together in agonizing struggles, and uttered soul-harrowing cries; and their countenances, as they gradually stiffened under the hand of death, were all turned towards me with glassy stare, while the lurid expression of their glistening eyes upbraided me with having been the cause of their untimely end.

"Never shall I forget these looks. They haunt me wherever I am—asleep and awake—night and day. I have kept this tale of horror secret till now, and do not know if I shall ever have courage to relate it again. The masts of the vessel projected above the surface of the sea for several months after she was lost, as if to keep me in recollection of the night in which so many human creatures perished, in consequence of my neglect and carelessness. Would to God I had no memory! I sometimes think I am getting mad. The past and present are equally dreadful to me; and I dare not anticipate the future."

I felt a sort of superstitious dread steal over me, while Morvalden related his story, and we continued walking the deck in silence till the period of his watch expired. I then went below, and took refuge in my berth, though I was but little inclined for sleep. The gloomy ideas and dark forebodings expressed by Morvalden weighed heavily upon my mind, without my knowing why; and my situation, which had at first seemed only dreary and depressing, began to have something indefinitely terrible in its aspect.

Next day, when Morvalden proceeded as usual to put the beacon in order, he called upon Angerstoff to come and assist him, which the latter peremptorily refused. Morvalden then went down to the cabin, where his companion was, and requested to know why his orders were not obeyed.

"Because I hate trouble," replied Angerstoff. "I am master here," said Morvalden, "and have been intrusted with the direction of everything. Do not attempt to trifle with me."

"Trifle with you!" exclaimed Angerstoff, looking contemptuously. "No, no, I am no trifler; and I advise you to walk upstairs again, lest I prove this to your cost."

"Why, husband," cried Marietta, "I believe there are no bounds to your laziness. You make this young man toil from morning to night, and take advantage of his good nature in the most shameful manner."

"Peace, infamous woman!" said Morvalden; "I know very well why you stand up in his defense; but I'll put a stop to the intimacy that exists between you. Go to your room instantly! You are my wife, and shall obey me." "Is this usage to be borne?" exclaimed Marietta. "Will no one step forward to protect me from his violence?" "Insolent fellow!" cried Angerstorff, "don't presume to insult my mistress."

"Mistress!" repeated Morvalden. "This to my face!" and struck him a severe blow.

Angerstorff sprung forward, with the intention of returning it, but I got between them, and prevented him. Marietta then began to shed tears, and applauded the generosity her paramour had evinced in sparing her husband, who immediately went upon deck, without speaking a word, and hurriedly resumed the work that had engaged his attention previous to the quarrel.

Neither of the two men seemed at all disposed for a reconciliation, and they had no intercourse during the whole day, except angry and revengeful looks. I frequently observed Marietta in deep consultation with Angerstoff, and easily perceived that the subject of debate had some relation to her injured husband, whose manner evinced much alarm and anxiety, although he endeavored to look calm and cheerful. He did not make his appearance at meals, but spent all his time upon deck. Whenever Angerstoff accidentally passed him, he shrank back with an expression of dread, and intuitively, as it were, caught hold of a rope, or any other object to which he could cling.

The day proved a wretched and fearful one to me, for I momentarily expected that some terrible affray would occur on board, and that I would be implicated in it. I gazed upon the surrounding sea almost without intermission, ardently hoping that some boat might approach near enough to afford me an opportunity of quitting the horrid and dangerous abode in which I was imprisoned.

It was Angerstoff's watch on deck till midnight; and as I did not wish to have any communication with him, I remained below. At twelve o'clock Morvalden got up and relieved him, and he came down to the cabin, and soon after retired to his berth. Believing, from this arrangement, that they had no hostile intentions, I lay down in bed with composure, and fell asleep.

It was not long before a noise overhead awakened me. I started up, and listened intently. The sound appeared to be that of two persons scuffling together, for a successsion of irregular footsteps beat the deck, and I could hear violent blows given at intervals. I got out of my berth, and entered the cabin, where I found Marietta standing alone, with a lamp in her hand.

"Do you hear that?" cried I.

"Hear what?" returned she; "I have had a dreadful dream—I am all trembling."

"Is Angerstoff below?" demanded I.

"No—yes, I mean," said Marietta. "Why do you ask that? He went upstairs."

"Your husband and he are fighting. We must part them instantly."

"How can that be?" answered Marietta; "Angerstoff is asleep."

"Asleep! Didn't you say he went upstairs?"

"I don't know," returned she; "I am hardly awake yet—Let us listen for a moment."

Everything was still for a few seconds; then a voice shrieked out, "Ah! that knife! you are murdering me! Draw it out! No help! Are you done? Now—now—now!" A heavy body fell suddenly along the deck, and some words were spoken in a faint tone, but the roaring of the sea prevented me from hearing what they were.

I rushed up the cabin stairs, and tried to push open the folding-doors at the head of them, but they resisted my utmost efforts. I knocked violently and repeatedly to no purpose.

"Some one is killed," cried I. "The person who barred these doors on the outside is guilty."

"I know nothing of that," returned Marietta. "We can't be of any use now.—Come here again!—how dreadfully quiet it is. My God!—a drop of blood has fallen through the skylight.—What faces are yon looking down upon us?—But this lamp is going out.—We must be going through the water at a terrible rate—how it rushes past us!—I am getting dizzy.—Do you hear these bells ringing? and strange voices—"

The cabin doors were suddenly burst open, and Angerstoff next moment appeared before us, crying out, "Morvalden has fallen overboard. Throw a rope to him!—he will be drowned." His hands and dress were marked with blood, and he had a frightful look of horror and confusion.

"You are a murderer!" exclaimed I, almost involuntarily.

"How do you know that?" said he, staggering back; "I'm sure you never saw—"

"Hush, hush," cried Marietta to him; "are you mad? Speak again!—What frightens you?—Why don't you run and help Morvalden?"

"Has anything happened to him?" inquired Angerstoff, with a gaze of consternation.

"You told us he had fallen overboard," returned Marietta; "must my husband perish?"

"Give me some water to wash my hands," said Angerstoff, growing deadly pale, and catching hold of the table for support.

I now hastened upon deck, but Morvalden was not there. I then went to the side of the vessel, and put my hands on the gunwale, while I leaned over, and looked downwards. On taking them off, I found them marked with blood. I grew sick at heart, and began to identify myself with Angerstoff the murderer.

The sea, the beacon, and the sky, appeared of a sanguine hue, and I thought I heard the dying exclamations of Morvalden sounding a hundred fathom below me, and echoing through the caverns of the deep. I advanced to the cabin door, intending to descend the stairs, but found that some one had fastened it firmly on the inside. I felt convinced that I was intentionally shut out, and a cold shuddering pervaded my frame. I covered my face with my hands, not daring to look around; for it seemed as if I was excluded from the company of the living, and doomed to be the associate of the spirits of drowned and murdered men.

After a little time, I began to walk hastily backwards and forwards; but the light of the lantern happened to flash on a stream of blood that ran along the deck, and I could not summon up resolution to pass the spot where it was a second time. The sky looked black and threatening—the sea had a fierceness in its sound and motions—and the wind swept over its bosom with melancholy sighs. Everything was somber and ominous; and I looked in vain for some object that would, by its soothing aspect, remove the dark impressions which crowded upon my mind.

While standing near the bows of the vessel, I saw a hand and arm rise slowly behind the stern, and wave from side to side. I started back as far as I could go in horrible affright, and looked again, expecting to behold the entire spectral figure of which I supposed they formed a part. But nothing more was visible. I struck my eyes till the light flashed from them, in hopes that my senses had been imposed upon by distempered vision. However, it was in vain, for the hand still motioned me to advance, and I rushed forwards with wild desperation, and caught hold of it.

I was pulled along a little way notwithstanding the resistance I made, and soon discovered a man stretched along the stern-cable, and clinging to it in a convulsive manner. It was Morvalden. He raised his head feebly, and said something, but I could only distinguish the words, "murdered—overboard—reached this rope—terrible death."

I stretched out my arms to support him, but at that moment the vessel plunged violently, and he was shaken off the cable, and dropped among the waves. He floated for an instant, and then disappeared under the keel.

I seized the first rope I could find, and threw one end of it over the stern, and likewise flung some planks into the sea, thinking that the unfortunate Morvalden might still retain strength enough to catch hold of them if they came within his reach. I continued on the watch for a considerable time, but at last abandoned all hopes of saving him, and made another attempt to get down to the cabin. The doors were now unfastened, and I opened them without any difficulty.

The first thing I saw on going below, was Angerstoff stretched along the floor, and fast asleep. His torpid look, flushed countenance, and uneasy respiration, convinced me that he had taken a large quantity of ardent spirits. Marietta was in her own apartment. Even the presence of a murderer appeared less terrible than the frightful solitariness of the deck, and I lay down upon a bench determining to spend the remainder of the night there. The lamp that hung from the roof soon went out, and left me in total darkness.

Imagination began to conjure up a thousand appalling forms, and the voice of Angerstoff, speaking in his sleep, filled my ears at intervals—"Hoist up the beacon!—the lamps won't burn—horrible!—they contain blood instead of oil. Is that a boat coming?—Yes, yes, I hear the oars. Damnation!—why is that corpse so long of sinking?—if it doesn't go down soon they'll find me out. How terribly the wind blows!—we are driving ashore—See! see! Morvalden is swimming after us—how he writhes in the water!"

Marietta now rushed from her room, with a light in her hand, and seizing Angerstoff by the arm, tried to awake him. He soon rose up with chattering teeth and shivering limbs, and was on the point of speaking, but she prevented him, and he staggered away to his berth, and lay down in it.

Next morning, when I went upon deck, after a short and perturbed sleep, I found Marietta dashing water over it, that she might efface all vestige of the transactions of the preceding night.

Angerstoff did not make his appearance till noon, and his looks were ghastly and agonized. He seemed stupefied with horror, and sometimes entirely lost all perception of the things around him for a considerable time. He suddenly came close up to me, and demanded, with a bold air, but quivering voice, what I had meant by calling him a murderer?

"Why, that you are one," replied I, after a pause,

"Beware what you say," returned he fiercely,—"you cannot escape my power now—I tell you, sir, Morvalden fell overboard."

"Whence, then, came that blood that covered the deck?" inquired I.

He grew pale, and then cried, "You lie—you lie infernally—there was none!"

"I saw it," said I. "I saw Morvalden himself—long after midnight. He was clinging to the stern-cable, and said—"

"Ha, ha, ha—devils!—curses!" exclaimed Angerstoff. "Did you hear me dreaming?—I was mad last night—Come, come, come!—We shall tend the beacon together—Let us make friends, and don't be afraid, for you'll find me a good fellow in the end."

He now forcibly shook hands with me, and then hurried down to the cabin.

In the afternoon, while sitting on deck, I discerned a boat far off, but I determined to conceal this from Angerstoff and Marietta, lest they should use some means to prevent its approach. I walked carelessly about, casting a glance upon the sea occasionally, and meditating how I could best take advantage of the means of deliverance which I had in prospect. After the lapse of an hour, the boat was not more than half a mile distant from us, but she suddenly changed her course, and bore away towards the shore.

I immediately shouted, and waved a handkerchief over my head, as signals for her to return. Angerstoff rushed from the cabin, and seized my arm, threatening at the same time to push me overboard if I attempted to hail her again. I disengaged myself from his grasp, and dashed him violently from me. The noise brought Marietta upon deck, who immediately perceived the cause of the affray, and cried:

"Does the wretch mean to make his escape? For Godsake, prevent the possibility of that!"

"Yes, yes," returned Angerstoff; "he never shall leave the vessel—He had as well take care, lest I do to him what I did to—"

"To Morvalden, I suppose you mean," said I.

"Well, well, speak it out," replied he ferociously; "there is no one here to listen to your damnable falsehoods, and I'll not be fool enough to give you an opportunity of uttering them elsewhere. I'll strangle you the next time you tell these lies about—"

"Come," interrupted Marietta, "don't be uneasy—the boat will soon be far enough way—If he wants to give you the slip, he must leap overboard."

I was irritated and disappointed beyond measure at the failure of the plan of escape I had formed, but thought it most prudent to conceal my feelings. I now perceived the rashness and bad consequences of my bold assertions respecting the murder of Morvalden; for Angerstoff evidently thought that his personal safety, and even his life, would be endangered, if I ever found an opportunity of accusing and giving evidence against him.

All my motions were now watched with double vigilance. Marietta and her paramour kept upon deck by turns during the whole day, and the latter looked over the surrounding ocean, through a glass, at intervals, to discover if any boat or vessel was approaching us. He often muttered threats as he walked past me, and, more than once, seemed waiting for an opportunity to push me overboard. Marietta and he frequently whispered together, and I always imagined I heard my name mentioned in the course of these conversations.

I now felt completely miserable, being satisfied that Angerstoff was bent upon my destruction. I wandered, in a state of fearful circumspection, from one part of the vessel to the other, not knowing how to secure myself from his designs. Every time he approached me, my heart palpitated dreadfully; and when night came on, I was agonized with terror, and could not remain in one spot, but hurried backwards and forwards between the cabin and the deck, looking wildly from side to side, and momentarily expecting to feel a cold knife entering my vitals.

My forehead began to burn, and my eyes dazzled; I became acutely sensitive, and the slightest murmur, or the faintest breath of wind, set my whole frame in a state of uncontrollable vibration. At first, I sometimes thought of throwing myself into the sea; but I soon acquired such an intense feeling of existence, that the mere idea of death was horrible to me.

Shortly after midnight I lay down in my berth, almost exhausted by the harrowing emotions that had careered through my mind during the past day. I felt a strong desire to sleep, yet dared not indulge myself; soul and body seemed at war. Every noise excited my imagination, and scarcely a minute passed, in the course of which I did not start up and look around. Angerstoff paced the deck overhead, and when the sound of his footsteps accidentally ceased at any time, I grew deadly sick at heart, expecting that he was silently coming to murder me.

At length I thought I heard some one near my bed. I sprung from it, and, having seized a bar of iron that lay on the floor, rushed into the cabin. I found Angerstoff there, who started back when he saw me, and said:

"What is the matter? Did you think that—I want you to watch the beacon, that I may have some rest. Follow me upon deck, and I will give you directions about it."

I hesitated a moment, and then went up the gangway stairs behind him. We walked forward to the mast together, and he showed how I was to lower the lantern when any of the lamps happened to go out, and bidding me beware of sleep, returned to the cabin. Most of my fears forsook me the moment he disappeared. I felt nearly as happy as if I had been set at liberty, and, for a time, forgot that my situation had anything painful or alarming connected with it. Angerstoff resumed his station in about three hours, and I again took refuge in my berth, where I enjoyed a short but undisturbed slumber.

Next day while I was walking the deck, and anxiously surveying the expanse of ocean around, Angerstoff requested me to come down to the cabin. I obeyed his summons, and found him there. He gave me a book, saying it was very entertaining, and would serve to amuse me during my idle hours; and then went above, shutting the doors carefully behind him. I was struck with his behavior, but felt no alarm, for Marietta sat at work near me, apparently unconscious of what had passed. I began to peruse the volume I held in my hand, and found it so interesting that I paid little attention to anything else, till the dashing of oars struck my ear.

I sprang from my chair, with the intention of hastening upon deck, but Marietta stopped me, saying, "It is of no use—the gangway doors are fastened."

Notwithstanding this information, I made an attempt to open them, but could not succeed. I was now convinced, by the percussion against the vessel, that a boat lay alongside, and I heard a strange voice addressing Angerstoff. Fired with the idea of deliverance, I leaped upon a table which stood in the middle of the cabin, and tried to push off the skylight, but was suddenly stunned by a violent blow on the back of my head. I staggered back and looked round. Marietta stood close behind me, brandishing an ax, as if in the act of repeating the stroke.

Her face was flushed with rage, and, having seized my arm, she cried, "Come down instantly, accursed villain! I know you want to betray us, but may we all go to the bottom if you find a chance of doing so."

I struggled to free myself from her grasp, but, being in a state of dizziness and confusion, I was unable to effect this, and she soon pulled me to the ground.

At that moment, Angerstoff hurriedly entered the cabin, exclaiming, "What noise is this? Oh, just as I expected! Has that devil—that spy—been trying to get above boards? Why haven't I the heart to dispatch him at once? But there's no time now. The people are waiting—Marietta, come and lend a hand."

They now forced me down upon the floor, and bound me to an iron ring that was fixed in it. This being done, Angerstoff directed his female accomplice to prevent me from speaking, and went up on deck again.

While in this state of bondage, I heard distinctly all that passed without. Some one asked Angerstoff how Morvalden did. "Well, quite well," replied the former; "but he's below, and so sick that he can't see any person." "Strange enough," said the first speaker, laughing. "Is he ill and in good health at the same time? he had as well be overboard as in that condition." "Overboard!" repeated

Angerstoff, "what!—how do you mean?—all false!—but listen to me,—Are there any news stirring ashore?" "Why," said the stranger, "the chief talk there just now is about a curious thing that happened this morning.

"A dead man was found upon the beach, and they suspect, from the wounds on his body, that he hasn't got fair play. They are making a great noise about it, and Government means to send out a boat, with an officer on board, who is to visit all the shipping round this, that he may ascertain if any of them has lost a man lately. 'Tis a dark business; but they'll get to the bottom of it, I warrant ye. Why, you look as pale as if you knew more about this matter than you choose to tell."

"No, no, no," returned Angerstoff; "I never hear of a murder but I think of a friend of mine who—but I won't detain you, for the sea is getting up—we'll have a blowy night, I'm afraid."

"So you don't want any fish to-day?" cried the stranger. "Then I'll be off—Good morning, good morning. I suppose you'll have the Government boat alongside by-and-by."

I now heard the sound of oars, and supposed, from the conversation having ceased, that the fisherman had departed. Angerstoff came down to the cabin soon after, and released me without speaking a word.

Marietta then approached him, and, taking hold of his arm, said, "Do you believe what that man has told you?"

"Yes, by the eternal hell!" cried he, vehemently; "I suspect I will find the truth of it soon enough."

"My God!" exclaimed she, "what is to become of us?—How dreadful! We are chained here and cannot escape."

"Escape what?" interrupted Angerstoff; "girl, you have lost your senses. Why should we fear the officers of justice? Keep a guard over your tongue."

"Oh," returned Marietta, "I talk without thinking, or understanding my own words; but come upon deck, and let me speak with you there."

They now went up the gangway stairs together, and continued in deep conversation for some time.

Angerstoff gradually became more agitated as the day advanced. He watched upon deck almost without intermission, and seemed irresolute what to do, sometimes sitting down composedly, and at other times hurrying backwards and forwards, with clenched hands and bloodless cheeks. The wind blew pretty fresh from the shore, and there was a heavy swell; and I supposed, from the anxious looks with which he contemplated the sky, that he hoped the threatening aspect of the weather would prevent the government boat from putting out to sea. He kept his glass constantly in his hand, and surveyed the ocean through it in all directions.

At length he suddenly dashed the instrument away, and exclaimed, "God help us! they are coming now!"

Marietta, on hearing this, ran wildly towards him, and put her hands in his, but he pushed her to one side, and began to pace the deck, apparently in deep thought.

After a little time, he started, and cried, "I have it now!—It's the only plan—I'll manage the business—yes, yes—I'll cut the cables, and off we'll go—that's settled!"

He then seized an ax, and first divided the hawser at the bows, and afterwards the one attached to the stern.

The vessel immediately began to drift away, and having no sails or helm to steady her, rolled with such violence that I was dashed from side to side several times. She often swung over so much that I thought she would not regain the upright position, and Angerstoff all the while unconsciously strengthened this belief, by exclaiming, "She will capsize! shift the ballast, or we must go to the bottom!"

In the midst of this, I kept my station upon deck, intently watching the boat, which was still several miles distant. I waited in fearful expectation, thinking that every new wave against which we were impelled would burst upon our vessel and overwhelm us, while our pursuers were too far off to afford any assistance. The idea of perishing when on the point of being saved was inexpressibly agonizing.

As the day advanced, the hopes I had entertained of the boat making up with us gradually diminished. The wind blew violently, and we drifted along at a rapid rate, and the weather grew so hazy that our pursuers soon became quite undistinguishable. Marietta and Angerstoff appeared to be stupefied with terror. They stood motionless, holding firmly by the bulwarks of the vessel; and though the waves frequently broke over the deck, and rushed down the gangway, they did not offer to shut the companion door, which would have remained open had I not closed it.

The tempest, gloom, and danger that thickened around us, neither elicited from them any expressions of mutual regard, nor seemed to produce the slightest sympathetic emotion in their bosoms. They gazed sternly at each other and at me, and every time the vessel rolled, clung with convulsive eagerness to whatever lay within their reach.

About sunset our attention was attracted by a dreadful roaring, which evidently did not proceed from the waves around us; but the atmosphere being very hazy, we were unable to ascertain the cause of it for a long time. At length we distinguished a range of high cliffs, against which the sea beat with terrible fury. Whenever the surge broke upon them, large jets of foam started up to a great height, and flashed angrily over their black and rugged surfaces, while the wind moaned and whistled with fearful caprice among the projecting points of rock. A dense mist covered the upper part of the cliffs, and prevented us from seeing if there were any houses upon their summits, though this point appeared of little importance, for we drifted towards the shore so fast that immediate death seemed inevitable.

We soon felt our vessel bound twice against the sand, and in a little time after a heavy sea carried her up the beach, where she remained imbedded and hard aground. During the ebb of the waves there was not more than two feet of water round her bows.

I immediately perceived this, and, watching a favorable opportunity, swung myself down to the beach by means of part of the cable that projected through the hawse-hole. I began to run towards the cliffs the moment my feet touched the ground, and Angerstoff attempted to follow me, that he might prevent my escape; but while in the act of descending from the vessel, the sea flowed in with such violence that he was obliged to spring on board again to save himself from being overwhelmed by its waters.

I hurried on and began to climb up the rocks, which were very steep and slippery; but I soon grew breathless from fatigue, and found it necessary to stop. It was now almost dark, and when I looked around, I neither saw anything distinctly, nor could form the least idea how far I had still to ascend before I reached the top of the cliffs. I knew not which way to turn my steps, and remained irresolute, till the barking of a dog faintly struck my ear. I joyfully followed the sound, and, after an hour of perilous exertion, discovered a light at some distance, which I soon found to proceed from the window of a small hut.

After I had knocked repeatedly, the door was opened by an old man, with a lamp in his hand. He started back on seeing me, for my dress was wet and disordered, my face and hands had been wounded while scrambling among the rocks, and fatigue and terror had given me a wan and agitated look. I entered the house, the inmates of which were a woman and a boy, and having seated myself near the fire, related to my host all that had occurred on board the floating beacon, and then requested him to accompany me down to the beach, that we might search for Angerstoff and Marietta.

"No, no," cried he; "that is impossible. Hear how the storm rages! Worlds would not induce me to have any communication with murderers. It would be impious to attempt it on such a night as this. The Almighty is surely punishing them now! Come here and look out."

I followed him to the door, but the moment he opened it the wind extinguished the lamp. Total darkness prevailed without, and a chaos of rushing, bursting and moaning sounds swelled upon the ear with irregular loudness. The blast swept round the hut in violent eddyings, and we felt the chilly spray of the sea driving upon our faces at intervals. I shuddered, and the old man closed the door, and then resumed his seat near the fire.

My entertainer made a bed for me upon the floor, but the noise of the tempest, and the anxiety I felt about the fate of Angerstoff and Marietta, kept me awake the greater part of the night. Soon after dawn my host accompanied me down to the beach. We found the wreck of the floating beacon, but were unable to discover any traces of the guilty pair whom I had left on board of it.

The Fate of the *Alida*

LOUIS BECKE

We were lying inside Funafuti Lagoon, in the Ellice Group. The last cask of oil had been towed off to the brig and placed under hatches, and we were to sail in the morning for our usual cruise among the Gilbert and Kingsmill Islands.

Our captain, a white trader from the shore, and myself were sitting on deck "yarning" and smoking. We lay about a quarter of a mile from the beach—such a beach, white as the driven snow, and sweeping in a great curve for five long miles to the north and a lesser distance to the south and west.

Right abreast of the brig, nestling like huge birds' nests in the shade of groves of coconut and breadfruit trees, were the houses of the principal village in Funafuti.

Presently the skipper picked up his glasses that lay beside him on the skylight, and looked away down to leeward, where the white sails of a schooner beating up to the anchorage were outlined against the line of palms that fringed the beach of Funafala—the westernmost island that forms one of the chain enclosing Funafuti Lagoon.

"It's Taplin's schooner, right enough," he said. "Let us go ashore and give him and his pretty wife a hand to pack up."

Taplin was the name of the only other white trader on Funafuti besides old Tom Humphreys, our own man. He had been two years on the island, and was trading in opposition to our trader, as agent for a foreign house—our owners were Sydney people—but his firm's unscrupulous method of doing business had disgusted him. So one day he told the supercargo of their vessel that he would trade for them no longer than the exact time he had agreed upon—two years. He had come to Funafuti from the Pelews, and was now awaiting the return of his firm's vessel to take him back there again. Getting into our boat we were pulled ashore and landed on the beach in front of the trader's house.

"Well, Taplin, here's your schooner at last," said old Tom, as we shook hands and seated ourselves in the comfortable, pleasant-looking room. "I see you're getting ready to go."

Taplin was a man of about thirty or so, with a quiet, impassive face and dark, deep-set eyes that gave to his features a somewhat gloomy look, except when he smiled, which was not often.

"Yes," he answered, "I am nearly ready. I saw the schooner at daylight, and I knew it was the *Alida*."

"Where do you think of going to, Taplin?" I asked.

"Back to the Carolines. Nerida belongs down that way, you know; and she is fretting to get back again—otherwise I wouldn't leave this island. I've done pretty well here, although the people I trade for are—well, you know what they are."

"Aye," assented old Humphreys, "there isn't one of 'em but what is the two ends and bight of a—scoundrel; and that supercargo with the yaller mustache and womany hands is the worst of the lot. I wonder if he's aboard this trip? I don't let him inside my house; I've got too many daughters, and they all think him a fine man."

Nerida, Taplin's wife, came out to us from an inner room. She was a native of one of the Pelew Islands, a tall, slenderly built girl, with pale olive skin and big, soft eyes. A flowing gown of yellow muslin—the favorite color of the Portuguese blooded natives of the Pelews—buttoned high up to her throat, draped her graceful figure. After putting her little hand in ours, and greeting us in the Funafuti dialect, she went over to Taplin, and touching his arm, pointed out the schooner that was now only a mile or so away, and a smile parted her lips, and the starlike eyes glowed and filled with a tender light.

I felt Captain Warren touch my arm as he rose and went outside. I followed.

"L——," said Warren, "can't we do something for Taplin ourselves? Isn't there a station any-where about Tonga or Wallis Island that would suit him?"

"Would he come, Warren? He—or rather, that pretty wife of his—seems bent upon going away in the schooner to the Carolines."

"Aye," said the skipper, "that's it. If it were any other vessel I wouldn't care." Then suddenly, "That fellow Motley (the supercargo) is a d——scoundrel—capable of any villainy where a woman is concerned. Did you ever hear about old Raymond's daughter, down at Mangareva?"

I had heard. Suffice it here to say that by means of a forged letter purporting to have been written by her father—an old English trader in the Gambier Group—Motley had lured the beautiful young half-blood away from a school in San Francisco, and six months afterwards turned her adrift on the streets of Honolulu. Raymond was a lonely man, and passionately attached to his only child; so no one wondered when, reaching California a year after and finding her gone, he shot himself in his room at a hotel.

"I will ask him, anyway," I said; and as we went back into the house the *Alida* shot past our line of vision through the coconuts, and brought up inside the brig.

"Taplin," I said, "would you care about taking one of our stations to the eastward? Name any island you fancy, and we will land you there with the pick of our 'trade' room."

"Thank you. I would be only too glad—but I cannot. I have promised Nerida to go back to Babelthouap or somewhere in the Pelews, and Motley has promised to land us at Ponape, in the Carolines. We can get away from there in one of the Dutch firm's vessels."

"I am very sorry, Taplin—" I commenced, when Captain Warren burst in with—"Look here, Taplin, we haven't got much time to talk. Here's the *Alida's* boat coming, with that (blank-blank) scoundrel Motley in it. Take my advice. Don't go away in the *Alida.*" And then he looked at Nerida and whispered something.

A red spark shone in Taplin's dark eyes, then he pressed Warren's hand.

"I know," he answered, "he's a most infernal villain—Nerida hates him too. But you see how I am fixed. The *Alida* is our only chance of getting back to the northwest. But he hasn't got old Raymond to deal with in me. Here they are."

Motley came in first, hat and fan in hand. He was a fine-looking man, with blue eyes and an unusually fair skin for an island supercargo, with a long, drooping, yellow mustache. Riedermann, the skipper, who followed, was stout, coarse, red-faced, and brutal.

"How are you, gentlemen?" said Motley, affably, turning from Taplin and his wife and advancing towards us.

Warren looked steadily at him for a moment, and then glanced at his outstretched hand.

"The pleasure isn't mutual, blarst you, Mr. Motley," he said coldly, and he put his hand in his pocket.

The supercargo took a step nearer to him with a savage glare in his blue eyes. "What do you mean by this, Captain Warren?"

"Mean," and the imperturbable Warren seated himself on a corner of the table, and gazed stolidly first at the handsome Motley and then at the heavy, vicious features of Riedermann. "Oh, anything you like. Perhaps it's because it's not pleasant to see white men landing at a quiet island like this with revolvers slung to their waists under their pajamas; looks a bit too much like Bully Hayes' style for me," and then his tone of cool banter suddenly changed to that of studied insolence. "I say, Motley, I was talking about you just now to Taplin *and* Nerida; do you want to know what I was saying? Perhaps I had better tell you. I was talking about Tita Raymond—and yourself?"

Motley put his right hand under his pajama jacket, but Taplin sprang forward, seized his wrist in a grip of iron, and drew him aside.

"The man who draws a pistol in my house, Mr. Motley, does a foolish thing," he said in quiet, contemptuous tones, as he threw the supercargo's revolver into a corner.

With set teeth and clenched hands Motley flung himself into a chair, unable to speak.

Warren, still seated on the table, swung his foot nonchalantly to and fro and then commenced at Riedermann.

"Why, how's this, Captain Riedermann? Don't you back up your supercargo's little quarrels, or have you left your pistol on board? Ah, no, you haven't. I can see it there right enough. Modesty forbids you putting a bullet into a man in the presence of a lady, eh?" Then slewing round again he addressed Motley, "By God, sir, it is well for you that we are in a white man's house and that that man is my friend and took away that pistol from your treacherous hand; if you had fired at me *I would have booted you from one end of Funafuti beach to the other*—and I've a damned good mind to do it now, but won't, as Taplin has to do some business with you."

"That will do, Warren," I said. "We don't want to make a scene in Taplin's house."

Still glaring angrily at Riedermann and Motley, Warren got down slowly from the table. Then we bade Taplin and Nerida good-by and went aboard.

At daylight we saw Taplin and his wife go off in the *Alida's* boat. They waved their hands to us in farewell as the boat pulled past the brig, and then the schooner hove-up anchor, and with all sail set stood away down to the northwest passage off the lagoon.

A year or so afterward we were on a trading voyage to the islands of the Tubuai Group, and were lying becalmed, in company with a New Bedford whaler. Her skipper came on board the brig, and we started talking of Taplin, whom the whaleship captain knew.

"Didn't you hear?" he said. "The *Alida* never showed up again. 'Turned turtle,' I suppose, somewhere in the islands, like all those slashing over-masted 'Frisco-built schooners do, sooner or later."

"Poor Taplin," said Warren, "I thought somehow we would never see him again."

Five years had passed. Honest old Warren, fiery-tempered and true-hearted, had long since died of fever in the Solomons, and I was supercargo with a smart young American skipper in the brigantine *Palestine*, when we one day sailed along the weather-side of a tiny little atoll in the Caroline Islands.

The *Palestine* was leaking, and Packenham, tempted by the easy passage into the beautiful lagoon, decided to run inside and discharge our cargo of copra to get at the leak.

The island had but very few inhabitants—perhaps ten or twelve men and double that number of women and children. No ship, they told us, had ever entered the lagoon but Bully Hayes's brig, and that was nine years before.

At the time of Hayes' visit the people were in sore straits, and on the brink of actual starvation, for although there were fish and turtle in plenty, they had not the strength to catch them. A few months before a cyclone had destroyed nearly all the coconut trees, and an epidemic followed it, and carried off half of the scanty population.

The jaunty sea-rover—than whom a kinder-hearted man to natives never sailed the South Seas—took pity on the survivors, especially the youngest and prettiest girls, and gave them a passage in the famous *Leonora* to another island where food was plentiful. There they remained for some years, till the inevitable *mal du pays* that is inborn to every Polynesian and Micronesian, became too strong to be resisted; and so, one day, a wandering sperm whaler brought them back again.

But in their absence strangers had come to the island. As the people landed from the boats of the whaleship, two brown men, a woman and a child, came out of one of the houses, and gazed at them. Then they fled to the farthest end of the island and hid.

Some weeks passed before the returned islanders found out the retreat of the strangers, who were armed with rifles, and called to them to "come out and be friends." They did so, and by some subtle treachery the two men were killed during the night. The woman, who was young and handsome, was spared, and, from what we could learn, had been well treated ever since.

"Where did the strangers come from?" we asked.

That they could not tell us. But the woman had since told them that the ship had anchored in the lagoon because she was leaking badly; and that the captain and crew were trying to stop the leak when she commenced to sink, and they had barely time to save a few things when she sank. In a few days the captain and crew left the island in the boat; and the two natives and the woman elected to remain on the island.

"That's a mighty fishy yarn," said Packenham to me. "We'll go ashore to-morrow and have a look round."

A little after sunset the skipper and I were leaning over the rail watching the figures of the natives as they moved to and fro in the glare of the fires lighted here and there along the beach.

"Hallo," said Packenham, "here's a canoe coming, with only a woman in it. By thunder, she's traveling, too, and coming straight for the ship."

A few minutes more and the canoe was alongside. The woman hastily picked up a little girl that was sitting in the bottom, looked up, and called out in English—

"Take my little girl, please."

A native sailor leaned over the bulwarks and lifted up the child, and the woman clambered after her. Then seizing the child from the sailor, she flew along the deck and into the cabin.

She was standing facing us as we followed and entered, holding the child tightly to her bosom. The soft light of the cabin lamp fell full upon her features, and we saw that she was very young and seemed wildly excited.

"Who are you?" began I, when she advanced, put out a trembling hand to me, and said, "Don't you know me, Mr. Supercargo? I am Nerida, Taplin's wife." Then she sank on a seat and sobbed violently.

We waited till she regained her composure somewhat, and then I said, "Nerida, where is Taplin?"

"Dead," she said in a voice scarce above a whisper, "only us two are left—I and little Teresa."

Packenham held out his hands to the child. With wondering, timid eyes, she came, and for a moment or two looked doubtingly upwards into the brown, handsome face of the skipper, and then nestled beside him.

"Nerida, how and where did Taplin die?"

"My husband was murdered at sea," she said; and then she covered her face with her hands.

"Don't ask her any more now," said Packenham, pityingly, "let her tell us to-morrow."

She raised her face. "Yes, I will tell you to-morrow. You will take me away with you, will you not, gentlemen—for my child's sake?"

"Of course," said the captain, promptly. And he stretched out his honest hand to her.

"She's a wonderful pretty woman," said Packenham, as we walked the poop later on, and he glanced down through the open skylight to where she and the child slept peacefully on the cushioned transoms. "How prettily she speaks English too; do you think she was fond of her husband, or was it merely excitement that made her cry?"

"I can only tell you, Packenham, that when I saw her last, five years ago, she was a graceful girl of eighteen, and as full of happiness as a bird is of song—she looks thirty now; and her face is thin and drawn. But I don't say all for love of Taplin."

"That will all wear off by and by," said the skipper, confidently.

"Yes," I thought, "and she won't be a widow long."

Next morning Nerida had an hour or two among the prints and muslin in the traderoom, and there was something of the old beauty about her when she sat down to breakfast with us. We were to sail at noon. The leak had been stopped, and Packenham was in high good-humor.

"Nerida," I inquired, unthinkingly, "do you know what became of the *Alida?* She never turned up again."

"Yes," she answered, "she is here, at the bottom of the lagoon. Will you come and look at her?"

After breakfast we lowered the dinghy, the captain and I pulling. Nerida steered us out to the north end of the lagoon till we reached a spot where the water suddenly deepened.

She held up her hands for us to back water, then she gazed over the side into the water.

"Look," she said, "there lies the *Alida.*"

We bent over the side of the boat. The waters of the lagoon were as smooth as glass and as clear. We saw two slender rounded columns that seemed to shoot up in a slanting direction from out the vague blue depths beneath, to within four or five fathoms of the surface of the water. Swarms of gorgeously-hued fish swam and circled in and about the masses of scarlet and golden weed that clothed the columns from their tops downward and swayed gently to and fro as they glided in and out.

"'Twas six years ago," said Nerida, as we raised our heads.

That night, as the *Palestine* sped noiselessly before the trade wind to the westward she told me, in the old Funafuti tongue, the tragedy of the *Alida*.

"The schooner," she said, "sailed very quickly, for on the fifteenth day out from Funafuti we saw the far-off peaks of Strong's Island. I was glad, for Kusaie is not many days' sail from Ponape—and I hated to be on the ship. The man with the blue eyes filled me with fear when he looked at me; and he and the captain and mate were forever talking amongst themselves in whispers.

"There were five native sailors on board—two were countrymen of mine, and three were Tafitos.

"One night we were close to a little island called Mokil, and Taplin and I were awakened by a loud cry on deck; my two countrymen were calling on him to help them. He sprang on deck, pistol in hand, and, behold! the schooner was laid to the wind with the land close to, and the boat alongside, and the three white men were binding my countrymen with ropes, because they would not get into the boat.

"'Help us, O friend!' they called to my husband in their own tongue; 'the white men say that if we go not ashore here at Mokil they will kill us. Help us—for they mean evil to thee and Nerida. He with the yellow mustache wants her for his wife.'

"There were quick, fierce words, and then my husband struck Motley on the head with his pistol and felled him, and then pointed it at the mate and the captain, and made them untie the men, and called to the two Tafito sailors who were in the boat to let her tow astern till morning.

"His face was white with the rage that burned in him, and all that night he walked to and fro and let me sleep on the deck near him.

"'To-morrow,' he said, 'I will make this captain land us on Mokil'—it was for that he would not let the sailors come up from the boat.

"At dawn I slept soundly. Then I awoke with a cry of fear, for I heard a shot, and then a groan, and my husband fell across me, and the blood poured out of his mouth and ran down my arms and neck. I struggled to rise and he tried to draw his pistol, but the man with yellow hair and blue eyes, who stood over him, stabbed him twice in the back. Then the captain and mate seized him by the arms and lifted him up. As his head fell back I saw there was blood streaming from a hole in his chest."

She ceased, and leaned her cheek against the face of the little girl, who looked in childish wonder at the tears that streamed down her mother's face.

"They cast him over into the sea with life yet in him—and ere he sank, Motley (that devil with the blue eyes) stood with one foot on the rail and fired another shot, and laughed when he saw the bullet strike. Then he and the other two talked.

"'Let us finish these Pelew men, ere mischief come of it,' said Riedermann, the captain.

"But the others dissuaded him. There was time enough, they said, to kill them. And if they killed them now, there would be but three sailors to work the ship. And Motley looked at me and laughed, and said he, for one, would do no sailor's work yet awhile.

"Then they all trooped below, and took me with them—me, with my husband's blood not yet dried on my hands and bosom. They made me get liquor for them to drink, and they drank and laughed, and Motley put his bloodied hand around my waist and kissed me, and the others laughed still more.

"In a little while Riedermann and the mate were so drunken that no words came from them, and they fell on the cabin floor. Then Motley, who could stand, but staggered as he walked, came and sat beside me and kissed me again, and said he had always loved me; but I pointed to the blood of my husband that stained my skin and clotted my hair together, and besought him to first let me wash it away.

"'Wash it there,' he said, and pointed to his cabin.

"'Nay,' said I, 'see my hair. Let me then go on deck, and I can pour water over my head.'

"But he held my hand tightly as we came up, and my heart died within me; for it was in my mind to spring overboard and follow my husband.

"He called to one of the Tafito men to bring water, but none came; for they, too, were drunken with liquor they had stolen from the hold.

"But my two countrymen were sober; one of them steered the ship, and the other stood beside him with an ax in his hand, for they feared the Tafito men, who are devils when they drink grog.

"'Get some water,' said Motley, to Juan—he who held the ax; and, as he brought it, he said, 'How is it, tattooed dog, that thou art so slow to move?' and he struck him in the teeth, and as he struck he fell.

"Ah! that was my time! Ere he could rise I sprang at him, and Juan raised the ax and struck off his right foot; and then Liro, the man who steered, handed me his knife. It was a sharp knife, and I stabbed him, even as he had stabbed my husband, till my arm was tired, and all my hate of him had died away in my heart.

"There was quick work then. My two countrymen went below into the cabin and took Motley's pistol from the table; . . . then I heard two shots.

"*Guk!* He was a fat, heavy man, that Riedermann, the captain, the three of us could scarce drag him up on deck and cast him over the side.

"Then Juan and Liro talked and said, 'Now for these Tafito men; they too must die.' They brought up rifles and went to the fore-part of the schooner where the Tafito men lay in a drunken sleep and shot them dead.

"In two more days we saw land—the island we have left but now, and because that there were no people living there—only empty houses could we see—Juan and Liro sailed the schooner into the lagoon.

"We took such things on shore as we needed, and then Juan and Liro cut away the topmasts and towed the schooner to the deep pool, where they made holes in her, so that she sank.

"Juan and Liro were kind to me, and when my child was born five months after we landed, they cared for me tenderly, so that I soon became strong and well.

"Only two ships did we ever see, but they passed far-off like clouds upon the sea-rim; and we thought to live and die there by ourselves. Then there came a ship, bringing back the people who had once lived there. They killed Juan and Liro, but let me and the child live. The rest I have told you . . . how is this captain named? . . . He is a handsome man and I like him."

We landed Nerida at Yap, in the Western Carolines. A year afterwards, when I left the *Palestine*, I heard that Packenham had given up the sea, was trading in the Pelew Group, and was permanently married, and that his wife was the only survivor of the ill-fated *Alida*.

A Glory Departed

C. ERNEST FAYLE

We were discussing, soberly enough, certain problems of trade and shipping when I happened to mention my one long voyage in a sailing vessel. "Ah yes," said Captain——with a new animation in his voice, "but she wasn't a flyer like my old ship." His tone was so full of pride and affection that it was with an eager interest I enquired her name. "*Cutty Sark*," he replied, "I was in her when she made her last run home with tea from China." It was like meeting a man who had known King Arthur intimately.

Even among those who have made no special study of the sea, the name of *Cutty Sark* is known as one of the fastest and smartest—many would say *the* fastest and smartest—of the wonderful clippers with whom the old order at sea culminated, and passed away. Too late for the great years of the tea races from Foochow, she was for many years the crack ship of the wool fleet from Australia which carried on, right into the nineties, so gallant a fight against the competition of the steamer; but like most of her consorts, she was at length 'sold foreign,' and until her recent purchase brought her back to the British register she had been knocking about under the Portuguese flag, forgotten by all but a few who had known and loved her. To-day, when the windjammer has ceased almost entirely to count as a factor in ocean trade, the glories of the old clippers have acquired an almost legendary savour, and this chance meeting with one who had served in *Cutty Sark* in the days of her greatness brought home with something of a shock the narrowness of the gulf that separates us from an era now irrevocably past.

It set me trying to fathom the secret of that romance which clings around the names of the China and Colonial clippers—*Ariel, Sir Lancelot, Thermopylæ, Salamis*—and is denied, fairly or unfairly, to their successors, the ocean greyhounds of to-day. We all know what Kipling's old Scotch engineer thought of the amateur yachtsman who asked him, "Mister MacAndrews, don't you think steam spoils romance at sea?" and the creator of MacAndrews has proved, if it needed proving, that poetry and romance can be found in the engine-room as well as on the skysail yard; yet for most of us the white-winged clipper has a charm and personality that we cannot so fully associate with the masterpieces of modern marine architecture. I do not know whether a man would be moved, as Captain——was moved, in saying "I was in the *Mauretania* when she won the blue riband of the Atlantic." I am sure we should not listen to him with the same thrill.

It is not merely, as has sometimes been suggested, a question of beauty. True, the towering canvas, the tapering spars, the clipper bow are gone; but the lines of an *Olympic* or a *Mauretania* have a beauty of their own, a beauty firmly based on essential rightness and fitness for purpose. It is not 'the taint of commercialism.' *Ariel* and *Cutty Sark* were run to pay, and though success in the race home with tea from China or with wool from Australia was a matter of personal pride to owner, master, and crew, the main object of the race was to reach London in time for the first sales of the season. A reputation as a flyer had its cash value in the freight markets.

There are many other causes that have been advanced for the passing of the glamour that surrounds the sailing ship—the substitution of the big impersonal company for the individual owner, the smaller opportunities for human contacts on board a mammoth liner, the lesser value of instinctive seamanship and long experience in a steamer's crew. Almost all of them connect themselves in some way with a loss of that personality which the sailing ship possessed, and to which Joseph Conrad has given imperishable expression. There is one factor in this loss of personality, however, which has perhaps been insufficiently emphasized. The quality in the steamer that has done most to dim the romance of the sea is that which, from every other point of view, is her crowning glory. She suffers from the defect of reliability.

A ship is built to-day for a speed of 12, 15, 20 knots, and though her actual performance may vary a little from voyage to voyage, she will make passage after passage, in the liner trades, to a fixed schedule of dates, and with a variation of only a few hours in her actual time at sea. It is her boast that she may be depended on with almost mathematical certainty to make her port on the appointed day. The ratio of her speed to that of her rivals is known and recorded.

In the old days it was not so. When the clipper left port, it was never safe to calculate within a week the date of her arrival. Her passage was a matter of pluck and luck. *Cutty Sark*, of course, was a marvel, and the average of all her wool passages between 1874 and 1890 works out at 77 days, only five days above her best passage between port and port during that period; but *Serica*, one of the three who came home from Foochow in 99 days in the great race of 1866, took 120 in the following year, and four consecutive runs of *Salamis* from Melbourne to London give 94, 100, and 77 days respectively. These records, picked out at random from Mr. Basil Lubbock's fascinating volumes, *The China Clippers* and *The Colonial Clippers*, are only stray instances of a variation between voyage and voyage which, apart altogether from port delays or accidents, frequently presented still greater contrasts.

It was partly a matter of handling, of the smartness of the crew, of the tenacity with which the master would 'carry on,' when the gale drove others to shorten sail, the skill with which he could take advantage of the slightest puff of wind in the 'doldrums,' the judgment with which he shaped his course. It was partly a matter of luck; a long succession of contrary winds or baffling calms might nullify the effects of the most beautiful model and the most skilful seamanship. Hence there could be no reckoning with certainty on either the actual or the comparative performances of the ships. The cracks raced year after year with varying and often alternate success; a change of master or the favour of the elements might bring the laggard of the fleet into the first flight.

This it was that gave to the old sailing tradition a large part of its vitality and thrill. The modern liner may have the satisfaction of lowering a record established by her predecessors, but the largest share of the glory goes to those who designed her hull and engines, and from the standard set on her maiden voyage she will show but small variation. To a great extent—for the argument must not be pushed too far—she is like a watch, which, once set and regularly wound, will keep time until it wears out. The clipper was like a high-metalled horse, responsive with the responsiveness of a living thing to the touch of her master, capable of being coaxed into surprising efforts, subject, as all living things are subject, to strange inconsistencies and reversals of fortune. For her, each voyage was a contest with other ships and with the elements, to the result of which neither her own previous performances, nor those of her rivals, afforded any sure pointer. For master, officers, and crew, each passage was one long struggle, calling for daring, skill, endurance and ceaseless vigilance.

This element of struggle is essential to romance. We can admire the skill by which victory is assured, but it is only so long as the event of a contest is uncertain that it stirs the blood, and the longer the odds, the greater the thrill. Set in a world where arduous effort and uncertain reward are the normal conditions of our existence, we cannot easily recognize a kinship to humanity in the effortless certainty with which the machine performs its work. We have come to love the struggle for its own sake and to think more of the effort than of the attainment.

The heart of man revolts against the finality of accomplishment. The development of the steamship is a triumph over the elements; it enables man to sail at his own will, not the wind's; but for this triumph a price has been paid. The true romance of steam was in the days when the elements were still imperfectly subdued, when every ship was experimental, and the possibility of an Atlantic steamship service was a matter of bitter controversy. Now that we know what we can do, some of the savour has gone out of the doing.

It is for this reason that so large a proportion of our energy and inventiveness, so much of youth and daring and enterprise, are to-day directed not to the sea, but to the air, where unknown possibilities still remain to be explored. It is for this reason that, while the perils of the seas still surround every voyage with a halo of adventure, we look back with a special affection and pride to the doings of the *Cutty Sark* and her contemporaries, in days when the race was not always to the swift, and either personality or fortune could still upset the most careful calculations.

The Yacht

ARNOLD BENNETT

When Mrs. Alice Thorpe, with her black Pomeranian, arrived at the Hard from the railway station she at once picked out a small motor-launch among the boats that were bobbing about the steps, and said:

"Is this Mr. Thorpe's?"

"Yes'm," said the sailor in charge of the launch.

She signalled to a lad who lingered in the rear with her valise perched on his head; the valise was dropped into the forward part of the launch, Mrs. Thorpe gave the boy sixpence, and placed herself and dog neatly in the stern-sheets; the engine suddenly began to fire and throb with great velocity and noise, and the launch threaded out from the concourse of craft into the middle of the creek, leaving a wake of boiling foam. There had been no delay, no misunderstanding, no bungling, no slip. The telegraphic arrangements for taking Mrs. Thorpe on board the yacht had worked to perfection. Efficiency reigned.

Aged twenty-seven, slim, not tall, Alice was a capable woman. Her eyes had the capable look which many men dislike, for while they appreciate the conveniences of efficiency in a girl they seem to prefer the efficiency to be modestly masked by an appearance of helplessness. Alice neither disguised nor flaunted the fact that she was capable. Her eyes had also the look of one accustomed to give orders that were obeyed. The dog was supposed to be the only Pomeranian on earth not given to habitual yapping; Alice had purged it of the hereditary Pomeranian curse by replying instantly to every yap with a sound smack on the head. She adored the dog, which was passionately and exclusively devoted to her, after the manner of Pomeranian ladies to their mistresses. This Pomeranian's mistress, if not beautiful, was attractive, especially in figure and in clothes. She was a fine dancer, with a body that always surprised her partners by its extraordinary yieldingness, responsiveness and flexibility. A man having danced with her for the first time would remember her physical elasticity for days—to say nothing of her sudden eager smiles that puckered all the skin round her eyes.

"Which is the yacht?" asked Alice of the sailor.

He was tidily dressed, but had an untidy mop of red hair escaping from his white cap, and a shapeless, ugly face; and his manner was somewhat gruff. She knew that he must be Peter, the steward and handy man, her husband's favourite, more than once referred to with laudation in her husband's letters. She did not care for him, and had already decided that he did not care for her. But she smiled amiably.

"Her's lying at the mouth of the creek, in the river," said Peter, pointing. "That's her, that ketch with the blue ensign at the mizzen."

Alice looked in vain along the vista of yachts and other craft in the creek. She did not know what a mizzen was, nor that the blue ensign was a flag—she fancied indeed that an ensign was a sort of three-cornered thing. Peter's incomprehensible indication, however, merely increased her sense of mystery and expectancy. The moment was thrilling for her.

She had met her husband when both of them were in uniform in France. She had married him in London impulsively because they were mad for each other. A week later he had been tragically swept off to Mesopotamia. Then, having got out of uniform, she had become organising secretary to a political body, and had had to go to America on its business. During her absence James Thorpe had received unexpected leave. But her tyrannous conscience would not allow her to depart from the United States until her work was done; and she exulted in her work. Some caprice of the political body ended it in an hour by cable. She had obtained a berth on a Liverpool-bound liner the very next day.

She might have cabled the grand news to her husband, but she found somewhere in her mind a piquant pleasure in the notion of surprising him. She surprised him by a telegram from Liverpool. She knew that he was out of the army and in business. The unconventional wording of his reply to her telegram enchanted her, besides providing diversion for telegraph operators (who are not easily diverted). He was yachting, alone. She remembered, vaguely, that he possessed a yacht (laid up for five years), and had spoken very enthusiastically of yachting. Of course he had been for meeting her in London; but she would have none of it. "You shall receive me on your yacht," she had telegraphed. As she was an expert organiser, and he was an expert organiser, the arrangements following this decision of hers were easy enough.

She was now afraid, and her fear was romantic and terrible. The creek was alarmingly short, the launch surged at an alarming speed through the dappled blue water. She had not seen her lover, who was incidentally her husband, for nearly two years. She knew him by his photographs, his handwriting, his turns of phrase, and the memory of his gestures and of the feel of his moustache—but did she know him? Would he prove on further acquaintance to be somebody quite other than the image established in her heart? The situation was acutely disconcerting as she approached it. She stroked the dog's silky hair, and the dog glanced up at her face.

"That's her," said Peter, to the composed and prim young lady opposite him, pointing again.

She almost exclaimed:

"It's a very small yacht, isn't it?" But restrained herself.

The yacht's stem was pointing up-creek, against the ebb-tide. Peter seemed to steer the launch very queerly. He was apparently passing the yacht. She caught sight of a name on a life-buoy hung in the yacht's rigging. The name was *Alice*.

"But I thought the yacht was called *Hermes*," she said.

"Guv'nor had her name changed last month," gloomily answered Peter, as it were with resentment. Peter was preoccupied with the manœuvring of the launch on the tide, and Alice perceived that he knew exactly what he was doing. The nose of the launch edged towards the yacht's side; the launch seemed to hang in the current; then it slowly swung round, the propeller stopped, and the whole affair came gently to rest against dazzlingly white cushiony fenders and a polished stairway, from the top of which hung two dazzlingly white ropes. The yacht had grown enormous. Its bulwark rose high above the tiny launch, and it was as solid and moveless as a rock.

"And now he's called it *Alice*," said Alice to herself; and the situation appeared to be rather disconcerting.

II

Her husband loomed perpendicularly over her.

"Hallo!" he cried, saluting.

She answered in a weak voice:

"Well?" Her face was burning.

She seized the white ropes and tripped neatly up the stairway, and the blanched deck of the yacht stretched out firm and vast; and tall Jim clutched at her hand.

"Come below and see the saloon," he murmured.

He pushed her to a mahogany staircase under the main boom, and no sooner were they out of sight of the deck than he kissed her with rather more than his old accustomed violence. And the situation was acutely disconcerting again, but differently.

There was a pattering of innumerable little feet on the staircase, and the dog, who under excitement produced in human ears the illusion that she was a centipede and not a quadruped, bounded into the saloon.

"Oh, Fifi! I'd forgotten you! . . . Jim, this is Fifi."

The dog sprang into her arms, and Jim praised the dog highly and stroked her.

Husband and wife sat side by side in the saloon, and talked rather self-consciously about nothing, which was rather strange, seeing that each of them had ten thousand exciting matters to impart to the other. Still, it was all right. Alice knew it was all right, and she knew that Jim knew it was all right. They were strangers in one way and the most intimate of intimates in another. It might be said that the saloon held four people, not two.

"Oh! What's that funny thing?" Alice demanded, pointing to a very complicated kind of dial with a finger on it that was screwed face downwards to the saloon ceiling.

"That? Oh! That's a compass so that I can see the course of the ship when I'm having my meals."

"But the finger's moving right round!"

"Then you may be sure the yacht's moving right round too."

"Then we are off—already?"

And Jim said in his stern, sardonic tone:

"Didn't you hear the anchor being hauled up? Can't you feel the propeller?"

The fact was that Alice had not noticed the loud clacking of the anchor chain, her powers of observation having been temporarily impaired by the surpassing interest of her own private sensations. As for the propeller, she had in a vague manner been aware of a general vibration, but had not attributed it to anything in particular; she did not even know that the yacht possessed a propeller. Jim took her by the shoulders and they ran up on deck. The yacht was gliding out to sea, magically, formidably, by its own secret force; for the sails were not yet set. The entire adventure was ecstatic, incredibly romantic. Alice had never been so happy, so troubled, so restless.

"I do want to see all the rooms," said she, like a curious child.

"You shall. Are you given to being seasick?"

"I have never been seasick in my life," the capable woman replied with confidence.

Jim's keen eyes wandered over her admiringly.

"No," he murmured. "You aren't the sort that's seasick, you aren't."

They descended again to the saloon. A beautiful tea, with real crockery and brilliant electro-plate and real cakes and real cream, all set out upon a brass tray, lay on the table.

"Oh! Pete's served the tea. Good! Will you pour out? You must. You're the mistress of this wigwam."

She poured out. As she leaned an elbow on the table, the table tipped downwards under the pressure of her arm. She gave a little squeal.

"All right! All right!" Jim reassured her grandly. "Pete's taken the pin out, you know. Leaves the table free to oscillate when the boat rolls. It's weighted with lead underneath, so it can't swing far."

"Oh! I see. Of course!" said Alice, who, however, was not completely reassured. Things were not after all quite what they seemed.

She admired tremendously the internal arrangements of the yacht—they were so cosy, they were so complete; the most home-like thing she had ever seen. She visited every bit of the home. There was the saloon, or drawing-room, and there were a large double sleeping-cabin and a small single one; also there was a tiny bathroom. The multiplicity of cupboards and drawers delighted her; only in Utopia could she have imagined there would be so many cupboards and drawers. And there was electric light. And there were electric bells. You rang a bell, and it was answered just as it would have been in a real house—but much more promptly. Indeed, life on the yacht might be described as playing at perfect housekeeping. Everything had a place, and everything had to be in its place; and every place was full—except the drawers and the mirrored wardrobe reserved for the use of the mistress of the floating home. In the pantry every cup was hung on a hook; every wine-glass was lightly wedged in a fitting so that it could not dash itself against another wine-glass; and the same with saucers and plates. One surmised that even if the yacht were to turn upside down nothing would break.

And the organism was complete in itself, and sufficient to itself. Before dinner Jim said:

"Like a cocktail, beloved infant?"

The notion of a cocktail appealed to her as something wild and wicked.

"Why not?" said she. And Jim rang a bell.

"Two cocktails, Pete."

In about two minutes Peter, in a white jacket, brought two cocktails out of the mysteries of the forecastle where the pantry was. If Jim had ordered two nectars doubtless Pete would have produced them.

The dinner was very sound. It was strictly plain—oxtail soup (tinned), herring, roast mutton, potatoes, rice pudding—but it was sound. Alice admitted that Pete, for all his defects, could not merely cook meat well—he could buy good meat.

But she pointed out to Jim that Pete did not know how to lay the table properly—the fellow had put the fish knife and fork within the meat knife and fork—and at Jim's suggestion she pointed out the sad lapse to Pete personally, with a bright smile. Pete received the correction with a tranquillity too perfect, indicating by his nonchalant demeanour that if it pleased madam to have the meat knife and fork within the fish knife and fork he had no objection to obliging her, but that for himself his soul was above trifles. Pete had been Jim's batman for nearly three years in the war, and Jim spoke with quiet enthusiasm of his qualities. Alice, however, did not quite see what that had to do with the knife-and-fork question. They went on deck. The yacht was now at anchor in another estuary, whose quiet waters were full of phosphorescence. A dinghy moving towards another yacht close by threw up marvellous silver fireworks at every stroke of the oars. The night was obscure and warm and incredible. A radiance came from the saloon skylight; and a brighter radiance, sharply rectangular, from the open hatch of the forecastle. The crew (four human beings) could be heard talking in the depths of the forecastle. The old skipper appeared and made an inspection in the gloom; and Jim addressed him as "Skipper" with affectionate respect, though he was naught but a fisherman in winter and spoke with a terrific Essex accent.

The skipper disappeared. When next Alice glanced round there was no radiance, and no sound, from the forecastle. The crew had gone to bed. She and Jim were alone in the vast and miraculous world, enveloped by the poetry of water and sky. . . .

III

Nevertheless the next morning, in the double cabin, when she awoke very early in the twilight, that singular young woman was not utterly happy. That is to say, she was utterly happy, but at the same time she was unhappy—her heart being a huge place where all kinds of contradictory emotions could roam in comfort without interfering with each other. Jim was not in his berth. Through the open skylight, across which a horizontal blue blind was drawn, she could hear him chatting with the skipper. Jim was disturbingly friendly with his crew. "Look lively with the tea, Pete," he cried out. "Very good, sir." In another minute she could hear him sipping tea in enormous sips. She had an impression that he was seated, in pyjamas and dressing-gown, on the very skylight itself.

The floating home, then, had already begun to function very perfectly for the day. It was precisely the perfect functioning of the organism that upset her. Every contrivance in it was a man's contrivance. Woman had had naught to do with its excellence. It would function with the same perfection whether she happened to be there or not. It was orderly, it was comfortable; it was luxurious; and men had accomplished it and were maintaining it all by themselves. And the five males appeared to have an understanding among themselves, as if they belonged to a secret monastic or masonic order. She was outside the understanding. She was a woman, ornamental no doubt, but unnecessary. Well, she resented this in her great happiness. And she petted Fifi, who was curled within her arm, and Fifi resented it also.

So that the next afternoon Alice had a headache. It was a genuine headache, of which the symptoms were genuine pain in the forehead and a general sense of impending calamity. Considering a headache to be the proper thing at this conjuncture, she had desired to have a headache, and she had a headache; for she was a capable and thoroughly efficient woman. Hence, with Fifi, she went and lay down in her bunk in the big cabin, and parted from Jim at the door thereof, telling him that she did not want him to tuck her up. She noticed that the general sense of impending calamity had already affected Jim's gaze, and she resented that. What justification had Jim to assume that all was not for the best on board of an ideal yacht, seeing that her behaviour towards him had been pluperfect? He had no justification. Therefore he was in the wrong.

In her happiness she gave herself up to unhappiness. And yet her second marriage—it must be deemed her second marriage to Jim, the first having been an experiment, a prelude, an overture to the authentic union—her second marriage was unquestionably a success. She was mad about him. He was mad about her. She admired his character. He admired hers. She knew that he was the man for her and she the woman for him. Nothing could have been more propitious, more delicious, more exciting, more solidly sure. But she gave herself up to unhappiness because she felt herself unnecessary to the smooth working of the material organism in which she lived, and also because she felt herself to be outside the monastic or masonic order of five mutually comprehending males. And here was the self-same woman who had commanded hundreds of fellow-creatures in France, saying to them Go and they went, and Come and they came; and who had positively frightened a British political body, and startled bigwigs in New York, by the calm, unsentimental power of her horse-sense. Most of the persons with whom she had come into contact would have been ready to assert that where a woman's heart usually is she carried a bundle of pure sagacity, and none would have admitted that she could be subject to fancies. If those people whose respect she had extorted could have seen the charming little creature as she lay all wires and springs and nerves in the bunk! And if they could have looked inside her head! Marriage is a most mysterious developer. The worst of it was that Fifi encouraged Alice in her morbidity. Fifi understood; she did not argue; she did not even yap; but the glance of her eyes was a plain statement of the thesis: "You are always right, and when the created universe is out of tune with you the created universe needs altering."

Then Alice became aware of a vibration, which increased till it affected the entire ship—the bunk, the water-glass, the skylight, the pillow, the mattress, her toes, her temples. The propeller was propelling! Never before had the propeller been set to work while Alice was lying in her bunk. Why was the propeller now propelling? The weather was magnificent; the sun slanted into the cabin; the water was calm. Did not everybody know that she had a headache and was trying to rest? It was an outrage that the propeller should be set to work in such circumstances. Soon the propeller was doing more than revolve behind the stern-post of the yacht; it was revolving right inside her poor head. She could not and would not stand it. She rang the bell. A red head appeared in the doorway.

"Come in, come in," she said pettishly.

But the red head, timid in spite of campaigns, would not come in.

"Yes'm?"

"Oh! Please ask Mr. Thorpe to have that propeller stopped."

Peter merely laughed—a sort of contemptuously amused grin—and shut the door.

The propeller was not stopped. In five minutes, which seemed rather like a century, there was nothing else on earth for Alice save the propeller. It became the sole mundane phenomenon. It was revolving not only in her head, but in every part of her lithe and attractive body. It monopolised her attention, her intelligence, and her emotions. It had been going on from everlasting, and it would go on to everlasting. As a method of torture it rivalled and surpassed the most devilish inventions of the Holy Office at Toledo. It was the very thing to manufacture lunatics. Why had not Jim had the propeller stopped? He owned the yacht. If you could not silence your own propeller, what point was there in owning a yacht? Enormous and inexplicable events were passing on deck—bumps, thuds, sudden rushes of feet, shouts, bangs, rattlings, thunderings, clackings. But none of the five members of the monastic or masonic order showed the least interest in Alice and her aching head. Ah! The door of the cabin opened.

"Better?" asked Jim, standing by the side of her bunk. He was perspiring.

"No," she said.

"Tea-time. Come and have tea on deck. Do you good."

"No," she said.

"Shall I bring it you here?"

"No," she said.

At that moment the propeller stopped.

"At last!" breathed Alice sardonically and even bitterly. "If you've got a headache it's the most horrible torment one can imagine. I rang for Peter hours ago and asked him to tell you to stop it."

"I'm so sorry, my dove. But you see the propeller couldn't be stopped. We were going up the Blackwater against the ebb. And it's some ebb, believe me. Wind fell to nothing. If we'd stopped the propeller we should certainly have drifted on to a mudbank—Blackwater's full of 'em—and stuck there till next tide. We might have heeled over and filled as the tide fell. Ticklish thing, a boat drawing eight feet odd on a falling tide in a river like the Blackwater."

"Well, I think some one might have told me. I'm quite capable of understanding, though perhaps you mayn't think it."

Jim's eyes glittered.

"My child, I never thought for a moment——

"Just so! Just so! And let me tell you your Peter's extremely rude. When I asked him, do you know what he did? He just laughed—his horrid sarcastic grin. And I'll thank you to speak to him about his manners to me."

Jim did a surprising thing. He laughed, heartily.

"Well, of course it *would* strike Peter as comic, asking for the propeller to be stopped in a dead calm against an ebb-tide in this old Blackwater. He laughed when he came on deck and told me. It appealed to his sense of humour."

"And I suppose you all laughed!" said Alice sharply, in a loud tone. "You would!" She raised herself too violently on one elbow, and her delightful, misguided head struck the ceiling above the bunk.

"Awfully sorry, darling!" said Jim, very quietly. But whether he was sorry about Peter's enormity, or sorry merely about the detail of the head-bumping, Alice could not decide. At any rate, the bumping of her head rendered her furious and—quaintly enough—quite cured the headache.

"Peter is a fool!" she almost shouted.

"Hush!" Jim murmured grimly and dangerously.

And at the same time the skipper's voice was heard on deck:

"Let out a couple o' fathoms more chain, Charlie."

Alice's brain grasped the great truth that if she could hear the skipper, the skipper and crew could hear her, and the still greater truth that voice-raising in anger was impossible on that yacht without open scandal. She would have given about ten pounds for the privilege of one unrestrained scream.

Jim whispered uncompromisingly:

"Pete certainly isn't a fool. Also, he's a particular friend of mine."

An awful silence descended upon the yacht, and in the silence the yacht's clock, placed over the saloon stairs, could be heard ticking with uncanny loudness. In the late afternoon and early evening Alice ranged and raged about the vessel, chewing the cud of the discovery that there was no real privacy aboard. There was privacy from eyes, and plenty of it; but there was absolutely no privacy from ears if you raised your tone beyond a certain degree. She wanted to do that more than she wanted to do anything else in the world. She examined the dispositions of the yacht again and again, with no satisfactory result. It was sixty feet from end to end of its wonderful deck, and it was full of secret compartments, but it held no compartment in which a grand quarrel, row, and upset could be comfortably conducted according to the rules of such encounters. As a honeymoon resort the yacht was merely absurd. None but an idiot could have had the preposterous notion of honeymooning on a fifty-ton yacht.

Alice did not reflect upon the dangerous folly and the bad form and the gross inefficiency of making a scene on the third day of your second honeymoon. She did not even reflect that man is held to be a reasoning animal. She reflected simply and exclusively upon her predicament, which was surely the most singular predicament that a bride had ever found herself in. But she did not disclose her thoughts. No, to external view she was a charming, capable, sensible little yachtswoman in an agreeable blue jumper and blue skirt, wandering to and fro in and on the yacht, interesting herself in its construction and its life, and behaving to all the men with the delicatest feminine sweetness. To Jim she was acquiescence embodied; the irritation shown in the bunk had completely vanished. Night fell, and a red eye shone forth from the land. She learned that it indicated a jetty on an island which, in mid-Blackwater, was devoted to the reclamation of habitual drunkards. She was suddenly inspired.

"Let's row ashore, shall we?" she suggested persuasively.

"But the island's private, you know," said Jim.

Here, referring to the affair of the propeller, she might have revolted, and said angrily:

"Of course you're against anything I want."

Many women in her place would have said just that. But Alice was determined to be efficient, and so she said with increased persuasiveness:

"Still, it would be a bit of a lark, wouldn't it?"

Jim gave the order to lower the launch, and they were taken ashore, and the launch instructed to return in an hour. Half an hour would have sufficed for Alice's purposes; but the captain and two of the crew were also in the launch and had to go down river to fill six beakers with fresh water from a well in the vicinity; which job could scarcely be accomplished in less than an hour.

IV

"Now," said Jim, "shall we take a stroll and look for reformed drunkards?"

"I think we'll just stay where we are," Alice answered. "I must have an understanding with you." She spoke firmly but quietly. The desire to make a noise seemed to have left her, now that she was free to make a noise without making a scandal. Both inside and out she was the self-possessed woman again, the model of efficiency and sagacity, not merely in appearance, but to her own secret judgment.

"Certainly," said Jim with calmness. "Let's understand."

She was nettled because she thought she detected irony in his powerful, almost brutal, masculine voice.

"I've already told you that I think Peter ought to apologise to me. He hasn't apologised to me. Quite the contrary."

"Ah!" Jim answered. "I knew that was on your mind. You're an Aɪ actress, but I'm an Aɪ dramatic critic." And he proceeded: "And what's more, I've already told you that Pete's a friend of mine, and I don't like to hear my wife call my friends fools."

She then burst out into one of the most voluptuous of human passions—over-righteous indignation. She didn't want any more to be self-possessed, efficient, sagacious; nor to be an exemplary wife, nor to teach a barbaric husband by the force of Christian example, nor to do any of the things that serious young wives very properly want to do. She just wanted to let herself go; and she did. The mysterious and terrible potion had been brewing for several hours; it now boiled over, surging magnificently upwards as a geyser shoots out of the ground. She was at last free of the captivity of the yacht. There was none to overhear and no eye to see except the red eye on the jetty.

"That's just like you," she cried. "That's just like you. You're ready to risk the whole of our married life in order to indulge your brutality. You once said you were a brute, and so you are. We've scarcely been three days together and yet you're spoiling for a row. You think you can browbeat me, you and your crew. You can't. You've all done nothing but laugh at me since I went on board. Look how you all stood round and smiled condescendingly when I steered. And heaven knows I only took the helm because you asked me to. You're all as thick as thieves together, and I'm nobody. I'm only a woman, a doll to be petted and laughed at. Do you imagine I wanted to steer your precious yacht? Indeed no! Give me an Atlantic liner, that's what I say. Your crew do what they like with you, and you're such a simpleton you can't see it. They flatter you, and you're so conceited you swallow it all. And shouldn't I just like to see the food bills for your precious yacht. Why, there's been as much meat cooked for us two in these three days as would keep a family for a fortnight. You pay your crew wages that include their food, and then instead of buying their own food they live on ours. It's as plain as a pikestaff."

In a short pause that followed Jim said:

"Don't let me interrupt you. Tell me when you've quite done, and then I'll make a short speech. But if you think I'm going to lose my temper, old woman, you're mistook."

Alice resumed.

"I said Peter was a fool. So he is. But he's also a lout. And what's worse, he's a thief. He steals your food."

Then Jim, taken unawares, lost his temper. The battle was joined. A big steam tug passed slowly up the river, a noisy but a noble phenomenon in the night. They did not notice it. They noticed nothing except their own dim forms, pale faces and glinting eyes; heard nothing but their own voices and the crunching of their restless feet on the caked mud of the foreshore. The old earth was whirling round with incredible velocity amid uncounted millions of starry bodies of which it was nearly the very least. The mystery of life was unfathomed the structure of society was shaken and cracked. Tens of thousands of children were starving in Europe. Frightful problems presented themselves on every side for solution. The future of the world was dark with fantastic menaces. And the great beauty and wistfulness of nature were unimpaired by all these horrors. But Alice and Jim ignored everything save the gratification of their base and petty instincts. They were indeed a shocking couple. The moon rose—the solemn lovely moon that was drawing incalculable volumes of water out of the ocean into the estuary of the Blackwater—and Alice snapped:

"What I say I stick to. And I tell you another thing—all red-headed men are the same."

A strange glow appeared on the yacht. They did not see it. Peter hailed faintly from the yacht. They did not hear him. They were indulging themselves after restraint. They had gone back to the neolithic age after too much civilisation. And the whole francas was due to the fact that, on a small yacht, everybody can hear everything. The ignoble altercation was suddenly cut short by the grating of a boat's keel on the muddy shingle—Peter in the dinghy.

"Yacht's afire, sir!" Peter called grimly.

So it was. They could see flames coiling like snakes about the region of the saloon hatch.

Jim came back to civilisation in an instant.

"Well, why haven't you put it out, you fool, instead of coming here to tell me? Do you want the bally ship to be burnt to the water's edge?"

"Can't find the extinguisher, sir. It's supposed to hang in the small cabin, but it isn't on its hook. And we've run out of water on account of missis's baths. . . . Not as canvas buckets would be much good."

"My dog!" cried Alice. "She'll be roasted alive."

"I've brought her ashore," said Peter, pitching the animal out of the dinghy.

"Ah!"

Jim rushed to the boat's nose, shoved her back into the water, and sprang aboard.

"Pull like the devil."

"Stop!" shouted Alice. "I know where the extinguisher is." She plunged, Fifi in her arms, into the dark water, and was dragged into the dinghy.

Not only had she transgressed the rules of the yacht by taking fresh-water baths, but she had moved the Pyrene extinguisher from its hook into a locker in order to get another hook for her dresses. The small cabin had been allotted to her for a tiring-room, and her attire was all over it. Wonderful it was how one small valise could carry all she wore. She had taken things from the valise and more and more things, in the manner of a conjurer taking drapers' shops, flower shops, and zoological gardens out of one small hat.

Once aboard the vessel, she plunged devotedly through smoke into the bowels thereof and ascended again with the extinguisher. In three minutes the fire was out. It appeared that someone with a British sense of humour had thrown a piece of burning rope from the tug. The rope had dropped on to the saloon hatch. The roof of the said hatch was severely damaged and the coat of the mainsail a little charred; but that was the limit of the catastrophe.

V

The yacht was speeding up the Blackwater in the moonlight towards Maldon, James Thorpe, with all the dark fire of his nature, having determined at once to hunt the flame-scattering tug and get the law of it. He was in possession of what he considered to be sound circumstantial evidence of the tug's guilt. James himself had taken the wheel. Alice reclined at his feet. Fifi reclined at Alice's feet. The captain and crew were forward. Alice was perfectly happy. She had never really been unhappy—and especially had she not been unhappy in her nervous outpouring of riotous temper. But now she was in a kind of bliss—a bliss which was heightened by certain pin-pricks. These pin-pricks came from the facts, one, that she had upset the marvellous functioning of the ship by misplacing the fire-extinguisher; two, that she had upset the marvellous economy of the ship by using fresh water instead of salt water for her baths; and three, that James, in his enormous magnanimity, had refrained from twitting her about these lapses.

She reflected that, owing to pressure of patriotic and other business, she had not lost her temper for several years, and probably would not lose it again for several years, and at any rate to have lost it and safely found it so early in marriage, and with such an agreeable result, was not a bad thing, for it had amounted to a desirable and successful experiment. Her powerful common sense told her that there was a process in marriage known as "settling down," that this process had to be gone through by all couples and that she and Jim were getting through it quickly and brightly. She knew that she need not apologise to Jim, and indeed that he would hate her for apologising to him. She apologised by a touch, a glance, a tone, and by sitting at his feet.

Peter came aft to the little deck-larder that was forward of the saloon skylight.

"Pete."

"Sir?"

"Don't buy any more meat to-morrow until you've spoken to the mistress about it."

"No, sir."

Peter departed.

Jim lowered his face and murmured:

"You know you've got to admit that old Pete isn't a fool."

Alice had already fully absorbed the truth that Peter was not a fool. A man who, placed as Peter was placed, had had the presence of mind to think of the dog and bring the dog to safety ashore—such a man could not possibly be a fool. As for being the other thing that she had called him, of course that was absurd, and she had not meant it. No! She fully admitted, in the privacy of her mind, that she had been hopelessly wrong to call Peter a fool. But what she murmured to Jim in reply was:

"Why! You called him a fool yourself!"

Jim pinched her arm cruelly, but she dared not cry out lest she should be overheard. Therefore she suffered in silence and enjoyed the suffering.

Mark Tapley at Sea

CHARLES DICKENS

Onward she comes, in gallant combat with the elements, her tall masts trembling, and her timbers starting on the strain; onward she comes, now high upon the curling billows, now low down in the hollows of the sea as hiding for the moment from its fury; and every storm-voice in the air and water, cries more loudly yet, "A ship!"

Still she comes striving on: and at her boldness and the spreading cry, the angry waves rise up above each other's hoary heads to look; and round about the vessel, far as the mariners on her decks can pierce into the gloom, they press upon her, forcing each other down, and starting up, and rushing forward from afar, in dreadful curiosity. High over her they break; and round her surge and roar; and giving place to others, moaningly depart, and dashing themselves to fragments in their baffled anger; still she comes onward bravely. And though the eager multitude crowd thick and fast upon her all the night, and dawn of day discovers the untiring train yet bearing down upon the ship in an eternity of troubled water, onward she comes, with dim lights burning in her hull, and people there, asleep; as if no deadly element were peering in at every seam and chink, and no drowned seaman's grave, with but a plank to cover it, were yawning in the unfathomable depths below.

Among these sleeping voyagers were Martin Chuzzlewit and Mark Tapley, who, rocked into heavy drowsiness by the unaccustomed motion, were as insensible to the foul air in which they lay, as to the uproar without. It was broad day, when the latter awoke with a dim idea that he was dreaming of having gone to sleep in a four-post bedstead which had turned bottom upwards in the course of the night. There was more reason in this too, than in the roasting of eggs; for the first objects Mr. Tapley recognised when he opened his eyes were his own heels—looking down at him, as he afterwards observed, from a nearly perpendicular elevation.

"Well!" said Mark, getting himself into a sitting posture, after various ineffectual struggles with the rolling of the ship. "This is the first time as I ever stood on my head all night."

"You shouldn't go to sleep upon the ground with your head to leeward, then," growled a man in one of the berths.

"With my head to *where*?" asked Mark. The man repeated his previous sentiment.

"No, I won't another time," said Mark, "when I know whereabouts on the map that country is. In the meanwhile I can give you a better piece of advice. Don't you nor any other friend of mine never go to sleep with his head in a ship, any more."

The man gave a grunt of discontented acquiescence, turned over in his berth, and drew his blanket over his head.

"—For," said Mr. Tapley, pursuing the theme by way of soliloquy, in a low tone of voice; "the sea is as nonsensical a thing as any going. It never knows what to do with itself. It hasn't got no employment for its mind, and is always in a state of vacancy. Like them Polar bears in the wild-beast shows as is constantly a-nodding their heads from side to side, it never *can* be quiet. Which is entirely owing to its uncommon stupidity."

"Is that you, Mark?" asked a faint voice from another berth.

"It's as much of me as is left, sir, after a fortnight of this work," Mr. Tapley replied. "What with leading the life of a fly, ever since I've been aboard—for I've been perpetually holding-on to something or other, in a upside-down position—what with that, sir, and putting a very little into myself, and taking a good deal out of myself, there an't too much of me to swear by. How do *you* find yourself this morning, sir?"

"Very miserable," said Martin, with a peevish groan. "*Ugh!* This is wretched, indeed!"

"Creditable," muttered Mark, pressing one hand upon his aching head and looking round him with a rueful grin. "That's the great comfort. It is creditable to keep up one's spirits here. Virtue's its own reward. So's jollity."

The Monkey

EDEN PHILLPOTTS

They sat together forward, under scant shadows, while the *Land Crab*, a little coasting schooner, lay nearly becalmed in the Caribbean. Her sails flapped idly; hot air danced over the deck and along the bulwarks. Now and then a spar creaked lazily, or a block went "chip, chip," as the *Land Crab* rolled on a swell. The sun blazed over the foreyard-arm, the heat was tremendous, but Pete and Pete basked in it and loved it. Neither saw necessity for a straw of head covering; indeed Pete the greater wore no clothes at all. He sat watching Pete the less; anon he put forth a small black hand for a banana; then, with forehead puckered into a world of wrinkles and furrows, he inspected his namesake's work; and later, tired of squatting in the sun, hopped on to the bulwark and up the mizzen shrouds.

Peter the greater was a brown monkey, treasured property of the skipper; and Pete the less, now cleaning some flying-fish for the cook, was a negro boy, treasured property of nobody—a small lad, with a lean body, more of which appeared than was hidden by the rags of his shirt, and great black eyes like a dog's. He was, in fact, a very dog-like boy. When the men cursed him he cowered, and hung his head, and slunk away, sometimes showing a canine tooth; when they were in merry mood he frisked and fawned and went mad with delight. But chance for joy seldom offered. He had a stern master, and an awful responsibility in the shape of Pete the greater. This active beast, under God and the skipper, was Pete's boss. The sailors said that he always touched his wool to it, and everybody knew that he talked to it for hours at a time. When the lad first came aboard, Captain Spicer put the matter in a nutshell.

"See here, nig—this monkey's your pigeon; you've just got to watch it, an' feed it, an' think of it all the time. And bear in mind as he's a darned sight more valuable than anything else aboard this ship. So keep your weather eye lifting, and remember there'll be hell round here if harm comes to Pete."

"I's call Pete too, Cap'n sar," the boy had answered, grinning at what had struck him as a grand joke.

"Are you? Well, you get pals with Pete number one. That's what you've got to do."

But apes are capricious, and Pete the less found his pigeon aboard the *Land Crab* no bed of roses. For that matter the rest of the hands suffered too. Nathan Spicer was a bald-headed old man with an evil temper—one blighted by sorrow and affliction, hard to please, bad to sail with. Dick Bent, the mate, had known his captain in past years, when the sun shone on him, and he explained the position from his former knowledge.

"It's like this 'ere—Nature filled the old sweep with the milk of human kindness; then she up and sent a thunderstorm of troubles and turned it sour. I've sailed on and off with him these twenty year, and I mind when he kept his foot on his temper, an' were a very tidy member o' seafarin' society. But after his missis died and his kid died, then he—what had married old and was wrapped up in the woman—why, then he cast off all holds, and chucked religion, and wished he could see the world in hell, and done his little best to help send it there. Men gets that way when things turn contraiwise. Not but what there's good hid in him too."

But Bent's shipmates—three mongrel negroes and two Englishmen—failed to find the buried treasure. Skipper Spicer was always the same, with painful monotony. Only the man, Duck Bent, and the monkey, Pete, could pull with him. The rest of the crew suffered variously, for the captain, though no longer young, was rough and powerful. He had outbursts of passion that presented a sorry sight for gods and men. Such paroxysms seemed likely enough to end life for him some day; and just as likely to end life for another.

The negro boy scraped out his flying-fish and cut off their tails and wings, then he peeled a pannikin of sweet potatoes and talked to his charge.

"Marse Pete," he said gravely, "you's a dam lucky gem'man, sar—de mose lucky gem'man aboard de *Lan' Crab*. You frens wid cap'n a'ways. He nebber sharp wid you—nebber; but he dat sharp wid me, sar, dat I'se sore all over de backside all de time. I fink you might say word to cap'n for me, Marse Pete, for I'se mighty kind nigger to you, sar."

The monkey was chewing another banana. It stripped off the skin with quick black fingers, filled its mouth, stuffed its cheeks, and then munched and munched and looked at Pete. It held its head on one side as though thinking and weighing each word, and Pete felt quite convinced that it understood him. The boy himself was ten years old. He had entered the world undesired and knew little of it, save that sugar-cane was sweet in the mouth but hard to come by, honestly or otherwise. Pete the greater lived in his master's cabin, and Pete the less often heard the skipper talking to him. If the captain could exchange ideas with his monkey, surely a nigger might do so; and it comforted the boy to chatter his miseries and empty his heart to the beast. Nobody on board had time or inclination to attend to him.

"I wish you was me and me was you, sar, for I has berry bad time aboard dis boat, but you has all b'nana an' no work—an'—an'—don't be so spry, Marse Pete!" as the monkey went capering aloft. "One day you run 'long dem spars too often and fall in de sea to Marse Shark. Den what de boss do wid me?"

It happened that Bent was lying full sprawl behind a hatchway, smoking and grinning, as he listened to these remarks. Now he lifted a funny, small head, with a red beard, and answered the question.

"Old man'd skin you, nig, and then throw you after the monkey," he answered.

"I guess he would, sar."

"So keep alive. Why, you might as well steal skipper's watch as let that animal there get adrift."

The skipper came on deck and both Petes saw him at the same moment. One touched his wool and ambled forward to the galley; the other came down the ratlines head first, and leapt chattering to the captain's shoulder, a favourite perch. His master had owned the monkey five years. It belonged once to his mulattress wife; and when she was dying, she specially mentioned it and made it over to him. That and his watch were the only treasures he had in the world. With his brown wife and his home in Tobago, the man had been happy, even God-fearing, but the first baby killed its mother and, dying also, left a wrecked life behind. Nathan Spicer cared for nothing now, and consequently feared nothing. It is their interest on earth, not the stake in eternity, that makes men cowards.

II

The *Land Crab*, delayed by light winds, was some days overdue at Trinidad, and the skipper exploded in successive volcanoes from dawn till dusk. He was always in a rage, and, as Bent observed:

"If this sight o' energy, and cussing and swearing and to helling the ship's comp'ny, was only shoved into the elements we'd 'a' had half a gale o' wind by now. The old man'll bust 'is biler, sure as death, 'fore he's done with it."

But the winds kept baffling, and swearing did not mend them, nor yet blows, nor yet footfall with Pete the boy. There is no reason to suppose that Skipper Spicer disliked Pete overmuch—not more than he hated any boy; but he was brutal, and needed something to kick at times. Moreover, a kick does not show on a negro, and many imagine that it is the only way of explaining that you disagree with him.

Once the mate ventured to intercede by virtue of his long acquaintance.

"We're old pals, Cap'n," he said, "and meanin' no disrespect, it's like this 'ere—you're killing that little black devil. 'E's small, and you do welt that 'ard. It's 'cause he's a good boy I mention it. If he was a bad 'un, then I'd say, 'lather on,' and I'd help. But he minds his pigeon."

"Which you'd better do likewise," answered the skipper.

"All right, boss. Only it's generally allowed now that nigs is human, same as us, and has workin' souls also."

"Drivel and rot! I don't have none of that twaddle aboard this ship. I know—nobody better'n me—'cause I was a psalm-singer myself among the best. And what's come of it? There ain't no God in these latitoods anyway, else why did he play it so dirty on me? If there's any manner of God at all, He killed my wife and my child for fun, and I don't take no stock in a God that could do that. I'll rip forrard my own way now, till He calls for my checks, which He's quite welcome to, any time—damn Him. But 'tis all bunkum and mumbo-jumbo. Nobody's got a soul no more'n my monkey, so there's a end of the argument."

"Soul or none, 'e's a deal of sense for sartin," admitted the mate, "a 'mazing deal of sense. An' he takes kind to t'other Pete. If 'e could talk now, I bet he'd say to give the boy a chance, off and on, to get a whole skin over his bones for a change."

"Which if he did," answered the other, "I should say to him as I do to you: to mind his own blasted bus'ness."

But the men were friends in half an hour, for a fair wind came up out of the sea at dusk, the *Land Crab* plodded along and Spicer quickly thawed.

"Darn the old tub, she makes some of them new-fangled boats look silly yet!" he said to Bent, as, a day later, they lumbered through the Dragon's Teeth to Port of Spain.

After leaving Trinidad, the little coaster proceeded to Tobago for a cargo of coconuts, and the crew viewed that circumstance with gratification, for the most heavy-witted amongst them never failed to notice how a visit to his former home softened the old man. On this occasion, as upon past trips, the palm-crowned mountains of Tobago brought a measure of peace into the skipper's heart, whilst a fair wind and a good cargo tended to improve that condition. All hands reaped benefit and to Dick Bent the captain grew more communicative than usual.

They walked the deck together one morning on the homeward passage to Barbados, and Spicer lifted a corner of the curtain hiding his past.

"Then it was good to live like, but when my missus went 'west,' and took the baby along with her, life changed. Now there's only two things in all creation I care a red cent about. One's a beast, t'other an old gold watch—pretty mean goods to set your heart on, but all as I've got in the whole world."

"It's a mighty fine watch," said Bent.

"It is, and chain too, for that matter. I was lookin' at 'em in my cabin only half an hour past." He brightened as he thought of the trinket, and continued, "I doubt there's many better'n me would fancy that chain across their bellies, but she—"

"Lord deliver us, look aft!" sang out the mate suddenly, interrupting and pointing to the hatch of the companion.

Spicer's monkey had just hopped up on deck, and from his black paw hung the skipper's watch and chain. Pete the greater ambled along towards the bulwark, and a sweat burst from his master's face as he called to the brute in a strange voice. But Pete was perverse. He reached the bulwark and the skipper's nerve died in him, while Bent dared not to take a step towards hastening the threatened catastrophe, or identifying himself therewith. It was a trying moment as the monkey made for his favourite perch on the mizzen rigging, and while he careered forward on all fours, the watch bumped, bumped against the ship's side. The sound brought the blood with a rush to Skipper Spicer's head. Patience was no virtue of his at the best, and he jumped forward with a curse. The man had his hand within six inches of the watch when Pete squeaked and dropped it into the sea. There was a splash, a gleam of gold, and the treasure sank, flashing and twinkling down through the blue, dwindling to a bright, submerged snake, then vanishing for ever. A great gust of passion shook the skipper and tied his tongue. He tried to swear, but could only hiss and growl like an angry beast. Then he seized the monkey by the scruff of the neck as it jumped for his shoulder, shook it and flung it overboard with a shower of oaths. A red light blinded him, he felt his temples bursting, and he reeled away below, not stopping to see a brown head rise from the foam of the splash where Pete had fallen. The monkey fought for it, as one may see a rat driven off shipboard into the deep water. Two terrified eyes gazed upwards at his home, while the *Land Crab* swept by him; his red mouth opened with a yell, and his black paws began beating the water hard as he fell astern. Presently Pete sank for the first time. Then he came up again and went on fighting.

But the skipper saw nothing. He only felt the hot blood surging through his head as he flung himself on his bunk, face downwards. For a moment he thought death had gripped him; but the threatened evil passed, and his consciousness did not depart. He guessed that he had been near apoplexy. Then thoughts came and flooded his brain with abomination of desolation. He lay with his bald head on his arms and turned his mind back into the past. He remembered so much, and every shaft of memory brought him back with a round turn to the present. There was the lemon-tree with Pete's perch on it. His wife had loved the monkey. He could see her now kissing its nose. And she had died with the gold watch ticking under her head. Her wedding ring was upon the chain of it. She had tried to put it on his little finger before she went, but it would not get over the second joint, so she had slipped it upon the watch-chain. Now God in heaven could tell what loathsome fish was nosing it under the sea. And her monkey, her last gift to him, a live meal for a shark. Now the wide world remained to him, empty—save for the thought of what he had done.

He lay needless of time for near three hours. Then he sat up and looked round the cabin. As he did so the door opened, Bent's small head peeped in and the mate spoke:

"Fit as a fiddle, boss; only a flea or two missing."

Then the man shut the cabin door again. But he left something behind. Pete the greater chattered and jumped to his perch in the corner, and from there on to his master's berth. He was dry, warm and much as usual apparently; and he bore no malice whatever. Spicer glared and his breath caught in his throat. Then he grabbed the brute to him till it squeaked, while Nathan snuffled horrible but grateful oaths.

There was only one soul aboard the *Land Crab* who would have gone into a shark-haunted sea to save a monkey, and he did not think twice about it. He came on deck too late to see the catastrophe, though in time to note Pete the greater in the jaws of death. Had he known how the monkey came into the Caribbean he might have doubted the propriety of attempting a rescue; but he did not know, and so he joined it, feeling they might as well die together as perish apart. The boy could swim like a duck, and as Bent lowered a boat smartly, and the sharks held off, it was not long before Pete and Pete came aboard again. But, meantime, their master in his bunk did not even know that the ship had been hove to.

They emptied the water out of Pete the monkey and dried him, and they gave Pete the negro some rum. Both were jolly in an hour; and Skipper Spicer chose to take peculiar views of the gravity of the incident. He never kicked his cabin-boy again.

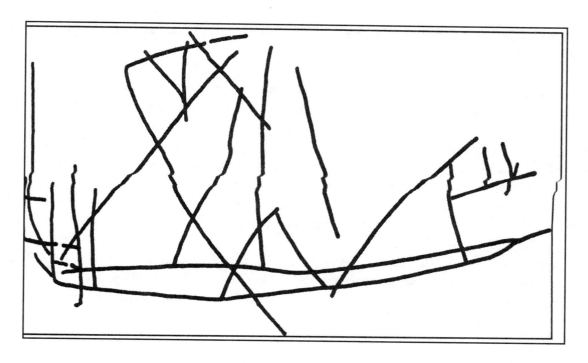

The Murderer

PERCEVAL GIBBON

From the open door of the galley, where the cross, sleepy cook was coaxing his stove to burn, a path of light lay across the deck, showing a slice of steel bulwark with ropes coiled on the pins, and above it the arched foot of the mainsail. In the darkness forward, where the port watch of the *Villingen* was beginning the sea day by washing down decks, the brooms swished briskly and the head-pump clacked like a great, clumsy clock.

The men worked in silence, though the mate was aft on the poop, and nothing prevented them from talking as they passed the buckets to and from the tub under the pump and drove their brooms along the planks. They laboured with the haste of men accustomed to be driven hard, with the shuffling, involuntary speed that has nothing in it of free strength or goodwill. The big German four-master had gathered from the boarding-houses of Philadelphia a crew representing all the nationalities which breed sailors, and carried officers skilled in the crude arts of getting the utmost out of it. And since the *lingua franca* of the sea, the tongue which has meaning for Swedish carpenters,

Finn sail-makers, and Greek fo'c'sle hands alike, is not German, orders aboard the *Villingen* were given and understood in English.

"A hand com' aft here!"

It was the mate's voice from the poop, robust and peremptory. Conroy, one of the two Englishmen in the port watch, laid down the bucket he was carrying and moved aft in obedience to the summons. As he trod into the slip of light by the galley door he was visible as a fair youth, long-limbed and slender, clad in a serge shirt, with dungaree trousers rolled up to the knees, and girt with a belt which carried the usual sheath-knife. His pleasant face had a hint of uncertainty; it was conciliatory and amiable; he was an able seaman of the kind which is manufactured by a boarding-master short of men out of a runaway apprentice. The others, glancing after him while they continued their work, saw him suddenly clear by the galley door, then dim again as he stepped beyond it. He passed out of sight towards the lee poop ladder.

The silent, hurried sailors pressed on with their work, while the big barque purred through the water to the drone of wind thrusting in the canvas. The brooms were abaft of the galley when the out-cry began which caused them to look apprehensively toward the poop without ceasing their business of washing down. First it was an oath in explosive German, the tongue which puts a cutting-edge on profanity; then the mate's roar:

"Is dat vat I tell you, you *verfluchter* fool? Vat? Vat? You don't understand ven I speak? I show you vat——"

The men who looked up were on the wrong side of the deck to make out what was happening, for the chart-house screened the drama from them. But they knew too well the meaning of that instantaneous silence which cut the words off. It was the mate biting in his breath as he struck. They heard the smack of the fist's impact and Conroy's faint, angry cry as he failed to guard it; then the mate again, bull-mouthed, lustful for cruelty: "Vat—you lift up your arm to me! You dog!" More blows, a rain of them, and then a noise as though Conroy had fallen or been knocked down. And after that a thud and a scream.

The men looked at one another, and nods passed among them. "He kicked him when he was down on the deck," the whisper went. The other Englishman in the watch swore in a low grunt and dropped his broom, meeting the wondering eyes of the "Dutchmen" and "Dagoes" with a scowl. He was white-haired and red-faced, a veteran among the nomads of the sea, the oldest man aboard, and the only one in the port watch who had not felt the weight of the mate's fist. Scowling still, as though in deep thought, he moved towards the ladder. The forlorn hope was going on a desperate enterprise of rescue.

It might have been an ugly business; there was a sense in the minds of his fellows of something sickening about to happen; but the mate had finished with Conroy. The youth came staggering and crying down the ladder, with tears and blood befouling his face, and stumbled as his foot touched the deck. The older man, Slade, saved him from falling, and held him by the upper arm with one gnarled, toil-roughened hand, peering at him through the early morning gloom.

"Kicked you when you was down, didn't he?" he demanded abruptly.

"Yes," blubbered Conroy, shivering and dabbing at his face. "With his sea-boots, too, the—the——"

Slade shook him. "Don't make that noise or he might kick you some more," he advised grimly. "You better go now an' swab that blood off your face."

"Yes," agreed Conroy tremulously, and Slade let him go.

The elder man watched him move forward on shambling and uncertain feet, with one hand pressed to his flank, where the mate's kick was still an agony. Slade was frowning heavily, with a tincture of thought in his manner, as though he halted on the brink of some purpose.

"Conroy," he breathed, and started after the other.

The younger man turned. Slade again put his hand on Conroy's arm.

"Say," he said, breathing short, "is that a knife in your belt?"

Conroy felt behind him, uncomprehending, for the sheath-knife which he wore, sailor fashion, in the middle of his back.

"What d'you mean?" he asked vacantly. "Here's my knife."

He drew it and showed it to Slade, the flat blade displayed in his palm.

The white-haired seaman thrust his keen old face toward Conroy's, so that the other could see the flash of the white of his eyes.

"And he kicked you, didn't he?" said Slade tensely. "You fool!"

He struck the knife to the deck, where it rattled and slid toward the scupper.

"Eh?" Conroy gaped, not understanding. "I don't see what——"

"Pick it up!" said Slade, with a gesture toward the knife. He spoke, as though he strangled an impulse to brandish his fists and scream, in a nasal whisper. "It's safe to kick you," he said. "A woman could do it."

"But——" Conroy flustered vaguely.

Slade drove him off with a wave of his arm and turned away with the abruptness of a man disgusted beyond bearing.

Conroy stared after him and saw him pick up his broom where he had dropped it and join the others. His intelligence limped; his thrashing had stunned him, and he could not think—he could only feel, like fire in his mind, the passion of the feeble soul resenting injustice and pain which it cannot resist or avenge. He stooped to pick up his knife and went forward to the tub under the head-pump, to wash his cuts in cold sea-water, the cheap balm for so many wrongs of cheap humanity.

It was an accident such as might serve to dedicate the day to the service of the owners of the *Villingen*. It was early and sudden; but, save in these respects, it had no character of the unusual. The men who plied the brooms and carried the buckets were not shocked or startled by it so much as stimulated; it thrust under their noses the always imminent danger of failing to satisfy the mate's ideal of seamanlike efficiency. They woke to a fresher energy, a more desperate haste, under its suggestion.

It was after the coffee interval, which mitigates the sourness of the morning watch, when daylight had brought its chill, grey light to the wide, wet decks, that the mate came forward to superintend the "pull all round," which is the ritual sequel to washing down.

"Lee fore-brace, dere!" his flat, voluminous voice ordered, heavy with the man's potent and dreaded personality. They flocked to obey, scurrying like scared rats, glancing at him in timid hate. He came striding along the weather side of the deck from the remote, august poop; he was like a dreadful god making a dreadful visitation upon his faithful. Short-legged, tending to bigness in the belly, bearded, vibrant with animal force and personal power, his mere presence cowed them. His gross face, the happy face of an egoist with a sound digestion, sent its lofty and sure regard over them; it had a kind of unconsciousness of their sense of humility, of their wrong and resentment—the innocence of an aloof and distant tyrant, who has not dreamed how hurt flesh quivers and seared minds rankle. He was bland and terrible; and they hated him after their several manners, some with dull fear, one or two—and Slade among them—with a ferocity that moved them like physical nausea.

He had left his coat on the wheel-box to go to his work, and was manifestly unarmed. The belief which had currency in the forecastle, that he came on watch with a revolver in his coat pocket, did not apply to him now; they could have seized him, smitten him on his blaspheming mouth, and hove him over the side without peril. It is a thing that has happened to a hated officer more than once or ten times, and a lie, solemnly sworn to by every man of the watch on deck, has been entered in the log, and closed the matter for all hands. He was barer of defence than they, for they had their sheath-knives; and he stood by the weather-braces, arrogant, tyrannical, overbearing, and commanded them. He seemed invulnerable, a thing too great to strike or defy, like the white squalls that swooped from the horizon and made of the vast *Villingen* a victim and a plaything. His full, boastful eye travelled over them absently, and they cringed like slaves.

"Belay, dere!" came his orders, overloud and galling to men surging with cowardly and insufferable hate. "Lower tobsail—haul! Belay! Ubber tobsail—haul, you sons of dogs! Haul, dere, blast you! You vant me to come over and show you?"

Servilely, desperately, they obeyed him, spending their utmost strength to placate him, while the naked spirit of murder moved in every heart among them. At the tail of the brace, Conroy, with his cuts stanched, pulled with them. His abject eyes, showing the white in sidelong glances, watched the great, squat figure of the mate with a fearful fascination.

Eight bells came at last, signalling the release of the port watch from the deck and the tension of the officer's presence. The forecastle received them, the stronghold of their brief and limited leisure. The unkempt, weather-stained men, to whom the shifting seas were the sole arena of their lives, sat about on chests and on the edges of the lower bunks, at their breakfast, while the pale sunlight travelled to and fro on the deck as the *Villingen* lurched in her gait. Conroy, haggard and drawn, let the coffee slop over the brim of his hook-pot as he found himself a seat.

"Well, an' what did he punch ye for this time?"

It was old Slade who put the question, seated on a chest with his back against the bulkhead. His pot was balanced on his knee, and his venerable, sardonic face, with the scanty white hair clinging about the temples, addressed Conroy with slow mockery.

Conroy hesitated. "It was over coilin' away some gear," he said. Slade waited, and he had to go on. He had misunderstood the mate's order to coil the ropes on the pins, where they would be out of the way of the deck-washing, and he had flemished them down on the poop instead. It was the mistake of a fool, and he knew it.

Slade nodded. "Ye-es," he drawled. "You earned a punch an' you got it. But he kicked you, too, didn't he?"

"Kicked me!" cried Conroy. "Why, I thought he was goin' to kill me! Look here—look at this, will you?"

With fumbling hands he cast loose his belt and flung it on the floor, and plucked his shirt up so as to leave his side bare. He stood up, with one arm raised above his head, showing his naked flank to the slow eyes of his shipmates. His body had still a boyish delicacy and slenderness; the labour of his trade had not yet built it and thickened it to a full masculinity of proportion. Measured by any of the other men in the watch, it was frail, immature, and tender. The moving sunlight that flowed around the door touched the fair skin and showed the great, puffed bruises that stood on it, swollen and horrid, like' some vampire fungus growing on the clean flesh.

A great Greek, all black hair and eyeball, clicked softly between his teeth.

"It looks like—a hell!" he said softly, in his purring voice.

"Dem is kicks, all right—*ja!*" said some one else, and yet another added the comment of a heavy oath.

Old Slade made no comment, but sat, balancing his hook-pot of coffee and watching the scene under his heavy white brows. Conroy lowered his arm and let the shirt fall to cover the bruises.

"You see?" he said to Slade.

"I see," answered the other, with a bitter twist of his old, malicious lips. Setting down the pot which he held, he stooped and lifted the belt which Conroy had thrown down. It seemed to interest him, for he looked at it for some moments.

"And here's yer knife," he said, reaching it to the youth, still with his manner of mockery. "There's some men it wouldn't be safe to kick, with a knife in their belts."

He and Conroy were the only Englishmen there; the rest were of the races which do not fight barehanded. The big Greek flashed a smile through the black, shining curls of his beard, and continued to smile without speaking. Through the tangle of incomprehensible conventions, he had arrived at last at a familiar principle.

Conroy flushed hotly, the blood rising hectic on his bruised and broken face.

"If he thinks it's safe with me," he cried, "he'll learn different. I didn't have a chance aft there; he came on me too quick, before I was expecting him, and it was dark, besides. Or else———"

"It'll be dark again," said Slade, with intent, significant eyes fixed on him, "and he needn't be expecting you. But—it don't do to talk too much. Talk's easy—talk is."

"I'll do more than talk," responded Conroy. "You'll see!"

Slade nodded. "Right, then; we'll see," he said, and returned to his breakfast.

His bunk was an upper one, lighted and aired by a brass-framed port-hole. Here, when his meal was at an end, he lay, his pipe in his mouth, his hands behind his head, smoking with slow relish, with his wry old face upturned, and the leathery, muscular forearms showing below the rolled shirtsleeves. His years had ground him to an edge; he had an effect, as he lay, of fineness, of subtlety, of keen and fastidious temper. Forty years of subjection to arbitrary masters had left him shrewd and secret, a Machiavelli of the forecastle.

Once Conroy, after seeming to sleep for an hour, rose on his elbow and stared across at him, craning his neck from his bunk to see the still mask of his face.

"Slade?" he said uncertainly.

"What?" demanded the other, unmoving.

Conroy hesitated. The forecastle was hushed; the seamen about them slumbered; the only noises were the soothing of the water overside, the stress of the sails and gear, and the irregular tap of a hammer aft. It was safe to speak, but he did not speak.

"Oh, nothing," he said, and lay down again. Slade smiled slowly, almost paternally.

It took less than eight hours for Conroy's rancour to wear dull, and he could easily have forgotten his threat against the mate in twelve, if only he had been allowed to. He was genuinely shocked when he found that his vapourings were taken as the utterance of a serious determination. Just before eight bells in the afternoon watch he went forward beneath the forecastle head in search of some rope-yarns, and was cutting an end off a bit of waste-line when the Greek, he of the curly beard and extravagant eyeballs, rose like a demon of pantomime from the forepeak. Conroy had his knife in his hand to cut the rope, and the Greek's sudden smile seemed to rest on that and nothing else.

"Sharp, eh?" asked the Greek, in a whisper that filled the place with dark drama.

Conroy paused, apprehending his meaning with a start.

"Oh, it's all right," he growled, and began to saw at the rope in his hand, while the Greek watched him with his fixed, bony smile.

"No," said the latter suddenly. "Dat-a not sharp—no! Look-a 'ere; you see dis?"

He drew his own knife, and showed it pointing toward Conroy in a damp, swarthy hand, whose knuckles bulged above the haft. His rough, spatulate thumb rasped along it, drawing from it the crepitation that proves an acute edge.

"Carve him like-a da pork," he said in his stage conspirator's whisper. "And da point—now, see!"

He glanced over his shoulder to be sure that none overlooked them; then, with no more than a jerk of his hand beside his hip, threw the keen blade toward the wooden door of the bo'sun's locker. It travelled through the air swiftly and stuck, quivering on its thin point, in the stout teak. The Greek turned his smile again for a moment on Conroy before he strode across and recovered it.

"You take 'im," he whispered. "Beter dan your little knife—yais."

By the mere urgency of his proffering it the exchange was made, and Conroy found himself with a knife in his hand that fell through the strands of the manila line as though they had been butter, an instrument made and perfected for a murder.

"Yes, but look here——" he began in alarm.

The broad, mirthless smile was turned on him.

"Just like-a da pork," purred the Greek, and nodded assuringly before he turned to go aft.

The bull-roar of the mate, who was awaiting his return with the rope-yarns, roused Conroy from a scared reverie over the knife. He started; the mate was bustling furiously forward in search of him, full of uproar and anger.

"Dam' lazy *Schwein*, you goin' to schleep dere? You vant me to come an' fetch you? You vant anodder schmack on de *Maul* to keep you avake—yes?"

He stamped into view round the forward house, while Conroy stood, convicted of idleness by the rope in his hand only half cut through. At the same moment a population of faces came into being behind him. A man who had been aloft shuffled down to the rail; a couple of others came into view on the deck; on top of the house, old Slade kneeled to see under the break of the forecastle head. It seemed as though a sceptical audience had suddenly been created out of his boast of the morning, every face threatening him with that shame which vanity will die rather than endure. In a panic of his faculties he took one step toward the mate.

"Hey?" The mate halted in his stride, with sheer amazement written on his face. "You vant yer head knocked off—yes?"

"No, I don't," said Conroy, out of a dry mouth.

According to the usage of ships, even that was defiance and a challenge.

He had forgotten the revolver with which the mate was credited; he had forgotten everything but the fact that eyes were on him. Even the knife in his hand passed from his mind; he was a mere tingling pretence at fortitude, expending every force to maintain his pose.

"Put dat knife avay!" ordered the mate suddenly.

He arrested an automatic movement to obey, fighting down a growing fear of his opponent.

"I've not finished with it yet," he answered.

The mate measured him with a practised eye. Though he had the crazy courage of a bulldog, he was too much an expert in warlike emergencies to overlook the risk of trying to rush a desperate man armed with a knife; the chances of the grapple were too ugly. There was something lunatic and strange in the youth's glare also; and it will sometimes happen that an oppressed and cowed man in his extremity will shrug his meekness from him and become, in a breath, a desperado. This had its place in the mate's considerations.

"Finish, den!" he rasped, with no weakening of his tone or manner. "You don't t'ink I'm goin' to vait all night for dem rope-yarns—hey?"

He turned his back at once lest Conroy should venture another retort, and make an immediate fight unavoidable. Before his eye the silent audience melted as swiftly as it had appeared, and Conroy was alone with his sick sense of having ventured too far, which stood him in place of the thrill of victory.

The thrill came later, in the forecastle, where he swelled to the adulation of his mates. They, at any rate, had been deceived by his attitude; they praised him by word and look; the big Greek infused a certain geniality into his smile. Only Slade said the wrong thing.

"I was ready for him as soon as he moved," Conroy was asserting. "And he knew it. You should ha' seen how he gaped when I wouldn't put the knife away."

The men were listening, crediting him. Old Slade, in the background, took his pipe from his lips.

"An' now I suppose you're satisfied," he inquired harshly.

"How d'you mean, satisfied?" demanded Conroy, colouring. "You saw what happened, didn't you?"

"You made him gape," said Slade. "That was because he made you howl, eh? Well, ain't you calling it quits, then—till the next time he kicks you?"

Some one laughed; Conroy raised his voice.

"He'll never kick me again," he cried. "His kicking days are over. He's kicked me once too often, he has. Quits—I guess not!"

Slade let a mouthful of smoke trickle between his lips; it swam in front of his face in a tenuous film of pale vapour.

"Well, talkin' won't do it, anyhow," he said.

"No," retorted Conroy, and collected all eyes to his gesture. "But this will!"

He showed them the thin-bladed knife which the Greek had given him, holding it before them by the hilt. He let a dramatic moment elapse.

"Like that!" he said, and stabbed at the air. "Like that—see? Like that!"

They came upon bad weather gradually, drawing into a belt of half-gales, with squalls that roared up from the horizon and made them for the time into whole gales. The *Villingen*, designed and built primarily for cargo capacity, was a wet ship, and upon any point of sailing had a way of scooping in water by the many tons. In nearly every watch came the roar, "Stand by yer to'gallant halliards!" Then the wait for ten seconds or ten minutes while the wind grew and the big four-masted barque lay over and bumped her bluff bows through racing seas, till the next order, shriller and more urgent, "Lower away!" and the stiff canvas fought and slatted as the yards came down. Sea-boots and oilskins were the wear for every watch; wet decks and the crash of water coming inboard over the rail, dull cold and the rasp of heavy, sodden canvas on numb fingers, became again familiar to the men, and at last there arrived the evening, gravid with tempest, on which all hands reefed topsails.

The mate had the middle watch, from midnight till four o'clock in the morning, and for the first two hours it was Conroy's turn on the look-out. The rest, in oilskins and sea-boots, were standing by under the break of the poop; save for the sleeping men in the shut forecastle, he had the fore part of the ship to himself. He leaned against the after rail of the forecastle head, where a ventilator somewhat screened him from the bitter wind that blew out of the dark, and gazed ahead at the murk. Now and again the big barque slid forward with a curtseying motion, and dipped up a sea that flowed aft over the anchors and cascaded down the ladders to the main-deck; spray that spouted aloft and drove across on the wind, sparkled red and green in the glare of the sidelights like brief fireworks.

The splash and drum of waters, the heavy drone of the wind in the sails, the clatter of gear aloft, were in his ears; he did not hear one bell strike from the poop, which he should have answered with a stroke on the big bell behind him and a shouted report on the lights.

"Hoy! You schleepin' up dere—hey?"

It was the mate, who had come forward in person to see why he had not answered. He was by the fore fife-rail, a mere black shape in the dark.

"Sleepin'—no, sir!"

"Don t you hear von bell shtrike?" cried the mate, slithering on the wet deck toward the foot of the ladder.

"No, sir," said Conroy, and stooped to strike the bell.

The mate came up the ladder, hauling himself by the handrails, for he was swollen beyond the ordinary with extra clothes under his long oilskin coat. A plume of spray whipped him in the face as he got to the top, and he swore shortly, wiping his eyes with his hands. At the same moment Conroy, still stooping to the bell-lanyard, felt the *Villingen* lower her nose and slide down in one of her disconcerting curtseys; he caught at the rail to steady himself. The dark water, marbled with white foam, rode in over the deck, slid across the anchors and about the capstan, and came aft toward the ladder and the mate. The ship rolled at the same moment.

Conroy saw what happened as a grotesque trick of circumstance. The mate, as the deck slanted, slipped and reached for the hand-rail with an ejaculation. The water flowed about his knees; he fell back against the hand-rail, which was just high enough for him to sit on. It was what, for one ridiculous moment, he seemed to be doing. The next, his booted feet swayed up and he fell over backward, amid the confusion of splashing water that leaped down the main-deck. Conroy heard him strike something below with a queer, smacking noise.

"Pity he didn't go overboard while he was about it," he said to himself, acting out his role. Really he was rather startled and dismayed.

He found the mate coiled in the scupper, very wet and still. He took hold of him to draw him under the forecastle head, where he would have shelter, and was alarmed at the inertness of the body under his hands.

"Sir!" he cried, "sir!—sir!"

He shook the great shoulders, but quickly desisted; there was something horrible, something that touched his nerves, in its irresponsiveness. He remembered that he might probably find matches in the lamp-locker, and staggered there to search. He had to grope in gross darkness about the place, touching brass and the uncanny smoothness of glass, before his hand fell on what he sought. At last he was on one knee by the mate's side, and a match shed its little illumination. The mate's face was odd in its quietude, and the sou'-wester of oilskin was still on his head, held there by the string under the chin. From under its edge blood flowed steadily, thickly, appallingly.

"But——" cried Conroy. The match-flame stung his fingers and he dropped it. "O Lord!" he said. It occurred to him then, for the first time, that the mate was dead.

The men aft, bunched up under the break of the poop, were aware of him as a figure that came sliding and tottering toward them and fell sprawling at the foot of the poop ladder. He floundered up and clutched the nearest of them, the Greek.

"The mate's dead," he broke out, in a kind of breathless squeal. "Somebody call the captain; the mate's dead."

There was a moment of silence; then a cackle of words from several of them together. The Greek's hands on his shoulders tightened. He heard the man's purring voice in his ear.

"How did you do it?"

Conroy thrust himself loose; the skies of his mind were split by a frightful lightning flash of understanding. He had been alone with the mate; he had seen him die; he was sworn to kill him. He could see the livid smile of the Greek bent upon him.

He fell over backward

"I didn't do it," he choked passionately, and struck with a wild, feeble hand at the smile. "You liar—I didn't do it."

"Hush!" The Greek caught him again and held him.

Some of the men had started forward; others had slipped into the alleyway to rouse the second mate and captain. The Greek had him clutched to his bosom in a strong embrace and was hushing him as one might hush a scared child. Slade was at his side.

"He slipped, I tell you; he slipped at the top of the ladder! She'd shipped a dollop of water and then rolled, and over he went. I heard his head go smack and went down to him. I never touched him. I swear it—I never touched him."

"Hush!" It was Slade this time. "And yer sure he's dead?"

"Yes, he's dead."

"Well——" the old man exchanged nods with the Greek. "All right. Only—don't tell the captain that tale; it ain't good enough."

"But——" began Conroy. A hug that crushed his face against the Greek's oilskin breast silenced him.

"Vat is all dis?"

It was the captain, tall, august, come full-dressed from his cabin. At his back the second mate, with his oilskin coat over his pyjamas, thrust forward his red, cheerful face.

Slade told the matter briefly. "And it's scared young Conroy all to bits, sir," he concluded.

"Come for'ard," bade the captain. "Get a lamp, some vun!"

They followed him along the wet, slippery deck slowly, letting him pass ahead out of earshot.

"It was a belayin'-pin, ye-es?" queried the Greek softly of Conroy.

"He might have hit his head against a pin," replied Conroy.

"Eh?" The Greek stopped. "Might 'ave—might 'ave 'it 'is 'ead! Ah, dat is fine! 'E might 'ave 'it 'is 'ead, Slade! You 'ear dat?"

"Yes, it ain't bad!" replied Slade, and Conroy, staring in a wild attempt to see their faces clearly, realised that they were laughing, laughing silently and heartily. With a gesture of despair he left them.

A globe-lamp under the forecastle head lighted the captain's investigations, gleaming on wet oilskins, shadow-pitted faces, and the curious, remote thing that had been the mate of the *Villingen*. Its ampler light revealed much that the match-flame had missed from its field—the manner in which the sou'-wester and the head it covered were caved in at one side, the cut in the sou'-wester through which clotted hair protruded, the whole ghastliness of death that comes by violence. With all that under his eyes, Conroy had to give his account of the affair, while the ring of silent, hard-breathing men watched him and marvelled at the clumsiness of his story.

"It is strange," said the captain. "Fell ofer backvards, you said. It is very strange! And vere did you find de body?"

The scupper and deck had been washed clean by successive seas; there was no trace there of blood, and none on the rail. Even while they searched, water spouted down on them. But what Conroy noted was that no pin stood in the rail where the mate had fallen, and the hole that might have held one was empty.

"Ah, vell!" said the captain at last. "De poor fellow is dead. I do not understand, quite, how he should fall like dat, but he is dead. Four of you get de body aft."

"Please, sir," accosted Conroy, and the tall captain turned.

"Vell, vat is it?"

"Can I go below, sir? It was me that found him, sir. I feel rather—rather bad."

"So!" The tall captain considered him inscrutably, he, the final arbiter of fates. "You feel bad— yes? Vell, you can go below!"

The little group that bore the mate's body shuffled aft, with the others following like a funeral procession. A man looked shivering out of the door of the starboard forecastle, and inquired in loud whispers: "*Was ist los? Sag' mal—was ist denn los?*" He put his inquiry to Conroy, who waved him off and passed to the port forecastle on the other side of the deckhouse.

The place was somehow strange, with its double row of empty bunks like vacant coffin-shelves in a vault, but solitude was what he desired. The slush-lamp swung and stank and made the shadows wander. From the other side of the bulkhead he could hear stirrings and a murmur of voices as the starboard watch grew aware that something had happened on deck. Conroy, with his oilskin coat half off, paused to listen for comprehensible words. The opening of the door behind him startled him, and he spun round to see Slade making a cautious entry. He recoiled.

"Leave me alone," he said, in a strangled voice, before the other could speak. "What are you following me for? You want to make me out a murderer. I tell you I never touched him."

The other stood just within the door, the upper half of his face shadowed by his sou'-wester, his thin lips curved in a faint smile. "No!" he said mockingly. "You didn't touch him? An' I make no doubts you'd take yer oath of it. But you shouldn't have put the pin back in the rail when you was through with it, all the same."

"There wasn't any pin there," said Conroy quickly. He had backed as far from Slade as he could, and was staring at him with horrified eyes.

"But there would ha' been if I hadn't took a look round while you were spinnin' your yarn to the Old Man," said Slade. "I knew you was a fool."

With a manner as of mild glee he passed his hand into the bosom of his coat, still keeping his sardonic gaze fixed on Conroy.

"Good thing you've got me to look after you," he went on. "Thinks I, 'He might easy make a mistake that 'ud cost him dear'; so I took a look round. An' I found this." From within his coat he brought forth an iron belaying-pin, and held it out to Conroy.

"See?" His finger pointed to it. "That's blood, that is—and that's hair. Look for yourself! *Now* I suppose you'll tell me you never touched him!"

"He hit his head against it when he fell," protested the younger man. "He did! Oh, God, I can't stand this!"

He sank to a seat on one of the chests and leaned his face against the steel plate of the wall.

"Hit his head!" snorted old Slade. "Couldn't you ha' fixed up a better yarn than that? What are you snivellin' at? D'ye think yer the only man as ever stove in a mate's head—an' him a murderin' man-driver? Keep them tales for the Old Man; he believes 'em seemingly; but don't you come them on me."

Conroy was moaning. "I never touched him; I never touched him!"

"Never touched him! Here, take the pin; it's yours!"

He shrank from it. "No, no!"

Slade pitched it to his bunk, where it lay on the blanket. "It's yours," he repeated. "If yer don't want it, heave it overboard yerself or stick it back in the rail. Never touched him—you make me sick with yer 'never touched him'!"

The door slammed on his scornful retreat; Conroy shuddered and sat up. The iron belaying-pin lay where it had fallen, on his bed, and even in that meagre light it carried the traces of its part in the mate's death. It had the look of a weapon rather than of a humble ship-fitting. It rolled a couple of inches where it lay as the ship leaned to a gust, and he saw that it left a mark where it had been, a stain.

He seized it in a panic and started for the door to be rid of it at once.

As if a malicious fate made him its toy, he ran full into the Greek outside.

"Ah!" The man's smile flashed forth, wise and livid "An' so you 'ad it in your pocket all de time, den!"

Conroy answered nothing. It was beyond striving against. He walked to the rail and flung the thing forth with hysterical violence to the sea.

The watch going below at four o'clock found him apparently asleep, with his face turned to the wall. They spoke in undertones, as though they feared to disturb him, but none of them mentioned the only matter which all had in mind. They climbed heavily to their bunks, there to smoke the brief pipe, and then to slumber. Only Slade, who slept little, would from time to time lean up on one elbow to look down and across to the still figure which hid its face throughout the night.

Conroy woke when the watch was called for breakfast by a man who thrust his head in and shouted. He had slept at last, and now as he sat up it needed an effort of mind to recall his trouble.

He looked out at his mates, who stood about the place pulling on their clothes, with sleep still heavy on them. They seemed as usual. It was his turn to fetch the coffee from the galley, he remembered, and he slipped out of his bunk to dress and attend to it.

"I won't be a minute," he said to the others, as he dragged on his trousers.

A shaggy young Swede near the door was already dressed.

"I vill go," he said. "You don't bother," and forthwith slipped out.

The others were looking at him now, glancing with a queer, sharp interest and turning away when they met his eyes. It was as though he were a stranger.

"That was a queer thing last night," he said to the nearest.

"Yes," the other agreed, with a kind of haste.

They sat about at their meal, when the coffee had been brought by the volunteer, under the same constraint. He could not keep silent; he had to speak and make them answer.

"Where is he?" he asked abruptly.

"On de gratings," he was told. And the Swede who fetched the coffee added, "Sails is sowin' him up now already."

"We'll see the last of him to-day," said Slade. "He won't kick nobody again!"

There was a mutter of agreement, and eyes turned on Conroy again. Slade smiled slowly.

"Yes, he keeck once too many times," said the Greek.

The shaggy young Swede wagged his head. "He t'ink it was safe to kick Conroy, but it aindt," he observed profoundly. "No, it aindt safe."

"He got vat he ask for. . . . Didn't know vat he go up againdst. . . . No, it aindt—it aindt safe. . . . Maybe vish he aindt so handy mit his feet now."

They were all talking; their mixed words came to Conroy in broken sentences. He stared at them a little wildly, realising the fact that they were admiring him, praising him, and afraid of him. The blood rose in his face hotly.

"You fellers talk," he began, and was disconcerted at the manner in which they all fell silent to hear him—"you talk as if I'd killed him."

"Well! . . . *Ach was!*"

He faced their smiles, their conciliatory gestures, with a frown.

"You better stop it," he said. "He fell—see? He fell an' stove his head in. An' any feller that says he didn't——"

His regard travelled from face to face, giving force to his challenge.

"Ve aindt goin' to say nodings!" they assured him mildly. "You don't need to be scared of us, Conroy."

"I'm not scared," he said with meaning. "But—look out, that's all."

When breakfast was over, it was his turn to sweep up. But there was almost a struggle for the broom and the privilege of saving him that trouble. It comforted him and restored him; it would have been even better but for the presence of Slade, sitting aloft in his bunk, smiling over his pipe with malicious understanding.

The *Villingen* was still under reefed upper topsails, walking into the seas on a taut bowline, with water coming aboard freely. There was little for the watch to do save those trivial jobs which never fail on a ship. Conroy and some of the others were set to scrubbing teak on the poop, and he had a view of the sail-maker at his work on the gratings under the break of the poop, stitching on his knees to make the mate presentable for his last passage. The sail-maker was a bearded Finn, with a heavy, darkling face and the secret eyes of a faun. He bent over his task, and in his attitude and the slow rhythm of his moving hand there was a suggestion of ceremonial, of an act mysterious and ritual.

Half-way through the morning Conroy was sent for to the cabin, there to tell his tale anew, to see it taken down, and to sign it. The captain even asked him if he felt better.

"Thank you, sir," replied Conroy. "It was a shock, findin' him dead like that."

"Yes, yes," agreed the captain. "I can understand—a great shock. Yes!"

He was bending over his papers at the table; Conroy smiled over his bowed head. Returning on deck, he winked to the man at the wheel, who smiled uncomfortably in return. Later he borrowed a knife to scrape some spots of paint off the deck; he did not want to spoil the edge of his own.

They buried the mate at eight bells; the weather was thickening, and it might be well to have the thing done. The hands stood around, bareheaded, with the grating in the middle of them, one edge resting on the rail, the other supported by two men. There was a dark smudge on the sky up to windward, and several times the captain glanced up from his book towards it. He read in German slowly, with a dwelling upon the sonorous passages, and towards the end he closed the book and finished without its aid.

Conroy was at the foot of the ladder; the captain was above him, reading mournfully, solemnly, without looking at the men. They were rigid, only their eyes moving. Conroy collected their glances irresistibly. When the captain had finished his reading he sighed and made a sign, lifting his hand like a man who resigns himself. The men holding the grating tilted it; the mate of the *Villingen*, with a little jerk, went over the side.

"Shtand by der tobs'l halliards!" roared the second mate.

Conroy, in the flurry, found himself next to a man of his watch. He jerked a thumb in the direction of the second mate, who was still vociferating orders.

"Hark at him!" he said. "Before we're through I'll teach *him* manners too."

And he patted his knife.

The Fair Exchange

ANNA MCMULLEN

I've never before realised what it means to me. Even the familiar things: the murmur of talk in the bar downstairs; the hum of conversation from the groups of people on the Hard—all those commonplace sounds I am hearing now. And behind them all, the sea, slapping softly at the boats as the rising tide creeps up the mud.

Ever since I can remember I have found here everything that is *necessary* for my life. This place has been all-sufficient. The sea, so vast, and yet so small and intimate where it gurgles in the little creeks among the saltings. The saltings, so grey and dun, and then so beautiful when they are purple with sea lavender, in the summer, and green with the queer transparent samphire. Even the mud can be lovely at low tide, with lights and shades, and the different greens of the seaweeds that grow on the harder parts. And the winds: the east wind that brings the pure sea smell, a *deep* sea smell, and raises white horses up the river; and the south-west wind that brings the mud smell at low tide, a mixed smell of flowers and hedgerows, and a warm smell of cattle on the marshes.

Winter and summer it changes, but I love it. I have seen it on November evenings, very grey and colourless, and very still; the water like a mirror, hazy with mist; the marshes lying low and quiet. A flock of great saddle-back gulls standing motionless on the mud, the silence only broken as one or another of them flies up with a flapping of wings and a harsh cry. And on cold, frosty mornings the water blue and dancing in the sunlight, and flocks of oxbird wheeling and turning in the clear sky, flashing silver as they turn their white undersides to the sun; the saltings sparkling with frost, the fleets on the marshes frozen hard enough for skating.

But I can never make any one understand what all this means to me. Except Peter; I think Peter would understand. With Peter I have never felt the need to explain, from the days when we used to wade after flounders up the creeks at low tide—feeling with our hands along the rill of water at the bottom. Then catching them and throwing them up on the mud. When the tide began to flow we would tramp along the mud to collect them, and stow them in Peter's canvas dinghy. I remember how our bare legs looked like long black stockings, and how we used to cut our feet on oyster shells.

Those days are still so vivid to me—the freedom and the timelessness. In fact, the only sort of time that mattered at all was the ebb and flow of the tides. Taking sandwiches, we would go out all day on the Old Barn Marsh. Walking till we were tired and hungry; then bathing in the creek over the seawall. After that we would eat our sandwiches; then lie on our backs in the sweet marsh grass, watching a heron flap slowly across the vast sky that stretches enormously from low horizon to horizon. And then we'd go to Holepenny Fleet, and creep up to the decoy to see how many duck we could surprise in it.

Or we'd take the dinghy and explore new, unknown creeks, following them right up to the end. Sometimes the tide would fall, leaving us stranded on the mud, with no choice but to get out and push the dinghy or wait until the water returned. And sometimes the creeks became so narrow at the end that we were squeezed between the banks of the saltings.

That was before Peter's father built me *The Fair Exchange*—cutter-rigged, eighteen feet long, and not very beautiful. But comfortable and easy to handle. He said she was only a fair exchange for my amusing Peter during his holidays. After that we could explore the larger and more distant creeks; could sail across the estuary to villages on the other side. And then, later still, I could sail *The Fair Exchange* in the club races, with Peter as crew.

Now I can hear Joe clearing the bar and father's voice saying good-night. I can hear other voices getting louder as they pass into the road. But to-night they are not so loud and cheerful as usual.

I cannot believe there might have come a time when all this would have gone on without me. When I could no longer have sat up here in my room at night, looking over the dark water, watching the yachts' lights and their shimmering reflections.

If I put my head out of the window I can see the few lights on the derelict tramp steamers lying up the river. Through the window comes the smell of the sea, and now and then a wailing cry from redshank on the marshes. Footsteps and voices are dying away now, some up the road and some down to the Hard. In a minute or two father will be coming upstairs. He will be very kind and tender.

He has always been kind and tender. Ever since my mother died and he retired from the navy. So simple in his kindness. Just as he is simple in his queer pride at being an innkeeper.

He was so pleased and proud when I became engaged to Ralph. He had always wanted me to be mistress of a comfortable home: of luxuries and possessions that he could never give me—and that I have never wanted. And he had always been afraid that I should marry Peter. Not that he wasn't fond of him, but Peter was only the son of a boatbuilder. Poor Peter.

It was a Saturday when Ralph first came—one of those soft, warm days we sometimes get in very early spring. I remember Peter and I had *The Fair Exchange* up on the Hard and were scraping and painting her. Ralph's friends had arranged for him to put up with us at the Lord Nelson. I remember father coming down to see how we were getting on, and telling us that an elder brother of Ralph's had served under him in the navy.

Ralph came down fairly often after that, and most week-ends his big grey car was in our garage. It is there now, I suppose. He seemed to enjoy coming, and was at first anxious for me to teach him to sail and to take him out in *The Fair Exchange*. By the end of May we were engaged; and to this day I don't know how it happened. I remember it only as part of the evening, for in itself it never seemed to make a real impression on me.

Father had been out of sorts all the week, depressed and anxious because business was slack; and I was worried about him. Ralph arrived in high spirits, and father seemed to cheer up at once. Somehow the sight of his big body with its strength and assurance relieved my worry. I was glad to listen to his jokes and talk at dinner. After dinner Ralph and I walked down the coast road to the old tarred wooden houses and ships' stores. Then on to the sea-wall that runs up the creek. The evening was warm and still. The thorn trees on Haye Island stood out black against a clear, green-blue sky. The tide was ebbing, the mud glimmering in the fading light. After walking along a little, we sat down on a derelict boat, upturned against the sea-wall. I think the beauty of the evening had stilled even Ralph's tongue—the silence was broken only by the gentle sucking noises the water makes as it runs out of the little creeks and holes in the saltings. Ralph turned to speak to me and I laid a finger on his rather full lips—I had always wanted to do that—and then I was in his arms. It was as if all my worry and tiredness were flowing away with the tide, leaving a sense of renewed strength that was yet peaceful and secure.

I don't remember feeling very different afterwards, or thinking much about it. Life went on as usual and father's health improved. He was in good spirits and especially affectionate to me. During the week I did my usual jobs about the house, bathed and walked, and sailed *The Fair Exchange*. The only difference was that I didn't see so much of Peter.

I used to look forward to the week-ends—to the strange, sweet excitement of being taken in Ralph's arms and kissed. I enjoyed taking him for walks, and out in *The Fair Exchange*, and trying to show him the ropes.

But he never had any sea sense. At first I think he genuinely tried to be interested and to like the things I liked. But he didn't like mud, and he didn't like getting wet and not having his meals at regular times. I think he was soon impatient of my preoccupation with it all, and would try to make me discuss the wedding and the house he was building for me. He liked to make me go out in the car with him instead of sailing. And yet he had only to touch me and I forgot all those things and would do as he liked.

Ralph came down last night. For the first time I was glad when he let me go. I don't know whether it was the faint smell of petrol on his clothes, or the strength with which he held me—he seemed so benevolently possessive. At dinner he began to plan a long drive for to-day. Father said it was a good idea, and would be a change for me. Somehow the fact of their both being in agreement made me resentful. I said it looked so fine that it would be a good opportunity to take Ralph for a long sail. He didn't like the idea, and was inclined to argue. But I had my way.

It is strange to think that it was only this morning we started out. It seems like something that happened a long time ago, or like a violent storm that has now drifted away.

The day was so fine when I woke this morning that I never gave Ralph a thought. It was a lovely day, and we were going sailing. I was up early, so that I could get my jobs done in good time and the food-basket ready. As I worked I whistled. Even Ralph seemed cheerful, and tried to help me in. his clumsy way.

We started down to the Hard, Ralph, in his clean white flannels, carrying the lunch-basket, and I carrying the oars and rowlocks for the dinghy, for since my new brass ones disappeared I have always brought the rowlocks up at night. I reckoned it would be high tide about 1.15, and I wondered whether last night I had left the dinghy anchor high enough up the beach to get it without wading.

I found the anchor without any trouble, and pulled the dinghy in against the stone part of the Hard so that Ralph and the lunch could embark without getting muddy. Then I pulled out from among the huddle of boats, and rowed to *The Fair Exchange*, rocking gently at her moorings in the middle of the creek.

I brought the dinghy alongside and went aboard, so that I could take the lunch-basket from Ralph, and make the dinghy fast. Ralph came aboard heavily, as he usually does, making both boats rock. I made him undo the tiers round the mainsail while I got the jib ready for hoisting. Then I gave him the tiller, and told him to keep her head to wind, and the mainsheet clear, while I hoisted the sails. I went forward and cast off from the buoy, ran back and took the tiller from Ralph, took in the jibsheet and mainsheet, and we were off, leaving the dinghy on the mooring. We had a soldier's wind down the creek—it was fair nearly all the way across the estuary to Stonewell, except for a short beat up Stonewell Creek.

Soon I forgot about Ralph. The boat was like a live thing under my hands, quivering as she forged ahead, the water slapping under herbow, and the wind thrumming through the stays. The smell of the sea was in my nostrils, and the wind in my hair.

It was about half-past twelve when we sailed up the creek to Stonewell, and brought up at the little tumbledown jetty, making fast to one of the wooden piles. I let down the sails, and we left *The Fair Exchange* snug and tidy and went ashore. As we walked along the grass lane to the Leather Bottle to buy beer, the sounds and smells were all of the country instead of the sea—the humming of insects and bees, the song of larks, and the smell of dusty roads and cow-dung. We ate our lunch and drank our beer in the shade of a haystack. It was soft and comfortable in the sweet-smelling hay, and I think I must have dozed for a moment after lunch, because when I closed my eyes Ralph was lighting a cigarette, and when I next opened them he was stubbing it out on the sole of his shoe.

We got up and shook the hay out of our clothes, and walked back to the jetty. The spring tide was at its height, the saltings covered, with only a tuft of coarse grass here and there standing up out of the water, which had risen right up to the sea-walls.

Ralph took my hand in his, and we stood looking over the water. I remember Ralph asked me about some gulls that got up and flew along the creek, and I told him they were cob-gulls, which get their black heads from March to September, so the fishermen say, by dipping them in March water.

The tide turned while we were standing there, and I noticed that the sky had clouded over and the sun gone in. The wind, that had freshened, blew rather chilly, and we decided to set off. We went aboard *The Fair Exchange*, ran up the sails, and got under way. As we came out of the creek into the estuary the wind was against the tide, and the sea was quite rough. *The Fair Exchange* put her nose into it once or twice, sending a shower of water over us. We sailed for home.

I suppose if I'd not decided to turn and run up West Creek it might never have happened. But *The Fair Exchange* goes so well in a strong breeze; it was still early; and I'd caught sight of Peter's sail round a bend in the creek. Ralph wasn't very wet but he hated the taste of salt on his lips. For some reason he was always afraid of gybing, so to save his feelings I wended round, and we set off up the creek after Peter.

The tide was racing out of West Creek against the wind, and even there it was choppy. We were running by the lee and I knew we should have to gybe at the bend, so I warned Ralph. He asked, why couldn't we wend, and I explained there wasn't room. There was a pretty strong gust of wind as we came to the bend. I said: " 'Ware gybe!" to Ralph, put up the helm, and started to gather in the mainsheet.

About what happened then I shall never know. I suppose Ralph either fouled the mainsheet accidentally or seized it in a panic. At the time all I knew was that we were over, the sail flat in the water, and I was automatically bracing my feet against the gunwale, trying, to stop any loose gear going overboard.

Then I was aware of Ralph's feet scrabbling violently on the bottom boards, as he tried to climb on to the top side of the overturned boat.

"Hurry up and get there, Ralph," I said. "You'll have the bottom boards out in a minute."

I glanced down the creek and saw Peter about three minutes away. He waved his arm to us, and I waved back.

The Fair Exchange was getting lower in the water.

I said to Ralph, "You'd better abandon ship and swim ashore, or potter about till Peter picks you up."

But he sat on, his face looking rather white.

"Hurry up, Ralph, do!" I said. "Your weight is sinking her."

He would not let go.

I said again, "Your weight is sinking her. What are you waiting for?"

But he still clung on.

Suddenly the look of panic in his eyes infuriated me. If he stayed there much longer he'd sink the boat. He'd only just got to drop into the water and swim about till Peter came; but there he sat like a great stuffed dummy, white and shivering.

"Go on, you fool!" I said, and gave him a push. He went into the water.

It was when I saw the look on his face and heard his frantic splashings that I first realised he couldn't swim. For a second or two I hesitated, amazed. Before I was in the water the race had caught him, and was sweeping him out of my reach.

When I had cleared the hair and water from my eyes I saw Peter dive in and seize him. Ralph was struggling furiously, and as Peter first caught hold of him they both went under. When they came up again they were farther from me, and as the tide hurried them along I heard Peter calling.

I swam with every ounce of energy I possessed—my lungs bursting, my clothes sodden and heavy. I can feel the ache in my limbs now. But I couldn't get near them, though I could see that Ralph had got Peter round the neck and was hanging on. I tried to shout, but my mouth was full of water and my hair was getting in my eyes. For a moment I thought I heard the chug-chug of a motor-boat. But soon that was drowned by the sound of water roaring in my ears.

The next thing I felt—as if to reassure me—was the familiar sensation of a boat under way. I was lying on the deck of a smack, while a fisherman tried to pour something down my throat. For a little I lay still, trying to remember. Then I remembered. I looked at his face and I knew they were gone.

I lay still and watched the top of the mast swaying against the sky. I listened to the throb of the engine and the wash of the dinghy astern. Overhead the gulls circled and screamed.

"Go on, you fool!"

It was on the mud they found them, at low tide, their bodies locked together. There was mud in their eyes and ears when they brought them ashore two hours ago. The mud that to Peter and me has always been a friendly and familiar sort of joke. But Ralph, he would have hated to be found like that. He hated the mud, the way it oozes round your bare feet in the water, the way it sticks and clings and spreads to everything you touch.

Now I can hear father shutting and bolting the door. Soon he will be coming upstairs. I shall see the pain and bewilderment in his eyes. He will be appalled at the idea of my grief. He will be kind and very gentle, thinking I am numbed with shock, fearing the moment when the full realisation of my grief will come.

But I can feel no grief. And I believe no grief *will* come. Perhaps I am utterly heartless. Perhaps in my soul I have committed murder. But now suddenly all things are plain and clear. They are both gone—Ralph whom I desired, and, at the last moment, hated, and Peter who was part of all those things I love. But those other things have been returned to me. And now they will never be taken from me. To me it seems a fair exchange. The only thing I can't understand is how I ever came to be in such danger—I mean the danger of marrying Ralph, of going away and losing everything.

Father is coming upstairs now. I don't think I have seen so fine a night this summer. There is a shifting mist on the marshes behind the sea-wall. The moonlight is shining through it, giving it the milky appearance of pearls. Pearls and diamonds. I suppose I can take this ring off now? I should like to throw it away. To-morrow I think I *shall* throw it away. Into the sea, perhaps. Yes, into the sea.

The Running Amok in the "Frank N. Thayer"

J. G. LOCKHART

The sea and the desert are akin in this—that each holds for those who travel it a supreme charm and a supreme danger. The charm is beyond debate, familiar to any one who has made even the shortest of voyages, or trod even the fringes of a desert. The danger is more elusive. I refer not to risks of shipwreck or drowning by sea, of thirst or loss of bearings by land, but to something psychological. A dreadful malady lingers about those great spaces. The French legionary with *le cafard*, who shoots his sergeant and then blows out his own brains, is fellow-sufferer to the Malay seaman who, without any warning, runs amok and knifes his comrades. We may not understand these things. We cannot explain them adequately, any more than we can deny them glibly. But they exist; and in them I find the only possible solution to the puzzling and horrible story of the *Frank N. Thayer*.

On the morning of Monday, January 14th, 1886, the small population of Jamestown, St. Helena, awoke to find that during the night an open boat containing seventeen castaways had come into harbour, freighted with as strange and gruesome a tale as any man could wish to hear. They were the survivors of the *Frank N. Thayer* of Boston, a fine American vessel of 1600 tons burden, sailing from Manila to New York with a cargo of hemp. The men had been taken to the office of the American Consul, Mr. McKnight, and, as details of their experiences leaked out, there was great excitement; the wildest rumours ran through the little town, and the truth, astounding though it was, became distorted beyond recognition. The account which I give here is taken from Mr. McKnight's report, following the official investigation which he held in the island.

Until the night of Saturday, January 2nd, when the *Frank N. Thayer* was about seven hundred miles south-east of St. Helena, her voyage had been entirely uneventful. There was not the least apprehension of impending danger in the minds either of Robert K. Clarke, her commander, or of his two officers. All was as it should be. Nothing unusual or disturbing had occurred. The officers knew their job and did it. The men were contented. The weather was fine. When the Captain went below at ten o'clock to join his wife and child in their cabin, all was shipshape aboard, the night was bright and starlit, and the *Frank N. Thayer* was bowling along under a fair, strong breeze. Two hours later the men on watch below had the first indication that something was amiss when, just before the change of watch, they noticed that a man of their number had gone on deck. This was one of two seamen shipped at Manila—they are described as Indian coolies—fine, stalwart fellows who had worked well and given no trouble. The irregularity was trifling, and none of the watch below was at all alarmed by the man's absence.

On deck the first and second mates were sitting and chatting on the booby hatch, when the two Manila men came up to them in the darkness, one of them beginning to explain that he had been taken ill. It was an odd hour at which to report sick, and the first mate was starting to question the man, when suddenly the Indians whipped out knives and fell upon their unarmed officers. A few yards away a white seaman, Maloney, was at the wheel. He saw everything that occurred, but was too terrified to utter a sound. The two mates were stabbed or slashed to death before his eyes.

The Captain, peacefully asleep below, awoke suddenly with a loud cry ringing in his ears. It was followed by a babble of voices as in altercation. He tumbled from his bunk and went out into the little passage to discover what had happened. He was clad in shirt and trousers; he was dazed with sleep; and he had a vague idea that one of the mates was calling him to see a vessel which had been ahead of them the previous evening and which they had been afraid of overhauling during the night. From the passage the deck was reached by a companion-way, and the Captain had hardly set foot on the lowest step when a man came tumbling down from above, cried out, "Captain Clarke! Captain Clarke!" in an agonised voice, and collapsed in a heap on the deck. It was the second mate. By the starlight which dropped through the open hatch the Captain could see that blood was pouring from him. Clarke's name was still on his lips when he died.

Had the Captain stopped to think he would now have gone back to his cabin and fetched his revolver. As it was, he seems to have been utterly bewildered by this sudden horror, and mounted the companionway unarmed. At the top some one stabbed him on the head and then seized him by the throat. Though nearly blinded by a rush of blood, he turned and knocked his assailant over with a blow between the eyes. Then at last he tried to retire to his cabin for a weapon, but the coolie was up in a moment and grappled with him, and the pair of them fell struggling down the companion. The coolie strove to use his knife and managed to wound the Captain severely in the left side. At the bottom Clarke recovered his foothold, but slipped on the bloodstained deck and fell back into the open door of his cabin. Whereupon the coolie stabbed him again and left him, thinking him dead, and doubtless intending to return a little later to ransack the cabin and deal with the woman and child.

The Captain, however, though badly hurt, was not quite out of action. With the help of his wife he got his revolver and crawled out again into the passage. It must be remembered that he had still no idea what the trouble was. Some one had killed the mate and attacked him. It was mutiny beyond a doubt; but how many of his men were in it, and how many loyal men remained alive, he did not know. His first impulse, therefore, was to secure his own quarters against further attack. Looking up through the open hatch he could see the man Maloney still at the wheel and still too paralysed by fear to give the alarm. He called to him to shut the door at the top of the companion-way.

"I can't, sir," the man called tremulously back.

"Why not?"

"There's somebody there," objected Maloney.

"Who is it?"

"I don't know, sir."

The man was useless, obviously unwilling to stir from the wheel. Possibly, thought the Captain, he was in the mutiny, or had been overawed by the mutineers. He himself was too weak from loss of blood to climb the companion-way, but he shut and locked the door of the after-cabin, leading into the passage, and also the door of the fore-cabin. Then he returned to his wife; but hardly had he done so when he heard some one floundering down the companion-way outside. He opened the door once more, to find one of his white seamen, Hendricsen by name, outside. The Captain covered him with his revolver and demanded to be told what had happened. The man was apparently mad with fright. He could only stammer, "Oh, hide me, Captain, hide me."

Clarke was dizzy, faint, and bewildered. Hendricsen might be genuinely afraid, but again he might be privy to this extraordinary, murderous conspiracy and be intending treachery. It was better to take no risks, and the Captain slammed his door on the cowering man, leaving him in the passage.

He then lay down on a mat in a corner of his cabin from which he could command with his revolver the door and the big portholes opening on to the deck outside, while Mrs. Clarke, who had behaved throughout with the greatest pluck and self control, washed and bandaged his wounds. The worst of these was the stab in his side, from which the lower lobe of the left lung protruded, but he had also some bad gashes on his head and temple; moreover, he was so exhausted from loss of blood that it was only by an effort of will that he could keep himself from fainting.

Mrs. Clarke was still dressing her husband's wounds when there was a further alarm. From one of the big portholes came a crash of shattered glass, and through the opening appeared the brown leg of one of the Indians. The Captain, who by now could hardly hold his revolver, fired twice, blindly and wide; but the shots served their purpose, for the coolie, who had supposed the Captain to be dead, was scared and quickly withdrew. In the cabin they heard the pair of mutineers go off cursing.

Silence followed, broken a little later by the noise of a scuffle and a single shrill scream from the deck. Half an hour later another scream rang out; and—at about five in the morning—yet another. The first was the death-cry of Maloney, the man at the wheel, whose timidity had not saved him; the second that of the carpenter, who was surprised and murdered while asleep in his shop; and the third that of the last man left alive on deck. The mutineers flung the three bodies overboard. These facts were afterwards elicited from Ah Say, the Chinese cook, who was a trembling witness of the crimes. The coolies spared his life because, as they explained, they wished him to cook for them.

What, meanwhile, had been happening elsewhere in the ship? Down in the fo'c'sle twelve men were asleep. When the watch was relieved a scuffle overhead was heard, and a moment later the first mate had tumbled in among them. He had taken advantage of the encounter between the Captain and the coolies to make his escape from the booby hatch where he had been surprised. He was desperately hurt, could give no clear account of what had passed, and, in fact, died three hours later. It was clear that something very serious had occurred, and while three of the men stayed with the mate, the other nine armed themselves with capstan-bars and went aft to investigate. Suddenly the two coolies appeared among them, cutting stabbing, slashing, and shouting that the Captain and mates were dead and the ship was now in their charge. In the darkness it was hard to distinguish friend from foe. There was a panic. The crew broke and fled in disorder back to the fo'c'sle. One man, Robert Sonnberg, alone remained outside. Cut off from safety, he made for the mizzen-rigging and climbed up to the cross-jack yard. From there he climbed along the stays towards the fo'c'sle, but by the time he reached it he found that the mutineers, following up the flying crew, had roughly barricaded them in. A little later, to his mortification, he saw the coolies return and make a sure job of it, battening down the hatch and securing it so strongly that it would be necessary for the men inside to hew a way out with axes.

Sonnberg returned to the rigging, from which he saw Maloney dragged shrieking from the wheel and butchered. The murder of Booth the carpenter followed; and worst of all was the death of Antonio Serrain, the third victim, who had often befriended the coolies during the voyage, and now pleaded hard for mercy; but none was shown him. The coolies then clad themselves in the carpenter's best clothes and called to Sonnberg to come down from the rigging, promising that if he did so they would not harm him. Sonnberg, wisely, remained aloft, and, detaching a block, tied it to a gasket, so that he might have a weapon of sorts. Thus he stayed through the long hours of Sunday.

Night fell once more, and at eight o'clock Sonnberg was nodding on his perch when he started awake as the rigging perceptibly shook. There, a couple of feet below, was the face of one of the mutineers, with a knife in his hand and murder in his eyes. Sonnberg dodged a blow and struck back at the man with his block. The coolie, baffled, returned to the deck, while Sonnberg climbed to the greater safety of the royal yard where he spent the rest of the night, descending to the topsail yard in the light of day.

Let us return to the cabin. All through Sunday the Captain was prostrate, nursed by his wife. The mutineers, beyond screening the portholes with timber to cover them from revolver-fire, left him alone. In the small hours of Monday morning he was so much stronger that he was able to undertake a reconnaissance outside. In his lavatory he found the man Hendricsen, who had rushed down the companion-way twenty-four hours before. From him he was at last able to obtain an account of what had happened. The Captain also found the Chinese steward hiding in one of the cabins. He armed both these men, and prepared to take the offensive against the mutineers.

First of all, the Captain tried to get a sight of the enemy. This was not easy, as all portholes and hatches had been blocked and he had to use the skylight. Through it he obtained occasional fleeting glimpses. Apparently one of the coolies was watching the cabin, the other the fo'c'sle; they had armed themselves with harpoons and knives lashed to the ends of sticks, to be flung at any one who showed himself, or to be used for probing at random through the skylight. The Captain and his two men now opened fire whenever a target appeared, and when they heard footsteps on the deck they discharged their revolvers blindly through the partitions. A lucky shot at last found a mark. There was a shriek of pain, followed by sounds of a hurried retreat forward. At that moment Sonnberg, watching events from the rigging, seized his opportunity and made for the fo'c'sle.

For meanwhile the men below had been stirred to belated action. During Sunday they had remained unaccountably passive, preferring the security of their prison to the risks of the deck. The first mate was dead, and, to the best of their belief, the Captain and second mate had also been murdered. What was there for them to do? Indeed, the crew might have stayed inactive even longer than they did, had not Ah Say, the Chinese cook, who had just been compelled to prepare a meal of coffee, chickens, and rice for the mutineers, contrived to smuggle an axe through the fo'c'sle window. This

Sonnberg struck at the man with his block

put spirit into the men, and they began to hack their way out. As they toiled below, Sonnberg, who had found an axe lying on the deck, started to smash away the barricading over the hatches. And at the same time the Captain and his helpers, encouraged by that one successful shot, were battering down the cabin door. The two parties emerged from their respective prisons almost simultaneously.

But the mutineers had realised that their fun was finished. One of them was badly wounded in the breast, and their plans had so far miscarried that an unmanageable number of men remained alive and were growing in aggression. They decided to make a bolt from the ship. They rushed a heavy boom to the side and flung it overboard, the wounded coolie jumping in after it. But one last blow was to be struck, so, just as the cabin and fo'c'sle parties met, the other coolie made a sudden dash for a ventilating hatch and sprang through it into the hold. The Captain sent Hendricsen and the steward below with revolvers to hunt the man out, but they were too late or too cautious to stop the mischief. The coolie had set alight the cargo in several places before they found him, and presently dense volumes of smoke began to pour through the hatch.

Presently, too the atmosphere of the hold became unendurable. After firing at and wounding their man, Hendricsen and the steward groped their way on deck half-suffocated. A moment later the coolie followed, smoked out like a rat. With a wild yell he made for the side and jumped over, joining his fellow-mutineer, who was already in the water.

By this time the men on board, maddened by the traces of bloodshed which met them everywhere, were in no mood for mercy. They opened fire on the two wretches in the sea, and went on shooting until they had sunk from sight.

The murderers were dead, but a new danger now threatened. The fire in the hold had got a very strong purchase, and, although the crew fought it stoutly for four hours, they were unable to extinguish it. Slowly it crept through the ship, eating out her vitals and—a most serious matter—destroying her spare sails and all the provisions in store except those which were kept in the boats ready for emergencies. When the Captain saw that it was impossible to save the ship, he gave orders to lower away two boats. One of them capsized, but seventeen people managed to pack themselves into the other. During Monday night they stood by the blazing vessel, hoping that some passing craft, attracted by the glare, would pick them up. But on Tuesday morning there was not a sail in sight, and the *Frank N. Thayer* was burned almost to the water's edge.

The survivors had now no option but to make for the nearest land, the island of St. Helena, which was still some hundreds of miles distant. To men in their condition a voyage of such length in an open boat must have been a stern ordeal, and has not had the attention it deserved. It lasted for nine days. The supply of food and water was very scanty. Five of the party were suffering from wounds. As neither mast nor sail had survived the fire, a couple of oars were lashed together and blankets were fastened to them. Fortunately the wind was favourable; had it been otherwise the boat could never have reached harbour as it did, on the night of January 13th, without another life being lost.

That was the end of a queer tale, not altogether creditable—in its early phases—to the crew of the *Frank N. Thayer*. Not much could have been expected of the Captain after the wounds he had received, and undoubtedly he made a plucky recovery. The amazing fact remains that a pair of determined coolies, without firearms, mastered a company of twenty, killed five, wounded four, and overawed the remainder for a period of forty-eight hours; and that eleven active men were quite content during that period to remain imprisoned below-deck while their comrades were being murdered above.

The cause of the outbreak remains a mystery; in any case, we have the evidence of only one side. Captain Clarke, in a statement which he made to the harbourmaster at St. Helena, expressed his belief that the two coolies had plotted to murder every one on board and then take to a boat, posing to any one who might pick them up as the innocent survivors of a mutiny. This explanation, of course, shirks the real issue. Why should two men, apparently contented with their lot, outwardly at amity with their fellows, suddenly launch so murderous an attack? If we may assume that we have all the evidence, there can be only one answer. Madness is plainly stamped on each episode. The plan itself was mad, its execution was mad, its end was mad. Sane men could hardly have conceived such a scheme; certainly sane men could never have carried it out.

The Voice in the Night

WILLIAM HOPE HODGSON

It was a dark, starless night. We were becalmed in the Northern Pacific. Our exact position I do not know; for the sun had been hidden during the course of a weary, breathless week, by a thin haze which had seemed to float above us, about the height of our mastheads, at whiles descending and shrouding the surrounding sea.

With there being no wind, we had steadied the tiller, and I was the only man on deck. The crew, consisting of two men and a boy, were sleeping forrard in their den; while Will—my friend, and the master of our little craft—was aft in his bunk on the port side of the little cabin.

Suddenly, from out of the surrounding darkness, there came a hail:—

"Schooner, ahoy!"

The cry was so unexpected that I gave no immediate answer, because of my surprise.

It came again—a voice curiously throaty and inhuman, calling from somewhere upon the dark sea away on our port broadside:—

"Schooner, ahoy!"

"Hullo!" I sung out, having gathered my wits somewhat. "What are you? What do you want?"

"You need not be afraid," answered the queer voice, having probably noticed some trace of confusion in my tone. "I am only an old—man."

The pause sounded oddly; but it was only afterwards that it came back to me with any significance.

"Why don't you come alongside, then?" I queried somewhat snappishly; for I liked not his hinting at my having been a trifle shaken.

"I—I—can't. It wouldn't be safe. I——" The voice broke off, and there was silence.

"What do you mean?" I asked, growing more and more astonished. "Why not safe? Where are you?"

I listened for a moment; but there came no answer. And then, a sudden indefinite suspicion, of I knew not what, coming to me, I stepped swiftly to the binnacle, and took out the lighted lamp. At the same time, I knocked on the deck with my heel to waken Will. Then I was back at the side, throwing the yellow funnel of light out into the silent immensity beyond our rail. As I did so, I heard a slight, muffled cry, and then the sound of a splash, as though some one had dipped oars abruptly. Yet I cannot say that I saw anything with certainty; save, it seemed to me, that with the first flash of the light, there had been something upon the waters, where now there was nothing.

"Hullo, there!" I called. "What foolery is this!"

But there came only the indistinct sounds of a boat being pulled away into the night.

Then I heard Will's voice, from the direction of the after scuttle:—

"What's up, George?"

"Come here, Will!" I said.

"What is it?" he asked, coming across the deck.

I told him the queer thing which had happened. He put several questions; then, after a moment's silence, he raised his hands to his lips, and hailed:—

"Boat, ahoy!"

From a long distance away, there came back to us a faint reply, and my companion repeated his call. Presently, after a short period of silence, there grew on our hearing the muffled sound of oars; at which Will hailed again.

This time there was a reply:—

"Put away the light."

"I'm damned if I will," I muttered; but Will told me to do as the voice bade, and I shoved it down under the bulwarks.

"Come nearer," he said, and the oar-strokes continued. Then, when apparently some half-dozen fathoms distant, they again ceased.

"Come alongside," exclaimed Will. "There's nothing to be frightened of aboard here!"

"Promise that you will not show the light?"

"What's to do with you," I burst out, "that you're so infernally afraid of the light?"

"Because——" began the voice, and stopped short.

"Because what?" I asked, quickly.

Will put his hand on my shoulder.

"Shut up a minute, old man," he said, in a low voice. "Let me tackle him."

He leant more over the rail.

"See here, Mister," he said, "this is a pretty queer business, you coming upon us like this, right out in the middle of the blessed Pacific. How are we to know what sort of a hanky-panky trick you're up to? You say there's only one of you. How are we to know, unless we get a squint at you—eh? What's your objection to the light, anyway?"

As he finished, I heard the noise of the oars again, and then the voice came; but now from a greater distance, and sounding extremely hopeless and pathetic.

"I am sorry—sorry! I would not have troubled you, only I am hungry, and—so is she."

The voice died away, and the sound of the oars, dipping irregularly, was borne to us.

"Stop!" sung out Will. "I don't want to drive you away. Come back! We'll keep the light hidden, if you don't like it."

He turned to me:—

"It's a damned queer rig, this; but I think there's nothing to be afraid of?"

There was a question in his tone, and I replied.

"No, I think the poor devil's been wrecked around here, and gone crazy."

The sound of the oars drew nearer.

"Shove that lamp back in the binnacle," said Will; then he leaned over the rail, and listened. I replaced the lamp, and came back to his side. The dipping of the oars ceased some dozen yards distant.

"Won't you come alongside now?" asked Will in an even voice. "I have had the lamp put back in the binnacle."

"I—I cannot," replied the voice. "I dare not come nearer. I dare not even pay you for the—the provisions."

"That's all right," said Will, and hesitated. "You're welcome to as much grub as you can take——" Again he hesitated.

"You are very good," exclaimed the voice. "May God, Who understands everything, reward you——" It broke off huskily.

"The—the lady?" said Will, abruptly. "Is she——"

"I have left her behind upon the island," came the voice.

"What island?" I cut in.

"I know not its name," returned the voice. "I would to God——!" it began, and checked itself as suddenly.

"Could we not send a boat for her?" asked Will at this point.

"No!" said the voice, with extraordinary emphasis. "My God! No!" There was a moment's pause; then it added, in a tone which seemed a merited reproach:—

"It was because of our want I ventured—Because her agony tortured me."

"I am a forgetful brute," exclaimed Will. "Just wait a minute, whoever you are, and I will bring you up something at once."

In a couple of minutes he was back again, and his arms were full of various edibles. He paused at the rail.

"Can't you come alongside for them?" he asked.

"No—I *dare not*," replied the voice, and it seemed to me that in its tones I detected a note of stifled craving—as though the owner hushed a mortal desire. It came to me then in a flash, that the poor old creature out there in the darkness, was *suffering* for actual need of that which Will held in his arms; and yet, because of some unintelligible dread, refraining from dashing to the side of our little schooner, and receiving it. And with the lightning-like conviction, there came the knowledge that the Invisible was not mad; but sanely facing some intolerable horror.

"Damn it, Will!" I said, full of many feelings, over which predominated a vast sympathy. "Get a box. We must float off the stuff to him in it."

This we did—propelling it away from the vessel, out into the darkness, by means of a boathook. In a minute, a slight cry from the Invisible came to us, and we knew that he had secured the box.

A little later, he called out a farewell to us, and so heartful a blessing, that I am sure we were the better for it. Then, without more ado, we heard the ply of oars across the darkness.

"Pretty soon off," remarked Will, with perhaps just a little sense of injury.

"Wait," I replied. "I think somehow he'll come back. He must have been badly needing that food."

"And the lady," said Will. For a moment he was silent; then he continued:—

"It's the queerest thing ever I've tumbled across, since I've been fishing."

"Yes," I said, and fell to pondering.

And so the time slipped away—an hour, another, and still Will stayed with me; for the queer adventure had knocked all desire for sleep out of him.

The third hour was three parts through, when we heard again the sound of oars across the silent ocean.

"Listen!" said Will, a low note of excitement in his voice.

"He's coming, just as I thought," I muttered.

The dipping of the oars grew nearer, and I noted that the strokes were firmer and longer. The food had been needed.

They came to a stop a little distance off the broadside, and the queer voice came again to us through the darkness:—

"Schooner, ahoy!"

"That you?" asked Will.

"Yes," replied the voice. "I left you suddenly; but—but there was great need."

"The lady?" questioned Will.

"The—lady is grateful now on earth. She will be more grateful soon in—in heaven."

Will began to make some reply, in a puzzled voice; but became confused, and broke off short. I said nothing. I was wondering at the curious pauses, and, apart from my wonder, I was full of a great sympathy.

The voice continued:—

"We—she and I, have talked, as we shared the result of God's tenderness and yours——"

Will interposed; but without coherence.

"I beg of you not to—to belittle your deed of Christian charity this night," said the voice. "Be sure that it has not escaped His notice."

It stopped, and there was a full minute's silence. Then it came again:—

"We have spoken together upon that which—which has befallen us. We had thought to go out, without telling any, of the terror which has come into our——lives. She is with me in believing that to-night's happenings are under a special ruling, and that it is God's wish that we should tell to you all that we have suffered since—since——"

"Yes?" said Will, softly.

"Since the sinking of the 'Albatross.'"

"Ah!" I exclaimed, involuntarily. "She left Newcastle for 'Frisco some six months ago, and hasn't been heard of since."

"Yes," answered the voice. "But some few degrees to the North of the line she was caught in a terrible storm, and dismasted. When the day came, it was found that she was leaking badly, and, presently, it falling to a calm, the sailors took to the boats, leaving—leaving a young lady—my fiancée—and myself upon the wreck.

"We were below, gathering together a few of our belongings, when they left. They were entirely callous, through fear, and when we came up upon the decks, we saw them only as small shapes afar off upon the horizon. Yet we did not despair, but set to work and constructed a small raft. Upon this we put such few matters as it would hold, including a quantity of water and some ship's biscuit. Then, the vessel being very deep in the water, we got ourselves on to the raft, and pushed off.

"It was later, when I observed that we seemed to be in the way of some tide or current, which bore us from the ship at an angle; so that in the course of three hours, by my watch, her hull became invisible to our sight, her broken masts remaining in view for a somewhat longer period. Then, towards evening, it grew misty, and so through the night. The next day we were still encompassed by the mist, the weather remaining quiet.

"For four days, we drifted through this strange haze, until, on the evening of the fourth day, there grew upon our ears the murmur of breakers at a distance. Gradually it became plainer, and, somewhat after midnight, it appeared to sound upon either hand at no very great space. The raft was raised upon a swell several times, and then we were in smooth water, and the noise of the breakers was behind.

"When the morning came, we found that we were in a sort of great lagoon; but of this we noticed little at the time; for close before us, through the enshrouding mist, loomed the hull of a large sailing-vessel. With one accord, we fell upon our knees and thanked God; for we thought that here was an end to our perils. We had much to learn.

"The raft drew near to the ship, and we shouted on them, to take us aboard; but none answered. Presently, the raft touched against the side of the vessel, and, seeing a rope hanging downwards, I seized it and began to climb. Yet I had much ado to make my way up, because of a kind of grey, lichenous fungus, which had seized upon the rope, and which blotched the side of the ship, lividly.

"I reached the rail, and clambered over it, on to the deck. Here, I saw that the decks were covered, in great patches, with the grey masses, some of them rising into nodules several feet in height; but at the time, I thought less of this matter than of the possibility of there being people aboard the ship. I shouted; but none answered. Then I went to the door below the poop deck. I opened it, and peered in. There was a great smell of staleness, so that I knew in a moment that nothing living was within, and with the knowledge, I shut the door quickly; for I felt suddenly lonely.

"I went back to the side, where I had scrambled up. My—my sweetheart was still sitting quietly upon the raft. Seeing me look down, she called up to know whether there were any aboard of the ship. I replied that the vessel had the appearance of having been long deserted; but that if she would wait a little, I would see whether there was anything in the shape of a ladder, by which she could ascend to the deck. Then we would make a search through the vessel together. A little later, on the opposite side of the decks, I found a rope side-ladder. This I carried across, and a minute afterwards, she was beside me.

"Together, we explored the cabins and apartments in the after-part of the ship; but nowhere was there any sign of life. Here and there, within the cabins themselves, we came across odd patches of that queer fungus; but this, as my sweetheart said, could be cleansed away.

"In the end, having assured ourselves that the after portion of the vessel was empty, we picked our ways to the bows, between the ugly grey nodules of that strange growth; and here we made a further search, which told us that there was indeed none aboard but ourselves.

"This being now beyond any doubt, we returned to the stern of the ship, and proceeded to make ourselves as comfortable as possible. Together, we cleared out and cleaned two of the cabins; and, after that, I made examination whether there was anything eatable in the ship. This I soon found was so, and thanked God in my heart for His goodness. In addition to this, I discovered the whereabouts of the freshwater pump, and having fixed it, I found the water drinkable, though somewhat unpleasant to the taste.

"For several days, we stayed aboard the ship, without attempting to get to the shore. We were busily engaged in making the place habitable. Yet even thus early, we became aware that our lot was even less to be desired than might have been imagined; for though, as a first step, we scraped away the odd patches of growth that studded the floors and walls of the cabins and saloon, yet they returned almost to their original size within the space of twenty-four hours, which not only discouraged us, but gave us a feeling of vague unease.

"Still, we would not admit ourselves beaten, so set to work afresh, and not only scraped away the fungus, but soaked the places where it had been, with carbolic, a can-full of which I had found in the pantry. Yet, by the end of the week, the growth had returned in full strength, and, in addition, it had spread to other places, as though our touching it had allowed germs from it to travel elsewhere.

"On the seventh morning, my sweetheart woke to find a small patch of it growing on her pillow, close to her face. At that, she came to me, so soon as she could get her garments upon her. I was in the galley at the time, lighting the fire for breakfast.

"'Come here, John,' she said, and led me aft. When I saw the thing upon her pillow, I shuddered, and then and there we agreed to go right out of the ship, and see whether we could not fare to make ourselves more comfortable ashore.

"Hurriedly, we gathered together our few belongings, and even among these, I found that the fungus had been at work; for one of her shawls had a little lump of it growing near one edge. I threw the whole thing over the side, without saying anything to her.

"The raft was still alongside; but it was too clumsy to guide, and I lowered down a small boat that hung across the stern, and in this we made our way to the shore. Yet, as we drew near to it, I became gradually aware that here the vile fungus, which had driven us from the ship, was growing riot. In places it rose into horrible, fantastic mounds, which seemed almost to quiver, as with a quiet life, when the wind blew across them. Here and there, it took on the forms of vast fingers, and in others it just spread out flat and smooth and treacherous. Odd places, it appeared as grotesque stunted trees, seeming extraordinarily kinked and gnarled——The whole quaking vilely at times.

"At first, it seemed to us that there was no single portion of the surrounding shore which was not hidden beneath the masses of the hideous lichen; yet, in this, I found we were mistaken; for somewhat later, coasting along the shore at a little distance, we descried a smooth white patch of what appeared to be fine sand, and there we landed. It was not sand. What it was, I do not know. All that I have observed, is that upon it, the fungus will not grow; while everywhere else, save where the sand-like earth wanders oddly, path-wise, amid the grey desolation of the lichen, there is nothing but that loathsome greyness.

"It is difficult to make you understand how cheered we were to find one place that was absolutely free from the growth, and here we deposited our belongings. Then we went back to the ship for such things as it seemed to us we should need. Among other matters, I managed to bring ashore with me one of the ship's sails, with which I constructed two small tents, which, though exceedingly rough-shaped, served the purposes for which they were intended. In these, we lived and stored our various necessities, and thus for a matter of some four weeks, all went smoothly and without particular unhappiness. Indeed, I may say with much of happiness——for—for we were together.

"It was on the thumb of her right hand, that the growth first showed. It was only a small circular spot, much like a little grey mole. My God! how the fear leapt to my heart when she showed me the place. We cleansed it, between us, washing it with carbolic and water. In the morning of the following day, she showed her hand to me again. The grey warty thing had returned. For a little while, we looked at one another in silence. Then, still wordless, we started again to remove it. In the midst of the operation, she spoke suddenly.

" 'What's that on the side of your face, Dear!" Her voice was sharp with anxiety. I put my hand up to feel.

" 'There! Under the hair by your ear.—A little to the front a bit.' My finger rested upon the place, and then I knew.

" 'Let us get your thumb done first' I said. And she submitted, only because she was afraid to touch me until it was cleansed. I finished washing and disinfecting her thumb, and then she turned to my face. After it was finished, we sat together and talked awhile of many things; for there had come into our lives sudden, very terrible thoughts. We were, all at once, afraid of something worse than death. We spoke of loading the boat with provisions and water, and making our way out on to the sea; yet we were helpless, for many causes, and—and the growth had attacked us already. We decided to stay. God would do with us what was His will. We would wait.

"A month, two months, three months passed, and the places grew somewhat, and there had come others. Yet we fought so strenuously with the fear, that its headway was but slow, comparatively speaking.

"Occasionally, we ventured off to the ship for such stores as we needed. There, we found that the fungus grew persistently. One of the nodules on the maindeck became soon as high as my head.

"We had now given up all thought or hope of leaving the island. We had realised that it would be unallowable to go among healthy humans, with the thing from which we were suffering.

"With this determination and knowledge in our minds, we knew that we should have to husband our food and water; for we did not know, at that time, but that we should possibly live for many years.

"This reminds me that I have told you that I am an old man. Judged by years this is not so. But—but——"

He broke off; then continued somewhat abruptly:—

"As I was saying, we knew that we should have to use care in the matter of food. But we had no idea then how little food there was left, of which to take care. It was a week later, that I made the discovery that all the other bread tanks—which I had supposed full—were empty, and that (beyond odd tins of vegetables and meat, and some other matters) we had nothing on which to depend, but the bread in the tank which I had already opened.

"After learning this, I bestirred myself to do what I could, and set to work at fishing in the lagoon; but with no success. At this, I was somewhat inclined to feel desperate, until the thought came to me to try outside the lagoon, in the open sea.

"Here, at times, I caught odd fish; but, so infrequently, that they proved of but little help in keeping us from the hunger which threatened. It seemed to me that our deaths were likely to come by hunger, and not by the growth of the thing which had seized upon our bodies.

"We were in this state of mind when the fourth month wore out. Then I made a very horrible discovery. One morning, a little before midday, I came off from the ship, with a portion of the biscuits which were left. In the mouth of her tent, I saw my sweetheart sitting, eating something.

" 'What is it, my Dear?' I called out as I leapt ashore. Yet, on hearing my voice, she seemed confused, and, turning, slyly threw something towards the edge of the little clearing. It fell short, and, a vague suspicion having arisen within me, I walked across and picked it up. It was a piece of the grey fungus.

"As I went to her, with it in my hand, she turned deadly pale; then a rose red.

"I felt strangely dazed and frightened.

" 'My Dear! My Dear!' I said, and could say no more. Yet, at my words, she broke down and cried bitterly. Gradually, as she calmed, I got from her the news that she had tried it the preceding day, and—and liked it. I got her to promise on her knees not to touch it again, however great our hunger. After she had promised, she told me that the desire for it had come suddenly, and that, until the moment of desire, she had experienced nothing towards it, but the most extreme repulsion.

"Later in the day, feeling strangely restless, and much shaken with the thing which I had discovered, I made my way along one of the twisted paths—formed by the white, sand-like substance—which led among the fungoid growth. I had, once before, ventured along there; but not to any great distance. This time, being involved in perplexing thought, I went much further than hitherto.

"Suddenly, I was called to myself, by a queer hoarse sound on my left. Turning quickly, I saw that there was movement among an extraordinarily shaped mass of fungus, close to my elbow. It was swaying uneasily, as though it possessed life of its own. Abruptly, as I stared, the thought came to me that the thing had a grotesque resemblance to the figure of a distorted human creature. Even as the fancy flashed into my brain, there was a slight, sickening noise of tearing, and I saw that one of the branch-like arms was detaching itself from the surrounding grey masses, and coming towards me. The head of the thing—a shapeless grey ball, inclined in my direction. I stood stupidly, and the vile arm brushed across my face. I gave out a frightened cry, and ran back a few paces. There was a sweetish taste upon my lips, where the thing had touched me. I licked them, and was immediately filled with an inhuman desire. I turned and seized a mass of the fungus. Then more, and—more. I was insatiable. In the midst of devouring, the remembrance of the morning's discovery swept into my mazed brain. It was sent by God. I dashed the fragment I held, to the ground. Then, utterly wretched and feeling a dreadful guiltiness, I made my way back to the little encampment.

"I think she knew, by some marvellous intuition which love must have given, so soon as she set eyes on me. Her quiet sympathy made it easier for me, and I told her of my sudden weakness; yet omitted to mention the extraordinary thing which had gone before. I desired to spare her all unnecessary terror.

"But, for myself, I had added an intolerable knowledge, to breed an incessant terror in my brain; for I doubted not but that I had seen the end of one of those men who had come to the island in the ship in the lagoon; and in that monstrous ending, I had seen our own.

"Thereafter, we kept from the abominable food, though the desire for it had entered into our blood. Yet, our drear punishment was upon us; for, day by day, with monstrous rapidity, the fungoid growth took hold of our poor bodies. Nothing we could do would check it materially, and so—and so—we who had been human, became—Well, it matters less each day. Only—only we had been man and maid!

"And day by day, the fight is more dreadful, to withstand the hunger-lust for the terrible lichen.

"A week ago we ate the last of the biscuit, and since that time I have caught three fish. I was out here fishing to-night, when your schooner drifted upon me out of the mist. I hailed you. You know the rest, and may God, out of His great heart, bless you for your goodness to a—a couple of poor outcast souls."

There was the dip of an oar—another. Then the voice came again, and for the last time, sounding through the slight surrounding mist, ghostly and mournful.

"God bless you! Good-bye!"

"Good-bye," we shouted together, hoarsely, our hearts full of many emotions.

I glanced about me. I became aware that the dawn was upon us.

The sun flung a stray beam across the hidden sea; pierced the mist dully, and lit up the receding boat with a gloomy fire. Indistinctly, I saw something nodding between the oars. I thought of a sponge—a great, grey nodding sponge——The oars continued to ply. They were grey—as was the boat—and my eyes searched a moment vainly for the conjunction of hand and oar. My gaze flashed back to the—head. It nodded forward as the oars went backward for the stroke. Then the oars were dipped, the boat shot out of the patch of light, and the—the thing went nodding into the mist.

J. Habakuk Jephson's Statement

A. CONAN DOYLE

In the month of December, 1873, the British ship *Dei Gratia* steered into Gibraltar, having in tow the derelict brigantine *Marie Celeste*, which had been picked up in latitude 30° 40' N., longitude 17° 15' W. There were several circumstances in connection with the condition and appearance of this abandoned vessel which excited considerable comment at the time, and aroused a curiosity which has never been satisfied.

What these circumstances were was summed up in an able article which appeared in the "Gibraltar Gazette." The curious can find it in the issue for January 4, 1874, unless my memory deceives me. For the benefit of those, however, who may be unable to refer to the paper in question, I shall subjoin a few extracts which touch upon the leading features of the case.

"We have ourselves," says the anonymous writer in the "Gazette," "been over the derelict *Marie Celeste*, and have closely questioned the officers of the *Dei Gratia* on every point which might throw light on the affair. They are of opinion that she had been abandoned several days, or perhaps weeks, before being picked up. The official log, which was found in the cabin, states that the vessel sailed from Boston to Lisbon starting upon October 16th. It is, however, most imperfectly kept, and affords little information. There is no reference to rough weather, and, indeed, the state of the vessel's paint and rigging excludes the idea that she was abandoned for any such reason.

"She is perfectly water-tight. No signs of a struggle or of violence are to be detected, and there is absolutely nothing to account for the disappearance of the crew. There are several indications that a lady was present on board, a sewing-machine being found in the cabin and some articles of female attire. These probably belonged to the captain's wife, who is mentioned in the log as having accompanied her husband. As an instance of the mildness of the weather, it may be remarked that a bobbin of silk was found standing upon the sewing-machine, though the least roll of the vessel would have precipitated it to the floor. The boats were intact and slung upon the davits; and the cargo, consisting of tallow and American clocks, was untouched.

"An old-fashioned sword of curious workmanship was discovered among some lumber in the forecastle, and this weapon is said to exhibit a longitudinal striation on the steel, as if it had been recently wiped. It has been placed in the hands of the police, and submitted to Doctor Monoghan, the analyst, for inspection. The result of his examination has not yet been published. We may remark, in conclusion, that Captain Dalton, of the *Dei Gratia*, an able and intelligent seaman, is of opinion that the *Marie Celeste* may have been abandoned a considerable distance from the spot at which she was picked up, since a powerful current runs up in that latitude from the African coast. He confesses his inability, however, to advance any hypothesis which can reconcile all the facts of the case. In the utter absence of a clew or grain of evidence, it is to be feared that the fate of the crew of the *Marie Celeste* will be added to those numerous mysteries of the deep which will never be solved until the great day when the sea shall give up its dead. If crime has been committed, as is much to be suspected, there is little hope of bringing the perpetrators to justice."

I shall supplement this extract from the "Gibraltar Gazette" by quoting a telegram from Boston, which went the round of the English papers, and represented the total amount of information which had been collected about the *Marie Celeste*.

"She was," it said, "a brigantine of one hundred and seventy tons burden, and belonged to White, Russell & White, wine importers, of this city. Captain J. W. Tibbs was an old servant of the firm, and was a man of known ability and tried probity. He was accompanied by his wife, aged thirty-one, and their youngest child, five years old. The crew consisted of seven hands, including two colored seamen and a boy.

"There were three passengers, one of whom was the well-known Brooklyn specialist on consumption, Doctor Habakuk Jephson, who was a distinguished advocate for Abolition in the early days of the movement, and whose pamphlet, entitled 'Where Is Thy Brother?' exercised a strong influence on public opinion before the war. The other passengers were Mr. J. Harton, a writer in the employ of the firm, and Mr. Septimus Goring, a half-caste gentleman from New Orleans. All investigations have failed to throw any light upon the fate of these fourteen human beings. The loss of Doctor Jephson will be felt both in political and scientific circles."

I have here epitomized, for the benefit of the public, all that has been hitherto known concerning the *Marie Celeste* and her crew, for the past ten years have not in any way helped to elucidate the mystery. I have now taken up my pen with the intention of telling all that I know of the ill-fated voyage. I consider that it is a duty which I owe to society, for symptoms which I am familiar with in others lead me to believe that before many months my tongue and hand may be alike incapable of conveying information. Let me remark, as a preface to my narrative, that I am Joseph Habakuk Jephson, Doctor of Medicine of the University of Harvard and ex-Consulting Physician of the Samaritan Hospital of Brooklyn.

Many will doubtless wonder why I have not proclaimed myself before, and why I have suffered so many conjectures and surmises to pass unchallenged. Could the ends of justice have been served in any way by my revealing the facts in my possession, I should unhesitatingly have done so.

It seemed to me, however, that there was no possibility of such a result; and when I attempted, after the occurrence, to state my case to an English official, I was met with such offensive incredulity that I determined never again to expose myself to the chance of such an indignity. I can excuse the discourtesy of the Liverpool magistrate, however, when I reflect upon the treatment which I received at the hands of my own relatives, who, though they knew my unimpeachable character, listened to my statement with an indulgent smile as if humoring the delusion of a monomaniac. This slur upon my veracity led to a quarrel between myself and John Vanburger, the brother of my wife, and confirmed me in my resolution to let the matter sink into oblivion—a determination which I have only altered through my son's solicitations. In order to make my narrative intelligible, I must run lightly over one or two incidents in my former life which throw light upon subsequent events.

My father, William K. Jephson, was a preacher of the sect called Plymouth Brethren, and was one of the most respected citizens of Lowell. Like most of the other Puritans of New England, he was a determined opponent to slavery, and it was from his lips that I received those lessons which tinged every action of my life. While I was studying medicine at Harvard University, I had already made a mark as an advanced Abolitionist, and when, after taking my degree, I bought a third share of the practice of Doctor Willis, of Brooklyn, I managed, in spite of my professional duties, to devote a considerable time to the cause which I had at heart, my pamphlet, "Where Is Thy Brother?" (Swarburgh, Lister & Co., 1859) attracting considerable attention.

When the war broke out, I left Brooklyn and accompanied the One Hundred and Thirteenth New York Regiment through the campaign. I was present at the second battle of Bull Run and at the battle of Gettysburg. Finally, I was severely wounded at Antietam, and would probably have perished on the field had it not been for the kindness of a gentleman named Murray, who had me carried to his house and provided me with every comfort. Thanks to his charity, and to the nursing which I received from his black domestics, I was soon able to get about the plantation with the help of a stick. It was during this period of convalescence that an incident occurred which is closely connected with my story.

Among the most assiduous of the negresses who had watched my couch during my illness there was one old crone who appeared to exert considerable authority over the others. She was exceedingly attentive to me, and I gathered from the few words that passed between us that she had heard of me, and that she was grateful to me for championing her oppressed race.

One day, as I was sitting alone in the veranda, basking in the sun and debating whether I should rejoin Grant's army, I was surprised to see this old creature hobbling toward me. After looking cautiously around to see that we were alone, she fumbled in the front of her dress and produced a small chamois-leather bag which was hung round her neck by a white cord.

"Massa," she said, bending down and croaking the words into my ear, "me die soon. Me very old woman. Not stay long on Massa Murray's plantation."

"You may live a long time yet, Martha," I answered. "You know I am a doctor. If you feel ill, let me know about it, and I will try to cure you."

"No wish to live—wish to die. I'm gwine to join the heavenly host." Here she relapsed into one of those half-heathenish rhapsodies in which negroes indulge. "But, massa, me have one thing must leave behind me when I go. No able to take it with me across the Jordan. That one thing very precious, more precious and more holy than all thing else in the world. Me, a poor old black woman, have this because my people, very great people, 'spose they was back in the old country. But you cannot understand this same as black folk could. My fader give it me, and his fader give it him, but now who shall I give it to? Poor Martha hab no child, no relation, nobody. All round I see black man very bad man. Black woman very stupid woman. Nobody worthy of the stone. And so I say, Here is Massa Jephson who writes books and fights for colored folk—he must be good man, and he shall have it, though he is white man, and nebber can know what it mean or where it came from."

Here the old woman fumbled in the chamois-leather bag and pulled out a flattish black stone with a hole through the middle of it. "Here, take it," she said, pressing it into my hand; "take it. No harm nebber come from anything good. Keep it safe—nebber lose it!" and with a warning gesture, the old crone hobbled away in the same cautious way as she had come, looking from side to side to see if we had been observed.

I was more amused than impressed by the old woman's earnestness, and was only prevented from laughing during her oration by the fear of hurting her feelings. When she was gone, I took a good look at the stone which she had given me. It was intensely black, of extreme hardness, and oval in shape—just such a flat stone as one would pick up on the seashore if one wished to throw a long way. It was about three inches long and an inch and a half broad at the middle, but rounded off at the extremities. The most curious parts about it were several well-marked ridges which ran in semicircles over its surface, and gave it exactly the appearance of a human ear.

Altogether I was rather interested in my new possession, and determined to submit it, as a geological specimen, to my friend Professor Shroeder of the New York Institute, upon the earliest opportunity. In the meantime I thrust it into my pocket, and rising from my chair, started off for a short stroll in the shrubbery, dismissing the incident from my mind.

As my wound had nearly healed by this time I took my leave of Mr. Murray shortly afterward. The Union armies were everywhere victorious and converging on Richmond, so that my assistance seemed unnecessary, and I returned to Brooklyn. There I resumed my practice, and married the second daughter of Josiah Vanburger, the well-known wood engraver. In the course of a few years I built up a good connection and acquired considerable reputation in the treatment of pulmonary complaints.

I still kept the old black stone in my pocket, and frequently told the story of the dramatic way in which I had become possessed of it. I also kept my resolution of showing it to Professor Shroeder, who was much interested both by the anecdote and the specimen. He pronounced it to be a piece of meteoric stone, and drew my attention to the fact that its resemblance to an ear was not accidental, but that it was most carefully worked into that shape. A dozen little anatomical points showed that the worker had been as accurate as he was skillful.

"I should not wonder," said the professor, "if it were broken off from some larger statue, though how such hard material could be so perfectly worked is more than I can understand. If there is a statue to correspond, I should like to see it!" So I thought at the time, but I have changed my opinion since.

The next seven or eight years of my life were quiet and uneventful. Summer followed spring, and spring followed winter, without any variation in my duties. As the practice increased, I admitted J. S. Jackson as partner, he to have one-fourth of the profits. The continued strain had told upon my constitution, however, and I became at last so unwell that my wife insisted upon my consulting Doctor Kavanagh Smith, who was my colleague at the Samaritan Hospital. That gentleman examined me, and pronounced the apex of my left lung to be in a state of consolidation, recommending me at the same time to go through a course of medical treatment and to take a long sea voyage.

My own disposition, which is naturally restless, predisposed me strongly in favor of the latter piece of advice, and the matter was clinched by my meeting young Russell, of the firm of White, Russell & White, who offered me a passage in one of his father's ships, the *Marie Celeste*, which was just starting from Boston. "She is a snug little ship," he said, "and Tibbs, the captain, is an excellent fellow. There is nothing like a sailing ship for an invalid." I was very much of the same opinion myself, so I closed with the offer on the spot.

My original plan was that my wife should accompany me on my travels. She has always been a very poor sailor, however, and there were strong family reasons against her exposing herself to any risk at the time, so we determined that she should remain at home. I am not a religious or an effusive man; but oh, thank God for that! As to leaving my practice, I was easily reconciled to it, as Jackson, my partner, was a reliable and hard-working man.

I arrived in Boston on October 12, 1873, and proceeded immediately to the office of the firm in order to thank them for their courtesy. As I was sitting in the counting-house waiting until they should be at liberty to see me, the words *Marie Celeste* suddenly attracted my attention. I looked round and saw a very tall, gaunt man, who was leaning across the polished mahogany counter asking some questions of the clerk at the other side.

His face was turned half toward me, and I could see that he had a strong dash of negro blood in him, being probably a quadroon or even nearer akin to the black. His curved aquiline nose and straight lank hair showed the white strain; but the dark, restless eyes, sensuous mouth and gleaming teeth all told of his African origin. His complexion was of a sickly, unhealthy yellow, and as his face was deeply pitted with smallpox, the general impression was so unfavorable as to be almost revolting. When he spoke, however, it was in a soft, melodious voice, and in well-chosen words, and he was evidently a man of some education.

"I wished to ask a few questions about the *Marie Celeste*," he repeated, leaning across to the clerk. "She sails the day after to-morrow, does she not?"

"Yes, sir," said the young clerk, awed into unusual politeness by the glimmer of a large diamond in the stranger's shirt front.

"Where is she bound for?"

"Lisbon."

"How many of a crew?"

"Seven, sir."

"Passengers?"

"Yes, two. One of our young gentlemen and a doctor from New York."

"No gentlemen from the South?" asked the stranger, eagerly.

"No, none, sir."

"Is there room for another passenger?"

"Accommodation for three more," answered the clerk.

"I'll go," said the quadroon, decisively; "I'll go; I'll engage my passage at once. Put it down, will you—Mr. Septimus Goring, of New Orleans."

The clerk filled up a form and handed it over to the stranger, pointing to a blank space at the bottom. As Mr. Goring stooped over to sign it, I was horrified to observe that the fingers of his right hand had been lopped off, and that he was holding the pen between his thumb and the palm. I have seen thousands slain in battle, and assisted at every conceivable surgical operation, but I cannot recall any sight which gave me such a thrill of disgust as that great brown spongelike hand with the single member protruding from it. He used it skillfully enough, however, for, dashing off his signature, he nodded to the clerk and strolled out of the office just as Mr. White sent out word that he was ready to receive me.

I went down to the *Marie Celeste* that evening and looked over my berth, which was extremely comfortable considering the size of the vessel. Mr. Goring, whom I had seen in the morning, was to have the one next mine. Opposite was the captain's cabin and a small berth for Mr. John Harton, a gentleman who was going out in the interests of the firm. These little rooms were arranged on each side of the passage which led from the main-deck to the saloon. The latter was a comfortable room, the paneling tastefully done in oak and mahogany, with a rich Brussels carpet and luxurious settees.

I was very much pleased with the accommodation, and also with Tibbs, the captain, a bluff, sailor-like fellow, with a loud voice and hearty manner, who welcomed me to the ship with effusion, and insisted upon our splitting a bottle of wine in his cabin. He told me that he intended to take his wife and youngest child with him on the voyage, and that he hoped with good luck to make Lisbon in three weeks. We had a pleasant chat and parted the best of friends, he warning me to make the last of my preparations next morning, as he intended to make a start by the midday tide, having now shipped all his cargo. I went back to my hotel, where I found a letter from my wife awaiting me, and, after a refreshing night's sleep, returned to the boat in the morning.

From this point I am able to quote from the journal which I kept in order to vary the monotony of the long sea voyage. If it is somewhat bald in places, I can at least rely upon its accuracy in details, as it was written conscientiously from day to day.

October 16*th*.—Cast off our warps at half-past two and were towed out into the bay, where the tug left us, and with all sail set we bowled along at about nine knots an hour. I stood upon the poop watching the low land of America sinking gradually upon the horizon until the evening haze hid it from my sight. A single red light, however, continued to blaze balefully behind us, throwing a long track like a trail of blood upon the water, and it is still visible as I write, though reduced to a mere speck. The captain is in a bad humor, for two of his hands disappointed him at the last moment, and he was compelled to ship a couple of negroes who happened to be on the quay. The missing men were steady, reliable fellows, who had been with him several voyages, and their non-appearance puzzled as well as irritated him.

Where a crew of seven men have to work a fair-sized ship, the loss of two experienced seamen is a serious one, for though the negroes may take a spell at the wheel or swab the decks, they are of little or no use in rough weather. Our cook is also a black man, and Mr. Septimus Goring has a little darky servant, so that we are rather a piebald community. The accountant, John Harton, promises to be an acquisition, for he is a cheery, amusing young fellow. Strange how little wealth has to do with happiness! He has all the world before him and is seeking his fortune in a far land, yet he is as transparently happy as a man can be. Goring is rich, if I am not mistaken, and so am I; but I know that I have a lung, and Goring has some deeper trouble still, to judge by his features. How poorly do we both contrast with the careless, penniless clerk!

October 17th.—Mrs. Tibbs appeared upon deck for the first time this morning—a cheerful, energetic woman, with a dear little child just able to walk and prattle. Young Harton pounced on it at once and carried it away to his cabin, where no doubt he will lay the seeds of future dyspepsia in the child's stomach. Thus medicine doth make cynics of us all! The weather is still all that could be desired, with a fine fresh breeze from the west-sou'-west. The vessel goes so steadily that you would hardly know that she was moving were it not for the creaking of the cordage, the bellying of the sails and the long white furrow in our wake. Walked the quarter-deck all morning with the captain, and I think the keen fresh air has already done my breathing good, for the exercise did not fatigue me in any way.

Tibbs is a remarkably intelligent man, and we had an interesting argument about Maury's observations on ocean currents, which we terminated by going down into his cabin to consult the original work. There we found Goring, rather to the captain's surprise, as it is not usual for passengers to enter that sanctum unless specially invited. He apologized for his intrusion, however, pleading his ignorance of the usages of ship life; and the good-natured sailor simply laughed at the incident, begging him to remain and favor us with his company.

Goring pointed to the chronometers, the case of which he had opened, and remarked that he had been admiring them. He has evidently some practical knowledge of mathematical instruments, as he told at a glance which was the most trustworthy of the three, and also named their price within a few dollars. He had a discussion with the captain, too, upon the variation of the compass, and when we came back to the ocean currents he showed a thorough grasp of the subject. Altogether he rather improves upon acquaintance, and is a man of decided culture and refinement. His voice harmonizes with his conversation, and both are the very antithesis of his face and figure.

The noonday observation shows that we have run two hundred and twenty miles. Toward evening the breeze freshened up, and the first mate ordered reefs to be taken in the topsails and topgallant sails in expectation of a windy night. I observe that the barometer has fallen to twenty-nine. I trust our voyage will not be a rough one, as I am a poor sailor, and my health would probably derive more harm than good from a stormy trip, though I have the greatest confidence in the captain's seamanship and in the soundness of the vessel. Played cribbage with Mrs. Tibbs after supper, and Harton gave us a couple of tunes on the violin.

October 18*th.*—The gloomy prognostications of last night were not fulfilled, as the wind died away again, and we are lying now in a long greasy swell, ruffled here and there by a fleeting catspaw which is insufficient to fill the sails. The air is colder than it was yesterday, and I have put on one of the thick woolen jerseys which my wife knitted for me. Harton came into my cabin in the morning, and we had a cigar together. He says that he remembers having seen Goring in Cleveland, Ohio, in '69. He was, it appears, a mystery then as now, wandering about without any visible employment, and extremely reticent on his own affairs. The man interests me as a psychological study.

At breakfast this morning I suddenly had that vague feeling of uneasiness which comes over some people when closely stared at, and, looking quickly up, I met his eyes bent upon me with an intensity which amounted to ferocity, though their expression instantly softened as he made some conventional remark upon the weather. Curiously enough, Harton says that he had a very similar experience yesterday upon deck. I observe that Goring frequently talks to the colored seamen as he strolls about—a trait which I rather admire, as it is common to find half-breeds ignore their dark strain and treat their black kinsfolk with greater intolerance than a white man would do. His little page is devoted to him, apparently, which speaks well for his treatment of him. Altogether, the man is a curious mixture of incongruous qualities, and, unless I am deceived in him, will give me food for observation during the voyage.

The captain is grumbling about his chronometers, which do not register exactly the same time. He says it is the first time that they have ever disagreed. We were unable to get a noonday observation on account of the haze. By dead reckoning we have done about a hundred and seventy miles in twenty-four hours. The dark seamen have proved, as the skipper prophesied, to be very inferior hands, but as they can both manage the wheel well, they are kept steering, and so leave the more experienced men to work the ship. These details are trivial enough, but a small thing serves as food for gossip aboard ship. The appearance of a whale in the evening caused quite a flutter among us. From its sharp back and forked tail I should pronounce it to have been a rorqual, or "finner," as they are called by the fishermen.

October 19*th.*—Wind was cold, so I prudently remained in my cabin all day, only creeping out for dinner. Lying in my bunk, I can, without moving, reach my books, pipes, or anything else I may want, which is one advantage of a small apartment. My old wound began to ache a little to-day, probably from the cold. Read Montaigne's "Essays" and nursed myself. Harton came in in the afternoon with Doddy, the captain's child, and the skipper himself followed, so that I held quite a reception.

October 20*th and* 21*st.*—Still cold, with a continual drizzle of rain, and I have not been able to leave the cabin. This confinement makes me feel weak and depressed. Goring came in to see me, but his company did not tend to cheer me up much, as he hardly uttered a word, but contented himself with staring at me in a peculiar and rather irritating manner. He then got up and stole out of the cabin without saying anything. I am beginning to suspect that the man is a lunatic. I think I mentioned that his cabin is next to mine. The two are simply divided by a thin wooden partition which is cracked in many places, some of the cracks being so large that I can hardly avoid, as I lie in my bunk, observing his motions in the adjoining room.

Without any wish to play the spy, I see him continually stooping over what appears to be a chart and working with a pencil and compasses. I have remarked the interest he displays in matters connected with navigation, but I am surprised that he should take the trouble to work out the course of the ship. However, it is a harmless amusement enough, and no doubt he verifies his results by those of the captain.

I wish the man did not run in my thoughts so much. I had a nightmare on the 20th, in which I thought my bunk was a coffin, that I was laid out in it, and that Goring was endeavoring to nail up the lid, which I was frantically pushing away. Even when I woke up I could hardly persuade myself that I was not in a coffin. As a medical man, I know that a nightmare is simply a vascular derangement of the cerebral hemispheres, and yet in my weak state I cannot shake off the morbid impression which it produces.

October 22nd.—A fine day, without a cloud in the sky, and a fresh breeze from the sou'-west which wafts us gayly on our way. There has evidently been some heavy weather near us, as there is a tremendous swell on, and the ship lurches until the end of the foreyard nearly touches the water. Had a refreshing walk up and down the quarter-deck, though I have hardly found my sea-legs yet. Several small birds—chaffinches, I think—perched in the rigging.

4.40 P.M.—While I was on deck this morning I heard a sudden explosion from the direction of my cabin, and, hurrying down, found that I had very nearly met with a serious accident. Goring was cleaning a revolver, it seems, in his cabin, when one of the barrels which he thought was unloaded went off. The ball passed through the side partition and imbedded itself in the bulwarks in the exact place where my head usually rests. I have been under fire too often to magnify trifles, but there is no doubt if I had been in the bunk it must have killed me. Goring, poor fellow, did not know that I had gone on deck that day, and must therefore have felt terribly frightened. I never saw such emotion on a man's face as when, on rushing out of his cabin with the smoking pistol in his hand, he met me face to face as I came down from the deck. Of course, he was profuse in his apologies, though I simply laughed at the incident.

11 P.M.—A misfortune has occurred so unexpected and so horrible that my little escape of the morning dwindles into insignificance. Mrs. Tibbs and her child have disappeared—utterly and entirely disappeared. I can hardly compose myself to write the sad details.

About half-past eight Tibbs rushed into my cabin with a very white face and asked me if I had seen his wife. I answered that I had not. He then ran wildly into the saloon and began groping about for any trace of her, while I followed him, endeavoring vainly to persuade him that his fears were ridiculous. We hunted over the ship for an hour and a half without coming on any sign of the missing woman or child. Poor Tibbs lost his voice completely from calling her name. Even the sailors, who are generally stolid enough, were deeply affected by the sight of him as he roamed bareheaded and disheveled about the deck, searching with feverish anxiety the most impossible places, and returning to them again and again with a piteous pertinacity.

The last time she was seen was about seven o'clock, when she took Doddy on to the poop to give him a breath of fresh air before putting him to bed. There was no one there at the time except the black seaman at the wheel, who denies having seen her at all. The whole affair is wrapped in mystery. My own theory is that while Mrs. Tibbs was holding the child and standing near the bulwarks it gave a spring and fell overboard, and that in her convulsive attempt to catch or save it, she followed it. I cannot account for the double disappearance in any other way.

It is quite feasible that such a tragedy should be enacted without the knowledge of the man at the wheel, since it was dark at the time, and the peaked skylights of the saloon screen the greater part of the quarter-deck. Whatever the truth may be, it is a terrible catastrophe, and has cast the darkest gloom upon our voyage. The mate has put the ship about, but of course there is not the slightest hope of picking them up. The captain is lying in a state of stupor in his cabin. I gave him a powerful dose of opium in his coffee, that for a few hours at least his anguish may be deadened.

October 23rd.—Woke with a vague feeling of heaviness and misfortune, but it was not until a few moments' reflection that I was able to recall our loss of the night before. When I came on deck I saw the poor skipper standing gazing back at the waste of waters behind us which contains everything dear to him upon earth. I attempted to speak to him, but he turned brusquely away and began pacing the deck with his head sunk upon his breast. Even now, when the truth is so clear, he cannot pass a boat or an unbent sail without peering under it. He looks ten years older than he did yesterday morning. Harton is terribly cut up, for he was fond of little Doddy, and Goring seems sorry too. At least he has shut himself up in his cabin all day, and when I got a casual glance at him his head was resting on his two hands, as if in a melancholy revery.

I fear we are about as dismal a crew as ever sailed. How shocked my wife will be to hear of our disaster! The swell has gone down now, and we are doing about eight knots with all sail set and a nice little breeze. Hyson is practically in command of the ship, as Tibbs, though he does his best to bear up and keep a brave front, is incapable of applying himself to serious work.

October 24th.—Is the ship accursed? Was there ever a voyage which began so fairly and which changed so disastrously? Tibbs shot himself through the head during the night. I was awakened about three o'clock in the morning by an explosion, and immediately sprang out of bed and rushed into the captain's cabin to find out the cause, though with a terrible presentiment in my heart.

Quickly as I went, Goring went more quickly still, for he was already in the cabin stooping over the dead body of the captain. It was a hideous sight, for the whole front of his face was blown in, and the little room was swimming in blood. The pistol was lying beside him on the floor, just as it had dropped from his hand. He had evidently put it to his mouth before pulling the trigger. Goring and I picked him reverently up and laid him on his bed. The crew had all clustered into his cabin, and the six white men were deeply grieved, for they were old hands who had sailed with him many years.

There were dark looks and murmurs among them, too, and one of them openly declared that the ship was haunted. Harton helped to lay the poor skipper out, and we did him up in canvas between us. At twelve o'clock the foreyard was hauled aback, and we committed his body to the deep, Goring reading the Church of England burial service. The breeze has freshened up, and we have done ten knots all day and sometimes twelve. The sooner we reach Lisbon and get away from this accursed ship the better pleased shall I be. I feel as though we were in a floating coffin. Little wonder that the poor sailors are superstitious when I, an educated man, feel it so strongly.

October 25th.—Made a good run all day. Feel listless and depressed.

October 26th.—Goring, Harton, and I had a chat together on deck in the morning. Harton tried to draw Goring out as to his profession and his object in going to Europe, but the quadroon parried all his questions and gave us no information. Indeed, he seemed to be slightly offended by Harton's pertinacity, and went down into his cabin. I wonder why we should both take such an interest in this man? I suppose it is his striking appearance, coupled with his apparent wealth, which piques our curiosity. Harton has a theory that he is really a detective, that he is after some criminal who has got away to Portugal, and that he has chosen this peculiar way of traveling that he may arrive unnoticed and pounce upon his quarry unawares.

I think the supposition is rather a far-fetched one, but Harton bases it upon a book which Goring left on deck, and which he picked up and glanced over. It was a sort of scrap-book, it seems, and contained a large number of newspaper cuttings. All these cuttings related to murders which had been committed at various times in the States during the last twenty years or so. The curious thing which Harton observed about them, however, was that they were invariably murders the authors of which had never been brought to justice. They varied in every detail, he says, as to the manner of execution and the social status of the victim, but they uniformly wound up with the same formula that the murderer was still at large, though, of course, the police had every reason to expect his speedy capture. Certainly the incident seems to support Harton's theory, though it may be a mere whim of Goring's, or, as I suggested to Harton, he may be collecting materials for a book which shall outvie De Quincey. In any case it is no business of ours.

October 27th, 28th.—Wind still fair, and we are making good progress. Strange how easily a human unit may drop out of its place and be forgotten! Tibbs is hardly ever mentioned now; Hyson has taken possession of his cabin, and all goes on as before. Were it not for Mrs. Tibbs's sewing-machine upon a side-table we might forget that the unfortunate family had ever existed.

Another accident occurred on board to-day, though fortunately not a very serious one. One of our white hands had gone down the after-hold to fetch up a spare coil of rope, when one of the hatches which he had removed came crashing down on the top of him. He saved his life by springing out of the way, but one of his feet was terribly crushed, and he will be of little use for the remainder of the voyage. He attributes the accident to the carelessness of his negro companion, who had helped him to shift the hatches. The latter, however, puts it down to the roll of the ship. Whatever be the cause, it reduces our short-handed crew still further. This run of ill-luck seems to be depressing Harton, for he has lost his usual good spirits and joviality. Goring is the only one who preserves his cheerfulness. I see him still working at his chart in his own cabin. His nautical knowledge would be useful should anything happen to Hyson—which God forbid!

October 29th, 30th.—Still bowling along with a fresh breeze. All quiet and nothing to chronicle.

October 31st.—My weak lungs, combined with the exciting episodes of the voyage, have shaken my nervous system so much that the most trivial incident affects me. I can hardly believe that I am the same man who tied the external iliac artery, an operation requiring the nicest precision, under a heavy rifle fire at Antietam. I am as nervous as a child. I was lying half dozing last night about four bells in the middle watch, trying in vain to drop into a refreshing sleep. There was no light inside my cabin, but a single ray of moonlight streamed in through the porthole, throwing a silvery flickering circle upon the door.

As I lay I kept my drowsy eyes upon this circle, and was conscious that it was gradually becoming less well defined as my senses left me, when I was suddenly recalled to full wakefulness by the appearance of a small dark object in the very center of the luminous disk.

I lay quietly and breathlessly watching it. Gradually it grew larger and plainer, and then I perceived that it was a human hand which had been cautiously inserted through the chink of the half-closed door—a hand which, as I observed with a thrill of horror, was not provided with fingers. The door swung cautiously backward, and Goring's head followed his hand. It appeared in the center of the moonlight, and was framed, as it were, in a ghastly, uncertain halo, against which his features showed out plainly. It seemed to me that I had never seen such an utterly fiendish and merciless expression upon a human face. His eyes were dilated and glaring, his lips drawn back so as to show his white fangs, and his straight black hair appeared to bristle over his low forehead like the hood of a cobra.

The sudden and noiseless apparition had such an effect upon me that I sprang up in bed, trembling in every limb, and held out my hand toward my revolver. I was heartily ashamed of my hastiness when he explained the object of his intrusion, as he immediately did in the most courteous language. He had been suffering from toothache, poor fellow! and had come in to beg some laudanum, knowing that I possessed a medicine chest. As to his sinister expression he is never a beauty, and what with my state of nervous tension and the effect of the shifting moonlight, it was easy to conjure up something horrible. I gave him twenty drops, and he went off again with many expressions of gratitude. I can hardly say how much this trivial incident affected me. I have felt unstrung all day.

A week's record of our voyage is here omitted, as nothing eventful occurred during the time, and my log consists merely of a few pages of unimportant gossip.

November 7th.—Harton and I sat on the poop all the morning, for the weather is becoming very warm as we come into southern latitudes. We reckon that we have done two-thirds of our voyage. How glad we shall be to see the green banks of the Tagus, and leave this unlucky ship forever! I was endeavoring to amuse Harton to-day and to while away the time by telling him some of the experiences of my past life. Among others I related to him how I came into the possession of my black stone, and as a finale I rummaged in the side pocket of my old shooting-coat and produced the identical object in question. He and I were bending over it together, I pointing out to him the curious ridges upon its surface, when we were conscious of a shadow falling between us and the sun, and looking round saw Goring standing behind us glaring over our shoulders at the stone.

For some reason or other he appeared to be powerfully excited, though he was evidently trying to control himself and to conceal his emotion. He pointed once or twice at my relic with his stubby thumb before he could recover himself sufficiently to ask what it was and how I obtained it—a question put in such a brusque manner that I should have been offended had I not known the man to be an eccentric. I told him the story very much as I had told it to Harton. He listened with the deepest interest, and then asked me if I had any idea what the stone was. I said I had not, beyond that it was meteoric. He asked me if I had ever tried its effect upon a negro. I said I had not. "Come," said he; "we'll see what our black friend at the wheel thinks of it." He took the stone in his hand and went across to the sailor, and the two examined it carefully.

I could see the man gesticulating and nodding his head excitedly, as if making some assertion, while his face betrayed the utmost astonishment, mixed, I think, with some reverence. Goring came across the deck to us presently, still holding the stone in his hand. "He says it is a worthless, useless thing," he said, "and fit only to be chucked overboard," with which he raised his hand and would most certainly have made an end of my relic had the black sailor behind him not rushed forward and seized him by the wrist. Finding himself secured, Goring dropped the stone and turned away with a very bad grace to avoid my angry remonstrances at his breach of faith. The black picked up the stone and handed it to me with a low bow and a sign of profound respect.

The whole affair is inexplicable. I am rapidly coming to the conclusion that Goring is a maniac or something very near one. When I compare the effect produced by the stone upon the sailor, however, with the respect shown to Martha on the plantation, and the surprise of Goring on its first production, I cannot but come to the conclusion that I have really got hold of some powerful talisman which appeals to the whole dark race. I must not trust it in Goring's hands again.

November 8th, 9th.—What splendid weather we are having! Beyond one little blow, we have had nothing but fresh breezes the whole voyage. These two days we have made better runs than any hitherto. It is a pretty thing to watch the spray fly up from our prow as it cuts through the waves. The sun shines through it and breaks it up into a number of miniature rainbows—"sun-dogs," the sailors call them. I stood on the foc's'le-head for several hours to-day watching the effect, and surrounded by a halo of prismatic colors. The steersman has evidently told the other blacks about my wonderful stone, for I am treated by them all with the greatest respect.

Talking about optical phenomena, we had a curious one yesterday evening which was pointed out to me by Hyson. This was the appearance of a triangular, well-defined object high up in the heavens to the north of us. He explained that it was exactly like the Peak of Teneriffe as seen from a great distance—the peak was, however, at that moment at least five hundred miles to the south. It may have been a cloud, or it may have been one of those strange reflections of which one reads. The weather is very warm. The mate says that he never knew it so warm in these latitudes. Played chess with Harton in the evening.

November 10th.—It is getting warmer and warmer. Some land birds came and perched in the rigging today, though we are still a considerable way from our destination. The heat is so great that we are too lazy to do anything but lounge about the decks and smoke. Goring came over to me to-day and asked me some more questions about my stone; but I answered him rather shortly, for I have not quite forgiven him yet for the cool way in which he attempted to deprive me of it.

November 11th, 12th.—Still making good progress. I had no idea Portugal was ever as hot as this, but no doubt it is cooler on land. Hyson himself seemed surprised at it, and so do the men.

November 13th.—A most extraordinary event has happened, so extraordinary as to be almost inexplicable. Either Hyson has blundered wonderfully, or some magnetic influence has disturbed our instruments. Just about daybreak the watch on the foc's'le-head shouted out that he heard the sound of surf ahead, and Hyson thought he saw the loom of land. The ship was put about, and, though no lights were seen, none of us doubted that we had struck the Portuguese coast a little sooner than we had expected.

What was our surprise to see the scene which was revealed to us at daybreak! As far as we could look on either side was one long line of surf, great green billows rolling in and breaking into a cloud of foam. But behind the surf what was there? Not the green banks nor the high cliffs of the shores of Portugal, but a great sandy waste which stretched away and away until it blended with the skyline.

To right and left, look where you would, there was nothing but yellow sand, heaped in some places into fantastic mounds, some of them several hundred feet high, while in other parts were long stretches as level apparently as a billiard board.

Harton and I, who had come on deck together, looked at each other in astonishment, and Harton burst out laughing. Hyson is exceedingly mortified at the occurrence, and protests that the instruments have been tampered with. There is no doubt that this is the mainland of Africa, and that it was really the Peak of Teneriffe which we saw some days ago upon the northern horizon. At the time when we saw the land birds we must have been passing some of the Canary Islands. If we continued on the same course, we are now to the north of Cape Blanco, near the unexplored country which skirts the great Sahara. All we can do is to rectify our instruments as far as possible and start afresh for our destination.

8.30 P.M.—Have been lying in a calm all day. The coast is now about a mile and a half from us. Hyson has examined the instruments, but cannot find any reason for their extraordinary deviation.

This is the end of my private journal, and I must make the remainder of my statement from memory. There is little chance of my being mistaken about facts which have seared themselves into my recollection. That very night the storm which had been brewing so long burst over us, and I came to learn whither all those little incidents were tending which I had recorded so aimlessly. Blind fool that I was not to have seen it sooner! I shall tell what occurred as precisely as I can.

I had gone into my cabin about half-past eleven, and was preparing to go to bed, when a tap came at my door. On opening it I saw Goring's little black page, who told me that his master would like to have a word with me on deck. I was rather surprised that he should want me at such a late hour, but I went up without hesitation. I had hardly put my foot on the quarter-deck before I was seized from behind, dragged down upon my back, and a handkerchief slipped round my mouth.

I struggled as hard as I could, but a coil of rope was rapidly and firmly wound round me, and I found myself lashed to the davit of one of the boats, utterly powerless to do or say anything, while the point of a knife, pressed to my throat, warned me to cease my struggles. The night was so dark that I had been unable hitherto to recognize my assailants; but as my eyes became accustomed to the gloom, and the moon broke out through the clouds that obscured it, I made out that I was surrounded by the two negro sailors, the black cook, and my fellow-passenger, Goring. Another man was crouching on the deck at my feet, but he was in the shadow and I could not recognize him.

All this occurred so rapidly that a minute could hardly have elapsed from the time I mounted the companion until I found myself gagged and powerless. It was so sudden that I could scarcely bring myself to realize it, or to comprehend what it all meant. I heard the gang round me speaking in short, fierce whispers to each other, and some instinct told me that my life was the question at issue. Goring spoke authoritatively and angrily—the others doggedly and all together, as if disputing his commands. Then they moved away in a body to the opposite side of the deck, where I could still hear them whispering, though they were concealed from my view by the saloon skylights.

All this time the voices of the watch on deck chatting and laughing at the other end of the ship was distinctly audible, and I could see them gathered in a group, little dreaming of the dark doings which were going on within thirty yards of them. Oh, that I could have given them one word of warning, even though I had lost my life in doing it! But it was impossible.

The moon was shining fitfully through the scattered clouds, and I could see the silvery gleam of the surge, and beyond it the vast, weird desert with its fantastic sand-hills. Glancing down, I saw that the man who had been crouching on the deck was still lying there, and as I gazed at him, a flickering ray of moonlight fell full upon his upturned face.

Great Heaven! even now, when more than twelve years have elapsed, my hand trembles as I write that, in spite of distorted features and projecting eyes, I recognized the face of Harton, the cheery young clerk who had been my companion during the voyage. It needed no medical eye to see that he was quite dead, while the twisted handkerchief round the neck and the gag in his mouth showed the silent way in which the hell-hounds had done their work. The clew which explained every event of our voyage came upon me like a flash of light as I gazed on poor Harton's corpse. Much was dark and unexplained, but I felt a dim perception of the truth.

I heard the striking of a match at the other side of the skylight, and then I saw the tall, gaunt figure of Goring standing up on the bulwarks and holding in his hands what appeared to be a dark lantern. He lowered this for a moment over the side of the ship, and, to my inexpressible astonishment, I saw it answered instantaneously by a flash among the sand-hills on shore, which came and went so rapidly that unless I had been following the direction of Goring's gaze I should never have detected it. Again he lowered the lantern, and again it was answered from the shore.

He then stepped down from the bulwarks, and in doing so slipped, making such a noise that for a moment my heart bounded with the thought that the attention of the watch would be directed to his proceedings. It was a vain hope. The night was calm and the ship motionless, so that no idea of duty kept them vigilant. Hyson, who after the death of Tibbs was in command of both watches, had gone below to snatch a few hours' sleep, and the boatswain who was left in charge was standing with the other two men at the foot of the foremast. Powerless, speechless, with the cords cutting into my flesh and the murdered man at my feet, I awaited the next act in the tragedy.

The four ruffians were standing up now at the other side of the deck. The cook was armed with some sort of a cleaver, the others had knives, and Goring had a revolver. They were all leaning against the rail and looking out over the water as if watching for something. I saw one of them grasp another's arm and point as if at some object, and following the direction, I made out the loom of a large moving mass making toward the ship.

As it emerged from the gloom I saw that it was a great canoe crammed with men and propelled by at least a score of paddles. As it shot under our stern the watch caught sight of it also, and raising a cry, hurried aft. They were too late, however. A swarm of gigantic negroes clambered over the quarter, and, led by Goring, swept down the deck in an irresistible torrent.

All opposition was overpowered in a moment, the unarmed watch were knocked over and bound, and the sleepers dragged out of their bunks and secured in the same manner. Hyson made an attempt to defend the narrow passage leading to his cabin, and I heard a scuffle, and his voice shouting for assistance. There was none to assist, however, and he was brought on to the poop with the blood streaming from a deep cut in his forehead. He was gagged like the others, and a council was held upon our fate by the negroes. I saw our black seamen pointing toward me and making some statement, which was received with murmurs of astonishment and incredulity by the savages.

One of them then came over to me, and plunging his hand into my pocket, took out my black stone and held it up. He then handed it to a man who appeared to be a chief, who examined it as minutely as the light would permit, and muttering a few words, passed it on to the warrior beside him, who also scrutinized it and passed it on until it had gone from hand to hand round the whole circle. The chief then said a few words to Goring in the native tongue, on which the quadroon addressed me in English. At this moment I seem to see the scene. The tall masts of the ship with the moonlight streaming down, silvering the yards and bringing the network of cordage into hard relief; the group of dusky warriors leaning on their spears; the dead man at my feet; the line of white-faced prisoners, and in front of me the loathsome half-breed, looking, in his white linen and elegant clothes, a strange contrast to his associates.

"You will bear me witness," he said in his softest accent, "that I am no party to sparing your life. If it rested with me you would die as these other men are about to do. I have no personal grudge against either you or them, but I have devoted my life to the destruction of the white race, and you are the first that has ever been in my power and has escaped me. You may thank that stone of yours for your life. Those poor fellows reverence it, and indeed, if it really be what they think it is, they have cause. Should it prove, when we get ashore, that they are mistaken, and that its shape and material is a mere chance, nothing can save your life. In the meantime we wish to treat you well, so if there are any of your possessions which you would like to take with you, you are at liberty to get them."

As he finished, he gave a sign, and a couple of the negroes unbound me, though without removing the gag. I was led down into the cabin, where I put a few valuables into my pockets, together with a pocket-compass and my journal of the voyage. They then pushed me over the side into a small canoe, which was lying beside the large one, and my guards followed me, and shoving off, began paddling for the shore. We had got about a hundred yards or so from the ship when our steersman held up his hand, and the paddlers paused for a moment and listened.

Then on the silence of the night I heard a sort of dull, moaning sound, followed by a succession of splashes in the water. That is all I know of the fate of my poor shipmates. Almost immediately afterward the large canoe followed us, and the deserted ship was left drifting about—a dreary, specter-like hulk. Nothing was taken from her by the savages. The whole fiendish transaction was carried through as decorously and temperately as though it were a religious rite.

The first gray of daylight was visible in the east as we passed through the surge and reached the shore. Leaving half a dozen men with the canoes, the rest of the negroes set off through the sand-hills, leading me with them, but treating me very gently and respectfully. It was difficult walking, as we sank over our ankles into the loose, shifting sand at every step, and I was nearly dead beat by the time we reached the native village, or town rather, for it was a place of considerable dimensions. The houses were conical structures not unlike beehives, and were made of compressed seaweed cemented over with a rude form of mortar, there being neither stick nor stone upon the coast nor anywhere within many hundreds of miles. As we entered the town, an enormous crowd of both sexes came swarming out to meet us, beating tom-toms and howling and screaming.

On seeing me they redoubled their yells and assumed a threatening attitude, which was instantly quelled by a few words shouted by my escort. A buzz of wonder succeeded the war-cries and yells of the moment before, and the whole dense mass proceeded down the broad central street of the town, having my escort and myself in the center.

My statement hitherto may seem so strange as to excite doubt in the minds of those who do not know me, but it was the fact which I am now about to relate which caused my own brother-in-law to insult me by disbelief. I can but relate the occurrence in the simplest words, and trust to chance and time to prove their truth. In the center of this main street there was a large building, formed in the same primitive way as the others, but towering high above them; a stockade of beautifully polished ebony rails was planted all round it, the framework of the door was formed by two elephant's tusks sunk in the ground on each side and meeting at the top, and the aperture was closed by a screen of native cloth richly embroidered in gold.

We made our way to this imposing-looking structure, but, on reaching the opening in the stockade, the multitude stopped and squatted down upon their hams, while I was led through into the inclosure by a few of the chiefs and elders of the tribe, Goring accompanying us, and in fact directing the proceedings. On reaching the screen which closed the temple—for such it evidently was—my hat and my shoes were removed, and I was then led in, a venerable old negro leading the way, carrying in his hand my stone, which had been taken from my pocket. The building was only lighted up by a few long slits in the roof, through which the tropical sun poured, throwing broad golden bars upon the clay floor, alternating with intervals of darkness.

The interior was even larger than one would have imagined from the outside appearance. The walls were hung with native mats, shells, and other ornaments, but the remainder of the great space was quite empty, with the exception of a single object in the center. This was the figure of a colossal negro, which I at first thought to be some real king or high priest of titanic size, but as I approached it I saw by the way in which the light was reflected from it that it was a statue admirably cut in jet-black stone. I was led up to this idol, for such it seemed to be, and looking at it closer, I saw that though it was perfect in every other respect, one of its ears had been broken short off. The gray-haired negro who held my relic mounted upon a small stool, and stretching up his arm, fitted Martha's black stone on to the jagged surface on the side of the statue's head. There could not be a doubt that the one had been broken off from the other.

The parts dovetailed together so accurately that when the old man removed his hand the ear stuck in its place for a few seconds before dropping into his open palm. The group round me prostrated themselves upon the ground at the sight with a cry of reverence, while the crowd outside, to whom the result was communicated, set up a wild whooping and cheering.

In a moment I found myself converted from a prisoner into a demi-god. I was escorted back through the town in triumph, the people pressing forward to touch my clothing and to gather up the dust on which my foot had trod. One of the largest huts was put at my disposal, and a banquet of every native delicacy was served me. I still felt, however, that I was not a free man, as several spearmen were placed as a guard at the entrance of my hut. All day my mind was occupied with plans of escape, but none seemed in any way feasible. On the one side was the great arid desert stretching away to Timbuctoo, on the other was a sea untraversed by vessels. The more I pondered over the problem the more hopeless did it seem. I little dreamed how near I was to its solution.

Night had fallen, and the clamor of the negroes had died gradually away. I was stretched on the couch of skins which had been provided for me, and was still meditating over my future, when Goring walked stealthily into the hut. My first idea was that he had come to complete his murderous holocaust by making away with me, the last survivor, and I sprang to my feet, determined to defend myself to the last. He smiled when he saw the action, and motioned me down again while he seated himself upon the other end of the couch.

"What do you think of me?" was the astonishing question with which he commenced our conversation.

"Think of you!" I almost yelled. "I think you the vilest, most unnatural renegade that ever polluted the earth. If we were away from these black devils of yours, I would strangle you with my hands!"

"Don't speak so loud," he said, without the slightest appearance of irritation. "I don't want our chat to be cut short. So you would strangle me, would you?" he went on, with an amused smile. "I suppose I am returning good for evil, for I have come to help you to escape."

"You!" I gasped, incredulously.

"Yes, I," he continued. "Oh, there is no credit to me in the matter. I am quite consistent. There is no reason why I should not be perfectly candid with you. I wish to be king over these fellows—not a very high ambition, certainly, but you know what Cæsar said about being first in a village in Gaul. Well, this unlucky stone of yours has not only saved your life, but has turned all their heads, so that they think you are come down from heaven, and my influence will be gone until you are out of the way. That is why I am going to help you to escape, since I cannot kill you"—this in the most natural and dulcet voice, as if the desire to do so were a matter of course.

"You would give the world to ask me a few questions," he went on, after a pause; "but you are too proud to do it. Never mind; I'll tell you one or two things, because I want your fellow white men to know them when you go back, if you are lucky enough to get back. About that cursed stone of yours, for instance. These negroes, or at least so the legend goes, were Mohammedans originally. While Mohammed himself was still alive, there was a schism among his followers, and the smaller party moved away from Arabia, and eventually crossed Africa. They took away with them, in their exile, a valuable relic of their old faith in the shape of a large piece of black stone of Mecca.

"The stone was a meteoric one, as you may have heard, and in its fall upon the earth it broke into two pieces. One of these pieces is still at Mecca. The larger piece was carried away to Barbary, where a skillful worker modeled it into the fashion which you saw to-day. These men are the descendants of the original seceders from Mohammed, and they have brought their relic safely through all their wanderings until they settled in this strange place, where the desert protects them from their enemies."

"And the ear?" I asked, almost involuntarily.

"Oh, that was the same story over again. Some of the tribe wandered away to the south a few hundred years ago, and one of them, wishing to have good luck for the enterprise, got into the temple at night and carried off one of the ears. There has been a tradition among the negroes ever since that the ear would come back some day. The fellow who carried it was caught by some slaver, no doubt, and that was how it got into America, and so into your hands—and you have had the honor of fulfilling the prophecy."

He paused for a few minutes, resting his head upon his hands, waiting apparently for me to speak. When he looked up again, the whole expression of his face had changed. His features were firm and set, and he changed the air of half levity with which he had spoken before for one of sternness and almost ferocity.

"I wish you to carry a message back," he said, "to the white race, the great dominating race whom I hate and defy. Tell them that I have battened on their blood for twenty years, that I have slain them until even I became tired of what had once been a joy, that I did this unnoticed and unsuspected in the face of every precaution which their civilization could suggest. There is no satisfaction in revenge when your enemy does not know who has struck him. I am not sorry, therefore, to have you as a messenger. There is no need why I should tell you how this great hate became born in me. See this," and he held up his mutilated hand; "that was done by a white man's knife. My father was white, my mother was a slave. When he died she was sold again, and I, a child then, saw her lashed to death to break her of some of the little airs and graces which her late master had encouraged her in. My young wife, too—oh, my young wife!" a shudder ran through his whole frame.

"No matter! I swore my oath, and I kept it. From Maine to Florida, and from Boston to San Francisco, you could track my steps by sudden deaths which baffled the police. I warred against the whole white race as they for centuries had warred against the black one. At last, as I tell you, I sickened of blood. Still, the sight of a white face was abhorrent to me, and I determined to find some bold, free black people and to throw in my lot with them, to cultivate their latent powers, and to form a nucleus for a great colored nation.

"This idea possessed me, and I traveled over the world for two years seeking for what I desired. At last I almost despaired of finding it. There was no hope of regeneration in the slave-dealing Soudanese, the debased Fantee, or the Americanized negro of Liberia. I was returning from my quest, when chance brought me in contact with this magnificent tribe of dwellers in the desert, and I threw in my lot with them. Before doing so, however, my old instinct of revenge prompted me to make one last visit to the United States, and I returned from it in the *Marie Celeste*.

"As to the voyage itself, your intelligence will have told you by this time, thanks to my manipulation, both compasses and chronometers were entirely untrustworthy. I alone worked out the course with correct instruments of my own, while the steering was done by my black friends under my guidance. I pushed Tibbs's wife overboard. What! You look surprised and shrink away. Surely you had guessed that by this time. I would have shot you that day through the partition, but unfortunately you were not there. I tried again afterward, but you were awake. I shot Tibbs. I think the idea of suicide was carried out rather neatly. Of course when once we got on the coast the rest was simple. I had bargained that all on board should die; but that stone of yours upset my plans. I also bargained that there should be no plunder. No one can say we are pirates. We have acted from principle, not from any sordid motive."

I listened in amazement to the summary of his crimes which this strange man gave me, all in the quietest and most composed of voices, as though detailing incidents of every-day occurrence. I still seem to see him sitting like a hideous nightmare at the end of my couch, with the single rude lamp flickering over his cadaverous features.

"And now," he continued, "there is no difficulty about your escape. These stupid adopted children of mine will say that you have gone back to heaven from whence you come. The wind blows off the land. I have a boat all ready for you, well stored with provisions and water. I am anxious to be rid of you, so you may rely that nothing is neglected. Rise up and follow me."

I did what he commanded, and he led me through the door of the hut. The guards had either been withdrawn, or Goring had arranged matters with them. We passed unchallenged through the town and across the sandy plain.

Once more I heard the roar of the sea, and saw the long white line of the surge. Two figures were standing upon the shore arranging the gear of a small boat. They were the two sailors who had been with us on the voyage. "See him safely through the surf," said Goring. The two men sprang in and pushed off, pulling me in after them. With mainsail and jib we ran out from the land and passed safely over the bar.

Then my two companions without a word of farewell sprang overboard, and I saw their heads like black dots on the white foam as they made their way back to the shore, while I scudded away into the blackness of the night. Looking back, I caught my last glimpse of Goring. He was standing upon the summit of a sand-hill, and the rising moon behind him threw his gaunt, angular figure into hard relief.

He was waving his arms frantically to and fro; it may have been to encourage me on my way, but the gestures seemed to me at the time to be threatening ones, and I've often thought that it was more likely that his old savage instinct had returned when he realized that I was out of his power. Be that as it may, it was the last that I ever saw or ever shall see of Septimus Goring.

There is no need for me to dwell upon my solitary voyage. I steered as well as I could for the Canaries, but was picked up upon the fifth day by the British and African Steam Navigation Company's boat *Monrovia*. Let me take this opportunity of tendering my sincerest thanks to Captain Stornoway and his officers for the great kindness which they showed me from that time till they landed me in Liverpool, where I was enabled to take one of the Guion boats to New York.

From the day on which I found myself once more in the bosom of my family I have said little of what I have undergone. The subject is still an intensely painful one to me, and the little which I have dropped has been discredited. I now put the facts before the public as they occurred, careless how far they may be believed, and simply writing them down because my lung is growing weaker, and I feel the responsibility of holding my peace longer.

I make no vague statement. Turn to your map of Africa. There above Cape Blanco, where the land trends away north and south from the westernmost point of the continent, there it is that Septimus Goring still reigns over his dark subjects, unless retribution has overtaken him; and there, where the long green ridges run swiftly in to roar and hiss upon the hot, yellow sand, it is there that Harton lies with Hyson and the other poor fellows who were done to death in the *Marie Celeste*.

Freedom

EDWIN L. SABIN

Wayburn, lately third mate of the Biddeford brig *Delight*, sat open-necked and perspiring in the humid dram booth facing the quay, and sipped his glass of Santa Cruz rum while he reflected upon the hazards of a lee shore. The day, of course, was hot, as August days always are in Matanzas of the Isle of Cuba; he was still weak from the recent illness which had laid him by, and he was a mate without a berth, a sailor without a ship, a Yankee merchantman marooned in a foreign port—a port all the more constricted in this, the yellow-fever season.

A small, nimble, biliously dark man approached him—a man attired in a beribboned round Panama hat, a dirty whitish shirt and sashed pantaloons, with dirk haft convenient. Bowing with a flourish of civility, the stranger accosted him in carefully accented English:

"I make you my good-day, señor."

"Good-day to you, sir," Wayburn cordially responded.

The man seated himself fussily at the table, with a beck and a word ordered a bottle and fresh glasses, and proceeded:

"You are a sailor; I have a ship. I am called Don Pedro Manegat and I need a first mate."

The breath of the free, live ocean, not that of this pent, pestilential harbor, swept Wayburn's nostrils again.

"Where is your ship, Captain?"

"She is here, in harbor, ready all except for mate. The American consul tell me of you. My first mate lies dead of the fever."

"What ship?"

"The schooner *Alice*, señor, of New Orleans. A fine, clean ship, very well found."

"Where bound, then?"

"From New Orleans, for Cape Palmas and near points of the windward coast, with lumber and iron-ware and trading goods."

"Palmas? That would be the West African coast?"

"Yes, señor. You know these waters?"

"No. I have been to the Canaries, but not south-'ard for the slave coast.'

With spread of soft hands Captain Manegat deprecated the tone.

"Ah, the 'slave coast'—that is so, my friend. But there are also the grain coast, the ivory coast, the gold coast—all there at Cape Palmas of the windward coast, all very good trader coast. Gold dust, ivory, oil, gums, dyewoods, wax, spices, bought with powder, muskets, rum, blue cloth, what-not."

"So I know," said Wayburn. "And flesh and blood is bought, too."

"If you like," Manegat granted. "More profit, yes; and more risk, very much yes. I am American citizen and lawful trader. The consul will tell you my papers are all right. Shall we talk terms over a glass of rum, my friend?"

They settled upon terms; and since Wayburn desperately wished to get out of these enervating doldrums—in fact, had worn threadbare his welcome at the consulate—he signed on as first mate of the American schooner *Alice*—American registry, Pedro Manegat of New Orleans, owner and Master—upon a trading voyage from port of New Orleans to Cape Palmas and the windward coast, West Africa.

It would take him far from Biddeford, Maine, but Biddeford men and Biddeford craft had been farther, and he had carried deep water in both pockets before.

His sea-chest followed him aboard the *Alice*. Baltimore-built, she was, as any sailor would note at a glance, by the lines of her hull and the rake of her sticks; of one hundred fifty tons burden, and like her sweet name she had been somebody's fancy, for abaft the mainmast there was much fine inlay and bright brasswork, bestowed upon wheel and binnacle and cabin.

Indeed, from stern to stem she was kept like a lady; which agreeably surprised him. He had his Down-East prejudices in the matter of Spanish gentry, sea or land, and for the African trade. But although the captain, second mate and crew of six, save one, were Spanish, and the schooner was for debatable latitudes and longitude, she certainly was well found, and tight and clean and happy.

As master, Pedro Manegat aspired to little navigation; he and the supercargoes Gama and Galliego minded rum in the cabin more than wind and weather above. It seemed that part of the lading was consigned to the supercargoes, Portuguese or Spanish, for the windward coast.

A true-blue schooner with a true-blue name deserved better than a mongrel crew, thought Wayburn; but thank the Lord, anyway, for the one other American. And seeking comfort in him, during watch one night when the *Alice* logged steadily eastward for that trader's Africa of gold dust, ivory, palm oil, fragrant gums, dyewoods, wax, spices and black "animates," he got quite the opposite.

The twain were alone, on deck aft, with Martin (an East Boston man) at the wheel and a half-moon riding the sky and dodging the mast-tips. Said Wayburn, glad of homely speech:

"She's a sailor's sweetheart, John."

"Ought to be, sir, with that name. But bein' as is, I'd wish her better business."

"How's that?"

"I reckoned you knowed, sir."

"What?"

"Why," said John, from the corner of his mouth, with an eye cocked to the luff of the sail, "ain't she made a hussy of, sir? What is she but a bloody yaller-crewed Guineaman, after a cargo of blackbirds?"

"A slaver?"

"Nothin' short, sir. You can see for yourself. Have you looked through the hold?"

"Lumber, iron-ware and notions; Manegat said they needed no overhauling."

"Lumber, sir? That's plankin' for slave-deck tiers, and staves and hoops for leaguers—the big water-casks, sir. Ironware is ankle shackles and the like, and notions will be includin' pannikins, and slave coppers for b'ilin' the rice. Oh, I know all the damn' tricks, sir."

"You've been in the African trade?"

"The blackbird trade, sir? I have—all along the West Coast from Sierry Leone to Frio. But I don't stomick it, though there's money for officers and crew if you can stand the stink. I shipped this time when I was in liquor, sir; and as soon as I clapped sober eyes on master and men I knowed our ratin'."

"But the ship is clean and sweet, and the papers are regular."

"She's sweet and clean going' out; she'll be foul as a drab comin' back. As for papers, sir, 'tis a common shift, as the African trade knows, for a ship to sail out with American clearance and ready to h'ist the American flag for a blind—and to sail back with different name and different papers. That's one way of dodgin' our own cruisers and them British channel-scourers."

"But that is piracy!"

"So is slave-carryin', sir, if you're ketched."

"Then you think we're bound after a black lading?"

"He's no sailor, sir, that Manegat! He's a slave factor, I'll wager, and them supercargoes are partners. There's no trouble pickin' up a cargo of blacks almost anywhere from Frio north to Senegal, four thousand miles of coast. But from what I've l'arned from the below-deck talk, we're bound for the mouth o' the Nun, in the Bay of Guinea, to refit a factory and take on a cargo of blacks for Cuby. Gold coast, ivory coast, grain coast—they're all slave coast; and any Africa trader is like to be a Guineaman."

Guineaman! Sea-lane argot of contempt! A slaver, a kidnaper, a panderer in human bondage in the persons of black men and women—a vocation ostracized by civil and social laws and made a byward, paralleled by only one trade upon the land. So this neat and pretty *Alice* was to be a procuress, a creature shunned by clean, uprightly folk!

The assertion of John gave Wayburn a sore shock. The slave-trade was a traffic condemned as piracy in the courts of the civilized world; yes. Nevertheless vessels and skippers took chances, and one successful round trip a year made a year's profits. But a craft like this beautiful schooner was to him a living form; he had the sailor's love for a tidy ship as for a tidy lass, and there was an Alice in Biddeford; there should be in every American and English sailor's port an Alice.

Aye, Alice was a home name, a true name, an honored name—that did not well accord with sluttishness, perfidy and degradation.

However, 'twould boot him little to accuse Manegat now!

Mysterious Africa loomed into the dawn's horizon. Landfall steadily raised, until on long tacks they went curtsying and careening down a never-ending coast of bulky headlands, snowy sands and whiter surf and waving palms and other tropic growth, of inlets, outlets, bays and bights and low villages, and of purplish mountain ranges receding until they rested over the vast unknown like a cloud. All day they could see Africa; all night they could smell Africa upon the warm jungle breeze; and at last, where through its great delta the River Quorra—by some called the Niger—discharged by the Nun, the Brass, the Bonny and many another mouth into the Gulf of Guinea, the Manegat glass picked out safety signals; whereupon the *Alice* crossed the Nun bar and slipping up a broad brackish channel, turgid with Africa and blotched with crocodiles, in the failing sea-breeze dropped anchor and canvas, well out between mangrove-covered shores.

Upon the left-hand shore above the muddy bank in the sultry clearing, that nucleus of thatches and palisades would be the slave factory (so-called); higher above the sodden reek of hot lagoons and decaying vegetation, that galleried, whitely gleaming hermitage would be the agent's quarters.

This, then, appeared to be the sorry business of the *Alice*. But Wayburn as mate had not yet accused his captain, to be told either truth or lie. His duty had been to sail the schooner; if he did not like her he could quit her, wherever practicable; but he could not quit her without proved occasion.

A boat had put out from shore, amid the bustle of coming to anchorage; the white occupant climbed up by the side ladder, to the hail of Manegat, and these two, with the supercargoes, sat a brief time in the cabin, drinking. Then they all went ashore, and the schooner's yawl, with whoever wished passage, went ashore also.

There was free intercourse between schooner and shore. Why not, after a six-weeks' voyage, here where no one could get farther? Festal drum-beat and shrill laughter sounded from the swarmed huts of the clearing. Those black folk were kindly.

Wayburn stood looking down into the barracoon—that palisade enclosure which penned the consignments for shipping. The open center, like a common, was of hard-baked earth; the only shelter from sun and dew was formed by the enskirting kennels of thatch, underneath which naked and near-naked men, women and children might lie.

The cast of features, the complexions and the forms varied; so did the temperaments—for he saw laughing, weeping, wonderment and despair, and heard outcries and barbaric chants. He saw scowls, and heard curses, also.

A finely erect, tawny young woman, with curling lip and flashing black eyes gazed up at the new faces gazing down, and delivered a tirade until silenced by a shout and the threatening motion of a musket from a black guard.

Manegat, beside Wayburn in the elevated guard-box, made explanation.

"A Foulah witch, they say. She is angry because we do not keep her child. But her people are glad to be rid of both—and a child under six is worth nothing."

—"Where is the child?" Wayburn asked.

"Oh, it will have died," said Manegat. "Who would want it? The mother is trouble enough. But we have a good lot, around thirty years. Not too many women. Women lose time, with children and sickness. You know blacks? Well, you will. I see Eboes, Ashantis, Cameroons, Foulahs, Mandingoes. They will all work."

"So your trade is the slave trade, is it?" Wayburn challenged. "You shipped me under false colors!"

Manegat laughed.

"A trading voyage. What matter if we trade goods for black men instead of for ivory? You object? When you pocket your pay from the profits you will forget to object, then. Everybody on board has his share per head."

"It's piracy."

Manegat laughed again.

"Bah! First we must be caught, with proof. American ship, right papers, American master, mate—warships of other nations dare do nothing. Going back—well, once outside, then our chance very good on the high seas, and we make landing at Cuba easy."

"It's a dirty, cruel traffic," Wayburn rasped.

"Whatever you say, my friend, do not think foolish," Manegat bade. "Black men and women are slaves, everywhere. All the black kings in this big country make other black people slaves. War prisoners and murderers and thieves and witches—instead of being killed they are sold to traders; we sell them to white masters, and they are much better off. Much better off to work alive in Cuba, America, Jamaica, than to be eaten dead in Africa."

"You intend to lade with all these in this stockade, do you?"

"All these? There are only two hundred and twenty. If we do not carry more than two blacks to the ton we lose money. When the *Alice* sails she will have four hundred between decks. But some, of course, will die during the voyage."

Shocked out of his judicious poise, Wayburn exclaimed: "Four hundred! In the schooner's hold?"

"Each full-grown will have his fourteen inches of width, and six feet of length," said Manegat. "Space to lie upon; what more is needed? Lopez the trader is due with another lot from upriver."

He turned to descend. "Be careful you do not fall down in there," he jocularly warned. "I see black men with filed teeth, ready to pick your bones."

Manegat left. Then almost under Wayburn's stand a voice supplicated in fairly clear accents:

"Master! You are white man, you are English. Help!"

"What's wanted?"

"See me, master. I am free negro. I am a Wangwana, of Zanzibar, East Coast. I am a Zanzibari, master; I am no slave."

"How come you here, then?" Wayburn asked of the black giant, woolly-headed, and intelligently countenanced, now standing upright, unclothed except for a makeshift loin-strip, and pleading so earnestly that his round dark face glistened with sweat.

"I have half-brother in a king's town, back from coast," replied the black. "I go to visit him, and in the night soldiers seize me and carry me to 'nother king. King give me to bigger king, master. Bigger king sell me to traders, master. Traders sell me to Guinea trader. Guinea trader bring me here. But I am free negro. In Zanzibar many years, master, interpreter to white men. I speak languages. My name is Jack. Everybody in Zanzibar know Jack Bimbo."

"I'm afraid I can't do anything for you," said Wayburn.

"Hear me, master!" The agony of this black man, clutching at hope as frail as straws, was pitiable. All the barracoon was murmurous. "How can I go as slave?" he urged. "I, a Wangwana, a born freeman who has own ground at Zanzibar—who walks the streets of Zanzibar—bery well known in Zanzibar—very much respected—a wearer of white shirts, master, not a naked wild man!"

"I will see," Wayburn promised. "Are there other free blacks?"

"Some say so of themselves; but they do not speak languages like I do, of Zanzibar. And there are bad men in here, master; black-meat eaters, and fighters, and jungle dwellers. I am afraid."

At that, a bronze-skinned savage with ring-hung ears and nose, who had been seated upon the ground in the entrance of a nearby kennel, as if censorious of the imploration suddenly rose to an imposing height and with a long stride, a long reach, and the accompaniement of angry voice, sent Jack Bimbo reeling from a hearty cuff.

The Zanzibar cowered affrightedly before the imperious figure, whose snarl revealed sharp, artificially serrated teeth; and leaving the scene, which appeared only to amuse the guards, Wayburn sought for Manegat. He found the captain drinking rum with the supercargoes and the agent.

They all smiled at the report.

"A common tale," Manegat remarked. "Is it not so, Felix?"

"It is so," the agent nodded. "Full of frauds, those blacks. They need only an attentive ear. Free? Certainly, until caught and sold—for some reason or other, which is nothing to us."

"This man has the manner of a free man, and speaks fair English," Wayburn argued.

"Likely a runaway slave who had served in some cultured household. He went back to his tribe and was caught again in the traders' net."

"He is not in favor among those barbarians. He may be killed."

"Oh, these Africans are like dogs," laughed Manegat. "Some bully, others cringe. They fight among themselves, even in the barracoons, until they know who is master. And one place in Africa fights another place in Africa, out of jealousy. If that filed-toothed fellow gets dangerous, and kills, we'll put him in irons. Carcasses are a loss."

"But if the English-speaking man can prove himself to be of Zanzibar of the East Coast, and a free man?"

The supercargo Gama, flabbily corpulent, and pudding-faced with eyes like two black currants, gave authoritative utterance.

"It is a long way to Zanzibar and another long way to Cuba. Where the traders get their shipments we do not care. In Cuba he will be worth fifty doubloons, which is more than any free black is worth in Zanzibar. Sit to a glass of rum, my friend, and never mind the lies of the barracoon."

But Wayburn excused himself upon plea of work to be done aboard the schooner; he avoided the barracoon which haunted him with its lassitudes, its terrors, its fevered implorations, its barbaric irrational mirths and its dully burning or explosive wraths.

The trade goods, of colored glass beads, cotton cloths, brass wire in coils, rum, cheap muskets, poor powder, and so forth, had been put ashore, and the schooner was in ballast; but through the main hold the extra slave deck had been laid with the fitted planks, the intermediate platforms or slave tiers had been installed, and the shackle-rails of heavy chain cable bolted fast; the great leaguers for fresh water had been cooperated, ready to be filled; and the slave coppers—the large kettles for the rations—had been set into their brick hearths abaft the foremast.

These preparations were completed none too soon. In mid-morning drum-beat and trumpet-blare announced the caravan that should cap the schooner's consignment. Here, however, not a caravan but a flotilla of canoes blackly crowded and paddled to the incitement of martial notes like victory's pæan, rounded the bend of the broad Nun, above the anchorage, and swept down, to throng against the muddy bank before the factory; thence a double file of coupled negroes, men and women, tethered fore and aft, neck to neck, with armed guards and whip-flourishing overseers beside, like file-closers, and a few children trotting, wended up through the mangroves of the seething shore and entered the barracoon, from which a jabber had wailed.

Late the same afternoon the lading began. Canoes as large as lighters, crammed with the figures of blacks, put out in turn, to take station under the port rail 'midships; and, urged up the long cleated gangplank, by dint of shout and gesture and shove, the chattel Africans, as naked as when born—naked regardless of habits—passed over the rail in a steady stream and, almost numb with terror, down the main hatchway: the women and the few children (none under six years) first, the men following.

Between decks, dociled by the mystery of their strange quarters, they were arrayed by the *Alice's* crew: the women and children in the steerage end, beyond a bulkhead barrier; the men forward of them; all stowed snugly upon their backs, in rows heads to soles, the women free of irons but the men anklelinked in pairs and at regular intervals chained to the shackle-rails also.

First the floor was covered; then the shelves or tiers elevated three feet above were called into play. The six-foot depth of the slave-deck hold was halved for that purpose.

This Wayburn knew, although as first mate he only had charge, under Manegat, of the main deck and the influx there, while the second mate and the sailors attended to the lading below hatches; but he had talked with John Martin.

He saw among the first of the men that strapping bronze fellow of the rings and the filed teeth; and propelled after him, Jack Bimbo, the alleged freeman of faraway Zanzibar; or he imagined that he saw them both, the one defiantly erect and shameless, the other bruised of lips, agonized and wildly staring. But there were many black or bronzy wooly-headed men, similar to all outward appearance; and there were cocoa-colored men, dull-sooty men and tattooed men, men well-featured and men ill-featured, Ethiop princes, warriors, satyrs and bandy-legged apes—samples of Africa, one would think, to confuse one.

As a last thing the full complement of fresh water had to be taken on. There could not be too much of that, when some four hundred extra gullets were allowed a half-pint pannikin each, every morning and every evening, and a six-weeks' voyage might be extended by days of unkind winds or festering calm.

The crew worked far into the dusk. Such as wished had shore leave this night; the schooner was to lift anchor before dawn and to have Africa low on her weather rail ere the hatch gratings were again raised. It was bad for the blacks to see their land recede. Some might jump over in a panic and be lost.

The parting celebration on the factory's palaver-ground drew all hands but Martin and the cook. On short cable the *Alice*, with Wayburn in charge, bided the return of the yawl.

The African night was thick with the damp of river and of vegetation; the schooner's one riding-light hung, however, above the rail as a guide to the side-ladder—glimmered murkily even from the deck, and the land breeze was hardly brisk enough to set the great sober African stars to twinkling in the black-velvet depths of the over-brooding sky.

She rode here, in midstream, like a plague-ship, silent, sinister and shamed, did this *Alice*, so fair to the eye without, so foul to the eye within. From beneath her main-hatch gratings there issued scarcely a sound; the cries of lamentation and fear and rage had waned and now the human lading, of forms laid shoulder to shoulder, thigh to thigh, was quiet with exhaustion and the smothering dark. But already the body stench—all the physical emanations of that closely-pent cargo of humans—welled up the hatchway and seemed to Wayburn to seep through the schooner from cabin to fore-castle. And of course there were sounds: groanings, gurglings, gusty spasms, as from the pit.

The sounds ashore were distinct and of a different kind. There, devils were making jubilation, as though over a successful haul. From the red nebula of a central fire the tom-tom rhythm of the African dance-drums went rolling through the night, carrying on its heated waves the shouts and shrieks and laughter of incited men and women.

The shore celebration apparently was near crescendo when the cabin clock struck six bells. Standing with John Martin, Wayburn had no need to issue spoken order. He and John were in accord, and a jerk of the head was sufficient. Together they turned, and stepping forward they pounced upon the cook, asleep in the doorway of his galley, gagged him and bound him and threw him into his bunk.

Wayburn locked the galley door. Then he and John, at the windlass, eased off the cable. The sluggish current of the Nun took link after link as the schooner floated freer; the clank and rasp merged with the festal hubbub beating upon the air, and the back men and women in the slave hold and the officers and crew at the jungle orgies were unaware that the *Alice* was stealing away.

Wayburn paused long enough to set the side lantern under cover. Then he and John let go all—the cable end rattled through the hawsehole and plunked into the water. They were adrift. They shook out jib enough for steerage way; as the schooner's head swung around before the languid breeze John ran for the wheel, and conscious of almost imperceptible motion, Wayburn seized the lantern and called down the main-hatch:

"Jack Bimbo! Hello! Jack Bimbo!"

His hail was thrown back into his face from the shallow depth packed and suffocating; but he had aroused a murmur and a confused jabbering, and the thick, far response:

"Jack Bimbo? Here Jack Bimbo. Who call Jack Bimbo?"

"White man friend. I am coming. No harm. Tell them all, no harm."

He sprang down into the prison reek, the unrest, and the darkness that but for the lantern would have been Stygian. A wild-beast den! His skin prickled while amid glitter of eyeballs and shimmer of teeth he picked his way, with pistol and lantern in hand, over the writhing floor, and between the feverish shelves.

By the voice he found Jack Bimbo, shackled low in the charnel quarters—aye, in space not so roomy as a coffin; found him frightened and fervently imploring, and reassured him: "No harm, I tell you. You tell these others no harm. Where's your ankle?" Applying the key, Wayburn unlocked the ankle cuff by which Bimbo was shackled to a neighbor. Then he flashed the lantern upon the neighbor's splendid bulk and serrated teeth not so splendid.

"Who is this man?" he asked.

"I nebber know him, master," Jack Bimbo bleated. "Bad man, master. Man-eating man, master! Bery careful!"

For safe anchorage again Wayburn clicked the empty cuff into the shackle-rail, and bade Bimbo:

"Go on up. Get out and be quick about it! You are free."

The naked Jack Bimbo stumbled out, assailed by imprecation, admonishment and appeal—babble the meaning of which could only be guessed at by Wayburn, following, sickened by the fœtor, and by the waving hands and beseeching voices—somewhat fearful, in spite of his pistol, and extremely anxious to be again in the open of the main deck.

It seemed to him that Martin had been up there a long time, alone in the darkness of a treacherous waterway and a drifting craft. He emerged right after Jack Bimbo.

"All right, John?" he hailed cautiously.

"All right, sir. Cook wants to get out. We're making way, by the feel of her. Could use more canvas. Shall I put the wheel in beckets and help you on a haul, sir?"

"No. I've the negro. Mind the currents till we give you more steerage. Here, Bimbo! Haul with me, on the rope. Understand?"

"Understand, master."

Reckless of creak and flap they hoisted the mainsail; the ripples were tinkling under the *Alice's* forefoot when with his helper Wayburn scurried on to the jibs.

With sheets tautened the schooner slipped along, down the broad Nun. The clamor ashore receded, but now the schooner herself was the offender. The dark bowels of her cried aloud with utterances wrung forth by the motion, and the cook was hammering upon the galley door, while the canvas occasionally fluttered, plucked at by ghostly crosscurrents of air.

Wayburn walked to the galley.

"What's the row in there?"

The Portuguese cook made profane counter-query.

"I'm in charge now," Wayburn informed him. "Quit your rumpus and you'll be let out in the morning. Try to give me trouble, and down you go among the blacks."

The cook subsided. Wayburn turned to the Zanzibar freeman.

"Jack! Can't you make those people below keep quiet?"

"I try, master. I speak Mandingo, Kiswahili. Most everybody known a little of dem. I tell 'em, 'Shut up! Sleep. No harm!' "

Whereupon Jack shouted into the hatchway; his words seemed to be repeated, and the lugubrious tumult stilled.

Wayburn continued aft for a sight of the compass and a word with John.

By the penciled chart in the cabin he had worked out the course. He would have preferred anchoring, or standing back and forth till daylight ere making the offing, but he had to reckon with pursuit by the yawl and canoes, and with the treachery of unknown currents ambushed in the darkness and the inky depths. The onward channel was wide and unobstructed, there should be good water in the exit bight, and a clearer firmament over; if the stars favored, the schooner ought to pass the bar and win into the open sea. If, however, with four hundred stowaway souls below, and only three or four actives above, he dared not risk passage at once, then he would more safely find holding-ground in the Nun mouth and wait for the first African dawn.

"Keep her as she is, John?"

"Aye, aye, sir. We've plenty water. I've been in this river before. I think we can feel our way out, sir."

"White-man master, please—where we going?" inquired Jack Bimbo humbly.

"Up the coast to Monrovia, where the American consul lives. He will take charge."

"Ship and black people and all?"

"Yes. You can tell them they are going to a good white man who will send them all home."

"No, no, please, master," Jack besought. "They no understand. White men all the same, all bad, to them. Please, master, do not let black men on deck, together more than two or three. Be bery glad to kill you."

"Mightn't there be boatmen among them?"

"Mebbe few Krus, master. But most all from far inside Africa; nebber have seen sea or big boat with wings, like this. They be much scared. But I, a Wangwana of Zanzibar," Jack continued, "know the sea and know ship and know the white men, and understand. I am not like that naked maneater king's son that I was chained to. The American consul at where we are going will take care of me; but what will he do with this man-eater and all those others who have been captured and have a long way to trabbel?"

"This Zanzibar nigger is right, sir," said John. "If once we let those blacks run foul of us on deck we're food for the fishes. They know no difference betwixt us and the Portuguese slave-drivers."

"Please, master," Jack Bimbo stammered, "bery bad black man I chained to. Bery bad place, too, down in that hold. Please to gib me a shirt, that I may feel like freeman again."

A garment was found, but the potentialities of four hundred hostile human animals caged underneath one's feet had to be contemplated. The cargo was a powder magazine, safest when kept closed; yet on the contrary it had to be broken out, assorted and re-stowed, every day: the men, women and children should be watered, fed, aired and exercised; and the nearest American consulate, at Monrovia, of Liberia, was three hundred leagues up the coast.

Wayburn was less concerned over what the consul would do with this embarrassment of black contraband delivered to him than over what might befall John and himself ere they obtained clearance and discharge. Could he have evicted his cargo at once, upon the banks of the Nun, he would have been vastly relieved.

The *Alice* jogged along, with sheets off, and the surf dully crashing in the night, ahead. When the African dawn burst redly she was well outside, and standing on close-hauled, was nosing northward; the Portuguese cook had been released for onerous duty; and with the assistance of Jack Bimbo the black women, and the black men in twos at a time, were passed up, for water, food, a little fresh air and a little exercise.

The land breeze faltered; to slat of canvas the sea breeze wafted in, and with lurch of booms and scurry of tackle the schooner met the change. But there was an ominous oiliness upon the wrinkled sea, and a brazen cast to the blue sky; and the distant coast-line, of white and brown and purple simmered hazily.

The sun rose higher, the breeze, perfunctory and fitful, lapsed and the sea smoothed into long glassy swells. By noon the schooner rolled in almost dead calm.

The third day, it was, of the calm. The schooner had drifted somewhat inshore. There were coco palms and breaking surf, plain through the glass. In the opposite direction, the southwest, there was the flick of a sail.

Under the awning stretched above the after-deck the heat nevertheless burned; and what the weather was between-decks in the slave quarters, nose and ears reported while the eyes shrank.

The fresh water was going fast—the blacks were constantly petitioning for more, more, as well for breath, space, change of posture: any easement from their inferno. John whistled for a breeze, the cook waxed morose, Jack Bimbo argued with the rebellious, miserable cargo, and Wayburn, sweltering and careworn, began to worry. Conditions were approaching the intolerable. Soon they would be passing up the dead, mingled with the living.

"My last cruise, the cap'n threw over one hundred and seventy-two," John remarked, "and we floated in the midst of 'em and sharks for a day and a night."

"That fellow seems to be moving on a course as if he had a whiff of air now and then," Wayburn said. "What do you make of him this time?"

So John squinted through the glass at the sail to wind'ard (had there been a windward in this doldrums latitude), and drawled:

"Looks a trifle like a sloop, sir, but the heat makes him blink. He might be a man-'o-war cutter, and I think he'd wish to overhaul us."

"He's welcome to. We'll show him our colors, and our manifest will declare itself. Climb aloft and see what you can make from there."

From the main-rigging John spied again. He came down rather sobered.

"That's no cutter, sir. He looks like a felucca rig and he's standing on as if he might be fetching his own breeze."

"A felucca rig!"

"Yes, sir. Lateen-rigged—Portuguese or Spanish. He's a coaster, and I don't believe you can expect much good of him, sir, in these parts."

"Pirate?"

"Well, ready to be, sir. There are plenty of 'em on the gold and ivory coasts."

"We've nothing for him."

"He doesn't know that; and he's not likely to know it till he gets to lu'ard of us and smells us, and he'll keep the wind of us if he can, sir. We look like a smart trader, 'stead of a stinkin' slaver. If he boards us—well, a scuttled ship tells no tales, sir."

"We'll have to find a breeze, John."

The schooner idly swung; limp canvas flapped, the jaws of the gaffs creaked against the masts; the blacks below cried out for drink, breath, food, space, easement. The few upon deck goggled, panted, supplicated, and dozed. All hated; one, especially, steeped his hate in a contemptuous silence save when he mandatorily rebuked the mass.

Wayburn had learned his voice. He was the strapping cannibal—the one-time yokefellow of Jack Bimbo; and a recognized personage. Through him Jack Bimbo appeared to convey orders and promises; he it was who, sometimes exasperated, briefly exhorted, and quelled the tumult to moans and passive despair. On deck he was inflexible, repellent, invisibly cuirassed with scorn and hate of ship and ship's-master, but no master accepted by him. Whether in darkness or in light he was, Wayburn felt, a force to be reckoned with.

Thus the calm aggravated one's anxieties: mutinous wild men and women below, unrestricted sea savages abeam.

At sunset the felucca was nearer, having come on unostentatiously before mysterious impulses favoring its rig; and following the sun there floated, from the land, a warm but stirring air, so that the *Alice* took heart and with lights doused and all canvas spread, stole away again.

But at midnight the breeze dropped. In the morning the shark-fins of the scavenger again cut the distant blue. The blacks were so restive that only two at a time were to be allowed upon deck; conditions below were sickening to the senses. And as if deceived by the schooner's brightwork and her smartness the felucca began to bear in.

The mystery of this was soon explained. The fellow was using sweeps.

In all the hot horizon there was not another sail. The vastly prostrate Atlantic lay lifeless save for leaping fish and swooping fowl, and this predatory rover—a corsair of the coast.

The air puffed, the sea wrinkled, and to twirl of wheel and draw of sail the *Alice* filled away; and reeved to the signal halyards the Stars and Stripes broke out from her main-peak. The felucca responded not at all with a flag.

That the felucca was in chase could not be doubted; that he was closing in could equally not be doubted. He had the wind, and the first airs, and between airs he used his sweeps.

The Portuguese cook, in the doorway of his galley, knew; and by his pallor, his shiftness, and his dubitative mutters little help could be expected of him. Jack Bimbo knew, John at the wheel knew, and beside him, Wayburn knew.

He prayed for a real breeze, that he might race for the weather-gauge and for the deep and tossing blue where feluccas should not venture.

"That fellow means to board us."

"Yes, sir," said John.

"He carries no guns, evidently."

"No, sir. With them thirty or forty oars, say a hundred men, and plenty small-arms and sharp steel, he aims at close quarters and quick work."

"Would he attack a slaver, you think?"

"All's grist to a shark's mill, sir, and slavers carry specie, frequent. Likely he's hopin' for a haul o' gold and ivory. If he's disapp'inted, he can cut throats."

"A black deck might sheer him off."

"A black deck might be as bad as a yaller deck, sir," John observed. "We're in sight of Africky; and it'd be us two white men above hatches with four hundred jungle-folk who lack only an inch and a word."

There was a rack of cutlasses against the bulkhead in the cabin; another of muskets, and a pistol locker. The *Alice* was munitioned to deal with insurrection, but Manegat had thriftily dispensed with deck guns. Her trade was her best protection. Few other craft would willingly lay courses for a laden Guineaman; and, light or heavy, her only defense from challenging cruisers was her speed.

Of what avail, however, would be cutlass and small-arm, in the hands of three or four holding bulwarks against a host swarming up the sides?

In the glass the felucca was coming on like a huge spraddly water-bug. He mustered, as John surmised, forty oars—twenty on a side, two masts, lateen rig, a cabin, its roof almost flush with the rails; he steered by a tiller, and from tiller forward to the beaked cut-water he was garish with brightly costumed, swarthy men.

Even if the breeze, such as it was, held for the schooner, he would be alongside in half an hour. The *Alice* could not jockey him out of that.

"We'll have to fit the remedy to the case, John," said Wayburn. And explained his idea.

"That sounds like a Yankee trick, sir," John conceded. "Well, there's nothin' like turning' curses into blessin's."

Wayburn went forward and spoke to Jack Bimbo.

"Who is some fighting-man among those black men that I may talk to?"

Jack looked alarmed.

"You want fighting-men, master?"

"Yes. You see that pirate. He means to board us."

"The man-eater king's son—he is the head fighting-man of them all down there, master. But he bery bad man. Full of hate. I think it no good to talk to him, master. Other fighting-men do as he say. As soon kill you as anybody. Please be careful, master."

"Go and fetch him up; and be quick about it," Wayburn ordered. "Are you afraid?"

"Oh, he be glad to come up again," Jack faltered. "But I be glad when he back down. Do not take his irons off, master."

Jack came up with the great naked, clanking bronzed fellow, who made swift, unbending survey of deck and sea, but betrayed emotion at nothing. Whether he deigned comprehension of the words translated for him by the despised Zanzibari, Wayburn could not know, until the answer: "Why should I or men of mine fight for a white man?"

Never was answer more cold with scorn, or more difficult of rebuttal.

"Wait!" Wayburn stepped to him. An instant, and the shackles of ankles and wrists (for he had been double-ironed) fell to the deck.

"Now! What is it that men of any race will fight for hardest? snapped Wayburn.

The savage stared. His mighty chest swelled, his hands clenched, his lips parted upon his hideous serrated teeth, and vehement utterance found vent: "Freedom!"

Wayburn laughed, well pleased.

"Listen, then." Through the Zanzibari he spoke in trenchant sentences, for time pressed. The black giant listened. "Get your fighting-men, and your canoe-men," Wayburn concluded. "There is Africa. Tell all, and make them ready. But be quick."

"Can I believe you?" the other demanded.

"When you have weapons in your hands, who can make you slaves again?" Wayburn retorted.

The great barbarian leaped high into the air, clapping his shanks together before landing. At the same time he shouted with reiterative syllables that might have been a battle-cry; and snatching the shackles key he plunged below with Jack Bimbo.

While at the arms rack in the cabin Wayburn heard from beyond the bulkhead a strange and stirring sound. It was the sound of deep-lunged intoning, like the fervid hum of hiving bees, so that, as seemed to him, the *Alice* trembled with the vibration, as if in a thrill of hope.

Jack Bimbo came with another stalwart black. The muskets, pistols and cutlasses were served out. Most of these, in number such as they were, vanished down the hatchway. They would have to be reinforced by anything and everything that could be called a weapon.

Before a freshening breeze, and plying the oars, the felucca now charged in avidly. He saw this defenseless trader caught between him and a lee shore, with a scant crew of whites and blacks showing, and never a gun.

In a fierce chorus from flashing teeth the rover spurted, swung broadside, and throwing grapnels and clinging with the very fingernails the horde scrambled by rope and by human ladders for the schooner's rail. Wayburn whistled shrilly, and the black men struck.

From along the bulwarks they sprang up and forward, meeting hanger and poniard, ax and blunderbuss with cutlass and musket-barrel, pistol-butt and belaying-pin; they opposed their naked bodies to blade and ball—they crowded on, and down, and in dark torrent up the main hatchway and across the deck and over the rail boiled those others—Ebo, Ashanti, Cameroon, Foulah, Mandingo—yelling, snarling, wielding fetters, splinters, leaguer staves, jagged pannikins, what-not—or empty-handed but still dangerous. The shrieking women followed.

By that time sheer weight and fury as impelled by hope had told. The sea around was cluttered with the quick and the dead; the schooner floated higher, the felucca floated lower; shouting, Wayburn and Jack Bimbo and the cook cast off the grapnels, John at the wheel put the helm hard up and as the *Alice* rapidly fell off, the space from the felucca widened.

They looked across. There were remnants of commotion; the mass of dark lading eddied hither and thither and forms, inanimate, or yet active, were being discharged over the side; but Kru men (West Coast seafarers) were at sheets and tiller, interior canoe-men were reducing the oars to paddles, and towering erect upon the house the gigantic "king's son" appeared to be directing all.

With Wave of hands and weapons, and a victory chant from high voices, the captured felucca veered for the African coast. Provisioned, armed, and triumphant, the company should make far. Who in Africa could stop it upon the road to freedom?

The Captain of the Onion Boat

WILLIAM HOPE HODGSON

Big John Carlos, captain of the *Santa*, stood looking up at the long tapered window in the otherwise great, grey blank of the convent wall, a dozen yards away.

The wall formed the background of the quay, and between it and the side of the vessel was a litter of unloaded gear and cargo. The Captain's face, as he stared upward at that one lonesome window, had an extraordinarily set expression; and his Mate, a little lop-shouldered man, very brown and lean, watched him over the coaming of the main hatchway, with a curious grimace of half-sympathy and half-curiosity.

"Old Man's got it bad as ever," he muttered, in an accent and language that spoke of the larger English. He transferred his gaze from the silent form of the skipper, standing, in the stern, to the long taper of the one window that broke the towering side of the convent.

Presently, the thing for which the two men watched, came into view, as it did twice daily, at morning and evening—a long line of half-veiled nuns, who were obviously ascending some stairway within the convent, on to which this solitary window threw light.

Most of the women went by the window quietly, with faces composed, and looking before them; but here and there a young nun would take this opportunity to glance out into the Carnal World which they had renounced for ever. Young, beautiful faces there were, that looked out momentarily, showing doubly human, because of the cold ascetic garb of renunciation which framed them; then were gone on from sight, in the long, steadily moving procession of silent figures.

It was about the middle of the procession, after a weary line of seeming mutes had gone past, that the Mate saw that for which he waited. For, suddenly, the great body of the Captain stiffened and became rigid, as the head of one of the moving figures turned and stared out on to the quay. The Mate saw her face clearly. It was still young and lovely, but seemed very white and hopeless. He noted the eager, hungry look in the eyes; and then the wonderful way in which they lit up, as with a strange inward fire, at sight of the big man standing there; and the whole face seemed to quiver into living emotion. Immediately afterwards, she was gone past, and more mutes were making the grey, ascending line.

"Gord! that's 'er!" said the Mate, and glanced towards his master. The face of the big skipper was still upturned and set with a fixed, intense stare, as though even now he saw her face at the long window. His body was yet rigid with intensity, and his great hands gripped tightly the front of his slack jumper, straining it, unconsciously, down upon his hips. For some moments longer, he stood like this, lost to all knowledge except the tellings of his memory, and stunned with his emotions. Then he relaxed abruptly, as if some string within him had been loosed, and turned towards the open hatchway, where the Mate bent once more to his work.

"W'y don't 'e get 'er out," the Mate remarked to himself. "They've bin doin' that years 'n years, from wot I can see an' 'ear, an' breakin' their blessed 'earts. W'y the 'ell don't 'e get 'er out! It's easy ter see she's a woman, a sight more'n a bloomin' nun!" In all of which the little crooked shouldered Mate showed a fund of common sense; but likewise an insufficient ability to realise how thoroughly a religious belief may sometimes prove a stumbling-block in the pathway to mere human happiness.

How a man of the stamp of Big John Carlos came to be running an onion boat, must be conjectured. His name is explained by his father having been a Spaniard and his mother an Englishwoman. Originally, Big John had been a merchant, of a kind, going to sea in his own ship, and trading abroad.

As a youth, he had become engaged to Marvonna Della, whose father had owned much property, farther up the coast. Her father had died, and she had been an heiress, sought by all the youths about; but he—Big John Carlos—had won her.

They were to have been married on his return from his next trading voyage; but the report went home to his sweetheart that he had been drowned at sea; and indeed he had truly fallen overboard; but had been picked up by a China-bound sailing-ship, and had been a little over a year lost to his friends, before he had managed to reach home, to carry the news that he still lived. For this was before the days of the telegraph, and his one letter had gone astray.

When at last, he reached home, it was to find sad changes. His sweetheart, broken-hearted, had become a nun at the great convent of St. Sebastian's, and had endowed it with all her wealth and lands. What attempts he made to have speech with her, I do not know; but if his religious scruples had allowed him to beg her to renounce her vows and retirement, and return to the world to be his wife, they had certainly been unsuccessful; though it is quite conceivable that no word had ever passed between them, since she had put the world behind her.

From then onward, through nine long years, Big John Carlos had traded along the coast. His former business, he had dropped, and now he wandered from port to port in his small craft. And twice in every year, he would come alongside of the little wharf opposite to the great, grey wall of the convent, and there lie for a week, watching year by year that long narrow window for the two brief glimpses daily of his lost sweetheart.

After a week, he would go. It was always a week that he stayed there by the old wharf. Then, as if that had exhausted his strength—as if the pain of the thing had grown in that time to be too dreadful to continue, he would haul out, and away, whatever the weather or the state of trade. All of this the little twisted Mate knew, more or less clearly in detail, having learned it in the previous visit, which he had made with Big John Carlos to the insignificant port where the convent stood.

And she—what can the young nun have thought and felt? How she must have fought to endure the grey weary months between the far-apart visits; and day by day glanced out of the tall stair-window, as she passed in the long, mute procession, for a sight of the little onion boat and the big man standing in the stern, watching—tense and silent—for that one brief glimpse of her, as she passed in the remorseless line of figures. And something of this also, the little crooked-shouldered Mate had realised, vaguely, and had achieved an instant though angry sympathy. But his point of view was limited and definite:—"W'y the 'ell don't 'e get 'er out!" was his brief formula. And that marked the limit of his imagination, and therefore of his understanding.

His own religious beliefs were of the kind that are bred in the docks (London docks, in his case), and fostered in dirty fo'cas'les; and now he was "come down to this onion shuntin'," as he would have worded it. Yet, whatever his religious lack, or even his carelessness on a point of ethics, he was thoroughly and masculinely human.

"W'y the 'ell——" he began again, in his continual grumble to himself; and had no power to conceive that the woman, having taken a certain step, might believe that step to be unretraceable—that usage, belief, and finally (bred of these two) Conscience might forbid even the thought, stamping it as a crime that would shut her out from the Joy of the Everlasting.

The Joy of the Everlasting! The little twisted man would have grinned at you, had you mentioned it. "W'y the 'ell don't 'e get 'er out!" would have been his reply, accompanied by a profuseness of tobacco-juice.

And yet, it is conceivable that the heart of the woman was, even this long while, grown strong to do battle for dear Happiness—her heart that had known, silently and secretly and dumbly, all along, the unnatural wickedness of her outrage of her Womanhood. Visit by visit, through the long years, her heart must have grown fiercely strong to end this torture which her brain (darkened with the Clouds of Belief) had put upon her, to endure through all her life.

And so, all unknowingly, because of the loyal brain *that would not be aware* of the growing victory of her heart, she was come to a condition in which her beliefs held her no more than if they had been cords that had rotted upon her, as indeed they might be said to have done. That she was free to come, the little Mate had seen, using his eyes and his heart and his wit. To him, it was merely a matter of ways and means—physical. "W'y the 'ell——!" that was his puzzle.

Why? With an angry impatience, that came near to verging upon the borderland of scorn, the little Mate would question inwardly. Was Big John Carlos bit wiv them religious notions, same as the other dagoes! He did not understand the complaint, or how it was achieved; but he knew, as an outside fact, that there was something of that kind which infected the peoples along the coasts he travelled. If Big John were not troubled in this way, "why the 'ell——" And so he would return to his accustomed formula, working furiously, in sheer irritation of mind:—"If 'e ain't religious, *wot* is it? Carn't 'e see the way 'er eyes blessed well looks at 'im! Carn't 'e see she's mad an' double mad to be out wiv 'im!"

Why did not John Carlos attempt to win back for himself the one thing that he desired in all the world? Maybe (and I think that it is very possible) in the early years of his return, he had so striven; but the young nun, shaken with the enormousness of the thought, hopelessly weighted with her vows, had not dared to think upon it—had retreated with horror from the suggestion; had turned with an intention of double ardour to seek in her religious duties, the calm and sweetness, the peace and joy, which she felt to be lost to her forever in any more earthly way.

And then had followed the long years, with her heart fighting silently and secretly—*secretly almost from herself*—unto victory. And the man (having lost the force of that first fierce unpenting of his intention to win her—and mayhap having been repulsed, as it would seem to his masculine mind, *hopelessly*) had fallen back under the sway of the religious beliefs, which ruled him in his more normal hours; and so, year by year, had withheld from any further attempt to win her; striving to content his soul with those two brief visits each year to the old wharf; each time to endure a mad week of those futile watchings for his beloved.

Yet, in him, as in the woman, there had been going forward, without his knowledge, that steady disruption of religious belief—the rotting and decaying of all arbitrary things, before the primal need of the human heart; so that the olden barriers of "Impossibility," were now but as shadows, that would be gone in a moment, when next the Force of his Need should urge him to take his heart's desire.

His first attempt—if there had ever been such—had been the outcome of his natural want—his Love—; but lacking the foundations of Sureness of Himself and of his Power to withstand the Future. Indeed, it is conceivable that had he succeeded at the first, and gained his desire, the two of them would have wilted in the afterblast of thought and fear-of-the-hereafter, and in the Fires of Scruples which would have burned in their path through all the years.

But now, whatever they might do, they would do—if it ever came to pass—with a calm and determined Intention; having done their thinking first, and weighed all known costs, and proved their strength, and learned the utterness of their need to be truly greater than all else that might be set as balance against it. And because of this, they were ripe—wanting only the final stimulus to set into action the ready Force that had concentrated through the years.

Yet, strangely, neither the man nor the woman *knew*, as I have shown, that they had developed to this. Their brains refused to know; their Consciences looked, each with its blind eye, at their hearts, and saw nothing to give cause of offence to the ethical in them; or, did Conscience catch an odd glimpse, with its seeing eye, of impossible wickedness, there followed hours of imagined repentance, deep and painful, resulting in a double assuredness, within the brain (and "Manufactured" Parts) of a conquered and chastened heart, and of fiercer resolutions for the future Torture of Salvation. But always, deep within, the unconquerable heart fought for the victory that was each year more assured.

And so, as you have already seen, these two, the man and the woman, were but waiting—the man for some outward stimulus, to put into action all the long-pent force in him, revealing to him his actual nature, developed and changed in the course of the long years of pain, until he should be scarcely likely to recognise himself in the first moments of his awakening to this reality. And the woman, waiting, subconsciously, for the action of the man to bring her to a knowledge of the realities—to an awaredness of the woman she had become, of the woman into which she had developed, unable any more to endure the bondage of aught save her heart that leaped to the ordering of Mother Nature. Nay, more, fiercely and steadfastly eager to take with both hands the forbidden joy of her Natural Birthright, and calm and resolute and unblinking to face the future, with its unsolvable problem of the Joy of the Everlasting.

And thus were these two standing, as it might be said, on the brink of their destinies; waiting, with blinded eyes, and as that they listened unknowingly for the coming of the unknown one who should give the little push forward, and so cause them to step over the borderland into all natural and long craved for happiness.

Who would be That One?

"W'y the 'ell don't 'e get 'er out?" the Mate had asked the First Hand, who knew all the story, having sailed years with Big John Carlos. But the First Hand had raised his arms in horror, and made plain in broken English his opinion of the sacrilege, though that was not how he had pronounced it.

"Sacrilege be jiggered!" the Mate had replied, humping his twisted shoulders. "I s'pose though there'd be a 'oly rumpus, hey?"

The First Hand had intimated very definitely that there would be a "rumpus," which, the Mate ferreted out, might involve some very unpleasant issues both for the man and the woman guilty of such a thing. The First Hand spoke (in broken English) as if he were the Religious Conscience of his nation. Such things could not be tolerated. His phraseology did not include such words; but he was sufficiently definite.

"Nice 'ealthy lot o' savages, *you!*" the Mate had explained, after listening to much intolerant jabbering. "Strike me! If you ain't canniballs!" And straightway saddled on to the unfortunate Catholic Faith the sins peculiar to a hot-blooded and emotional People, whose enthusiasms and prejudices would have been just as apparent, had they been called forth by some other force than their Faith, or by a Faith differently shaped and Denominated.

It was the little crooked Mate who was speaking to Big John Carlos, in the evening of the sixth day of their stay beside the old wharf. And the big man was listening, in a stunned kind of silence. Through those six days the little man had watched the morning and evening tragedy, and the sanity of his free thoughts had been as a yeast in him. Now he was speaking, unlading all the things that he *had* to say.

"W'y the 'ell don't you take 'er out?" he had asked in so many words. And to him it had seemed, that very evening, that the woman's eyes had been saying the same thing to the Captain, as she looked her brief, dumb agony of longing across the little space that had lain between; yet which, as it were, was in verity the whole width of Eternity. And now the little Mate was putting it all into definite words—standing there, an implement of Fate or Providence or the Devil, according to the way that you may look at it, his twisted shoulder heaving with the vehemence of his speech:—

"You didn't orter do it, Capting," he said. "You're breakin' 'er up, an' you're breakin' *you* up; an' no good to it. W'y the 'ell don't you do somefink! Rescue 'er, or keep away. If it's 'ell for you, it's just 's much 'ell for 'er! She'll come like a little bloomin' bird. See 'ow she looks at you. She's fair askin' you to come an' take 'er out of it all—an' you just standin' there! My Gord!"

"What can I do," said the Captain, hoarsely; and put his hands suddenly to his head. He did not ask a question, or voice any hopelessness; but just gave out the words, as so many sounds, mechanically; for he was choked, suffocating during those first few moments, with the vast surge of hope that rose and beat upward in him, as the little twisted Mate's words crashed ruthlessly through the shrouding films of Belief.

And suddenly he *knew.* He knew that he could do this thing; that all scruples, all bonds of belief, of usage, of blind fears for the future, and *of* the Hereafter, were all fallen from him, as so much futile dust. Until that moment, as I have shown to you before, he had *not* known that he could do it—had not known of his steady and silent development. But now, suddenly, all his soul and being, lighted with Hope, he looked inward, and saw himself, as the man he was—the man to which he had grown and come to be. He knew. *He knew.*

"Would she. . . would she?" The question came unconsciously from his lips; but the little twisted man took it up.

"Arsk 'er! Arsk 'er!" he said, vehemently. "I knows she'll come. I seen it in 'er eyes to-night w'en she looked out at you. She was sayin' as plain as your 'at, 'W'y the 'ell don't you take me out? W'y the 'ell don't you?' You arsk 'er, an' she'll come like a bird."

The little Mate spoke with the eagerness of conviction, and indulged in no depressing knowledge of incongruities. "Arsk 'er!" was his refrain. "You arsk 'er!"

"How?" said the Captain, coming suddenly to realities.

The little man halted, and stumbled over his unreadiness. He had no plan; nothing but his feelings. He sought around in his mind, and grasped at an idea.

"Write it on an 'atch cover, wiv chalk," he said, triumphant. "Lean the 'atch cover by you. W'en 'she comes, point to it, 'n she'll read it."

"Ha!" said the Captain, in a strange voice, as if he both approved, and, at the same time, had remembered something.

"Then she'll nod," continued the little man. "No one else ever looks outer that winder, scarcely, not to think to read writin', anyway. An' you can cover it, till she's due to show. Then we'll plan 'ow to get 'er out."

All that night, Big John Carlos paced the deck of his little craft, alone, thinking, and thrilling with great surges of hope and maddened determination.

In the morning, he put the plan to the test; only that he wrote the question on the hatch-cover in peculiar words, that he had not used all those long grey years; for he made use of a quaint but simple transposition of letters, which had been a kind of love-language between them, in the olden days. This was why he had called "Ha!" so strangely, being minded suddenly of it, and to have the sweetness of using it to that one particular purpose.

Slowly, the line of grey moving figures came into view, descending. Big John Carlos kept the hatch-cover turned to him, and counted; for well he knew just when she would appear. The one hundred and ninth mute would pass, and the one hundred and tenth would show the face of his Beloved. The order never changed through the years, in that changeless world within.

As the hundred and seventh figure passed the narrow window, he turned the hatch-cover, so that the writing was exposed, and pointed down to it, so that his whole attitude should direct her glance instantly to his question, that she might have some small chance to read it, in the brief moment that was hers as she went slowly past the narrow panes. The hundred and ninth figure passed down from sight, and then he was looking dumbly into her face, as she moved into view, her eyes already strained to meet his. His heart was beating with a dull, sickening thudding, and there seemed just the faintest of mists before his vision; but he knew that her glance had flown eagerly to the message, and that her white face had flashed suddenly to a greater whiteness, disturbed by the battle of scores of emotions loosed in one second of time. Then she was gone downward out of his sight, and he let the hatch-cover fall, gripping the shrouds with his left hand.

The little twisted man stole up to him.

"She *saw*, Capting! She 'adn't time to answer. Not to know if she was on 'er 'ead or 'er 'eels. Look out to-night. She'll nod then." He brought it all out in little whispered jerks, and the big man, wiping his forehead, nodded.

Within the convent, a woman (outwardly a nun) was even then descending the stairs, with shaking knees, and a brain that had become in a few brief instants a raging gulf of hope. Before she had descended three steps below the level of the window, even whilst her sight-memory still held the message out for her brain to read and comprehend, she had realised that spiritually she was clothed only with the ashes of Belief and Fear and Faith. The original garment had become charred to nothing in the Fire of Love and Pain, with which the years had enveloped her. No bond held her; no fear held her; nothing in all the world mattered, except to be his for all the rest of her life. She took and realised the change in her character, in a moment of time. Eight long years had the yeast of love been working in her, which had bred the chemistry of pain; but only in that instant did she *know* and comprehend that she was developed so extensively, as to be changed utterly from the maid of eight years gone. Yet, in the next few steps she took, she had adapted herself to the new standpoint of her fresh knowledge of herself. She had no pause or doubt; but acknowledged with an utter startled joyfulness that she would go—that all was as nothing to her, now, except that she go to him. Willing, beyond all words that might express her willingness, to risk (aye, even to *exchange*) the unknown Joy of the Everlasting for this *certain* "mess of pottage" that was so desired of her hungry heart. And having acknowledged to *herself* that she was utterly *willing*, she had no thought of anything but to pass on the knowledge of her altered state to the man who would be waiting there in the little onion boat at sunset.

That evening, just before the dusk, Big John Carlos saw the hundred and tenth grey figure nod swiftly to him, in passing; and he held tightly to the shroud, until the suffocation of his emotion passed from him.

After all, the Rescue—if it can be named by a term so heroic—proved a ridiculously easy matter. It was the spiritual prison that had held the woman so long—the Physical expression of the same, was easily made to give up its occupant.

In the morning, expectant, she read in her fleeting glance at the onion boat, a message written on the hatch-cover. She was to be at the window at midnight. That evening, as she ascended in the long grey line of mutes for the last weary time, she nodded her utter agreement and assent.

After night had fallen thickly on the small, deserted wharf, the little twisted Mate and the Captain reared a ladder against the convent side. By midnight, they had cut out entirely the lead framing of all the lower part of the window.

A few minutes later, the woman came. The Captain held out his big hands, in an absolute silence, and lifted the trembling figure gently down on to the ladder. He steadied her firmly, and they climbed down to the wharf, and were presently aboard the vessel, with no word yet between them to break the ten years of loneliness and silence; for it was ten years, as you will remember, since Big John Carlos had sailed on that voyage of dismay.

And now, full grown man and woman, they stood near to each other, in a dream-quietness, who had lived on the two sides of Eternity so long. And still they had no word. Youth and Maiden they had parted with tears; Man and Woman they met in a great silence—too grown and developed to have words over-easily at such a moment-of-life. Yet their very quiet, held a speech too full and subtle, aye and subtile, for made-words of sound. It came from them, almost as it were a soul-fragrance, diffused around them, and made visible only in the quiet trembling of hands——that reached unknowing unto the hands of the other. For the two were full-grown, as I have said, and had come nigh to the complete *awaredness* of life, and the taste of the brine of sorrow was yet in them. They had been ripened in the strange twin Suns of Love and Pain—that ripen the unseen fruit of the soul. Their hands met, trembling, and gripped a long, long while, till the little twisted Mate came stumbling aft, uneasy to be gone. Then the big man and the fragile woman stood apart, the woman dreaming, while the big man went to give the little Mate a hand.

Together, the two men worked to get the sail upon the small vessel, and the ropes cast off. They left the First and Second Hands sleeping. Presently, with light airs from the land, they moved out-ward to the sea.

There was no pursuit. All the remainder of that night, the small onion boat went outward into the mystery of the dark, the big man steering, and the woman close beside him; and for a long while the constant silence of communion.

As I have said, there was no pursuit, and at dawn the little twisted man wondered. He searched the empty sea, and found only their own shadow upon the almost calm waters. Perhaps the First Hand had held a wrong impression. The Peoples of the Coast may have been shocked, when they learned. Maybe they never learned. Convents, like other institutions, can keep their secrets, odd whiles. Possibly this was one of those times. Perhaps they remembered, with something of worldly wisdom, that they held the Substance; wherefore trouble overmuch concerning the shadow—of a lost nun. Certainly, not to the bringing of an ill-name upon their long holiness. Surely, Satan can be trusted, etc. We can all finish the well-hackneyed thought. Or, maybe, there were natural human hearts in diverse places, that—knowing something of the history of this love-tale—held sympathy in silence, and silence in sympathy. Is this too much to hope?

That evening, the man and the woman stood in the stern, looking into the wake, whilst the Second-Hand steered. Forrard, in the growing dusk, there was a noise of scuffling. The little humped Mate was having a slight difference of opinion with the First Hand, who had incautiously made use of a parallel word for "Sacrilege," for the second time. The scuffling continued; for the little twisted man was emphatic:—

"Sacrilege be jiggered! Wot the 'ell——"

The physical sounds of his opinion, drowned the monotonous accompaniment of his speech. The small craft sailed on into the sunset, and the two in the stern stared blindly into distances, holding hands like two little children.

At Sea

GUY DE MAUPASSANT

The following lines recently appeared in the press:

"Boulogne-Sur-Mer, January 22.

"From our correspondent.

"A frightful disaster has occurred which throws into consternation our maritime population, so grievously afflicted for the last two years. The fishing boat, commanded by Captain Javel, entering into port, was carried to the west, and broken upon the rocks of the breakwater near the pier. In spite of the efforts of the life-boat, and of life-lines shot out to them, four men and a cabin boy perished. The bad weather continues. Further wrecks are feared."

Who is this Captain Javel? Is he the brother of the one-armed Javel? If this poor man tossed by the waves, and dead perhaps, under the *débris* of his boat cut in pieces, is the one I think he is, he witnessed, eighteen years ago, another drama, terrible and simple as are all the formidable dramas of the sea.

Javel senior was then master of a smack. The smack is the fishing boat *par excellence*. Solid, fearing no kind of weather, with round body, rolled incessantly by the waves, like a cork, always lashed by the harsh, salty winds of the Channel, it travels the sea indefatigably, with sail filled, carrying in its wake a net which reaches the bottom of the ocean, detaching all the sleeping creatures from the rocks, the flat fishes glued to the sand, the heavy crabs with their hooked claws, and the lobster with his pointed mustaches.

When the breeze is fresh and the waves choppy, the boat puts about to fish. A rope is fastened to the end of a great wooden shank tipped with iron, which is let down by means of two cables slipping over two spools at the extreme end of the craft. And the boat, driving under wind and current, drags after her this apparatus, which ravages and devastates the bottom of the sea.

Javel had on board his younger brother, four men, and a cabin boy. He had set out from Boulogne in fair weather to cast the nets. Then, suddenly, the wind arose and a squall drove the boat before the wind. It reached the coast of England; but a tremendous sea was beating against the cliffs and the shore so that it was impossible to enter port. The little boat put to sea again and returned to the coast of France. The storm continued to make the piers unapproachable, enveloping with foam, noise and danger every place of refuge.

The fishing boat set out again, running along the tops of the billows, tossed about, shaken up, streaming, buffeted by mountains of water, but game in spite of all, accustomed to heavy weather, which sometimes kept it wandering for five or six days between the two countries, unable to land in the one or the other.

Finally, the hurricane ceased, when they came out into open sea, and although the sea was still high, the Old Man ordered them to cast the net. Then the great fishing tackle was thrown overboard, and two men at one side and two at the other began to unwind from windlasses the cable which held it. Suddenly it touched the bottom, but a high wave tipped the boat forward. Javel junior, who was in the prow directing the casting of the net, tottered and found his arm caught between the cable, slackened an instant by the motion, and the wood on which it was turning. He made a desperate effort with his other hand to lift the cable, but the net was dragging again and the taut cable would not yield.

Rigid with pain, he called. Every one ran to him. His brother left the helm. They threw their full force upon the rope, forcing it away from the arm it was grinding. It was in vain. "We must cut it," said a sailor, and he drew from his pocket a large knife which could, in two blows, save young Javel's arm. But to cut was to lose the net, and the net meant money, much money—fifteen hundred francs; it belonged to the elder Javel, who was keen on his property.

In anguish he cried out: "No, don't cut; I'll luff the ship." And he ran to the wheel, putting the helm about. The boat scarcely obeyed, paralyzed by the net, which counteracted its power, and driven besides by the force of the leeway and the wind.

Young Javel fell to his knees with set teeth and haggard eyes. He said nothing. His brother returned, still anxious about the sailor's knife.

"Wait! wait!" he said, "don't cut; we must cast anchor."

The anchor was thrown overboard, all the chain paid out, and they then tried to take a turn around the capstan with the cables in order to loosen them from the weight of the net. The cables finally relaxed, and they released the arm, which hung inert under a sleeve of bloody woolen cloth.

Young Javel seemed to have lost his mind. They removed his jersey, and then saw something horrible; a mass of bruised flesh, from which the blood was gushing, as if it were forced by a pump. The man himself looked at his arm and murmured: "Done for."

Then, as the hæmorrhage made a pool on the deck of the boat, the sailors cried: "He'll lose all his blood. We must bind the artery!"

They then took some twine, thick, black, tarred twine, and, twisting it around the limb above the wound, bound it with all their strength. Little by little the jets of blood stopped, and finally ceased altogether.

Young Javel arose, his arm hanging by his side. He took it by the other hand, raised it, turned it, shook it. Everything was broken; the bones were crushed completely; only the muscles held it to his body. He looked at it thoughtfully, with sad eyes. Then he seated himself on a folded sail, and his comrades came around him, advising him to soak it continually to prevent gangrene.

They put a bucket near him and every moment he would dip into it with a glass and bathe the horrible wound by letting a thin stream of clear water fall upon it.

"You would be better down below," said his brother. He went down, but after an hour he came up again, feeling better not to be alone. And then, he preferred the open air. He sat down again upon the sail and continued bathing his arm.

The fishing was good. The huge fish with white bodies were lying beside him, shaken by the spasms of death. He looked at them without ceasing to sprinkle the mangled flesh.

When they started to return to Boulogne, another gale of wind began to blow. The little boat resumed its mad course, bounding, and tumbling, shaking the poor wounded man.

Night came on. The weather was heavy until daybreak. At sunrise, they could see England again, but as the sea was a little less rough, they turned toward France, beating against the wind.

Toward evening, young Javel called his comrades and showed them black traces and the hideous signs of decay around that part of his arm which was no longer joined to his body.

The sailors looked at it, giving advice: "That must be gangrene," said one.

"It must have salt water on it," said another.

Then they brought salt water and poured it on the wound. The wounded man became livid, grinding his teeth, and twisting with pain; but he uttered no cry.

When the burning grew less, he said to his brother: "Give me your knife." The brother gave it to him.

"Hold this arm up for me, and pull it."

His brother did as he was asked.

Then he began to cut. He cut gently, with caution, severing the last tendons with the blade as sharp as a razor. Soon he had only a stump. He heaved a deep sigh and said: "That had to be done. Otherwise, it would be all up."

He seemed relieved and breathed energetically. He continued to pour water on the part of his arm remaining to him.

The night was still bad and they could not land. When the day appeared, young Javel took his severed arm and examined it carefully. Putrefaction had begun. His comrades came also and examined it, passing it from hand to hand, touching it, turning it over, and smelling it.

His brother said: "It's about time to throw that into the sea."

Young Javel was angry; he replied: "No, oh! no! I will not. It is mine, isn't it? Since it is my arm—" He took it and held it between his legs.

"It won't grow any less putrid," said the elder.

Then an idea came to the wounded man. In order to keep the fish when they remained a long time at sea, they had with them barrels of salt. "Couldn't I put it in there in the brine?" he asked.

"That's so," declared the others.

Then they emptied one of the barrels, already full of fish from the last few days, and, at the bottom, they deposited the arm. Then they turned salt upon it and replaced the fishes, one by one.

One of the sailors made a little joke: "Take care we don't happen to sell it at the fish market."

And everybody laughed except the Javel brothers.

The wind still blew. They beat about in sight of Boulogne until the next day at ten o'clock. The wounded man still poured water on his arm. From time to time he would get up and walk from one end of the boat to the other. His brother, who was at the wheel, shook his head and followed him with his eye.

Finally, they came into port.

The doctor examined the wound and declared it was doing well. He dressed it properly and ordered rest. But Javel could not go to bed without having his arm again, and went quickly back to the dock to find the barrel, which he had marked with a cross.

They emptied it in front of him, and he found his arm well preserved in the salt, wrinkled and in good condition. He wrapped it in a napkin brought for this purpose, and took it home.

His wife and children examined carefully this fragment of their father, touching the fingers, taking up the grains of salt that had lodged under the nails. Then they sent for the carpenter, who measured it for a little coffin.

The next day the complete crew of the fishing smack followed the funeral of the severed arm. The two brothers, side by side, conducted the ceremony. The parish beadle held the coffin under his arm.

Javel junior gave up going to sea. He obtained a small position in port, and, later, whenever he spoke of the accident, he would say to his auditor, in a low tone: "If my brother had been willing to cut the net, I should still have my arm, for certain. But he was thinking of his valuable property."

Davy Jones's Gift

JOHN MASEFIELD

"Once upon a time," said the sailor, "the Devil and Davy Jones came to Cardiff, to the place called Tiger Bay. They put up at Tony Adams's, not far from Pier Head, at the corner of Sunday Lane. And all the time they stayed there they used to be going to the rum-shop, where they sat at a table, smoking their cigars, and dicing each other for different persons' souls. Now you must know that the Devil gets landsmen, and Davy Jones gets sailor-folk; and they get tired of having always the same, so then they dice each other for some of another sort.

"One time they were in a place in Mary Street, having some burnt brandy, and playing red and black for the people passing. And while they were looking out on the street and turning the cards, they saw all the people on the sidewalk breaking their necks to get into the gutter. And they saw all the shop-people running out and kowtowing, and all the carts pulling up, and all the police saluting. 'Here comes a big nob,' said Davy Jones. 'Yes,' said the Devil; 'it's the Bishop that's stopping with the Mayor.' 'Red or black?' said Davy Jones, picking up a card. 'I don't play for bishops,' said the Devil. 'I respect the cloth,' he said. 'Come on, man,' said Davy Jones. 'I'd give an admiral to have a bishop. Come on, now; make your game. Red or black?' 'Well, I say red,' said the Devil. 'It's the ace of clubs,' said Davy Jones 'I win; and it's the first bishop ever I had in my life.' The Devil was mighty angry at that—at losing a bishop. 'I'll not play any more,' he said; 'I'm off home. Some people gets too good cards for me. There was some queer shuffling when that pack was cut, that's my belief.'

" 'Ah, stay and be friends, man,' said Davy Jones. 'Look at what's coming down the street. I'll give you that for nothing.'

"Now, coming down the street there was a reefer—one of those apprentice fellows. And he was brass-bound fit to play music. He stood about six feet, and there were bright brass buttons down his jacket, and on his collar, and on his sleeves. His cap had a big gold badge, with a house-flag in seven different colours in the middle of it, and a gold chain cable of a chinstay twisted round it. He was wearing his cap on three hairs, and he was walking on both the sidewalks and all the road. His trousers were cut like wind-sails round the ankles. He had a fathom of red silk tie rolling out over his chest. He'd a cigarette in a twisted clay holder a foot and a half long. He was chewing tobacco over his shoulders as he walked. He'd a bottle of rum-hot in one hand, a bag of jam tarts in the other, and his pockets were full of love-letters from every port between Rio and Callao, round by the East.

" 'You mean to say you'll give me that?' said the Devil. 'I will,' said Davy Jones, 'and a beauty he is. I never see a finer.' 'He is, indeed, a beauty,' said the Devil. 'I take back what I said about the cards. I'm sorry I spoke crusty. What's the matter with some more burnt brandy?' 'Burnt brandy be it,' said Davy Jones. So then they rang the bell, and ordered a new jug and clean glasses.

"Now the Devil was so proud of what Davy Jones had given him, he couldn't keep away from him. He used to hang about the East Bute Docks, under the red-brick clock-tower, looking at the barque the young man worked aboard. Bill Harker his name was. He was in a West Coast barque, the *Coronel*, loading fuel for Hilo. So at last, when the *Coronel* was sailing, the Devil shipped himself aboard her, as one of the crowd in the fo'c'sle, and away they went down the Channel. At first he was very happy, for Bill Harker was in the same watch, and the two would yarn together. And though he was wise when he shipped, Bill Harker taught him a lot. There was a lot of things Bill Harker knew about. But when they were off the River Plate, they got caught in a pampero, and it blew very hard, and a big green sea began to run. The *Coronel* was a wet ship, and for three days you could stand upon her poop, and look forward and see nothing but a smother of foam from the break of the poop to the jib-boom. The crew had to roost on the poop. The fo'c'sle was flooded out. So while they were like this the flying jib worked loose. 'The jib will be gone in half a tick,' said the mate. 'Out there, one of you, and make it fast, before it blows away.' But the boom was dipping under every minute, and the waist was four feet deep, and green water came aboard all along her length. So none of the crowd would go forward. Then Bill Harker shambled out, and away he went forward, with the green seas smashing over him, and he lay out along the jib-boom and made the sail fast, and jolly nearly drowned he was. 'That's a brave lad, that Bill Harker,' said the Devil. 'Ah, come off,' said the sailors. 'Them reefers, they haven't got souls to be saved.' It was that that set the Devil thinking.

"By and by they came up with the Horn; and if it had blown off the Plate, it now blew off the roof. Talk about wind and weather. They got them both for sure aboard the *Coronel*. And it blew all the sails off her, and she rolled all her masts out, and the seas made a breach of her bulwarks, and the ice knocked a hole in her bows. So watch and watch they pumped the old *Coronel*, and the leak gained steadily, and there they were hove to under a weather cloth, five and a half degrees to the south of anything. And while they were like this, just about giving up hope, the old man sent the watch below, and told them they could start prayers. So the Devil crept on to the top of the half-deck, to look through the scuttle, to see what the reefers were doing, and what kind of prayers Bill Harker was putting up. And he saw them all sitting round the table, under the lamp, with Bill Harker at the head. And each of them had a hand of cards, and a length of knotted rope-yarn, and they were playing able-whackets. Each man in turn put down a card, and swore a new blasphemy, and if his swear didn't come as he played the card, then all the others hit him with their teasers. But they never once had a chance to hit Bill Harker. 'I think they were right about his soul,' said the Devil. And he sighed, like he was sad.

"Shortly after that the *Coronel* went down, and all hands drowned in her, saving only Bill and the Devil. They came up out of the smothering green seas, and saw the stars blinking in the sky, and heard the wind howling like a pack of dogs. They managed to get aboard the *Coronel's* hen-house, which had come adrift, and floated. The fowls were all drowned inside, so they lived on drowned hens. As for drink, they had to do without, for there was none. When they got thirsty they splashed their faces with salt water; but they were so cold they didn't feel thirst very bad. They drifted three days and three nights, till their skins were all cracked and salt-caked. And all the Devil thought of was whether Bill Harker had a soul. And Bill kept telling the Devil what a thundering big feed they would have as soon as they fetched to port, and how good a rum-hot would be, with a lump of sugar and a bit of lemon peel.

"And at last the old hen-house came bump on to Terra del Fuego, and there were some natives cooking rabbits. So the Devil and Bill made a raid of the whole jing bang, and ate till they were tired. Then they had a drink out of a brook, and a warm by the fire, and a pleasant sleep, 'Now,' said the Devil, 'I will see if he's got a soul. I'll see if he give thanks.' So after an hour or two Bill took a turn up and down and came to the Devil. 'It's mighty dull on this forgotten continent,' he said. 'Have you got a ha'penny?' 'No,' said the Devil. 'What in joy d'ye want with a ha'penny?' 'I might have played you pitch and toss,' said Bill. 'It was better fun on the hen-coop than here.' 'I give you up,' said the Devil; 'you've no more soul than the inner part of an empty barrel.' And with that the Devil vanished in a flame of sulphur.

"Bill stretched himself, and put another shrub on the fire. He picked up a few round shells, and began a game of knucklebones."

"Blow Up with the Brig!"

WILKIE COLLINS

I have got an alarming confession to make. I am haunted by a Ghost.

If you were to guess for a hundred years, you would never guess what my ghost is. I shall make you laugh to begin with—and afterward I shall make your flesh creep. My Ghost is the ghost of a Bedroom Candlestick.

Yes, a bedroom candlestick and candle, or a flat candlestick and candle—put it which way you like—that is what haunts me. I wish it was something pleasanter and more out of the common way; a beautiful lady, or a mine of gold and silver, or a cellar of wine and a coach and horses, and such like. But, being what it is, I must take it for what it is, and make the best of it; and I shall thank you kindly if you will help me out by doing the same.

I am not a scholar myself, but I make bold to believe that the haunting of any man with any thing under the sun begins with the frightening of him. At any rate, the haunting of me with a bedroom candlestick and candle began with the frightening of me with a bedroom candlestick and candle—the frightening of me half out of my life; and, for the time being, the frightening of me altogether out of my wits. That is not a very pleasant thing to confess before stating the particulars; but perhaps you will be the readier to believe that I am not a downright coward, because you find me bold enough to make a clean breast of it already, to my own great disadvantage so far.

Here are the particulars, as well as I can put them:

I was apprenticed to the sea when I was about as tall as my own walking-stick; and I made good enough use of my time to be fit for a mate's berth at the age of twenty-five years.

It was in the year eighteen hundred and eighteen or nineteen, I am not quite certain which, that I reached the before-mentioned age of twenty-five. You will please to excuse my memory not being very good for dates, names, numbers, places, and such like. No fear, though, about the particulars I have undertaken to tell you of; I have got them all shipshape in my recollection; I can see them, at this moment, as clear as noonday in my own mind. But there is a mist over what went before, and, for the matter of that, a mist likewise over much that came after—and it's not very likely to lift at my time of life, is it?

Well, in eighteen hundred and eighteen, or nineteen, when there was peace in our part of the world—and not before it was wanted, you will say—there was fighting, of a certain scampering, scrambling kind, going on in that old battle-field which we seafaring men know by the name of the Spanish Main.

The possessions that belonged to the Spaniards in South America had broken into open mutiny and declared for themselves years before. There was plenty of bloodshed between the new Government and the old; but the new had got the best of it, for the most part, under one General Bolivar—a famous man in his time, though he seems to have dropped out of people's memories now. Englishmen and Irishmen with a turn for fighting, and nothing particular to do at home, joined the general as volunteers; and some of our merchants here found it a good venture to send supplies across the ocean to the popular side. There was risk enough, of course, in doing this; but where one speculation of the kind succeeded, it made up for type? at the least, that failed. And that's the true principle of trade, wherever I have met with it, all the world over.

Among the Englishmen who were concerned in this Spanish-American business, I, your humble servant, happened, in a small way, to be one.

I was then mate of a brig belonging to a certain firm in the City, which drove a sort of general trade, mostly in queer out-of-the-way places, as far from home as possible; and which freighted the brig, in the year I am speaking of, with a cargo of gunpowder for General Bolivar and his volunteers. Nobody knew anything about our instructions, when we sailed, except the captain; and he didn't half seem to like them. I can't rightly say how many barrels of powder we had on board, or how much each barrel held—I only know we had no other cargo. The name of the brig was the *Good Intent*—a queer name enough, you will tell me, for a vessel laden with gunpowder, and sent to help a revolution. And as far as this particular voyage was concerned, so it was. I mean that for a joke, and I hope you will encourage me by laughing at it.

The *Good Intent* was the craziest tub of a vessel I ever went to sea in, and the worst found in all respects. She was two hundred and thirty, or two hundred and eighty tons burden, I forget which; and she had a crew of eight, all told—nothing like as many as we ought by rights to have had to work the brig. However, we were well and honestly paid our wages; and we had to set that against the chance of foundering at sea, and, on this occasion, likewise the chance of being blown up into the bargain.

In consideration of the nature of our cargo, we were harassed with new regulations, which we didn't at all like, relative to smoking our pipes and lighting our lanterns; and, as usual in such cases, the captain, who made the regulations, preached what he didn't practise. Not a man of us was allowed to have a bit of lighted candle in his hand when he went below—except the skipper; and he used his light, when he turned in, or when he looked over his charts on the cabin table, just as usual.

This light was a common kitchen candle or "dip," and it stood in an old battered flat candlestick, with all the japan worn and melted off, and all the tin showing through. It would have been more seaman-like and suitable in every respect if he had had a lamp or a lantern; but he stuck to his old candlestick; and that same old candlestick has ever afterward stuck to *me*. That's another joke, if you please, and a better one than the first, in my opinion.

Well (I said "well" before, but it's a word that helps a man on like), we sailed in the brig, and shaped our course, first, for the Virgin Islands, in the West Indies; and, after sighting them, we made for the Leeward Islands next, and then stood on due south, till the lookout at the masthead hailed the deck and said he saw land. That land was the coast of South America. We had had a wonderful voyage so far. We had lost none of our spars or sails, and not a man of us had been harassed to death at the pumps. It wasn't often the *Good Intent* made such a voyage as that, I can tell you.

I was sent aloft to make sure about the land, and I did make sure of it.

When I reported the same to the skipper, he went below and had a look at his letter of instructions and the chart. When he came on deck again, he altered our course a trifle to the eastward—I forget the point on the compass, but that don't matter. What I do remember is, that it was dark before we closed in with the land. We kept the lead going, and hove the brig to in from four to five fathoms water, or it might be six—I can't say for certain. I kept a sharp eye to the drift of the vessel, none of us knowing how the currents ran on that coast. We all wondered why the skipper didn't anchor; but he said No, he must first show a light at the foretopmast-head, and wait for an answering light on shore. We did wait, and nothing of the sort appeared. It was starlight and calm. What little wind there was came in puffs off the land. I suppose we waited, drifting a little to the westward, as

I made it out, best part of an hour before anything happened—and then, instead of seeing the light on shore, we saw a boat coming toward us, rowed by two men only.

We hailed them, and they answered "Friends!" and hailed us by our name. They came on board. One of them was an Irishman, and the other was a coffee-coloured native pilot, who jabbered a little English.

The Irishman handed a note to our skipper, who showed it to me. It informed us that the part of the coast we were off was not oversafe for discharging our cargo, seeing that spies of the enemy (that is to say, of the old Government) had been taken and shot in the neighbourhood the day before. We might trust the brig to the native pilot; and he had his instructions to take us to another part of the coast. The note was signed by the proper parties; so we let the Irishman go back alone in the boat, and allowed the pilot to exercise his lawful authority over the brig. He kept us stretching off from the land till noon the next day—his instructions, seemingly, ordering him to keep up well out of sight of the shore. We only altered our course in the afternoon, so as to close in with the land again a little before midnight.

This same pilot was about as ill-looking a vagabond as ever I saw; a skinny, cowardly, quarrel-some mongrel, who swore at the men in the vilest broken English, till they were every one of them ready to pitch him overboard. The skipper kept them quiet, and I kept them quiet; for the pilot being given us by our instructions, we were bound to make the best of him. Near nightfall, however, with the best will in the world to avoid it, I was unlucky enough to quarrel with him.

He wanted to go below with his pipe, and I stopped him, of course, because it was contrary to orders. Upon that he tried to hustle by me, and I put him away with my hand. I never meant to push him down, but somehow I did. He picked himself up as quick as lightning, and pulled out his knife. I snatched it out of his hand, slapped his murderous face for him, and threw his weapon overboard. He gave me one ugly look, and walked aft. I didn't think much of the look then, but I remembered it a little too well afterward.

We were close in with the land again, just as the wind failed us, between eleven and twelve that night, and dropped our anchor by the pilot's directions.

It was pitch-dark, and a dead, airless calm. The skipper was on deck, with two of our best men for watch. The rest were below, except the pilot, who coiled himself up, more like a snake than a man, on the forecastle. It was not my watch till four in the morning. But I didn't like the look of the night, or the pilot, or the state of things generally, and I shook myself down on deck to get my nap there, and be ready for anything at a moment's notice. The last I remember was the skipper whispering to me that he didn't like the look of things either, and that he would go below and consult his instructions again. That is the last I remember, before the slow, heavy, regular roll of the old brig on the ground-swell rocked me off to sleep.

I was awoke by a scuffle on the forecastle and a gag in my mouth. There was a man on my breast and a man on my legs, and I was bound hand and foot in half a minute.

The brig was in the hands of the Spaniards. They were swarming all over her. I heard six heavy splashes in the water, one after another. I saw the captain stabbed to the heart as he came running up the companion, and I heard a seventh splash in the water. Except myself, every soul of us on board had been murdered and thrown into the sea. Why I was left I couldn't think, till I saw the pilot stoop over me with a lantern, and look, to make sure of who I was. There was a devilish grin on his face, and he nodded his head at me, as much as to say, *You* were the man who hustled me down and slapped my face, and I mean to play the game of cat and mouse with you in return for it!

I could neither move nor speak, but I could see the Spaniards take off the main hatch and rig the purchases for getting up the cargo. A quarter of an hour afterward I heard the sweeps of a schooner, or other small vessel, in the water. The strange craft was laid alongside of us, and the Spaniards set to work to discharge our cargo into her. They all worked hard except the pilot; and he came from time to time, with his lantern, to have another look at me, and to grin and nod, always in the same devilish way. I am old enough now not to be ashamed of confessing the truth, and I don't mind acknowledging that the pilot frightened me.

The fright, and the bonds, and the gag, and the not being able to stir hand or foot, had pretty nigh worn me out by the time the Spaniards gave over work. This was just as the dawn broke. They had shifted a good part of our cargo on board their vessel, but nothing like all of it, and they were sharp enough to be off with what they had got before daylight.

I need hardly say that I had made up my mind by this time to the worst I could think of. The pilot, it was clear enough, was one of the spies of the enemy, who had wormed himself into the confidence of our consignees without being suspected. He, or more likely his employers, had got knowledge enough of us to suspect what our cargo was; we had been anchored for the night in the safest berth for them to surprise us in; and we had paid the penalty of having a small crew, and consequently an insufficient watch. All this was clear enough—but what did the pilot mean to do with *me?*

On the word of a man, it makes my flesh creep now, only to tell you what he did with me.

After all the rest of them were out of the brig, except the pilot and two Spanish seamen, these last took me up, bound and gagged as I was, lowered me into the hold of the vessel, and laid me along on the floor, lashing me to it with ropes' ends, so that I could just turn from one side to the other, but could not roll myself fairly over, so as to change my place. They then left me. Both of them were the worse for liquor; but the devil of a pilot was sober—mind that!—as sober as I am at the present moment.

I lay in the dark for a little while, with my heart thumping as if it was going to jump out of me. I lay about five minutes or so when the pilot came down into the hold alone.

He had the captain's cursed flat candlestick and a carpenter's awl in one hand, and a long thin twist of cotton yarn, well oiled, in the other. He put the candlestick, with a new "dip" candle lighted in it, down on the floor about two feet from my face, and close against the side of the vessel. The light was feeble enough; but it was sufficient to show a dozen barrels of gunpowder or more left all round me in the hold of the brig. I began to suspect what he was after the moment I noticed the barrels. The horrors laid hold of me from head to foot, and the sweat poured off my face like water.

I saw him go next to one of the barrels of powder standing against the side of the vessel in a line with the candle, and about three feet, or rather better, away from it. He bored a hole in the side of the barrel with his awl, and the horrid powder came trickling out, as black as hell, and dripped into the hollow of his hand, which he held to catch it. When he had got a good handful, he stopped up the hole by jamming one end of his oiled twist of cotton-yarn fast into it, and he then rubbed the powder into the whole length of the yarn till he had blackened every hair-breadth of it.

The next thing he did—as true as I sit here, as true as the heaven above us all—the next thing he did was to carry the free end of his long, lean, black, frightful slow-match to the lighted candle alongside my face. He tied it (the bloody-minded villain!) in several folds round the tallow dip, about a third of the distance down, measuring from the flame of the wick to the lip of the candlestick. He did that; he looked to see that my lashings were all safe; and then he put his face close to mine, and whispered in my ear, "Blow up with the brig!"

He was on deck again the moment after, and he and the two others shoved the hatch on over me. At the farthest end from where I lay they had not fitted it down quite true, and I saw a blink of daylight glimmering in when I looked in that direction. I heard the sweeps of the schooner fall into the water—splash! splash! fainter and fainter, as they swept the vessel out in the dead calm, to be ready for the wind in the offing. Fainter and fainter, splash, splash! for a quarter of an hour or more.

While those receding sounds were in my ears, my eyes were fixed on the candle.

It had been freshly lighted. If left to itself, it would burn for between six and seven hours. The slow-match was twisted round it about a third of the way down, and therefore the flame would be about two hours reaching it. There I lay, gagged, bound, lashed to the floor; seeing my own life burning down with the candle by my side—there I lay, alone on the sea, doomed to be blown to atoms, and to see that doom drawing on, nearer and nearer with every fresh second of time, through nigh on two hours to come; powerless to help myself, and speechless to call for help to others. The wonder to me is that I didn't cheat the flame, the slow-match, and the powder, and die of the horror of my situation before my first half-hour was out in the hold of the brig.

I can't exactly say how long I kept the command of my senses after I had ceased to hear the splash of the schooner's sweeps in the water. I can trace back everything I did and everything I thought up to a certain point; but, once past that, I get all abroad, and lose myself in my memory now, much as I lost myself in my own feelings at the time.

The moment the hatch was covered over me, I began, as every other man would have begun in my place, with a frantic effort to free my hands. In the mad panic I was in, I cut my flesh with the lashings as if they had been knife blades, but I never stirred them. There was less chance still of freeing my legs, or of tearing myself from the fastenings that held me to the floor. I gave in when I was all but suffocated for want of breath. The gag, you will be pleased to remember, was a terrible enemy to me; I could only breathe freely through my nose—and that is but a poor vent when a man is straining his strength as far as ever it will go.

I gave in and lay quiet, and got my breath again, my eyes glaring and straining at the candle all the time.

While I was staring at it, the notion struck me of trying to blow out the flame by pumping a long breath at it suddenly through my nostrils. It was too high above me, and too far away from me, to be reached in that fashion. I tried, and tried, and tried; and then I gave in again, and lay quiet again, always with my eyes glaring at the candle, and the candle glaring at *me.* The splash of the schooner's sweeps was very faint by this time. I could only just hear them in the morning stillness. Splash! splash!—fainter and fainter—splash! splash!

Without exactly feeling my mind going, I began to feel it getting queer as early as this. The snuff of the candle was growing taller and taller, and the length of tallow between the flame and the slow-match, which was the length of my life, was getting shorter and shorter. I calculated that I had rather less than an hour and a half to live.

An hour and a half! Was there a chance in that time of a boat pulling off to the brig from shore? Whether the land near which the vessel was anchored was in possession of our side, or in possession of the enemy's side, I made out that they must, sooner or later, send to hail the brig merely because she was a stranger in those parts. The question for *me* was, how soon? The sun had not risen yet, as I could tell by looking through the chink in the hatch. There was no coast village near us, as we all knew, before the brig was seized, by seeing no lights on shore. There was no wind, as I could tell by listening, to bring any strange vessel near. If I had had six hours to live, there might have been a chance for me, reckoning from sunrise to noon. But with an hour and a half, which had dwindled to an hour and a quarter by this time—or, in other words, with the earliness of the morning, the uninhabited coast, and the dead calm all against me—there was not the ghost of a chance. As I felt that, I had another struggle—the last—with my bonds, and only cut myself the deeper for my pains.

I gave in once more, and lay quiet, and listened for the splash of the sweeps.

Gone! Not a sound could I hear but the blowing of a fish now and then on the surface of the sea, and the creak of the brig's crazy old spars, as she rolled gently from side to side with the little swell there was on the quiet water.

An hour and a quarter. The wick grew terribly as the quarter slipped away, and the charred top of it began to thicken and spread out mushroom-shape. It would fall off soon. Would it fall off red-hot, and would the swing of the brig cant it over the side of the candle and let it down on the slow-match? If it would, I had about ten minutes to live instead of an hour.

This discovery set my mind for a minute on a new tack altogether. I began to ponder with myself what sort of a death blowing up might be. Painful! Well, it would be, surely, too sudden for that. Perhaps just one crash inside me, or outside me, or both; and nothing more! Perhaps not even a crash; that and death and the scattering of this living body of mine into millions of fiery sparks, might all happen in the same instant! I couldn't make it out; I couldn't settle how it would be. The minute of calmness in my mind left it before I had half done thinking; and I got all abroad again.

When I came back to my thoughts, or when they came back to me (I can't say which), the wick was awfully tall, the flame was burning with a smoke above it, the charred top was broad and red, and heavily spreading out to its fall.

My despair and horror at seeing it took me in a new way, which was good and right, at any rate, for my poor soul. I tried to pray—in my own heart, you will understand, for the gag put all lip-praying out of my power. I tried, but the candle seemed to burn it up in me. I struggled hard to force my eyes from the slow, murdering flame, and to look up through the chink in the hatch at the blessed daylight. I tried once, tried twice; and gave it up. I next tried only to shut my eyes, and keep them shut—once—twice—and the second time I did it. "God bless old mother, and sister Lizzie; God keep them both, and forgive me." That was all I had time to say, in my own heart, before my eyes opened again, in spite of me, and the flame of the candle flew into them, flew all over me, and burned up the rest of my thoughts in an instant.

I couldn't hear the fish blowing now; I couldn't hear the creak of the spars; I couldn't think; I couldn't feel the sweat of my own death agony on my face—I could only look at the heavy, charred top of the wick. It swelled, tottered, bent over to one side, dropped—red-hot at the moment of its fall—black and harmless, even before the swing of the brig had canted it over into the bottom of the candlestick.

I caught myself laughing.

Yes! laughing at the safe fall of the bit of wick. But for the gag, I should have screamed with laughter. As it was, I shook with it inside me—shook till the blood was in my head, and I was all but suffocated for want of breath. I had just sense enough left to feel that my own horrid laughter at that awful moment was a sign of my brain going at last. I had just sense enough left to make another struggle before my mind broke loose like a frightened horse, and ran away with me.

One comforting look at the blink of daylight through the hatch was what I tried for once more. The fight to force my eyes from the candle and to get that one look at the daylight was the hardest I had had yet; and I lost the fight. The flame had hold of my eyes as fast as the lashings had hold of my hands. I couldn't look away from it. I couldn't even shut my eyes, when I tried that next, for the second time. There was the wick growing tall once more. There was the space of unburned candle between the light and the slow-match shortened to an inch or less.

How much life did that inch leave me? Three-quarters of an hour? Half an hour? Fifty minutes? Twenty minutes? Steady! an inch of tallow candle would burn longer than twenty minutes. An inch of tallow! the notion of a man's body and soul being kept together by an inch of tallow! Wonderful! Why, the greatest king that sits on a throne can't keep a man's body and soul together; and here's an inch of tallow that can do what the king can't! There's something to tell mother when I get home which will surprise her more than all the rest of my voyages put together. I laughed inwardly again at the thought of that, and shook and swelled and suffocated myself, till the light of the candle leaped in through my eyes, and licked up the laughter, and burned it out of me, and made me all empty and cold and quiet once more.

Mother and Lizzie. I don't know when they came back; but they did come back—not, as it seemed to me, into my mind this time, but right down bodily before me, in the hold of the brig.

Yes: sure enough, there was Lizzie, just as lighthearted as usual, laughing at me. Laughing? Well, why not? Who is to blame Lizzie for thinking I'm lying on my back, drunk in the cellar, with the beer barrels all round me? Steady! she's crying now—spinning round and round in a fiery mist, wringing her hands, screeching out for help—fainter and fainter, like the splash of the schooner's sweeps. Gone—burned up in the fiery mist! Mist? fire? no; neither one nor the other. It's mother makes the light—mother knitting, with ten flaming points at the ends of her fingers and thumbs, and slow-matches hanging in bunches all round her face instead of her own grey hair. Mother in her old armchair, and the pilot's long skinny hands hanging over the back of the chair, dripping with gunpowder. No! no gunpowder, no chair, no mother—nothing but the pilot's face, shining red-hot, like a sun, in the fiery mist; turning upside down in the fiery mist; running backward and forward along the slow-match, in the fiery mist; spinning millions of miles in a minute, in the fiery mist—spinning itself smaller and smaller into one tiny point, and that point darting on a sudden straight into my head—and then, all fire and all mist—no hearing, no seeing, no thinking, no feeling—the brig, the sea, my own self, the whole world, all gone together!

After what I've just told you, I know nothing and remember nothing, till I woke up (as it seemed to me) in a comfortable bed, with two rough-and-ready men like myself sitting on each side of my pillow, and a gentleman standing watching me at the foot of the bed. It was about seven in the morning. My sleep (or what seemed like my sleep to me) had lasted better than eight months—I was among my own countrymen in the island of Trinidad—the men at each side of my pillow were my keepers, turn and turn about—and the gentleman standing at the foot of the bed was the doctor. What I said and did in those eight months I never have known, and never shall. I woke out of it as if it had been one long sleep—that's all I know.

It was another two months or more before the doctor thought it safe to answer the questions I asked him.

An American vessel, becalmed in the offing, had made out the brig as the sun rose; and the captain, seeing her anchored where no vessel had any reason to be, had manned one of his boats and sent his mate to look into the matter and report of what he saw.

What he saw, when he and his men found the brig deserted and boarded her, was a gleam of candlelight through the chink in the hatchway. The flame was within about a thread's breadth of the slow-match when he lowered himself into the hold; and if he had not had the sense and coolness to cut the match in two with his knife before he touched the candle, he and his men might have been blown up along with the brig as well as me. The match caught, and turned into sputtering red fire, in the very act of putting the candle out. . . .

What became of the Spanish schooner and the pilot I have never heard from that day to this.

As for the brig, the Yankees took her, as they took me, to Trinidad, and claimed their salvage, and got it, I hope, for their own sakes. I was landed just in the same state as when they rescued me from the brig—that is to say, clean out of my senses. But please to remember, it was a long time ago; and, take my word for it, I was discharged cured, as I have told you. Bless your hearts, I'm all right now, as you may see. I'm a little shaken by telling the story, as is only natural—a little shaken, my good friends, that's all.

The Admiral

O. HENRY

Spilled milk draws few tears from an Anchurian administration. Many are its lacteal sources; and the clock's hands point for ever to milking time. Even the rich cream skimmed from the treasury by the bewitched Miraflores did not cause the newly-installed patriots to waste time in unprofitable regrets. The government philosophically set about supplying the deficiency by increasing the import duties and by "suggesting" to wealthy private citizens that contributions according to their means would be considered patriotic and in order. Prosperity was expected to attend the reign of Losada, the new president. The ousted office-holders and military favourites organised a new "Liberal" party, and began to lay their plans for a re-succession. Thus the game of Anchurian politics began, like a Chinese comedy, to unwind slowly its serial length. Here and there Mirth peeps for an instant from the wings and illumines the florid lines.

A dozen quarts of champagne in conjunction with an informal sitting of the president and his cabinet led to the establishment of the navy and the appointment of Felipe Carrera as its admiral. Next to the champagne the credit of the appointment belongs to Don Sabas Placido, the newly confirmed Minister of War.

The president had requested a convention of his cabinet for the discussion of questions politic and for the transaction of certain routine matters of state. The session had been signally tedious; the business and the wine prodigiously dry. A sudden, prankish humour of Don Sabas, impelling him to the deed, spiced the grave affairs of state with a whiff of agreeable playfulness.

In the dilatory order of business had come a bulletin from the coast department of Orilla del Mar reporting the seizure by the customs-house officers at the town of Coralio of the sloop *Estrella del Noche* and her cargo of dry goods, patent medicines, granulated sugar and three-star brandy. Also six Martini rifles and a barrel of American whisky. Caught in the act of smuggling, the sloop with its cargo was now, according to law, the property of the republic.

The Collector of Customs, in making his report, departed from the conventional forms so far as to suggest that the confiscated vessel be converted to the use of the government. The prize was the first capture to the credit of the department in ten years. The collector took opportunity to pat his department.

It often happened that government officers required transportation from point to point along the coast, and means were usually lacking. Furthermore, the sloop could be manned by a loyal crew and employed as a coast guard to discourage the pernicious art of smuggling. The collector also ventured to nominate one to whom the charge of the boat could be safely entrusted—a young man of Coralio, Felipe Carrera—not, be it understood, one of extreme wisdom, but loyal and the best sailor along the coast.

It was upon this hint that the Minister of War acted, executing a rare piece of drollery that so enlivened the tedium of executive session.

In the constitution of this small, maritime banana republic was a forgotten section that provided for the maintenance of a navy. This provision—with many other wiser ones—had lain inert since the establishment of the republic. Anchuria had no navy and had no use for one. It was characteristic of Don Sabas—a man at once merry, learned, whimsical and audacious—that he should have disturbed the dust of this musty and sleeping statute to increase the humour of the world by so much as a smile from his indulgent colleagues.

With delightful mock seriousness the Minister of War proposed the creation of a navy. He argued its need and the glories it might achieve with such gay and witty zeal that the travesty overcame with its humour even the swart dignity of President Losada himself.

The champagne was bubbling trickily in the veins of the mercurial statesmen. It was not the custom of the grave governors of Anchuria to enliven their sessions with a beverage so apt to cast a veil of disparagement over sober affairs. The wine had been a thoughtful compliment tendered by the agent of the Vesuvius Fruit Company as a token of amicable relations—and certain consummated deals—between that company and the republic of Anchuria.

The jest was carried to its end. A formidable, official document was prepared, encrusted with chromatic seals and jaunty with fluttering ribbons, bearing the florid signatures of state. This commission conferred upon *el Señor* Don Felipe Carrera the title of Flag Admiral of the Republic of Anchuria. Thus within the space of a few minutes and the dominion of a dozen "extra dry" the country took its place among the naval powers of the world, and Felipe Carrera became entitled to a salute of nineteen guns whenever he might enter port.

The southern races are lacking in that particular kind of humour that finds entertainment in the defects and misfortunes bestowed by Nature. Owing to this defect in their constitution they are not moved to laughter (as are their northern brothers) by the spectacle of the deformed, the feeble-minded or the insane.

Felipe Carrera was sent upon earth with but half his wits. Therefore, the people of Coralio called him "*El pobrecito loco*"—"the poor little crazed one"—saying that God had sent but half of him to earth, retaining the other half.

A sombre youth, glowering, and speaking only at the rarest times, Felipe was but negatively "loco." On shore he generally refused all conversation. He seemed to know that he was badly handicapped on land, where so many kinds of understanding are needed; but on the water his one talent set him equal with most men. Few sailors whom God had carefully and completely made could handle a sail-boat as well. Five points nearer the wind than the best of them he could sail his sloop. When the elements raged and set other men to cowering, the deficiencies of Felipe seemed of little importance. He was a perfect sailor, if an imperfect man. He owned no boat, but worked among the crews of the schooners and sloops that skimmed the coast, trading and freighting fruit out to the steamers where there was no harbour. It was through his famous skill and boldness on the sea, as well as for the pity felt for his mental imperfections, that he was recommended by the collector as a suitable custodian of the captured sloop.

When the outcome of Don Sabas' little pleasantry arrived in the form of the imposing and preposterous commission, the collector smiled. He had not expected such prompt and overwhelming response to his recommendation. He dispatched a *muchacho* at once to fetch the future admiral.

The collector waited in his official quarters. His office was in the Calle Grande, and the sea-breezes hummed through its windows all day. The collector, in white linen and canvas shoes, philandered with papers on an antique desk. A parrot, perched on a pen rack, seasoned the official tedium with a fire of choice Castilian imprecations. Two rooms opened into the collector's. In one the clerical force of young men of variegated complexions transacted with glitter and parade their several duties. Through the open door of the other room could be seen a bronze babe, guiltless of clothing, that rollicked upon the floor. In a grass hammock a thin woman, tinted a pale lemon, played a guitar and swung contentedly in the breeze. Thus surrounded by the routine of his high duties and the visible tokens of agreeable domesticity, the collector's heart was further made happy by the power placed in his hands to brighten the fortunes of the "innocent" Felipe.

Felipe came and stood before the collector. He was a lad of twenty, not ill-favoured in looks, but with an expression of distant and pondering vacuity. He wore white cotton trousers, down the seams of which he had sewn red stripes with some vague aim of military decoration. A flimsy blue shirt fell open at his throat; his feet were bare; he held in his hand the cheapest of straw hats from the States.

"*Señor* Carrera," said the collector gravely, producing the showy commission, "I have sent for you at the president's bidding. This document that I present to you confers upon you the title of Admiral of this great republic, and gives you absolute command of the naval forces and fleet of our country. You may think, friend Felipe, that we have no navy—but yes! The sloop the *Estrella del Noche*, that my brave men captured from the coast smugglers, is to be placed under your command. The boat is to be devoted to the services of your country. You will be ready at all times to convey officials of the government to points along the coast where they may be obliged to visit. You will also act as a coast-guard to prevent, as far as you may be able, the crime of smuggling. You will uphold the honour and prestige of your country at sea, and endeavour to place Anchuria among the proudest naval powers of the world. These are your instructions as the Minister of War desires me to convey them to you. *Por Dios!* I do not know how all this is to be accomplished, for not one word did the letter contain in respect to a crew or to the expenses of this navy. Perhaps you are to provide a crew yourself, *Señor* Admiral—I do not know—but it is a very high honour that has descended upon you. I now hand you your commission. When you are ready for the boat I will give orders that she shall be made over into your charge. That is as far as my instructions go."

Felipe took the commission that the collector handed to him. He gazed through the open window at the sea for a moment, with his customary expression of deep but vain pondering. Then he turned without having spoken a word, and walked swiftly away through the hot sand of the street.

"*Pobrecito loco!*" sighed the collector; and the parrot on the pen racks screeched, "Loco!—loco!—loco!"

The next morning a strange procession filed through the streets to the collector's office. At its head was the admiral of the navy. Somewhere Felipe had raked together a pitiful semblance of a military uniform—a pair of red trousers, a dingy blue short jacket heavily ornamented with gold braid, and an old fatigue cap that must have been cast away by one of the British soldiers in Belize and brought away by Felipe on one of his coasting voyages. Buckled around his waist was an ancient ship's cutlass contributed to his equipment by Pedro Lafitte, the baker, who proudly asserted its inheritance from his ancestor, the illustrious buccaneer. At the admiral's heels tagged his newly-shipped crew—three grinning, glossy, black Caribs, bare to the waist, the sand spurting in showers from the spring of their naked feet.

Briefly and with dignity Felipe demanded his vessel of the collector. And now a fresh honour awaited him. The collector's wife, who played the guitar and read novels in the hammock all day, had more than a little romance in her placid, yellow bosom. She had found in an old book an engraving of a flag that purported to be the naval flag of Anchuria. Perhaps it had so been designed by the founders of the nation; but, as no navy had ever been established, oblivion had claimed the flag. Laboriously with her own hands she had made a flag after the pattern—a red cross upon a blue-and-white ground. She presented it to Felipe with these words: "Brave sailor, this flag is of your country. Be true, and defend it with your life. Go you with God."

For the first time since his appointment the admiral showed a flicker of emotion. He took the silken emblem, and passed his hand reverently over its surface. "I am an admiral," he said to the collector's lady. Being on land he could bring himself to no more exuberant expression of sentiment. At sea with the flag at the masthead of his navy, some more eloquent exposition of feelings might be forthcoming.

Abruptly the admiral departed with his crew. For the next three days they were busy giving the *Estrella del Noche* a new coat of white paint trimmed with blue. And then Felipe further adorned himself by fastening a handful of brilliant parrot's plumes in his cap. Again he tramped with his faithful crew to the collector's office and formally notified him that the sloop's flame had been changed to *El Nacional*.

During the next few months the navy had its troubles. Even an admiral is perplexed to know what to do without any orders. But none came. Neither did any salaries. *El Nacional* swung idly at anchor.

When Felipe's little store of money was exhausted he went to the collector and raised the question of finances.

"Salaries!" exclaimed the collector, with hands raised; "*Valgame Dios!* not one *centavo* of my own pay have I received for the last seven months. The pay of an admiral, do you ask? *Quién sabe?* Should it be less than three thousand *pesos?* *Mira!* you will see a revolution in this country very soon. A good sign of it is when the government calls all the time for *pesos, pesos, pesos,* and pays none out."

Felipe left the collector's office with a look almost of content on his sombre face. A revolution would mean fighting, and then the government would need his services. It was rather humiliating to be an admiral without anything to do, and have a hungry crew at your heels begging for *reales* to buy plantains and tobacco with.

When he returned to where his happy-go-lucky Caribs were waiting they sprang up and saluted, as he had drilled them to do.

"Come, *muchachos*," said the admiral; "it seems that the government is poor. It has no money to give us. We will earn what we need to live upon. Thus we will serve our country. Soon"—his heavy eyes almost lighted up—"it may gladly call upon us for help."

Thereafter *El Nacional* turned out with the other coast craft and became a wage-earner. She worked with the lighters freighting bananas and oranges out to the fruit steamers that could not approach nearer than a mile from the shore. Surely a self-supporting navy deserves red letters in the budget of any nation.

After earning enough at freighting to keep himself and his crew in provisions for a week, Felipe would anchor the navy and hang about the little telegraph office, looking like one of the chorus of an insolvent comic opera troupe besieging the manager's den. A hope for orders from the capital was always in his heart. That his services as admiral had never been called into requirement hurt his pride and patriotism. At every call he would inquire, gravely and expectantly, for dispatches. The operator would pretend to make a search, and then reply:

"Not yet, it seems, *Senor el Almirante—poco tiempo!*"

Outside in the shade of the lime trees the crew chewed sugarcane or slumbered, well content to serve a country that was contented with so little service.

One day in the early summer the revolution predicted by the collector flamed out suddenly. It had long been smouldering. At the first note of alarm the admiral of the navy force and fleet made all sail for a larger port on the coast of a neighbouring republic, where he traded a hastily collected cargo of fruit for its value in cartridges for the five Martini rifles, the only guns that the navy could boast. Then to the telegraph office sped the admiral. Sprawling in his favourite corner, in his fast-decaying uniform, with his prodigious sabre distributed between his red legs, he waited for the long-delayed, but now soon expected, orders.

"Not yet, *Señor el Almirante*," the telegraph clerk would call to him—"*poco tiempo!*"

At the answer the admiral would plump himself down with a great rattling of scabbard to await the infrequent tick of the little instrument on the table.

"They will come," would be his unshaken reply; "I am the admiral."

At Moro Castle

MICHAEL SCOTT

When the day broke, with a strong breeze and a fresh shower, the *Firebrand* was about two miles off the Moro Castle, at the entrance of Santiago de Cuba.

I went aloft to look round me. The sea breeze blew strong until it reached within half a mile of the shore, where it stopped short, shooting in cat's-paws occasionally into the smooth belt of water beyond, where the long unbroken swell rolled like molten silver in the rising sun, without a ripple on its surface, until it dashed its gigantic undulations against the face of the precipitous cliffs on the shore and flew up in smoke. The entrance to the harbour is very narrow, and looked from my perch like a zigzag chasm in the rock, inlaid at the bottom with polished blue steel; so clear and calm and pellucid was the still water, wherein the frowning rocks, and magnificent trees on the banks, and the white Moro, rising with its grinning tiers of cannon, battery above battery, were reflected, as if it had been in a mirror.

We had shortened sail and fired a gun, and the signal for a pilot was flying, when the captain hailed me. "Does the sea breeze blow into the harbour yet, Mr. Cringle?"

"Not yet, sir; but it is creeping in fast."

"Very well. Let me know when we can run in. Mr. Yerk, back the main-topsail and heave the ship to."

Presently the pilot canoe, with the Spanish flag flying in the stern, came alongside; and the pilot, a tall brown man, a *Moreno*, as the Spaniards say, came on board. He wore a glazed cocked hat, rather an out-of-the-way finish to his figure, which was rigged in a simple Osnaburg shirt and pair of trousers. He came on the quarter-deck, and made his bow to the captain with all the ease in the world, wished him a good-morning, and taking his place by the quartermaster at the conn, he took charge of the ship. "Señor," quoth he to me, "is de harbour blow up yet? I mean, you see de *viento* walking into him?—de terral—dat is land wind—has he cease?"

"No," I answered; "the belt of smooth water is growing narrower fast; but the sea breeze does not blow into the channel yet. Now it has reached the entrance."

"Ah, den make sail, Señor Capitan; fill de main-topsail." We stood in, the scene becoming more and more magnificent as we approached the land.

The fresh green shores of this glorious island lay before us, fringed with white surf, as the ever-lasting ocean in its approach to it gradually changed its dark blue colour, as the water shoaled, into a bright joyous green under the blazing sun, before it tumbled in shaking thunders on the reefs. The undulating hills in the vicinity were all either cleared, and covered with the greenest verdure that imagination can picture, over which strayed large herds of cattle, or with forests of gigantic trees from amongst which, every now and then, peeped out some palm-thatched mountain settlement, with its small thread of blue smoke floating up into the calm clear morning air, while the blue hills in the distance rose higher and higher, and more and more blue, and dreamy, and indistinct, until their rugged summits could not be distinguished from the clouds through the glimmering hot haze of the tropics.

"By the mark seven," sung out the leadsman in the starboard, chains. "Quarter less three," responded he in the larboard, showing the inequalities of the surface at the bottom of the sea.

By this time, on our right hand, we were within pistol-shot of the Moro, where the channel is not above fifty yards across; indeed there is a chain, made fast to a rock on the opposite side, that can be hove up by a capstan until is is level with the water, so as to constitute an insurmountable obstacle to any attempt to force an entrance in time of war. As we stood in, the golden flag of Spain rose slowly on the staff at the Water Battery, and cast its large sleepy folds abroad in the breeze; but, instead of floating over mail-clad men, or Spanish soldiers in warlike array, three poor devils of half-naked mulattoes stuck their heads out of an embrasure under its shadow. We were mighty close upon leaving the bones of the old ship here, by the by; for at the very instant of entering the harbour's mouth, the land-wind checked us off, and very nearly hove us broadside on upon the rocks below the castle, against which the swell was breaking in thunder.

"Let go the anchor," sung out the captain.

"All gone, sir," promptly responded the boatswain from the forecastle. And as he spoke we struck once, twice, and very heavily the third time. But the breeze coming in strong, we fetched way again; and as the cable was promptly cut, we got safely off. However, on weighing the anchor afterwards, we found the water had been so shoal under the bows that the ship when she stranded had struck it and broken the stock short off by the ring.

The only laughable part of the story consisted in the old cook, an Irishman, with one leg and half an eye, scrambling out of the galley nearly naked, in his trousers, shirt, and greasy nightcap, and sprawling on all fours after two tubsful of yams, which the third thump had capsized all over the deck. "Oh, you scurvy-looking tief," said he, eyeing the pilot; "if it was running us ashore you were set on, why the blazes couldn't ye wait until the yams were in the copper, bad luck to ye—and them all scraped too! I do believe, *if they even had been taties it would have been all the same to you.*"

We stood on, the channel narrowing still more—the rocks rising to a height of a least five hundred feet from the water's edge, as sharply as if they had only yesterday been split asunder.

Noble trees shot out in all directions wherever they could find a little earth and a crevice to hold on by, almost meeting overhead in several places, and alive with all kinds of birds and beasts incidental to the climate; parrots of all sorts, great and small, *clomb*, and hung, and fluttered amongst the branches; and pigeons of numberless varieties; and the glancing woodpecker, with his small hammerlike *tap, tap, tap*; and the West India nightingale, and humming-birds of all hues; while cranes, black, white, and grey, frightened from their fishing-stations, stalked and peeped about, as awkwardly as a warrant-officer in his long-skirted coat on a Sunday; while whole flocks of ducks flew across the mastheads and through the rigging; and the dragon-like guanas, and lizards of many kinds, disported themselves amongst the branches.

And then the dark, transparent crystal depth of the pure waters under foot, reflecting all nature so steadily and distinctly, that in the hollows, where the overhanging foliage of the laurel-like bushes darkened the scene, you could not for your life tell where the elements met, so blended were earth and sea.

"Starboard," said I. I had now come on deck. "Starboard, or the main-topgallant-masthead *will be foul of the limb of that tree.* Foretop, there—lie out on the larboard foreyard-arm, and be ready to shove her off if she sheers too close."

"Let go the anchor," struck in the first lieutenant.

Splash—the cable rumbled through the hawse-hole.

"Now here are we brought up in paradise," quoth the doctor.

"Curukity coo—curukity coo," sung out a great bushy-whiskered sailor from the crows' nest, our old friend Timothy Tailtackle. "Here am I, Jack, a booby amongst the singing-birds," crowed he to one of his messmates in the maintop, as he clutched a branch of a tree in his hand, and swung himself up into it. But the ship, as Old Nick would have it, at the very instant dropped astern a few yards in swinging to her anchor, and that so suddenly, that she left him on his perch in the tree, converting his jest, poor fellow, into melancholy earnest.

"Oh Lord, sir!" sung out Timotheus, in a great quandary. "Captain, do heave ahead a bit—Murder—I shall never get down again! Do, Mr. Yerk, if you please, sir!" And there he sat twisting and craning himself about, and screwing his features into combinations evincing the most comical perplexity.

The captain, by way of a bit of fun, pretended not to hear him.

"Maintop, there," quoth he.

The midshipman in the top answered him, "Ay, ay, sir."

"Not you, Mr. Reefpoint; the captain of the top I want."

"He is not in the top, sir," responded little Reefpoint, chuckling like to choke himself.

"Where the devil is he, sir?"

"*Here*, sir," squealed Timothy, his usual gruff voice spindling into a small *cheep* through his great perplexity. "*Here*, sir."

"What are you doing there, sir? Come down this moment, sir. Rig out the main-topmast-studding-sail-boom, Mr. Reefpoint, and tell him to slew himself down by that long water-withe."

To hear was to obey. Poor Timothy clambered down to the fork of the tree, from which the withe depended, and immediately began to warp himself down, until he reached within three or four yards of the starboard fore-topsail-yard-arm; but the corvette *still* dropped astern, so that, after a vain attempt to hook on by his feet, he swung off into mid-air, hanging by his hands.

It was no longer a joke. "Here, you black fellows in the pilot canoe," shouted the captain, as he threw them a rope himself. "Pass the end of that line round the stump yonder—that one below the cliff, there—now pull like devils, pull."

They did not understand a word he said; but, comprehending his gestures, did what he wished.

"Now haul on the line, men—gently, that will do. Missed it again," continued the skipper, as the poor fellow once more made a fruitless attempt to swing himself on to the yard.

"Pay out the warp again," sung out Tailtackle—"quick, quick, let the ship swing from under, and leave me scope to dive, or I shall be obliged to let go, and be killed on the deck."

"God bless me, yes," said Transon, "stick out the warp, let her swing to her anchor."

In an instant all eyes were again fastened with intense anxiety on the poor fellow, whose strength was fast failing, and his grasp plainly relaxing.

"See all clear to pick me up, messmates."

Tailtackle slipped down to the extreme end of the black withe, that looked like a scorched snake, pressed his legs close together, pointing his toes downwards, and then steadying himself for a moment, with his hands right above his head, and his arms at the full stretch, he dropped, struck the water fairly, entering its dark blue depths without a splash, and instantly disappeared, leaving a white frothy mark on the surface.

"Did you ever see anything better done?" said Yerk. "Why, he clipped into the water with the speed of light, as clean and clear as if he had been a marlinspike."

"Thank heaven!" gasped the captain; for if he had struck the water horizontally, or fallen head-long, he would have been shattered in pieces—every bone would have been broken—he would have been as completely smashed as if he had dropped upon one of the limestone rocks on the ironbound shore.

"Ship, ahoy!" We were all breathlessly looking over the side where he fell, expecting to see him rise again; but the hail came from the water on t'other side. "Ship, ahoy—throw me a rope, good people—a rope, if you please. Do you mean to careen the ship, that you have all run to the starboard side, leaving me to be drowned to port here?"

"Ah, Tailtackle! well done, old boy," sung out a volley of voices, men and officers rejoiced to see the honest fellow alive. He clambered on board, in the bight of one of twenty ropes that were hove to him.

When he came on deck the captain slyly said, "I don't think you'll go a bird-nesting in a hurry again, Tailtackle."

Tim looked with a most quizzical expression at his captain all blue and breathless and dripping as he was; and then sticking his tongue slightly in his cheek, he turned away, without addressing him directly, but murmuring as he went, "A glass of grog now."

The captain, with whom he was a great favourite, took the hint. "Go below now, and turn in till eight bells, Tailtackle. Mafame," to his steward, "send him a glass of hot brandy grog."

Our instructions were to lie at St. Jago until three British ships, then loading, were ready for sea, and then to convoy them through the Caicos, or windward passage. As our stay was therefore likely to be ten days or a fortnight at the shortest, the boats were hoisted out, and we made our little arrange-ments and preparations for taking all the recreation in our power; and our worthy skipper, taut and stiff as he was at sea, always encouraged all kinds of fun and larking, both amongst the men and the officers, on occasions like the present.

Amongst his other pleasant qualities, he was a great boat-racer, constantly building and altering gigs and pulling-boats at his own expense, and matching the men against each other for small prizes. He had just finished what the old carpenter considered his *chef-d'œuvre*, and a curious affair this same masterpiece was. In the first place it was forty-two feet long over all, and only three and a half feet beam—the planking was not much above an eighth of an inch in thickness, so that if one of the crew had slipped his foot off the stretcher it must have gone through the bottom. There was a standing order that no man was to go into it with shoes on. She was to pull six oars, and her crew were the captains of the tops, the primest seamen in the ship, and the steersman, no less a character than the skipper himself.

Her name, for I love to be particular, was the *Dragonfly*; she was painted out and in of a bright red, amounting to a flame colour—oars red—the men wearing trousers and shirts of red flannel, and red net nightcaps—which common uniform the captain himself wore. I think I have said before that he was a very handsome man, but if I have not I say so now, and when he had taken his seat, and the *gigs*, all fine men, were seated each with his oar held upright upon his knees ready to be dropped into the water at the same instant, the craft and her crew formed to my eye as pretty a plaything for grown children as ever was seen.

"Give way, men," the oars dipped as clean as so many knives, without a sparkle, the gallant fellows stretched out, and away shot the *Dragonfly* like an arrow, the green water foaming into white smoke at the bows, and hissing away in her wake.

She disappeared in a twinkling round a reach of the canal where we were anchored, and we, the officers, for we must needs have our boat also, were making ready to be off, to have a shot at some beautiful cranes that, floating on there large pinions, slowly passed us with their long legs stuck straight out astern, and their longer necks gathered into their crops when we heard a loud shouting in the direction where the captain's boat had vanished.

Presently the *Devil's Darning Needle* as the Scottish part of the crew loved to call the *Dragonfly* stuck her long snout round the headland and came spinning along with a Spanish canoe manned by four negroes, and steered by an elderly gentleman, a sharp acute-looking little man in a gingham coat, in her wake, also pulling very fast; however, the Don seemed dead beat, and the captain was in great glee.

By this time both boats were alongside, and the old Spaniard, Don Ricardo Campana, addressed the captain, judging that he was one of the seamen. "Is the captain on board?" said he in Spanish. The captain, who understood the language, but did not speak it, answered him in French, which Don Ricardo seemed to speak fluently.

"No, sir, the captain is not on board; but there is Mr. Yerk, the first lieutenant, at the gangway." He had come for the letter-bag, he said, and if we had any newspapers, and could spare them, it would be conferring a great favour on him.

He got his letters and newspapers handed down, and very civilly gave the captain a dollar, who touched his cap, tipped the money to the men, and winking slightly to old Yerk and the rest of us, addressed himself to shove off. The old Don, drawing up his eyebrows a little (I *guess* he rather saw who was who, for all his make-believe innocence) bowed to the officers at the gangway, sat down, and desiring his people to use their broad-bladed, clumsy-looking oars, or paddles, began to move awkwardly away. We, that is, the gunroom officers, all except the second lieutenant, who had the watch, and the master, now got into our own gig also, rowed by ourselves, and away we all went in a covey; the purser and doctor, and three of the middies forward, Thomas Cringle, gent., pulling the stroke-oar, with old Moses Yerk as coxswain; and as the Dragonflies were all red, so we were all sea-green, boat, oars, trousers, shirts, and nightcaps.

We soon distanced the cumbrous-looking Don, and the strain was between the *Devil's Darning Needle* and our boat the *Watersprite*, which was making capital play, for although we had not the bottom of the topmen, yet we had more blood, so to speak, and we had already beaten them, in their last gig, all to sticks. But the *Dragonfly* was a new boat, and now in the water for the first time.

We were both of us so intent on our own match, that we lost sight of the Spaniard altogether, and the captain and the first lieutenant were bobbing in the stern-sheets of their respective gigs like a couple of *souple Tams*, as intent on the game as if all our lives had depended on it, when in an instant the long black dirty prow of the canoe was thrust in between us, the old Don singing out, "*Dexa mi lugar, paysanos, dexa mi lugar, mis hijos*" ("Leave me room, countrymen—leave me room, my children").

We kept away right and left, to look at the miracle; and there lay the canoe, rumbling and splashing, with her crew walloping about, and grinning and yelling like incarnate fiends, and as naked as the day they were born, and the old Don himself, so staid and so sedate and drawly as he was a minute before, now all alive, shouting "*Tira diablitos, tira!*" ("Pull, you devils, pull!"), flourishing a small paddle, with which he steered, about his head like a wheel, and dancing and jumping about in his seat.

"Zounds," roared the skipper—"why, topmen—why, gentlemen, give way for the honour of the ship—Gentlemen, stretch out—Men, pull like devils; twenty pounds if you beat him."

We pulled, and they pulled, and the water roared, and the men strained their muscles and sinews to cracking; and all was splash, splash, and *whiz, whiz*, and *pech, pech*, about us, *but it would not do*—the canoe headed us like a shot, and in passing, the cool old Don again subsided into a calm as suddenly as he had been roused from it, and sitting once more, stiff as a poker, turned round and touched his *sombrero*, "I will tell that you are coming, gentlemen."

It was now the evening, near nightfall, and we had been so intent on beating our awkward-looking opponent, that we had none of us time to look at the splendid scene that burst upon our view, on rounding a precipitous rock, from the crevices of which some magnificent trees shot up—their gnarled trunks and twisted branches overhanging the canal where we were pulling and anticipating the fast-falling darkness that was creeping over the fair face of nature; and there we floated, in the deep shadow of the cliff and trees—Dragonflies and Watersprites—motionless and silent, the boats floating so lightly that they scarcely seemed to touch the water, the men resting on their oars, and all of us rapt with the magnificence of the scenery around us, beneath us, and above us.

The left or western bank of the narrow entrance to the harbour from which we were now debouching, ran out in all its precipitousness and beauty (with its dark evergreen bushes overshadowing the deep blue waters, and its gigantic trees shooting forth high into the glowing western sky), until it joined the northern shore, when it sloped away gradually towards the east; the higher parts of the town sparkled in the evening sun, on this dun ridge, like golden turrets on the back of an elephant, while the houses that were in the shade covered the declivity with their dark masses, until it sank down to the water's edge.

On the right hand the haven opened boldly out into a basin about four miles broad by seven long, in which the placid waters spread out beyond the shadow of the western bank into one vast sheet of molten gold, with the canoe tearing along the shining surface, her side glancing in the sun, and her paddles flashing back his rays, and leaving a long train of living fire sparkling in her wake.

It was now about six o'clock in the evening; the sun had set to us, as we pulled along under the frowsing brow of the cliff, where the birds were fast settling on their nightly perches with small happy twitterings, and the lizards and numberless other chirping things began to send forth their evening hymn to the great Being who made them and us, and a solitary white-sailing owl would every now and then flit spectre-like from one green tuft, across the bald face of the cliff, to another, and the small divers around us were breaking up the black surface of the waters into little sparkling circles as they fished for their suppers. All was becoming brown and indistinct near us; but the level beams of the setting sun still lingered with a golden radiance upon the lovely city and the shipping at anchor before it, making their sails, where loosed to dry, glance like leaves of gold.

One half of every object, shipping, houses, trees, and hills, was gloriously illuminated; but even as we looked, the lower part of the town gradually sank into darkness, and faded from our sight—the deepening gloom cast by the high bank above us, like the dark shadow of a bad spirit, gradually crept on and on, and extended farther and farther; the sailing water-fowl in regular lines no longer made the water flash up like flame; the russet mantle of eve was fast extending over the entire hemisphere; the glancing minarets, and the tallest trees, and the topgallant-yards and masts of the shipping, alone flashed back the dying effulgence of the glorious orb, which every moment grew fainter and fainter, and redder and redder, until it shaded into purple, and the loud deep bell of the convent of La Merced swung over the still waters, announcing the arrival of evensong and the departure of day.

"Had we not better pull back to supper, sir?" quoth Moses Yerk to the captain. We all started, the men dipped their oars, our dreams were dispelled, the charm was broken—"Confound the matter-of-fact blockhead," or something very like it, grumbled the captain—"but give way, men," fast followed, and we returned towards the ship.

We had not pulled fifty yards, when we heard the distant rattle of the muskets of the sentries at the gangways, as they discharged them at sundown, and were remarking, as we were rowing leisurely along, upon the strange effect produced by the reports, as they were frittered away amongst the over-hanging cliffs in chattering reverberations, when the captain suddenly sang out, "Oars!" All hands lay on them. "Look there," he continued—"There—between the gigs—saw you ever anything like that, gentlemen?" We all leant over; and although the boats, from the *way* they had, were skimming along nearer seven than five knots, *there* lay a large shark—he must have been twelve feet long at the shortest—swimming right in the middle, and equidistant from both, and keeping *way* with us most accurately.

He was distinctly visible, from the strong and vivid phosphorescence excited by his rapid motion through the sleeping waters of the dark creek, which lit up his jaws, head, and whole body; his eyes were especially luminous, while a long wake of sparkles streamed astern of him from the lashing of his tail. As the boats lost speed, the luminousness of his appearance faded gradually as he shortened sail also, until he disappeared altogether. He was then at rest, and suspended motionless in the water; and the only thing that indicated his proximity was an occasional sparkle from the motion of a fin.

We brought the boats nearer together, after pulling a stroke or two, but he seemed to sink as we closed, until at last we could merely perceive an indistinct halo far down in the clear black profound. But as we separated, and resumed our original position, he again rose near the surface; and although the ripple and dip of the oars rendered him invisible while we were pulling, yet the moment we again rested on them, there was the monster, like a persecuting fiend, once more right between us, glaring on us, and apparently watching every motion. It was a terrible spectacle.

"A water-kelpie," murmured one of the captain's gigs, a Scotsman, "an evil sprite."

The men were evidently alarmed. "Stretch out, men; never mind the shark. He can't jump into the boat surely," said the skipper. "What the deuce are you afraid of?"

We arrived within pistol-shot of the ship. As we approached, the sentry hailed, "Boat, ahoy!"

"Firebrand," sang out the skipper, in reply.

"Man the side—gangway lanterns there," quoth the officer on duty; and by the time we were close to, there were two sides-men over the side with the man-ropes ready stuck out to our grasp, and two boys with lanterns above them. We got on deck, the officers touching their hats, and speedily the captain dived down the ladder, saying, as he descended, "Mr. Yerk, I shall be happy to see you and your boat's-crew at supper, or rather to a late dinner, at eight o'clock; but come down a moment as you are. Tailtackle, bring the gigs into the cabin to get a glass of grog, will you?"

"Ay, ay, sir," responded Timothy. "Down with you, you flaming thieves."

So down we all trundled into the cabin, masters and men.

The Phantom Ship

CAPTAIN MARRYAT

The ship was ready to sail for Europe; and Philip Vanderdecken went on board—hardly caring whither he went. To return to Terneuse was not his object; he could not bear the idea of revisiting the scene of so much happiness and so much misery. Amine's form was engraven on his heart, and he looked forward with impatience to the time when he should be summoned to join her in the land of spirits.

He had awakened as from a dream, after so many years of aberration of intellect. He was no longer the sincere Catholic that he had been; for he never thought of religion without his Amine's cruel fate being brought to his recollection. Still he clung on to the relic—he believed in that—and that only. It was his god—his creed—his everything—the passport for himself and for his father into the next world—the means whereby he should join his Amine—and for hours would he remain holding in his hand that object so valued—gazing upon it—recalling every important event in his life, from the death of his poor mother, and his first sight of Amine; to the last dreadful scene. It was to him a journal of his existence, and on it were fixed all his hopes for the future.

"When! oh, when is it to be accomplished!" was the constant subject of his reveries. "Blessed, indeed, will be the day when I leave this world of hate, and seek that other in which 'the weary are at rest.'"

The vessel on board of which Philip was embarked as a passenger was the *Nostra Señora da Monte*, a brig of three hundred tons, bound for Lisbon. The captain was an old Portuguese, full of superstition, and fond of arrack—a fondness rather unusual with the people of his nation. They sailed from Goa, and Philip was standing abaft, and sadly contemplating the spire of the Cathedral, in which he had last parted with his wife, when his elbow was touched, and he turned round.

"Fellow-passenger again!" said a well-known voice—it was that of the pilot Schriften.

There was no alteration in the man's appearance; he showed no marks of declining years; his one eye glared as keenly as ever.

Philip started, not only at the sight of the man, but at the reminiscences which his unexpected appearance brought to his mind. It was but for a second, and he was again calm and pensive.

"You here again, Schriften?" observed Philip. "I trust your appearance forebodes the accomplishment of my task."

"Perhaps it does," replied the pilot; "we both are weary."

Philip made no reply; he did not even ask Shriften in what manner he had escaped from the fort; he was indifferent about it; for he felt that the man had a charmed life.

"Many are the vessels that have been wrecked, Philip Vanderdecken, and many the souls summoned to their account by meeting with your father's ship, while you have been so long shut up," observed the pilot.

"May our next meeting with him be more fortunate—may it be the last!" replied Philip.

"No, no! rather may he fulfil his doom, and sail till the day of judgment," replied the pilot with emphasis.

"Vile caitiff! I have a foreboding that you will not have your detestable wish. Away!—leave me! or you shall find that although this head is blanched by misery, this arm has still some power."

Schriften scowled as he walked away; he appeared to have some fear of Philip, although it was not equal to his hate. He now resumed his former attempts of stirring up the ship's company against Philip, declaring that he was a Jonas, who would occasion the loss of the ship, and that he was connected with the *Flying Dutchman*. Philip very soon observed that he was avoided; and he resorted to counter-statements, equally injurious to Schriften, whom he declared to be a demon. The appearance of Schriften was so much against him, while that of Philip, on the contrary, was so prepossessing, that the people on board hardly knew what to think. They were divided: some were on the side of Philip—some on that of Schriften; the captain and many others looking with equal horror upon both, and longing for the time when they could be sent out of the vessel.

The captain, as we have before observed, was very superstitious, and very fond of his bottle. In the morning he would be sober and pray; in the afternoon he would be drunk, and swear at the very saints whose protection he had invoked but a few hours before.

"May Holy Saint Antonio preserve us, and keep us from temptation," said he, on the morning after a conversation with the passengers about the Phantom Ship. "All the saints protect us from harm," continued he, taking off his hat reverentially, and crossing himself. "Let me but rid myself of these two dangerous men without accident, and I will offer up a hundred wax candles, of three ounces each, to the shrine of the Virgin, upon my safe anchoring off the tower of Belem." In the evening he changed his language.

"Now, if that Maldetto Saint Antonio don't help us, may he feel the coals of hell yet; damn him and his pigs too; if he has the courage to do his duty, all will be well; but he is a cowardly wretch, he cares for nobody, and will not help those who call upon him in trouble. Carambo! that for you," exclaimed the captain, looking at the small shrine of the saint at the bittacle, and snapping his fingers at the image—"that for you, you useless wretch, who never help us in our trouble. The Pope must canonise some better saints for us, for all we have now are worn out. They could do something formerly, but now I would not give two ounces of gold for the whole calendar; as for you, you lazy old scoundrel," continued the captain, shaking his fist at poor Saint Antonio.

The ship had now gained off the southern coast of Africa, and was about one hundred miles from the Lagullas coast; the morning was beautiful, a slight ripple only turned over the waves, the breeze was light and steady, and the vessel was standing on a wind, at the rate of about four miles an hour.

"Blessed be the holy saints," said the captain, who had just gained the deck; "another little slant in our favour, and we shall lay our course. Again I say, blessed be the holy saints, and particularly our worthy patron Saint Antonio, who has taken under his peculiar protection the *Nostra Señora da Monte*. We have a prospect of fine weather; come, signors, let us down to breakfast, and after breakfast we will enjoy our cigarros upon the deck."

But the scene was soon changed; a bank of clouds rose up from the eastward, with a rapidity that, to the seamen's eyes, was unnatural, and it soon covered the whole firmament; the sun was obscured, and all was one deep and unnatural gloom; the wind subsided, and the ocean was hushed. It was not exactly dark, but the heavens were covered with one red haze, which gave an appearance as if the world was in a state of conflagration.

In the cabin the increased darkness was first observed by Philip, who went on deck; he was followed by the captain and passengers, who were in a state of amazement. It was unnatural and incomprehensible. "Now, holy Virgin, protect us—what can this be?" exclaimed the captain in a fright. "Holy Saint Antonio, protect us—but this is awful."

"There! there!" shouted the sailors, pointing to the beam of the vessel. Every eye looked over the gunnel to witness what had occasioned such exclamations. Philip, Schriften, and the captain were side by side. On the beam of the ship, not more than two cables' length distant, they beheld, slowly rising out of the water, the tapering mast-head and spars of another vessel. She rose, and rose gradually; her topmasts and top-sail yards, with the sails set, next made their appearance; higher and higher she rose up from the element. Her lower masts and rigging, and, lastly, her hull showed itself above the surface. Still she rose up till her ports, with her guns, and at last the whole of her floatage was above water, and there she remained close to them, with her main-yard squared, and hove-to.

"Holy Virgin!" exclaimed the captain, breathless; "I have known ships to *go down*, but never to *come up* before. Now will I give one thousand candles, of ten ounces each, to the shrine of the Virgin to save us in this trouble. One thousand wax candles! Hear me, blessed lady; ten ounces each. Gentlemen," cried the captain to the passengers, who stood aghast, "why don't you promise? Promise, I say; *promise*, at all events."

"The Phantom Ship—*The Flying Dutchman*," shrieked Schriften; "I told you so, Philip Vanderdecken; there is your father. He! he!"

Philip's eyes had remained fixed on the vessel; he perceived that they were lowering down a boat from her quarter. "It is possible," thought he, "I shall now be permitted!" and Philip put his hand into his bosom and grasped the relic.

The gloom now increased, so that the strange vessel's hull could but just be discovered through the murky atmosphere. The seamen and passengers threw themselves down on their knees, and invoked their saints. The captain ran down for a candle, to light before the image of St. Antonio, which he took out of its shrine, and kissed with much apparent affection and devotion, and then replaced.

Shortly afterwards the splash of oars was heard alongside, and a voice calling out, "I say, my good people, give us a rope from forward."

No one answered, or complied with the request. Schriften only went up to the captain, and told him that if they offered to send letters they must not be received or the vessel would be doomed, and all would perish.

A man now made his appearance from over the gunnel, at the gangway. "You might as well have let me had a side rope, my hearties," said he, as he stepped on deck; "where is the captain?"

"Here," replied the captain, trembling from head to foot. The man who accosted him appeared a weather-beaten seaman, dressed in a fur cap and canvas petticoats; he held some letters in his hand.

"What do you want?" at last screamed the captain.

"Yes—what do you want?" continued Schriften. "He! he!"

"What, you here, pilot?" observed the man; "well—I thought you had gone to Davy's locker, long enough ago."

"He! he!" replied Schriften, turning away.

"Why, the fact is, captain, we have had very foul weather, and we wish to send letters home; I do believe that we shall never get round this Cape."

"I can't take them," cried the captain.

"Can't take them! well, it's very odd—but every ship refuses to take our letters; it's very unkind—seamen should have a feeling for brother seamen, especially in distress. God knows, we wish to see our wives and families again; and it would be a matter of comfort to them, if they only could hear from us."

"I cannot take your letters—the saints preserve us," replied the captain.

"We have been a long while out," said the seaman, shaking his head.

"How long?" inquired the captain, not knowing what to say.

"We can't tell; our almanack was blown overboard, and we have lost our reckoning. We never have our latitude exact now for we cannot tell the sun's declination for the right day."

"Let *me* see your letters," said Philip, advancing, and taking them out of the seaman's hands.

"They must not be touched," screamed Schriften.

"Out, monster!" replied Philip, "who dares interfere with me?"

"Doomed—doomed—doomed!" shrieked Schriften, running up and down the deck, and then breaking into a wild fit of laughter.

"Touch not the letters," said the captain, trembling as if in an ague fit.

Philip made no reply, but held out his hand for the letters.

"Here is one from our second mate, to his wife at Amsterdam, who lives on Waser Quay."

"Waser Quay has long been gone, my good friend; there is now a large dock for ships where it once was," replied Philip.

"Impossible!" replied the man; "here is another from the boatswain to his father, who lives in the old market-place."

"The old market-place has long been pulled down, and there now stands a church upon the spot."

"Impossible!" replied the seaman; "here is another from myself to my sweetheart, Vrow Ketser—with money to buy her a new brooch."

Philip shook his head—"I remember seeing an old lady of that name buried some thirty years ago."

"Impossible! I left her young and blooming. Here's one for the house of Slutz & Co., to whom the ship belongs."

"There's no such house now," replied Philip; "but I have heard that many years ago there was a firm of that name."

"Impossible! you must be laughing at me. Here is a letter from our captain to his son—"

"Give it me," cried Philip, seizing the letter, he was about to break the seal when Schriften snatched it out of his hand, and threw it over the lee gunnel.

"That's a scurvy trick for an old shipmate," observed the seaman. Schriften made no reply, but catching up the other letters which Philip had laid down on the capstan, he hurled them after the first.

The strange seaman shed tears, and walked again to the side. "It is very hard—very unkind," observed he, as he descended; "the time may come when you may wish that your family should know your situation." So saying, he disappeared—in a few seconds was heard the sound of the oars, retreating from the ship.

"Holy St. Antonio!" exclaimed the captain, "I am lost in wonder and fright. Steward, bring me up the arrack."

The steward ran down for the bottle; being as much alarmed as his captain, he helped himself before he brought it up to his commander. "Now," said the captain, after keeping his mouth for two minutes to the bottle, and draining it to the bottom, "what is to be done next?"

"I'll tell you," said Schriften, going up to him. "That man there has a charm hung round his neck; take it from him and throw it overboard, and your ship will be saved; if not, it will be lost, with every soul on board."

"Yes, yes, it's all right, depend upon it," cried the sailors.

"Fools," replied Philip, "do you believe that wretch? Did you not hear the man who came on board recognise him, and call him shipmate? He is the party whose presence on board will prove so unfortunate."

"Yes, yes," cried the sailors, "it's all right, the man did call him shipmate."

"I tell you it's all wrong," cried Schriften; "that is the man, let him give up the charm."

"Yes, yes; let him give up the charm," cried the sailors, and they rushed upon Philip.

Philip started back to where the captain stood. "Madmen, know ye what ye are about? It is the holy cross that I wear round my neck. Throw it overboard if you dare, and your souls are lost for ever": and Philip took the relic from his bosom and showed it to the captain.

"No, no, men," exclaimed the captain, who was now more settled in his nerves; "that won't do—the saints protect us."

The seamen, however, became clamorous; one portion were for throwing Schriften overboard, the other for throwing Philip; at last, the point was decided by the captain, who directed the small skiff, hanging astern, to be lowered down, and ordered both Philip and Schriften to get into it. The seamen approved of this arrangement, as it satisfied both parties. Philip made no objection; Schriften screamed and fought, but he was tossed into the boat. There he remained trembling in the stern sheets, while Philip, who had seized the sculls, pulled away from the vessel in the direction of the Phantom Ship.

In a few minutes the vessel which Philip and Schriften had left was no longer to be discerned through the thick haze; the Phantom Ship was still in sight, but at a much greater distance from them than she was before. Philip pulled hard towards her, but although hove-to, she appeared to increase her distance from the boat. For a short time he paused on his oars to regain his breath, when Schriften rose up and took his seat in the stern sheets of the boat. "You may pull and pull, Philip Vanderdecken," observed Schriften; "but you will not gain that ship—no, no, that cannot be—we may have a long cruise together, but you will be as far from your object at the end of it as you are now at the commencement. Why don't you throw me overboard again? You would be all the lighter—He! he!"

"I threw you overboard in a state of frenzy," replied Philip, "when you attempted to force from me my relic."

"And have I not endeavoured to make others take it from you this very day?—Have I not— He! he!"

"You have," rejoined Philip; "but I am now convinced, that you are as unhappy as myself, and that in what you are doing, you are only following your destiny, as I am mine. Why and wherefore I cannot tell, but we are both engaged in the same mystery;—if the success of my endeavours depends upon guarding the relic, the success of yours depends upon your obtaining it, and defeating my purpose by so doing. In this matter we are both agents, and you have been, as far as my mission is concerned, my most active enemy. But, Schriften, I have not forgotten, and never will, that you kindlily *did advise* my poor Amine; that you prophesied to her what would be her fate, if she did not listen to your counsel; that you were no enemy of hers, although you have been, and are still mine. Although my enemy, for her sake I *forgive you*, and will not attempt to harm you."

"You do then *forgive your enemy*, Philip Vanderdecken?" replied Schriften, mournfully, "for such, I acknowledge myself to be."

"I do, with *all my heart, with all my soul*," replied Philip.

"Then you have conquered me, Philip Vanderdecken; you have now made me your friend, and your wishes are about to be accomplished. You would know who I am. Listen:—when your father, defying the Almighty's will, in his rage took my life, he was vouchsafed a chance of his doom being cancelled, through the merits of his son. I had also my appeal, which was for *vengeance*; it was granted that I should remain on earth, and thwart your will. That as long as we were enemies, you should not succeed; but that when you had conformed to the highest attribute of Christianity, proved on the holy cross, that of *forgiving your enemy*, your task should be fulfilled. Philip Vanderdecken, you have forgiven your enemy, and both our destinies are now accomplished."

With their hands raised to heaven.

As Schriften spoke, Philip's eyes were fixed upon him. He extended his hand to Philip—it was taken; and as it was pressed, the form of the pilot wasted as it were into the air, and Philip found himself alone.

"Father of Mercy, I thank Thee," said Philip, "that my task is done, and that I again may meet my Amine."

Philip then pulled towards the Phantom Ship, and found that she no longer appeared to leave him; on the contrary, every minute he was nearer and nearer, and at last he threw in his oars, climbed her sides, and gained her deck.

The crew of the vessel crowded round him.

"Your captain," said Philip; "I must speak with your captain."

"Who shall I say, sir?" demanded one, who appeared to be the first mate.

"Who?" replied Philip. "Tell him his son would speak to him, his son Philip Vanderdecken."

Shouts of laughter from the crew followed this answer of Philip's; and the mate, as soon as they ceased, observed with a smile:

"You forget, sir, perhaps you would say his father."

"Tell him his son, if you please," replied Philip; "take no note of grey hairs."

"Well, sir, here he is coming forward," replied the mate, stepping aside, and pointing to the captain.

"What is all this?" inquired the captain.

"Are you Philip Vanderdecken, the captain of this vessel?"

"I am, sir," replied the other.

"You appear not to know me! But how can you? You saw me but when I was only three years old; yet may you remember a letter which you gave to your wife."

"Ha!" replied the captain; "and who then are you?"

"Time has stopped with you, but with those who live in the world he stops not! and for those who pass a life of misery, he hurries on still faster. In me, behold your son, Philip Vanderdecken, who has obeyed your wishes; and after a life of such peril and misery as few have passed, has at last fulfilled his vow, and now offers to his father the precious relic that he required to kiss."

Philip drew out the relic, and held it towards his father. As if a flash of lightning had passed through his mind, the captain of the vessel started back, clasped his hands, fell on his knees, and wept.

"My son, my son!" exclaimed he, rising, and throwing himself into Philip's arms, "my eyes are opened—the Almighty knows how long they have been obscured." Embracing each other, they walked aft, away from the men, who were still crowded at the gangway.

"My son, my noble son, before the charm is broken—before we resolve, as we must into the elements oh! let me kneel in thanksgiving and contrition: my son, my noble son, receive a father's thanks," exclaimed Vanderdecken. Then with tears of joy and penitence he humbly addressed himself to that Being whom he once so awfully defied.

The elder Vanderdecken knelt down: Philip did the same; still embracing each other with one arm, while they raised on high the other, and prayed.

For the last time the relic was taken from the bosom of Philip and handed to his father—and his father raised his eyes to heaven and kissed it. And as he kissed it, the long, tapering, upper spars of the Phantom vessel, the yards and sails that were set, fell into dust, fluttered in the air and sank upon the wave. Then mainmast, foremast, bowsprit, everything above the deck, crumbled into atoms and disappeared.

Again he raised the relic to his lips and the work of destruction continued, the heavy iron guns sank through the decks and disappeared; the crew of the vessel (who were looking on) crumbled down into skeletons, and dust, and fragments of ragged garments; and there were none left on board the vessel in the semblance of life but the father and the son.

Once more did he put the sacred emblem to his lips, and the beams and timber separated, the decks of the vessel slowly sank, and the remnants of the hull floated upon the water; and as the father and son—the one young and vigorous, the other old and decrepit—still kneeling, still embracing, with their hands raised to heaven, sank slowly under the deep blue wave the lurid sky was for a moment illumined by a lightning cross.

Then did the clouds which obscured the heavens roll away swift as thought—the sun again burst out in all his splendour—the rippling waves appeared to dance with joy. The screaming seagull again whirled in the air, and the scared albatross once more slumbered on the wing. The porpoise tumbled and tossed in his sportive play, the albicore and dolphin leaped from the sparkling sea. All nature smiled as if it rejoiced that the charm was dissolved for ever, and that "THE PHANTOM SHIP" WAS NO MORE.

The Seed of McCoy

JACK LONDON

The *Pyrenees*, her iron sides pressed low in the water by her cargo of wheat, rolled sluggishly, and made it easy for the man who was climbing aboard from out a tiny outrigger canoe. As his eyes came level with the rail, so that he could see inboard, it seemed to him that he saw a dim, almost indiscernible haze. It was more like an illusion, like a blurring film that had spread abruptly over his eyes. He felt an inclination to brush it away, and the same instant he thought that he was growing old and that it was time to send to San Francisco for a pair of spectacles.

As he came over the rail he cast a glance aloft at the tall masts, and next, at the pumps. They were not working. There seemed nothing the matter with the big ship, and he wondered why she had hoisted the signal of distress. He thought of his happy islanders, and hoped it was not disease. Perhaps the ship was short of water or provisions. He shook hands with the captain, whose gaunt face and careworn eyes made no secret of the trouble, whatever it was. At the same moment the new-comer was aware of a faint, indefinable smell. It seemed like that of burnt bread, but different.

He glanced curiously about him. Twenty feet away a weary-faced sailor was caulking the deck. As his eye lingered on the man, he saw suddenly arise from under his hands a faint spiral of haze that curled and twisted and was gone. By now he had reached the deck. His bare feet were pervaded by a dull warmth that quickly penetrated the thick calluses. He knew now the nature of the ship's distress. His eyes roved swiftly forward, where the full crew of weary-faced sailors regarded him eagerly. The glance from his liquid brown eyes swept over them like a benediction, soothing them, wrapping them about as in the mantle of a great peace. "How long has she been afire, captain?" he asked, in a voice so gentle and unperturbed that it was as the cooing of a dove.

At first the captain felt the peace and content of it stealing in upon him; then the consciousness of all that he had gone through and was going through smote him, and he was resentful. By what right did this ragged beach-comber, in dungaree trousers and a cotton shirt, suggest such a thing as peace and content to him and his overwrought, exhausted soul? The captain did not reason this; it was the unconscious process of emotion that caused his resentment.

"Fifteen days," he answered shortly. "Who are you?"

"My name is McCoy," came the answer, in tones that breathed tenderness and compassion.

"I mean, are you the pilot?"

McCoy passed the benediction of his gaze over the tall, heavy-shouldered man with the haggard, unshaven face who had joined the captain.

"I am as much a pilot as anybody," was McCoy's answer. "We are all pilots here, captain, and I know every inch of these waters."

But the captain was impatient.

"What I want is some of the authorities. I want to talk with them, and blame quick."

"Then I'll do just as well."

Again that insidious suggestion of peace, and his ship a raging furnace beneath his feet! The captain's eyebrows lifted impatiently and nervously, and his fist clenched as if he were about to strike a blow with it.

"Who the blazes are you?" he demanded.

"I am the chief magistrate," was the reply, in a voice that was still the softest and gentlest imaginable.

The tall, heavy-shouldered man broke out in a harsh laugh that was partly amusement, but mostly hysterical. Both he and the captain regarded McCoy with incredulity and amazement. That this barefooted beach-comber should possess such high-sounding dignity was inconceivable. His cotton shirt, unbuttoned, exposed a grizzled chest and the fact that there was no undershirt beneath. A worn straw hat failed to hide the ragged grey hair. Half-way down his chest descended an untrimmed patriarchal beard. In any slop-shop, two shillings would have outfitted him complete as he stood before them.

"Any relation to the McCoy of the *Bounty*?" the captain asked.

"He was my great grand-father."

"Oh," the captain said, then bethought himself. "My name is Davenport, and this is my first mate, Mr. Konig."

They shook hands.

"And now to business." The captain spoke quickly, the urgency of a great haste pressing his speech. "We've been on fire for over two weeks. She's ready to break all hell loose any moment. That's why I held for Pitcairn. I want to beach her, or scuttle her, and save the hull."

"Then you made a mistake, captain," said McCoy. "You should have slacked away for Mangareva. There's a beautiful beach there, in a lagoon where the water is like a mill-pond."

"But we're here, ain't we?" the first mate demanded. "That's the point. We're here, and we've got to do something."

McCoy shook his head kindly.

"You can do nothing here. There is no beach. There isn't even anchorage."

"Gammon!" said the mate. "Gammon!" he repeated loudly, as the captain signalled him to be more soft-spoken. "You can't tell me that sort of stuff. Where d'ye keep your own boats, hey—your schooner, or cutter, or whatever you have? Hey? Answer me that."

McCoy smiled as gently as he spoke. His smile was a caress, an embrace that surrounded the tired mate and sought to draw him into the quietude and rest of McCoy's tranquil soul.

"We have no schooner or cutter," he replied. "And we carry our canoes to the top of the cliff."

"You've got to show me," snorted the mate. "How d'ye get around to the other islands, hey? Tell me that."

"We don't get around. As governor of Pitcairn, I sometimes go. When I was younger I was away a great deal—sometimes on the trading schooners, but mostly on the missionary brig. But she's gone now, and we depend on passing vessels. Sometimes we have had as high as six calls in one year. At other times, a year, and even longer, has gone by without one passing ship. Yours is the first in seven months."

"And you mean to tell me——" the mate began.

But Captain Davenport interfered.

"Enough of this. We're losing time. What is to be done, Mr. McCoy?"

The old man turned his brown eyes, sweet as a woman's, shoreward, and both captain and mate followed his gaze around from the lonely rock of Pitcairn to the crew clustering forward and waiting anxiously for the announcement of a decision. McCoy did not hurry. He thought smoothly and slowly, step by step, with the certitude of a mind that was never vexed or outraged by life.

"The wind is light now," he said finally. "There is a heavy current setting to the westward."

"That's what made us fetch to leeward," the captain interrupted, desiring to vindicate his seamanship.

"Yes, that is what fetched you to leeward," McCoy went on. "Well, you can't work up against this current to-day. And if you did, there is no beach. Your ship will be a total loss."

He paused, and captain and mate looked despair at each other.

"But I will tell you what you can do. The breeze will freshen to-night around midnight—see those tails of cloud and that thickness to windward, beyond the point there? That's where she'll come from, out of the south-east, hard. It is three hundred miles to Mangareva. Square away for it. There is a beautiful bed for your ship there."

The mate shook his head.

"Come into the cabin and we'll look at the chart," said the captain.

McCoy found a stifling, poisonous atmosphere in the pent cabin. Stray waftures of invisible gases bit his eyes and made them sting. The deck was hotter, almost unbearably hot to his bare feet. The sweat poured out of his body. He looked almost with apprehension about him. This malignant, internal heat was astounding. It was a marvel that the cabin did not burst into flames. He had a feeling as of being in a huge bake-oven where the heat might at any moment increase tremendously and shrivel him up like a blade of grass.

As he lifted one foot and rubbed the hot sole against the leg of his trousers, the mate laughed in a savage, snarling fashion.

"The anteroom of hell," he said. "Hell herself is right down there under your feet."

"It's hot!" McCoy cried involuntarily, mopping his face with a bandana handkerchief.

"Here's Mangareva," the captain said, bending over the table and pointing to a black speck in the midst of the white blankness of the chart. "And here, in between, is another island. Why not run for that?"

McCoy did not look at the chart.

"That's Crescent Island," he answered. "It is uninhabited, and it is only two or three feet above water. Lagoon, but no entrance. No, Mangareva is the nearest place for your purpose."

"Mangareva it is, then," said Captain Davenport, interrupting the mate's growling objection. "Call the crew aft, Mr. Konig."

The sailors obeyed, shuffling wearily along the deck and painfully endeavouring to make haste. Exhaustion was evident in every movement. The cook came out of his galley to hear, and the cabin-boy hung about near him.

When Captain Davenport had explained the situation and announced his intention of running for Mangareva, an uproar broke out. Against a background of throaty rumbling arose inarticulate cries of rage, with here and there a distinct curse, or word, or phrase. A shrill Cockney voice soared and dominated for a moment, crying, "'Ear 'im! After bein 'in 'ell for fifteen days—an' now 'e wants us to sail this floatin' 'ell to sea again!"

The captain could not control them, but McCoy's gentle presence seemed to rebuke and calm them, and the muttering and cursing died away, until the full crew, save here and there an anxious face directed at the captain, yearned dumbly towards the green-clad peaks and beetling coast of Pitcairn.

Soft as a spring zephyr was the voice of McCoy:

"Captain, I thought I heard some of them say they were starving."

"Aye," was the answer, "and so we are. I've had a sea-biscuit and a spoonful of salmon in the last two days. We're on whack. You see, when we discovered the fire, we battened down immediately to suffocate the fire. And then we found how little food there was in the pantry. But it was too late. We didn't dare break out the lazarette. Hungry? I'm just as hungry as they are."

He spoke to the men again, and again the throat-rumbling and cursing arose, their faces convulsed and animal-like with rage. The second and third mates had joined the captain, standing behind him at the break of the poop. Their faces were set and expressionless; they seemed bored, more than anything else, by this mutiny of the crew. Captain Davenport glanced questioningly at his first mate, and that person merely shrugged his shoulders in token of his helplessness.

"You see," the captain said to McCoy, "you can't compel sailors to leave the safe land and go to sea on a burning vessel. She has been their floating coffin for over two weeks now. They are worked out, and starved out, and they've got enough of her. We'll beat up for Pitcairn."

But the wind was light, the *Pyrenees'* bottom was foul, and she could not beat up against the strong westerly current. At the end of two hours she had lost three miles. The sailors worked eagerly, as if by main strength they could compel the *Pyrenees* against the adverse elements. But steadily, port tack and starboard tack, she sagged off to the westward. The captain paced restlessly up and down, pausing occasionally to survey the vagrant smoke-wisps and to trace them back to the portions of the deck from which they sprang. The carpenter was engaged constantly in attempting to locate such places, and, when he succeeded, in caulking them tighter and tighter.

"Well, what do you think?" the captain finally asked McCoy, who was watching the carpenter with all a child's interest and curiosity in his eyes.

McCoy looked shoreward, where the land was disappearing in the thickening haze.

"I think it would be better to square away for Mangareva. With that breeze that is coming, you'll be there to-morrow evening."

"But what if the fire breaks out? It is liable to do it any moment."

"Have your boats ready in the falls. The same breeze will carry your boats to Mangareva if the ship burns out from under."

Captain Davenport debated for a moment, and then McCoy heard the question he had not wanted to hear, but which he knew was surely coming.

"I have no chart of Mangareva. On the general chart it is only a fly-speck. I would not know where to look for the entrance into the lagoon. Will you come along and pilot her in for me?"

McCoy's serenity was unbroken.

"Yes, captain," he said, with the same quiet unconcern with which he would have accepted an invitation to dinner, "I'll go with you to Mangareva."

Again the crew was called aft, and the captain spoke to them from the break of the poop.

"We've tried to work her up, but you see how we've lost ground. She's setting off in a two-knot current. This gentleman is the Honourable McCoy, Chief Magistrate and Governor of Pitcairn Island. He will come along with us to Mangareva. So you see the situation is not so dangerous. He would not make such an offer if he thought he was going to lose his life. Besides, whatever risk there is, if he of his own free will come on board and take it, we can do no less. What do you say for Mangareva?"

This time there was no uproar. McCoy's presence, the surety and calm that seemed to radiate from him, had had its effect. They conferred with one another in low voices. There was little arguing. They were virtually unanimous, and they shoved the Cockney out as their spokesman. That worthy was overwhelmed with consciousness of the heroism of himself and his mates, and with flashing eyes he cried:

"If 'e will, we will!"

The crew mumbled its assent and started forward.

"One moment, captain," McCoy said, as the other was turning to give orders to the mate. "I must go ashore first."

Mr. Konig was thunderstruck, staring at McCoy as if he were a madman.

"Go ashore!" the captain cried. "What for? It will take you three hours to get there in your canoe."

McCoy measured the distance of the land away and nodded.

"Yes; it is six now. I won't get ashore till nine. The people cannot be assembled earlier than ten. As the breeze freshens up to-night, you can begin to work up against it, and pick me up at daylight to-morrow morning."

"In the name of reason and common sense," the captain burst forth, "what do you want to assemble the people for? Don't you realise that my ship is burning beneath me?"

McCoy was as placid as a summer sea, and the other's anger produced not the slightest ripple upon it.

"Yes, captain," he cooed in his dovelike voice, "I do realise that your ship is burning. That is why I am going with you to Mangareva. But I must get permission to go with you. It is our custom. It is an important matter when the governor leaves the island. The people's interests are at stake, and so they have the right to vote their permission or refusal. But they will give it, I know that."

"Are you sure?"

"Quite sure."

"Then if you know they will give it, why bother with getting it? Think of the delay—a whole night."

"It is our custom," was the imperturbable reply. "Also, I am the governor, and I must make arrangements for the conduct of the island during my absence."

"But it is only a twenty-four hour run to Mangareva," the captain objected. "Suppose it took you six times that long to return to windward that would bring you back by the end of a week."

McCoy smiled his large, benevolent smile.

"Very few vessels come to Pitcairn, and when they do, they are usually from San Francisco or from around the Horn. I shall be fortunate if I get back in six months. I may be away a year, and I may have to go to San Francisco in order to find a vessel that will bring me back. My father once left Pitcairn to be gone three months, and two years passed before he could get back. Then, too, you are short of food. If you have to take to the boats, and the weather comes up bad, you may be days in reaching land. I can bring off two canoe loads of food in the morning. Dried bananas will be best. As the breeze freshens, you beat up against it. The nearer you are, the bigger loads I can bring off. Good-bye."

He held out his hand. The captain shook it, and was reluctant to let go. He seemed to cling to it as a drowning sailor clings to a lifebuoy.

"How do I know you will come back in the morning?" he asked.

"Yes, that's it!" cried the mate. "How do we know but what he's skinning out to save his own hide?"

McCoy did not speak. He looked at them sweetly and benignantly, and it seemed to them that they received a message from his tremendous certitude of soul.

The captain released his hand, and, with a last sweeping glance that embraced the crew in its benediction, McCoy went over the rail and descended into his canoe.

The wind freshened, and the *Pyrenees*, despite the foulness of her bottom, won half a dozen miles away from the westerly current. At daylight, with Pitcairn three miles to windward, Captain Davenport made out two canoes coming off to him. Again McCoy clambered up the side and dropped over the rail to the hot deck. He was followed by many packages of dried bananas, each package wrapped in dry leaves.

"Now, captain," he said, "swing the yards and drive for dear life. You see, I am no navigator," he explained a few minutes later, as he stood by the captain aft, the latter with gaze wandering from aloft to overside as he estimated the *Pyrenees'* speed. "You must fetch her to Mangareva. When you have picked up the land, then I will pilot her in. What do you think she is making?"

"Eleven," Captain Davenport answered, with a final glance at the water rushing past.

"Eleven. Let me see, if she keeps up that gait, we'll sight Mangareva between eight and nine o'clock to-morrow morning. I'll have her on the beach by ten, or by eleven at latest. And then your troubles will be all over."

It almost seemed to the captain that the blissful moment had already arrived, such was the persuasive convincingness of McCoy. Captain Davenport had been under the fearful strain of navigating his burning ship for over two weeks, and he was beginning to feel that he had had enough.

A heavier flaw of wind struck the back of his neck and whistled by his ears. He measured the weight of it, and looked quickly overside.

"The wind is making all the time," he announced. "The old girl's doing nearer twelve than eleven right now. If this keeps up, we'll be shortening down to-night."

All day the *Pyrenees*, carrying her load of living fire, tore across the foaming sea. By nightfall, royals and topgallant-sails were in, and she flew on into the darkness, with great crested seas roaring after her. The auspicious wind had had its effect, and fore and aft a visible brightening was apparent. In the second dog-watch some careless soul started a song, and by eight bells the whole crew was singing.

Captain Davenport had his blankets brought up and spread on top of the house.

"I've forgotten what sleep is," he explained to McCoy. "I'm all in. But give me a call at any time you think necessary."

At three in the morning he was aroused by a gentle tugging at his arm. He sat up quickly, bracing himself against the skylight, stupid yet from his heavy sleep. The wind was thrumming its war-song in the rigging, and a wild sea was buffeting the *Pyrenees*. Amidships she was wallowing first one rail under and then the other, flooding the waist more often than not. McCoy was shouting something he could not hear. He reached out, clutched the other by the shoulder, and drew him close so that his own ear was close to the other's lips.

"It's three o'clock," came McCoy's voice, still retaining its dovelike quality, but curiously muffled, as if from a long way off. "We've run two hundred and fifty. Crescent Island is only thirty miles away, somewhere there dead ahead. There's no lights on it. If we keep running, we'll pile up, and lose ourselves as well as the ship."

"What d'ye think—heave to?"

"Yes; heave to till daylight. It will only put us back four hours."

So the *Pyrenees*, with her cargo of fire, was hove to, biting the teeth of the gale, and fighting, and smashing the pounding seas. She was a shell, filled with a conflagration, and on the outside of the shell, clinging precariously, the little motes of men, by pull and haul, helped her in the battle.

"It is most unusual, this gale," McCoy told the captain, in the lee of the cabin. "By rights there should be no gale at this time of the year. But everything about the weather has been unusual. There has been a stoppage of the trades, and now it's howling right out of the trade quarter." He waved his hand into the darkness, as if his vision could dimly penetrate for hundreds of miles. "It is off to the westward. There is something big making off there somewhere—a hurricane or something. We're lucky to be so far to the eastward. But this is only a little blow," he added. "It can't last. I can tell you that much."

By daylight the gale had eased down to normal. But daylight revealed a new danger. It had come on thick. The sea was covered by a fog, or, rather, by a pearly mist that was fog-like in density in so far as it obstructed vision, but that was no more than a film on the sea, for the sun shot through it and filled it with a glowing radiance.

The deck of the *Pyrenees* was making more smoke than on the preceding day, and the cheerfulness of officers and crew had vanished. In the lee of the galley the cabin-boy could be heard whimpering. It was his first voyage, and the fear of death was at his heart. The captain wandered about like a lost soul, nervously chewing his moustache, scowling, unable to make up his mind what to do.

"What do you think?" he asked, pausing by the side of McCoy, who was making a breakfast off fried bananas and a mug of water.

McCoy finished the last banana, drained the mug, and looked slowly around. In his eyes was a smile of tenderness as he said:

"Well, captain, we might as well drive as burn. Your decks are not going to hold out for ever. They are hotter this morning. You haven't a pair of shoes I can wear? It is getting uncomfortable for my bare feet."

The *Pyrenees* shipped two heavy seas as she was swung off and put once more before it, and the first mate expressed a desire to have all that water down in the hold, if only it could be introduced without taking off the hatches. McCoy ducked his head into the binnacle and watched the course set.

"I'd hold her up some more, captain," he said. "She's been making drift when hove to."

"I've set it to a point higher already," was the answer. "Isn't that enough?"

"I'd make it two points, captain. This bit of a blow kicked that westerly current ahead faster than you imagine."

Captain Davenport compromised on a point and a half, and then went aloft, accompanied by McCoy and the first mate, to keep a look-out for land. Sail had been made, so that the *Pyrenees* was doing ten knots. The following sea was dying down rapidly. There was no break in the pearly fog, and by ten o'clock Captain Davenport was growing nervous. All hands were at their stations, ready, at the first warning of land ahead, to spring like fiends to the task of bringing the *Pyrenees* up on the wind. That land ahead, a surf-washed outer reef, would be perilously close when it revealed itself in such a fog.

Another hour passed. The three watchers aloft stared intently into the pearly radiance.

"What if we miss Mangareva?" Captain Davenport asked abruptly.

McCoy, without shifting his gaze, answered softly:

"Why, let her drive, captain. That is all we can do. All the Paumotus are before us. We can drive for a thousand miles through reefs and atolls. We are bound to fetch up somewhere."

"Then drive it is." Captain Davenport evidenced his intention of descending to the deck. "We've missed Mangareva. God knows where the next land is. I wish I'd held up that other half-point," he confessed a moment later. "This cursed current plays the devil with a navigator."

"The old navigators called the Paumotus the Dangerous Archipelago," McCoy said when they had partly regained the poop. "This very current was partly responsible for that name."

"I was talking with a sailor chap in Sydney once," said Mr. Konig. "He'd been trading in the Pautomus. He told me insurance was eighteen per cent. Is that right?"

McCoy smiled and nodded.

"Except that they don't insure," he explained. "The owners write off twenty per cent of the cost of their schooners each year."

Captain Davenport groaned. "That makes the life of a schooner only five years!" He shook his head sadly, murmuring, "Bad waters! bad waters!"

Again they went into the cabin to consult the big general chart; but the poisonous vapours drove them coughing and gasping on deck.

"Here is Moerenhout Island." Captain Davenport pointed it out on the chart, which he had spread on the house. "It can't be more than a hundred miles to leeward."

"A hundred and ten." McCoy shook his head doubtfully. "It might be done, but it is very difficult. I might beach her, and then, again, I might put her on the reef. A bad place, a very bad place."

"We'll take the chance," was Captain Davenport's decision, as he set about working out the course.

Sail was shortened early in the afternoon, to avoid running past in the night; and in the second dog-watch the crew manifested its regained cheerfulness. Land was so very near, and their troubles would be over in the morning.

But morning broke clear, with a blazing tropic sun. The south-east trade had swung around to the eastward, and was driving the *Pyrenees* through the water at an eight-knot clip. Captain

Davenport worked up his dead reckoning, allowing generously for drift, and announced Moerenhout Island to be not more than ten miles off. The *Pyrenees* sailed the ten miles; she sailed ten miles more; and the look-outs at the three mastheads saw naught but the naked, sun-washed sea.

"But the land is there, I tell you," Captain Davenport shouted to them from the poop.

McCoy smiled soothingly, but the captain glared about him like a madman, fetched his sextant, and took a chronometer sight.

"I knew I was right," he almost shouted, when he had worked up the observation. "Twenty-one, fifty-five, south; one-thirty-six, two, west. There you are. We're eight miles to windward yet. What did you make it out, Mr. Konig?"

The first mate glanced at his own figures, and said in a low voice:

"Twenty-one, fifty-five all right; but my longitude's one-thirty-six, forty-eight. That puts us considerably to leeward——"

But Captain Davenport ignored his figures with so contemptuous a silence as to make Mr. Konig grit his teeth and curse savagely under his breath.

"Keep her off," the captain ordered the man at the wheel. "Three points—steady there, as she goes!"

Then he returned to his figures and worked them over. The sweat poured from his face. He chewed his moustache, his lips, and his pencil, staring at the figures as a man might at a ghost. Suddenly, with a fierce, muscular outburst, he crumpled the scribbled paper in his fist and crushed it under foot. Mr. Konig grinned vindictively and turned away, while Captain Davenport leaned against the cabin and for half an hour spoke no word, contenting himself with gazing to leeward with an expression of musing hopelessness on his face.

"Mr. McCoy," he broke silence abruptly. "The chart indicates a group of islands, but not how many, off there to the north'ard, or nor'-nor'-westward, about forty miles—the Acteon Islands. What about them?"

"There are four, all low," McCoy answered. "First, to the south-east is Matueri—no people, no entrance to the lagoon. Then comes Tenarunga. There used to be about a dozen people there, but they may be all gone now. Anyway, there is no entrance for a ship—only a boat entrance, with a fathom of water. Vehauga and Teua-raro are the other two. No entrances, no people, very low. There is no bed for the *Pyrenees* in that group. She would be a total wreck."

"Listen to that!" Captain Davenport was frantic. "No people! No entrances! What in the devil are islands good for?

"Well, then," he barked suddenly, like an excited terrier, "the chart gives a whole mess of islands off to the nor'-west. What about them? What one has an entrance where I can lay my ship?"

McCoy calmly considered. He did not refer to the chart. All these islands, reefs, shoals, lagoons, entrances, and distances were marked on the chart of his memory. He knew them as the city dweller knows his buildings, streets, and alleys.

"Papakena and Vanavana are off there to the westward, or west-nor'-westward, a hundred miles, and a bit more," he said. "One is uninhabited, and I heard that the people on the other had gone off to Cadmus Island. Anyway, neither lagoon has an entrance. Ahunui is another hundred miles on to the nor'-west. No entrance, no people."

"Well, forty miles beyond them are two islands?" Captain Davenport queried, raising his head from the chart.

McCoy shook his head.

"Paros and Manuhungi—no entrances, no people. Nengo-Nengo is forty miles beyond them, in turn, and it has no people and no entrance. But there is Hao Island. It is just the place. The lagoon is thirty miles long and five miles wide. There are plenty of people. You can usually find water. And any ship in the world can go through the entrance."

He ceased, and gazed solicitously at Captain Davenport, who, bending over the chart with a pair of dividers in hand, had just emitted a low groan.

"Is there any lagoon with an entrance anywhere nearer than Hao Island?" he asked.

"No, captain; that is the nearest."

"Well, it's three hundred and forty miles." Captain Davenport was speaking very slowly, with decision. "I won't risk the responsibility of all these lives. I'll wreck her on the Acteons. And she's a good ship, too," he added regretfully, after altering the course, this time making more allowance than ever for the westerly current.

An hour later the sky was overcast. The south-east trade still held, but the ocean was a checker-board of squalls.

"We'll be there by one o'clock," Captain Davenport announced confidently—"by two o'clock at the outside. McCoy, you put her ashore on the one where the people are."

The sun did not appear again, nor, at one o'clock, was any land to be seen. Captain Davenport looked astern at the *Pyrenees'* canting wake.

"Good Lord!" he cried. "An easterly current! Look at that!"

Mr. Konig was incredulous. McCoy was non-committal, though he said that in the Paumotus there was no reason why it should not be an easterly current. A few minutes later a squall robbed the *Pyrenees* temporarily of all her wind, and she was left rolling heavily in the trough.

"Where's that deep lead? Over with it, you there!" Captain Davenport held the lead-line and watched it sag off to the north-east. "There, look at that! Take hold of it for yourself."

McCoy and the mate tried it, and felt the line thrumming and vibrating savagely to the grip of the tidal stream.

"A four-knot current," said Mr. Konig.

"An easterly current instead of a westerly," said Captain Davenport, glaring accusingly at McCoy, as if to cast the blame for it upon him.

"That is one of the reasons, captain, for insurance being eighteen per cent in these waters," McCoy answered cheerfully. "You never can tell. The currents are always changing. There was a man who wrote books, I forget his name, in the yacht *Casco*. He missed Takaroa by thirty miles and fetched Tikei, all because of the shifting currents. You are up to windward now, and you'd better keep off a few points."

"But how much has this current set me?" the captain demanded irately. "How am I to know how much to keep off?"

"I don't know, captain," McCoy said with great gentleness.

The wind returned, and the *Pyrenees*, her deck smoking and shimmering in the bright grey light, ran off dead to leeward. Then she worked back, port tack and starboard tack, crisscrossing her track, combing the sea for the Acteon Islands, which the masthead look-outs failed to sight.

Captain Davenport was beside himself. His rage took the form of sullen silence, and he spent the afternoon in pacing the poop or leaning against the weather-shrouds. At nightfall, without even consulting McCoy, he squared away and headed into the north-west. Mr. Konig, surreptitiously consulting chart and binnacle, and McCoy, openly and innocently consulting the binnacle, knew that they were running for Hao Island. By midnight the squalls ceased, and the stars came out. Captain Davenport was cheered by the promise of a clear day.

"I'll get an observation in the morning," he told McCoy, "though what my latitude is, is a puzzler. But I'll use the Sumner method and settle that. Do you know the Sumner line?"

And thereupon he explained it in detail to McCoy.

The day proved clear, the trade blew steadily out of the east, and the *Pyrenees* just as steadily logged her nine knots. Both the captain and mate worked out the position on a Sumner line, and agreed, and at noon agreed again, and verified the morning sights by the noon sights.

"Another twenty-four hours and we'll be there," Captain Davenport assured McCoy. "It's a miracle the way the old girl's decks hold out. But they can't last. They can't last. Look at the smoke, more and more every day. Yet it was a tight deck to begin with, fresh-caulked in 'Frisco. I was surprised when the fire first broke out and we battened down. Look at that!"

He broke off to gaze with dropped jaw at a spiral of smoke that coiled and twisted in the lee of the mizzen-mast twenty feet above the deck.

"Now, how did that get there?" he demanded indignantly.

Beneath it there was no smoke. Crawling up from the deck, sheltered from the wind by the mast, by some freak it took form and visibility at that height. It writhed away from the mast, and for a moment overhung the captain like some threatening portent. The next moment the wind whisked it away, and the captain's jaw returned to place.

"As I was saying, when we first battened down, I was surprised. It was a tight deck, yet it leaked smoke like a sieve. And we've caulked and caulked ever since. There must be tremendous pressure underneath to drive so much smoke through."

That afternoon the sky became overcast again, and squally, drizzly weather set in. The wind shifted back and forth between south-east and north-east, and at midnight the *Pyrenees* was caught aback by a sharp squall from the south-west, from which point the wind continued to blow intermittently.

"We won't make Hao until ten or eleven," Captain Davenport complained at seven in the morning, when the fleeting promise of the sun had been erased by hazy cloud masses in the eastern sky. And the next moment he was plaintively demanding, "And what are the currents doing?"

Look-outs at the mastheads could report no land, and the day passed in drizzling calms and violent squalls. By nightfall a heavy sea began to make from the west. The barometer had fallen to 29.50. There was no wind, and still the ominous sea continued to increase. Soon the *Pyrenees* was rolling madly in the huge waves that marched in an unending procession from out of the darkness of the west. Sail was shortened as fast as both watches could work, and when a tired crew had finished, its grumbling and complaining voices, peculiarly animal-like and menacing, could be heard in the darkness. Once the starboard watch was called aft to lash down and make secure, and the men openly advertised their sullenness and unwillingness. Every slow movement was a protest and a threat. The atmosphere was moist and sticky like mucilage, and in the absence of wind all hands seemed to pant and gasp for air. The sweat stood out on faces and bare arms, and Captain Davenport for one, his face more gaunt and careworn than ever, and his eyes troubled and staring, was oppressed by a feeling of impending calamity.

"It's off to the westward," McCoy said encouragingly. "At worst, we'll only be on the edge of it."

But Captain Davenport refused to be comforted, and by the light of a lantern read up the chapter in his *Epitome* that related to the strategy of shipmasters in cyclonic storms. From somewhere amidships the silence was broken by a low whimpering from the cabin-boy.

"Oh, shut up!" Captain Davenport yelled suddenly and with such force as to startle every man on board and to frighten the offender into a wild wail of terror.

"Mr. Konig," the captain said in a voice that trembled with rage and nerves, "will you kindly step for'ard and stop that brat's mouth with a deck mop?"

But it was McCoy who went forward, and in a few minutes had the boy comforted and asleep.

Shortly before daybreak the first breath of air began to move from out the south-east, increasing swiftly to a stiff and stiffer breeze. All hands were on deck waiting for what might be behind it.

"We're all right now, captain," said McCoy, standing close to his shoulder. "The hurricane is to the west'ard, and we are south of it. This breeze is the in-suck. It won't blow any harder. You can begin to put sail on her."

"But what's the good? Where shall I sail? This is the second day without observations, and we should have sighted Hao Island yesterday morning. Which way does it bear, north, south, east, or what? Tell me that, and I'll make sail in a jiffy."

"I am no navigator, captain," McCoy said in his mild way.

"I used to think I was one," was the retort, "before I got into these Paumotus."

At midday the cry of "Breakers ahead!" was heard from the look-out. The *Pyrenees* was kept off and sail after sail was loosed and sheeted home. The *Pyrenees* was sliding through the water and fighting a current that threatened to set her down upon the breakers. Officers and men were working like mad, cook and cabin-boy, Captain Davenport himself, and McCoy all lending a hand. It was a close shave. It was a low shoal, a bleak and perilous place over which the seas broke unceasingly, where no man could live, and on which not even sea-birds could rest. The *Pyrenees* was swept within a hundred yards of it before the wind carried her clear, and at this moment the panting crew, its work done, burst out in a torrent of curses upon the head of McCoy—of McCoy who had come on board, and proposed the run to Mangareva, and lured them all away from the safety of Pitcairn Island to certain destruction in this baffling and terrible stretch of sea. But McCoy's tranquil soul was undisturbed. He smiled at them with simple and gracious benevolence, and, somehow, the exalted goodness of him seemed to penetrate to their dark and sombre souls, shaming them, and from very shame stilling the curses vibrating in their throats.

"Bad waters! bad waters!" Captain Davenport was murmuring as his ship forged clear; but he broke off abruptly to gaze at the shoal which should have been dead astern, but which was already on the *Pyrenees'* weather-quarter and working up rapidly to windward.

He sat down and buried his face in his hands. And the first mate saw, and McCoy saw, and the crew saw, what he had seen. South of the shoal an easterly current had set them down upon it; north of the shoal an equally swift westerly current had clutched the ship and was sweeping her away.

"I've heard of these Paumotus before," the captain groaned, lifting his blanched face from his hands. "Captain Moyendale told me about them after losing his ship on them. And I laughed at him behind his back. God forgive me, I laughed at him. What shoal is that?" he broke off to ask McCoy.

"I don't know, captain."

"Why don't you know?"

"Because I never saw it before, and because I never heard of it. I do know that it is not charted. These waters have never been thoroughly surveyed."

"Then you don't know where we are?"

"No more than you do," McCoy said gently.

At four in the afternoon coco-nut trees were sighted, apparently growing out of the water. A little later the low land of an atoll was raised above the sea.

"I know where we are now, captain." McCoy lowered the glasses from his eyes. "That's Resolution Island. We are forty miles beyond Hao Island, and the wind is in our teeth."

"Get ready to beach her, then. Where's the entrance?"

"There's only a canoe passage. But now that we know where we are, we can run for Barclay de Tolley. It is only one hundred and twenty miles from here, due nor'-nor'-west. With this breeze we can be there by nine o'clock to-morrow morning."

Captain Davenport consulted the chart and debated with himself.

"If we wreck her here," McCoy added, "we'd have to make the run to Barclay de Tolley in the boats just the same."

The captain gave his orders, and once more the *Pyrenees* swung off for another run across the inhospitable sea.

And the middle of the next afternoon saw despair and mutiny on her smoking deck. The current had accelerated, the wind had slackened, and the *Pyrenees* had sagged off to the west. The look-out sighted Barclay de Tolley to the eastward, barely visible from the masthead, and vainly and for hours the *Pyrenees* tried to beat up to it. Ever, like a mirage, the coco-nut trees hovered on the horizon, visible only from the masthead. From the deck they were hidden by the bulge of the world.

Again Captain Davenport consulted McCoy and the chart. Makemo lay seventy-five miles to the south-west. Its lagoon was thirty miles long, and its entrance was excellent. When Captain Davenport gave his orders, the crew refused duty. They announced that they had had enough of hell-fire under their feet. There was the land. What if the ship could not make it? They could make it in the boats. Let her burn, then. Their lives amounted to something to them. They had served faithfully the ship, now they were going to serve themselves.

They sprang to the boats, brushing the second and third mates out of the way, and proceeded to swing the boats out and to prepare to lower away. Captain Davenport and the first mate, revolvers in hand, were advancing to the break of the poop, when McCoy, who had climbed on top of the cabin, began to speak.

He spoke to the sailors, and at the first sound of his dovelike, cooing voice they paused to hear. He extended to them his own ineffable serenity and peace. His soft voice and simple thoughts flowed out to them in a magic stream, soothing them against their wills. Long-forgotten things came back to them, and some remembered lullaby songs of childhood and the content and rest of the mother's arm at the end of the day. There was no more trouble, no more danger, no more irk, in all the world. Everything was as it should be, and it was only a matter of course that they should turn their backs upon the land and put to sea once more with hell-fire hot beneath their feet.

McCoy spoke simply; but it was not what he spoke. It was his personality that spoke more eloquently than any word he could utter. It was an alchemy of soul occultly subtle and profoundly deep—a mysterious emanation of the spirit, seductive, sweetly humble, and terribly imperious. It was illumination in the dark crypts of their souls, a compulsion of purity and gentleness vastly greater than that which resided in the shining death-spitting revolvers of the officers.

The men wavered reluctantly where they stood, and those who had loosed the turns made them fast again. Then one, and then another, and then all of them, began to sidle awkwardly away.

McCoy's face was beaming with childlike pleasure as he descended from the top of the cabin. There was no trouble. For that matter there had been no trouble averted. There never had been any trouble, for there was no place for such in the blissful world in which he lived.

"You hypnotised 'em," Mr. Konig grinned at him, speaking in a low voice.

"Those boys are good," was the answer. "Their hearts are good. They have had a hard time, and they have worked hard, and they will work hard to the end."

Mr. Konig had no time to reply. His voice was ringing out orders, the sailors were springing to obey, and the *Pyrenees* was paying slowly off from the wind until her bow should point in the direction of Makemo.

The wind was very light, and after sun-down almost ceased. It was insufferably warm, and fore and aft men sought vainly to sleep. The deck was too hot to lie upon, the poisonous vapours, oozing through the seams, crept like evil spirits over the ship, stealing into the nostrils and windpipes of the unwary and causing fits of sneezing and coughing. The stars blinked lazily in the dim vault overhead; and the full moon, rising in the east, touched with its light the myriads of wisps and threads and spidery films of smoke that intertwined and writhed and twisted along the deck, over the rails, and up the masts and shrouds.

"Tell me," Captain Davenport said, rubbing his smarting eyes, "what happened with that *Bounty* crowd after they reached Pitcairn? The account I read said they burnt the *Bounty*, and that they were not discovered until many years later. But what happened in the meantime? I've always been curious to know. They were men with their necks in the rope. There were some native men, too. And then there were women. That made it look like trouble right from the jump."

"There was trouble," McCoy answered. "They were bad men. They quarrelled about the women right away. One of the mutineers, Williams, lost his wife. All the women were Tahitian women.

His wife fell from the cliffs when hunting sea-birds. Then he took the wife of one of the native men away from him. All the native men were made very angry by this, and they killed off nearly all the mutineers. Then the mutineers that escaped killed off all the native men. The women helped. And the natives killed each other. Everybody killed everybody. They were terrible men.

"Timiti was killed by two other natives while they were combing his hair in friendship. The white men had sent them to do it. Then the white men killed them. The wife of Tullaloo killed him in a cave because she wanted a white man for husband. They were very wicked. God had hidden His face from them. At the end of two years all the native men were murdered, and all the white men except four. They were Young, John Adams, McCoy, who was my great-grandfather, and Quintal. He was a very bad man too. Once, just because his wife did not catch enough fish for him, he bit off her ear."

"They were a bad lot!" Mr. Konig exclaimed.

"Yes, they were very bad," McCoy agreed, and went on serenely cooing of the blood and lust of his iniquitous ancestry. "My great-grandfather escaped murder in order to die by his own hand. He made a still and manufactured alcohol from the roots of the ti-plant. Quintal was his chum, and they got drunk together all the time. At last McCoy got delirium tremens, tied a rock to his neck, and jumped into the sea.

"Quintal's wife, the one whose ear he bit off, also got killed by falling from the cliffs. Then Quintal went to Young and demanded his wife, and went to Adams and demanded his wife. Adams and Young were afraid of Quintal. They knew he would kill them. So they killed him, the two of them together, with a hatchet. Then Young died. And that was about all the trouble they had."

"I should say so," Captain Davenport snorted. "There was nobody left to kill."

"You see, God had hidden His face," McCoy said.

By morning no more than a faint air was blowing from the eastward, and, unable to make appreciable southing by it, Captain Davenport hauled up full-and-by on the port tack. He was afraid of that terrible westerly current which had cheated him out of so many ports of refuge. All day the calm continued, and all night, while the sailors, on a short ration of dried banana, were grumbling. Also, they were growing weak, and complaining of stomach pains caused by the straight banana diet. All day the current swept the *Pyrenees* to the westward, while there was no wind to bear her south. In the middle of the first dog-watch, coco-nut trees were sighted due south, their tufted heads rising above the water and marking the low-lying atoll beneath.

"That is Taenga Island," McCoy said. "We need a breeze to-night, or else we'll miss Makemo."

"What's become of the south-east trade?" the captain demanded. "Why don't it blow? What's the matter?"

"It is the evaporation from the big lagoons—there are so many of them," McCoy explained. "The evaporation upsets the whole system of trades. It even causes the wind to back up and blow gales from the south-west. This is the Dangerous Archipelago, captain."

Captain Davenport faced the old man, opened his mouth, and was about to curse, but paused and refrained. McCoy's presence was a rebuke to the blasphemies that stirred in his brain and trembled in his larynx. McCoy's influence had been growing during the many days they had been together. Captain Davenport was an autocrat of the sea, fearing no man, never bridling his tongue, and now he found himself unable to curse in the presence of this old man with the feminine brown eyes and the voice of a dove. When he realized this, Captain Davenport experienced a distinct shock. This old man was merely the seed of McCoy, of McCoy of the *Bounty*, the mutineer fleeing from the hemp that waited him in England, the McCoy who was a power for evil in the early days of blood and lust and violent death on Pitcairn Island.

Captain Davenport was not religious, yet in that moment he felt a mad impulse to cast himself at the other's feet—and to say he knew not what. It was an emotion that so deeply stirred him, rather than a coherent thought, and he was aware in some vague way of his own unworthiness and smallness in the presence of this other man who possessed the simplicity of a child and the gentleness of a woman.

Of course he could not humble himself so before the eyes of his officers and men. And yet the anger that had prompted the blasphemy still raged in him. He suddenly smote the cabin with his clenched hand and cried:

"Look here, old man, I won't be beaten. These Paumotus have cheated and tricked me and made a fool of me. I refuse to be beaten. I am going to drive this ship, and drive and drive and drive clear through the Paumotus to China but what I find a bed for her. If every man deserts, I'll stay by her. I'll show the Paumotus. They can't fool me. She's a good girl, and I'll stick by her as long as there's a plank to stand on. You hear me?"

"And I'll stay with you, captain," McCoy said.

During the night, light, baffling airs blew out of the south, and the frantic captain, with his cargo of fire, watched and measured his westward drift, and went off by himself at times to curse softly so that McCoy should not hear.

Daylight showed more palms growing out of the water to the south.

"That's the leeward point of Makemo," McCoy said. "Katiu is only a few miles to the west. We may make that."

But the current, sucking between the two islands, swept them to the north-west, and at one in the afternoon they saw the palms of Katiu rise above the sea and sink back into the sea again.

A few minutes later, just as the captain had discovered that a new current from the north-east had gripped the *Pyrenees*, the masthead look-outs raised coco-nut palms in the north-west.

"It is Raraka," said McCoy. "We won't make it without wind. The current is drawing us down to the south-west. But we must watch out. A few miles farther on a current flows north and turns in a circle to the north-west. This will sweep us away to Fakarava, and Fakarava is the place for the *Pyrenees* to find her bed."

"They can sweep all they—all they well please," Captain Davenport remarked with heat. "We'll find a bed for her somewhere just the same."

But the situation on the *Pyrenees* was reaching a culmination. The deck was so hot that it seemed an increase of a few degrees would cause it to burst into flames. In many places even the heavy-soled shoes of the men were no protection, and they were compelled to step lively to avoid scorching their feet. The smoke had increased and grown more acrid. Every man on board was suffering from inflamed eyes, and they coughed and strangled like a crew of tuberculosis patients. In the afternoon the boats were swung out and equipped. The last several packages of dried bananas were stored in them, as well as the instruments of the officers. Captain Davenport even put the chronometer into the long-boat, fearing the blowing up of the deck at any moment.

All night this apprehension weighed heavily on all, and in the first morning light, with hollow eyes and ghastly faces, they stared at one another as if in surprise that the, *Pyrenees* still held together and that they still were alive.

Walking rapidly at times, and even occasionally breaking into an undignified hop-skip-and-run, Captain Davenport inspected his ship's deck.

"It is a matter of hours now, if not of minutes," he announced on his return to the poop.

The cry of land came down from the masthead. From the deck the land was invisible, and McCoy went aloft, while the captain took advantage of the opportunity to curse some of the bitterness out of his heart. But the cursing was suddenly stopped by a dark line on the water which he sighted to the north-east. It was not a squall, but a regular breeze—the disrupted trade-wind, eight points out of its direction, but resuming business once more.

"Hold her up, captain," McCoy said as soon as he reached the poop. "That's the easterly point of Fakarava, and we'll go in through the passage full tilt, and wind abeam, and every sail drawing."

At the end of an hour, the coco-nut trees and the low-lying land were visible from the deck. The feeling that the end of the *Pyrenees'* resistance was imminent weighed heavily on everybody. Captain Davenport had the three boats lowered and dropped short astern, a man in each to keep them apart. The *Pyrenees* closely skirted the shore, the surf-whitened atoll a bare two cable-lengths away.

"Get ready to wear her, captain," McCoy warned.

And a minute later the land parted, exposing a narrow passage and the lagoon beyond, a great mirror, thirty miles in length and a third as broad.

"Now, captain."

For the last time the yards of the *Pyrenees* swung around as she obeyed the wheel and headed into the passage. The turns had scarcely been made, and nothing had been coiled down, when the men and mates swept back to the poop in panic terror. Nothing had happened, yet they averred that something was going to happen. They could not tell why. They merely knew that it was about to happen. McCoy started forward to take up his position on the bow in order to con the vessel in; but the captain gripped his arm and whirled him around.

"Do it from here," he said. "That deck's not safe. What's the matter?" he demanded the next instant. "We're standing still."

McCoy smiled.

"You are bucking a seven-knot current, captain," he said. "That is the way the full ebb runs out of this passage."

At the end of another hour the *Pyrenees* had scarcely gained her length, but the wind freshened and she began to forge ahead.

"Better get into the boats, some of you," Captain Davenport commanded.

His voice was still ringing, and the men were just beginning to move in obedience, when the amidship deck of the *Pyrenees*, in a mass of flame and smoke, was flung upward into the sails and rigging, part of it remaining there and the rest falling into the sea. The wind being abeam was what had saved the men crowded aft. They made a blind rush to gain the boats, but McCoy's voice, carrying its convincing message of vast calm and endless time, stopped them.

"Take it easy," he was saying. "Everything is all right. Pass that boy down somebody, please."

The man at the wheel had forsaken it in a funk, and Captain Davenport had leaped and caught the spokes in time to prevent the ship from yawing in the current and going ashore.

"Better take charge of the boats," he said to Mr. Konig. "Tow one of them short, right under the quarter. . . . When I go over, it'll be on the jump."

Mr. Konig hesitated, then went over the rail and lowered himself into the boat.

"Keep her off half a point, captain."

Captain Davenport gave a start. He had thought he had the ship to himself.

"Ay, ay; half a point it is," he answered.

Amidships, the *Pyrenees* was an open, flaming furnace, out of which poured an immense volume of smoke which rose high above the masts and completely hid the forward part of the ship. McCoy, in the shelter of the mizzen-shrouds, continued his difficult task of conning the ship through the intricate channel. The fire was working aft along the deck from the seat of explosion, while the soaring tower of canvas on the mainmast went up and vanished in a sheet of flame. Forward, though they could not see them, they knew that the headsails were still drawing.

"If only she don't burn all her canvas off before she makes inside," the captain groaned.

"She'll make it," McCoy assured him with supreme confidence. "There is plenty of time. She is bound to make it. And once inside, we'll put her before it; that will keep the smoke away from us and hold back the fire from working aft."

A tongue of flame sprang up the mizzen, reached hungrily for the lowest tier of canvas, missed it, and vanished. From aloft a burning shred of ropestuff fell square on the back of Captain Davenport's neck. He acted with the celerity of one stung by a bee as he reached up and brushed the offending fire from his skin.

"How is she heading, captain?"

"Nor'-west by west."

"Keep her west-nor'-west."

Captain Davenport put the wheel up and steadied her.

"West by north, captain."

"West by north she is."

"And now west."

Slowly, point by point, as she entered the lagoon, the *Pyrenees* described the circle that put her before the wind; and point by point, with all the calm certitude of a thousand years of time to spare, McCoy chanted the changing course.

"Another point, captain."

"A point it is."

Captain Davenport whirled several spokes over suddenly reversing and coming back one to check her.

"Steady."

"Steady she is—right on it."

Despite the fact that the wind was now astern, the heat was so intense that Captain Davenport was compelled to steal sidelong glances into the binnacle, letting go the wheel, now with one hand, now with the other, to rub or shield his blistering cheeks. McCoy's beard was crinkling and shrivelling, and the smell of it, strong in the other's nostrils, compelled him to look toward McCoy with sudden solicitude. Captain Davenport was letting go the spokes alternately with his hands in order to rub their blistering backs against his trousers. Every sail on the mizzen-mast vanished in a rush of flame, compelling the two men to crouch and shield their faces.

"Now," said McCoy, stealing a glance ahead at the low shore, "four points up, captain, and let her drive."

Shreds and patches of burning rope and canvas were falling about them and upon them. The tarry smoke from a smouldering piece of rope at the captain's feet set him off into a violent coughing fit, during which he still clung to the spokes.

The *Pyrenees* struck, her bow lifted, and she ground ahead gently to a stop. A shower of burning fragments, dislodged by the shock, fell about them. The ship moved ahead again and struck a second time. She crushed the fragile coral under her keel, drove on, and struck a third time.

"Hard over," said McCoy. "Hard over?" he questioned gently, a minute later.

"She won't answer," was the reply.

"All right. She is swinging around." McCoy peered over the side. "Soft, white sand. Couldn't ask better. A beautiful bed."

As the *Pyrenees* swung around, her stern away from the wind, a fearful blast of smoke and flame poured aft. Captain Davenport deserted the wheel in blistering agony. He reached the painter of the boat that lay under the quarter, then looked for McCoy, who was standing aside to let him go down.

"You first," the captain cried, gripping him by the shoulder and almost throwing him over the rail. But the flame and smoke were too terrible, and he followed hard after McCoy, both men wriggling on the rope and sliding down into the boat together. A sailor in the bow, without waiting for orders, slashed the painter through with his sheath-knife. The oars, poised in readiness, bit into the water, and the boat shot away.

"A beautiful bed, captain," McCoy murmured, looking back.

"Ay, a beautiful bed, and all thanks to you," was the answer.

The three boats pulled away for the white beach of pounded coral, beyond which, on the edge of a coco-nut grove, could be seen a half-dozen grasshouses, and a score or more of excited natives, gazing wide-eyed at the conflagration that had come to land.

The boats grounded and they stepped out on the white beach.

"And now," said McCoy, "I must see about getting back to Pitcairn."

BOOK XII of Homer's Odyssey

SAMUEL BUTLER

After we were clear of the river Oceanus, and had got out into the open sea, we went on till we reached the Aeaean island where there is dawn and sunrise as in other places. We then drew our ship on to the sands and got out of her on to the shore, where we went to sleep and waited till day should break.

"Then, when the child of morning, rosy-fingered Dawn, appeared, I sent some men to Circe's house to fetch the body of Elpenor. We cut firewood from a wood where the headland jutted out into the sea, and after we had wept over him and lamented him we performed his funeral rites. When his body and armor had been burned to ashes, we raised a cairn, set a stone over it, and at the top of the cairn we fixed the oar that he had been used to row with.

"While we were doing all this, Circe, who knew that we had got back from the house of Hades, dressed herself and came to us as fast as she could; and her maidservants came with her bringing us bread, meat, and wine. Then she stood in the midst of us and said, 'You have done a bold thing in going down alive to the house of Hades, and you will have died twice, to other people's once. Now, then, stay here for the rest of the day, feast your fill, and go on with your voyage at daybreak tomorrow morning. In the meantime I will tell Odysseus about your course, and will explain everything to him so as to prevent your suffering from misadventure either by land or sea.'

"We agreed to do as she had said, and feasted through the livelong day to the going down of the sun, but when the sun had set and it came on dark, the men laid themselves down to sleep by the stern cables of the ship. Then Circe took me by the hand and bade me be seated away from the others, while she reclined by my side and asked me all about our adventures.

" 'So far so good,' said she, when I had ended my story, 'and now pay attention to what I am about to tell you—heaven itself, indeed, will recall it to your recollection. First you will come to the Sirens who enchant all who come near them. If anyone unwarily draws in too close and hears the singing of the Sirens, his wife and children will never welcome him home again, for they sit in a green field and warble him to death with the sweetness of their song. There is a great heap of dead men's bones lying all around, with the flesh still rotting off them. Therefore pass these Sirens by, and stop your men's ears with wax that none of them may hear; but if you like you can listen yourself, for you may get the men to bind you as you stand upright on a cross-piece halfway up the mast, and they must lash the rope's ends to the mast itself, that you may have the pleasure of listening. If you beg and pray the men to unloose you, then they must bind you faster.

" 'When your crew have taken you past these Sirens, I cannot give you coherent directions as to which of two courses you are to take; I will lay the two alternatives before you, and you must consider them for yourself. On the one hand there are some overhanging rocks against which the deep blue waves of Amphitrite beat with terrific fury; the blessed gods call these rocks the Wanderers. Here not even a bird may pass, no, not even the timid doves that bring ambrosia to Father Zeus, but the sheer rock always carries off one of them, and Father Zeus has to send another to make up their number. No ship that ever yet came to these rocks has got away again, but the waves and whirlwinds of fire are freighted with wreckage and with the bodies of dead men. The only vessel that ever sailed and got through was the famous Argo on her way from the house of Aeetes, and she too would have gone against these great rocks, only that Hera piloted her past them for the love she bore to Jason.

" 'Of these two rocks the one reaches heaven and its peak is lost in a dark cloud. This never leaves it, so that the top is never clear not even in summer and early autumn. No man, though he had twenty hands and twenty feet, could get a foothold on it and climb it, for it runs sheer up, as smooth as though it had been polished. In the middle of it there is a large cavern, looking west and turned towards Erebus; you must take your ship this way, but the cave is so high up that not even the stoutest archer could send an arrow into it. Inside it Scylla sits and yelps with a voice that you might take to be that of a young hound, but in truth she is a dreadful monster and no one—not even a god—could face her without being terror-struck. She has twelve misshapen feet, and six necks of the most prodigious length; and at the end of each neck she has a frightful head with three rows of teeth in each, all set very close together, so that they would crunch anyone to death in a moment. She sits deep within her shady cell thrusting out her heads and peering all round the rock, fishing for dolphins or dogfish or any larger monster that she can catch, of the thousands with which Amphitrite teems. No ship ever yet got past her without losing some men, for she shoots out all her heads at once, and carries off a man in each mouth.

" 'You will find the other rock lies lower, but they are so close together that there is not more than a bow-shot between them. A large fig tree in full leaf grows upon it, and under it lies the sucking whirlpool of Charybdis. Three times in the day does she vomit forth her waters, and three times she sucks them down again. See that you be not there when she is sucking, for if you are, Poseidon himself could not save you; you must hug the Scylla side and drive your ship by as fast as you can, for you had better lose six men than your whole crew.'

" 'Is there no way,' said I, 'of escaping Charybdis, and at the same time keeping Scylla off when she is trying to harm my men?'

" 'You daredevil,' replied the goddess, 'you are always wanting to fight somebody or something; you will not let yourself be beaten even by the immortals. For Scylla is not mortal; moreover she is savage, extreme, rude, cruel and invincible. There is no help for it; your best chance will be to get by her as fast as ever you can, for if you dawdle about her rock while you are putting on your armor, she may catch you with a second cast of her six heads, and snap up another half dozen of your men. So drive your ship past her at full speed, and roar out lustily to Crataiis who is Scylla's dam, bad luck to her; she will then stop her from making a second raid upon you.

" 'You will now come to the Thrinacian island, and here you will see many herds of cattle and flocks of sheep belonging to the sun-god—seven herds of cattle and seven flocks of sheep, with fifty head in each flock. They do not breed, nor do they become fewer in number, and they are terided by the goddesses Phaethusa and Lampetie, who are children of the sun-god Hyperion by Neaera. Their mother, when she had borne them and had done suckling them, sent them to the Thrinacian island, which was a long way off, to live there and look after their father's flocks and herds. If you leave these flocks unharmed, and think of nothing but getting home, you may yet after much hardship reach Ithaca. But if you harm them, then I forewarn you of the destruction both of your ship and of your comrades; and even though you may yourself escape, you will return late, in bad plight, after losing all your men.'

"Here she ended, and dawn enthroned in gold began to show in heaven, whereon she returned inland. I then went on board and told my men to loose the ship from her moorings; so they at once got into her, took their places, and began to smite the gray sea with their oars. Presently the great and cunning goddess Circe befriended us with a fair wind that blew dead aft, and stayed steadily with us, keeping our sails well filled, so we did whatever wanted doing to the ship's gear, and let her go as wind and helmsman headed her.

"Then, being much troubled in mind, I said to my men, 'My friends, it is not right that one or two of us alone should know the prophecies that Circe has made me, I will therefore tell you about them, so that whether we live or die we may do so with our eyes open. First she said we were to keep clear of the Sirens, who sit and sing most beautifully in a field of flowers; but she said I might hear them myself so long as no one else did. Therefore, take me and bind me to the crosspiece halfway up the mast; bind me as I stand upright, with a bond so fast that I cannot possibly break away, and lash the rope's ends to the mast itself. If I beg and pray you to set me free, then bind me more tightly still.'

"I had hardly finished telling everything to the men before we reached the island of the two Sirens, for the wind had been very favorable. Then all of a sudden it fell dead calm; there was not a breath of wind or a ripple upon the water, so the men furled the sails and stowed them; then taking to their oars they whitened the water with the foam they raised in rowing. Meanwhile I took a large wheel of wax and cut it up small with my sword. Then I kneaded the wax in my strong hands till it became soft, which it soon did between the kneading and the rays of the sun-god son of Hyperion. Then I stopped the ears of all my men, and they bound me hands and feet to the mast as I stood upright on the crosspiece; but they went on rowing themselves. When we had got within earshot of the land, and the ship was going at a good rate, the Sirens saw that we were getting in shore and began with their singing.

" 'Come here,' they sang, 'renowned Odysseus, honor to the Achaean name, and listen to our two voices. No one ever sailed past as without staying to hear the enchanting sweetness of our song—and he who listens will go on his way not only charmed, but wiser, for we know all the ills that the gods laid upon the Argives and Trojans before Troy, and can tell you everything that is going to happen over the whole world.'

"They sang these words most musically, and as I longed to hear them further I made signs by frowning to my men that they should set me free; but they quickened their stroke, and Eurylochus and Perimedes bound me with still stronger bonds till we had got out of hearing of the Sirens' voices. Then my men took the wax from their ears and unbound me.

"Immediately after we had got past the island I saw a great wave from which spray was rising, and I heard a loud roaring sound. The men were so frightened that they loosed hold of their oars, for the whole sea resounded with the rushing of the waters, but the ship stayed where it was, for the men had left off rowing. I went round, therefore, and exhorted them man by man not to lose heart.

" 'My friends,' said I, 'this is not the first time that we have been in danger, and we are in nothing like so bad a case as when the Cyclops shut us up in his cave; nevertheless, my courage and wise counsel saved us then, and we shall live to look back on all this as well. Now, therefore, let us all do as I say, trust in Zeus and row on with might and main. As for you, coxswain, these are your orders—attend to them, for the ship is in your hands: turn her head away from these steaming rapids and hug the rock, or she will give you the slip and be over yonder before you know where you are, and you will be the death of us.'

"So they did as I told them; but I said nothing about the awful monster Scylla, for I knew the men would not go on rowing if I did, but would huddle together in the hold. In one thing only did I disobey Ciree's strict instructions—I put on my armor. Then seizing two strong spears I took my stand on the ship's bows, for it was there that I expected first to see the monster of the rock, who was to do my men so much harm; but I could not make her out anywhere, though I strained my eyes with looking the gloomy rock all over and over.

"Then we entered the Straits[1] in great fear of mind, for on the one hand was Scylla, and on the other dread Charybdis kept sucking up the salt water. As she vomited it up, it was like the water in a cauldron when it is boiling over upon a great fire, and the spray reached the top of the rocks on either side. When she began to suck again, we could see the water all inside whirling round and round, and it made a deafening sound as it broke against the rocks. We could see the bottom of the whirlpool all black with sand and mud, and the men were at their wits ends for fear. While we were taken up with this, and were expecting each moment to be our last, Scylla pounced down suddenly upon us and snatched up my six best men. I was looking at once after both ship and men, and in a moment I saw their hands and feet ever so high above me, struggling in the air as Scylla was carrying them off, and I heard them call out my name in one last despairing cry. As a fisherman, seated, spear in hand, upon some jutting rock,[2] throws bait into the water to deceive the poor little fishes, and spears them with the ox's horn with which his spear is shod, throwing them gasping on to the land as he catches them one by one—even so did Scylla land these panting creatures on her rock and munch them up at the mouth of her den, while they screamed and stretched out their hands to me in their mortal agony. This was the most sickening sight that I saw throughout all my voyages.

"When we had passed the [Wandering] rocks, with Scylla and terrible Charybdis, we reached the noble island of the sun-god, where were the goodly cattle and sheep belonging to the sun Hyperion. While still at sea in my ship I could hear the cattle lowing as they came home to the yards, and the sheep bleating. Then I remembered what the blind Theban prophet Teiresias had told me, and how carefully Aeaean Circe had warned me to shun the island of the blessed sun-god. So being much troubled, I said to the men, 'My men, I know you are hard pressed, but listen while I tell you the prophecy that Teiresias made me, and how carefully Aeaean Circe warned me to shun the island of the blessed sun-god, for it was here, she said, that our worst danger would lie. Head the ship, therefore, away from the island.'

---

[1] These straits are generally understood to be the Straits of Messina.

[2] In the islands of Favognana and Marettimo off Sicily I have seen men fish exactly as here described. They chew bread into a paste and throw it into the sea to attract the fish, which they then spear. No line is used. (B.)

"The men were in despair at this, and Eurylochus at once gave me an insolent answer. 'Odysseus,' said he, 'you are cruel. You are very strong yourself and never get worn out; you seem to be made of iron, and now, though your men are exhausted with toil and want of sleep, you will not let them land and cook themselves a good supper upon this island, but bid them put out to sea and go faring fruitlessly on through the watches of the flying night. It is by night that the winds blow hardest and do so much damage. How can we escape should one of those sudden squalls spring up from southwest or west, which so often wreck a vessel when our lords the gods are unpropitious? Now, therefore, let us obey the behests of night and prepare our supper here hard by the ship; tomorrow morning we will go on board again and put out to sea.'

"Thus spoke Eurylochus, and the men approved his words. I saw that heaven meant us a mischief and said, 'You force me to yield, for you are many against one, but at any rate each one of you must take his solemn oath that if he meet with a herd of cattle or a large flock of sheep, he will not be so mad as to kill a single head of either, but will be satisfied with the food that Circe has given us.'

"They all swore as I bade them, and when they had completed their oath we made the ship fast in a harbor that was near a stream of fresh water, and the men went ashore and cooked their suppers. As soon as they had had enough to eat and drink, they began talking about their poor comrades whom Scylla had snatched up and eaten; this set them weeping, and they went on crying till they fell off into a sound sleep.

"In the third watch of the night when the stars had shifted their places, Zeus raised a great gale of wind that blew a hurricane so that land and sea were covered with thick clouds, and night sprang forth out of the heavens. When the child of morning, rosy-fingered Dawn, appeared, we brought the ship to land and drew her into a cave wherein the sea-nymphs hold their courts and dances, and I called the men together in council.

" 'My friends,' said I, 'we have meat and drink in the ship, let us mind, therefore, and not touch the cattle, or we shall suffer for it; for these cattle and sheep belong to the mighty sun, who sees and gives ear to everything.' And again they promised that they would obey.

"For a whole month the wind blew steadily from the south, and there was no other wind, but only south and east.[3] As long as corn and wine held out the men did not touch the cattle when they were hungry. When, however, they had eaten all there was in the ship, they were forced to go further afield, fishing with hook and line, catching birds, and taking whatever they could lay their hands on, for they were starving. One day, therefore, I went up inland that I might pray heaven to show me some means of getting away. When I had gone far enough to be clear of all my men, and had found a place

---

[3] The writer evidently regards Odysseus as on a coast that looked east at no great distance south of the Straits of Messina somewhere, say, near Tauromeniuin, now Taormina. (B.)

that was well sheltered from the wind, I washed my hands and prayed to all the gods in Olympus till by and by they sent me off into a sweet sleep.

"Meanwhile Eurylochus had been giving evil counsel to the men. 'listen to me,' said he, 'my poor comrades. All deaths are bad enough, but there is none so bad as famine. Why should not we drive in the best of these cows and offer them in sacrifice to the immortal gods? If we ever get back to Ithaca, we can build a fine temple to the sun-god and enrich it with every kind of ornament. If, however, he is determined to sink our ship out of revenge for these horned cattle, and the other gods are of the same mind, I for one would rather drink salt water once for all and have done with it than be starved to death by inches in such a desert island as this is.'

"Thus spoke Eurylochus, and the men approved his words. Now the cattle, so fair and goodly, were feeding not far from the ship; the men, therefore, drove in the best of them, and they all stood round them saying their prayers, and using young oak-shoots instead of barley meal, for there was no barley left. When they had done praying they killed the cows and dressed their carcasses; they cut out the thighbones, wrapped them round in two layers of fat, and set some pieces of raw meat on the top of them. They had no wine with which to make drink offerings over the sacrifice while it was cooking, so they kept pouring on a little water from time to time while the inward meats were being grilled. Then, when the thigh bones were burned and they had tasted the inward meats, they cut the rest up small and put the pieces upon the spits.

"By this time my deep sleep had left me, and I turned back to the ship and to the seashore. As I drew near I began to smell hot roast meat, so I groaned out a prayer to the immortal gods. 'Father Zeus,' I exclaimed, 'and all you other gods who live in everlasting bliss, you have done me a cruel mischief by the sleep into which you have sent me. See what fine work these men of mine have been making in my absence.'

"Meanwhile Lampetie went straight off to the sun and told him we had been killing his cows, whereon he flew into a great rage, and said to the immortals, 'Father Zeus, and all you other gods who live in everlasting bliss, I must have vengeance on the crew of Odysseus' ship. They have had the insolence to kill my cows, which were the one thing I loved to look upon, whether I was going up heaven or down again. If they do not square accounts with me about my cows, I will go down to Hades and shine there among the dead.'

"'Sun,' said Zeus, 'go on shining upon us gods and upon mankind over the fruitful earth. I will shiver their ship into little pieces with a bolt of white lightning as soon as they get out to sea.'

"I was told all this by Calypso, who said she had heard it from the mouth of Hermes.

"As soon as I got down to my ship and to the seashore, I rebuked each one of the men separately, but we could see no way out of it, for the cows were dead already. And indeed the gods began at once to show signs and wonders among us, for the hides of the cattle crawled about, and the joints upon the spits began to low like cows, and the meat, whether cooked or raw, kept on making a noise just as cows do.

"For six days my men kept driving in the best cows and feasting upon them, but when Zeus the son of Cronus had added a seventh day, the fury of the gale abated; we therefore went on board, raised our masts, spread sail, and put out to sea. As soon as we were well away from the island, and could see nothing but sky and sea, the son of Cronus raised a black cloud over our ship, and the sea grew dark beneath it. We did not get on much further, for in another moment we were caught by a terrific squall from the west that snapped the forestays of the mast so that it fell aft, while all the ship's gear tumbled about at the bottom of the vessel. The mast fell upon the head of the helmsman in the ship's stern, so that the bones of his head were crushed to pieces, and he fell overboard as though he were diving, with no more life left in him.

"Then Zeus let fly with his thunderbolts, and the ship went round and round, and was filled with fire and brimstone as the lightning struck it. The men all fell into the sea; they were carried about in the water round the ship, looking like so many sea gulls, but the god presently deprived them of all chance of getting home again.

"I stuck to the ship till the sea knocked her sides from her keel (which drifted about by itself) and struck the mast out of her in the direction of the keel; but there was a backstay of stout ox-thong still hanging about it, and with this I lashed the mast and keel together, and getting astride of them was carried wherever the winds chose to take me.

"The gale from the west had now spent its force, and the wind got into the south again, which frightened me lest I should be taken back to the terrible whirlpool of Charybdis. This indeed was what actually happened, for I was borne along by the waves all night, and by sunrise had reached the rock of Scylla, and the whirlpool. She was then sucking down the salt sea water, but I was carried aloft toward the fig tree, which I caught hold of and clung on to like a bat. I could not plant my feet anywhere so as to stand securely, for the roots were a long way off and the boughs that overshadowed the whole pool were too high, too vast, and too far apart for me to reach them; so I hung patiently on, waiting till the pool should discharge my mast and raft again—and a very long while it seemed. A juryman is not more glad to get home to supper, after having been long detained in court by troublesome cases, than I was to see my raft beginning to work its way out of the whirlpool again. At last I let go with my hands and feet, and fell heavily into the sea, hard by my raft on to which I then got, and began to row with my hands. As for Scylla, the father of gods and men would not let her get further sight of me—otherwise I should have certainly been lost.

"Hence I was carried along for nine days till on the tenth night the gods stranded me on the Ogygian island, where dwells the great and powerful goddess Calypso. She took me in and was kind to me, but I need say no more about this, for I told you and your noble wife all about it yesterday, and I hate saying the same thing over and over again."

The First Lowering

HERMAN MELVILE

The phantoms, for so they then seemed, were flitting on the other side of the deck, and, with a noiseless celerity, were casting loose the tackles and bands of the boat which swung there. This boat had always been deemed one of the spare boats, though technically called the captain's, on account of its hanging from the starboard quarter. The figure that now stood by its bows was tall and swart, with one white tooth evilly protruding from its steel-like lips. A rumpled Chinese jacket of black cotton funereally invested him, with wide black trowsers of the same dark stuff. But strangely crowning his ebonness was a glistening white plaited turban, the living hair braided and coiled round and round upon his head. Less swart in aspect, the companions of this figure were of that vivid, tiger-yellow complexion peculiar to some of the aboriginal natives of the Manillas;—a race notorious for a certain diabolism of subtilty, and by some honest white mariners supposed to be the paid spies and secret confidential agents on the water of the devil, their lord, whose counting-room they suppose to be elsewhere.

While yet the wondering ship's company were gazing upon these strangers, Ahab cried out to the white-turbaned old man at their head, 'All ready there, Fedallah?'

'Ready,' was the half-hissed reply.

'Lower away then; d'ye hear?' shouting across the deck. 'Lower away there, I say.'

Such was the thunder of his voice, that spite of their amazement the men sprang over the rail; the sheaves whirled round in the blocks; with a wallow, the three boats dropped into the sea; while, with a dexterous, off-handed daring, unknown in any other vocation, the sailors, goat-like, leaped down the rolling ship's side into the tossed boats below.

Hardly had they pulled out from under the ship's lee, when a fourth keel, coming from the windward side, pulled round under the stern, and showed the five strangers rowing Ahab, who, standing erect in the stern, loudly hailed Starbuck, Stubb, and Flask, to spread themselves widely, so as to cover a large expanse of water but with all their eyes again riveted upon the swart Fedallah and his crew, the inmates of the other boats obeyed not the command.

'Captain Ahab?—' said Starbuck.

'Spread yourselves,' cried Ahab; 'give way, all four boats. Thou, Flask, pull out more to leeward!'

'Aye, aye, sir,' cheerily cried little King-Post, sweeping round his great steering oar. 'Lay back!' addressing his crew. 'There!—there!—there again! There she blows right ahead, boys! — lay back!'

'Never heed yonder yellow boys, Archy.'

'Oh, I don't mind 'em, sir,' said Archy; 'I knew it all before now. Didn't I hear 'em in the hold? And didn't I tell Cabaco here of it? What say ye, Cabaco? They are stowaways, Mr. Flask.'

'Pull, pull, my fine hearts-alive; pull, my children; pull, my little ones,' drawingly and soothingly sighed Stubb to his crew, some of whom still showed signs of uneasiness. 'Why don't you break your backbones, my boys? What is it you stare at? Those chaps in yonder boat? Tut! They are only five more hands come to help us—never mind from where—the more the merrier. Pull, then, do pull; never mind the brimstone—devils are good fellows enough. So, so; there you are now; that's the stroke for a thousand pounds; that's the stroke to sweep the stakes! Hurrah for the gold cup of sperm oil, my heroes! Three cheers, men—all hearts alive! Easy, easy; don't be in a hurry—don't be in a hurry. Why don't you snap your oars, you rascals? Bite something, you dogs! So, so, so, then;—softly, softly! That's it—that's it! long and strong. Give way there, give way! The devil fetch ye, ye ragamuffin rapscallions; ye are all asleep. Stop snoring, ye sleepers, and pull. Pull, will ye? pull, can't ye? pull, won't ye? Why in the name of gudgeons and ginger-cakes don't ye pull?—pull and break something! pull, and start your eyes out! Here! whipping out the sharp knife from his girdle; every mother's son of ye draw his knife, and pull with the blade between his teeth. That's it—that's it. Now ye do something; that looks like it, my steel-bits. Start her—start her, my silver-spoons! Start her, marling-spikes!'

Stubb's exordium to his crew is given here at large, because he had rather a peculiar way of talking to them in general, and especially in inculcating the religion of rowing. But you must not suppose from this specimen of his sermonizings that he ever flew into downright passions with his congregation. Not at all; and therein consisted his chief peculiarity. He would say the most terrific things to his crew, in a tone so strangely compounded of fun and fury, and the fury seemed so calculated merely as a spice to the fun, that no oarsman could hear such queer invocations without pulling for dear life, and yet pulling for the mere joke of the thing. Besides he all the time looked so easy and indolent himself, so loungingly managed his steering-oar, and so broadly gaped—open-mouthed at times—that the mere sight of such a yawning commander, by sheer force of contrast, acted like a charm upon the crew. Then again, Stubb was one of those odd sort of humorists, whose jollity is sometimes so curiously ambiguous, as to put all inferiors on their guard in the matter of obeying them.

In obedience to a sign from Ahab, Starbuck was now pulling obliquely across Stubb's bow; and when for a minute or so the two boats were pretty near to each other, Stubb hailed the mate.

'Mr. Starbuck! larboard boat there, ahoy! a word with ye, sir, if ye please!'

'Halloa!' returned Starbuck, turning round not a single inch as he spoke; still earnestly but whisperingly urging his crew; his face set like a flint from Stubb's.

'What think ye of those yellow boys, sir!'

'Smuggled on board, somehow, before the ship sailed. (Strong, strong, boys!') in a whisper to his crew, then speaking out loud again: 'A sad business, Mr. Stubb! (seethe her, seethe her, my lads!) but never mind, Mr. Stubb, all for the best. Let all your crew pull strong, come what will. (Spring, my men, spring!) There's hogsheads of sperm ahead, Mr. Stubb, and that's what ye came for. (Pull, my boys!) Sperm, sperm's the play! This at least is duty; duty and profit hand in hand!'

'Aye, aye, I thought as much,' soliloquized Stubb, when the boats diverged, 'as soon as I clapt eye on 'em, I thought so. Aye, and that's what he went into the after hold for, so often, as Dough-Boy long suspected. They were hidden down there. The White Whale's at the bottom of it. Well, well, so be it! Can't be helped! All right! Give way, men! It ain't the White Whale to-day! Give way!'

Now the advent of these outlandish strangers at such a critical instant as the lowering of the boats from the deck, this had not unreasonably awakened a sort of superstitious amazement in some of the ship's company; but Archy's fancied discovery having some time previous got abroad among them, though indeed not credited then, this had in some small measure prepared them for the event. It took off the extreme edge of their wonder; and so what with all this and Stubb's confident way of accounting for their appearance, they were for the time freed from superstitious surmisings; though the affair still left abundant room for all manner of wild conjectures as to dark Ahab's precise agency in the matter from the beginning. For me, I silently recalled the mysterious shadows I had seen creeping on board the Pequod during the dim Nantucket dawn, as well as the enigmatical hintings of the unaccountable Elijah.

Meantime, Ahab, out of hearing of his officers, having sided the furthest to windward, was still ranging ahead of the other boats; a circumstance bespeaking how potent a crew was pulling him. those tiger yellow creatures of his seemed all steel and whale-bone; like five trip-hammers they rose and fell with regular strokes of strength, which periodically started the boat along the water like a horizontal burst boiler out of a Mississippi steamer. As for Fedallah, who was seen pulling the harpooneer oar, he had thrown aside his black jacket, and displayed his naked chest with the whole part of his body above the gunwale, clearly cut against the alternating depressions of the watery horizon; while at the other end of the boat Ahab, with one arm, like a fencer's, thrown half backward into the air, as if to counterbalance any tendency to trip: Ahab was seen steadily managing his steering oar as in a thousand boat lowerings ere the White Whale had torn him. All at once the out-stretched arm gave a peculiar motion and then remained fixed, while the boat's five oars were seen simultaneously peaked. Boat and crew sat motionless on the sea. Instantly the three spread boats in the rear paused on their way. The whales had irregularly settled bodily down into the blue, thus giving no distantly discernible token of the movement, though from his closer vicinity Ahab had observed it.

'Every man look out along his oars!' cried Starbuck. 'Thou, Queequeg, stand up!'

Nimbly springing up on the triangular raised box in the bow, the savage stood erect there, and with intensely eager eyes gazed off towards the spot where the chase had last been descried. Likewise upon the extreme stern of the boat where it was also triangularly platformed level with the gunwale, Starbuck himself was seen coolly and adroitly balancing himself to the jerking tossings of his chip of a craft, and silently eyeing the vast blue eye of the sea.

Not very far distant Flask's boat was also lying breathlessly still; its commander recklessly standing upon the top of the loggerhead, a stout sort of post rooted in the keel, and rising some two feet above the level of the stern platform. it is used for catching turns with the whale line. Its top is not more spacious than the palm of a man's hand, and standing upon such a base as that, Flask seemed perched at the mast-head of some ship which had sunk to all but her trucks. But little King-Post was small and short, and at the same time little King-Post was full of a large and tall ambition, so that this loggerhead stand-point of his did by no means satisfy King-Post.

'I can't see three seas off; tip us up an oar there, and let me on to that.'

Upon this, Daggoo, with either hand upon the gunwale to steady his way, swiftly slid aft, and then erecting himself volunteered his lofty shoulders for a pedestal.

'Good a mast-head as any, sir. Will you mount?'

'That I will, and thank ye very much, my fine fellow; only I wish you fifty feet taller.'

Whereupon planting his feet firmly against two opposite planks of the boat, the gigantic negro, stooping a little, presented his flat palm to Flask's foot, and then putting Flask's hand on his hearse-plumed head and bidding him spring as he himself should toss, with one dexterous fling landed the little man high and dry on his shoulders. And here was Flask now standing, Daggoo with one lifted arm furnishing him with a breast-band to lean against and steady himself by.

At any time it is a strange sight to the tyro to see with what wondrous habitude of unconscious skill the whaleman will maintain an erect posture in his boat, even when pitched about by the most riotously perverse and cross-running seas. Still more strange to see him giddily perched upon the loggerhead itself, under such circumstances. But the sight of little Flask mounted upon gigantic Daggoo was yet more curious; for sustaining himself with a cool, indifferent, easy, unthought of, barbaric majesty, the noble negro to every roll of the sea harmoniously rolled his fine form. On his broad back, flaxen-haired flask seemed a snow-flake. The bearer looked nobler than the rider. Though truly vivacious, tumultuous, ostentatious little Flask would now and then stamp with impatience; but not one added heave did he thereby give to the negro's lordly chest. So have I seen Passion and Vanity stamping the living magnanimous earth, but the earth did not alter her tides and her seasons for that.

Meanwhile Stubb, the third mate, betrayed no such far-gazing solicitudes. The whales might have made one of their regular soundings, not a temporary dive from mere fright; and if that were the case, Stubb, as his wont in such cases, it seems, was resolved to solace the languishing interval with his pipe. He withdrew it from his hatband, where he always wore it aslant like a feather. He loaded it, and rammed home the loading with his thumb-end; but hardly had he ignited his match across the rough sand-paper of his hand, when Tashtego, his harpooneer, whose eyes had been setting to windward like two fixed stars, suddenly dropped like light from his erect attitude to his seat, crying out in a quick phrensy of hurry, 'Down, down all, and give way!—there they are!'

To a landsman, no whale, nor any sign of a herring, would have been visible at that moment; nothing but a troubled bit of greenish white water, and thin scattered puffs of vapor hovering over it, and suffusingly blowing off to leeward, like the confused scud from white rolling billows. The air around suddenly vibrated and tingled, as it were, like the air over intensely heated plates of iron. Beneath this atmospheric waving and curling, and partially beneath a thin layer of water, also, the whales were swimming. Seen in advance of all the other indications, the puffs of vapor they spouted, seemed their forerunning couriers and detached flying outriders.

All four boats were now in keen pursuit of that one spot of troubled water and air. But it bade far to outstrip them; it flew on and on, as a mass of interblending bubbles borne down a rapid stream from the hills.

'Pull, pull, my good boys,' said Starbuck, in the lowest possible but intensest concentrated whisper to his men; while the sharp fixed glance from his eyes darted straight ahead of the bow, almost seemed as two visible needles in two unerring binnacle compasses. He did not say much to his crew, though, nor did his crew say anything to him. Only the silence of the boat was at intervals startlingly pierced by one of his peculiar whispers, now harsh with command, now soft with entreaty.

How different the loud little King-Post. 'Sing out and say something, my hearties. Roar and pull, my thunderbolts! Beach me, beach me on their black backs, boys; only do that for me, and I'll sign over to you my Martha's Vineyard plantation, boys; including wife and children, boys. Lay me on—lay me on! O Lord, Lord! but I shall go stark, staring mad: See! see that white water!' And so shouting, he pulled his hat from his head, and stamped up and down on it; then picking it up, flirted it far off upon the sea; and finally fell to rearing and plunging in the boat's stern like a crazed colt from the prairie.

'Look at that chap now,' philosophically drawled Stubb, who, with his unlighted short pipe, mechanically retained between his teeth, at a short distance, followed after—'He's got fits, that Flask has. Fits? yes, give him fits—that's the very word—pitch fits into 'em. Merrily, merrily, hearts-alive. Pudding for supper, you know;—merry's the word. Pull, babes—pull, sucklings—pull, all. But what the devil are you hurrying about? Softly, softly, and steadily, my men. Only pull, and keep pulling; nothing more. Crack all your backbones, and bite your knives in two—that's all. Take it easy—why don't ye take it easy, I say, and burst all your livers and lungs!'

But what it was that inscrutable Ahab said to that tiger-yellow crew of his—these were words best omitted here; for you live under the blessed light of the evangelical land.

Only the infidel sharks in the audacious seas may give ear to such words, when, with tornado brow, and eyes of red murder, and foam-glued lips, Ahab leaped after his prey.

Meanwhile, all the boats tore on. The repeated specific allusions of Flask to 'that whale', as he called the fictitious monster which he declared to be incessantly tantalizing his boat's bow with its tail—these allusions of his were at times so vivid and life-like, that they would cause some one or two of his men to snatch a fearful look over the shoulder. But this was against all rule; for the oarsmen must put out their eyes, and ram a skewer through their necks; usage pronouncing that they must have no organs but ears, and no limbs but arms, in these critical moments.

It was a sight full of quick wonder and awe! The vast swells of the omnipotent sea; the surging, hollow roar they made, as they rolled along the eight gunwales, like gigantic bowls in a boundless bowling-green; the brief suspended agony of the boat, as it would tip for an instant on the knife-like edge of the sharper waves, that almost seemed threatening to cut it in two; the sudden profound dip into the watery glens and hollows; the keen spurrings and goadings to gain the top of the opposite hill; the headlong, sled-like slide down its other side;—all these, with the cries of the headsmen and harpooneers, and the shuddering gasps of the oarsmen, with the wondrous sight of the ivory Pequod bearing down upon her boats with outstretched sails, like a wild hen after her screaming brood;—all this was thrilling. Not the raw recruit, marching from the bosom of his wife into the fever heat of his first battle; not the dead man's ghost encountering the first unknown phantom in the other world;—neither of these can feel stranger and stronger emotions than that man does, who for the first time finds himself pulling into the charmed, churned circle of the hunted Sperm Whale.

The dancing white water made by the chase was now becoming more and more visible, owing to the increasing darkness of the dun cloud-shadows flung upon the sea. The jets of vapor no longer blended, but tilted everywhere to right and left; the whales seemed separating their wakes. The boats were pulled more apart; Starbuck giving chase to three whales running dead to leeward. Our sail was now set, and, with the still rising wind, we rushed along; the boat going with such madness through the water, that the lee oars could scarcely be worked rapidly enough to escape being torn from the row-locks.

Soon we were running through a suffusing wide veil of mist; neither ship nor boat to be seen.

'Give way, men,' whispered Starbuck, drawing still further aft the sheet of his sail; 'there is time to kill a fish yet before the squall comes. There's white water again!—close to! Spring!'

Soon after, two cries in quick succession on each side of us denoted that the other boats had got fast; but hardly were they overheard, when with a lightning-like hurtling whisper Starbuck said: 'Stand up!' and Queequeg, harpoon in hand, sprang to his feet.

Though not one of the oarsmen was then facing the life and death peril so close to them ahead, yet with their eyes on the intense countenance of the mate in the stern of the boat, they knew that the imminent instant had come; they heard, too, an enormous wallowing sound as of fifty elephants stirring in their litter. Meanwhile the boat was still booming through the mist, the waves curling and hissing around us like the erected crests of enraged serpents.

'That's his hump. There, there, give it to him!' whispered Starbuck.

A short rushing sound leaped out of the boat; it was the darted iron of Queequeg. Then all in one welded commotion came an invisible push from astern, while forward the boat seemed striking on a ledge; the sail collapsed and exploded; a gush of scalding vapor shot up near by; something rolled and tumbled like an earthquake beneath us. The whole crew were half suffocated as they were tossed helter-skelter into the white curdling cream of the squall. Squall, whale, and harpoon had all blended together; and the whale, merely grazed by the iron, escaped.

Though completely swamped, the boat was nearly unharmed. Swimming round it we picked up the floating oars, and lashing them across the gunwale, tumbled back to our places. There we sat up to our knees in the sea, the water covering every rib and plank, so that to our downward gazing eyes the suspended craft seemed a coral boat grown up to us from the bottom of the ocean.

The wind increased to a howl; the waves dashed their bucklers together; the whole squall roared, forked, and crackled around us like a white fire upon the prairie, in which, unconsumed, we were burning; immortal in these jaws of death! In vain we hailed the other boats; as well roar to the live coals down the chimney of a flaming furnace as hail those boats in that storm. Meanwhile the driving scud, rack, and mist, grew darker with the shadows of night; no sign of the ship could be seen. The rising sea forbade all attempts to bale out the boat. The oars were useless as propellers, performing now the office of life-preservers. So, cutting the lashing of the water-proof match keg, after many failures Starbuck contrived to ignite the lamp in the lantern; then stretching it on a waif pole, handed it to Queequeg as the standard-bearer of this forlorn hope. There, then, he sat, holding up that imbecile candle in the heart of that almighty forlornness. There, then, he sat, the sign and symbol of a man without faith, hopelessly holding up hope in the midst of despair.

Wet, drenched through, and shivering cold, despairing of ship or boat, we lifted up our eyes as the dawn came on. The mist still spread over the sea, the empty lantern lay crushed in the bottom of the boat. Suddenly Queequeg started to his feet, hollowing his hand to his ear. We all heard a faint creaking, as of ropes and yards hitherto muffled by the storm. The sound came nearer and nearer; the thick mists were dimly parted by a huge, vague form. Affrighted, we all sprang into the sea as the ship at last loomed into view, bearing right down upon us within a distance of not much more than its length.

Floating on the waves we saw the abandoned boat, as for one instant it tossed and gaped beneath the ship's bows like a chip at the base of a cataract; and then the vast hull rolled over it, and it was seen no more till it came up weltering astern. Again we swam for it, were dashed against it by the seas, and were at last taken up and safely landed on board. Ere the squall came close to, the other boats had cut loose from their fish and returned to the ship in good time. The ship had given us up, but was still cruising, if haply it might light upon some token of our perishing,—an oar or a lance pole.

Youth

JOSEPH CONRAD

This could have occurred nowhere but in England, where men and sea interpenetrate, so to speak—the sea entering into the life of most men, and the men knowing something or everything about the sea, in the way of amusement, of travel, or of bread-winning.

We were sitting round a mahogany table that reflected the bottle, the claret-glasses, and our faces as we leaned on our elbows. There was a director of companies, an accountant, a lawyer, Marlow, and myself. The director had been a *Conway* boy, the accountant had served four years at sea, the lawyer—a fine crusted Tory, High Churchman, the best of old fellows, the soul of honour—had been chief officer in the P. & O. service in the good old days when mail-boats were square-rigged at least on two masts, and used to come down the China Sea before a fair monsoon with stun'-sails set alow and aloft. We all began life in the merchant service. Between the five of us there was the strong bond of the sea, and also the fellowship of the craft, which no amount of enthusiasm for yachting, cruising, and so on can give, since one is only the amusement of life and the other is life itself.

Marlow (at least I think that is how he spelt his name) told the story, or rather the chronicle, of a voyage:—

"Yes, I have seen a little of the Eastern seas; but what I remember best is my first voyage there. You fellows know there are those voyages that seem ordered for the illustration of life, that might stand for a symbol of existence. You fight, work, sweat, nearly kill yourself, sometimes do kill yourself, trying to accomplish something—and you can't. Not from any fault of yours. You simply can do nothing, neither great nor little—not a thing in the world—not even marry an old maid, or get a wretched 600-ton cargo of coal to its port of destination.

"It was altogether a memorable affair. It was my first voyage to the East, and my first voyage as second mate; it was also my skipper's first command. You'll admit it was time. He was sixty if a day; a little man, with a broad, not very straight back, with bowed shoulders and one leg more bandy than the other, he had that queer twisted-about appearance you see so often in men who work in the fields. He had a nut-cracker face—chin and nose trying to come together over a sunken mouth—and it was framed in iron-gray fluffy hair, that looked like a chin-strap of cotton-wool sprinkled with coal-dust. And he had blue eyes in that old face of his, which were amazingly like a boy's, with that candid expression some quite common men preserve to the end of their days by a rare internal gift of simplicity of heart and rectitude of soul. What induced him to accept me was a wonder. I had come out of a crack Australian clipper, where I had been third officer, and he seemed to have a prejudice against crack clippers as aristocratic and high-toned. He said to me, 'You know, in this ship you will have to work.' I said I had to work in every ship I had ever been in. 'Ah, but this is different, and you gentlemen out of them big ships; . . . but there! I dare say you will do. Join to-morrow.'

"I joined to-morrow. It was twenty-two years ago; and I was just twenty. How time passes! It was one of the happiest days of my life. Fancy! Second mate for the first time—a really responsible officer! I wouldn't have thrown up my new billet for a fortune. The mate looked me over carefully. He was also an old chap, but of another stamp. He had a Roman nose, a snow-white, long beard, and his name was Mahon, but he insisted that it should be pronounced Mann. He was well connected; yet there was something wrong with his luck, and he had never got on.

"As to the captain, he had been for years in coasters, then in the Mediterranean, and last in the West Indian trade. He had never been round the Capes. He could just write a kind of sketchy hand, and didn't care for writing at all. Both were thorough good seamen of course, and between those two old chaps I felt like a small boy between two grandfathers.

"The ship also was old. Her name was the *Judea*. Queer name, isn't it? She belonged to a man Wilmer, Wilcox—some name like that; but he has been bankrupt and dead these twenty years or more, and his name don't matter. She had been laid up in Shadwell basin for ever so long. You may imagine her state. She was all rust, dust, grime—soot aloft, dirt on deck. To me it was like coming out of a palace into a ruined cottage. She was about 400 tons, had a primitive windlass, wooden latches to the doors, not a bit of brass about her, and a big square stern. There was on it, below her name in big letters, a lot of scrollwork, with the gilt off, and some sort of a coat of arms, with the motto 'Do or Die' underneath. I remember it took my fancy immensely. There was a touch of romance in it, something that made me love the old thing—something that appealed to my youth:

"We left London in ballast—sand ballast—to load a cargo of coal in a northern port for Bankok. Bankok! I thrilled. I had been six years at sea, but had only seen Melbourne and Sydney, very good places, charming places in their way—but Bankok!

"We worked out of the Thames under canvas, with a North Sea pilot on board. His name was Jermyn, and he dodged all day long about the galley drying his handkerchief before the stove. Apparently he never slept. He was a dismal man, with a perpetual tear sparkling at the end of his nose, who either had been in trouble, or was in trouble, or expected to be in trouble—couldn't be happy unless something went wrong. He mistrusted my youth, my common-sense, and my seamanship, and made a point of showing it in a hundred little ways. I dare say he was right. It seems to me I knew very little then, and I know not much more now; but I cherish a hate for that Jermyn to this day.

"We were a week working up as far as Yarmouth Roads, and then we got into a gale—the famous October gale of twenty-two years ago. It was wind, lightning, sleet, snow, and a terrific sea. We were flying light, and you may imagine how bad it was when I tell you we had smashed bulwarks and a flooded deck. On the second night she shifted her ballast into the lee bow, and by that time we had been blown off somewhere on the Dogger Bank. There was nothing for it but go below with shovels and try to right her, and there we were in that vast hold, gloomy like a cavern, the tallow dips stuck and flickering on the beams, the gale howling above, the ship tossing about like mad on her side; there we all were, Jermyn, the captain, every one, hardly able to keep our feet, engaged on that gravedigger's work, and trying to toss shovelfuls of wet sand up to windward. At every tumble of the ship you could see vaguely in the dim light men falling down with a great flourish of shovels. One of the ship's boys (we had two), impressed by the weirdness of the scene, wept as if his heart would break. We could hear him blubbering somewhere in the shadows.

"On the third day the gale died out, and by and by a north-country tug picked us up. We took sixteen days in all to get from London to the Tyne! When we got into dock we had lost our turn for loading, and they hauled us off to a tier where we remained for a month. Mrs. Beard (the captain's name was Beard) came from Colchester to see the old man. She lived on board. The crew of runners had left, and there remained only the officers, one boy and the steward, a mulatto who answered to the name of Abraham. Mrs. Beard was an old woman, with a face all wrinkled and ruddy like a winter apple, and the figure of a young girl. She caught sight of me once, sewing on a button, and insisted on having my shirts to repair. This was something different from the captains' wives I had known on board crack clippers. When I brought her the shirts, she said: 'And the socks? They want mending, I am sure, and John's—Captain Beard's—things are all in order now. I would be glad of something to do.' Bless the old woman. She overhauled my outfit for me, and meantime I read for the first time *Sartor Resartus* and Burnaby's *Ride to Khiva*. I didn't understand much of the first then; but I remember I preferred the soldier to the philosopher at the time; a preference which life has only confirmed. One was a man, and the other was either more—or less. However, they are both dead and Mrs. Beard is dead, and youth, strength, genius, thoughts, achievements, simple hearts—all die. . . . No matter.

"They loaded us at last. We shipped a crew. Eight able seamen and two boys. We hauled off one evening to the buoys at the dock-gates, ready to go out, and with a fair prospect of beginning the voyage next day. Mrs. Beard was to start for home by a late train. When the ship was fast we went to tea. We sat rather silent through the meal—Mahon, the old couple, and I. I finished first, and slipped away for a smoke, my cabin being in a deck-house just against the poop. It was high water, blowing fresh with a drizzle; the double dock-gates were opened, and the steam-colliers were going in and out in the darkness with their lights burning bright, a great plashing of propellers, rattling of winches, and a lot of hailing on the pier-heads. I watched the procession of head-lights gliding high and of green lights gliding low in the night, when suddenly a red gleam flashed at me, vanished, came into view again, and remained. The fore-end of a steamer loomed up close. I shouted down the cabin, 'Come up, quick!' and then heard a startled voice saying afar in the dark, 'Stop her, sir.' A bell jingled. Another voice cried warningly, 'We are going right into that barque, sir.' The answer to this was a gruff 'All right,' and the next thing was a heavy crash as the steamer struck a glancing blow with the bluff of her bow about our fore-rigging. There was a moment of confusion, yelling, and running about. Steam roared. Then somebody was heard saying, 'All clear, sir.' . . . 'Are you all right?' asked the gruff voice. I had jumped forward to see the damage, and hailed back, 'I think so.' 'Easy astern,' said the gruff voice. A bell jingled. 'What steamer is that?' screamed Mahon. By that time she was no more to us than a bulky shadow manœuvring a little way off. They shouted at us some name—a woman's name, Miranda or Melissa—or some such thing. 'This means another month in this beastly hole,' said Mahon to me, as we peered with lamps about the splintered bulwarks and broken braces. 'But where's the captain?'

'We had not heard or seen anything of him all that time. We went aft to look. A doleful voice arose hailing somewhere in the middle of the dock, '*Judea* ahoy!' . . . How the devil did he get there? . . . 'Hallo!' we shouted. 'I am adrift in our boat without oars,' he cried. A belated water-man offered his services, and Mahon struck a bargain with him for half-a-crown to tow our skipper alongside; but it was Mrs. Beard that came up the ladder first. They had been floating about the dock in that mizzly cold rain for nearly an hour. I was never so surprised in my life.

"It appears that when he heard my shout 'Come up' he understood at once what was the matter, caught up his wife, ran on deck, and across, and down into our boat, which was fast to the ladder. Not bad for a sixty-year-old. Just imagine that old fellow saving heroically in his arms that old woman—the woman of his life. He set her down on a thwart, and was ready to climb back on board when the painter came adrift somehow, and away they went together. Of course in the confusion we did not hear him shouting. He looked abashed. She said cheerfully, 'I suppose it does not matter my losing the train now?' 'No, Jenny—you go below and get warm,' he growled. Then to us: 'A sailor has no business with a wife—I say. There I was, out of the ship. Well, no harm done this time. Let's go and look at what that fool of a steamer smashed.'

"It wasn't much, but it delayed us three weeks. At the end of that time, the captain being engaged with his agents, I carried Mrs. Beard's bag to the railway-station and put her all comfy into a third-class carriage. She lowered the window to say, 'You are a good young man. If you see John—Captain Beard—without his muffler at night, just remind him from me to keep his throat well wrapped up.' 'Certainly, Mrs. Beard,' I said. 'You are a good young man; I noticed how attentive you are to John—to Captain——' The train pulled out suddenly; I took my cap off to the old woman: I never saw her again. . . Pass the bottle.

"We went to sea next day. When we made that start for Bankok we had been already three months out of London. We had expected to be a fortnight or so—at the outside.

"It was January, and the weather was beautiful—the beautiful sunny winter weather that has more charm than in the summer-time, because it is unexpected, and crisp, and you know it won't, it can't, last long. It's like a windfall, like a godsend, like an unexpected piece of luck.

"It lasted all down the North Sea, all down Channel; and it lasted till we were three hundred miles or so to the westward of the Lizards: then the wind went round to the sou'west and began to pipe up. In two days it blew a gale. The *Judea*, hove to, wallowed on the Atlantic like an old candle-box. It blew day after day: it blew with spite, without interval, without mercy, without rest. The world was nothing but an immensity of great foaming waves rushing at us, under a sky low enough to touch with the hand and dirty like a smoked ceiling. In the stormy space surrounding us there was as much flying spray as air. Day after day and night after night there was nothing round the ship but the howl of the wind, the tumult of the sea, the noise of water pouring over her deck. There was no rest for her and no rest for us. She tossed, she pitched, she stood on her head, she sat on her tail, she rolled, she groaned, and we had to hold on while on deck and cling to our bunks when below, in a constant effort of body and worry of mind.

One night Mahon spoke through the small window of my berth. It opened right into my very bed, and I was lying there sleepless, in my boots, feeling as though I had not slept for years, and could not if I tried. He said excitedly—

" 'You got the sounding-rod in here, Marlow? I can't get the pumps to suck. By God! it's no child's play.'

"I gave him the sounding-rod and lay down again, trying to think of various things—but I thought only of the pumps. When I came on deck they were still at it, and my watch relieved at the pumps. By the light of the lantern brought on deck to examine the sounding-rod I caught a glimpse of their weary, serious faces. We pumped all the four hours. We pumped all night, all day, all the week—watch and watch. She was working herself loose, and leaked badly—not enough to drown us at once, but enough to kill us with the work at the pumps. And while we pumped the ship was going from us piecemeal: the bulwarks went, the stanchions were torn out, the ventilators smashed, the cabin-door burst in. There was not a dry spot in the ship. She was being gutted bit by bit. The long-boat changed, as if by magic, into matchwood where she stood in her gripes. I had lashed her myself, and was rather proud of my handiwork, which had withstood so long the malice of the sea. And we pumped. And there was no break in the weather. The sea was white like a sheet of foam, like a caldron of boiling milk; there was not a break in the clouds, no—not the size of a man's hand—no, not for so much as ten seconds. There was for us no sky, there were for us no stars, no sun, no universe—nothing but angry clouds and an infuriated sea. We pumped watch and watch, for dear life; and it seemed to last for months, for years, for all eternity, as though we had been dead and gone to a hell for sailors. We forgot the day of the week, the name of the month, what year it was, and whether we had ever been ashore. The sails blew away, she lay broadside on under a weather-cloth, the ocean poured over her, and we did not care. We turned those handles, and had the eyes of idiots. As soon as we had crawled on deck I used to take a round turn with a rope about the men, the pumps, and the mainmast, and we turned, we turned incessantly, with the water to our waists, to our necks, over our heads. It was all one. We had forgotten how it felt to be dry.

"And there was somewhere in me the thought: By Jove! this is the deuce of an adventure—something you read about; and it is my first voyage as second mate—and I am only twenty—and here I am lasting it out as well as any of these men, and keeping my chaps up to the mark. I was pleased. I would not have given up the experience for worlds. I had moments of exultation. Whenever the old dismantled craft pitched heavily with her counter high in the air, she seemed to me to throw up, like an appeal, like a defiance, like a cry to the clouds without mercy, the words written on her stern: 'Judea, London. Do or Die.'

"O youth! The strength of it, the faith of it, the imagination of it! To me she was not an old rattletrap carting about the world a lot of coal for a freight—to me she was the endeavour, the test, the trial of life I think of her with pleasure, with affection, with regret—as you would think of someone dead you have loved. I shall never forget her. . . Pass the bottle.

"One night when tied to the mast, as I explained, we were pumping on, deafened with the wind, and without spirit enough in us to wish ourselves dead, a heavy sea crashed aboard and swept clean over us. As soon as I got my breath I shouted, as in duty bound, 'Keep on, boys!' when suddenly I felt something hard floating on deck strike the calf of my leg. I made a grab at it and missed. It was so dark we could not see each other's faces within a foot—you understand.

"After that thump the ship kept quiet for a while, and the thing, whatever it was, struck my leg again. This time I caught it—and it was a saucepan. At first, being stupid with fatigue and thinking of nothing but the pumps, I did not understand what I had in my hand. Suddenly it dawned upon me, and I shouted, 'Boys, the house on deck is gone. Leave this, and let's look for the cook.'

"There was a deck-house forward, which contained the galley, the cook's berth, and the quarters of the crew. As we had expected for days to see it swept away, the hands had been ordered to sleep in the cabin—the only safe place in the ship. The steward, Abraham, however, persisted in clinging to his berth, stupidly, like a mule—from sheer fright I believe, like an animal that won't leave a stable falling in an earthquake. So we went to look for him. It was chancing death, since once out of our lashings we were as exposed as if on a raft. But we went. The house was shattered as if a shell had exploded inside. Most of it had gone overboard—stove, men's quarters, and their property, all was gone; but two posts, holding a portion of the bulkhead to which Abraham's bunk was attached, remained as if by a miracle. We groped in the ruins and came upon this, and there he was, sitting in his bunk, surrounded by foam and wreckage, jabbering cheerfully to himself. He was out of his mind; completely and for ever mad, with this sudden shock coming upon the fag-end of his endurance. We snatched him up, lugged him aft, and pitched him head-first down the cabin companion. You understand there was no time to carry him down with infinite precautions and wait to see how he got on. Those below would pick him up at the bottom of the stairs all right. We were in a hurry to go back to the pumps. That business could not wait. A bad leak is an inhuman thing.

"One would think that the sole purpose of that fiendish gale had been to make a lunatic of that poor devil of a mulatto. It eased before morning, and next day the sky cleared, and as the sea went down the leak took up. When it came to bending a fresh set of sails the crew demanded to put back—and really there was nothing else to do. Boats gone, decks swept clean cabin gutted, men without a stitch but what they stood in, stores spoiled, ship strained. We put her head for home, and—would you believe it? The wind came east right in our teeth. It blew fresh, it blew continuously. We had to beat up every inch of the way, but she did not leak so badly, the water keeping comparatively smooth. Two hours' pumping in every four is no joke—but it kept her afloat as far as Falmouth.

"The good people there live on casualties of the sea, and no doubt were glad to see us. A hungry crowd of shipwrights sharpened their chisels at the sight of that carcass of a ship. And, by Jove! they had pretty pickings off us before they were done. I fancy the owner was already in a tight place. There were delays. Then it was decided to take part of the cargo out and caulk her topsides. This was done, the repairs finished, cargo reshipped; a new crew came on board, and we went out—for Bankok. At the end of a week we were back again. The crew said they weren't going to Bankok—a hundred and fifty days' passage—in a something hooker that wanted pumping eight hours out of the twenty-four; and the nautical papers inserted again the little paragraph: '*Judea*. Barque. Tyne to Bankok; coals; put back to Falmouth leaky and with crew refusing duty.'

"There were more delays—more tinkering. The owner came down for a day, and said she was as right as a little fiddle. Poor old Captain Beard looked like the ghost of a Geordie skipper—through the worry and humiliation of it. Remember he was sixty, and it was his first command. Mahon said it was a foolish business, and would end badly. I loved the ship more than ever, and wanted awfully to get to Bankok. To Bankok! Magic name, blessed name. Mesopotamia wasn't a patch on it. Remember I was twenty, and it was my first second-mate's billet, and the East was waiting for me.

"We went out and anchored in the outer roads with a fresh crew—the third. She leaked worse than ever. It was as if those confounded shipwrights had actually made a hole in her. This time we did not even go outside. The crew simply refused to man the windlass.

"They towed us back to the inner harbour, and we became a fixture, a feature, an institution of the place. People pointed us out to visitors as 'That 'ere barque that's going to Bankok—has been here six months—put back three times.' On holidays the small boys pulling about in boats would hail, '*Judea*, ahoy!' and if a head showed above the rail shouted, 'Where you bound to?—Bankok?' and jeered. We were only three on board. The poor old skipper mooned in the cabin. Mahon undertook the cooking, and unexpectedly developed all a Frenchman's genius for preparing nice little messes. I looked languidly after the rigging. We became citizens of Falmouth. Every shopkeeper knew us. At the barber's or tobacconist's they asked familiarly. 'Do you think you will ever get to Bankok?' Meantime the owner, the underwriters, and the charterers squabbled amongst themselves in London, and our pay went on. . . . Pass the bottle.

"It was horrid. Morally it was worse than pumping for life. It seemed as though we had been forgotten by the world, belonged to nobody, would get nowhere; it seemed that, as if bewitched, we would have to live for ever and ever in that inner harbour, a derision and a byword to generations of long-shore loafers and dishonest boatmen. I obtained three months' pay and a five days' leave, and made a rush for London. It took me a day to get there and pretty well another to come back—but three months' pay went all the same. I don't know what I did with it. I went to a music-hall, I believe, lunched, dined, and supped in a swell place in Regent Street, and was back to time, with nothing but a complete set of Byron's works and a new railway rug to show for three months' work. The boat-man who pulled me off to the ship said: 'Hallo! I thought you had left the old thing. *She* will never get to Bankok.' 'That's all *you* know about it,' I said scornfully—but I didn't like that prophecy at all.

"Suddenly a man, some kind of agent to somebody, appeared with full powers. He had grog-blossoms all over his face, an indomitable energy, and was a jolly soul. We leaped into life again. A hulk came alongside, took our cargo, and then we went into dry dock to get our copper stripped. No wonder she leaked. The poor thing, strained beyond endurance by the gale, had, as if in disgust, spat out all the oakum of her lower seams. She was recaulked, new coppered, and made as tight as a bottle. We went back to the hulk and reshipped our cargo.

"Then, on a fine moonlight night, all the rats left the ship.

"We had been infested with them. They had destroyed our sails, consumed more stores than the crew, affably shared our beds and our dangers, and now, when the ship was made seaworthy, concluded to clear out. I called Mahon to enjoy the spectacle. Rat after rat appeared on our rail, took a last look over his shoulder, and leaped with a hollow thud into the empty hulk. We tried to count them, but soon lost the tale. Mahon said: 'Well, well! don't talk to me about the intelligence of rats. They ought to have left before, when we had that narrow squeak from foundering. There you have the proof how silly is the superstition about them. They leave a good ship for an old rotten hulk, where there is nothing to eat, too, the fools! . . . I don't believe they know what is safe or what is good for them, any more than you or I.'

"And after some more talk we agreed that the wisdom of rats had been grossly overrated, being in fact no greater than that of men.

"The story of the ship was known, by this, all up the Channel from Land's End to the Forelands, and we could get no crew on the south coast. They sent us one all complete from Liverpool, and we left once more—for Bankok.

"We had fair breezes, smooth water right into the tropics, and the old *Judea* lumbered along in the sunshine. When she went eight knots everything cracked aloft, and we tied our caps to our heads; but mostly she strolled on at the rate of three miles an hour. What could you expect? She was tired—that old ship. Her youth was where mine is—where yours is—you fellows who listen to this yarn; and what friend would throw your years and your weariness in your face? We didn't grumble at her. To us aft, at least, it seemed as though we had been born in her, reared in her, had lived in her for ages, had never known any other ship. I would just as soon have abused the old village church at home for not being a cathedral.

"And for me there was also my youth to make me patient. There was all the East before me, and all life, and the thought that I had been tried in that ship and had come out pretty well. And I thought of men of old who, centuries ago, went that road in ships that sailed no better, to the land of palms, and spices, and yellow sands, and of brown nations ruled by kings more cruel than Nero the Roman, and more splendid than Solomon the Jew. The old bark lumbered on, heavy with her age and the burden of her cargo, while I lived the life of youth in ignorance and hope. She lumbered on through an interminable procession of days; and the fresh gilding flashed back at the setting sun, seemed to cry out over the darkening sea the words painted on her stern, '*Judea*, London. Do or Die.'

"Then we entered the Indian Ocean and steered northerly for Java Head. The winds were light. Weeks slipped by. She crawled on, do or die, and people at home began to think of posting us as overdue.

"One Saturday evening, I being off duty, the men asked me to give them an extra bucket of water or so—for washing clothes. As I did not wish to screw on the fresh-water pump so late, I went forward whistling, and with a key in my hand to unlock the forepeak scuttle, intending to serve the water out of a spare tank we kept there.

"The smell down below was as unexpected as it was frightful. One would have thought hundreds of paraffin-lamps had been flaring and smoking in that hole for days. I was glad to get out. The man with me coughed and said, 'Funny smell, sir.' I answered negligently, 'It's good for the health they say,' and walked aft.

"The first thing I did was to put my head down the square of the midship ventilator. As I lifted the lid a visible breath, something like a thin fog, a puff of faint haze, rose from the opening. The ascending air was hot, and had a heavy, sooty, paraffiny smell. I gave one sniff, and put down the lid gently. It was no use choking myself. The cargo was on fire.

"Next day she began to smoke in earnest. You see it was to be expected, for though the coal was of a safe kind, that cargo had been so handled, so broken up with handling, that it looked more like smithy coal than anything else. Then it had been wetted—more than once. It rained all the time we were taking it back from the hulk, and now with this long passage it got heated, and there was another case of spontaneous combustion.

"The captain called us into the cabin. He had a chart spread on the table, and looked unhappy. He said, 'The coast of West Australia is near, but I mean to proceed to our destination. It is the hurricane month, too; but we will just keep her head for Bankok, and fight the fire. No more putting back anywhere, if we all get roasted. We will try first to stifle this 'ere damned combustion by want of air.'

"We tried. We battened down everything, and still she smoked. The smoke kept coming out through imperceptible crevices; it forced itself through bulkheads and covers; it oozed here and there and everywhere in slender threads, in an invisible film, in an incomprehensible manner. It made its way into the cabin, into the forecastle; it poisoned the sheltered places on the deck, it could be sniffed as high as the mainyard. It was clear that if the smoke came out the air came in. This was disheartening. This combustion refused to be stifled.

"We resolved to try water, and took the hatches off. Enormous volumes of smoke, whitish, yellowish, thick, greasy, misty, choking, ascended as high as the trucks. All hands cleared out aft.

Then the poisonous cloud blew away, and we went back to work in a smoke that was no thicker now than that of an ordinary factory chimney.

"We rigged the force-pump, got the hose along, and by and by it burst. Well, it was as old as the ship—a prehistoric hose, and past repair. Then we pumped with the feeble head-pump, drew water with buckets, and in this way managed in time to pour lots of Indian Ocean into the main hatch. The bright stream flashed in sunshine, fell into a layer of white crawling smoke, and vanished on the black surface of coal. Steam ascended mingling with the smoke. We poured salt water as into a barrel without a bottom. It was our fate to pump in that ship, to pump out of her, to pump into her; and after keeping water out of her to save ourselves from being drowned, we frantically poured water into her to save ourselves from being burnt.

"And she crawled on, do or die, in the serene weather. The sky was a miracle of purity, a miracle of azure. The sea was polished, was blue, was pellucid, was sparkling like a precious stone, extending on all sides, all round to the horizon—as if the whole terrestrial globe had been one jewel, one colossal sapphire, a single gem fashioned into a planet. And on the lustre of the great calm waters the *Judea* glided imperceptibly, enveloped in languid and unclean vapours, in a lazy cloud that drifted to leeward, light and slow; a pestiferous cloud defiling the splendour of sea and sky.

"All this time of course we saw no fire. The cargo smouldered at the bottom somewhere. Once Mahon, as we were working side by side, said to me with a queer smile: 'Now, if she only would spring a tidy leak—like that time when we first left the Channel—it would put a stopper on this fire. Wouldn't it?' I remarked irrelevantly, 'Do you remember the rats?'

"We fought the fire and sailed the ship too as carefully as though nothing had been the matter. The steward cooked and attended on us. Of the other twelve men, eight worked while four rested. Everyone took his turn, captain included. There was equality, and if not exactly fraternity, then a deal of good feeling. Sometimes a man, as he dashed a bucketful of water down the hatchway, would yell out, 'Hurrah for Bankok!' and the rest laughed. But generally we were taciturn and serious—and thirsty. Oh! how thirsty! And we had to be careful with the water. Strict allowance. The ship smoked, the sun blazed. . . Pass the bottle.

"We tried everything. We even made an attempt to dig down to the fire. No good, of course. No man could remain more than a minute below. Mahon, who went first, fainted there, and the man who went to fetch him out did likewise. We lugged them out on deck. Then I leaped down to show how easily it could be done. They had learned wisdom by that time, and contented themselves by fishing for me with a chain-hook tied to a broom-handle, I believe. I did not offer to go and fetch up my shovel, which was left down below.

"Things began to look bad. We put the long-boat into the water. The second boat was ready to swing out. We had also another, a 14-foot thing, on davits aft, where it was quite safe.

"Then, behold, the smoke suddenly decreased. We redoubled our efforts to flood the bottom of the ship. In two days there was no smoke at all. Everybody was on the broad grin. This was on a Friday. On Saturday no work, but sailing the ship of course, was done. The men washed their clothes and their faces for the first time in a fortnight, and had a special dinner given them. They spoke of spontaneous combustion with contempt, and implied *they* were the boys to put out combustions. Somehow we all felt as though we each had inherited a large fortune. But a beastly smell of burning hung about the ship. Captain Beard had hollow eyes and sunken cheeks. I had never noticed so much before how twisted and bowed he was. He and Mahon prowled soberly about hatches and ventilators, sniffing. It struck me suddenly poor Mahon was a very, very old chap. As to me, I was as pleased and proud as though I had helped to win a great naval battle. O! Youth!

"The night was fine. In the morning a homeward-bound ship passed us hull down—the first we had seen for months; but we were nearing the land at last, Java Head being about 190 miles off, and nearly due north.

"Next day it was my watch on deck from eight to twelve. At breakfast the captain observed, 'It's wonderful how that smell hangs about the cabin.' About ten, the mate being on the poop, I stepped down on the main-deck for a moment. The carpenter's bench stood abaft the mainmast: I leaned against it sucking at my pipe, and the carpenter, a young chap, came to talk to me. He remarked, 'I think we have done very well, haven't we?' and then I perceived with annoyance the fool was trying to tilt the bench. I said curtly, 'Don't, Chips,' and immediately became aware of a queer sensation, of an absurd delusion,—I seemed somehow to be in the air. I heard all round me like a pent-up breath released—as if a thousand giants simultaneously had said Phoo!—and felt a dull concussion which made my ribs ache suddenly. No doubt about it—I was in the air, and my body was describing a short parabola. But short as it was, I had the time to think several thoughts in, as far as I can remember, the following order: 'This can't be the carpenter—What is it?—Some accident—Submarine volcano?—Coals, gas!—By Jove! we are being blown up—Everybody's dead—I am falling into the after-hatch—I see fire in it.'

"The coal-dust suspended in the air of the hold had glowed dull-red at the moment of the explosion. In the twinkling of an eye, in an infinitesimal fraction of a second since the first tilt of the bench, I was sprawling full length on the cargo. I picked myself up and scrambled out. It was quick like a rebound. The deck was a wilderness of smashed timber, lying crosswise like trees in a wood after a hurricane; an immense curtain of soiled rags waved gently before me—it was the mainsail blown to strips. I thought, The masts will be toppling over directly; and to get out of the way bolted on all-fours towards the poop-ladder. The first person I saw was Mahon, with eyes like saucers, his mouth open, and the long white hair standing straight on end round his head like a silver halo. He was just about to go down when the sight of the main-deck stirring, heaving up, and changing into splinters before his eyes, petrified him on the top step. I stared at him in unbelief, and he stared at me with a queer kind of shocked curiosity. I did not know that I had no hair, no eyebrows, no eyelashes, that my young moustache was burnt off, that my face was black, one cheek laid open, my nose cut, and my chin bleeding. I had lost my cap one of my slippers, and my shirt was torn to rags. Of all this I was not aware. I was amazed to see the ship still afloat, the poop-deck whole—and, most of all, to see anybody alive. Also the peace of the sky and the serenity of the sea were distinctly surprising. I suppose I expected to see them convulsed with horror. . . Pass the bottle.

"There was a voice hailing the ship from somewhere—in the air, in the sky—I couldn't tell. Presently I saw the captain—and he was mad. He asked me eagerly, 'Where's the cabin-table?' and to hear such a question was a frightful shock. I had just been blown up, you understand, and vibrated with that experience,—I wasn't quite sure whether I was alive. Mahon began to stamp with both feet and yelled at him, 'Good God! don't you see the deck's blown out of her?' I found my voice, and stammered out as if conscious of some gross neglect of duty, 'I don't know where the cabin-table is.' It was like an absurd dream.

"Do you know what he wanted next? Well, he wanted to trim the yards. Very placidly, and as if lost in thought, he insisted on having the foreyard squared. 'I don't know if there's anybody alive,' said Mahon, almost tearfully. 'Surely,' he said, gently, 'there will be enough left to square the foreyard.'

"The old chap, it seems, was in his own berth winding up the chronometers, when the shock sent him spinning. Immediately it occurred to him—as he said afterwards—that the ship had struck something, and he ran out into the cabin. There, he saw, the cabin-table had vanished somewhere. The deck being blown up, it had fallen down into the lazarette of course. Where we had our breakfast that morning he saw only a great hole in the floor. This appeared to him so awfully mysterious, and impressed him so immensely, that what he saw and heard after he got on deck were mere trifles in comparison. And, mark, he noticed directly the wheel deserted and his barque off her course—and his only thought was to get that miserable, stripped, undecked, smouldering shell of a ship back again with her head pointing at her port of destination. Bankok! That's what he was after. I tell you this quiet, bowed, bandy-legged, almost deformed little man was immense in the singleness of his idea and in his placid ignorance of our agitation. He motioned us forward with a commanding gesture, and went to take the wheel himself.

"Yes; that was the first thing we did—trim the yards of that wreck! No one was killed, or even disabled, but everyone was more or less hurt. You should have seen them! Some were in rags, with black faces, like coal-heavers, like sweeps, and had bullet heads that seemed closely cropped, but were in fact singed to the skin. Others, of the watch below, awakened by being shot out from their collapsing bunks, shivered incessantly, and kept on groaning even as we went about our work. But they all worked. That crew of Liverpool hard cases had in them the right stuff. It's my experience they always have. It is the sea that gives it—the vastness, the loneliness surrounding their dark stolid souls. Ah! Well! we stumbled, we crept, we fell, we barked our shins on the wreckage, we hauled. The masts stood, but we did not know how much they might be charred down below. It was nearly calm, but a long swell ran from the west and made her roll. They might go at any moment. We looked at them with apprehension. One could not foresee which way they would fall.

"Then we retreated aft and looked about us. The deck was a tangle of planks on edge, of planks on end, of splinters, of ruined woodwork. The masts rose from that chaos like big trees above a matted undergrowth. The interstices of that mass or wreckage were full of something whitish, sluggish, stirring—of something that was like a greasy fog. The smoke of the invisible fire was coming up again, was trailing, like a poisonous thick mist in some valley choked with dead wood. Already lazy wisps were beginning to curl upwards amongst the mass of splinters. Here and there a piece of timber, stuck upright, resembled a post. Half of a fife-rail had been shot through the foresail, and the sky made a patch of glorious blue in the ignobly soiled canvas. A portion of several boards holding together had fallen across the rail, and one end protruded overboard, like a gangway leading upon nothing, like a gangway leading over the deep sea, leading to death—as if inviting us to walk the plank at once and be done with our ridiculous troubles. And still the air, the sky—a ghost, something invisible was hailing the ship.

"Someone had the sense to look over, and there was the helmsman, who had impulsively jumped overboard, anxious to come back. He yelled and swam lustily like a merman, keeping up with the ship. We threw him a rope, and presently he stood amongst us streaming with water and very crestfallen. The captain had surrendered the wheel, and apart, elbow on rail and chin in hand, gazed at the sea wistfully. We asked ourselves, What next? I thought, Now, this is something like. This is great. I wonder what will happen. O youth!

"Suddenly Mahon sighted a steamer far astern. Captain Beard said, 'We may do something with her yet.' We hoisted two flags, which said in the international language of the sea, 'On fire. Want immediate assistance.' The steamer grew bigger rapidly, and by and by spoke with two flags on her foremast, 'I am coming to your assistance.'

"In half an hour she was abreast, to windward, within hail, and rolling slightly, with her engines stopped. We lost our composure, and yelled all together with excitement, 'We've been blown up'. A man in a white helmet, on the bridge, cried, 'Yes! All right! all right!' and he nodded his head, and smiled, and made soothing motions with his hand as though at a lot of frightened children. One of the boats dropped in the water, and walked towards us upon the sea with her long oars. Four Calashes pulled a swinging stroke. This was my first sight of Malay seamen. I've known them since, but what struck me then was their unconcern: they came alongside, and even the bowman standing up and holding to our main-chains with the boat-hook did not deign to lift his head for a glance. I thought people who had been blown up deserved more attention.

"A little man, dry like a chip and agile like a monkey, clambered up. It was the mate of the steamer. He gave one look, and cried, 'O boys—you had better quit.'

"We were silent. He talked apart with the captain for a time—seemed to argue with him. Then they went away together to the steamer.

"When our skipper came back we learned that the steamer was the *Somerville*, Captain Nash, from West Australia to Singapore *via* Batavia with mails, and that the agreement was she should tow us to Anjer or Batavia, if possible, where we could extinguish the fire by scuttling, and then proceed on our voyage—to Bankok! The old man seemed excited. 'We will do it yet,' he said to Mahon, fiercely. He shook his fist at the sky. Nobody else said a word.

"At noon the steamer began to tow. She went ahead slim and high, and what was left of the *Judea* followed at the end of seventy fathom of tow-rope,—followed her swiftly like a cloud of smoke with mast-heads protruding above. We went aloft to furl the sails. We coughed on the yards, and were careful about the bunts. Do you see the lot of us there, putting a neat furl on the sails of that ship doomed to arrive nowhere? There was not a man who didn't think that at any moment the masts would topple over. From aloft we could not see the ship for smoke, and they worked carefully, passing the gaskets with even turns. 'Harbour furl—aloft there!' cried Mahon from below.

"You understand this? I don't think one of those chaps expected to get down in the usual way. When we did I heard them saying to each other, 'Well, I thought we would come down overboard, in a lump—sticks and all—blame me if I didn't.' 'That's what I was thinking to myself,' would answer wearily another battered and bandaged scarecrow. And, mind, these were men without the drilled-in habit of obedience. To an onlooker they would be a lot of profane scallywags without a redeeming point. What made them do it—what made them obey me when I, thinking consciously how fine it was, made them drop the bunt of the foresail twice to try and do it better? What? They had no professional reputation—no examples, no praise. It wasn't a sense of duty; they all knew well enough how to shirk, and laze, and dodge—when they had a mind to it—and mostly they had. Was it the two pounds ten a-month that sent them there? They didn't think their pay half good enough. No; it was something in them, something inborn and subtle and everlasting. I don't say positively that the crew of a French or German merchantman wouldn't have done it, but I doubt whether it would have been done in the same way. There was a completeness in it, something solid like a principle, and masterful like an instinct—a disclosure of something secret—of that hidden something, that gift of good or evil that makes racial difference, that shapes the late of nations.

"It was that night at ten that, for the first time since we had been fighting it, we saw the fire. The speed of the towing had fanned the smouldering destruction. A blue gleam appeared forward, shining below the wreck of the deck. It wavered in patches, it seemed to stir and creep like the light of a glowworm. I saw it first, and told Mahon. 'Then the game's up,' he said. 'We had better stop this towing, or she will burst out suddenly fore and aft before we can clear out.' We set up a yell; rang bells to attract their attention; they towed on. At last Mahon and I had to crawl forward and cut the rope with an axe. There was no time to cast off the lashings. Red tongues could be seen licking the wilderness of splinters under our feet as we made our way back to the poop.

"Of course they very soon found out in the steamer that the rope was gone. She gave a loud blast of her whistle, her lights were seen sweeping in a wide circle, she came up ranging close along-side, and stopped. We were all in a tight group on the poop looking at her. Every man had saved a little bundle or a bag. Suddenly a conical flame with a twisted top shot up forward and threw upon the black sea a circle of light, with the two vessels side by side and heaving gently in its centre. Captain Beard had been sitting on the gratings still and mute for hours, but now he rose slowly and advanced in front of us, to the mizzen-shrouds. Captain Nash hailed: 'Come along! Look sharp. I have mail-bags on board. I will take you and your boats to Singapore.'

" 'Thank you! No!' said our skipper. 'We must see the last of the ship.'

" 'I can't stand by any longer,' shouted the other. 'Mails—you know.'

" 'Ay! ay! We are all right.'

" 'Very well! I'll report you in Singapore. . . Good-bye!'

"He waved his hand. Our men dropped their bundles quietly. The steamer moved ahead, and passing out of the circle of light, vanished at once from our sight, dazzled by the fire which burned fiercely. And then I knew that I would see the East first as commander of a small boat. I thought it fine; and the fidelity to the old ship was fine. We should see the last of her. Oh, the glamour of youth! Oh, the fire of it, more dazzling than the flames of the burning ship, throwing a magic light on the wide earth, leaping audaciously to the sky, presently to be quenched by time, more cruel, more piti-less, more bitter than the sea—and like the flames of the burning ship surrounded by an impenetrable night.

"The old man warned us in his gentle and inflexible way that it was part of our duty to save for the underwriters as much as we could of the ship's gear. Accordingly we went to work aft, while she blazed forward to give us plenty of light. We lugged out a lot of rubbish. What didn't we save? An old barometer fixed with an absurd quantity of screws nearly cost me my life: a sudden rush of smoke came upon me, and I just got away in time. There were various stores, bolts of canvas, coils of rope; the poop looked like a marine bazaar, and the boats were lumbered to the gunwales. One would have thought the old man wanted to take as much as he could of his first command with him. He was very, very quiet, but off his balance evidently. Would you believe it? He wanted to take a length of old stream-cable and a kedge-anchor with him in the long-boat. We said, 'Ay, ay, sir,' deferentially,

and on the quiet let the things slip overboard. The heavy medicine-chest went that way, two bags of green coffee, tins of paint—fancy, paint!—a whole lot of things. Then I was ordered with two hands into the boats to make a stowage and get them ready against the time it would be proper for us to leave the ship.

"We put everything straight, stepped the long-boat's mast for our skipper, who was to take charge of her, and I was not sorry to sit down for a moment. My face felt raw, every limb ached as if broken, I was aware of all my ribs, and would have sworn to a twist in the backbone. The boats, fast astern, lay in a deep shadow, and all around I could see the circle of the sea lighted by the fire. A gigantic flame arose forward straight and clear. It flared fierce, with noises like the whirr of wings, with rumbles as of thunder. There were cracks, detonations, and from the cone of flame the sparks flew upwards, as man is born to trouble, to leaky ships, and to ships that burn.

"What bothered me was that the ship, lying broadside to the swell and to such wind as there was—a mere breath—the boats would not keep astern where they were safe, but persisted, in a pig-headed way boats have, in getting under the counter and then swinging alongside. They were knocking about dangerously and coming near the flame, while the ship rolled on them, and, of course, there was always the danger of the masts going over the side at any moment. I and my two boat-keepers kept them off as best we could, with oars and boat-hooks; but to be constantly at it became exasperating, since there was no reason why we should not leave at once. We could not see those on board, nor could we imagine what caused the delay. The boatkeepers were swearing feebly, and I had not only my share of the work but also had to keep at it two men who showed a constant inclination to lay themselves down and let things slide.

"At last I hailed, 'On deck there,' and someone looked over. 'We're ready here,' I said. The head disappeared, and very soon popped up again. 'The captain says, All right, sir, and to keep the boats well clear of the ship.'

"Half an hour passed. Suddenly there was a frightful racket, rattle, clanking of chain, hiss of water, and millions of sparks flew up into the shivering column of smoke that stood leaning slightly above the ship. The cat-heads had burned away, and the two red-hot anchors had gone to the bottom, tearing out after them two hundred fathom of red-hot chain. The ship trembled, the mass of flame swayed as if ready to collapse, and the fore top-gallant-mast fell. It darted down like an arrow of fire, shot under, and instantly leaping up within an oar's-length of the boats, floated quietly, very black on the luminous sea. I hailed the deck again. After some time a man in an unexpectedly cheerful but also muffled tone, as though he had been trying to speak with his mouth shut, informed me, 'Coming directly, sir,' and vanished. For a long time I heard nothing but the whirr and roar of the fire. There were also whistling sounds. The boats jumped, tugged at the painters, ran at each other playfully, knocked their sides together, or, do what we would, swung in a bunch against the ship's side. I couldn't stand it any longer, and swarming up a rope, clambered aboard over the stern.

"It was as bright as day. Coming up like this, the sheet of fire facing me was a terrifying sight, and the heat seemed hardly bearable at first. On a settee cushion dragged out of the cabin Captain Beard, his legs drawn up and one arm under his head, slept with the light playing on him. Do you know what the rest were busy about? They were sitting on deck right aft, round an open case, eating bread and cheese and drinking bottled stout.

"On the background of flames twisting in fierce tongues above their heads they seemed at home like salamanders, and looked like a band of desperate pirates. The fire sparkled in the whites of their eyes, gleamed on patches of white skin seen through the torn shirts. Each had the marks as of a battle about him—bandaged heads, tied-up arms, a strip of dirty rag round a knee—and each man had a bottle between his legs and a chunk of cheese in his hand. Mahon got up. With his handsome and disreputable head, his hooked profile, his long white beard, and with an uncorked bottle in his hand, he resembled one of those reckless sea-robbers of old making merry amidst violence and disaster. 'The last meal on board,' he explained solemnly. 'We had nothing to eat all day, and it was no use leaving all this.' He flourished the bottle and indicated the sleeping skipper. 'He said he couldn't swallow anything, so I got him to lie down,' he went on; and as I stared, 'I don't know whether you are aware, young fellow, the man had no sleep to speak of for days—and there will be dam' little sleep in the boats.' 'There will be no boats by-and-by if you fool about much longer,' I said, indignantly. I walked up to the skipper and shook him by the shoulder. At last he opened his eyes, but did not move. 'Time to leave her, sir,' I said quietly.

"He got up painfully, looked at the flames, at the sea sparkling round the ship, and black, black as ink farther away; he looked at the stars shining dim through a thin veil of smoke in a sky black, black as Erebus.

" 'Youngest first,' he said.

"And the ordinary seaman, wiping his mouth with the back of his hand, got up, clambered over the taffrail, and vanished. Others followed. One, on the point of going over, stopped short to drain his bottle, and with a great swing of his arm flung it at the fire. 'Take this!' he cried.

"The skipper lingered disconsolately, and we left him to commune alone for a while with his first command. Then I went up again and brought him away at last. It was time. The ironwork on the poop was hot to the touch.

"Then the painter of the long-boat was cut, and the three boats, tied together, drifted clear of the ship. It was just sixteen hours after the explosion when we abandoned her. Mahon had charge of the second boat, and I had the smallest—the 14-foot thing. The longboat would have taken the lot of us; but the skipper said we must save as much property as we could—for the underwriters—and so

I got my first command. I had two men with me, a bag of biscuits, a few tins of meat, and a breaker of water. I was ordered to keep close to the long-boat, that in case of bad weather we might be taken into her.

"And do you know what I thought? I thought I would part company as soon as I could. I wanted to have my first command all to myself. I wasn't going to sail in a squadron if there were a chance for independent cruising. I would make land by myself. I would beat the other boats. Youth! All youth! The silly, charming, beautiful youth.

"But we did not make a start at once. We must see the last of the ship. And so the boats drifted about that night, heaving and setting on the swell. The men dozed, waked, sighed, groaned. I looked at the burning ship.

"Between the darkness of earth and heaven she was burning fiercely upon a disc of purple sea shot by the blood-red play of gleams; upon a disc of water glittering and sinister. A high, clear flame, an immense and lonely flame, ascended from the ocean, and from its summit the black smoke poured continuously at the sky. She burned furiously; mournful and imposing like a funeral pile kindled in the night, surrounded by the sea, watched over by the stars. A magnificent death had come like a grace, like a gift, like a reward to that old ship at the end of her laborious days. The surrender of her weary ghost to the keeping of stars and sea was stirring like the sight of a glorious triumph. The masts fell just before daybreak, and for a moment there was a burst and turmoil of sparks that seemed to fill with flying fire the night patient and watchful, the vast night lying silent upon the sea. At daylight she was only a charred shell, floating still under a cloud of smoke and bearing a glowing mass of coal within.

"Then the oars were got out, and the boats forming in a line moved round her remains as if in procession—the long-boat leading. As we pulled across her stern a slim dart of fire shot out viciously at us, and suddenly she went down, head first, in a great hiss of steam. The unconsumed stern was the last to sink; but the paint had gone, had cracked, had peeled off, and there were no letters, there was no word, no stubborn device that was like her soul, to flash at the rising sun her creed and her name.

"We made our way north. A breeze sprang up, and about noon all the boats came together for the last time. I had no mast or sail in mine, but I made a mast out of a spare oar and hoisted a boat-awning for a sail, with a boat-hook for a yard. She was certainly over-masted, but I had the satisfaction of knowing that with the wind aft I could beat the other two. I had to wait for them. Then we all had a look at the captain's chart, and, after a sociable meal of hard bread and water, got our last instructions. These were simple: steer north, and keep together as much as possible. 'Be careful with that jury-rig, Marlow,' said the captain; and Mahon, as I sailed proudly past his boat, wrinkled his curved nose and hailed, 'You will sail that ship of yours under water, if you don't look out, young fellow.' He was a malicious old man—and may the deep sea where he sleeps now rock him gently, rock him tenderly to the end of time!

"Before sunset a thick rain-squall passed over the two boats, which were far astern, and that was the last I saw of them for a time. Next day I sat steering my cockle-shell—my first command—with nothing but water and sky around me. I did sight in the afternoon the upper sails of a ship far away, but said nothing, and my men did not notice her. You see I was afraid she might be homeward bound, and I had no mind to turn back from the portals of the East. I was steering for Java—another blessed name—like Bankok, you know. I steered many days.

"I need not tell you what it is to be knocking about in an open boat. I remember nights and days of calm, when we pulled, we pulled, and the boat seemed to stand still, as if bewitched within the circle of the sea horizon. I remember the heat, the deluge of rainsqualls that kept us baling for dear life (but filled our water-cask), and I remember sixteen hours on end with a mouth dry as a cinder and a steering-oar over the stern to keep my first command head on to a breaking sea. I did not know how good a man I was till then. I remember the drawn faces, the dejected figures of my two men, and I remember my youth and the feeling that will never come back any more—the feeling that I could last for ever, outlast the sea, the earth, and all men; the deceitful feeling that lures us on to joys, to perils, to love, to vain effort—to death; the triumphant conviction of strength, the heat of life in the handful of dust, the glow in the heart that with every year grows dim, grows cold, grows small, and expires—and expires, too soon, too soon—before life itself.

"And this is how I see the East. I have seen its secret places and have looked into its very soul; but now I see it always from a small boat, a high outline of mountains, blue and afar in the morning; like faint mist at noon; a jagged wall of purple at sunset. I have the feel of the oar in my hand, the vision of a scorching blue sea in my eyes. And I see a bay, a wide bay, smooth as glass and polished like ice, shimmering in the dark. A red light burns far off upon the gloom of the land, and the night is soft and warm. We drag at the oars with aching arms, and suddenly a puff of wind, a puff faint and tepid and laden with strange odours of blossoms, of aromatic wood, comes out of the still night—the first sigh of the East on my face. That I can never forget. It was impalpable and enslaving, like a charm, like a whispered promise of mysterious delight.

"We had been pulling this finishing spell for eleven hours. Two pulled, and he whose turn it was to rest sat at the tiller. We had made out the red light in that bay and steered for it, guessing it must mark some small coasting port. We passed two vessels, outlandish and high-sterned, sleeping at anchor, and, approaching the light, now very dim, ran the boat's nose against the end of a jutting wharf. We were blind with fatigue. My men dropped the oars and fell off the thwarts as if dead. I made fast to a pile. A current rippled softly. The scented obscurity of the shore was grouped into vast masses, a density of colossal clumps of vegetation, probably—mute and fantastic shapes. And at their foot the semicircle of a beach gleamed faintly, like an illusion. There was not a light, not a stir, not a sound. The mysterious East faced me, perfumed like a flower, silent like death, dark like a grave.

"And I sat weary beyond expression, exulting like a conqueror, sleepless and entranced as if before a profound, a fateful enigma.

"A splashing of oars, a measured dip reverberating on the level of water, intensified by the silence of the shore into loud claps, made me jump up. A boat, a European boat, was coming in. I invoked the name of the dead; I hailed: *Judea* ahoy! A thin shout answered.

"It was the captain. I had beaten the flagship by three hours, and I was glad to hear the old man's voice again, tremulous and tired. 'Is it you, Marlow?' 'Mind the end of that jetty, sir,' I cried.

"He approached cautiously, and brought up with the deep-sea lead-line which we had saved—for the underwriters. I eased my painter and fell alongside. He sat, a broken figure at the stern, wet with dew, his hands clasped in his lap. His men were asleep already. 'I had a terrible time of it,' he murmured. 'Mahon is behind—not very far.' We conversed in whispers, in low whispers, as if afraid to wake up the land. Guns, thunder, earthquakes would not have awakened the men just then.

"Looking round as we talked, I saw away at sea a bright light travelling in the night. 'There's a steamer passing the bay,' I said. She was not passing, she was entering, and she even came close and anchored. 'I wish,' said the old man, 'you would find out whether she is English. Perhaps they could give us a passage somewhere.' He seemed nervously anxious. So by dint of punching and kicking I started one of my men into a state of somnambulism, and giving him an oar, took another and pulled towards the lights of the steamer.

"There was a murmur of voices in her, metallic hollow clangs of the engine-room, footsteps on the deck. Her ports shone, round like dilated eyes. Shapes moved about, and there was a shadowy man high up on the bridge. He heard my oars.

"And then, before I could open my lips, the East spoke to me, but it was in a Western voice. A torrent of words was poured into the enigmatical, the fateful silence; outlandish, angry words, mixed with words and even whole sentences of good English, less strange but even more surprising. The voice swore and cursed violently; it riddled the solemn peace of the bay by a volley of abuse. It began by calling me Pig, and from that went crescendo into unmentionable adjectives—in English. The man up there raged aloud in two languages, and with a sincerity in his fury that almost convinced me I had, in some way, sinned against the harmony of the universe. I could hardly see him, but began to think he would work himself into a fit.

"Suddenly he ceased, and I could hear him snorting and blowing like a porpoise. I said—

" 'What steamer is this, pray?'

" 'Eh? What's this? And who are you?'

" 'Castaway crew of an English barque burnt at sea. We came here to-night. I am the second mate. The captain is in the long-boat, and wishes to know if you would give us a passage somewhere.'

" 'Oh, my goodness! I say. . . This is the *Celestial* from Singapore on her return trip. I'll arrange with your captain in the morning. . . and. . . I say. . . did you hear me just now?'

" 'I should think the whole bay heard you.'

" 'I thought you were a shore-boat. Now, look here—this infernal lazy scoundrel of a caretaker has gone to sleep again—curse him. The light is out, and I nearly ran foul of the end of this damned jetty. This is the third time he plays me this trick. Now, I ask you, can anybody stand this kind of thing? It's enough to drive a man out of his mind. I'll report him. . . . I'll get the Assistant Resident to give him the sack, by. . . ! See—there's no light. It's out, isn't it? I take you to witness the light's out. There should be a light, you know. A red light on the——'

" 'There was a light,' I said, mildly.

" 'But it's out, man! What's the use of talking like this? You can see for yourself it's out—don't you? If you had to take a valuable steamer along this Godforsaken coast you would want a light, too. I'll kick him from end to end of his miserable wharf. You'll see if I don't. I will——'

" 'So I may tell my captain you'll take us?' I broke in.

" 'Yes, I'll take you. Good-night,' he said, brusquely

"I pulled back, made fast again to the jetty, and then went to sleep at last. I had faced the silence of the East. I had heard some of its language. But when I opened my eyes again the silence was as complete as though it had never been broken. I was lying in a flood of light, and the sky had never looked so far, so high, before. I opened my eyes and lay without moving.

"And then I saw the men of the East—they were looking at me. The whole length of the jetty was full of people. I saw brown, bronze, yellow faces, the black eyes, the glitter, the colour of an Eastern crowd. And all these beings stared without a murmur, without a sigh, without a movement. They stared down at the boats, at the sleeping men who at night had come to them from the sea. Nothing moved. The fronds of palms stood still against the sky. Not a branch stirred along the shore, and the brown roofs of hidden houses peeped through the green foliage, through the big leaves that hung shining and still like leaves forged of heavy metal. This was the East of the ancient navigators, so old, so mysterious, resplendent and sombre, living and unchanged, full of danger and promise. And these were the men. I sat up suddenly. A wave of movement passed through the crowd from end to end, passed along the heads, swayed the bodies, ran along the jetty like a ripple on the water, like a breath of wind on a field—and all was still again. I see it now—the wide sweep of the bay, the glittering sands, the wealth of green infinite and varied, the sea blue like the sea of a dream, the crowd of attentive faces, the blaze of vivid colour—the water reflecting it all, the curve of the shore, the jetty, the high-sterned outlandish craft floating still, and the three boats with the tired men from the West sleeping, unconscious of the land and the people and of the violence of sunshine. They slept thrown across the thwarts, curled on bottom-boards, in the careless attitudes of death. The head of the old skipper, leaning back in the stern of the long-boat, had fallen on his breast, and he looked as though he would never wake. Farther out old Mahon's face was upturned to the sky, with the long white beard spread out on his breast, as though he had been shot where he sat at the tiller; and a man, all in a heap in the bows of the boat, slept with both arms embracing the stem-head and with his cheek laid on the gunwale. The East looked at them without a sound.

"I have known its fascination since; I have seen the mysterious shores, the still water, the lands of brown nations, where a stealthy Nemesis lies in wait, pursues, overtakes so many of the conquering race, who are proud of their wisdom, of their knowledge, of their strength. But for me all the East is contained in that vision of my youth. It is all in that moment when I opened my young eyes on it. I came upon it from a tussle with the sea—and I was young—and I saw it looking at me. And this is all that is left of it! Only a moment; a moment of strength, of romance, of glamour—of youth! A flick of sunshine upon a strange shore, the time to remember, the time for a sigh, and—good-bye!—Night—Good-bye!"

He drank.

"Ah! The good old time—the good old time. Youth and the sea. Glamour and the sea! The good, strong sea, the salt, bitter sea, that could whisper to you and roar at you and knock your breath out of you."

He drank again.

"By all that's wonderful it is the sea, I believe, the sea itself—or is it youth alone? Who can tell? But you here—you all had something out of life: money, love—whatever one gets on shore—and, tell me, wasn't that the best time, that time when we were young at sea; young and had nothing, on the sea that gives nothing, except hard knocks—and sometimes a chance to feel your strength—that only—what you all regret?"

And we all nodded at him: the man of finance, the man of accounts, the man of law, we all nodded at him over the polished table that like a still sheet of brown water reflected our faces, lined, wrinkled; our faces marked by toil, by deceptions, by success, by love; our weary eyes looking still, looking always, looking anxiously for something out of life, that while it is expected is already gone—has passed unseen, in a sigh, in a flash—together with the youth, with the strength with the romance of illusions.

PART III

Lea Shores, Wrecks, and other Catastrophes

The Singular Fate of the Brig Polly

RALPH D. PAINE

Steam has not banished from the deep sea the ships that lift tall spires of canvas to win their way from port to port. The gleam of their topsails recalls the centuries in which men wrought with stubborn courage to fashion fabrics of wood and cordage that should survive the enmity of the implacable ocean and make the winds obedient. Their genius was unsung, their hard toil forgotten, but with each generation the sailing ship became nobler and more enduring, until it was a perfect thing. Its great days live in memory with a peculiar atmosphere of romance. Its humming shrouds were vibrant with the eternal call of the sea, and in a phantom fleet pass the towering East Indiaman, the hard-driven Atlantic packet, and the gracious clipper that fled before the Southern trades.

A hundred years ago every bay and inlet of the New England coast was building ships which fared bravely forth to the West Indies, to the roadsteads of Europe, to the mysterious havens of the Far East. They sailed in peril of pirate and privateer, and fought these rascals as sturdily as they battled with wicked weather. Coasts were unlighted, the seas uncharted, and navigation was mostly by guesswork, but these seamen were the flower of an American merchant marine whose deeds are heroic in the nation's story. Great hearts in little ships, they dared and suffered with simple, uncomplaining fortitude. Shipwreck was an incident, and to be adrift in lonely seas or cast upon a barbarous shore was sadly commonplace. They lived the stuff that made fiction after they were gone.

Your fancy may be able to picture the brig *Polly* as she steered down Boston harbour in December, 1811, bound to Santa Cruz with lumber and salted provisions for the slaves of the sugar plantations. She was only a hundred and thirty tons burden and perhaps eighty feet long. Rather clumsy to look at and roughly built was the *Polly* as compared with the larger ships that brought home the China tea and silks to the warehouses of Salem. Such a ship was a community venture. The blacksmith, the rigger, and the calker took their pay in shares, or 'pieces.' They became part owners, as did likewise the merchant who supplied stores and material; and when the brig was afloat, the master, the mate, and even the seamen were allowed cargo space for commodities that they might buy and sell to their own advantage. A voyage directly concerned a whole neighbourhood.

Every coastwise village had a row of keel-blocks sloping to the tide. In winter weather too rough for fishing, when the farms lay idle, the Yankee Jack-of-all-trades plied with his axe and adze to shape the timbers and peg together such a little vessel as the *Polly*, in which to trade to London or Cadiz or the Windward Islands. Hampered by an unfriendly climate, hard put to it to grow sufficient food, with land immensely difficult to clear, the New Englander was between the devil and the deep sea, and he sagaciously, chose the latter. Elsewhere, in the early days, the forest was an enemy to be destroyed with great pains. The pioneers of Massachusetts, New Hampshire, and Maine regarded it with favour as the stuff with which to make stout ships and the straight masts they 'stepped' in them.

Nowadays, such a little craft as the *Polly* would be rigged as a schooner. The brig is obsolete, along with the quaint array of scows, ketches, pinks, brigantines and sloops which once filled the harbours and hove their hempen cables short to the clank of the windlass or capstan-pawl, while the brisk seamen sang a chanty to help the work along. The *Polly* had yards on both masts, and it was a bitter task to lay out in a gale of wind and reef the unwieldy single topsails. She would try for no record passages, but jogged sedately, and snugged down when the weather threatened.

On this tragic voyage she carried a small crew, Captain W. L. Cazneau, a mate, four sailors, and a cook who was a native Indian. No mention is to be found of any ill omens that forecasted disaster, such as a black cat, or a cross-eyed Finn in the forecastle. Two passengers were on board, "Mrs. J. S. Hunt and a negro girl nine years old." We know nothing whatever about Mr. Hunt, who may have been engaged in some trading 'adventure' of his own. Perhaps his kinsfolk had waved him a fare-ye-well from the pier-head when the *Polly* warped out of her berth.

The lone piccaninny is more intriguing. She appeals to the imagination and inspires conjecture. Was she a waif of the slave traffic whom some benevolent merchant of Boston was sending to Santa Cruz to find a home beneath kindlier skies? Had she been entrusted to the care of Mr. Hunt? She is unexplained, a pitiful atom visible for an instant on the tide of human destiny. She amused the sailors, no doubt, and that austere, copper-hued cook may have unbent to give her a doughnut when she grinned at the galley-door.

Four days out from Boston, on December 15, the *Polly* had cleared the perilous sands of Cape Cod and the hidden shoals of the Georges. Mariners were profoundly grateful when they, had safely worked off shore in the wintertime and were past Cape Cod, which bore a very evil repute in those days of square-rigged vessels. Captain Cazneau could recall that sombre day of 1802 when three fine ships, the *Ulysses, Brutus,* and *Volusia,* sailing together from Salem for European ports, were wrecked next day on Cape Cod. The fate of those who were washed ashore alive was most melancholy. Several died of the cold, or were choked by the sand which covered them after they fell exhausted.

As in other regions where shipwrecks were common, some of the natives of Cape Cod regarded a ship on the beach as their rightful plunder. It was old Parson Lewis of Wellfleet, who, from his pulpit window, saw a vessel drive ashore on a stormy Sunday morning. "He closed his Bible, put on his outside garment, and descended from the pulpit, not explaining his intention until he was in the aisle, and then he cried out 'Start fair' and took to his legs. The congregation understood and chased pell-mell after him."

The brig *Polly* laid her course to the southward and sailed into the safer, milder waters of the Gulf Stream. The skipper's load of anxiety was lightened. He had not been sighted and molested by the British men-of-war that cruised off Boston and New York to hold up Yankee merchantmen and impress stout seamen. This grievance was to flame in a righteous war only a few months later. Many a voyage was ruined, and ships had to limp back to port short-handed, because their best men had been kidnapped to serve in British ships. It was an age when might was right on the sea.

The storm which overwhelmed the brig *Polly* came out of the south-east, when she was less than a week on the road to Santa Cruz. To be dismasted and water logged was no uncommon fate. It happens often nowadays, when little schooners creep along the coast, from Maine and Nova Scotia ports, and dare the winter blows to earn their bread. Men suffer in open boats, as has been the seafarer's hard lot for ages, and they drown with none to hear their cries, but they are seldom adrift more than a few days. The story of the *Polly* deserves to be rescued from oblivion because, so far as I am able to discover, it is unique in the spray-swept annals of maritime disaster.

Seamanship was helpless to ward off the attack of the storm that left the brig a sodden hulk. Courageously her crew shortened sail and made all secure when the sea and sky presaged a change of weather. There were no green hands, but men seasoned by the continual hazards of their calling. The wild gale smote them in the darkness of the night. They tried to heave the vessel to, but she was battered and wrenched without mercy. Stout canvas was whirled away in fragments. The seams of the hull opened as she laboured, and six feet of water flooded the hold. Leaking like a sieve, the *Polly* would never see port again.

Worse was to befall her. At midnight she was capsized, or thrown on her beam-ends, as the sailor's lingo has it. She lay on her side while the clamorous seas washed clean over her. The skipper, the mate, the four seamen, and the cook somehow clung to the rigging and grimly refused to be drowned. They were of the old breed, "every hair a rope-yarn and every finger a fish-hook." They even managed to find an axe and grope their way to the shrouds in the faint hope that the brig might right if the masts went overside. They hacked away, and came up to breathe now and then, until the foremast and mainmast fell with a crash, and the wreck rolled level. Then they slashed with their knives at the tangle of spars and ropes until they drifted clear. As the waves rush across a half-tide rock, so they broke over the shattered brig, but she no longer wallowed on her side.

At last the stormy daylight broke. The mariners had survived, and they looked to find their two passengers, who had no other refuge than the cabin. Mr. Hunt was gone, blotted out with his affairs and his ambitions, whatever they were. The coloured child they had vainly tried to find in the night. When the sea boiled into the cabin and filled it, she had climbed to the skylight in the roof, and there she clung like a bat. They hauled her out through a splintered gap, and sought tenderly to shelter her in a corner of the streaming deck, but she lived no more than a few hours. It was better that this bit of human flotsam should flutter out in this way than to linger a little longer in this forlorn derelict of a ship. The *Polly* could not sink, but she drifted as a mere bundle of boards with the ocean winds and currents, while seven men tenaciously fought off death and prayed for rescue.

The gale blew itself out, the sea rolled blue and gentle, and the wreck moved out into the Atlantic, having veered beyond the eastern edge of the Gulf Stream. There was raw salt pork and beef to eat, nothing else, barrels of which they fished out of the cargo. A keg of water which had been lashed to the quarter-deck was found to contain thirty gallons. This was all there was to drink, for the other water-casks had been smashed or carried away. The diet of meat pickled in brine aggravated the thirst of these castaways. For twelve days they chewed on this salty raw stuff, and then the Indian cook, Moho by name, actually succeeded in kindling a fire by rubbing two sticks together in some abstruse manner handed down by his ancestors. By splitting pine spars and a bit of oaken rail he was able to find in the heart of them wood which had not been dampened by the sea, and he sweated and grunted until the great deed was done. It was a trick which he was not at all sure of repeating unless the conditions were singularly favourable. Fortunately for the hapless crew of the *Polly*, their Puritan grandsires had failed in their amiable endeavour to extinguish the aborigine.

The tiny galley, or 'camboose' as they called it, was lashed to ring-bolts in the deck, and had not been washed into the sea when the brig was swept clean. So now they patched it up and got a blaze going in the brick oven. The meat could be boiled, and they ate it without stint, assuming that a hundred barrels of it remained in the hold. It had not been discovered that the stern-post of the vessel was staved in under water and all of the cargo excepting some of the lumber had floated out.

The cask of water was made to last eighteen days by serving out a quart a day to each man. Then an occasional rain-squall saved them for a little longer from perishing of thirst. At the end of the forty days they had come to the last morsel of salt meat. The *Polly* was following an aimless course to the eastward, drifting slowly under the influence of ocean winds and currents. These gave her also a southerly slant, so that she was caught by the vast movement of water which is known as the Gulf Stream Drift. It sets over toward the coast of Africa and sweeps into the Gulf of Guinea.

The derelict was moving away from the routes of trade to Europe into the almost trackless spaces beneath the tropic sun, where the sea glittered empty to the horizon. There was a remote chance that she might be descried by a low-hulled slaver crowding for the West Indies under a mighty press of sail, with her human freightage jammed between decks to endure the unspeakable horrors of the Middle Passage. Although the oceans were populous with ships a hundred years ago, trade flowed on habitual routes. Moreover, a wreck might pass unseen two or three miles away. From the quarter-deck of a small sailing ship there was no such circle of vision as extends from the bridge of a steamer forty or sixty feet above the water, where the officers gaze through high-powered binoculars.

The crew of the *Polly* stared at skies which yielded not the merciful gift of rain. They had strength to build them a sort of shelter of lumber, but whenever the weather was rough, they were drenched by the waves which played over the wreck. At the end of fifty days of this hardship and torment the seven were still alive, but then the mate, Mr. Paddock, languished and died. It surprised his companions, for, as the old record runs,

> he was a man of robust constitution who had spent his life in fishing on the Grand Banks, was accustomed to endure privations, and appeared the most capable of standing the shocks of misfortune of any of the crew. In the meridian of life, being about thirty-five years old, it was reasonable to suppose that, instead of the first, he would have been the last to fall a sacrifice to hunger and thirst and exposure, but Heaven ordered it otherwise.

Singularly enough, the next to go was a young seaman, spare and active, who was also a fisherman by trade. His name was Howe. He survived six days longer than the mate, and "likewise died delirious and in dreadful distress." Fleeting thunder-showers had come to save the others, and they had caught a large shark by means of a running bowline slipped over his tail while he nosed about the weedy hull. This they cut up and doled out for many days. It was certain, however, that unless they could obtain water to drink they would soon all be dead men on the *Polly*.

Captain Cazneau seems to have been a sailor of extraordinary resource and resolution. His was the unbreakable will to live and to endure which kept the vital spark flickering in his shipmates. Whenever there was strength enough among them, they groped in the water in the hold and cabin in the desperate hope of finding something to serve their needs. In this manner they salvaged an iron tea-kettle and one of the captain's flint-lock pistols. Instead of flinging them away, he sat down to cogitate, a gaunt, famished wraith of a man who had kept his wits and knew what to do with them.

At length he took an iron pot from the galley, turned the tea-kettle upside down on it, and found that the rims failed to fit together. Undismayed, the skipper whittled a wooden collar with a seaman's sheath-knife, and so joined the pot and the kettle. With strips of cloth and pitch scraped from the deck-beams, he was able to make a tight union where his round wooden frame set into the flaring rim of the pot. Then he knocked off the stock of the pistol and had the long barrel to use for a tube. This he rammed into the nozzle of the tea-kettle, and calked them as well as he could. The result was a crude apparatus for distilling sea-water, when placed upon the bricked oven of the galley.

Imagine those three surviving seamen and the stolid redskin of a cook watching the skipper while he methodically tinkered and puttered! It was absolutely the one and final chance of salvation. Their lips were black and cracked and swollen, their tongues lolled, and they could no more than wheeze when they tried to talk. There was now a less precarious way of making fire than by rubbing dry sticks together. This had failed them most of the time. The captain had saved the flint and steel from the stock of his pistol. There was tow or tarry oakum to be shredded fine and used for tinder. This smouldered and then burst into a tiny blaze when the sparks flew from the flint, and they knew that they would not lack the blessed boon of fire.

Together they lifted the precious contrivance of the pot and the kettle and tottered with it to the galley. There was an abundance of fuel from the lumber, which was hauled through a hatch and dried on deck. Soon the steam was gushing from the pistol-barrel, and they poured cool salt water over the upturned spout of the tea-kettle to cause condensation. Fresh water trickled from the end of the pistol-barrel, and they caught it in a tin cup. It was scarcely more than a drop at a time, but they stoked the oven and lugged buckets of salt water, watch and watch, by night and day. They roused in their sleep to go on with the task with a sort of dumb instinct. They were like wretched automatons.

So scanty was the allowance of water obtained that each man was limited to "four small wine glasses" a day, perhaps a pint. It was enough to permit them to live and suffer and hope. In the warm seas which now cradled the *Polly* the barnacles grew fast. The captain, the cook, and the three seamen scraped them off and for some time had no other food. They ate these shell-fish mostly raw, because cooking interfered with that tiny trickle of condensed water.

The faithful cook was the next of the five to succumb. He expired in March, after they had been three months adrift, and the manner of his death was quiet and dignified, as befitted one who might have been a painted warrior in an earlier day. The account says of him:

On the 15th of March, according to their computation, poor Moho gave up the ghost, evidently from want of water, though with much less distress than the others, and in full exercise of his reason. He very devoutly prayed and appeared perfectly resigned to the will of God who had so sorely afflicted him.

The story of the *Polly* is unstained by any horrid episode of cannibalism, which occurs now and then in the old chronicles of shipwreck. In more than one seaport the people used to point at some weather-beaten mariner who was reputed to have eaten the flesh of a comrade. It made a marked man of him, he was shunned, and the unholy notoriety followed him to other ships and ports. The sailors of the *Polly* did cut off a leg of the poor, departed Moho, and used it as bait for sharks, and they actually caught a huge shark by so doing.

It was soon after this that they found the other pistol of the pair, and employed the barrel to increase the capacity of the still. By lengthening the tube attached to the spout of the tea-kettle, they gained more cooling surface for condensation, and the flow of fresh water now amounted to "eight junk bottles full" every twenty-four hours. Besides this, wooden gutters were hung at the eaves of the galley and of the rough shed in which they lived, and whenever rain fell, it ran into empty casks.

The crew was dwindling fast. In April, another seaman, Johnson by name, slipped his moorings and passed on to the haven of Fiddler's Green, where the souls of all dead mariners may sip their grog and spin their yarns and rest from the weariness of the sea. Three men were left aboard the *Polly*, the captain and two sailors.

The brig drifted into that fabled area of the Atlantic that is known as the Sargasso Sea, which extends between 16° and 38° North, between the Azores and the Antilles. Here the ocean currents are confused and seem to move in circles, with a great expanse of stagnant ocean, where the seaweed floats in tangled patches of red and brown and green. It was an old legend that ships once caught in the Sargasso Sea were unable to extricate themselves, and so rotted miserably and were never heard of again. Columbus knew better, for his caravels sailed through these broken carpets of weed, where the winds were so small and fitful that the Genoese sailors despaired of reaching anywhere. The myth persisted, and it was not dispelled until the age of steam. The doldrums of the Sargasso Sea were the dread of sailing ships.

The days and weeks of blazing calms in this strange wilderness of ocean mattered not to the blindly errant wreck of the *Polly*. She was a dead ship that had outwitted her destiny. She had no masts and sails to push her through these acres of leathery kelp and bright masses of weed which had drifted from the Gulf and the Caribbean to come to rest in this solitary, watery waste. And yet to the captain and his two seamen this dreaded Sargasso Sea was beneficent. The stagnant weed swarmed with fish and gaudy crabs and molluscs. Here was food to be had for the mere harvesting of it. They hauled masses of weed over the broken bulwarks and picked off the crabs by hundreds. Fishing gear was an easy problem for these handy sailor-men. They had found nails enough; hand-forged and malleable. In the galley they heated and hammered them to make fish-hooks, and the lines were of small stuff 'unrove' from a length of halyard. And so they caught fish, and cooked them while the oven could be spared. Otherwise they ate them raw, which was not distasteful after they had become accustomed to it. The natives of the Hawaiian Islands prefer their fish that way. Besides this, they split a large number of small fish and dried them in the hot sun upon the roof of the shelter. The sea-salt which collected in the bottom of the still was rubbed into the fish. It was a bitter condiment, but it helped to preserve them against spoiling.

The season of spring advanced until the derelict *Polly* had been four months afloat and wandering, and the end of the voyage was a long way off. The minds and bodies of the castaways had adjusted themselves to the intolerable situation. The most amazing aspect of the experience is that these men remained sane. They must have maintained a certain order and routine of distilling water, of catching fish, of keeping track of the indistinguishable procession of the days and weeks. Captain Cazneau's recollection was quite clear when he came to write down his account of what had happened. The one notable omission is the death of another sailor, name unknown, which must have occurred after April. The only seaman who survived to keep the skipper company was Samuel Badger.

By way of making the best of it, these two indomitable seafarers continued to work on their rough deckhouse, "which by constant improvement had become much more commodious." A few bundles of hewn shingles were discovered in the hold, and a keg of nails was found lodged in a corner of the forecastle. The shelter was finally made tight and water-proof, but, alas! there was no need of having it "more commodious." It is obvious, also, that "when reduced to two only, they had a better supply of water." How long they remained in the Sargasso Sea it is impossible to ascertain. Late in April it is recounted that "no friendly breeze wafted to their side the sea-weed from which they could obtain crabs or insects."

The mysterious impulse of the currents plucked at the keel of the *Polly* and drew her clear of this region of calms and of ancient, fantastic sea-tales. She moved in the open Atlantic again, without guidance or destination, and yet she seemed inexplicably to be following an appointed course, as though fate decreed that she should find rescue waiting somewhere beyond the horizon.

The brig was drifting toward an ocean more frequented, where the Yankee ships bound out to the River Plate sailed in a long slant far over to the African coast to take advantage of the booming trade-winds. She was also wallowing in the direction of the route of the East India-men, which departed from English ports to make the far-distant voyage around the Cape of Good Hope. None of them sighted the speck of a derelict, which floated almost level with the sea and had no spars to make her visible. Captain Cazneau and his companion saw sails glimmer against the sky-line during the last thousand miles of drift, but they vanished like bits of cloud, and none passed near enough to bring salvation.

June found the *Polly* approaching the Canary Islands. The distance of her journey had been about two thousand miles, which would make the average rate of drift something more than three hundred miles a month, or ten miles per day. The season of spring and its apple blossoms had come and gone in New England, and the brig had long since been mourned as missing with all hands. It was on the 20th of June that the skipper and his companion—two hairy, ragged apparitions—saw three ships which appeared to be heading in their direction. This was in latitude 28° North and longitude 13° West, and if you will look at a chart you will note that the wreck would soon have stranded on the coast of Africa. The three ships, in company, bore straight down at the pitiful little brig, which trailed fathoms of sea-growth along her hull. She must have seemed uncanny to those who beheld her and wondered at the living figures that moved upon the weather-scarred deck. She might have inspired "The Ancient Mariner."

Not one ship, but three, came bowling down to hail the derelict. They manned the braces and swung the main-yards aback, beautiful, tall ships and smartly handled, and presently they lay hove to. The captain of the nearest one shouted a hail through his brass trumpet, but the skipper of the *Polly* had no voice to answer back. He sat weeping upon the coaming of a hatch. Although not given to emotion, he would have told you that it had been a hard voyage. A boat was dropped from the davits of this nearest ship, which flew the red ensign from her spanker-gaff. A few minutes later Captain Cazneau and Samuel Badger, able seaman, were alongside the good ship *Fame* of Hull, Captain Featherstone, and lusty arms pulled them up the ladder. It was six months to a day since the *Polly* had been thrown on her beam-ends and dismasted.

The three ships had been near together in light winds for several days, it seemed, and it occurred to their captains to dine together on board of the *Fame*. And so the three skippers were there to give the survivors of the *Polly* a welcome and to marvel at the yarn they spun. The *Fame* was homeward bound from Rio Janeiro. It is pleasant to learn that Captain Cazneau and Samuel Badger "were received by these humane Englishmen with expressions of the most exalted sensibility." The musty old narrative concludes:

> Thus was ended the most shocking catastrophe which our seafaring history has recorded for many years, after a series of distresses from December 20 to the 20th of June, a period of one hundred and ninety-two days. Every attention was paid to the sufferers that generosity warmed with pity and fellow-feeling could dictate, on board the *Fame*. They were transferred from this ship to the brig *Dromio* and arrived in the United States in safety.

Here the curtain falls. I for one should like to hear more incidents of this astonishing cruise of the derelict *Polly* and also to know what happened to Captain Cazneau and Samuel Badger after they reached the port of Boston. Probably they went to sea again, and more than likely in a privateer to harry British merchantmen, for the recruiting officer was beating them up to the rendezvous with fife and drum, and in August of 1812 the frigate *Constitution,* with ruddy Captain Isaac Hull walking the poop in a gold-laced coat, was pounding the *Guerrière* to pieces in thirty minutes, with broadsides whose thunder echoed round the world.

"Ships are all right. It is the men in them," said one of Joseph Conrad's wise old mariners. This was supremely true of the little-brig that endured and suffered so much, and among the humble heroes of blue water by no means the least worthy to be remembered are Captain Cazneau and Samuel Badger, able seaman, and Moho, the Indian cook.

The Storm at Yarmouth

CHARLES DICKENS

As we struggled on, nearer and nearer to the sea, from which this mighty wind was blowing dead on shore, its force became more and more terrific. Long before we saw the sea, its spray was on our lips, and showered salt rain upon us. The water was out, over miles and miles of the flat country adjacent to Yarmouth; and every sheet and puddle lashed its banks, and had its stress of little breakers setting heavily towards us. When we came within sight of the sea, the waves on the horizon, caught at intervals above the rolling abyss, were like glimpses of another shore with towers and buildings. When at last we got into the town, the people came out to their doors, all aslant, and with streaming hair, making a wonder of the mail that had come through such a night.

I put up at the old inn, and went down to look at the sea; staggering along the street, which was strewn with sand and seaweed, and with flying blotches of sea-foam; afraid of falling slates and tiles; and holding by people I met, at angry corners. Coming near the beach, I saw, not only the boatmen, but half the people of the town, lurking behind buildings; some, now and then braving the fury of the storm to look away to sea, and blown sheer out of their courses in trying to get zigzag back.

Joining these groups, I found bewailing women whose husbands were away in herring or oyster boats, which there was too much reason to think might have foundered before they could run in anywhere for safety. Grizzled old sailors were among the people, shaking their heads, as they looked from water to sky, and muttering to one another; ship-owners, excited and uneasy; children huddling together, and peering into older faces; even stout mariners, disturbed and anxious, levelling their glasses at the sea from behind places of shelter, as if they were surveying an enemy.

The tremendous sea itself, when I could find sufficient pause to look at it, in the agitation of the blinding wind, the flying stones and sand, and the awful noise, confounded me. As the high watery walls came rolling in, and, at their highest, tumbled into surf, they looked as if the least would engulf the town. As the receding wave swept back with a hoarse roar, it seemed to scoop out deep caves in the beach, as if its purpose were to undermine the earth. When some white-headed billows thundered on, and dashed themselves to pieces before they reached the land, every fragment of the late whole seemed possessed by the full might of its wrath, rushing to be gathered to the composition of another monster. Undulating hills were changed to valleys, undulating valleys (with a solitary storm-bird sometimes skimming through them) were lifted up to hills; masses of water shivered and shook the beach with a booming sound; every shape tumultuously rolled on, as soon as made, to change its shape and place, and beat another shape and place away; the ideal shore on the horizon, with its towers and buildings, rose and fell; the clouds flew fast and thick; I seemed to see a rending and upheaving of all nature.

I went back to the inn; and when I had washed and dressed, and tried to sleep, but in vain, it was five o'clock in the afternoon. I had not sat five minutes by the coffee-room fire, when the waiter coming to stir it, as an excuse for talking, told me that two colliers had gone down, with all hands, a few miles away; and that some other ships had been seen labouring hard in the Roads, and trying, in great distress, to keep off shore. Mercy on them, and on all poor sailors, said he, if we had another night like the last!

I could not eat, I could not sit still, I could not continue steadfast to anything. Something within me, faintly answering to the storm without, tossed up the depths of my memory, and made a tumult in them. Yet, in all the hurry of my thoughts, wild running with the thundering sea,—the storm and my uneasiness regarding Ham were always in the foreground.

My dinner went away almost untasted; and I tried to refresh myself with a glass or two of wine. In vain. I fell into a dull slumber before the fire, without losing my consciousness, either of the uproar out of doors, or of the place in which I was. Both became overshadowed by a new and indefinable horror; and when I awoke—or rather when I shook off the lethargy that bound me in my chair—my whole frame thrilled with objectless and unintelligible fear.

It was reassuring, on such a night, to be told that some of the inn-servants had agreed together to sit up until morning. I went to bed, exceedingly weary and heavy; but, on my lying down, all such sensations vanished, as if by magic, and I was broad awake, with every sense refined.

For hours I lay there, listening to the wind and water; imagining, now, that I heard shrieks out at sea; now, that I distinctly heard the firing of signal guns; and now, the fall of houses in the town. I got up, several times, and looked out; but could see nothing, except the reflection in the window-panes of the faint candle I had left burning, and on my own haggard face looking in at me from the black void.

At length, my restlessness attained to such a pitch, that I hurried on my clothes, and went downstairs. In the large kitchen, where I dimly saw bacon and ropes of onions hanging from the beams, the watchers were clustered together, in various attitudes, about a table, purposely moved away from the great chimney, and brought near the door. A pretty girl, who had her ears stopped with her apron, and her eyes upon the door, screamed when I appeared, supposing me to be a spirit; but the others had more presence of mind, and were glad of an addition to their company. One man, referring to the topic they had been discussing, asked me whether I thought the souls of the collier-crews who had gone down, were out in the storm?

I remained there, I dare say, two hours. Once, I opened the yard-gate, and looked into the empty street. The sand, the seaweed, and the flakes of foam were driving by; and I was obliged to call for assistance before I could shut the gate again, and make it fast against the wind.

There was a dark gloom in my solitary chamber, when I at length returned to it; but I was tired now, and, getting into bed again, fell—off a tower and down a precipice—into the depths of sleep. I have an impression that for a long time, though I dreamed of being elsewhere and in a variety of scenes, it was always blowing in my dream. At length, I lost that feeble hold upon reality, and was engaged with two dear friends, but who they were I don't know, at the siege of some town in a roar of cannonading.

The thunder of the cannon was so loud and incessant, that I could not hear something I much desired to hear, until I made a great exertion and awoke. It was broad day—eight or nine o'clock; the storm raging, in lieu of the batteries; and some one knocking and calling at my door.

"What is the matter?" I cried.

"A wreck! Close by!"

I sprung out of bed and asked, "What wreck?"

"A schooner, from Spain or Portugal, laden with fruit and wine. Make haste, sir, if you want to see her! It's thought, down on the beach, she'll go to pieces every moment."

The excited voice went clamouring along the staircase, and I wrapped myself in my clothes as quickly as I could, and ran into the street.

Numbers of people were there before me, all running in one direction, to the beach. I ran the same way, outstripping a good many, and soon came facing the wild sea.

The wind might by this time have lulled a little, though not more sensibly than if the cannonading I had dreamed of had been diminished by the silencing of half a dozen guns out of hundreds. But the sea, having upon it the additional agitation of the whole night, was infinitely more terrific than when I had seen it last. Every appearance it had then presented, bore the expression of being *swelled*; and the height to which the breakers rose, and, looking over one another, bore one another down, and rolled in, in interminable hosts, was most appalling.

In the difficulty of hearing anything but wind and waves, and in the crowd, and the unspeakable confusion, and my first breathless efforts to stand against the weather, I was so confused that I looked out to sea for the wreck, and saw nothing but the foaming heads of the great waves. A half-dressed boatman, standing next me, pointed with his bare arm (a tattoo'd arrow on it, pointing in the same direction) to the left. Then, O great Heaven, I saw it, close in upon us!

One mast was broken short off, six or eight feet from the deck, and lay over the side, entangled in a maze of sail and rigging; and all that ruin, as the ship rolled and beat—which she did without a moment's pause, and with a violence quite inconceivable—beat the side as if it would stave it in. Some efforts were even then being made, to cut this portion of the wreck away; for, as the ship, which was broadside on, turned towards us in her rolling, I plainly descried her people at work with axes, especially one active figure with long curling hair, conspicuous among the rest. But a great cry, which was audible even above the wind and water, rose from the shore at this moment; the sea, sweeping over the rolling wreck, made a clean breach, and carried men, spars, casks, bulwarks, heaps of such toys, into the boiling surge.

The second mast was yet standing, with the rags of a rent sail, and a wild confusion of broken cordage flapping to and fro. The ship had struck once, the same boatman hoarsely said in my ear, and then lifted in and struck again. I understood him to add that she was parting amidships, and I could readily suppose so, for the rolling and the beating were too tremendous for any human work to suffer long. As he spoke, there was another great cry of pity from the beach; four men arose with the wreck out of the deep, clinging to the rigging of the remaining mast; uppermost, the active figure with the curling hair.

There was a bell on board; and as the ship rolled and dashed, like a desperate creature driven mad, now showing us the whole sweep of her deck, as she turned on her beam-ends towards the shore, now nothing but her keel, as she sprung wildly over and turned towards the sea, the bell rang; and its sound, the knell of those unhappy men, was borne towards us on the wind. Again we lost her, and again she rose. Two men were gone. The agony on shore increased. Men groaned, and clasped their hands; women shrieked, and turned away their faces. Some ran wildly up and down along the beach, crying for help where no help could be. I found myself one of these, frantically imploring a knot of sailors whom I knew, not to let those two lost creatures perish before our eyes.

They were making out to me, in an agitated way—I don't know how, for the little I could hear I was scarcely composed enough to understand—that the life-boat had been bravely manned an hour ago, and could do nothing; and that as no man would be so desperate as to attempt to wade off with a rope, and establish a communication with the shore, there was nothing left to try; when I noticed that some new sensation moved the people on the beach, and saw them part, and Ham come breaking through them to the front.

I ran to him—as well as I know—to renew my appeal for help. But, distracted though I was, by a sight so new to me and terrible, the determination in his face, and his look, out to sea, awoke me to a knowledge of his danger. I held him back with both arms; and implored the men with whom I had been speaking, not to listen to him, not to do murder, not to let him stir from off that sand!

Another cry arose on shore; and looking to the wreck, we saw the cruel sail, with blow on blow, beat off the lower of the men, and fly up in triumph round the active figure left alone upon the mast.

Against such a sight, and against such determination as that of the calmly desperate man who was already accustomed to lead half the people present, I might as hopefully have entreated the wind. "Mas'r Davy," he said, cheerily grasping me by both hands, "if my time is come, 'tis come. If 'tain't, I'll bide it. Lord above bless you, and bless all! Mates, make me ready! I'm agoing off!"

I was swept away, but not unkindly, to some distance, where the people around me made me stay; urging, as I confusedly perceived, that he was bent on going, with help or without, and that I should endanger the precautions for his safety by troubling those with whom they rested. I don't know what I answered, or what they rejoined; but, I saw hurry on the beach, and men running with ropes from a capstan that was there, and penetrating into a circle of figures that hid him from me. Then, I saw him standing alone, in a seaman's frock and trousers: a rope in his hand, or slung to his wrist: another round his body: and several of the best men holding, at a little distance, to the latter, which he laid out himself, slack upon the shore, at his feet.

The wreck, even to my unpractised eye, was breaking up. I saw that she was parting in the middle, and that the life of the solitary man upon the mast hung by a thread. Still, he clung to it. He had a singular red cap on—not like a sailor's cap, but of a finer colour; and as the few yielding planks between him and destruction rolled and bulged, and his anticipative death-knell rung, he was seen by all of us to wave it. I saw him do it now, and thought I was going distracted, when his action brought an old remembrance to my mind of a once dear friend.

Ham watched the sea, standing alone, with the silence of suspended breath behind him, and the storm before, until there was a great retiring wave, when, with a backward glance at those who held the rope which was made fast round his body, he dashed in after it, and in a moment was buffeting with the water; rising with the hills, falling with the valleys, lost beneath the foam; then drawn again to land. They hauled in hastily.

He was hurt. I saw blood on his face, from where I stood; but he took no thought of that. He seemed hurriedly to give them some directions for leaving him more free—or so I judged from the motion of his arm—and was gone as before.

And now he made for the wreck, rising with the hills, falling with the valleys, lost beneath the rugged foam, borne in towards the shore, borne on towards the ship, striving hard and valiantly. The distance was nothing, but the power of the sea and wind made the strife deadly. At length he neared the Wreck. He was so near, that with one more of his vigorous strokes he would be clinging to it, when a high, green, vast hill-side of water, moving on shoreward, from beyond the ship, he seemed to leap up into it with a mighty bound, and the ship was gone!

Some eddying fragments I saw in the sea, as if a mere cask had been broken, in running to the spot where they were hauling in. Consternation was in every face. They drew him to my very feet—insensible—dead. He was carried to the nearest house; and, no one preventing me now, I remained near him, busy, while every means of restoration were tried; but he had been beaten to death by the great wave, and his generous heart was stilled for ever.

As I sat beside the bed, when hope was abandoned and all was done, a fisherman, who had known me when Emily and I were children, and ever since, whispered my name at the door.

"Sir," said he, with tears starting to his weatherbeaten face, which, with his trembling lips, was ashy pale, "will you come over yonder?"

The old remembrance that had been recalled to me, was in his look. I asked him, terror-stricken, leaning on the arm he held out to support me:

"Has a body come ashore?"

He said, "Yes."

"Do I know it?" I asked then.

He answered nothing.

But, he led me to the shore. And on that part of it where she and I had looked for shells, two children—on that part of it where some lighter fragments of the old boat, blown down last night, had been scattered by the wind—among the ruins of the home he had wronged—I saw him lying with his head upon his arm, as I had often seen him lie at school.

From "David Copperfield"

The Strange Story of the *Emily Brand*

ANDREW HUSSEY ALLEN

I hardly suppose that any one will believe this story. Indeed I would hesitate to tell it were it not that its principal events are to be found recorded in the correspondence of the Department of State at Washington, and in the official reports of the Vice-Admiralty Court at Gibraltar, both of which sources of verification are, I have no doubt, accessible to the reader. I have myself seen the dispatches of our consul at Gibraltar and can vouch for their substantial correctness.

I was at Nice, where I had been sent a month earlier a tardy and restless convalescent, when, on the morning of November 20th, I found among my letters at breakfast one from my old friend Jack Drayton, dated two days earlier "On board the *Nomad*, Marseilles Harbor," and begging me to go for a cruise to the Azores with him. His fellow-voyagers, he wrote, had deserted him at Malta to go crusading to Jerusalem with some friends they had met there, and he urged me to go on this cruise with him as well on account of my health as on his account.

I called on my doctor, who agreed with Drayton that the voyage would set me squarely on my feet again, and as I knew of nothing that I would like better, I decided to go. I packed my trunks, took the early train for Marseilles, and boarded the yacht on the afternoon of the next day at five o'clock, and by eight the following morning we were under way.

The *Nomad* was a schooner of 230 tons, stanchly built for ocean cruising, and luxuriously equipped and furnished. Besides the captain, two mates, steward, cook, and Jack Drayton's servant, she carried a crew of seventeen men. Her owner was himself an able seaman, and his yacht was his home. He and I were such old friends and had lived together for so many years that we not only did not fear tiring of each other, but were reasonably sure of very good company.

On this occasion, however, we had a companion in Roy, a thoroughbred English mastiff that Drayton, who was very fond of animals, had taken to sea with him for the two preceding years. I never had appreciated before this cruise how much of a companion a dog could be. Roy quite won my heart. Unprejudiced by my affection for him, I think he was the noblest animal I have ever known. Stately, high-bred, intelligent, and lovable, he was "a gentleman and a scholar" from the jet of his handsome muzzle to the tip of his tawny tail.

We ran down the Mediterranean to the Straits with a fair, fast wind, feeling, as we passed the fortress, that we were well started on our voyage. But outside, on the ocean, Æolus became capricious, as is his wont, and bestowed his favors elsewhere. From that time on, until the fifth of December, we loitered sadly and uneventfully, with light northerly winds.

On the morning of that day, however, the breeze freshened somewhat, the smooth surface of the sea began to glitter with little ripples, our spirits rose with the prospect, and soon after nine o'clock we sighted a sail about three points off the port bow—the only thing in sight on the broad expanse of blue, shining ocean. By noon we had approached the stranger near enough to see that she was a brigantine under short sail, and in a little while we were within hailing distance.

Taking the glass, I made her out to be a smart-looking and beautifully modeled craft, and after a few minutes I read the name in gilt letters on her quarter as *Emily Brand.* Except her jib and a staysail, she had not a stitch of canvas set. As I looked she impressed me with a sense of deathlike stillness, desolation, and mystery, and I could see that her wheel was loose, and that there was no one on her deck. The slight breeze that still prevailed was from the north, and the brigantine was on the starboard tack, while the yacht, as she had been for several days, was on the port tack.

I handed the glass to Drayton, who, after a short survey, told Captain Parker to hail. The captain, as we neared her, called repeatedly in stentorian tones, but no answer came, and no sign of life appeared on board the strange vessel. Finally, when within three hundred yards of her, we shortened sail, had a boat lowered away, and Drayton and I, with the first mate of the *Nomad* and two seamen, rowed alongside.

Slowly drifting to leeward, she was barely moving, and Jamieson, the mate, clambered aboard by the gear of the bowsprit. He threw us a line, and, making the boat fast, we quickly followed him. He and the two men went forward, while Drayton and I, crossing the deck to the companionway, which we found open, entered the cabin. It was empty. The men forward likewise finding no one, we all five searched the vessel fore and aft, and high and low. There was not a living being besides ourselves on board. She had evidently been deserted. But why?

She was seemingly perfectly sound, and we failed to discover the least apparent cause for her abandonment. Her hold was exceptionally dry, there not being as much bilge in it as would fill a hogshead. Her cargo consisted of casks marked as containing alcohol, all of which were stowed in good order and condition except one, which had been started. The exterior of the hull above the water line did not exhibit the slightest trace of damage, nor was there the least evidence on the interior that the vessel had been repaired in any way or was at that time in need of any repairs.

Among the seamen's effects were found a number of articles of not inconsiderable value, going to show that the men were comparatively well-to-do and apparently in a great measure free from the too common prodigality of their class. We also found that the vessel was amply provisioned and that she had plenty of good water in her casks.

Of her cabin I must say that I had no idea there was a merchantman afloat so comfortably and attractively equipped in this respect. The apartment was large, high, and well lighted, with four state-rooms opening from it—two forward and two aft. On either side, along the bunks, were broad, thick hair cushions of crimson stuff. In the center the table with leaves was stationary, while in the space between the staterooms forward was a harmonium, open; and aft, in the corresponding space, stood a sewing-machine, also uncovered. On a chair beside the harmonium lay several music books and loose sheets of music, and on the sewing-machine we found a pattern in muslin, evidently a child's garment in process of making, besides a small phial of machine oil, a spool of cotton, and a thimble, all three in a perpendicular position: a fact which afforded additional proof that the vessel could not have encountered any stress of weather—not even enough, indeed, to upset these lightly balanced articles.

In the forward port stateroom, under the berth, we found an open box containing panes of glass packed in hay and unbroken. Hanging on the partition opposite the berth, in the starboard stateroom forward, we found a cutlass of somewhat ancient pattern, which, on extracting it from its scabbard, I discovered to be stained with what seemed to me to be blood.

I called Drayton's attention to this, and, after examining it, he agreed with me and concluded that we had perhaps found a clew to the mystery. Later along we discovered marks on the main rail, apparently of blood, but by that time we had been forced to give up the idea that there had been any violence on board the vessel, by the perfect order in which we had found everything on board. The remaining articles of furniture in the cabin were two large easy-chairs upholstered in leather, and several smaller, lighter chairs. The carpet was a heavy Brussels, and the woodwork was painted a pale, soft gray, with bluish trimmings. All the brass mountings and the lamps were bright and shining, and, in fact, the apartment was pervaded no less by an air of quiet order than of mystery. It was clear that it had been occupied in part by a woman and child, and these we naturally supposed to be the wife and child of the captain.

Our charts showed that we had boarded the derelict in latitude 38° 20' north, longitude 17° 15' west. In its proper place we found her log-book, but her chronometer, manifest, and bills of lading were missing. The log showed that the last day's work of the vessel had been on the twenty-fourth of November, sea time, when the weather had allowed an observation to be taken that placed her in latitude 36° 56' north, longitude 27° 20' west.

The entries on her slate log were, however, carried down to eight o'clock of the morning of the twenty-fifth, at which hour she had passed from west to east to the north of the island of St. Mary's

(Azores), the eastern point of which then bore south-southwest, six miles distant. The distance in longitude from the island of St. Mary's to the point at which we fell in with the *Emily Brand* is 7° 54'; the corrected distance of the latitude from the position last indicated in the log is 1° 18' north; and the brigantine had apparently held on her course for ten days after the twenty-fifth of November, the wheel being loose all the time.

But during the period from the twenty-fifth of November to the fifth of December the wind had been more or less from the north continuously, and it appeared to us impossible that the derelict could have covered within that time a distance of 7° 54' east, at any rate on the starboard tack. The obvious inference was, therefore, that she had not been abandoned until several days after the last entry made in the log.

Drayton, who was nothing if not practical when occasion required, at once set about making his arrangements to work our prize to Gibraltar. He dispatched the mate and the two men back to the yacht with orders to have Parker select five men from the crew, one to be in authority as sailing master, and send them aboard the brigantine prepared to take up their quarters. Meanwhile he returned to the cabin to look over the log-book again, and some papers we had found in the captain's room, and I went forward to poke about in the seamen's quarters, which were to be occupied by the *Nomad's* men.

Fifteen minutes later, standing by the foremast facing aft, I struck a match to light my cigar. As I raised my eyes from doing so, I distinctly saw a man step from the rail at the port quarter, move quickly across the deck, and disappear in the companionway.

At the moment I caught but the briefest glimpse of his face and figure; but they were not to be forgotten. He seemed to have clambered aboard from the sea, for he was dripping wet and hatless, and his light hair was matted or glued about his head and face by the water, while his clothes clung to his body and limbs, and glistened and dripped in the sunlight. His figure was gigantic. His face and trunk were bloated or distended, like those of a man who has been drowned, and the former, without a vestige of color, was ghastly horrible and expressionless, even to the eyes, beyond the possibility of description.

I was naturally startled and shocked by the suddenness of his appearance and his extraordinary condition; but not so much so that I failed to shout "Hallo there!" as I got sight of him. He neither answered nor hesitated; he did not even look towards me, but, almost as I uttered the words, disappeared, as I have said, down the companionway. I hurried aft and entered the cabin. There alone, with his feet on a chair before him and the log-book on his knees, was Drayton, quite calm, and half-facing the companionway. I looked around, saw no one else (all the stateroom doors were wide open), and exclaimed in amazement, "Where is he?"

"Where is who?" drawled Drayton.

"The fellow," I replied, "who just came in here. Wake up, Jack! I saw the man come in here this moment. He is here somewhere," I added, searching from room to room in vain, and trying to open a door in the forward starboard stateroom, leading, as I supposed, into the between-decks space. The door was fast, and bolted on my side of it. No one had gone through there.

I turned back to the cabin, where my companion stood gazing at me curiously. He stepped towards me, looked at me very closely, and then said sharply:

"What's the matter with you, old man; are you out of your mind? How could any one have come in here without my seeing him?"

I described the man, and added that I could swear I had seen him enter the cabin three seconds before me.

Finally, somewhat impressed by my positiveness, Drayton, in spite of himself, went on deck, I following, and hailing the yacht, he called out: "Let the men, when the boat comes over, bring the dog with them." And then, to me, "If there is any one on board here Roy will find him though we can't."

As we turned back to the cabin I noticed that that part of the deck over which I had seen the stranger pass, dripping with water, five minutes before, was perfectly dry, as were also the brass plates on the companion-ladder down which I had seen him disappear. This discovery bothered me not a little, as may be readily imagined. Still I remained firm in my conviction that I had actually seen the man, and had not, as Drayton evidently believed, simply suffered an optical illusion.

I paced the deck until the yacht's boat arrived with the men and Roy. When they had boarded the brigantine Drayton came on deck again, and we made another thorough search of her with the dog running on ahead and with the aid of two bull's-eye lanterns that the men had brought over. This second search was as fruitless of result as the first. By the time we had finished it was after five o'clock, and we were at the point of returning to the yacht, to prepare for dinner, when we decided that it would be best to lock the cabin. We entered it for that purpose, and after having secured the doors of the staterooms, and closed the ports, we turned to leave it, Drayton preceding me towards the deck.

Halfway up the companionway it suddenly occurred to me that I had left my cigar-case on the table, and I returned to get it. As I again stepped into the apartment I saw, clearly defined, at the upper end of the bunk on the starboard side upon the partition, close by the stateroom door, the shadow in profile of the face and figure of a man. The shadow appeared to be cast by some very tall person sitting on the bunk to my right, forward; but there was no one there, as a matter of course. I began to doubt the evidence of my senses, and stood for a moment looking about me in bewilderment.

Recovering myself, however, I approached the corner, convinced that the dark gray shadow was a stain upon the paint. Apparently it was not. From the chair near the harmonium I took a loose sheet of music, and, holding it between the shadow and the light, I looked behind it and perceived that that portion of the shadow—a part of the head and face—between which and the light I had interposed the obstacle had been obliterated. On looking at the surface of the paper in my hand, I beheld the missing portion of the shadow clearly silhouetted thereon.

Having thus satisfied myself that it was a shadow, and one cast by some (to me) invisible and impalpaole thing or substance, I hardly need add that I became somewhat excited. I shouted to Drayton, who immediately ran back into the cabin, followed by the dog. His examination of the phenomenon resulted exactly as mine had. On turning, at its conclusion, to speak to Roy, we found to our surprise that he had left us. Although we tried our best, neither by persuasion nor command could we move him to enter the cabin again.

We looked at each other nonplused, Drayton and I, and I am willing to confess that mingled with my feeling of triumph at having thus convinced him that there were others at work besides ourselves aboard the mysterious derelict, was an uncomfortable consciousness that the weird annoyance was beginning to tell on my nerves and to excite my imagination disagreeably as to what was to come next.

Still I entertained not the least doubt that we were the victims of some vulgar jugglery practiced upon us for some unexplained reason by hidden human agents. I was morally positive that this was the case. I had not, of course, had time to reason with myself as to the logic of the conclusion, but it was the only natural one, and certainly no other explanation of what I had seen occurred to me. Consideration of possible supernatural causes or solutions was out of the question with both of us. Jack Drayton was as free from all superstitious fancies as he was incapable of fear, and I may claim to have been his counterpart in the former respect.

Slowly, as we looked upon it, the strange shadow faded out. After a vain search of half an hour, and fruitless experiments with the lights and shadows of the cabin, we locked the companionway and returned to the yacht to dine.

By eight o'clock, having completed our arrangements, we went back to the brigantine to pass the night in her cabin. Roy received us on deck, and we tried again, but in vain, to induce him to enter the apartment with us. His refusal annoyed us both. It was incomprehensible. We, however, prepared ourselves for the night. Drayton established himself in the forward starboard corner on the bunk, looking after—the shadow's corner. I made myself comfortable in the port corner aft, diagonally opposite and facing him. We thus between us commanded a full view of the cabin and the four staterooms, the doors of which we had reopened.

The dog roamed restlessly about the decks until a little before midnight, when I heard him lie down across the entrance to the companionway.

At a quarter to one o'clock—I looked at my watch at the moment—without any premonition, the three cabin lamps—one over Drayton's head, one over mine, and one in the center over the table—suddenly became dim. This was surprising, as we had carefully filled and trimmed them all before lighting them. I got up to examine that nearest me, turning my back to Drayton.

As I did so I heard the peculiar double click of the hammer of a pistol. Turning again, I saw my companion, with his cocked revolver in hand, step to the floor.

His face was pale and rigid, and his eyes fierce and fixed. He moved to the table and raised the weapon. With an indescribable sensation of dread I looked in the direction of his aim, and there, not five feet from where I stood, on the inside edge of one of the ports, I saw a large, coarse, bloated hand clinging, and behind it, outside, at the shoulder, the ghastly, brutal face of the man I had seen cross the deck in the afternoon.

The dull, lead-colored eyes seemed peering into the cabin. Almost overcome by mingled horror and disgust (I can convey no idea of the loathesomeness of this man's appearance), I was somewhat relieved by the cold, clear tones of Drayton's voice, as I heard him say:

"Now, my man, I have you in range. I'm a passable shot, and if you move, I shall fire. Who are you? and what deviltry are you engaged in here?"

There was no reply. After a pause, Drayton spoke again:

"I intend to have an answer. If you don't speak up before I say three, I shall fire, anyway. We are not to be trifled with."

Still there was no reply; and after a pause of about ten seconds, Drayton counted very slowly, "one—two—three," and then followed the flash and report of a pistol.

The man at the porthole did not move. Drayton, with wonderful nerve, raised the weapon again; but even as he did so the face and hand disappeared. Not instantly; but, as if drawn slowly back, they seemed to be swallowed up in the darkness without. As they faded away, the light in the cabin waned again; and crying to me, "Stay where you are, and keep the dog with you" (the dog had bounded into the cabin, half involuntarily, I suppose, at the report of the pistol), Drayton hurried on deck.

I seized Roy's collar, and, at the moment, the doors of all four staterooms, although there was not the slightest lurch of the vessel, slowly but steadily swung and silently closed, as did also the skylights, the ports, and the sliding hatch and doors of the companionway, shutting me in alone with the dog.

My recollection of what followed is perfectly clear—nay, vivid—but it is not in my power to write an adequate description of it. All I can do is to relate what occurred as I actually saw and felt it. Appreciation of the horror of my position I must leave, with but an intimation of it, to the imagination of the reader.

On finding myself thus closed in, my first undefined idea, naturally, was to reach the deck and call Drayton. I was startled, but I do not think that I was afraid at first. Some new trick was about to be played upon us, and I wanted him to see what it was with me. It did not occur to me that the companion-hatch could have been made fast, so I turned to the steps, the dog accompanying me closely—too closely, in fact. As I raised my foot I felt that I was unable to place it on the first stair. It was as though the exit from the cabin had been walled up. A second attempt was equally in vain.

I endeavored to precipitate myself into the companionway. I might as well have tried to walk through a wall of solid rock, and still, in extending my hands and looking before me, I felt nothing but a soft though forbidding pressure, and saw nothing but the open stairway. I cannot say whether my sensation was one of terror or bewilderment—perhaps it was a mingling of the two.

I called aloud with the full strength of my lungs, but the sound of my voice seemed strangely muffled, even while I was perfectly conscious that I had full possession of my senses. During all this time the dog had been pressing close against me, trembling like a leaf, shuddering. I laid my hand on his head. It was hot to the touch. I looked down at him. With his ears laid back, his eyes protruding, and his tongue hanging out, he was the picture of terror—such a picture as I hope never to see again. A great, fearless, noble mastiff utterly abject, and cowering like any little cur.

And now the cabin lamps were suddenly extinguished, and only a small lantern left burning on the table. The atmosphere became oppressively hot, and a musty, moldy odor pervaded the apartment. In the deepened darknss I turned to look behind me with an added foreboding—if my horror may be said not to have reached its acme already. Beneath the door of the starboard stateroom, forward, I saw a brilliant line of light, and in the same place as before, the weird shadow of the afternoon, now bent over as though he who cast it there were listening at the door.

With my hand still on the mastiff's head, and impelled by some power not my own and stronger than my will, I moved towards the shade. My third step placed me directly in front of one of the large leather lounging chairs, which was so situated as to squarely face the dreadful corner. Into this chair I sank not only involuntarily, but seemingly by physical compulsion, the dog standing against it beside me. As again I laid my hand upon him I felt that he was rigid and strained in every muscle.

As I gazed at the shadow it slowly became upright and huge, and cast itself clearly upon the door, which immediately swung open without sound. With this phenomenon an indefinable sensation of almost intolerable pressure came upon me. I felt as though bound with iron or encased in lead. The chair seemed to hold me in a vise-like embrace. All power of motion left me. I tried to speak. I was dumb. The silence was awful; my sense of loneliness appalling. My mind, however, was most active and acute, and after a moment, every faculty seemed to be concentrated upon attention to what was going on before me.

Within the stateroom I saw a short, thick-set man seated on a camp-stool beside the berth, under a hanging lamp which shed a brilliant light. With his face in his hands and his head leaning against the partition before him, he seemed asleep; but I could not see that he breathed.

Behind him and half turned from me, I saw one standing who seemed to me to be the original of the shadow, and who, as I looked, raised his right arm in the air, and dealt the sleeping man a terrible blow at the back of the head with a heavy marline-spike, crushing the skull and killing the victim instantly.

No blood followed the stroke, and, although, as I have said, the room was brilliantly illuminated, I saw no shadows. The murderer seized the dead man's body before it fell to the floor, and opening the forward door of the stateroom, which led into the between-decks space, passed out, dragging the corpse with him, and disappeared in the darkness. Almost at once, however, he returned, and as he came towards me into the cabin, I again recognized the horrible face of the giant I had seen cross the deck above in the afternoon—the face of the man at whose hand I believed that Drayton with unerring aim had fired in the open porthole a little while before.

He entered the apartment, and, following with my eyes the direction of his movements, I saw him extend his hand and take up from the bunk, where he might have been sitting a few moments earlier, what appeared to me to be a carpenter's chisel or screw-driver. With this he again vanished into the darkness between decks. As he did so the forward door of the stateroom closed behind him, and simultaneously the light within went out, and the lamps in the cabin were relighted, while the doors and portholes, skylight, and companion-hatch were, I felt, reopened.

My hand being still upon the dog, I perceived a tremor or shudder pass through his entire frame, as with a deep sigh he instantly thereafter dashed from the cabin to the deck.

I heard Drayton's voice call loudly, "Roy! Roy!" and then a splash in the silent sea.

Freed from the terrible pressure, I now arose blindly to make my own way to the deck from the stifling atmosphere of the cabin; but the walls and furniture seemed to whirl and spin around and around me—and I remembered no more.

When I recovered consciousness I was again seated in the heavy chair, the cabin was cool, and there was the odor of brandy about. Drayton was standing over me with his hand on my forehead, and I heard the tramp of feet on the deck above. I looked at my watch, which I had laid open on the table several hours earlier, and it told me that I had been in the cabin alone with the dog but ten minutes at the uttermost.

From my companion I learned that after leaving me he had called the forward watch and one of the men from the deckhouse, and searched fruitlessly for a trace of the man at the porthole. As he had approached the companionway, the dog had dashed from it, foaming at the mouth, and in his madness leaped into the sea. Every effort was made to save him, but we never saw the poor fellow again.

The remaining hours of the night passed without incident. I related to Drayton what I had seen in the cabin, and we agreed that whatever the power that was exhibiting itself on board the brigantine—whether human or superhuman, natural or supernatural—it was one that we certainly could not account for, theorize as we might. Drayton, however, held to his purpose of taking the vessel to Gibraltar, there to turn her over, with as much of her story as we could tell, to the Vice-Admiralty Court for investigation.

In the morning we made an examination of the room in which I had seen the phantom murder committed (if I may describe as "phantom" those who seemed no less real flesh and blood than myself) and of the between-decks space forward of it, but we discovered nothing. At the edge of the porthole, however, at the spot where the hand had been, we found the bullet from the revolver buried in the wood.

By this time the seamen had gotten an inkling of the character of the ship's mystery; but as none of them had actually seen anything (nor, strangely enough, had heard the shot) Drayton's good sense and firmness triumphed over their superstition, and we were enabled to work the derelict to port without difficulty and without further incident. A second night passed in her cabin by both of us was quiet and uneventful in every way, but we were satisfied that we had discovered the cause of her abandonment. The sailors would have said that she was haunted.

We made Gibraltar on the morning of the thirteenth of December, and immediately reporting the circumstances under which we had found the *Emily Brand* we turned her over to the authorities.

The Queen's Proctor in Admiralty at once ordered a special survey of the vessel by the surveyor of shipping, assisted by the marshal of the court and an expert diver. The result of this survey was a report substantially embodying the facts as to the finding of the vessel and her condition here related by me. In addition to this, however, the stains on the old cutlass and on the vessel's rail were subjected to a chemical analysis by which it was proved that they were not bloodstains, and this fact was made an item of the report.

Upon this unsatisfactory conclusion Drayton and I determined to communicate to the authorities an account of the almost incredible events of our first day and night aboard the mysterious vessel. This we were enabled to do without making ourselves ridiculous, through the good offices of the governor of the fortress, to whom Drayton was well known. Thereupon a second survey was ordered, during which the entire cargo was removed.

At the request of one of the officials engaged in this second survey, I accompanied him aboard the brigantine for the purpose of pointing out the movements of the phantom murderer. This official developed a rather remarkable detective ingenuity. He subjected me, in the course of our conversation, to a close cross-examination concerning the chisel or screw-driver, for which the assassin had returned after the murder. On my remaining firm in my conviction as to what the tool appeared to be, he confided to me his theory of the terrible mock murder I had witnessed.

He believed, he told me, that the crime which had caused the vessel's abandonment had been revealed to me "by the spirits," as he expressed it, "of the principal actors." Proceeding on this theory, he personally (permitting me to accompany him) made a careful examination of the fatal stateroom and of the now empty between-decks space forward, his object being to discover some evidence of the use of such a tool, to the appearance of which he attached the greatest importance.

At a point about fifteen feet distant from the stateroom he found a narrow strip of oak about an inch in thickness and five feet in length, projecting, by its thickness, beyond the smooth surface of the vessel's inner shell. On scrutinizing it closely we perceived that it had been fixed in its place by means of five screws, apparently of brass, as the heads were incrusted with bright green rust or mold. We immediately summoned assistance, procured a screw-driver, and removed the strip. Having accomplished this, we discovered that the strip had been affixed over a perpendicular succession of the joints of the narrow planks of the vessel's interior hull, which sprang outward as they were released, far enough for my companion to insert his fingers behind them.

Wrenching them off, we found to our horror, wedged in the inner space, the grinning skeleton of a man, upon which hung shreds of clothing. As this skeleton was lifted out, something dropped to the deck with a metallic sound, and rolled to my feet. I stooped and picked it up. It was a plain band of gold—a ring. On the inside was engraved: "From H. M. to J. B."

The clothing of the unfortunate man appeared to have been partially eaten by rats. At the time it seemed to me a fortunate thing that it had not been entirely destroyed, as otherwise the ring, which had been retained in one of the folds, would long before have slipped from the bony finger to the bottom of the hold, and rendered positive identification, perhaps, impossible. The skeleton was clean, dry, and white, and on further examination we found that the back of the skull had been fractured, apparently by a blow from a club.

Since our arrival at Gibraltar, and about a week before the finding of the skeleton, Drayton had written to the owners of the brigantine at New York, having learned who they were from the surveyor of shipping, to whom her missing captain had been well and favorably known. In his letter to these gentlemen Drayton had asked for such a history of the *Emily Brand* as her owners were willing and prepared to give. He particularly required a full account of her missing company, and the details of any mutiny or other crime that might have occurred on board within their knowledge, with a description of the participants.

At the end of about three weeks from the date on which the skeleton was found (we in the meanwhile having had a run up the Mediterranean and back) a new captain and new crew arrived from New York, sent out by Messrs. Barnes and Spaulding, to take the brigantine on to Genoa, for which port she had been originally bound. The captain, Mr. Church, presented himself on board the *Nomad* the day of his arrival, as the bearer of a long letter to Drayton from Mr. Barnes, the senior member of the owning firm. From that letter I transcribed the ensuing account of the *Emily Brand.*

"The brigantine was built for us about two years ago at Portland, Maine. Including her present voyage she has made four in all. The first two were prosperous, and on neither of them did anything out of the ordinary run occur. A year ago last November, however, she sailed from this port, with a miscellaneous cargo, for Lisbon, taken out by Captain James Blaisdel, who had been in our employ for many years, and who had commanded her on her two preceding voyages.

"Among her crew was a Swede or Norwegian of the name of Peterson, a gigantic, ill-favored fellow, who had been injured in our service some time before by a fall from the rigging, in which he sustained a severe contusion of the brain. For several months he lay in the hospital here, in what was believed to be a hopeless condition of imbecility; but finally, having recovered, or apparently recovered, he applied for a berth on the *Emily Brand.*

"On the eleventh of December we received news by cable from Mr. Riggs, the mate, of the death of Captain Blaisdel and the man Peterson. On the twenty-sixth a letter came, giving the particulars, which were briefly as follows: About the eighth day out from New York Peterson developed symptoms of a relapse of this disease (caused by the fall), which seemed, however, to affect his mind only with a sort of intermittent stupor. He exhibited no signs of mania or violence, and was capable of performing his light duties about one half the time. He was accordingly not confined, and the master did what he could for him, treating him with the utmost kindness, and advising him to lay off from his work. This he did for several days, but apparently without beneficial effect.

"On the night of December 5, Mr. Blaisdel turned in at eight bells (twelve o'clock). The weather was clear, the wind over the port quarter, and the moon lighted up the deck. The vessel was then about latitude 38° north, longitude 17° west, near the point at which you picked her up. Just before two bells (one o'clock) the man at the wheel saw Peterson, whom he recognized by his great size, cross the deck amidship to the starboard rail and throw something into the sea. On being hailed by this man, Peterson went aft, and said that he had thrown a pair of old shoes overboard. He was in his stocking feet.

"In the morning the master failed to appear, and after waiting a reasonable time the steward knocked at his door. Receiving no response, he called Mr. Riggs, the mate, who entered the stateroom and found it empty. The berth had not been occupied. When after a search it became evident that the captain could not be found, Miller, the man who had taken the wheel at midnight, told the mate of Peterson's appearance and his conversation with him. Peterson was sent for, and found in his bunk, apparently sleeping. He was aroused, and brought on deck in a very excited condition, and on being interrogated by Mr. Riggs he became incoherent and violent.

"The mate thereupon ordered two of the men to seize him; but as they approached to do so, he eluded them, and darting to the vessel's side, went overboard. They put her about and lowered a boat immediately, but he was never seen again. It seems clear that in a fit of insanity he murdered the captain and threw his body into the sea during the night. How this was accomplished no one knows, for no noise was heard, nor were any traces of violence found about the vessel.

"On her present voyage Mr. Riggs, the former mate, went as master of the vessel. He was, I believe, thirty-six years of age, married, and had one child—a little girl of five or six years. It is our custom to allow our masters to purchase an interest in the vessels they command, and Mr. Riggs and his wife owned two-sixteenths of the *Emily Brand*. He was a man of the highest character and thoroughly competent to go as master. On this last voyage his wife and child accompanied him.

"I cannot form the slightest conjecture concerning the strange disappearance of poor Riggs and his family, with all on board, and I have but little belief that they will ever be heard of again."

From this letter it became evident that the skeleton found up in the between-decks space was that of Captain James Blaisdel, with whose name the initials engraved in the ring corresponded.

The remains thus identified were interred at Gibraltar.

Some hope of the rescue of the castaways was for a time entertained, as it was learned that the boat (the brigantine had but one) in which they were presumed to have left the vessel was a lifeboat, new, light, and incapable of sinking. Moreover, it was known that they could not have encountered any bad weather for many days after parting from the *Emily Brand*.

Accordingly the widest publicity was given to the fact of their having disappeared, and for more than a year the civilized world was searched throughout with all the facilities at the disposal of our own government and that of England, upon the chance that they had made some land or had been picked up by some passing vessel. But no trace of the lifeboat or of any of its occupants was ever discovered.

Jonah

THE BIBLE

Jonah, 1

1: Now the word of the LORD came unto Jonah the son of Amittai, saying,

2: Arise, go to Nineveh, that great city, and cry against it; for their wickedness is come up before me.

3: But Jonah rose up to flee unto Tarshish from the presence of the LORD, and went down to Joppa; and he found a ship going to Tarshish: so he paid the fare thereof, and went down into it, to go with them unto Tarshish from the presence of the LORD.

4: But the LORD sent out a great wind into the sea, and there was a mighty tempest in the sea, so that the ship was like to be broken.

5: Then the mariners were afraid, and cried every man unto his god, and cast forth the wares that were in the ship into the sea, to lighten it of them. But Jonah was gone down into the sides of the ship; and he lay, and was fast asleep.

6: So the shipmaster came to him, and said unto him, What meanest thou, O sleeper? arise, call upon thy God, if so be that God will think upon us, that we perish not.

7: And they said every one to his fellow, Come, and let us cast lots, that we may know for whose cause this evil is upon us. So they cast lots, and the lot fell upon Jonah.

8: Then said they unto him, Tell us, we pray thee, for whose cause this evil is upon us; What is thine occupation? and whence comest thou? what is thy country? and of what people art thou?

9: And he said unto them, I am an Hebrew; and I fear the LORD, the God of heaven, which hath made the sea and the dry land.

10: Then were the men exceedingly afraid, and said unto him, Why hast thou done this? For the men knew that he fled from the presence of the LORD, because he had told them.

11: Then said they unto him, What shall we do unto thee, that the sea may be calm unto us? for the sea wrought, and was tempestuous.

12: And he said unto them, Take me up, and cast me forth into the sea; so shall the sea be calm unto you: for I know that for my sake this great tempest is upon you.

13: Nevertheless the men rowed hard to bring it to the land; but they could not: for the sea wrought, and was tempestuous against them.

14: Wherefore they cried unto the LORD, and said, We beseech thee, O LORD, we beseech thee, let us not perish for this man's life, and lay not upon us innocent blood: for thou, O LORD, hast done as it pleased thee.

15: So they took up Jonah, and cast him forth into the sea: and the sea ceased from her raging.

16: Then the men feared the LORD exceedingly, and offered a sacrifice unto the LORD, and made vows.

17: Now the LORD had prepared a great fish to swallow up Jonah. And Jonah was in the belly of the fish three days and three nights.

Jonah, 2

1: Then Jonah prayed unto the LORD his God out of the fish's belly,

2: And said, I cried by reason of mine affliction unto the LORD, and he heard me; out of the belly of hell cried I, and thou heardest my voice.

3: For thou hadst cast me into the deep, in the midst of the seas; and the floods compassed me about: all thy billows and thy waves passed over me.

4: Then I said, I am cast out of thy sight; yet I will look again toward thy holy temple.

5: The waters compassed me about, even to the soul: the depth closed me round about, the weeds were wrapped about my head.

6: I went down to the bottoms of the mountains; the earth with her bars was about me for ever: yet hast thou brought up my life from corruption, O LORD my God.

7: When my soul fainted within me I remembered the LORD: and my prayer came in unto thee, into thine holy temple.

8: They that observe lying vanities forsake their own mercy.

9: But I will sacrifice unto thee with the voice of thanksgiving; I will pay that that I have vowed. Salvation is of the LORD.

10: And the LORD spake unto the fish, and it vomited out Jonah upon the dry land.

A Nightmare of the Doldrums

W. CLARK RUSSELL

The *Justitia* was a smart little barque of 395 tons. I had viewed her with something of admiration as she lay in midstream in the Hooghly—somewhere off the Coolie Bazaar.

I—representing in those days a large Birmingham firm of dealers in the fal-lal industries—had wished to make my way from Calcutta to Capetown. I saw the *Justitia* and took a fancy to her; I admired the long, low, piratic run of her hull, as she lay with straining hawsepipes on the rushing stream of the Hooghly; upon which, as you watched, there might go by in the space of an hour some halfscore at least of dead natives made ghastly canoes of by huge birds, erect upon the corpses, burying their beaks as they sailed along.

I called upon the agents, was told that the *Justitia* was not a passenger ship, but that I could hire a cabin for the run to Capetown if I chose; a sum in rupees, trifling compared with the cost of transit by steam, was named. I went on board, found the captain walking up and down under the awning, and agreeably killed an hour in a chat with as amiable a seaman as ever it was my good fortune to meet.

We sailed in the middle of July. Nothing worth talking about happened during our run down the Bay of Bengal. The crew aforemast were all of them Englishmen; there were twelve, counting the cook and steward. The captain was a man named Cayzer; the only mate of the vessel was one William Perkins. The boatswain, a rough, short, hairy, immensely strong man, acted as second mate and kept a look-out when Perkins was below. But he was entirely ignorant of navigation, and owned to me that he read with difficulty words of one syllable, and could not write.

I was the only passenger. My name, I may as well say here, is Thomas Barron. Our run to the south Ceylon parallels was slow and disappointing. The monsoon was light and treacherous, sometimes dying out in a sort of laughing, mocking gust till the whole ocean was a sheet-calm surface, as though the dependable trade wind was never again to blow.

"Oh, yes," said Captain Cayzer to me, "we're used to the unexpected hereabouts. Monsoon or no monsoon, I'll tell you what: you're always safe in standing by for an Irishman's hurricane down here."

"And what sort of breeze is that?" I asked.

"An up-and-down calm," said he; "as hard to know where it begins as to guess where it'll end."

However, thanks to the frequent trade puffs and other winds, which tasted not like the monsoon, we crawled through those latitudes which Ceylon spans and fetched within a few degrees of the Equator.

I left my cabin one morning some hours after the sun had risen, by which time the decks had been washed down, and were already dry, with a salt sparkle as of bright white sand on the face of the planks, so roasting was it. I went into the head to get a bath under the pump there.

It was a true tropic morning. The courses swung to the swell without response to the breathings of the air; and on high the light cotton-white royals were scarcely curved by the delicate passage of the draught.

Yet the barque had steerage way. When I looked through the grating at her metalled forefoot I saw the ripples plentiful as harpstrings threading aft, and whilst I dried myself I watched the slow approach of a piece of timber hoary with barnacles and venerable with long hairs of seaweed, amid and around which a thousand little fish were sporting, many-colored as though a rainbow had been shivered.

I returned to my cabin, dressed, and stepped on to the quarter-deck, where I found some men spreading the awning, and the captain viewing an object out upon the water through a telescope, and talking to the boatswain, who stood alongside.

"What do you see?" I asked.

"Something that resembles a raft," answered the captain.

The thing he looked at was about a mile distant, some three points on the starboard bow. On pointing the telescope, I distinctly made out the fabric of a raft, fitted with a short mast, to which midway a bundle—it resembled a parcel—was attached. A portion of the raft was covered by a white sheet or cloth, whence dangled a short length of something chocolate-coloured, indistinguishable even with the glass, lifting and sinking as the raft rose and fell upon the flowing heave of the sea.

"This ocean," said the captain, taking the glass from me, "is a big volume of tragic stories, and the artist who illustrates the book does it in that fashion," and he nodded in the direction of the raft.

"What do you make of it, boatswain?" I asked.

"It looks to me," he answered in his strong, harsh, deep voice, "like a religious job—one of them rafts the Burma covies float away their dead on. I never see one afore, sir, but I've heard tell of such things."

We sneaked stealthily towards the raft. It was seven bells—half-past seven—and the sailors ate their breakfast on the forecastle, that they might view the strange contrivance. The mate, Mr. Perkins, came on deck to relieve the boatswain, and, after inspecting the raft through the telescope, gave it as his opinion that it was a Malay floating bier—"a Mussulman trick of ocean burial, anyhow," said he. "There should be a jar of water aboard the raft, and cakes and fruit for the corpse to regale on, if he ha'n't been dead long."

The steward announced breakfast; the captain told him to hold it back awhile. He was as curious as I to get a close view of the queer object, but the wind was nearly gone, the barque scarcely responded to the motion of her rudder, the thread-like lines at the cutwater had faded, and a roasting, oppressive calm was upon the water, whitening it out into a tingling sheen of quicksilver with a fiery shaft of blinding dazzle, solitary and splendid.

The raft was about six cables' lengths off us when the barque came to a dead stand, with a soft, universal hollowing in of her canvas from royal to course, as though, like something sentient, she delivered one final sigh before the swoon of the calm seized her. But now we were near enough to resolve the floating thing with the naked eye into details.

It was a raft formed of bamboo canes. A mast about six feet tall was erected upon it; the dark thing over the edge proved a human leg, and, when the fabric lifted with the swell and raised the leg clear, we saw that the foot had been eaten away by fish, a number of which were swimming about the raft, sending little flashes of foam over the pale surface as they darted along with their back or dorsal fins exposed. They were all little fish; I saw no sharks. The body to which the leg belonged was covered by a white cloth. The captain called my attention to the parcel attached to the mast, and said that it possibly contained the food which the Malays leave beside their dead after burial.

"But let's go to breakfast now, Mr. Barron," said he, with a slow, reproachful, impatient look round the breathless scene of ocean. "If there's any amusement to be got out of that thing yonder there's a precious long, quiet day before us, I fear, for the entertainment."

We breakfasted, and in due course returned on deck. The slewing of the barque had caused the raft to shift its bearings, otherwise its distance remained as it was when we went below.

"Mr. Perkins," said the captain, "lower a boat and bring aboard that parcel from the raft's jury-mast, and likewise take a peep at the figure under the cloth, and report its sex and what it looks like."

I asked leave to go in the boat, and when she was lowered, with three men in her, I followed Mr. Perkins and we rowed over to the raft. All about the frail bamboo contrivance the water was beautiful with the colors and movements of innumerable fish. As we approached we were greeted by an evil smell. The raft seemed to have been afloat for a considerable period; its submerged portion was green with marine adhesions or growths. The fellow in the bows of the boat, maneuvering with the boathook, cleverly snicked the parcel from the jury-mast and handed it along to the mate, who put it beside him without opening it, for that was the captain's privilege.

"Off with that cloth," said Mr. Perkins, "and then back water a bit out of this atmosphere."

The bowman jerked the cloth clear of the raft with his boathook; the white sheet floated like a snowflake upon the water for a few breaths, then slowly sank. The body exposed was stark-naked and tawny. It was a male. I saw nothing revolting in the thing; it would have been otherwise perhaps had it been white. The hair was long and black, the nose aquiline, the mouth puckered into the aspect of a harelip; the gleam of a few white teeth painted a ghastly contemptuous grin upon the dead face. The only shocking part was the footless leg.

"Shall I hook him overboard, sir?" said the bowman.

"No, let him take his ease as he lies," answered the mate, and with that we returned to the barque.

We climbed over the side, the boat was hoisted to the davits, and Mr. Perkins took the parcel out of the stern-sheets and handed it to the captain. The cover was a kind of fine canvas, very neatly stitched with white thread. Captain Cayzer ripped through the stitching with his knife and exposed a couple of books bound in some kind of skin or parchment. They were probably the Koran, but the characters none of us knew. The captain turned them about for a bit, and I stood by looking at them; he then replaced them in their canvas cover and put them down upon the skylight, and, by and by, on his leaving the deck, he took them below to his cabin.

There had not been a stir of wind all day; not the faintest breathing of breeze had tarnished the sea down to the hour of midnight when, feeling weary, I withdrew to my cabin. I slept well, spite of the heat and the cockroaches, and rose at seven. I found the steward in the cabin. His face wore a look of concern; and on seeing me he instantly exclaimed:

"The captain seems very ill, sir. Might you know anything of physic? Neither Mr. Perkins nor me can make out what's the matter."

"I know nothing of physic," I answered, "but I'll look in on him."

I stepped to the door, knocked and entered. Captain Cayzer lay in a bunk under a middling-sized porthole; the cabin was full of the morning light. I started and stood at gaze, scarce crediting my sight, so shocked and astounded was I by the dreadful change which had happened in the night in the poor man's appearance.

His face was blue, and I remarked a cadaverous sinking in of the eyeballs; the lips were livid, the hands likewise blue, but strangely wrinkled like a washerwoman's. On seeing me he asked in a husky whispering voice for a drink of water. I handed him a full pannikin, which he drained feverishly, and then began to moan and cry out, making some weak, miserable efforts to rub first one arm, then the other, then his legs.

The steward stood in the doorway. I turned to him, sensible that my face was ashen, and asked some questions. I then said, "Where is Mr. Perkins?"

He was on deck. I bade the steward attend to the captain, and passed through the hatch to the quarterdeck, where I found the mate.

"Do you know that the captain is very ill?" said I.

"Do I know it, sir? Why, yes. I've been sitting by him chafing his limbs and giving him water to drink, and attending to him in other ways. What is it, d'ye know, sir?"

"*Cholera!*" said I.

"Oh, my God, I hope not!" he exclaimed. "How could it be cholera? How could cholera come aboard?"

"A friend of mine died of cholera at Rangoon when I was there," said I. "I recognize the looks and will swear to the symptoms."

"But how could it have come aboard?" he exclaimed in a voice low but agitated.

My eyes, as he asked the question, were upon the raft. I started and cried, "Is that thing still there?"

"Ay," said the mate, "we haven't budged a foot all night."

The suspicion rushed upon me whilst I looked at the raft and ran my eyes over the bright, hot morning sky and the burnished surface of sea, sheeting into dimness in the misty junction of heaven and water.

"I shouldn't be surprised," said I, "to discover that we brought the cholera aboard with us yesterday from that dead man's raft yonder."

"How is cholera to be caught in that fashion?" exclaimed Mr. Perkins, pale and a bit wild in his way of staring at me.

"We may have brought the poison aboard in the parcel of books."

"Is cholera to be caught so?"

"Undoubtedly. The disease may be propagated by human intercourse. Why not then by books which have been handled by cholera-poisoned people, or by the atmosphere of a body dead of the plague?" I added, pointing at the raft.

"No man amongst us is safe, then, now?" cried the mate.

"I'm no doctor," said I; "but I know this, that contagious poisons such as scarlet fever, glanders, and so on may retain their properties in a dormant state for years. I've heard tell of scores of instances of cholera being propagated through articles of dress. Depend upon it," said I, "that we brought the poison aboard with us yesterday from that accursed death-raft yonder."

"Aren't the books in the captain's cabin?" said the mate.

"Are they?"

"He took them below yesterday, sir."

"The sooner they're overboard the better," I exclaimed, and returned to the cabin.

I went to the captain and found the steward rubbing him. The disease appeared to be doing its work with horrible rapidity; the eyes were deeply sunk and red; every feature had grown sharp and pinched as after a long wasting disease; the complexion was thick and muddy. Those who have watched beside cholera know that terrific changes may take place in a few minutes. I cast my eyes about for the parcel of books, and, spying it, took a stick from a corner of the berth, hooked up the parcel, and, passing it through the open porthole, shook it overboard.

The captain lived till the evening, and seldom spoke save to call upon God to release him. I had found an opportunity to tell him that he was ill of the cholera, and explained how it happened that the horrible distemper was on board, for I was absolutely sure we had brought it with us in that parcel of books; but his anguish was so keen, his death so close then, that I cannot be sure he understood me. He died shortly after seven o'clock, and I have since learned that that time is one of the critical hours in cholera.

When the captain was dead I went to the mate and advised him to cast the body overboard at once. He called to some of the hands. They brought the body out just as the poor fellow had died, and, securing weight to the feet, they lifted the corpse over the rail and dropped it. No burial service was read. We were all too panic-stricken for reverence.

We got rid of the body quickly, the men handling the thing as though they felt the death in it stealing into them through their fingers—hoping and praying that with it the cholera would go. It was almost dark when this hurried funeral was ended. I stood beside the mate, looking round the sea for the shadow of wind in any quarter. The boatswain, who had been one of the men that handled the body, came up to us.

"Ain't there nothing to be done with that corpus out there?" he exclaimed, pointing with a square hand to the raft. "The men are agreed that there'll come no wind whilst that there dead blackie keeps afloat. And ain't he enough to make a disease of the hatmosphere itself, from horizon to horizon?"

I waited for the mate to answer. He said gloomily, "I'm of the poor captain's mind. You'll need to make something fast to the body to sink it. Who's to handle it? I'll ask no man to do what I wouldn't do myself, and rat me if I'd do *that!*"

"We brought the poison aboard by visiting the raft, bo'sun," said I. "Best leave the thing alone. The corpse is too far off to corrupt the air, as you suppose; though the imagination's nigh as bad as the reality," said I, spitting.

"If there's any of them game to sink the thing, may they do it?" said the boatswain. "For if there's ne'er a breeze of wind to come while it's there—"

"Chaw!" said the mate. "But try 'em, if you will. They may take the boat when the moon's up, should there come no wind first."

An hour later the steward told me that two of the sailors were seized with cramps and convulsions. After this no more was said about taking the boat and sinking the body. The mate went into the forecastle. On his return he begged me to go and look at the men.

"Better make sure that it's cholera with them too, sir," said he. "You know the signs;" and folding his arms, he leaned against the bulwarks in a posture of profound dejection.

I went forward and descended the forescuttle, and found myself in a small cave. The heat was overpowering; there was no air to pass through the little hatch; the place was dimly lighted by an evil-smelling lamp hanging under a beam, but, poor as the illumination was, I could see by it, and when I looked at the two men and spoke to them, I saw how it was, and came away sick at heart, and half dead with the hot foul air of the forecastle, and in deepest distress of mind, moreover, through perceiving that the two men had formed a part of the crew of the boat when we visited the raft.

One died at six o'clock next morning and the other at noon; but before this second man was dead three others had been attacked, and one of them was the mate. And still never a breath of air stirred the silver surface of the sea.

The mate was a strong man, and his fear of death made the conflict dreadful to behold. I was paralyzed at first by the suddenness of the thing and the tremendous character of our calamity, and, never doubting that I must speedily prove a victim as being one who had gone in the boat, I cast myself down upon a sofa in the cabin and there sat, waiting for the first signal of pain.

But a keen and biting sense of my cowardice came to my rescue. I sprang to my feet and went to the mate's berth, and nursed him till he died, which was shortly before midnight of the day of his seizure—so swift and sure was the poison we had brought from the raft.

He was dropped over the side, and in a few hours later he was followed by three others. I cannot be sure of my figures; it was a time of delirium, and I recall some details of it with difficulty, but I am pretty sure that by the morning of the fourth day of our falling in with the accursed raft the ship's company had been reduced to the boatswain and five men, making, with myself, seven survivors of fifteen souls who had sailed from Calcutta.

It was some time about the middle of the fifth day—two men were then lying stricken in the forecastle—the boatswain and a couple of seamen came aft to the quarter-deck where I was standing. The ocean floated in liquid glass; the smell of frying paint, bubbled into cinders by the roasting rays, rose like the stench of a second plague to the nostrils.

They had been drinking; no doubt they had broached the rum casks below. The boatswain carried a heavy weight of some sort, bound in canvas, with a long lanyard attached to it. He flung the parcel into the quarter-boat and roared out:

"If that don't drag the blistered cuss out of sight I'll show the fired carcass the road myself. Cholera or no cholera, here goes!"

"What are you going to do?" said I.

"Do?" he cried. "Why, sink that there plague out of it, so as to give us the chance of a breeze. Ain't this hell's delight? What's a-going to blow us clear whilst *he* keeps watch?" And he nodded with a fierce drunken gesture towards the raft.

"You'll have to handle the body to sink it," said I. "You're well, men, now; keep well, won't you? The two who are going may be the last taken."

The three of them roared out drunkenly together, so muddling their speech with oaths that I did not understand them. I walked aft, not liking their savage looks. Shouting and cursing plentifully, they lowered the boat, got into her by descending the falls, and shoved off for the raft.

They drew alongside the bamboo contrivance, and I looked to see the boat capsize, so wildly did they sway her in their wrath and drink as they fastened the weight to the foot of the body, sank it, and with the loom of their oars, hammered at the raft till the bamboos were scattered like a sheaf of walking-sticks cut adrift. They then returned to the barque, clambered aboard, and hoisted the boat.

The two sick men in the forecastle were at this time looked after by a seaman named Archer. I have said it was the fifth day of the calm; of the ship's company the boatswain and five men were living, but two were dying, and that, not counting me, left three as yet well and able to get about.

This man Archer, when the boatswain and his companions went forward, came out of the forecastle and drank at the scuttle-butt in the waist. He walked unsteadily, with that effort after stateliness which is peculiar to tipsy sailors; his eyes wandered, and he found some difficulty in hitting the bunghole with the dipper. Yet he was a civil sort of man when sober; I had occasionally chatted with him during his tricks at the wheel; and, feeling the need of some one to talk to about our frightful situation, I walked up to him and asked how the sick men did.

"Dying fast," he answered, steadying himself by leaning against the scuttle-butt, "and a-ravin' like screech-owls."

"What's to be done, Archer?"

"Oh, God alone He knows!" answered the man, and here he put his knuckles into his eyes and began to cry and sob.

"Is it possible that this calm can last much longer?"

"It may last six weeks," he answered, whimpering. "Down here, when the wind's drawed away by the sun, it may take six weeks afore it comes on to blow. Six weeks of calm down here ain't thought nothen of," and here he burst out blubbering again.

"Drinking 'll not help you," said I; "you'll all be the likelier to catch the malady for drinking. This is a sort of time, I should think, when a man most wants his senses. A breeze may come, and we ought to decide where to steer the barque to. The vessel's under all plain sail, too, and here we are, four men and a useless passenger, should it come on to blow suddenly—"

"We didn't sign on under you," he interrupted, with a tipsy scowl, "and as ye ain't no good either as sailor or doctor, you can keep your blooming sarmons to yourself till they're asked for."

I had now not only to fear the cholera but to dread the men. My mental distress was beyond all power of words to convey; I wonder it did not quickly drive me crazy and hurry me overboard. I lurked in the cabin to be out of sight of the fellows, and all the while my imagination was tormenting me with the first pangs of the cholera, and every minute I was believing I had the mortal malady. Sometimes I would creep up the companion steps and cautiously peer around, and always I beheld the same dead, faint blue surface of sea stretching like an ocean in a dream into the faint indefinable distances.

But shocking as that calm was to me, I very well knew there was nothing wonderful or preternatural in it. Our forefoot five days before had struck the equatorial zone called the Doldrums, and at a period of the year when a fortnight or even a month of atmospheric lifelessness might be as confidently looked for as the rising and setting of the sun.

At nine o'clock that night I was sitting at the cabin table with biscuit and a little weak brandy and water before me, when I was hailed by some one at the open skylight above. It was a black night, though the sky was glorious with stars; the moon did not rise till after eleven. I had lighted the cabin lamp, and the sheen of it was upon the face of Archer.

"The two men are dead and gone," said he, "and now the bo'sun and Bill are down. There's Jim dead drunk in his hammock. I can't stand the cries of sick men. What with liquor and pain, the air below suffocates me. Let me come aft, sir, and keep along with you. I'm sober, now. Oh, Christ, have mercy upon me! It's my turn next, ain't it?"

I passed a glass of brandy to him through the skylight, then joined him on deck, and told him that the two dead bodies must be thrown overboard and the sick men looked to. For some time he refused to go forward with me, saying that he was already poisoned and deadly sick, and a dying man, and that I had no right to expect that one dying man should wait upon another.

However, I was determined to turn the dead out of the ship in any case, for in freeing the vessel of the remains of the victims might lie my salvation. He consented to help me at last, and we went into the forecastle and between us got the bodies out of their bunks and dropped them, weighted, over the rail.

The boatswain and the other men lay groaning and writhing and crying for water; cursing at intervals. A coil of black smoke went up from the lamp-flame to the blackened beam under which the light was burning. The atmosphere was horrible. I bade Archer help me to carry a couple of mattresses on to the forecastle, and we got the sick men through the hatch, and they lay there in the coolness with plenty of cold water beside them and a heaven of stars above, instead of a low-pitched ceiling of grimy beam and plank dark with processions of cockroaches and dim with the smoke of the stinking slush lamp.

All this occupied us till about half-past ten. When I went aft I was seized with nausea, and, sinking upon the skylight, dabbled my brow in the dew betwixt the lifted lids for the refreshment of the moisture.

I believed that my time had come, and that this sickness was the cholera. Archer followed me, and seeing me in a posture of torment, as he supposed, concluded that I was a dead man. He flung himself upon the deck with a groan, and lay motionless, crying out at intervals, "God have mercy! God have mercy!" and that was all.

In about half an hour's time the sensation of sickness passed. I went below for some brandy, swallowed half a glass, and returned with a dram for Archer, but the man had either swooned or fallen asleep, and I let him lie. I had my senses perfectly, but felt shockingly weak in body. Indeed, the capacity of realization grew unendurably poignant. I imagined too well, I figured too clearly. I pictured myself as lying dead upon the deck of the barque, found a corpse by some passing vessel after many days; and so I dreamed, often breaking away from my horrible imaginations with moans and starts, then pacing the deck to rid me of the nightmare hag of thought till I was in a fever, then cooling my head by laying my cheek upon the dew-covered skylight.

By and by the moon rose, and I sat watching it. In half an hour she was a bright light in the east, and the shaft of silver that slept under her stretched to the barque's side. It was just then that one of the two sick men on the forecastle sent up a yell. The dreadful note rang through the vessel and dropped back to the deck in an echo from the canvas.

A moment after I saw a figure get on to the forecastle rail and spring overboard. I heard the splash of his body, and, bounding over to Archer, who lay on the deck, I pulled and hauled at him, roaring out that one of the sick men had jumped overboard, and then rushed forward and looked over into the water in the place where the man had leaped, but saw nothing, not even a ripple.

I turned and peered close at the man who lay on the forecastle, and discovered that the fellow who had jumped was the boatswain. I went again to the rail to look, and lifted a coil of rope from a pin, ready to fling the fakes to the man, should he rise. The moonlight was streaming along the ocean on this side of the ship, and now, when I leaned over the rail for the second time, I saw a figure close under the bows.

I stared a minute or two; the color of the body blended with the gloom, yet the moonlight was upon him too, and then it was that after looking awhile and observing the thing to lie motionless, I perceived that it was the body that had been upon the raft! No doubt the extreme horror raised in me by the sight of the poisonous thing beheld in that light and under such conditions crazed me.

I have a recollection of laughing wildly and of defying the dark floating shape in insane language. I remember that I shook my fist and spat at it, and that I turned to seek for something to hurl at the body, and it may have been that in the instant of turning my senses left me, for after this I can recall no more.

The sequel to this tragic and extraordinary experience will be found in the following statement made by the people of the ship *For fars hire*, from Calcutta to Liverpool:

"When in latitude 2° 15' N. and longitude 79° 40' E. we sighted a barque under all plain sail, apparently abandoned. The breeze was very scanty, and though we immediately shifted our helm for her on judging that she was in distress, it took us all the morning to approach her within hailing distance.

"Everything looked right with her aloft, but the wheel was deserted, and there were no signs of anything living in her. We sent a boat in charge of the second officer, who returned and informed us that the barque was the *Justitia*, of London.

"We knew that she was from Calcutta, for we had seen her lying in the river. The second officer stated that there were three dead bodies aboard, one in a hammock in the forecastle, a second on a mattress on the forecastle, and a third against the coamings of the main-hatch; there was also a fourth man lying at the heel of the port cathead—he did not seem to be dead.

"On this, Dr. Davison was requested to visit the barque, and he was put aboard by the second officer.

"He returned quickly with one of the men, whom he instantly ordered to be stripped and put into a warm bath and his clothes thrown overboard. He said that the dead showed unmistakable signs of having died from cholera.

"We proceeded, not deeming it prudent to have anything further to do with the ill-fated craft. The person we had rescued remained insensible for two days; his recovery was then slow, but sure, thanks to the skillful treatment of Dr. Davison. There were fifteen souls when the vessel left Calcutta, and all perished except the passenger, Thomas Barron."

Off the Horn[1]

BASIL LUBBOCK

Monday, October 16, 1899
    Lat. 56° 9' S., long. 77° 4' W.
    Course—S. 60 E. Run 222 miles.

Blowing harder than ever, and a mountainous sea running. It is really awe-inspiring, and the captain told me it is the biggest sea he has ever seen, which is saying a good deal, as this is his thirtieth passage round the Horn.

---

[1] From "Round the Horn before the Mast", by permission. Copyright by E. P. Dutton & Company.

In the forenoon watch, our watch below, the main upper-topsail split from top to bottom, so that sail and the lower-topgallant above it were made fast, and now we are running before the gale under three lower-topsails and foresail.

We are now well to the southward of the Horn, and the weather is as bad as any weather can be; hail squalls blow up at minute intervals, and Cape Horn greybeards, a mile or two long, with white shaggy crests, chase us like birds of prey.

The weather is so bad that there are no albatrosses about, they are all away to the nor'ard; there are, however, a few Cape pigeons and molly-hawks, upon which the weather seems to have very little effect.

It is very cold, and Don and I are wearing our oilskins over our Klondyke fur coats at night.

The huge seas are beginning to poop her very badly now, especially when the port watch are on deck, as their helmsmen are a very indifferent lot.

Ever and anon in our watch below we hear a terrific crash on the deck above us as a sea falls on to the poop, to pour in a roaring cascade on to the main-deck.

No sailor likes his ship to be constantly pooped liked this, and I can see that many of the men are beginning to get anxious and uneasy, especially the dagos.

Just as Mac, Loring, and I got on to the poop at eight bells, an immense sea pooped her. The mate, who was standing to leeward of the chart-house, trying to get a sight, was carried off his legs, and only the poop-rail saved him from being swept down on to the main-deck. He kept his presence of mind, however, as every sailor does, and clung on to his precious sextant, picking himself up as the water poured off, very little the worse for his mishap, which might have so easily ended seriously.

"If the old man does not heave her to soon, he'll never be able to heave her to," said Mac to me as we stood in the lee of the chart-house, "as on the ship coming up to the wind in a sea like this, it would roll her over and over."

He was evidently getting uneasy at the terrific sea and the constant pooping of the ship, and started yarning about the number of ships which had been lost with all hands from running too long before a storm.

I rather enjoyed the fun myself, it was so stupendous, so magnificent, so terrific.

When on top of one of the great Cape Horners, looking forward was like looking from the top of a mountain; first smaller mountains, then hills, until what looked like the valley, seemed miles away in the distance.

I am very certain that it was a good deal nearer two miles than one mile from crest to crest of these enormous seas, and I don't believe any vessel under 500 tons could have lived in them for five minutes.

The main-deck is often out of sight now for some minutes, even the hatches being covered, and as the ship rolls it becomes a roaring, hissing, boiling cauldron.

In the midship-house they are almost as badly off as we are in the half-deck, and the bosun, who is thoroughly scared, would give worlds, I am sure, to be safe and sound on his Californian farm again.

The old man, with all the care on his shoulders, seems the least anxious man on the ship, and is ably backed up by the two mates, who, with nerves of steel, send no one where they dare not go themselves.

All of a sudden, as I watch I catch sight of the topsails of a ship on our port quarter.

"Sail ho!" I cry.

You could only see her when both were on the top of a sea; she was a three-master, running before it like ourselves, under three lower-topsails and reefed foresail.

The old man said she was probably a wool-clipper from Australia. A sail is a cheering sight at all times; but at a time like this, in such a sea, she was watched with great eagerness, as we scanned her through the old ship's telescope and the captain's glasses.

I think the sight of her relieved the old man of a good deal of anxiety, as he got very cheerful and spun us several amusing yarns; so much so, that I forgot about four bells, and I am afraid struck them nearly ten minutes late, to the great disgust of the tired helmsman.

A landsman has no idea of the various noises on board a wind-jammer in a storm. Every part of the ship groans; up above the gale roars, sings, and whistles through the rigging; one backstay produces a deep note, and one could fancy an organ was being played aloft; others shriek shrilly, like telegraph wires; some hum, some ring, others twang like banjo strings; and above all is the crash of the seas falling on the main-deck, and the clang of the hardly-used ports as they are banged first open and then shut by each succeeding wave.

I am afraid the ends of the gear are badly mauled about, as they get washed off the pins and dragged through the ports.

We have to be very careful going in and out of the half-deck, as the break of the poop is filled up every other wave.

Some of these tremendous seas fall aboard the whole length of the weather rail, and even the forecastles are inches deep in water, though not to be compared with the awful state of the half-deck.

Indeed, it is really beginning to be dangerous in the half-deck; any moment an extra big sea may break in the doors, and the watch below would be drowned like rats in a trap.

In the second dog watch, whilst the second mate was below at his tea, there was a slight lull in the gale, and the mate ordered the fore upper-top sail to be reefed and set.

This was, no doubt, a great error of judgment on the mate's part; the glass was exceedingly low, and from the look of the sky, it was evidently going to blow harder than ever.

Perhaps he thought he would try and put more speed on to her, as the seas were pooping her so badly.

The old man was snatching a few moments for a snooze; but from what we have seen, the mate is even a bigger terror than the old man at carrying on—at any rate, in this instance, I thought him reckless to the verge of insanity.

But orders must be obeyed.

Two reef-earings were got ready, and away we went aloft and lay out on the yard.

I went out on the weather yardarm with Jamieson, and we soon had the earing passed.

"Ready?" shouted Mac from the bunt.

"Aye, aye, sir!"

"Haul out to windward!"

"Eh-hai-ai! Oh-oh! Oh-ho-oh!" we chorused.

"Far enough, sir!"

"Haul out leeward!"

"That'll do!"

"Tie her up, and don't miss any reef points!" We soon had the reef points tied, and Mac sings out, "Lay down from aloft, and set the sail!"

We took the halliards to the small capstan forward, and mastheaded the yard to the chanty of *Away for Rio!* Jamieson singing the solo. It was pretty bad weather for chantying, but there is nothing like a chanty to put new life into a man, and we roared out the chorus at the top of our pipes.

The dagos in the port watch looked out of our forecastle at us in amazement, just in time to let a sea in, which pretty well swamped them out, and did its best to wash us away from the capstan.

Of all the chanties, I think *Away for Rio!* is one of the finest, and I cannot refrain from giving you the words.

Away for Rio!

Solo. Oh, the anchor is weigh'd, and the sails they are set,
    Chorus. Away, Rio!
Solo. The maids that we're leaving we'll never forget,
    Chorus. For we're bound for Rio Grande,
        And away, Rio! aye, Rio!

Sing fare-ye-well, my bonny young girl,
We're bound for Rio Grande!

Solo. So man the good capstan, and run it around,
    Chorus. Away, Rio!
Solo. We'll heave up the anchor to this jolly sound,
    Chorus. For we're bound for Rio Grande,
        And away, Rio! etc.

Solo. We've a jolly good ship, and a jolly good crew,
    Chorus. Away, Rio!
Solo. A jolly good mate, and a good skipper too,
    Chorus. For we're bound for Rio Grande,
        And away, Rio! etc.

Solo. We'll sing as we heave to the maidens we leave,
    Chorus. Away, Rio!
Solo. You know at this parting how sadly we grieve,
    Chorus. For we're bound for Rio Grande,
        And away, Rio! etc.

Solo. Sing good-bye to Sally and good-bye to Sue,
    Chorus. Away, Rio!
Solo. And you who are listening, good-bye to you,
    Chorus. For we're bound for Rio Grande,
        And away, Rio! etc.

Solo. Come heave up the anchor, let's get it aweigh,
    Chorus. Away, Rio!
Solo. It's got a firm grip, so heave steady, I say,
    Chorus. For we're bound for Rio Grande,
        And away, Rio! etc.

Solo. Heave with a will, and heave long and strong,
    Chorus. Away, Rio!
Solo. Sing a good chorus, for 'tis a good song,
    Chorus. For we're bound for Rio Grande,
        And away, Rio! etc.

Solo. Heave only one pawl, then vast heaving, belay!
   Chorus. Away, Rio!
Solo. Heave steady, because we say farewell to-day,
   Chorus. For we're bound for Rio Grande,
      And away, Rio! etc.

Solo. The chain's up and down, now the bosun did say,
   Chorus. Away, Rio!
Solo. Heave up to the hawse-pipe, the anchor's aweigh!
   Chorus. For we're bound for Rio Grande,
      And away, Rio! aye, Rio!
      Sing fare-ye-well, my bonny young girl,
      We're bound for Rio Grande!

Of course the words are not exactly appropriate in the present occasion, but the chorus is one of the best I have heard, with its wild, queer wail.

It would have been a grand picture for a painter; the struggling ship surrounded by foam, the great, greeny-grey seas, the wild, stormy sky just tinged with yellow where the sun was setting, the wet, glistening decks, and the ring of toiling men heaving round the capstan.

With the extra cloth, the poor old *Royalshire* labored terribly, and seemed to make worse weather of it than ever.

Mac, Loring, and I managed to get along the main-deck and on to the poop without being washed overboard, and there found the second mate, the mate having gone below on being relieved, staring in consternation at the reefed topsail.

I asked Jamieson to-day whether he called the *Royalshire* a wet ship. He said that no iron ship could expect to be anything but a half-tide rock in such a terrific sea, and that he had been on ships which before now would have had their boats and everything on deck swept away by the weight of water. But the *Royalshire* has everything of the best, and all for strength.

"Great snakes, here comes a sea!" cried Loring all of a sudden.

I gave one look astern, and there, towering high above us, was a huge monster, roaring and hissing as it curled its top; it looked as if it must break full on to the poop, and was a sight to strike terror into the stoutest heart.

Would she rise to it, or was this our last moment on earth?

"Hang on for your lives!" roared the second mate.

Up, up, up, went the *Royalshire*, good old ship, she was going to top it after all; but though she did her best, the heavy weight aft held her down, and she did not quite get there.

When a deafening thud, the top of the monster curled into boiling surf and fell upon us, overwhelming the helmsman, who clung desperately to the wheel, and dipping us to the waist as we hung in the weather jigger-rigging.

In a roaring torrent it poured across the poop and then, like an earthquake wave, fell aboard the whole length of the port rail. Such a height was it, that it toppled over in a terrible breaker upon the top of the midship-house; the gig's sides and bottom fell out, as if hit by a thunderbolt, the lamp-locker door was smashed down, and all the lamps washed out (luckily Don was not inside this time, or he would have certainly been drowned), and it filled the main-deck high above the hatches until the water was on a level with the poop.

The poor old ship gave a sickly roll under the terrible weight of water, and dipped Loring and myself up to our necks in the next sea as we clung on to the port jigger-backstays.

All the life seemed struck out of her; she swung nearly five points off her course, and old Foghorn, Jennings, and the second mate were working like demons as they hove the wheel up.

"If she gets another on top of this, she'll go down like a stone!" yelled Mac in my ear.

"What price the watch below," I returned. "I thought the half-deck doors would go to a certainty."

"Yes, they held out well; that lamp-locker door's torn clean off its hinges, and is smashed in like a rotten apple. Just look at the lamps washing about; we must get them somehow, and put them down in the cabin as soon as the water clears off a bit."

"Aye, aye!"

"Did you hear the dagos yelling in the port-forecastle? I guess they thought they were half-way to Davy Jones' locker!"

Gradually the gallant ship shook herself clear, and the hatches showed their tops once more above the water.

Down Mac, Loring, and I dashed on to the main-deck until we were up to our waists in water, and started retrieving the lamps.

Meanwhile, a howling hail squall came down upon us, and the second mate rushed for the captain.

As we splashed about removing the lamps from the wrecked locker, Mac said grimly, "If another sea comes along and catches us two in here, we're gorners."

"I should think the betting's two to one on. Let's hope old Wilson won't let her run off; she's steering vile, though," I reply.

At that moment Loring, who was on the poop ladder passing the lamps up, shrieked at us,

"On the poop for your lives. God Almighty! look sharp, or you're caught!"

We made a wild rush for the ladder, a lamp under each arm; the invading sea leaping madly at us, tried its best to catch us, but in vain, we reached the poop in safety. The poop ladder was now working loose and wanted relashing, or it would go adrift.

At this moment the old man came on deck, and giving one glance round, turned to the second mate and said,

"Call all hands and get the sail off her, I must heave her to."

"Aye, aye, sir!"

I ran down to call the mate and found him dozing.

"It's all hands, sir; the captain's going to heave her to."

"What's that; is the weather worse?" he asked, as he struggled into his oilskins.

"It's blowing harder than ever, sir, and she shipped a very bad sea just now," I answered, and ran on deck again.

"All hands! all hands on deck!" yelled the second mate and Mac, as we splashed forward.

The port watch turned out sharply, looking pretty scared.

"How did you like the big sea in the half-deck?" I asked of Don.

"It poured in like a watershute, and your bunk was under water in double-quick time, my boy."

"Well, that don't matter much; I don't suppose I shall get much chance to sleep in it to-night."

"Henderson, go and get your side lights and binnacles lighted," called the second mate.

"What's become of them, sir; my lamp-locker's washed bare as a bone?"

"They are all down in the cabin."

Away went Don aft, to run the gauntlet of the furious seas until he reached the safety of the poop.

"Fore upper-topsail first!" called the mate. "Tail on to the spilling-lines all hands, and show what you can do!"

"Now then, starboard watch!" cried the second mate, "up with your sail, and give the port watch a dressing down!"

"Lively, boys; haul, and show your spunk!" yelled Mac.

"Yo-ho! Yo-hay! Yo-ho-oh! Up she goes!"

Crash! and a sea broke over us. One gasp and a splutter, and we were under water; swept off our feet, and knocked helter-skelter edgeways, we lay in tangled knots of yellow humanity. Some one tried to cram his foot down my throat, whilst my knee was gouging out his eyes. As the water poured off, it left us bruised, battered, breathless, but undaunted.

Scrambling to our feet, at it we went again, working like fiends and no skulkers.

"Haul, and bust yourselves; haul till you break!" yelled Mac.

"One more pull and she'll do!" cries the mate.

"Oh-ho! Oh-ha!"

"Turn that!"

"All fast, sir!"

"Up aloft, and roll up the sail!"

"Now then, starbowlines, give her hell and show your grit!" shouts the second mate as he dashes aloft at the head of us, as active as a monkey, whilst the port watch, led by Scar and Don, take the port rigging.

As we sprang into the shrouds, she rolled her rail under until we were dipped deep below the surface. But we hung on like grim death, and not a man was washed away.

Up we went over the futtock shrouds and on to the yard. It was pitch black now, and spitting hailstones as big as marbles.

The wind blew up aloft with an edge to it that froze one's extremities into ice. The sail was as stiff as a board, and it seemed a matter of impossibility to pick it up.

We hit it, we scratched at it, we clutched at it with hooked fingers until the blood gushed from our nails.

"Catch hold of her, dig your fingers in!" cries Mac. "You there, Bower, blast you, are you going to sleep on the damned yard, or what the devil do you think you are doing?"

Frenzied men tore at the sail with both hands, hanging on by their eyelids, whilst we out at the yardarm had the hardest task of all.

"Up with her!" roared the second mate at the bunt. "Now then, all together—oh-ho!—and she comes! on to the yard with her—oh-hay!—and roll her up!"

Truly a sailor must have each finger a fishhook, as they say.

Well, we got it on to the yard somehow, and made a fair stow of it.

Meanwhile the port watch were all at sixes and sevens, doing nothing much but hang on and swear in five languages. Don's language up aloft is enough to scare the devil, though he's the best man on a yard in the watch.

"Lay down from aloft!" cries the second mate, and we gain the deck glowing in triumph, for our last man is out of the rigging before they have picked up their sail.

But now comes a great tussle—the foresail had to come in, and it is a new sail.

Some of the men were pretty well coopered by the hard work, cold, wet, and strain of it all. Poor old Higgins could hardly stand on his legs, Bower was not much better, and as for the wretched port watch, their struggles on the upper-topsail yard had quite worn them out. Don and the red-haired third mate were hoarse with swearing, though both were still full of beans; the Arab was a miserable object, whose teeth rattled like castanets, and eyeballs rolled their whites in a frenzy of terror.

"Port buntlines and clew-garnets first!" yells the mate, whilst the second mate takes the ticklish job of easing away the sheet.

In the small space round the fife-rail, we were very cramped up and crowded out, and it was difficult to get the whole weight into the pull, so some of us got on to the fife-rail and hauled from above until the blocks came down too low.

Difficulties of all sorts cropped up: the blocks jammed, the buntlines twisted up and had to be unrove, and ever and anon the wash of a sea swept over us.

Men lost their balance and cannoned against each other, men slipped, and half a watch fell on their backs cursing, but the mate gave them no time to think.

"Up you get there, no skulking, or you won't know what hit you!" snarls Scar at the prostrate group. "You damned dagos, what good are ye?—hell, you ain't worth thumping."

"Dat no right, mistar, we do our dam level best, dat's true!" whimpers one.

"Oh, curse you for the worst watch I ever sailed with!" roars Scar in a frenzy of rage. "Here, you there, you blasted bandylegged Turk, haul, can't you! Don't look at me like that, damn ye!"

Inch by inch, with incredible labour, we hauled the sail up. The strongest of us got our fighting second wind, and the icy blast of the south wind only put new breath into our nostrils.

"Take some of your best hands to the braces and spill the sail, Mr. Knowles!" called the mate.

Mac, Don, Jamieson, Rooning, Loring, and myself followed the second mate.

"Jamieson and you, Bally, come with me to the weather braces; you, Mac, take the other three and get in the slack as we give it you."

This was as dangerous a bit of work as anyone could want; the sea swept in a continuous cascade over the rail where we were working, and more than half the time we were under water, hanging on for our lives.

One blunder and the yards might take charge. Inch by inch we let out, and those to leeward took in, watching our chance as the vessel rolled.

The second mate was like a bull for strength, and Jamieson a very tiger for energy.

"Take it off! Carefully does it—that's it—keep a turn in, and ease away gently." Then, as a huge black mountain of water appears above us:

"Hitch it, and hang on all. God Almighty! quick, for your lives!"

At last we have the fore-yards braced up fairly well.

"That'll do!" yells the mate above the shrieking of the storm, and we dash forward again.

The foresail was now fairly well hauled up. "Are you going to reef it, sir?" asked Scar. "No, furl it," answered the mate. "Away you go aloft, and take a yardarm at a time."

There were a goodish crowd of us when both watches were out on one yardarm, and we did not have as much trouble as we expected with the sail.

The lower yards are so big that it requires two men to pass a gasket; one sits down on the foot-ropes and catches the gasket, whilst the other man, hanging above the yard, swings it to him.

On the fore-yard the white tops of the huge seas seemed on a level with us as they rolled by in great mountains of ink, leaving a trail behind like the wash of a Kootenay stern-wheeler.

The sight was truly grand, illumined as it was by a small wisp of a moon which peeped out every now and then from behind the scudding clouds.

With the foresail furled, we had now the three lower-topsails alone set; but even this was too much, and the main lower-topsail had to come in before the old man dared bring her up to the wind.

The most dangerous work of the lot came now, as we had to haul up the main lower-topsail right amidships; here the water was up to our waists between the seas, and every moment the whole ship's company was under water.

It was a wonder nobody was lost, and a still greater wonder that no limbs were broken.

The second mate, Scar, Jamieson, and myself, hauling up the port clew-line, had a rare time of it.

Whenever we did get our heads above the water we managed to get a few short, strong pulls in; but mostly we had to work like divers.

If we saw a sea coming in time, we took a turn, and all four dashed for safety, one into the rigging, another on to the skids, a third up the iron ladder on to the midshiphouse, and the fourth on to the main fife-rail.

At last we had the sail hauled up, and away we went aloft to furl it.

Directly we had got the sail on to the yard and were making it fast, the helm was put down.

It was an exciting moment as her head came slowly up to the wind.

A huge sea rose up, before us until the spume off its boiling crest was blown into our faces, high up as we were, then down it swooped aboard, sweeping her fore and aft.

Over and over went the poor old *Royalshire*, until the lower yardarms were dipping into the whirl of broken water to leeward.

The main lower-topsail yard was almost straight up and down, and we hung on like so many frightened flies.

"She'll turn turtle!" yelled some one.

One of the dagos gave a wild shriek, which rang like the cry of a wild bird above the roar of the tempest, and in absolute terror would have fallen off the yard if the man next him had not hauled him back by the scuff of his neck.

"Hell, are you all going to sleep up here!" came the thundering voice of the second mate at the bunt.

"Tie up the sail and get a move on, or there'll be trouble." Nothing was able to dismay his indomitable spirit.

Mechanically we turned again to our work. Seconds passed like hours as we felt the ship heeling over, ever over.

Was she going? She was almost on her beam ends now! We could not see the decks; between them and us was a curtain of boiling, hissing spray and broken water, into which the masts were stuck half-way up to the lower yards.

After some terrible moments of suspense, we all felt that she had stopped going over, and lay steady almost on her beam ends.

Long before this point had been reached, ten or twenty years ago, the men would have been gathered in groups round the masts and standing rigging, with axes ready, waiting the order from the captain to "Cut away!"

But in a modern wind-jammer, with masts of iron and shrouds of the strongest twisted wire, this is impossible, and you can no longer save your ship by cutting away the masts.

Presently a lull came, and we could once more see the deck beneath us.

The *Royalshire* was lying over with her lee rail dipped, so that the fair-heads were level with the water, the hatches were half submerged, and the lee side of the poop was under water.

As we came down from aloft, the sprays were thick, as high as the main-yard, and it was like going into a boiling cauldron with the steam rising from it, with the difference that its embrace was icy cold.

Nothing more could be done now; the ship lay hove-to, though she was a good many points off. Our watch was sent below for a short hour and a half before coming on deck for the middle watch, and the port watch went on to the poop.

Wrecked in the Antarctic

W. CLARK RUSSELL

I lay for a long while insensible; and that I should have recovered my mind instead of dying in that swoon I must ever account as the greatest wonder of a life that has not been wanting in the marvellous. I had no sooner sat up than all that had happened and my present situation instantly came to me. My hair was stiff with ice; there was no more feeling in my hands than had they been of stone; my clothes weighed upon me like a suit of armour, so inflexibly hard were they frozen. Yet I got upon my legs, and found that I could stand and walk, and that life flowed warm in my veins, for all that I had been lying motionless for an hour or more, laved by water that would have become ice had it been still.

It was intensely dark; the binnacle lamp was extinguished, and the light in the cabin burned too dimly to throw the faintest colour upon the hatchway. One thing I quickly noticed, that the gale had broken and blew no more than a fresh breeze. The sea still ran very high, but though every surge continued to hurl its head of snow, and the heavens to resemble ink from contrast with the passage, as it seemed, close under them of these pallid bodies, there was less spite in its wash, less fury in its blow. The multitudinous roaring of the heaving blackness had sobered into a hard and sullen growling, a sound as of thunder among mountains heard in a valley.

The brig pitched and rolled heavily. Much of the buoyancy of her earlier dance was gone out of her. Nevertheless, I could not persuade myself that this sluggishness was altogether due to the water she had taken in. It was wonderful, however, that she should still be afloat. No man could have heard the rending and grating of her side against the ice without supposing that every plank in it was being torn out.

Finding that I had the use of my voice, I halloaed as loudly as I could, but no human note responded. Three or four times I shouted, giving some of the people their names, but in vain. Father of mercy! I thought, what has come to pass? Is it possible that all my companions have been washed overboard? Certainly, five men at least were living before we fouled the ice. And again I cried out, "Is there any one alive?" looking wildly along the black decks, and putting so much force into my voice with the consternation that the thought of my being alone raised in me, that I had like to have burst a blood-vessel.

My loneliness was more terrible to me than any other condition of my situation. It was dreadful to be standing, nearly dead with cold, in utter darkness, upon the flooded decks of a hull wallowing miserably amid the black hollows and eager foaming peaks of the labouring sea, convinced that she was slowly filling, and that at any moment she might go down with me; it was dreadful, I say, to be thus placed, and to feel that I was in the heart of the rudest, most desolate space of sea in the world, into which the commerce of the earth dispatched but few ships all the year round. But no feature of my lamentable situation so affrighted me, so worked upon the passions of my mind, as my loneliness. Oh, for one companion, even one only, to make me an echo for mine own speech! Nay, God Himself, the merciful Father of all, even He seemed not! The blackness lay like a pall upon the deep, and upon my soul. Misery and horror were within that shadow, and beyond it nothing that my spirit could look up to!

I stood for some moments as one stunned, and then my manhood—trained to some purpose by the usage of the sea—reasserted itself; and maybe I also got some slender comfort from observing that, dull and heavy as was the motion of the brig, there was yet the buoyancy of vitality in her manner of mounting the seas, and that, after all, her case might not be so desperate as was threatened by the way in which she had been torn and precipitated past the iceberg. At moments when she plunged the whiteness of the water creaming upon the surges on either hand threw out a phantom light of sufficient power to enable me to see that the forward part of the brig was littered with wreckage, which served to a certain extent as a breakwater by preventing the seas, which washed on to the forecastle, from cascading with their former violence aft; also that the whole length of the main and top masts lay upon the larboard rail and over the side, held in that position by the gear attached to them. This was all that I could distinguish, and of this only the most elusive glimpse was to be had.

Feeling as though the very marrow in my bones were frozen, I crawled to the companion and, pulling open the door, descended. The lamp in the companion burnt faintly. There was a clock fixed to a beam over the table; my eyes directly sought it, and found the time twenty minutes after ten. This signified that I had ten or eleven hours of darkness before me!

I took down the lamp, trimmed it, and went to the lazarette hatch at the after end of the cabin. Here were kept the stores for the crew. I lifted the hatch and listened, and could hear the water in the hold gurgling and rushing with every lift of the brig's bows; and I could not question from the volume of water which the sound indicated that the vessel was steadily taking it in, but not rapidly. I swallowed half a pannikin of the hollands for the sake of the warmth and life of the draught, and entering my cabin, put on thick dry stockings, first chafing my feet till I felt the blood in them; and I then, with a seaman's dispatch, shifted the rest of my apparel, and cannot express how greatly I was comforted by the change, though the jacket and trousers I put on were still damp with the soaking of previous days. To render myself as waterproof as possible—for it was the wet clothes against the skin that made the cold so cruel—I took from the captain's cabin a stout cloak and threw it over me, enveloping my head, which I had cased in a warm fur cap, with the hood of it; and thus equipped I lighted a small hand-lantern that was used on dark nights for heaving the log, that is, for showing how the sand runs in the glass, and carried it on deck.

The lantern made the scene a dead, grave-like black outside its little circle of illumination; nevertheless its rays suffered me to guess at the picture of ruin the decks offered. The main mast was snapped three or four feet above the deck, and the stump of it showed as jagged and barbed as a wild beast's teeth. But I now noticed that the weight of the hamper being on the larboard side, balanced the list the vessel took from her shifted ballast, and that she floated on a level keel with her bows fair at the sea, whence I concluded that a sort of sea-anchor had been formed ahead of her by the wreckage, and that it held her in that posture, otherwise she must certainly have fallen into the trough.

I moved with extreme caution, casting the lantern light before me, sometimes starting at a sound that resembled a groan, then stopping to steady myself during some particular wild leap of the hull; until, coming abreast of the main hatch, the rays of the lantern struck upon a man's body, which, on my bringing the flame to his face, proved to be Captain Rosy. There was a wound over his right brow; and as if that had not sufficed to slay him, the fall of the masts had in some wonderful manner whipped a rope several times round his body, binding his arms and encircling his throat so tightly, that no executioner could have gone more artistically to work to pinion and choke a man.

Under a mass of rigging in the larboard scuppers lay two bodies, as I could just faintly discern; it was impossible to put the lantern close enough to either one of them to distinguish his face, nor had I the strength even if I had possessed the weapons to extricate them, for they lay under a whole body of shrouds, complicated by a mass of other gear, against which leaned a portion of the caboose. I viewed them long enough to satisfy my mind that they were dead, and then with a heart of lead turned away.

I crossed to the starboard side, where the deck was comparatively clear, and found the body of a seaman named Abraham Wise near the fore-hatch. This man had probably been stunned and drowned by the sea that filled the deck after I loosed the staysail. These were all of our people that I could find; the others I supposed had been washed by the water or knocked by the falling spars overboard.

I returned to the quarter-deck, and sat down in the companion-way for the shelter of it and to think. No language that I have command of could put before you the horror that possessed me as I sat meditating upon my situation and recalling the faces of the dead. The wind was rapidly falling, and with it the sea, but the motion of the brig continued very heavy, a large swell having been set running by the long, fierce gale that was gone; and there being no uproar of tempest in the sky to confound the senses, I could hear a hundred harsh and melancholy groaning and straining sounds rising from the hull, with now and again a mighty blow as from some spar or lump of ice alongside, weighty enough, you would have supposed, to stave the ship. But though the *Laughing Mary* was not a new vessel, she was one of the stoutest of her kind ever launched, built mainly of oak, and put together by an honest artificer. Nevertheless her continuing to float in her miserably torn and mangled condition was so great a miracle, that, spite of my poor shipmates having perished and my own state being as hopeless as the sky was starless, I could not but consider that God's hand was very visible in this business.

I will not pretend to remember how I passed the hours till the dawn came. I recollect of frequently stepping below to lift the hatch of the lazarette, to judge by the sound of the quantity of water in the vessel. That she was filling I knew well, yet not leaking so rapidly but that, had our crew been preserved, we might easily have kept her free, and made shift to rig up jury masts and haul us as best we could out of these desolate parallels. There was, however, nothing to be done till the day broke. I had noticed the jolly-boat bottom up near the starboard gangway, and so far as I could make out by throwing the dull lantern light upon her she was sound; but I could not have launched her without seeing what I was doing, and even had I managed this, she stood to be swamped and I to be drowned. And, in sober truth, so horrible was the prospect of going adrift in her without preparing for the adventure with oars, sail, mast, provisions, and water—most of which, by the lamplight only, were not to be come at amid the hideous muddle of wreckage—that sooner than face it I was perfectly satisfied to take my chance of the hulk sinking with me in her before the sun rose.

II

The east grew pale and grey at last. The sea rolled black as the night from it, with a rounded smooth-backed swell; the wind was spent; only a small air, still from the north-east, stirred. There were a few stars dying out in the dark west; the atmosphere was clear, and when the sun rose I knew he would turn the sable pall overhead into blueness.

The hull lay very deep. I had at one time, during the black hours, struck into a mournful calculation, and reckoned that the brig would float some two or three hours after sunrise; but when the glorious beam flashed out at last, and transformed the ashen hue of dawn into a cerulean brilliance and a deep of rolling sapphire, I started with sudden terror to observe how close the covering-board sat upon the water, and how the head of every swell ran past as high as the bulwark rail.

Yet for a few moments I stood contemplating the scene of ruin. It was visible now to its most trifling detail. The foremast was gone smooth off at the deck; it lay over the starboard bow; and the topmast floated ahead of the hull, held by the gear. Many feet of bulwarks were crushed level; the pumps had vanished; the caboose was gone! A completer nautical ruin I had never viewed.

One extraordinary stroke I quickly detected. The jolly-boat had lain stowed in the long-boat; it was thus we carried those boats, the little one lying snugly enough in the other. The sea that had flooded our decks had floated the jolly-boat out of the long-boat, and swept it bottom up to the gangway where it lay, as though God's mercy designed it should be preserved for my use; for, not long after it had been floated out, the brig struck the berg, the masts fell—and there lay the long-boat crushed into staves!

This signal and surprising intervention filled my heart with thankfulness, though my spirits sank again at the sight of my poor drowned shipmates. But, unless I had a mind to join them, it was necessary I should speedily bestir myself. So after a minute's reflection I whipped out my knife, and cutting a couple of blocks away from the raffle on deck, I rove a line through them, and so made a tackle, by the help of which I turned the jolly-boat over: I then with a handspike prised her nose to the gangway, secured a bunch of rope on either side her to act as fenders or buffers when she should be launched and lying alongside, ran her midway out by the tackle, and, attaching a line to a ring-bolt in her bow, shoved her over the side, and she fell with a splash, shipping scarce a hatful of water.

I found her mast and sail—the sail furled to the mast, as it was used to lie in her—close against the stump of the mainmast; but though I sought with all the diligence that hurry would permit for her rudder, I nowhere saw it, but I met with an oar that had belonged to the other boat, and this with the mast and sail I dropped into her, the swell lifting her up to my hand when the blue fold swung past.

My next business was to victual her. I ran to the cabin, but the lazarette was full of water, and none of the provisions in it to be come at. I thereupon ransacked the cabin, and found a whole Dutch cheese, a piece of raw pork, half a ham, eight or ten biscuits, some candles, a tinder-box, several lemons, a little bag of flour, and thirteen bottles of beer. These things I rolled up in a cloth and placed them in the boat, then took from the captain's locker four jars of spirits, two of which I emptied that I might fill them with fresh water. I also took with me from the captain's cabin a small boat compass.

The heavy, sluggish, sodden movement of the hull advised me to make haste. She was now barely lifting to the swell that came brimming in broad liquid blue brows to her stem. It seemed as though another ton of water would sink her; and if the swell fell over her bows and filled the decks, down she would go. I had a small parcel of guineas in my chest, and was about to fetch this money, when a sort of staggering sensation in the upward slide of the hull gave me a fright, and, watching my chance, I jumped into the boat and cast the line that held her adrift.

The sun was an hour above the horizon. The sea was a deep blue, heaving very slowly, though you felt the weight of the mighty ocean in every fold; and eastwards, the shoulders of the swell, catching the glorious reflection of the sun, hurled the splendour along, till all that quarter of the sea looked to be a mass of leaping dazzle. Upon the eastern sea-line lay a range of white clouds, compact as the chalk cliffs of Dover; threads, crescents, feather-shapes of vapour of the daintiest sort, shot with pearly lustre, floated overhead very high. It was in truth a fair and pleasant morning—of an icy coldness indeed, but the air being dry, its shrewdness was endurable. Yet was it a brightness to fill me with anguish by obliging me to reflect how it would have been with us had it dawned yesterday instead of to-day. My companions would have been alive, and yonder sinking ruined fabric a trim ship capable of bearing us stoutly into warm seas and to our homes at last.

I threw the oar over the stern of the boat to keep her near to the brig, not so much because I desired to see the last of her, as because of the shrinking of my soul within me from the thought of heading in my loneliness into those prodigious leagues of ocean which lay stretched under the sky. Whilst the hull floated she was something to hold on to, so to say, something for the eye amid the vastness of water to rest upon, something to take out of the insufferable feeling of solitude the poisonous sting of conviction.

But her end was at hand. I had risen to step the boat's mast, and was standing and grasping it whilst I directed a slow look round the horizon in God knows what vain hope of beholding a sail, when my eye coming to the brig, I observed that she was sinking. She went down very slowly; there was a horrible gurgling sound of water rushing into her, and her main deck blew up with a loud clap or blast of noise. I could follow the line of her bulwarks fluctuating and waving in the clear dark blue when she was some feet under. A number of whirlpools spun round over her, but the slowness of her foundering was solemnly marked by the gradual descent of the ruins of masts and yards which were attached to the hull by their rigging, and which she dragged down with her. On a sudden, when the last fragment of mast had disappeared, and when the hollows of the whirlpools were flattening to the level surface of the sea, up rose a body, with a sort of leap. It was the sailor that had lain drowned on the starboard side of the forward deck. Being frozen stiff he rose in the posture in which he had expired, that is, with his arms extended; so that, when he jumped to the surface, he came with his hands lifted up to heaven, and thus he stayed a minute, sustained by the eddies which also revolved him.

The shock occasioned by this melancholy object was so great, it came near to causing me to swoon. He sank when the water ceased to twist him, and I was unspeakably thankful to see him vanish, for his posture had all the horror of a spectral appeal, and such was the state of my mind that imagination might quickly have worked the apparition, had it lingered, into an instrument for the unsettling of my reason.

I rose from the seat on to which I had sunk and loosed the sail, and hauling the sheet aft, put the oar over the stern, and brought the little craft's head to an easterly course. The draught of air was extremely weak, and scarce furnished impulse enough to the sail to raise a bubble alongside. The boat was about fifteen feet long; she would be but a small boat for summer pleasuring in English July lake-waters, yet here was I in her in the heart of a vast ocean, many leagues south and west of the stormiest, most inhospitable point of land in the world, with distances before me almost infinite for such a boat as this to measure ere I could heave a civilised coast or a habitable island into view!

At the start I had a mind to steer north-west and blow, as the wind would suffer, into the South Sea, where perchance I might meet a whaler or a Southseaman from New Holland; but my heart sank at the prospect of the leagues of water which rolled between me and the islands and the western American seaboard. Indeed I understood that my only hope of deliverance lay in being picked up; and that, though by heading east I should be clinging to the stormy parts, I was more likely to meet with a ship hereabouts than by sailing into the great desolation of the north-west. The burden of my loneliness weighed down upon me so crushingly that I cannot but consider my senses must have been somewhat dulled by suffering, for had they been active to their old accustomed height, I am persuaded my heart must have broken and that I should have died of grief.

Faintly as the wind blew, it speedily wafted me out of sight of the floating relics of the wreck, and then all was bare, bald, swelling sea and empearled sky, darkening in lagoons of azure down to the soft mountainous masses of white vapour lying like the coast of a continent on the larboard horizon. But one living thing there was besides myself a grey-breasted albatross, of a princely width of pinion. I had not observed it till the hull went down, and then, lifting my eyes with involuntary sympathy in the direction pointed to by the upraised arms of the sailor, I observed the great royal bird hanging like a shape of marble directly over the frothing eddies. It was as though the spirit of the deep had taken form in the substance of the noblest of all the fowls of its dominions, and, poised on tremorless wings, was surveying with the cold curiosity of an intelligence empty of human emotion the destruction of one of those fabrics whose unequal contests and repeated triumphs had provoked its haughty surprise. The bird quitted the spot of the wreck after a while and followed me. Its eyes had the sparkling blood-red gleam of rubies. It was as silent as a phantom, and with arched neck and motionless plumes seemed to watch me with an earnestness that presently grew insufferable. So far from finding any comfort of companionship in the creature, methought if it did not speedily break from the motionless posture in which it rested on its seat of air, and remove its piercing gaze, it would end in crazing me. I felt a sudden rage, and, jumping up, shouted and shook my fist at it. This frightened the thing. It uttered a strange salt cry—the very note of a gust of wind splitting upon a rope—flapped its wings, and after a turn or two sailed away into the north.

I watched it till its figure melted into the blue atmosphere; and then sank trembling into the sternsheets of the boat.

III

Four days did I pass in that little open boat.

The first day was fine till sunset; it then blew fresh from the north-west, and I was obliged to keep the boat before the wind. The next day was dark and turbulent, with heavy falls of snow and a high swell from the north, and the wind a small gale. On the third day the sun shone, and it was a fair day, but horribly cold, and I saw two icebergs like clouds upon the far western sea-line. There followed a cruel night of clouded skies, sleet and snow, and a very troubled sea; and then broke the fourth day, as softly brilliant as an English May day, but cold—great God, how cold!

Thus might I epitomise this passage; and I do so to spare you the weariness of a relation of uneventful suffering.

In those four days I mainly ran before the wind, and in this way drove many leagues south, though whenever a chance offered I hauled my sheet for the east. I know not, I am sure, how the boat lived. I might pretend it was due to my clever management—I do not say I had no share in my own preservation, but to God belongs all the praise.

In the blackness of the first night the sea boiled all about me. The boat leapt into hollows in which the sail slapped the mast. One look behind me at the high dark curl of the oncoming surge had so affrighted me that I never durst turn my head again lest the sight should deprive me of the nerve to hold the oar with which I steered. I sat as squarely as the task of steering would suffer, trusting that if a sea should tumble over the stern my back would serve as a breakwater, and save the boat from being swamped. The whole sail was on her, and I could not help myself; for it would have been certain death to quit the steering oar for an instant. It was this that saved me, perhaps; for the boat blew along with such prodigious speed, running to the height of a sea as though she meant to dart from that eminence into the air, that the slope of each following surge swung like a pendulum under her, and though her sail was becalmed in the trough, her momentum was so great that she was speeding up the acclivity and catching the whole weight of the wind afresh before there was time for her to lose way.

I was nearly dead with cold and misery when the morning came, but the sparkling sun and the blue sky cheered me, and as wind and sea fell with the soaring of the orb, I was enabled to flatten aft the sheet and let the boat steer herself whilst I beat my arms about for warmth and broke my fast. When I look back I wonder that I should have taken any pains to live. That it is possible for the human mind at any period of its existence to be absolutely hopeless, I do not believe; but I can very honestly say that when I gazed round upon the enormous sea I was in, and considered the size of my boat, the quantity of my provisions, and my distance (even if I was heading that way) from the nearest point of land, I was not sensible of the faintest stirring of hope, and viewed myself as a dead man.

No bird came near me. Once I spied the back of a great black fish about a quarter of a mile off. The wetness of it caught the sunshine and reflected it like a mirror of polished steel, and the flash was so brilliant it might have passed for a bed of white fire floating on the blue heavings. But nothing more that was living did I meet, and such was the vastness of the sea over which my little keel glided, in the midst of which I sat abandoned by the angels, that for utter loneliness I might have been the very last of the human race.

When the third night came down with sullen blasts sweeping into a steady storming of wind, that swung a strong melancholy howl through the gloom, it found me so weak with cold, watching and anxiety, and the want of space wherein to rid my limbs of the painful cramp which weighted them with an insupportable leaden sensation, that I had barely power to control the boat with the oar. I pined for sleep; one hour of slumber would, I felt, give me new life, but I durst not close my eyes. The boat was sweeping through the dark and seething seas, and her course had to be that of an arrow, or she would capsize and be smothered in a breath.

Maybe I fell something delirious, for I had many strange and frightful fancies. Indeed I doubt not it was the spirit of madness—that is certainly tonical when small—which furnished strength enough to my arm to steer with. It was like the action of a powerful cordial in my blood, and the very horrors it fed my brain with were an animation to my physical qualities. The gale became a voice; it cried out my name, and every shout of it past my ear had the sound of the word "Despair!" I witnessed the forms of huge phantoms flying over the boat; I watched the beating of their giant wings of shadow and heard the thunder of their laughter as they fled ahead, leaving scores of like monstrous shapes to follow. There was a faint lightning of phosphor in the creaming heads of the ebon surges, and my sick imagination twisted that pallid complexion into the dim reflection of the lamps of illuminated pavilions at the bottom of the sea; mystic palaces of green marble, radiant cities in the measureless kingdoms of the ocean gods. I had a fancy of roofs of pearl below, turrets of milk-white coral, pavements of rainbow lustre like to the shootings and dartings of the hues of shells inclined and trembled to the sun. I thought I could behold the movements of shapes as indeterminable as the forms which swarm in dreams, human brows crowned with gold, the cold round emerald eyes of fish, the creamy breasts of women, large outlines slowly floating upwards, making a deeper blackness upon the blackness like the dye of the electric storm upon the velvet bosom of midnight. Often would I shrink from side to side, starting from a fancied apparition leaping into terrible being out of some hurling block of liquid obscurity.

Once a light shone upon the masthead. At any other time I should have known this to be a St. Elmo's fire, a corposant, the ignis fatuus of the deep, and hailed it with a seaman's faith in its promise of gentle weather. But to my distempered fancy it was a lanthorn hung up by a spirit hand; I traced the dusky curve of an arm and observed the busy twitching of visionary fingers by the rays of the ghostly light; the outline of a large face of a bland and sorrowful expression, pallid as any foam flake whirling past, came into the sphere of those graveyard rays. I shrieked and shut my eyes, and when I looked again the light was gone.

Long before daybreak I was exhausted. Mercifully, the wind was scant; the stars shone very gloriously; on high sparkled the Cross of the southern world. A benign influence seemed to steal into me out of its silver shining; the craze fell from me, and I wept.

Shortly afterwards, worn out by three days and nights of suffering, I fell into a deep sleep, and when I awoke my eyes opened right upon the blinding sun.

This was the morning of the fourth day. I was without a watch. By the height of the sun I reckoned the hour to be ten. I threw a languid glance at the compass and found the boat's head pointing north-west; she fell off and came to, being without governance, and was scarcely sailing therefore. The wind was west, a very light breeze just enough to put a bright twinkling into the long, smooth folds of the wide and weighty swell that was rolling up from the north-east. I tried to stand, but was so benumbed that many minutes passed before I had the use of my legs. Brightly as the sun shone there was no more warmth in his light than you find in a moonbeam on a frosty night, and the bite in the air was like the pang of ice itself pressed against the cheek. My right hand suffered most; I had fallen asleep clasping the loom of the steering oar, and when I awoke my fingers still gripped it, so that, on withdrawing them, they remained curved like talons, and I believed I had lost their use, and even reckoned they would snap off and so set up a mortification, till by much diligent rubbing I grew sensible of a small glow which, increasing, ended in rendering the joints supple.

I stood up to take a view of the horizon, and the first sight that met my eye forced a cry from me. Extending the whole length of the south-west seaboard lay what I took to be a line of white coast melting at either extremity into the blue airy distance. Even at the low elevation of the boat my eye seemed to measure thirty miles of it. It was not white as chalk is; there was something of a crystalline complexion upon the face of its solidity. It was too far off to enable me to remark its outline; yet on straining my sight—the atmosphere being very exquisitely clear—I thought I could distinguish the projections of peaks, of rounded slopes, and aerial angularities in places which, in the refractive lens of the air, looked, with their hue of glassy azure, like the loom of high land behind the coastal line.

The notion that it was ice came into my head after the first prospect of it; and then I returned to my earlier belief that it was land. Methought if it were ice, it must be the borderland of the Antarctic circle, the limits of the unfrozen ocean, for it was incredible that so mighty a body could signify less than the capes and terraces of a continent of ice glazing the circumference of the pole for leagues and leagues; but then I also knew that, though first the brig and then my boat had been for days steadily blown south, I was still to the north of the South Shetland parallels, and many degrees therefore removed from the polar barrier. Hence I concluded that what I saw was land, and that the peculiar crystal shining of it was caused by the snow that covered it.

But what land? Some large island that had been missed by the explorers and left uncharted? I put a picture of the map of this part of the world before my mind's eye, and fell to an earnest consideration of it, but could recollect of no land hereabouts, unless indeed we had been wildly wrong in our reckoning aboard the brig, and I in the boat had been driven four or five times the distance I had calculated—things not to be entertained.

Yet even as a mere break in the frightful and enduring continuity of the sea-line—even as something that was not sea nor sky nor the cold silent and mocking illusion of clouds—it took a character of blessedness in my eyes; my gaze hung upon it joyously, and my heart swelled with a new impulse of life in my breast. It would be strange, I thought, if on approaching it something to promise me deliverance from this dreadful situation did not offer itself—some whaler or trader at anchor, signs of habitation and of the presence of men, nay, even a single hut to serve as a refuge from the pitiless cold, the stormy waters, the black, lonely, delirious watches of the night, till help should heave into view with the white canvas of a ship.

I put the boat's head before the wind, and steered with one hand whilst I got some breakfast with the other. I thanked God for the brightness of the day and for the sight of that strange white line of land, that went in glimmering blobs of faintness to the trembling horizon where the southern end of it died out. The swell rose full and brimming ahead, rolling in sapphire hills out of the north-east, as I have said, whence I inferred that that extremity of the land did not extend very much farther than I could see it, otherwise there could not have been so much weight of water as I found in the heaving.

The breeze blew lightly and was the weaker for my running before it; but the little line of froth that slipped past either side the boat gave me to know that the speed would not be less than four miles in the hour; and as I reckoned the land to be but a few leagues distant, I calculated upon being ashore some little while before sundown.

In this way two hours passed. By this time the features of the coast were tolerably distinct. Yet I was puzzled. There was a peculiar sheen all about the irregular skyline; a kind of pearly whitening, as it were, of the heavens beyond, like to the effect produced by the rising of a very delicate soft mist melting from a mountain's brow into the air. This dismayed me. Still I cried to myself, "It must be land! All that whiteness is snow, and the luminous tinge above it is the reflection of the glaring sunshine thrown upwards from the dazzle. It cannot be ice! 'tis too mighty a barrier. Surely no single iceberg ever reached to the prodigious proportions of that coast. And it cannot be an assemblage of bergs, for there is no break—it is leagues of solid conformation. Oh, yes, it is land, sure enough! some island whose tops and seaboard are covered with snow. But what of that? It may be populated all the same. Are the northern kingdoms of Europe bare of life because of the winter rigours?" And then I thought to myself, if that island have natives, I would rather encounter them as the savages of an icebound country than as the inhabitants of a land of sunshine and spices and radiant vegetation; for it is the denizens of the most gloriously fair ocean seats in the world who are man-eaters; not the Patagonian, giant though he be, nor the blubber-fed anatomies of the ice-climes.

Thus I sought to reassure and comfort myself. Meanwhile my boat sailed quietly along, running up and down the smooth and foamless hills of water very buoyantly, and the sun slided into the north-west sky and darted a reddening beam upon the coast towards which I steered.

The Wreck of the Deutschland

GERARD MANLEY HOPKINS

To the happy memory of five Franciscan Nuns exiles by the Falk Laws drowned between midnight and morning of Dec. 7th. 1875

Part the First

1

    THOU mastering me
      God! giver of breath and bread;
  World's strand, sway of the sea;
      Lord of living and dead;

Thou hast bound bones and veins in me, fastened me flesh,   5
And after it almost unmade, what with dread,
   Thy doing: and dost thou touch me afresh?
Over again I feel thy finger and find thee.

2

   I did say yes
   O at lightning and lashed rod;   10
   Thou heardst me truer than tongue confess
   Thy terror, O Christ, O God;
Thou knowest the walls, altar and hour and night:
The swoon of a heart that the sweep and the hurl of thee trod
   Hard down with a horror of height: 15
And the midriff astrain with leaning of, laced with fire of stress.

3

   The frown of his face
   Before me, the hurtle of hell
   Behind, where, where was a, where was a place?
   I whirled out wings that spell   20
And fled with a fling of the heart to the heart of the Host.
My heart, but you were dovewinged, I can tell,
   Carrier-witted, I am bold to boast,
To flash from the flame to the flame then, tower from the grace to the grace.

4

   I am soft sift   25
   In an hourglass—at the wall
   Fast, but mined with a motion, a drift,
   And it crowds and it combs to the fall;
I steady as a water in a well, to a poise, to a pane,

But roped with, always, all the way down from the tall   *30*
    Fells or flanks of the voel, a vein
Of the gospel proffer, a pressure, a principle, Christ's gift.

5

    I kiss my hand
      To the stars, lovely-asunder
   Starlight, wafting him out of it; and   *35*
      Glow, glory in thunder;
  Kiss my hand to the dappled-with-damson west:
 Since, tho' he is under the world's splendour and wonder,
   His mystery must be instressed, stressed;
For I greet him the days I meet him, and bless when I understand.   *40*

6

    Not out of his bliss
      Springs the stress felt
   Nor first from heaven (and few know this)
      Swings the stroke dealt—
  Stroke and a stress that stars and storms deliver,   *45*
 That guilt is hushed by, hearts are flushed by and melt—
   But it rides time like riding a river
(And here the faithful waver, the faithless fable and miss).

7

    It dates from day
      Of his going in Galilee;   *50*
   Warm-laid grave of a womb-life grey;
      Manger, maiden's knee;
  The dense and the driven Passion, and frightful sweat;
 Thence the discharge of it, there its swelling to be,

Though felt before, though in high flood yet—   *55*
What none would have known of it, only the heart, being hard at bay,

8

Is out with it! Oh,
    We lash with the best or worst
Word last! How a lush-kept plush-capped sloe
    Will, mouthed to flesh-burst,   *60*
Gush!—flush the man, the being with it, sour or sweet,
Brim, in a flash, full!—Hither then, last or first,
    To hero of Calvary, Christ, 's feet—
Never ask if meaning it, wanting it, warned of it—men go.   *65*

9

Be adored among men,
    God, three-numberèd form;
Wring thy rebel, dogged in den,
    Man's malice, with wrecking and storm.
Beyond saying sweet, past telling of tongue,
    Thou art lightning and love, I found it, a winter and warm;   *70*
    Father and fondler of heart thou hast wrung:
Hast thy dark descending and most art merciful then.

10

With an anvil-ding
    And with fire in him forge thy will
Or rather, rather then, stealing as Spring   *75*
    Through him, melt him but master him still:
Whether at once, as once at a crash Paul,
Or as Austin, a lingering-out sweet skill,
    Make mercy in all of us, out of us all
Mastery, but be adored, but be adored King.   *80*

Part the Second

11

'Some find me a sword; some
  The flange and the rail; flame,
Fang, or flood' goes Death on drum,
  And storms bugle his fame.
But wé dream we are rooted in earth—Dust!   *85*
Flesh falls within sight of us, we, though our flower the same,
  Wave with the meadow, forget that there must
The sour scythe cringe, and the blear share come.

12

On Saturday sailed from Bremen,
  American-outward-bound,   *90*
Take settler and seamen, tell men with women,
  Two hundred souls in the round—
O Father, not under thy feathers nor ever as guessing
The goal was a shoal, of a fourth the doom to be drowned;
  Yet did the dark side of the bay of thy blessing   *95*
Not vault them, the million of rounds of thy mercy not reeve even them in?

13

Into the snows she sweeps,
  Hurling the haven behind,
The Deutschland, on Sunday; and so the sky keeps,
  For the infinite air is unkind,   *100*
And the sea flint-flake, black-backed in the regular blow,
Sitting Eastnortheast, in cursed quarter, the wind;
  Wiry and white-fiery and whirlwind-swivellèd snow
Spins to the widow-making unchilding unfathering deeps.

14

She drove in the dark to leeward, 105
 She struck—not a reef or a rock
But the combs of a smother of sand: night drew her
 Dead to the Kentish Knock;
And she beat the bank down with her bows and the ride of her keel:
The breakers rolled on her beam with ruinous shock; 110
 And canvas and compass, the whorl and the wheel
Idle for ever to waft her or wind her with, these she endured.

15

Hope had grown grey hairs,
 Hope had mourning on,
Trenched with tears, carved with cares, 115
 Hope was twelve hours gone;
And frightful a nightfall folded rueful a day
Nor rescue, only rocket and lightship, shone,
 And lives at last were washing away:
To the shrouds they took,—they shook in the hurling and horrible airs. 120

16

One stirred from the rigging to save
 The wild woman-kind below,
With a rope's end round the man, handy and brave—
 He was pitched to his death at a blow,
For all his dreadnought breast and braids of thew: 125
They could tell him for hours, dandled the to and fro
 Through the cobbled foam-fleece, what could he do
With the burl of the fountains of air, buck and the flood of the wave?

17

They fought with God's cold—
    And they could not and fell to the deck   *130*
(Crushed them) or water (and drowned them) or rolled
    With the sea-romp over the wreck.
  Night roared, with the heart-break hearing a heart-broke rabble,
The woman's wailing, the crying of child without check—
    Till a lioness arose breasting the babble,   *135*
A prophetess towered in the tumult, a virginal tongue told.

18

Ah, touched in your bower of bone
    Are you! turned for an exquisite smart,
Have you! make words break from me here all alone,
    Do you!—mother of being in me, heart.   *140*
  O unteachably after evil, but uttering truth,
Why, tears! is it? tears; such a melting, a madrigal start!
    Never-eldering revel and river of youth,
What can it be, this glee? the good you have there of your own?

19

Sister, a sister calling   *145*
    A master, her master and mine!—
And the inboard seas run swirling and hawling;
    The rash smart sloggering brine
  Blinds her; but she that weather sees one thing, one;
Has one fetch in her: she rears herself to divine   *150*
    Ears, and the call of the tall nun
To the men in the tops and the tackle rode over the storm's brawling.

20

She was first of a five and came
   Of a coifèd sisterhood.   155
(O Deutschland, double a desperate name!
     O world wide of its good!
But Gertrude, lily, and Luther, are two of a town,
Christ's lily and beast of the waste wood:
   From life's dawn it is drawn down,
Abel is Cain's brother and breasts they have sucked the same.)   160

21

Loathed for a love men knew in them,
   Banned by the land of their birth,
   Rhine refused them. Thames would ruin them;
     Surf, snow, river and earth
Gnashed: but thou art above, thou Orion of light;   165
Thy unchancelling poising palms were weighing the worth,
   Thou martyr-master: in thy sight
Storm flakes were scroll-leaved flowers, lily showers—sweet heaven was astrew in them.

22

Five! the finding and sake
   And cipher of suffering Christ.   170
   Mark, the mark is of man's make
   And the word of it Sacrificed.
But he scores it in scarlet himself on his own bespoken,
Before-time-taken, dearest prizèd and priced—
   Stigma, signal, cinquefoil token   175
For lettering of the lamb's fleece, ruddying of the rose-flake.

23

Joy fall to thee, father Francis,
    Drawn to the Life that died;
  With the gnarls of the nails in thee, niche of the lance, his
    Lovescape crucified   *180*
And seal of his seraph-arrival! and these thy daughters
And five-livèd and leavèd favour and pride,
  Are sisterly sealed in wild waters,
To bathe in his fall-gold mercies, to breathe in his all-fire glances.

24

Away in the loveable west,   *185*
    On a pastoral forehead of Wales,
I was under a roof here, I was at rest,
    And they the prey of the gales;
She to the black-about air, to the breaker, the thickly
Falling flakes, to the throng that catches and quails   *190*
    Was calling 'O Christ, Christ, come quickly':
The cross to her she calls Christ to her, christens her wild-worst Best.

25

The majesty! what did she mean?
    Breathe, arch and original Breath.
Is it love in her of the being as her lover had been?   *195*
    Breathe, body of lovely Death.
They were else-minded then, altogether, the men
Woke thee with a *we are perishing* in the weather of Gennesareth.
    Or is it that she cried for the crown then,
The keener to come at the comfort for feeling the combating keen?   *200*

26

For how to the heart's cheering
The down-dugged ground-hugged grey
Hovers off, the jay-blue heavens appearing
Of pied and peeled May!
Blue-beating and hoary-glow height: or night, still higher,   *205*
With belled fire and the moth-soft Milky Way,
What by your measure is the heaven of desire,
The treasure never eyesight got, nor was ever guessed what for the hearing?

27

No, but it was not these.
The jading and jar of the cart,   *210*
Time's tasking, it is fathers that asking for ease
Of the sodden-with-its-sorrowing heart,
Not danger, electrical horror; then further it finds
The appealing of the Passion is tenderer in prayer apart:
Other, I gather, in measure her mind's   *215*
Burden, in wind's burly and beat of endragonèd seas.

28

But how shall I . . . make me room there:
Reach me a . . . Fancy, come faster—
Strike you the sight of it? look at it loom there,
Thing that she . . . there then! the Master,   *220*
Ipse, the only one, Christ, King, Head:
He was to cure the extremity where he had cast her;
Do, deal, lord it with living and dead;
Let him ride, her pride, in his triumph, despatch and have done with his doom there.

29

Ah! there was a heart right!   *225*
   There was single eye!
  Read the unshapeable shock night
   And knew the who and the why;
Wording it how but by him that present and past,
Heaven and earth are word of, worded by?—   *230*
  The Simon Peter of a soul! to the blast
Tarpeian-fast, but a blown beacon of light.

30

Jesu, heart's light,
   Jesu, maid's son,
  What was the feast followed the night   *235*
   Thou hadst glory of this nun?—
Feast of the one woman without stain.
For so conceivèd, so to conceive thee is done;
  But here was heart-throe, birth of a brain,
Word, that heard and kept thee and uttered thee outright.   *240*

31

Well, she has thee for the pain, for the
   Patience; but pity of the rest of them!
  Heart, go and bleed at a bitterer vein for the
   Comfortless unconfessed of them—
No not uncomforted: lovely-felicitous Providence   *245*
Finger of a tender of; O of a feathery delicacy, the breast of the
  Maiden could obey so, be a bell to, ring of it, and
Startle the poor sheep back! is the shipwrack then a harvest, does tempest carry the grain for thee?

32

I admire thee, master of the tides,
  Of the Yore-flood, of the year's fall;   *250*
  The recurb and the recovery of the gulf's sides,
    The girth of it and the wharf of it and the wall;
Stanching, quenching ocean of a motionable mind;
Ground of being, and granite of it: past all
  Grasp God, throned behind   *255*
Death with a sovereignty that heeds but hides, bodes but abides;

33

With a mercy that outrides
  The all of water, an ark
  For the listener; for the lingerer with a love glides
    Lower than death and the dark;   *260*
A vein for the visiting of the past-prayer, pent in prison,
The-last-breath penitent spirits—the uttermost mark
  Our passion-plungèd giant risen,
The Christ of the Father compassionate, fetched in the storm of his strides.

34

Now burn, new born to the world,   *265*
  Doubled-naturèd name,
  The heaven-flung, heart-fleshed, maiden-furled
    Miracle-in-Mary-of-flame,
Mid-numbered He in three of the thunder-throne!
Not a dooms-day dazzle in his coming nor dark as he came;   *270*
  Kind, but royally reclaiming his own;
A released shower, let flash to the shire, not a lightning of fire hard-hurled.

35

Dame, at our door
    Drowned, and among our shoals,
      Remember us in the roads, the heaven-haven of the Reward: *275*
    Our King back, oh, upon English souls!
Let him easter in us, be a dayspring to the dimness of us, be a crimson-cresseted east,
More brightening her, rare-dear Britain, as his reign rolls,
    Pride, rose, prince, hero of us, high-priest,
Our hearts' charity's hearth's fire, our thoughts' chivalry's throng's Lord.   *280*

The Plague Ship

HERMAN MELVILLE

"Mammy! mammy! come and see the sailors eating out of little troughs, just like our pigs at home." Thus exclaimed one of the steerage children, who at dinner-time was peeping down into the forecastle, where the crew were assembled, helping themselves from the "kids", which, indeed, resemble hog-troughs not a little.

"Pigs, is it?" coughed Jackson, from his bunk, where he sat presiding over the banquet, but not partaking, like a devil who had lost his appetite by chewing sulphur.—"Pigs, is it?—And the day is close by, ye spalpeens, when you'll want to be after taking a sup at our troughs!"

This malicious prophecy proved true.

As day followed day without glimpse of shore or reef, and head-winds drove the ship back, as hounds a deer; the improvidence and shortsightedness of the passengers in the steerage, with regard to their outfits for the voyage, began to be followed by the inevitable results.

Many of them at last went aft to the mate, saying that they had nothing to eat, their provisions were expended, and they must be supplied from the ship's stores, or starve.

This was told to the captain, who was obliged to issue a ukase from the cabin, that every steerage passenger, whose destitution was demonstrable, should be given one sea-biscuit and two potatoes a day; a sort of substitute for a muffin and a brace of poached eggs.

But this scanty ration was quite insufficient to satisfy their hunger: hardly enough to satisfy the necessities of a healthy adult. The consequence was, that all day long, and all through the night, scores of the emigrants went about the decks, seeking what they might devour. They plundered the chicken-coop; and disguising the fowls, cooked them at the public galley. They made inroads upon the pig-pen in the boat, and carried off a promising young shoat: *him* they devoured raw, not venturing to make an incognito of his carcass; they prowled about the cook's caboose, till he threatened them with a ladle of scalding water; they waylaid the steward on his regular excursions from the cook to the cabin; they hung round the forecastle, to rob the bread-barge; they beset the sailors, like beggars in the streets, craving a mouthful in the name of the Church.

At length, to such excesses were they driven, that the Grand Russian, Captain Riga, issued another ukase, and to this effect: Whatsoever emigrant is found guilty of stealing, the same shall be tied into the rigging and flogged.

Upon this, there were secret movements in the steerage, which almost alarmed me for the safety of the ship; but nothing serious took place, after all; and they even acquiesced in, or did not resent, a singular punishment which the captain caused to be inflicted upon a culprit of their clan, as a substitute for a flogging. For no doubt he thought that such rigorous discipline as *that* might exasperate five hundred emigrants into an insurrection.

A head was fitted to one of the large deck-tubs—the half of a cask; and into this head a hole was cut; also, two smaller holes in the bottom of the tub. The head—divided in the middle, across the diameter of the orifice—was now fitted round the culprit's neck; and he was forthwith coopered up into the tub, which rested on his shoulders, while his legs protruded through the holes in the bottom.

It was a burden to carry; but the man could walk with it; and so ridiculous was his appearance, that in spite of the indignity, he himself laughed with the rest at the figure he cut.

"Now, Pat, my boy," said the mate, "fill that big wooden belly of yours, if you can."

Compassionating his situation, our old "doctor" used to give him alms of food, placing it upon the cask-head before him; till at last, when the time for deliverance came, Pat protested against mercy, and would fain have continued playing Diogenes in the tub for the rest of this starving voyage.

Although fast-sailing ships, blest with prosperous breezes, have frequently made the run across the Atlantic in eighteen days; yet, it is not uncommon for other vessels to be forty, or fifty, and even sixty, eighty, and ninety days, in making the same passage. Though in these cases, some signal calamity or incapacity must occasion so great a detention. It is also true, that generally the passage out from America is shorter than the return; which is to be ascribed to the prevalence of westerly winds.

We had been outside of Cape Clear upward of twenty days, still harassed by head-winds, though with pleasant weather upon the whole, when we were visited by a succession of rain-storms, which lasted the greater part of a week.

During the interval, the emigrants were obliged to remain below; but this was nothing strange to some of them; who, not recovering, while at sea, from their first attack of seasickness, seldom or never made their appearance on deck, during the entire passage.

During the week, now in question, fire was only once made in the public galley. This occasioned a good deal of domestic work to be done in the steerage, which otherwise would have been done in the open air. When the lulls of the rain-storms would intervene, some unusually cleanly emigrant would climb to the deck, with a bucket of slops, to toss into the sea. No experience seemed sufficient to instruct some of these ignorant people in the simplest, and most elemental principles of ocean-life. Spite of all lectures on the subject, several would continue to shun the leeward side of the vessel, with their slops. One morning, when it was blowing very fresh, a simple fellow pitched over a gallon or two of something to windward. Instantly it flew back in his face; and also, in the face of the chief mate, who happened to be standing by at the time. The offender was collared, and shaken on the spot; and ironically commanded, never, for the future, to throw anything to windward at sea, but fine ashes and scalding hot water.

During the frequent hard blows we experienced, the hatchways on the steerage were, at intervals, hermetically closed; sealing down in their noisome den, those scores of human beings. It was something to be marvelled at, that the shocking fate, which, but a short time ago, overtook the poor passengers in a Liverpool steamer in the Channel, during similar stormy weather, and under similar treatment, did not overtake some of the emigrants of the *Highlander*.

Nevertheless, it was, beyond question, this noisome confinement in so close, unventilated, and crowded a den: joined to the deprivation of sufficient food, from which many were suffering; which, helped by their personal uncleanliness, brought on a malignant fever.

The first report was, that two persons were affected. No sooner was it known, than the mate promptly repaired to the medicine-chest in the cabin: and with the remedies deemed suitable, descended into the steerage. But the medicines proved of no avail; the invalids rapidly grew worse; and two more of the emigrants became infected.

Upon this, the captain himself went to see them; and returning, sought out a certain alleged physician among the cabin-passengers; begging him to wait upon the sufferers; hinting that, thereby, he might prevent the disease from extending into the cabin itself. But this person denied being a physician; and from fear of contagion—though he did not confess that to be the motive—refused even to enter the steerage.

The cases increased: the utmost alarm spread through the ship: and scenes ensued, over which, for the most part, a veil must be drawn; for such is the fastidiousness of some readers, that, many times, they must lose the most striking incidents in a narrative like mine.

Many of the panic-stricken emigrants would fain now have domiciled on deck; but being so scantily clothed, the wretched weather—wet cold, and tempestuous—drove the best part of them again below. Yet any other human beings, perhaps, would rather have faced the most outrageous storm, than continued to breathe the pestilent air of the steerage. But some of these poor people must have been so used to the most abasing calamities, that the atmosphere of a lazar-house almost seemed their natural air.

The first four cases happened to be in adjoining bunks; and the emigrants who slept in the farther part of the steerage, threw up a barricade in front of those bunks; so as to cut off communication. But this was no sooner reported to the captain, than he ordered it to be thrown down; since it could be of no possible benefit; but would only make still worse, what was already direful enough.

It was not till after a good deal of mingled threatening and coaxing, that the mate succeeded in getting the sailors below, to accomplish the captain's order.

The sight that greeted us, upon entering, was wretched indeed. It was like entering a crowded jail. From the rows of rude bunks, hundreds of meagre, begrimed faces were turned upon us; while seated upon the chests, were scores of unshaven men, smoking tea-leaves, and creating a suffocating vapour. But this vapour was better than the native air of the place, which from almost unbelievable causes, was fetid in the extreme. In every corner, the females were huddled together, weeping and lamenting; children were asking bread from their mothers, who had none to give; and old men, seated upon the floor, were leaning back against the heads of the water-casks, with closed eyes and fetching their breath with a gasp.

At one end of the place was seen the barricade, hiding the invalids; while—notwithstanding the crowd—in front of it was a clear area, which the fear of contagion had left open.

"That bulkhead must come down," cried the mate, in a voice that rose above the din. "Take hold of it, boys."

But hardly had we touched the chests composing it, when a crowd of palefaced, infuriated men rushed up; and with terrific howls, swore they would slay us, if we did not desist.

"Haul it down!" roared the mate.

But the sailors fell back, murmuring something about merchant seamen having no pensions in case of being maimed, and they had no out shipped to fight fifty to one. Further efforts were made by the mate who at last had recourse to entreaty; but it would not do; and we were obliged to depart, without achieving our object.

About four o'clock that morning, the first four died. They were all men; and the scenes which ensued were frantic in the extreme. Certainly, the bottomless profound of the sea, over which we were sailing, concealed nothing more frightful.

Orders were at once passed to bury the dead. But this was unnecessary. By their own countrymen, they were torn from the clasp of their wives, rolled in their own bedding, with ballast-stones, and with hurried rites, were dropped into the ocean.

At this time, ten more men had caught the disease; and with a degree of devotion worthy all praise, the mate attended them with his medicines; but the captain did not again go down to them.

It was all-important now that the steerage should be purified; and had it not been for the rains and squalls, which would have made it madness to turn such a number of women and children upon the wet and unsheltered decks, the steerage passengers would have been ordered above, and their den have been given a thorough cleansing. But, for the present, this was out of the question. The sailors peremptorily refused to go among the defilements to remove them; and so besotted were the greater part of the emigrants themselves, that though the necessity of the case was forcibly painted to them, they would not lift a hand to assist in what seemed their own salvation.

The panic in the cabin was now very great; and for fear of contagion to themselves, the cabin passengers would fain have made a prisoner of the captain, to prevent him from going forward beyond the mainmast. Their clamours at last induced him to tell the two mates that for the present they must sleep and take their meals elsewhere than in their old quarters, which communicated with the cabin.

On land, a pestilence is fearful enough; but there, many can flee from an infected city; whereas, in a ship, you are locked and bolted in the very hospital itself. Nor is there any possibility of escape from it; and in so small and crowded a place, no precaution can effectually guard against contagion.

Horrible as the sights of the steerage now were, the cabin, perhaps, presented a scene equally despairing. Many, who had seldom prayed before, now implored the merciful heavens, night and day, for fair winds and fine weather. Trunks were opened for Bibles; and at last, even prayer-meetings were held over the very table across which the loud jest had been so often heard.

Strange, though almost universal, that the seemingly nearer prospect of that death which anybody at any time may die, should produce these spasmodic devotions, when an everlasting Asiatic Cholera is forever thinning our ranks; and die by death we all must at last.

On the second day, seven died, one of whom was the little tailor; on the third, four; on the fourth, six, of whom one was the Greenland sailor, and another, a woman in the cabin, whose death, however, was afterward supposed to have been purely induced by her fears. These last deaths brought the panic to its height; and sailors, officers, cabin-passengers, and emigrants—all looked upon each other like lepers. All but the only true leper among us—the mariner Jackson, who seemed elated with the thought, that for *him*—already in the deadly clutches of another disease—no danger was to be apprehended from a fever which only swept off the comparatively healthy. Thus, in the midst of the despair of the healthful, this incurable invalid was not cast down; not, at least, by the same considerations that appalled the rest.

And still, beneath a gray, gloomy sky, the doomed craft beat on; now on this tack, now on that; battling against hostile blasts, and drenched in rain and spray; scarcely making an inch of progress toward her port.

On the sixth morning, the weather merged into a gale, to which we stripped our ship to a storm-stay-sail. In ten hours' time, the waves ran in mountains; and the *Highlander* rose and fell like some vast buoy on the water. Shrieks and lamentations were driven to leeward and drowned in the roar of the wind among the cordage; while we gave to the gale the blackened bodies of five more of the dead.

But as the dying departed, the places of two of them were filled in the rolls of humanity, by the birth of two infants, whom the plague, panic, and gale had hurried into the world before their time. The first cry of one of these infants, was almost simultaneous with the splash of its father's body in the sea. Thus we come and we go. But, surrounded by death, both mothers and babes survived.

At midnight, the wind went down; leaving a long, rolling sea; and, for the first time in a week, a clear, starry sky.

In the first morning-watch, I sat with Harry on the windlass, watching the billows; which, seen in the night, seemed real hills, upon which fortresses might have been built; and real valleys, in which villages, and groves, and gardens, might have nestled. It was like a landscape in Switzerland; for down into those dark, purple glens, often tumbled the white foam of the wavecrests, like avalanches; while the seething and boiling that ensued, seemed the swallowing up of human beings.

By the afternoon of the next day this heavy sea subsided; and we bore down on the waves, with all our canvas set; stun'-sails alow and aloft; and our best steersman at the helm; the captain himself at his elbow;— bowling along, with a fair, cheering breeze over the taffrail.

The decks were cleared, and swabbed bone-dry; and then, all the emigrants who were not invalids, poured themselves out on deck, snuffing the delightful air, spreading their damp bedding in the sun, and regaling themselves with the generous charity of the captain, who of late had seen fit to increase their allowance of food. A detachment of them now joined a band of the crew, who proceeding into the steerage, with buckets and brooms, gave it a thorough cleansing, sending on deck, I know not how many bucketsful of defilements. It was more like cleaning out a stable than a retreat for men and women. This day we buried three; the next day one, and then the pestilence left us, with seven convalescent; who, placed near the opening of the hatchway, soon rallied under the skilful treatment, and even tender care of the mate.

But even under this favorable turn of affairs, much apprehension was still entertained, lest in crossing the Grand Banks of Newfoundland, the fogs, so generally encountered there, might bring on a return of the fever. But, to the joy of all hands, our fair wind still held on; and we made a rapid run across these dreaded shoals, and southward steered for New York.

Our days were now fair and mild, and though the wind abated, yet we still ran our course over a pleasant sea. The steerage-passengers—at least by far the greater number—wore a still, subdued aspect, though a little cheered by the genial air, and the hopeful thought of soon reaching their port. But those who had lost fathers, husbands, wives, or children, needed no crêpe, to reveal to others who they were. Hard and bitter indeed was their lot; for with the poor and desolate, grief is no indulgence of mere sentiment, however sincere, but a gnawing reality, that eats into their vital beings; they have no kind condo-lers, and bland physicians, and troops of sympathizing friends; and they must toil, though to-morrow be the burial and their pallbearers throw down the hammer to lift up the coffin.

How, then, with these emigrants, who, three thousand miles from home, suddenly found them-selves deprived of brothers and husbands, with but a few pounds, or perhaps but a few shillings, to buy food in a strange land?

As for the passengers in the cabin, who now so jocund as they, drawing nigh, with their long purses and goodly portmanteaus to the promised land, without fear of fate? One and all were gener-ous and gay, the jelly-eyed old gentleman, before spoken of, gave a shilling to the steward.

One lady who had died, was an elderly person, an American, returning from a visit to an only brother in London. She had no friend or relative on board, hence, as there is little mourning for a stranger dying among strangers, her memory had been buried with her body.

But the thing most worthy of note among these now light-hearted people in feathers, was the gay way in which some of them bantered others, upon the panic into which nearly all had been thrown.

And since, if the extreme fear of a crowd in a panic of peril, proves grounded on causes sufficient, they must then indeed come to perish;—therefore it is, that at such times they must make up their minds either to die, or else survive to be taunted by their fellow-men with their fear. For except in extraordinary instances of exposure, there are few living men, who, at bottom, are not very slow to admit that any other living men have ever been very much nearer death than themselves. Accordingly, *craven* is the phrase too often applied to anyone who, with however good reason, has been appalled at the prospect of sudden death, and yet lived to escape it. Though, should he have perished in con-formity with his fears, not a syllable of *craven* would you hear. This is the language of one, who more than once has beheld the scenes, whence these principles have been deduced. The subject invites much subtle speculation; for in every being's ideas of death, and his behavior when it suddenly men-aces him, lies the best index to his life and his faith. Though the Christian era had not then begun, Socrates died the death of the Christian; and though Hume was not a Christian in theory, yet he, too, died the death of the Christian—humble, composed, without bravado; and thought the most skepti-cal of philosophical skeptics, yet full of that firm, creedless faith, that embraces the spheres. Seneca died dictating to posterity; Petronius lightly discoursing of essences and love-songs; and Addison, calling upon Christendom to behold how calmly a Christian could die; but not even the last of these three, perhaps, died the best death of the Christian.

The cabin passenger who had used to read prayers while the rest kneeled against the transoms and settees, was one of the merry young sparks, who had occasioned such agonies of jealousy to the, poor tailor, now no more. In his rakish vest, and dangling watch-chain, this same youth, with all the awfulness of fear, had led the earnest petitions of his companions, supplicating mercy, where before he had never solicited the slightest favour. More than once had he been seen thus engaged by the observant steersman at the helm: who looked through the little glass in the cabin bulk-head.

But this youth was an April man; the storm had departed; and now he shone in the sun, none braver than he.

One of his jovial companions ironically advised him to enter into holy orders upon his arrival in New York.

"Why so?" said the other, "have I such an orotund voice?"

"No;" profanely returned his friend—"but you are a coward—just the man to be a parson, and pray."

However this narrative of the circumstances attending the fever among the emigrants on the *Highlander* may appear; and though these things happened so long ago; yet just such events, nevertheless, are perhaps taking place to-day. But the only account you obtain of such events, is generally contained in a newspaper paragraph, under the shipping-head. *There* is the obituary of the destitute dead, who die on the sea. They die, like the billows that break on the shore, and no more are heard or seen. But in the events, thus merely initialized in the catalogue of passing occurrences, and but glanced at by the readers of news, who are more taken up with paragraphs of fuller flavour; what a world of life and death, what a world of humanity and its woes, lies shrunk into a three-worded sentence!

You see no plague-ship driving through a stormy sea; you hear no groans of despair; you see no corpses thrown over the bulwarks; you mark not the wringing hands and torn hair of widows and orphans:—all is a blank. And one of these blanks I have but filled up, in recounting the details of the *Highlander's* calamity.

Hurricane

WILLIAM WATSON

One day it fell dead calm, and about noon a large circle was observed round the sun of a purple colour, which some of the men declared indicated the approach of a heavy gale, and that we might in a short time look out for a violent norther. Anything would be a relief to this suspense, and a norther would be welcomed if it did not come too severe.

As it was about dead calm, sails were taken down, and every strop, hook, and cringle examined and made as secure as possible. Flying jib and small sails stowed, and everything about deck firmly lashed and made snug. Double reefs put in mainsail and foresail, and single reef in jib, and sails hoisted again, and we looked for the change in the weather.

We did not have long to wait. About 3 P.M. the sky darkened all round, and by 4 P.M. it was fearfully dark, the sky to the northward being black as ink. There was now no mistake but that we were going to have a heavy gale, but whether it was going to be a West India hurricane or a Texas norther we did not know.

It was not just yet the season for the regular northers, but there were often in those latitudes heavy gales about the equinox which sometimes took the form of northers, and blew with great violence, but they were generally of short duration, and might be said to be something between the Texas norther and the West India hurricane.

There could now be seen under the black cloud to the northward what appeared to be snow hillocks on the horizon, which soon spread out, and was coming towards us. This of course was the sea lashed into a foam by the fury of the wind, but still not a breath of wind had reached us, and the vessel still rolled in a dead calm.

It soon came on, however, direct from the north, and first a few drops of rain struck the vessel, and then the cold wind which indicated, to all appearance at least, it was a norther. It struck the vessel with such violence that I thought it would have torn the masts out of her before she gathered headway.

I was not sure how the *Rob Roy* would lay to under a close-reefed I foresail, and I determined, as the wind was fair for us, to make the best of it, and scud before it.

The vessel was now rushing through the water at a great rate, but when the full force of the gale came up it struck her with such violence that it seemed as if it would tumble her stern overhead.

"Get the mainsail off her," I cried.

This was easier said than done. The sheet had been eased off to run before the wind, and the belly of the sail was pressing against the shrouds, and with the awful force of the wind it was impossible to move it. To ease her in the meantime the peak purchase was cast off, and the peak dropped. This did ease her a little, but the gale kept increasing in violence, and the mainsail must come off her.

To handle such a large sail in such a tempest was no easy task, and as the boom was eased off it must be got aboard. No strength could haul it in against the force of such wind; the vessel must be rounded to.

"Hard down your helm!" was the word. The helm was put hard down, but the peak having been dropped she would not come up, but rushed along in the trough of the sea with the full force of the hurricane on her beam. That she did not lose her masts or capsize showed great strength and stability.

"Let go the jib halliards." This was done and the jib hauled down. This had the desired effect, and she came up into the wind. The fore sheet was hauled in, and she was held up till the main sheet could be hauled in, the sail lowered and stowed securely.

The gale had now become terrific, and the wind being directly against the current of the Gulf Stream, the waves rose very fast and to a great height. While we had the vessel thus rounded to, we thought to try if she would lay to in the gale, but the seas having got to a great height, and coming with great force, and the vessel having such a light hold on the water, she was thrown back stern on with every wave, causing her to fall heavily on her rudder, which I feared might be carried away; we thought it best to scud before the wind under a close reefed foresail.

The last reef was then put in the foresail, the jib tack hauled to windward, and part of the jib run up. She payed off quickly, and bounded off before the wind. The jib was then taken down and cleared so as to be run up quickly in case of necessity.

She now scudded along beautifully, but the wind increased far beyond our imagination, and was something appalling, but it did not vary a point in its direction. We steered about due south; everything depended upon the steersman; to have broached to would have been destruction.

The night was very dark, and the terrible roaring of the wind and the hissing of the spray off the tops of the waves seemed at times high over our heads. No one sought to sleep that night; the men were gathered aft, where they stood in silence with their eyes alternately upon the foresail and the man at the helm. Sometimes the silence would be broken by the expression—"Well, that is blowing pretty stiff."

Up till midnight all went well enough, but there was no abatement of the gale; it was rather increasing, and the seas were breaking more. Our only fears were for the foresail splitting.

About 1 A.M. a tremendous sea caused the vessel to yaw a little, and the foreboom jibed from starboard to port like the shot of a cannon, and as she recovered herself it jibed back again with the same force. This was dangerous work, as each time it struck against the fore-shrouds, and might have carried them away. I went with the mate to examine, but found no harm done. The fore-sheet, which worked in a traveller on deck, was taut as a bar, although the boom was pressing hard against the shrouds. Thinking to ease the boom off the shrouds a little, we got all hands to try a pull on the fore-sheet, but such was the pressure of the wind on the sail that we could not gain an inch. To have put a back-tackle on the boom to prevent it jibing would have been madness. So the hauling part of the sheet was made fast to the block at the traveller, and the boom allowed to have its play, and every one warned to keep out from the sweep of the boom, as one blow from it would have sent them beyond hail.

Shortly after this the boom jibed again with a loud report, and as quickly jibed back again, but in jibing back the jaw rope parted, and the boom unshipped from the mast, and lay across ship, with one end pressing against the mast, and the other against the fore-shrouds.

This was a bad state of things, but it was impossible to do anything with it, as such was the force of the wind, and the boom adrift and flying about, that it was dangerous to go near it.

It was evident that we were going to lose the foresail, and as our last resource we must try and get the jib upon her; but just as the men were trying to get forward to loose the jib a tremendous sea came rolling up astern, and a large body of water, detached from the top of it by the fury of the wind, fell on board right amidships, filling the large boat with water, and causing the vessel to reel over almost on her beam end. She quickly recovered herself again, but singularly and fortunately the sudden jerk started the foreboom from where it lay pressing against the mast and shrouds, and shipped it back into its place again. Lucky event!

"Well done, *Rob Roy!*" shouted the mate, as he seized a short piece of rope used as a stopper and darted forward to secure the boom in its place. I was quickly with him with more hands, warning them to keep forward of the mast out of the sweep of the boom. The rope was quickly passed round the neck of the boom, and brought round the mast to hold it in its place till a new jaw rope was got ready, when as many of the purls as could be picked up were strung upon it, and it was rove in its place, and the boom was all right again.

The vessel was now found to be staggering under the weight of the large boat full of water on deck. This must be emptied out; to bail it out would be dangerous work, as the boat was just under the sweep of the fore-boom. The mate remembered that there was a large plug in the boat, but the stopper was in. We tried to get the stopper out, but there were difficulties in the way. It could not be got at from the outside for the deck-load, and the fowls having been all used up, the then coop had been broken up, and an empty water-cask placed in the boat where it had been. This water-cask was right over the stopper, and the foreboom was just above the water-cask, so that it could not be moved.

The water-cask must be sacrificed. A hammer was got, and the cask knocked to pieces, and the mate, to avoid a stroke of the boom, sprawled along in the water, dived down and withdrew the stopper, and the water rushed out, and very soon the vessel was relieved of that unsteady top weight, and she bounded on all right again.

The gale had now reached its height, but still blew steady from the same point, and we began to imagine that it was abating a little.

As daylight began to appear we observed a small slit in the foresail, which, on being examined from the back or lee side of the sail, was found to be one of the seams which was just beginning to open. A piece of strong canvas was got, which, with a bent needle, was stitched strongly over the back of the place to help it a little.

When daylight broke clear the scene was truly grand. The most experienced man on board had never seen such a sea, but though the o waves were tremendously high it could not be called a dangerous cross chop of a sea. It was perfectly regular, and if from our position in it we could not afford to call it sublimely beautiful, we had at least to admit that it was grand and awful.

It seemed like a succession of mountain ridges perfectly straight and parallel to each other, rolling furiously in one direction, and between each a level plain about an eighth of a mile wide covered with white foam. This, I presume, was caused by the violent gale blowing steady from one point directly against the Gulf Stream.

About half-past seven the gale had somewhat abated, and soon after the cook managed to have some breakfast ready. Father Ryan, who had been up most of the night, was gazing on the scene.

"What do you think of that gale, Father Ryan?" said I.

"Awful! Truly awful," said he. "What kind of a gale do you call that? Is that a hurricane?"

"It blows hard enough for one," said I, "although it is too steady from one point for that. I think it is a sort of equinoctial norther. What do you think of that sea?"

"Oh, that is terrible," said he. "I would not think it safe for a small vessel like this."

"Many would think the same, and it is hard enough upon her, but she is buoyant, and rises finely upon it, and has come through it very well so far, and the worst is now past, for the gale has about spent itself."

"Oh, yes," said he, "it is calming down now, but when I looked out upon that awful sea this morning and thought of the calm sea of yesterday, I said, 'Surely awful are the works of the Almighty, and how suddenly He can send on the calmest sea such a storm as will raise it into angry mountains, and yet with the same hand He can guide safely through it a small, helpless vessel like this.'"

I agreed with him, and said we ought to be grateful.

By 9 A.M. the gale had much abated, and the morning, which up till now had been dark and cloudy, began to clear up, and soon after the sun broke through, and I got an observation, and assuming our latitude, found our longitude to be about 97° 20', which placed us about thirty miles from the coast of Mexico.

We now got more sail upon the vessel, and soon after we observed that the northerly wind of the gale had entirely spent itself, and we were into a light steady breeze from the eastward, although there was still a heavy swell from the northward. This indicated that the gale had not extended much further south, and we were now into the usual weather again.

The danger from the seas being for the time past, the old standing danger again cropped up, which was danger from the enemy, and, as we were now getting near to Tampico, it was exceedingly probable that some of their cruisers would be hovering in the neighbourhood with the view of picking up any blockade runner bound for that port. We, therefore, stood more to the westward, intending to sight the land, and then crawl down along the coast as we had done last trip.

We now began to wonder how it had fared with the *Mary Elizabeth*, which must have caught the gale at the same time with us. I knew that in point of management she would not lack, as she had a master and crew well experienced in these seas and in the management of this class of vessels. She was better provided in that respect than the *Roy Roy*, but she was a smaller vessel, and I knew that her sails were not of the same strength. We looked in all directions from the mast-head, but could see nothing of her.

As we stood to the westward, we saw something that looked like wreckage, but on steering towards it we found it to be large trees floating, which appeared to have been quite recently brought down some river, indicating that there had been heavy rain and floods in the northern parts of Mexico.

I may here anticipate, and say that of the *Mary Elizabeth* nothing was ever heard. Captain Shaeffer's brother afterwards called upon me in Havana to get the last and only information that he could ever obtain, and that was of her being seen by us on the day before the gale, and I have no doubt but that she foundered in that gale; and though she was larger, a better sea-boat, better found, and better managed than a great many of the craft which engaged in that rough and reckless trade, it was, strange to say, the only instance I ever knew of one of them being lost at sea. There was no doubt, however, that the gale, so far as it extended, was the heaviest which had been for some years.

We soon sighted the land, and at noon I got the latitude, and found that we were about fifteen miles to the northward of Tampico River, and we arrived off the mouth of the river about 3 P.M.

We found anchored there two vessels, both schooners. One of them was just such a vessel as the *Sylvia*, which we had met here six months before, and, like her, was from St. John with a cargo of lumber for Tampico. The other was a larger vessel, but she seemed light, as in ballast, and was anchored further out, some little distance away.

The former vessel we sailed up to and spoke with. I cannot remember her name, but will call her the *St. John*, as she was from that port. She had passed to the south of Cuba, and came in from the eastward, and had experienced nothing of the gale, but judged from the swell from the northward that there had been a heavy gale in that direction. They drew about six feet of water, and they wished to cross the bar and go up to Tampico Town.

The pilot's boat had been off in the morning, but it was impossible to take them over the bar at that time owing to the very high sea caused by the heavy swell from the northward, meeting in the channel the strong current of the Tampico River, which was then very high owing to great floods in the interior. The pilots had promised, however, to come out again in the afternoon, when, if the swell had gone down a little, they would be able to take them over.

As this bar at Tampico is of shifting quicksand, the channel through it keeps constantly changing, and it is necessary for the pilots to take soundings regularly—almost every day. It is sometimes very crooked and difficult to pass through, and if a vessel gets on to the shoal it is generally a total loss, and if it should be rough weather it is often attended with the loss of all hands, as no boat can live in the breakers. The entrance to this channel from seaward was supposed at this time to be about half a mile to the southward of where it was when we were here six months before, but it was very difficult to define the exact place.

As the pilots had promised to take over in the afternoon the *St. John,* which drew six feet of water, I conceived they could have no difficulty with the *Rob Roy,* which drew only four feet nine inches. We, therefore, dropped anchor and signalled for a pilot. After waiting about an hour there was no appearance of any pilot-boat coming off, and the sky had suddenly changed, and towards the north-east looked black and threatening. This was alarming.

Any one who knows anything of Tampico Roads knows what a dangerous place it is in a heavy north-easterly wind. A very high sea sets in, and with such violence that no amount of ground-tackling will I hold the vessel; and I have known large steamers with both anchors down and working propellers at full speed scarcely able to hold against it and keep off the breakers, while with a sailing vessel it is impossible to claw off.

As soon as I saw this appearance of a change in the weather I set about getting the anchor up to try and get out to sea, and I saw the other vessels doing the same, but it was too late. We had scarcely got sails set when it was down upon us. We set every bit of canvas, and gave full centre-board to see if we could weather the reefs to the southward, but we soon saw that we could not clear them on that stretch, and we tacked and stood to the northward as far as we could reach for the breakers, and then stood back to try again to weather the reefs to the southward; but to our dismay we found that we had not gained an inch, and the sea was now getting up and throwing us more to leeward, and we saw that the other two vessels were not making any more of it than ourselves.

This was something terrible to realize so suddenly and unexpected. To leeward and on each side were the shoals which hemmed us in, and on them the mountainous waves broke with great fury; to windward was the threatening cloud which betokened a heavy gale, and coming it was with certainty, and not the slightest chance of a lull or change in the wind, and night coming on. The gale did not come on with such violence as on the previous day, but it mattered little in the position we were in; it was sufficient to bring on our destruction, and that with certainty and in a very short time, and what would we not have given for the same sea room we had last night, even with the gale in all its fury.

What to do I did not know. The men looked at me, but no one spoke. I pointed to the deck-load of cotton.

"Men," said I, "the charge of every life is mine. Do you think it would help us any to throw over that deckload? If you think so, we will throw it over at once."

"It will do no good," they cried out together; "it eases her aloft and gives her a better hold on the water; and if at last we go on the bar there is a chance of saving our lives by clinging to bales of cotton."

"Then," said I, "we cannot claw off. The gale is increasing, night is upon us, and, do our best, we will be in these breakers before an hour. Now, I propose to make an attempt to run the gauntlet.

I have been observing with the glass, and I fancy I see what I take to be the opening to the channel, and I propose to make the attempt to cross the bar. I know it is a desperate and dangerous undertaking, but it is the only chance for our lives. What do you all say?"

"I say try it," said the mate; "it is our only chance."

The men all acquiesced, and said they were ready to obey.

One man then spoke up, and said: "I am ready to leave it to your own judgment, Captain; but if you take my advice when crossing you will steer through where you see the highest seas and the bluest water."

"I believe you are right," I said, "and I intend to do so."

Father Ryan, who stood with an expression something between composure and anxiety on his countenance, looked at me seriously and said, "Try it, Captain, and may the hand of God guide you."

For once at least in my life, I implored the aid of a higher hand. I went to the cabin and took the chronometer and cushioned it in one of the beds; as is usually done in crossing bars, in case of a sudden touch on the ground shaking it, and, going on deck, told the men that everything now depended upon their coolness and prompt action.

The greatest difficulty in crossing a bar through a narrow channel before a heavy sea was to keep the vessel straight in the channel, and prevent her stern being swung round by the heavy seas rolling up astern.

In placing the men, the first point to be determined was who was the best steersman. This was accorded to Hagan. To the cook was assigned the charge of the centre-board, the bar of which being near the door of the galley he had been accustomed to work, and lower or raise as required. The mate would take charge aft, with another man at the peak purchase, and be ready to drop the peak of the mainsail if a heavy sea rolling up astern swung her stern round; while two men would be stationed at the jibsheet to haul to windward and make her pay off, and I would take my station on the top of the cotton amidships, and with my glass look out ahead for the best water, and direct with my hand to the right or left the pourse to steer. The helmsman would keep his eye on me and steer by the direction of my hand. The mate would also be ready to assist the man at the helm, or to take the helm in case of the steersman being knocked down by a heavy sea coming over the stern. Father Ryan wished to know where he could be of service. I directed him to watch the companion doors, and keep them shut to prevent a sea going down in the cabin.

The most important part was to find the proper entrance to the channel; and we were now approaching the place which I supposed to be the entrance, and as soon as it was under our lee the gaff-topsail was taken in, but everything else was carried full.

Every man now took his place, and I got upon the top of the cotton with my glass and directed with my hand. As we approached the place, it looked awful; the waves toppled up like the walls of a fortress. Sheets were eased off, and under a full pressure of canvas the vessel rushed at it. She plunged violently, every spar and timber seemed to quiver. There was evidently a strong current against her, while the tremendous seas breaking on each side seemed above our heads. Sometimes I thought we were completely locked in, but still some higher and bluer waves gave indication of the deepest water. Sometimes a tremendous sea would come rolling up astern and throw her stern forward and bring her almost broadside on across the channel; but the peak would be quickly dropped and jib hauled to windward, and she payed off again before another sea came, when the same thing was repeated. We were nearly to the midst of it, but we were not making fast progress owing to the strong current of the river against us. This, however, made her steer better, and convinced me that we were in the right channel; but I feared that the shallowest and worst-defined part of it would be the end next the shore, and often the flying spray blinded me and dimmed the glass in my hand so that I had to keep wiping it with my handkerchief. I could only see ahead when lifted on the top of a huge wave, as, when that passed on, the mountain of water shut off for a time the view forward.

I fancied that the water was getting shallower on each side, the breakers worse, and the channel less defined. When looking forward my eye caught the shore in the distance, and I saw a Mexican flag—the pilot's flag—and I saw they were waving directions. First inclined to the north, we altered course to the north, then held up straight—steady; then inclined to the south. We altered course to the south, then up straight again—steady.

I had now some hopes. We continued on, and soon after all in front seemed breakers, and I saw no appearance of a channel or deep water; but the pilot's flag was held up steady to come straight on. It looked fearful, but on we must go. Several heavy broken waves came up, two of which came over our stern. Another heavier one came up, and, nearly burying us, carried us forward some distance, and when it passed she touched the ground, but it was just lightly and for a moment. She payed off again. Another heavy and broken wave followed, and a violent gust of wind at the same time carried us along through a mass of foam into the deep and smooth water inside of the bar.

"Round her to, haul down staysail and jib, and let go anchor," said I.

This was soon done. The men stood round, but said nothing. Father Ryan, whose hat had blown overboard, came up to me bareheaded, drenched with salt-water, and with tears in his eyes. He grasped me warmly by the hand, and said seriously, "Captain, the finger of God was there."

"It was," I said; and I never said two words with more sincerity in all my life. Of the many incidents in my somewhat adventurous life I do not think that any made a greater impression on me than the fortune of the last twenty-four hours, and especially this last hour.

The Loss of the "White Ship"

CHARLES DICKENS

One of the most famous wrecks in English history is that of the "White Ship" in which Prince William, son and heir of King Henry 1, was lost.

Henry the First went over to Normandy with Prince William and a great retinue, to have the Prince acknowledged as his successor by the Norman nobles, and to contract the promised marriage—this was one of the many promises the King had broken—between him and the daughter of the Count of Anjou. Both these things were triumphantly done, with great show and rejoicing; and on the 25th of November, in the year 1120, the whole retinue prepared to embark at the port of Barfleur, on the voyage home.

On that day, and at that place, there came to the King, Fitz-Stephen, a sea captain, and said:

"My liege, my father served your father all his life upon the sea. He steered the ship with the golden boy upon the prow, in which your father sailed to conquer England. I beseech you to grant me the same office. I have a fair vessel in the harbour here, called the *White Ship*, manned by fifty sailors of renown. I pray you, sire, to let your servant have the honour of steering you in the *White Ship* to England!"

"I am sorry, friend," replied the King, "that my vessel is already chosen, and that I cannot, therefore, sail with the son of the man who served my father. But the Prince and all his company shall go along with you, in the fair *White Ship*, manned by the fifty sailors of renown."

An hour or two afterwards, the King set sail in the vessel he had chosen, accompanied by other vessels, and sailing all night with a fair and gentle wind, arrived upon the coast of England in the morning. While it was yet night, the people in some of those ships heard a faint, wild cry come over the sea, and wondered what it was.

Now, the Prince was a young man of eighteen, who bore no love to the English, and had declared that, when he came to the throne, he would yoke them to the plough like oxen. He went aboard the *White Ship*, with one hundred and forty youthful nobles like himself, among whom were eighteen noble ladies of the highest rank. All this gay company, with their servants and the fifty sailors, made three hundred souls aboard the fair *White Ship*.

"Give three casks of wine, Fitz-Stephen," said the Prince, "to the fifty sailors of renown! My father the King has sailed out of the harbour. What time is there to make merry here, and yet reach England with the rest?"

"Prince," said Fitz-Stephen, "before morning, my fifty and the *White Ship* shall overtake the swiftest vessel in attendance on your father, the King, if we sail at midnight!"

Then the Prince commanded to make merry; and the sailors drank out the three casks of wine; and the Prince and all the noble company danced in the moonlight on the deck of the *White Ship*.

When, at last, she shot out of the harbour of Barfleur, there was not a sober seaman on board. But the sails were all set, and the oars all going merrily. Fitz-Stephen had the helm. The gay young nobles and the beautiful ladies, wrapped in mantles of various bright colours to protect them from the cold, talked, laughed, and sang. The Prince encouraged the fifty sailors to row harder yet, for the honour of the *White Ship*.

Crash! A terrific cry broke from three hundred hearts. It was the cry the people in the distant vessels of the King heard faintly on the water. The *White Ship* had struck upon a rock—was filling—going down.

Fitz-Stephen hurried the Prince into a boat, with some few nobles.

"Push off," he whispered, "and row to the land. It is not far, and the sea is smooth. The rest of us must die."

But, as they rowed away fast from the sinking ship, the Prince heard the voice of his sister Marie, the Countess of Perche, calling for help. He never in his life had been so good as he was then.

"Row back at any risk! I cannot bear to leave her!" he cried.

They rowed back. As the Prince held out his arms to catch his sister such numbers leaped in, that the boat was overset. And in the same instant the *White Ship* went down.

Only two men floated. They both clung to the main yard of the ship, which had broken from the mast, and now supported them. One asked the other who he was. He said:

"I am a nobleman, Godfrey by name, the son of Gilbert de l'Aigle. And you?"

"I am Berold, a poor butcher of Rouen," was the answer.

Then they said together, "Lord be merciful to us both!" and tried to encourage one another, as they drifted in the cold, benumbing sea on that unfortunate November night.

By-and-by, another man came swimming towards them, whom they knew, when he pushed aside his long wet hair, to be Fitz-Stephen.

"Where is the Prince?" said he.

"Gone! Gone!" the two cried together. "Neither he, nor his brother, nor his sister, nor the King's niece, nor her brother, nor any one of all the brave three hundred, noble or commoner, except we three, has risen above the water!"

Fitz-Stephen, with a ghastly face, cried, "Woe! Woe to me!" and sank to the bottom.

The other two clung to the yard for some hours. At length the young noble said faintly:

"I am exhausted, and chilled with the cold, and can hold no longer. Farewell, good friend! God preserve you!"

So, he dropped and sank; and of all the brilliant crowd, the poor butcher of Rouen alone was saved. In the morning some fishermen saw him floating in his sheepskin coat, and got him into their boat—the sole relater of the dismal tale.

For three days, no one dared to carry the intelligence to the King. At length, they sent into his presence a little boy, who, weeping bitterly and kneeling at his feet, told him that the *White Ship* was lost with all on board. The King was never afterwards seen to smile.

Man Overboard

W. H. G. KINGSTON

We were on our return home, by the way of the Cape of Good Hope, when, on the 8th of May of that year, we were off Cape L'Agullus. It was blowing a heavy gale of wind, with a tremendous sea running, such a sea as one rarely meets with anywhere but off the Cape, when just at nightfall, as we were taking another reef in the top-sails, a young seaman, a mizen-topman, James Miles by name, fell from the mizen-topsail-yard, and away he went overboard. In his descent he came across the chain-span of the weather-quarter davits, and with such force that he actually broke it. I could scarcely have supposed that he would have escaped being killed in his fall; but as the ship flew away from him, he was seen rising on the crest of a foaming wave, apparently unhurt. The life-buoy was let go as soon as possible, but by that time the ship had already got a considerable distance from him; and even could he reach it, I felt that the prospect of saving him was small indeed, as I had no hope, should we find him, of being able to pick him out of that troubled sea; and I had strong fears that a boat would be unable to swim to go to his rescue, should I determine to lower one. I was very doubtful as to what was my duty. I might, by allowing a boat to be lowered, sacrifice the lives of the officer and crew, who would, I was very certain, at all events volunteer to man her. It was a moment of intense anxiety. I instantly, however, wore the ship round; and while we stood towards the spot, as far as we could guess, where the poor fellow had fallen, the thoughts I have mentioned passed through my mind. The sad loss of the gallant Lieutenant Gore and a whole boat's crew a short time before, about the same locality, was present to my thoughts. To add to the chances of our not finding the man, it was now growing rapidly dusk. As we reached the spot, every eye on board was straining through the gloom to discern the object of our search, but neither Miles nor the life-buoy were to be seen. Still, I could not bring myself to leave him to one of the most dreadful of fates. He was a good swimmer, and those who knew him best asserted that he would swim to the last. For my part, I almost hoped that the poor fellow had been stunned, and would thus have sunk at once, and been saved the agony of despair he must be feeling were he still alive. Of one thing I felt sure, from the course we had steered, that we were close to the spot where he had fallen. Anxiously we waited,—minute after minute passed by,—still no sound was heard; not a speck could be seen to indicate his position. At least half an hour had passed by. The strongest man alive could not support himself in such a sea as this for so long, I feared. Miles must long before this have sunk, unless he could have got hold of the life-buoy, and of that I had no hope. I looked at my watch by the light of the binnacle lamp. "It is hopeless," I thought, "we must give the poor fellow up." When I had come to this melancholy resolve, I issued the orders for wearing ship in somewhat a louder voice than usual, as under the circumstances was natural, to stifle my own feelings. Just then I thought I heard a human voice borne down upon the gale. I listened; it was, I feared, but the effect of imagination; yet I waited a moment. Again the voice struck my ear, and this time several of the ship's company heard it. "There he is, sir! There he is away to windward!" exclaimed several voices; and then in return they uttered a loud hearty cheer, to keep up the spirits of the poor fellow. Now came the most trying moment; I must decide whether I would allow a boat to be lowered. "If I refuse," I felt, "my crew will say that I am careless of their lives. It is not their nature to calculate the risk they themselves must run." At once, Mr. Christopher, one of my lieutenants, nobly volunteered to make the attempt, and numbers of the crew came forward anxious to accompany him. At last, anxiety to save a drowning man prevailed over prudence, and I sanctioned the attempt.

The boat, with Mr. Christopher and a picked crew, was lowered, not without great difficulty and, sad to say, with the loss of one of the brave fellows. He was the bowman; and, as he stood up with his boathook in his hand to shove off, the boat give a terrific pitch and sent him over the bow. He must have struck his head against the side of the ship, for he went down instantly, and was no more seen. Thus, in the endeavour to save the life of one man, another was already sent to his long account. With sad forebodings for the fate of the rest of the gallant fellows, I saw the boat leave the ship's side. Away she pulled into the darkness, where she was no longer visible; and a heavy pull I knew she must have of it in that terrible sea, even if she escaped destruction. It was one of the most trying times of my life. We waited in suspense for the return of the boat; the minutes, seeming like hours, passed slowly by, and she did not appear. I began at length to dread that my fears would be realized, and that we should not again see her, when, after half an hour had elapsed since she had left the ship's side on her mission of mercy, a cheer from her gallant crew announced her approach with the success of their bold enterprise. My anxiety was not, however, entirely relieved till the falls were hooked on, and she and all her crew were hoisted on board, with the rescued man Miles. To my surprise I found that he was perfectly naked. As he came up the side, also, he required not the slightest assistance, but dived below at once to dry himself and to get out of the cold. I instantly ordered him to his hammock, and, with the doctor's permission, sent him a stiff glass of grog. I resolved also to relieve him from duty, believing that his nervous system would have received a shock from which it would take long to recover. After I had put the ship once more on her course, being anxious to learn the particulars of his escape, as soon as I heard that he was safely stowed away between the blankets, I went below to see him. His voice was as strong as ever; his pulse beat as regularly, and his nerves seemed as strong as usual. After pointing out to him how grateful he should feel to our Almighty Father for his preservation from an early and dreadful death, I begged him to tell me how he had contrived to keep himself so long afloat. He replied to me in the following words:—"Why, sir, you see as soon as I came up again, after I had first struck the water, I looked out for the ship, and, getting sight of her running away from me, I remembered how it happened I was there, and knew there would be no use swimming after her or singing out. Then, sir, I felt very certain you would not let me drown without an attempt to pick me up, and that there were plenty of fine fellows on board who would be anxious to man a boat to come to my assistance, if you thought a boat could swim. Then, thinks I to myself, a man can die but once, and if it's my turn to-day, why, there's no help for it. Yet I didn't think all the time that I was likely to lose the number of my mess, do ye see, sir. The next thought that came to me was, if I am to drown, it's as well to drown without clothes as with them; and if I get them off, why, there's a better chance of my keeping afloat till a boat can be lowered to pick me up; so I kicked off my shoes; then I got off my jacket, and then, waiting till I could get hold of the two legs at once, I drew off my trousers in a moment. My shirt was soon off me, but I took care to roll up the tails, so as not to get them over my face. As I rose on the top of the sea, I caught sight of the ship as you wore her round here, and that gave me courage, for I felt I was not to be deserted; indeed, I had no fear of that. Then I knew that there would be no use swimming; so all I did was to throw myself on my back and float till you came up to me. I thought the time was somewhat long, I own. When the ship got back, I saw her hove to away down to leeward, but I did not like to sing out for fear of tiring myself, and thought you would not hear me; and I fancied also that a boat would at once have been lowered to come and look for me. Well, sir, I waited, thinking the time was very long, and hearing no sound, yet still I could see the ship hove to, and you may be sure I did not take my eyes from off her; when at last I heard your voice give the order to wear ship again. Then thinks I to myself, now or never's the time to sing out. And, raising myself as high as I could out of the water, I sang out at the top of my voice. There was a silence on board, but no answer, and I did begin to feel that there was a chance of being lost after all. 'Never give in, though,' thinks I; so I sang out again, as loud, you may be sure, as I could sing. This time the answering cheers of my shipmates gave me fresh spirits; but still I knew full well that I wasn't safe on board yet. If I had wanted to swim, there was too much sea on to make any way; so I kept floating on my back as before, just keeping an eye to leeward to see if a boat was coming to pick me up. Well, sir, when the boat did come at last, with Mr. Christopher and the rest in her, I felt strong and hearty, and was well able to help myself on board. I now can scarcely fancy I was so long in the water."

I was much struck with the extraordinary coolness of Miles. He afterwards had another escape, which was owing less to his own self-possession, though he took it as coolly as the first. On our passage home, the ship was running with a lightish breeze and almost calm sea across the Bay of Biscay, when Miles was sent on the fore-top-gallant-yard. By some carelessness he fell completely over the yard, and those aloft expected to see him dashed to pieces on the forecastle. Instead of that, the foresail at that moment swelled out with a sudden breeze, and, striking the bulge of the sail, he was sent forward clear of the bows and hove into the water. A rope was towing overboard. He caught hold of it, and, hauling himself on board, was again aloft within a couple of minutes attending to his duty, which had so suddenly been interrupted. On his arrival in England, Lieutenant Christopher received the honorary silver medal from the Royal Humane Society for his gallant conduct on the occasion of saving Miles' life.

Through the Vortex of a Cyclone

WILLIAM HOPE HODGSON

(The Cyclone—"The most fearful enemy which the mariner's perilous calling obliges him to encounter.")

It was in the middle of November that the four-masted barque, *Golconda*, came down from Crockett and anchored off Telegraph Hill, San Francisco. She was loaded with grain, and was homeward bound round Cape Horn. Five days later she was towed out through the Golden Gates, and cast loose off the Heads, and so set sail upon the voyage that was to come so near to being her last.

For a fortnight we had baffling winds; but after that time, got a good slant that carried us down to within a couple of degrees of the Line. Here it left us, and over a week passed before we had managed to tack and drift our way into the Southern Hemisphere.

About five degrees South of the Line, we met with a fair wind that helped us Southward another ten or twelve degrees, and there, early one morning, it dropped us, ending with a short, but violent, thunder storm, in which, so frequent were the lightning flashes, that I managed to secure a picture of one, whilst in the act of snapshotting the sea and clouds upon our port side.

During the day, the wind, as I have remarked, left us entirely, and we lay becalmed under a blazing hot sun. We hauled up the lower sails to prevent them from chafing as the vessel rolled lazily on the scarce perceptible swells, and busied ourselves, as is customary on such occasions, with much swabbing and cleaning of paint-work.

As the day proceeded, so did the heat seem to increase; the atmosphere lost its clear look, and a low haze seemed to lie about the ship at a great distance. At times, the air seemed to have about it a queer, unbreathable quality; so that one caught oneself breathing with a sense of distress.

And, hour by hour, as the day moved steadily onward, the sense of oppression grew ever more acute.

Then, it was, I should think, about three-thirty in the afternoon, I became conscious of the fact that a strange, unnatural, dull, brick-red glare was in the sky. Very subtle it was, and I could not say that it came from any particular place; but rather it seemed to shine *in* the atmosphere. As I stood looking at it, the Mate came up beside me. After about half a minute, he gave out a sudden exclamation:—

"Hark!" he said. "Did you hear that?"

"No, Mr. Jackson," I replied. "What was it like?"

"Listen!" was all his reply, and I obeyed; and so perhaps for a couple of minutes we stood there in silence.

"There!——There it is again!" he exclaimed, suddenly; and in the same instant I heard it . . . a sound like low, strange growling far away in the North-East. It lasted for about fifteen seconds, and then died away in a low, hollow, moaning noise, that sounded indescribably dree.

After that, for a space longer, we stood listening; and so, at last, it came again . . . a far, faint, wild-beast growling, away over the North-Eastern horizon. As it died away, with that strange hollow note, the Mate touched my arm:—

"Go and call the Old Man," he said, meaning the Captain. "And while you're down, have a look at the barometer."

In both of these matters I obeyed him, and in a few moments the Captain was on deck, standing beside the Mate—listening.

"How's the glass?" asked the Mate, as I came up.

"Steady," I answered, and at that, he nodded his head, and resumed his expectant attitude. Yet, though we stood silent, maybe for the better part of half an hour, there came no further repetition of that weird, far-off growling, and so, as the glass was steady, no serious notice was taken of the matter.

That evening, we experienced a sunset of quite indescribable gorgeousness, which had, to me, an unnatural glow about it, especially in the way in which it lit up the surface of the sea, which was, at this time, stirred by a slight evening breeze. Evidently, the Mate was of the opinion that it foreboded something in the way of ill weather; for he gave orders for the watch on deck to take the three royals off her.

By the time the men had got down from aloft, the sun had set, and the evening was fading into dusk; yet, despite that, all the sky to the North-East was full of the most vivid red and orange; this being, it will be remembered, the direction from which we had heard earlier that sullen growling.

It was somewhat later, I remember, that I heard the Mate remark to the Captain that we were in for bad weather, and that it was his belief a Cyclone was coming down upon us; but this, the Captain—who was quite a young fellow—poo-poohed; telling him that he pinned *his* faith to the barometer, which was perfectly steady. Yet, I could see that the Mate was by no means so sure; but forebore to press further his opinion against his superior's.

Presently, as the night came down upon the world, the orange tints went out of the sky, and only a sombre, threatening red was left, with a strangely bright rift of white light running horizontally across it, about twenty degrees above the North-*Eastern* horizon.

This lasted for nigh on to half an hour, and so did it impress the crew with a sense of something impending, that many of them crouched, staring over the port rail, until long after it had faded into the general greyness.

That night, I recollect, it was my watch on deck from midnight until four in the morning. When the boy came down to wake me, he told me that it had been lightning during the past watch. Even as he spoke, a bright, bluish glare lit up the porthole; but there was no succeeding thunder.

I sprang hastily from my bunk, and dressed; then, seizing my camera, ran out on deck. I opened the shutter, and the next instant—flash! a great stream of electricity sprang out of the zenith.

Directly afterwards, the Mate called to me from the break of the poop to know whether I had managed to secure *that* one. I replied, Yes, I thought I had, and he told me to come up on to the poop, beside him, and have a further try from there; for he, the Captain and the Second Mate were much interested in my photographic hobby, and did all in their power to aid me in the securing of successful snaps.

That the Mate was uneasy, I very soon perceived; for, presently, a little while after he had relieved the Second Mate, he ceased his pacing of the poop deck, and came and leant over the rail, alongside of me.

"I wish to goodness the Old Man would have her shortened right down to lower topsails," he said, a moment later, in a low voice. "There's some rotten, dirty weather knocking around. I can smell it." And he raised his head, and sniffed at the air.

"Why not shorten her down, on your own?" I asked him.

"Can't!" he replied. "The Old Man's left orders not to touch anything; but to call him if any change occurs. He goes *too* d——n much by the barometer, to suit me, and won't budge a rope's end, because it's steady."

All this time, the lightning had been playing at frequent intervals across the sky; but now there came several gigantic flashes, seeming extraordinarily near to the vessel, pouring down out of a great rift in the clouds—veritable torrents of electric fluid. I switched open the shutter of my camera, and pointed the lens upward; and the following instant, I secured a magnificent photograph of a great flash, which, bursting down from the same rift, divided to the East and West in a sort of vast electric arch.

For perhaps a minute afterwards, we waited, thinking that such a flash *must* be followed by thunder; but none came. Instead, from the darkness to the North-East, there sounded a faint, far-drawn-out wailing noise, that seemed to echo queerly across the quiet sea. And after that, silence.

The Mate stood upright, and faced round at me.

"Do you know," he said, "only once before in my life have I heard anything like that, and that was before the Cyclone in which the *Lancing* and the *Eurasian* were lost, in the Indian Ocean."

"Do you think then there's *really* any danger of a Cyclone now?" I asked him, with something of a little thrill of excitement.

"I think——" he began, and then stopped, and swore suddenly. "Look!" he said, in a loud voice. "Look! 'Stalk' lightning, as I'm a living man!" And he pointed to the North-East. "Photograph that, while you've got the chance; you'll never have another as long as you live!"

I looked in the direction which he indicated, and there, sure enough, were great, pale, flickering streaks and tongues of flame *rising apparently out of the sea.* They remained steady for some ten or fifteen seconds, and in that time I was able to take a snap of them.

This photograph, as I discovered when I came to develop the negative, has not, I regret to say, taken regard of a strange, indefinable dull-red glare that lit up the horizon at the same time; but, as it is, it remains to me a treasured record of a form of electrical phenomenon but seldom seen, even by those whose good, or ill, fortune has allowed them to come face to face with a Cyclonic Storm. Before leaving this incident, I would once more impress upon the reader that this strange lightning was *not* descending from the atmosphere; but *rising from the sea.*

It was after I had secured this last snap, that the Mate declared it to be his conviction that a great Cyclonic Storm was coming down upon us from the North-East, and, with that—for about the twentieth time that watch—he went below to consult the barometer.

He came back in about ten minutes, to say that it was still steady; but that he had called the Old Man, and told him about the upward "Stalk" lightning; yet the Captain, upon hearing from him that the glass was still steady, had refused to be alarmed, but had promised to come up and take a look round. This, in a while, he did; but, as Fate would have it, there was no further display of the "Stalk" lightning, and, as the other kind had now become no more than an occasional dull glare behind the clouds to the North-East, he retired once more, leaving orders to be called if there were any change either in the glass or the weather.

With the sunrise there came a change, a low, slow-moving scud driving down from the North-East, and drifting across the face of the newly-risen sun, which was shining with a queer, unnatural glare. Indeed, so stormy and be-burred looked the sun, that I could have applied to it with truth the line:—

"And the red Sun all bearded with the Storm," to describe its threatening aspect.

The glass also showed a change at last, rising a little for a short while, and then dropping about a tenth, and, at that, the Mate hurried down to inform the Skipper, who was speedily up on deck.

He had the fore and mizzen t'gallants taken off her; but nothing more; for he declared that he wasn't going to throw away a fine fair wind for any Old Woman's fancies.

Presently, the wind began to freshen; but the orange-red burr about the sun remained, and also it seemed to me that the tint of the water had a "bad weather" look about it. I mentioned this to the Mate, and he nodded agreement; but said nothing in so many words, for the Captain was standing near.

By eight bells (4 A.M.) the wind had freshened so much that we were lying over to it, with a big cant of the decks, and making a good twelve knots, under nothing higher than the main t'gallant.

We were relieved by the other watch, and went below for a short sleep. At eight o'clock, when again I came on deck, I found that the sea had begun to rise somewhat; but that otherwise the weather was much as it had been when I left the decks; save that the sun was hidden by a heavy squall to windward, which was coming down upon us.

Some fifteen minutes later, it struck the ship, making the foam fly, and carrying away the main topsail sheet. Immediately upon this, the heavy iron ring in the clew of the sail began to thrash and beat about, as the sail flapped in the wind, striking great blows against the steel yard; but the clewline was manned, and some of the men went aloft to repair the damage, after which the sail was once more sheeted home, and we continued to carry on.

About this time, the Mate sent me down into the saloon to take another look at the glass, and I found that it had fallen a further tenth. When I reported this to him, he had the main t'gallant taken in; but hung on to the mainsail, waiting for eight bells, when the whole crowd would be on deck to give a hand.

By that time, we had begun to ship water, and most of us were speedily very thoroughly soused; yet, we got the sail off her, and she rode the easier for the relief.

A little after one o'clock in the afternoon, I went out on deck to have a final "squint" at the weather, before turning-in for a short sleep, and found that the wind had freshened considerably, the seas striking the counter of the vessel at times, and flying to a considerable height in foam.

At four o'clock, when once more I appeared on deck, I discovered the spray flying over us with a good deal of freedom, and the solid water coming aboard occasionally in odd tons.

Yet, so far there was, *to a sailorman*, nothing worthy of note in the severity of the weather. It was merely blowing a moderately heavy gale, before which, under our six topsails and foresail, we were making a good twelve knots an hour to the Southward. Indeed, it seemed to me, at this time, that the Captain was right in his belief that we were not in for any very dirty weather, and I said as much to the Mate; whereat he laughed somewhat bitterly.

"Don't you make any sort of mistake!" he said, and pointed to leeward, where continual flashes of lightning darted down from a dark bank of cloud. "We're already within the borders of the Cyclone We are travelling, so I take it, about a knot slower an hour to the South than the bodily forward movement of the Storm; so that you may reckon it's overtaking us at the rate of something like a mile an hour. Later on, I expect, it'll get a move on it, and then a torpedo boat wouldn't catch it! This bit of a breeze that we're having now"—and he gestured to windward with his elbow—"is only fluff—nothing more than the outer fringe of the advancing Cyclone! Keep your eye lifting to the North-East, and keep your ears open. Wait until you hear the thing yelling at you as loud as a million mad tigers!"

He came to a pause, and knocked the ashes out of his pipe; then he slid the empty "weapon" into the side pocket of his long oilskin coat. And all the time, I could see that he was ruminating.

"Mark my words," he said, at last, and speaking with great deliberation. "Within twelve hours it'll be upon us!"

He shook his head at me. Then he added:—

"Within twelve hours, my boy, you and I and every other soul in this blessed packet may be down there in the cold!" And the brute pointed downward into the sea, and grinned cheerfully at me.

It was our watch that night from eight to twelve; but, except that the wind freshened a trifle, hourly, nothing of note occurred during our watch. The wind was just blowing a good fresh gale, and giving us all we wanted, to keep the ship doing her best under topsails and foresail.

At midnight, I went below for a sleep. When I was called at four o'clock, I found a very different state of affairs. The day had broken, and showed the sea in a very confused state, with a tendency to run up into heaps, and there was a good deal less wind; but what struck me as most remarkable, and brought home with uncomfortable force the Mate's warning of the previous day, was the colour of the sky, which seemed to be everywhere one great glare of gloomy, orange-coloured light, streaked here and there with red. So intense was this glare that the seas, as they rose clumsily into heaps, caught and reflected the light in an extraordinary manner, shining and glittering gloomily, like vast moving mounds of liquid flame. The whole presenting an effect of astounding and uncanny grandeur.

I made my way up on to the poop, carrying my camera. There, I met the Mate.

"You'll not want that pretty little box of yours," he remarked, and tapped my camera. "I guess you'll find a coffin more useful."

"Then it's coming?" I said.

"Look!" was all his reply, and he pointed into the North-East.

I saw in an instant what it was at which he pointed. It was a great black wall of cloud that seemed to cover about seven points of the horizon, extending almost from North to East, and reaching upward some fifteen degrees towards the zenith. The intense, solid blackness of this cloud was astonishing, and threatening to the beholder, seeming, indeed, to be more like a line of great black cliffs standing out of the sea, than a mass of thick vapour.

I glanced aloft, and saw that the other watch were securing the mizzen upper topsail. At the same moment, the Captain appeared on deck, and walked over to the Mate.

"Glass has dropped another tenth, Mr. Jackson," he remarked, and glanced to windward. "I think we'd better have the fore and main upper topsails off her."

Scarcely had he given the order, before the Mate was down on the maindeck, shouting:—"Fore and main topsail hal'yards! Lower away! Man clewlines and spillinglines!" So eager was he to have the sail off her.

By the time that the upper topsails were furled, I noted that the red glare had gone out of the greater part of the sky to windward, and a stiffish looking squall was bearing down upon us. Away more to the North, I saw that the black rampart of cloud had disappeared, and, in place thereof, it seemed to me that the clouds in that quarter were assuming a hard, tufted appearance, and changing their shapes with surprising rapidity.

The sea also at this time was remarkable, acting uneasily, and hurling up queer little mounds of foam, which the passing squall caught and spread.

All these points, the Mate noted; for I heard him urging the Captain to take in the foresail and mizzen lower topsail. Yet, this, the Skipper seemed unwilling to do; but finally agreed to have the mizzen topsail off her. Whilst the men were up at this, the wind dropped abruptly in the tail of the squall, the vessel rolling heavily, and taking water and spray with every roll.

Now, I want the Reader to try and understand exactly how matters were at this particular and crucial moment. The wind had dropped entirely, and, with the dropping of the wind, a thousand different sounds broke harshly upon the ear, sounding almost unnatural in their distinctness, and impressing the ear with a sense of discomfort. With each roll of the ship, there came a chorus of creaks and groans from the swaying masts and gear, and the sails slatted with a damp, disagreeable sound. Beyond the ship, there was the constant, harsh murmur of the seas, occasionally changing to a low roar, as one broke near us. One other sound there was that punctuated all these, and that was the loud, slapping blows of the seas, as they hove themselves clumsily against the ship; and, for the rest, there was a strange sense of silence.

Then, as sudden as the report of a heavy gun, a great bellowing came out of the North and East, and died away into a series of monstrous grumbles of sound. It was not thunder. *It was the Voice of the approaching Cyclone.*

In the same instant, the Mate nudged my shoulder, and pointed, and I saw, with an enormous feeling of surprise, that a large waterspout had formed about four hundred yards astern, and was coming towards us. All about the base of it, the sea was foaming in a strange manner, and the whole thing seemed to have a curious luminous quality.

Thinking about it now, I cannot say that I perceived it to be in rotation; but nevertheless, I had the impression that it was revolving swiftly. Its general onward motion seemed to be about as fast as would be attained by a well-manned gig.

I remember, in the first moments of astonishment, as I watched it, hearing the Mate shout something to the Skipper about the foresail, then I realised suddenly that the spout was coming straight for the ship. I ran hastily to the taffrail, raised my camera, and snapped it, and then, as it seemed to tower right up above me, gigantic, I ran backwards in sudden fright. In the same instant, there came a blinding flash of lightning, almost in my face, followed instantaneously by a tremendous roar of thunder, and I saw that the thing had burst within about fifty yards of the ship. The sea, immediately beneath where it had been, leapt up in a great hummock of solid water, and foam, as though something as great as a house had been cast into the ocean. Then, rushing towards us, it struck the stern of the vessel, flying as high as our topsail yards in spray, and knocking me backwards on to the deck.

As I stood up, and wiped the water hurriedly from my camera, I heard the Mate shout out to know if I were hurt, and then, in the same moment, and before I could reply, he cried out:—

"It's coming! Up helium! Up hellum! Look out everybody! Hold on for your lives!"

Directly afterwards, a shrill, yelling noise seemed to fill the whole sky with a deafening, piercing sound. I glanced hastily over the port quarter. *In that direction the whole surface of the ocean seemed to be torn up into the air in monstrous clouds of spray.* The yelling sound passed into a vast scream, and the next instant the Cyclone was upon us.

Immediately, the air was so full of flying spray that I could not see a yard before me, and the wind slapped me back against the teak companion, pinning me there for a few moments, helpless. The ship heeled over to a terrible angle, so that, for some seconds, I thought we were going to capsize. Then, with a sudden lurch, she hove herself upright, and I became able to see about me a little, by switching the water from my face, and shielding my eyes. Near to me, the helmsman—a little Dago—was clinging to the wheel, looking like nothing so much as a drowned monkey, and palpably frightened to such an extent that he could hardly stand upright.

From him, I looked round at so much of the vessel as I could see, and up at the spars, and so, presently, I discovered how it was that she had righted. The mizzen topmast was gone just below the heel of the t'gallantmast, and the fore topmast a little above the cap. The main topmast alone stood. It was the losing of these spars which had eased her, and allowed her to right so suddenly. Marvellously enough, the foresail—a small, new, No. 1 canvas stormsail—had stood the strain, and was now bellying out, with a high foot, the sheets evidently having surged under the wind pressure. What was more extraordinary, was that the fore and main lower topsails were standing and this, despite the fact that the bare upper spars, on both the fore and mizzen masts, had been carried away.

And now, the first awful burst of the Cyclone having passed with the righting of the vessel, the three sails stood, though tested to their utmost, and the ship, under the tremendous urging force of the Storm, was tearing forward at a high speed through the seas.

I glanced down now at myself and camera. Both were soaked; yet, as I discovered later, the latter would still take photographs. I struggled forward to the break of the poop, and stared down on to the maindeck. The seas were breaking aboard every moment, and the spray flying over us continually in huge white clouds. And in my ears was the incessant, wild, roaring-scream of the monster Whirl-Storm.

Then I saw the Mate. He was up against the lee rail, chopping at something with a hatchet. At times the water left him visible to his knees; anon he was completely submerged; but ever there was the whirl of his weapon amid the chaos of water, as he hacked and cut at the gear that held the mizzen t'gallant mast crashing against the side.

I saw him glance round once, and he beckoned with the hatchet to a couple of his watch who were fighting their way aft along the streaming decks. He did not attempt to shout; for no shout could have been heard in the incredible roaring of the wind. Indeed, so vastly loud was the noise made by this element, that I had not heard even the topmasts carry away; though the sound of a large spar breaking will make as great a noise as the report of a big gun. The next instant, I had thrust my camera into one of the hencoops upon the poop, and turned to struggle aft to the companionway; for I knew it was no use going to the Mate's aid without axes.

Presently, I was at the companion, and had the fastenings undone; then I opened the door, and sprang in on to the stairs. I slammed-to the door, bolted it, and made my way below, and so, in a minute, had possessed myself of a couple of axes. With these, I returned to the poop, fastening the companion doors carefully behind me, and, in a little, was up to my neck in water on the maindeck, helping to clear away the wreckage. The second axe, I had pushed into the hands of one of the men.

Presently, we had the gear cleared away.

Then we scrambled away forrard along the decks, through the boiling swirls of water and foam that swept the vessel, as the seas thundered aboard; and so we came to the assistance of the Second

Mate, who was desperately busied, along with some of his watch, in clearing away the broken fore-topmast and yards that were held by their gear, thundering against the side of the ship.

Yet, it must not be supposed that we were to manage this piece of work, without coming to some harm; for, just as we made an end of it, an enormous sea swept aboard, and dashed one of the men against the spare topmast that was lashed along, inside the bulwarks, below the pin-rail. When we managed to pull the poor senseless fellow out from underneath the spar, where the sea had jammed him, we found that his left arm and collar-bone were broken. We took him forrard to the fo'cas'le, and there, with rough surgery, made him so comfortable as we could; after which we left him, but half conscious, in his bunk.

After that, several wet, weary hours were spent in rigging rough preventer-stays. Then the rest of us, men as well as officers, made our way aft to the poop; there to wait, desperately ready to cope with any emergency where our poor, futile human strength might aid to our salvation.

With great difficulty, the Carpenter had managed to sound the well, and, to our delight, had found that we were not making any water; so that the blows of the broken spars had done us no vital harm.

By midday, the following seas had risen to a truly formidable height, and two hands were working half naked at the wheel; for any carelessness in steering would, most certainly, have had horrible consequences.

In the course of the afternoon, the Mate and I went down into the saloon to get something to eat, and here, out of the deafening roar of the wind, I managed to get a short chat with my senior officer.

Talking about the waterspout which had so immediately preceded the first rush of the Cyclone, I made mention of its luminous appearance; to which he replied that it was due probably to a vast electric action going on between the clouds and the sea.

After that, I asked him why the Captain did not heave to, and ride the Storm out, instead of running before it, and risking being pooped, or broaching to.

To this, the Mate made reply that we were right in the line of translation; in other words, that we were directly in the track of the vortex, or centre, of the Cyclone, and that the Skipper was doing his best to edge the ship to leeward, before the centre, with the awful Pyramidal Sea, should overtake us.

"If we can't manage to get out of the way," he concluded, grimly, "you'll probably have a chance to photograph something that you'll never have time to develop!"

I asked him how he knew that the ship was directly in the track of the vortex, and he replied that the facts that the wind was not hauling, but getting steadily worse, with the barometer constantly falling, were sure signs.

And soon after that we returned to the deck.

As I have said, at midday, the seas were truly formidable; but by four P.M. they were so much worse that it was impossible to pass fore or aft along the decks, the water breaking aboard, as much as a hundred tons at a time, and sweeping all before it.

All this time, the roaring and *howling* of the Cyclone was so incredibly loud, that no word spoken, or shouted, out on deck—even though right into one's ear—could be heard distinctly, so that the utmost we could do to convey ideas to one another, was to make signs. And so, because of this, and to get for a little out of the painful and exhausting pressure of the wind, each of the officers would, in turn (sometimes singly and sometimes two at once), go down to the saloon, for a short rest and smoke.

It was in one of these brief "smoke-ohs" that the Mate told me the vortex of the Cyclone was probably within about eighty or a hundred miles of us, and coming down on us at something like twenty or thirty knots an hour, which—as this speed enormously exceeded ours—made it probable that it would be upon us before midnight.

"Is there no chance of getting out of the way?" I asked. "Couldn't we haul her up a trifle, and cut across the track a bit quicker than we are doing?"

"No," replied the Mate, and shook his head, thoughtfully. "The seas would make a clean breach over us, if we tried that. It's a case of 'run till you're blind, and pray till you bust'!" he concluded, with a certain despondent brutalness.

I nodded assent; for I knew that it was true. And after that we were silent. A few minutes later, we went up on deck. There we found that the wind had increased, and blown the foresail bodily away; yet, despite the greater weight of the wind, there had come a rift in the clouds, through which the sun was shining with a queer brightness.

I glanced at the Mate, and smiled; for it seemed to me a good omen; but he shook his head, as one who should say:— "It is no good omen; but a sign of something worse coming."

That he was right in refusing to be assured, I had speedy proof; for within ten minutes the sun had vanished, and the clouds seemed to be right down upon our mast-heads—great bellying webs of black vapour, that seemed almost to mingle with the flying clouds of foam and spray. The wind appeared to gain strength minute by minute, rising into an abominable scream, so piercing at times as to seem to pain the ear drums.

In this wise an hour passed, the ship racing onward under her two topsails, seeming to have lost no speed with the losing of the foresail; though it is possible that she was more under water forrard than she had been.

Then, about five-thirty P.M., I heard a louder roar in the air above us, so deep and tremendous that it seemed to daze and stun one; and, in the same instant, the two topsails were blown out of the bolt-ropes, and one of the hen-coops was lifted bodily off the poop, and hurled into the air, descending with an *inaudible* crash on to the maindeck. Luckily, it was not the one into which I had thrust my camera.

With the losing of the topsails, we might be very truly described as running under bare poles; for now we had not a single stitch of sail set anywhere. Yet, so furious was the increasing wind, so tremendous the weight of it, that the vessel, though urged forward only by the pressure of the element upon her naked spars and hull, managed to keep ahead of the monstrous following seas, which now were grown to truly awesome proportions.

The next hour or two, I remember only as a time that spread out monotonously. A time miserable and dazing, and dominated always by the deafening, roaring scream of the Storm. A time of wetness and dismalness, in which I knew, more than saw, that the ship wallowed on and on through the interminable seas. And so, hour by hour, the wind increased as the Vortex of the Cyclone—the "Death-Patch"—drew nearer and ever nearer.

Night came on early, or, if not night, a darkness that was fully its equivalent. And now I was able to see how tremendous was the electric action that was going on all about us. There seemed to be no lightning flashes; but, instead, there came at times across the darkness, queer luminous shudders of light. I am not acquainted with any word that better describes this extraordinary electrical phenomenon, than 'shudders' of light—broad, dull shudders of light, that came in undefined belts across the black, thunderous canopy of clouds, which seemed so low that our main-truck must have "puddled" them with every roll of the ship.

A further sign of electric action was to be seen in the "corpse candles," which ornamented every yard-arm. Not only were they upon the yardarms; but occasionally several at a time would glide up and down one or more of the fore and aft stays, at whiles swinging off to one side or the other; as the ship rolled. The sight having in it a distinct touch of weirdness.

It was an hour or so later, I believe a little after nine P.M., that I witnessed the most striking manifestation of electrical action that I have ever seen; this being neither more nor less than a display of Aurora Borealis lightning—a sight dree and almost frightening, with the sense of unearthliness and mystery that it brings.

I want you to be very clear that I am *not* talking about the Northern Lights—which, indeed, could never be seen at that distance to the Southward—; but of an extraordinary electrical phenomenon which occurred when the vortex of the Cyclone was within some twenty or thirty miles of the ship. It occurred suddenly. First, a ripple of "Stalk" lightning showed right away over the oncoming seas to the Northward; then, abruptly, a red glare shone out in the sky, and, immediately afterwards, vast streamers of greenish flame appeared above the red glare. These lasted, perhaps, half a minute, expanding and contracting over the sky with a curious quivering motion. The whole forming a truly awe-inspiring spectacle.

And then, slowly, the whole thing faded, and only the blackness of the night remained, slit in all directions by the phosphorescent crests of the seas.

I don't know whether I can convey to you any vivid impression of our case and chances at this time. It is so difficult—unless one had been through a similar experience—even to comprehend fully the incredible loudness of the wind. Imagine a noise as loud as the loudest thunder you have ever heard; then imagine this noise to last hour after hour, without intermission, and to have in it a hideously threatening hoarse note, and, blending with this, a constant yelling scream that rises at times to such a pitch that the very ear drums seem to experience pain, and then, perhaps, you will be able to comprehend merely the amount of *sound* that has to be endured during the passage of one of these Storms. And then, the *force* of the wind! Have you ever faced a wind so powerful that it splayed your lips apart, whether you would or not, laying your teeth bare to view? This is only a little thing; but it may help you to conceive something of the strength of a wind that will play such antics with one's mouth. The sensation it gives is extremely disagreeable—a sense of foolish impotence, is how I can best describe it.

Another thing; I learned that, with my face to the wind, I could not breathe. This is a statement baldly put; but it should help me somewhat in my endeavour to bring home to you the force of the wind, as exemplified in the minor details of my experience.

To give some idea of the wind's power, as shown in a larger way, one of the lifeboats on the after skids was up-ended against the mizzen mast, and there crushed flat by the wind, as though a monstrous invisible hand had pinched it. Does this help you a little to gain an idea of wind-force never met with in a thousand ordinary lives?

Apart from the wind, it must be borne in mind that the gigantic seas pitch the ship about in a most abominable manner. Indeed, I have seen the stern of a ship hove up to such a height that I could see the seas ahead over the fore topsail yards, and when I explain that these will be something like seventy to eighty feet above the deck, you may be able to imagine what manner of Sea is to be met with in a great Cyclonic Storm.

Regarding this matter of the size and ferocity of the seas, I possess a photograph that was taken about ten o'clock at night. This was photographed by the aid of flashlight, an operation in which the Captain assisted me. We filled an old, percussion pistol with flashlight powder, with an air-cone of paper down the centre. Then, when I was ready, I opened the shutter of the camera, and pointed it over the stern into the darkness. The Captain fired the pistol, and, in the instantaneous great blaze of light that followed, I saw what manner of sea it was that pursued us. To say it was a mountain, is to be futile. *It was like a moving cliff.*

As I snapped-to the shutter of my camera, the question flashed into my brain:—"Are we going to live it out, after all?" And, suddenly, it came home to me that I was a little man in a little ship, in the midst of a very great sea.

And then fresh knowledge came to me; I knew, abruptly, that it would not be a difficult thing to be very much afraid. The knowledge was new, and took me more in the stomach than the heart. Afraid! I had been in so many storms that I had forgotten they might be things to fear. Hitherto, my sensation at the thought of bad weather had been chiefly a feeling of annoyed repugnance, due to many memories of dismal wet nights, in wetter oilskins; with everything about the vessel reeking with damp and cheerless discomfort. But *fear*——No! A sailor has no more normal fear of bad weather, than a steeple-jack fears height. It is, as you might say, his vocation. And now this hateful sense of insecurity!

I turned from the taffrail, and hurried below to wipe the lens and cover of my camera; for the whole air was full of driving spray, that soaked everything, and hurt the face intolerably; being driven with such force by the storm.

Whilst I was drying my camera, the Mate came down for a minute's breathing space.

"Still at it?" he said.

"Yes," I replied, and I noticed, half-consciously, that he made no effort to light his pipe, as he stood with his arm crooked over an empty, brass candle bracket.

"You'll never develop them," he remarked.

"Of course I shall!" I replied, half-irritably; but with a horrid little sense of chilliness at his words, which came so unaptly upon my mind, so lately perturbed by uncomfortable thoughts.

"You'll see," he replied, with a sort of brutal terseness. "We shan't be above water by midnight!"

"You *can't* tell," I said. "What's the use of meeting trouble! Vessels have lived through worse than this?"

"Have they?" he said, very quietly. "Not many vessels have lived through worse than what's to come. I suppose you realise we expect to meet the Centre in less than an hour?"

"Well," I replied, "anyway, I shall go on taking photos. I guess if we come through all right, I shall have something to show people ashore."

He laughed, a queer, little, bitter laugh.

"You may as well do that as anything else," he said. "We can't do anything to help ourselves. If we're not pooped before the Centre reaches us, *IT*'ll finish us in quick time!"

Then that cheerful officer of mine turned slowly, and made his way on deck, leaving me, as may be imagined, particularly exhilarated by his assurances. Presently, I followed, and, having barred the companion-way behind me, struggled forward to the break of the poop, clutching blindly at any holdfast in the darkness.

And so, for a space, we waited in the Storm—the wind bellowing fiendishly, and our maindecks one chaos of broken water, swirling and roaring to and fro in the darkness.

It was a little later that some one plucked me hard by the sleeve, and, turning, I made out with difficulty that it was the Captain, trying to attract my attention. I caught his wrist, to show that I comprehended what he desired, and, at that, he dropped on his hands and knees, and crawled aft along the streaming poop deck, I following, my camera held between my teeth by the handle.

He reached the companion-way, and unbarred the starboard door; then crawled through, and I followed after him. I fastened the door, and made my way, in his wake, to the saloon. Here he turned to me. He was a curiously devil-may-care sort of man, and I found that he had brought me down to explain that the Vortex would be upon us very soon, and that I should have the chance of a life-time to get a snap of the much talked of Pyramidal Sea. And, in short, that he wished me to have everything prepared, and the pistol ready loaded with flashlight powder; for, as he remarked:—

"*If* we get through, it'll be a rare curiosity to show some of those unbelieving devils ashore."

In a little, we had everything ready, and then we made our way once more up on deck; the Captain placing the pistol in the pocket of his silk oilskin coat.

There, together, under the after weather-cloth, we waited. The Second Mate, I could not see; but occasionally I caught a vague sight of the First Mate, standing near the after binnacle, and obviously watching the steering. Apart from the puny halo that emanated from the binnacle, all else was blind darkness, save for the phosphorescent lights of the overhanging crests of the seas.

And above us and around us, filling all the sky with sound, was the incessant mad yowling of the Cyclone; the noise so vast, and the volume and mass of the wind so enormous that I am impressed now, looking back, with a sense of having been in a semi-stunned condition through those last minutes.

I am conscious now that a vague time passed. A time of noise and wetness and lethargy and immense tiredness. Abruptly, a tremendous flash of lightning burst through the clouds. It was followed, almost directly, by another, which seemed to rive the sky apart. Then, so quickly that the succeeding thunderclap was *audible* to our wind-deafened ears, the wind ceased, and, in the comparative, but hideously unnatural, silence, I caught the Captain's voice shouting:—

"The Vortex—quick!"

Even as I pointed my camera over the rail, and opened the shutter, my brain was working with a preternatural avidity, drinking in a thousand uncanny sounds and echoes that seemed to come upon me from every quarter, brutally distinct against the background of the Cyclone's distant howling. There were the harsh, bursting, frightening, intermittent noises of the seas, making tremendous, slopping crashes of sound; and, mingling with these, the shrill, hissing scream of the foam; the dismal sounds, that suggested dankness, of water swirling over our decks; and, oddly, the faintly-heard creaking of the gear and shattered spars; and then—*Flash*, in the same instant in which I had taken in these varied impressions, the Captain had fired the pistol, and I saw the Pyramidal Sea. . . . A sight never to be forgotten. A sight rather for the Dead than the Living. A sea such as I could never have imagined. Boiling and bursting upward in monstrous hillocks of water and foam as big as houses. I heard, without knowing I heard, the Captain's expression of amazement. Then a thunderous roar was in my ears. One of those vast, flying hills of water had struck the ship, and, for some moments, I had a sickening feeling that she was sinking beneath me. The water cleared, and I found myself clinging to the iron weather-cloth staunchion; the weather-cloth itself had gone. I wiped my eyes, and coughed dizzily for a little; then I stared round for the Captain. I could see something dimly up against the rail; something that moved and stood upright. I sung out to know whether it was the Captain, and whether he was all right? To which he replied, heartily enough, but with a gasp, that he was all right so far.

From him, I glanced across to the wheel. There was no light in the binnacle, and, later, I found that it had been washed away, and with it one of the helmsmen. The other man also was gone; but we discovered him, nigh an hour later, jammed half through the rail that ran round the poop. To leeward, I heard the Mate singing out to know whether we were safe; to which both the Captain and I shouted a reply, so as to assure him. It was then I became aware that my camera had been washed out of my hands. I found it eventually among a tangle of ropes and gear to leeward.

Again and again the great hills of water struck the vessel, seeming to rise up on every side at once—towering, live pyramids of brine, in the darkness, hurling upward with a harsh unceasing roaring.

From her taffrail to her knight-heads, the ship was swept, fore and aft, so that no living thing could have existed for a moment down upon the main-deck, which was practically submerged. Indeed, the whole vessel seemed at times to be lost beneath the chaos of water that thundered down and over her in clouds and cataracts of brine and foam, so that each moment seemed like to be our last.

Occasionally, I would hear the hoarse voice of the Captain or the Mate, calling through the gloom to one another, or to the figures of the clinging men. And then again would come the thunder of water, as the seas burst over us. And all this in an almost impenetrable darkness, save when some unnatural glare of lightning sundered the clouds, and lit up the thirty-mile cauldron that had engulfed us.

And, anon, all this while, round about, seeming to come from every point of the horizon, sounded a vast, but distant, bellowing and screaming noise, that I caught sometimes above the harsh, slopping roarings of the bursting water-hills all about us. The sound appeared now to be growing louder upon our port beam. It was the Storm circling far round us.

Some time later, there sounded an intense roar in the air above the ship, and then came a far-off shrieking, that grew rapidly into a mighty whistling-scream, and a minute afterwards a most tremendous gust of wind struck the ship on her port side, hurling her over on to her starboard broadside. For many minutes she lay there, her decks under water almost up to the coamings of the hatches. Then she righted, sullenly and slowly, freeing herself from, maybe, half a thousand tons of water.

Again there came a short period of windlessness and then once more the yelling of an approaching gust. It struck us; but now the vessel had paid off before the wind, and she was not again forced over on to her side.

From now onward, we drove forward over vast seas, with the Cyclone bellowing and wailing over us in one unbroken roar. . . . *The Vortex had passed*, and, could we but last out a few more hours, then might we hope to win through.

With the return of the wind, the Mate and one of the men had taken the wheel; but, despite the most careful steering, we were pooped several times; for the seas were hideously broken and confused, we being still in the wake of the Vortex, and the wind not having had time as yet to smash the Pyramidal Sea into the more regular storm waves, which, though huge in size, give a vessel a chance to rise to them.

It was later that some of us, headed by the Mate—who had relinquished his place at the wheel to one of the men—ventured down on to the main-deck with axes and knives, to clear away the wreckage of some of the spars which we had lost in the Vortex. Many a grim risk was run in that hour; but we cleared the wreck, and after that, scrambled back, dripping, to the poop, where the Steward, looking woefully white and scared, served out rum to us from a wooden deck-bucket.

It was decided now that we should bring her head to the seas, so as to make better weather of it. To reduce the risk as much as possible, we had already put out two fresh oil-bags, which we had prepared, and which, indeed, we ought to have done earlier; for though they were being constantly washed aboard again, we had begun at once to take less water.

Now, we took a hawser from the bows, outside of everything, and right away aft to the poop, where we bent on our sea-anchor, which was like an enormous log-bag, or drogue, made of triple canvas.

We bent on our two oil-bags to the sea-anchor, and then dropped the whole business over the side. When the vessel took the pull of it, we put down our helm, and came up into the wind, very quick, and without taking any great water. And a risk it was; but a deal less than some we had come through already.

Slowly, with an undreamt of slowness, the remainder of the night passed, minute by minute, and at last the day broke in a weary dawn; the sky full of a stormy, sickly light. One very side tumbled an interminable chaos of seas. And the vessel herself——! A wreck, she appeared. The mizzenmast had gone, some dozen feet above the deck; the main-topmast had gone, and so had the jigger-topmast. I struggled forrard to the break of the poop, and glanced along the decks. The boats had gone. All the iron scupper-doors were either bent, or had disappeared. On the starboard side, opposite to the stump of the mizzenmast, was a great ragged gap in the steel bulwarks, where the mast must have struck, when it carried away. In several other places, the t'gallant rail was smashed or bent, where it had been struck by falling spars. The side of the teak deck-house had been stove, and the water was roaring in and out with each roll of the ship. The sheep-pen had vanished, and so—as I discovered later—had the pigsty.

Further forrard, my glance went, and I saw that the sea had breached the bulkshead, across the after end of the fo'cas'le, and, with each biggish sea that we shipped, a torrent of water drove in, and then flowed out, sometimes bearing with it an odd board, or perhaps a man's boot, or some article of wearing apparel. In two places on the maindeck, I saw men's sea-chests, washing to and fro in the water that streamed over the deck. And, suddenly, there came into my mind a memory of the poor fellow who had broken his arm when we were cutting loose the wreck of the fore-topmast.

Already, the strength of the Cyclone was spent, so far, at least, as we were concerned; and I was thinking of making a try for the fo'cas'le, when, close beside me, I heard the Mate's voice. I turned, with a little start. He had evidently noticed the breach in the bulkshead; for he told me to watch a chance, and see if we could get forrard.

This, we did; though not without a further thorough sousing; as we were still shipping water by the score of tons. Moreover, the risk was considerably greater than might be conceived; for the door-less scupper-ports offered uncomfortable facilities for gurgling out into the ocean, along with a ton or two of brine from the decks.

We reached the fo'cas'le, and pulled open the lee door. We stepped inside. It was like stepping into a dank, gloomy cavern. Water was dripping from every beam and staunchion. We struggled across the slippery deck, to where we had left the sick man in his bunk. In the dim light, we saw that man and bunk, everything, had vanished; only the bare steel sides of the vessel remained. Every bunk and fitting in the place had been swept away, and all of the men's sea-chests. Nothing remained, save, it might be, an odd soaked rag of clothing, or a sodden bunk-board.

The Mate and I looked at one another, in silence.

"Poor devil!" he said. He repeated his expression of pity, staring at the place where had been the bunk. Then, grave of face, he turned to go out on deck. As he did so, a heavier sea than usual broke aboard; flooded roaring along the decks, and swept in through the broken bulkshead and the lee doorway. It swirled round the sides, caught us, and threw us down in a heap; then swept out through the breach and the doorway, carrying the Mate with it. He managed to grasp the lintel of the doorway, else, I do believe, he would have gone out through one of the open scupper traps. A doubly hard fate, after having come safely through the Cyclone.

Outside of the fo'cas'le, I saw that the ladders leading up to the fo'cas'le head had both gone; but I managed to scramble up. Here, I found that both anchors had been washed away, and the rails all round; only the bare staunchions remaining.

Beyond the bows, the jibboom had gone, and all the gear was draggled inboard over the fo'cas'le head, or trailing in the sea.

We made our way aft, and reported; then the roll was called, and we found that one else was missing, besides the two I have already mentioned, and the man we found jammed half through the poop rails, who was now under the Steward's care.

From that time on, the sea went down steadily, until, presently, it ceased to threaten us, and we proceeded to get the ship cleared up a bit; after which, one watch turned-in on the floor of the saloon, and the other was told to "stand easy."

Hour by hour, through that day and the next, the sea went down, until it was difficult to believe that we had so lately despaired for our lives. And so the second evening came, calm and restful, the wind no more than a light summer's breeze, and the sea calming steadily.

About seven bells that second night, a big steamer crossed our stern, and slowed down to ask us if we were in need of help; for, even by moonlight, it was easy to see our dismantled condition. This offer, however, the Captain refused; and with many good wishes, the big vessel swung off into the moon-wake, and so, presently, we were left alone in the quiet night; safe at last, and rich in a completed experience.

Shipwreck

CAPTAIN JAMES RILEY

We set sail from the bay of Gibraltar on the 23rd of August, 1815, intending to go by way of the Cape de Verd Islands, to complete the lading of the vessel with salt. We passed Capt Spartel on the morning of the 24th, giving it a birth of from ten to twelve leagues, and steered off to the W. S. W. I intended to make the Canary Islands, and pass between Teneriffe and Palma, having a fair wind; but it being very thick and foggy weather, though we got two observations at noon, neither could be much depended upon. On account of the fog, we saw no land, and found, by good meridian altitudes on the twenty-eighth, that we were in the latitude of 27. 30. N. having differed our latitude by the force of current, one hundred and twenty miles; thus passing the Canaries without seeing any of them. I concluded we must have passed through the intended passage without discovering the land on either side, particularly, as it was in the night, which was very dark, and black as pitch; nor could I believe otherwise from having had a fair wind all the way, and having steered one course ever since we took our departure from Cape Spartel. Soon after we got an observation on the 28th, it became as thick as ever, and the darkness seemed (if possible) to increase. Towards evening I got up my reckoning, and examined it all over, to be sure that I had committed no error, and caused the mates to do the same with theirs. Having thus ascertained that I was correct in calculation, I altered our course to S. W. which ought to have carried us nearly on the course I wished to steer, that is, for the easternmost of the Cape de Verds; but finding the weather becoming more foggy towards night, it being so thick that we could scarcely see the end of the jib-boom, I rounded the vessel to, and sounded with one hundred and twenty fathoms of line, but found no bottom, and continued on our course, still reflecting on what should be the cause of our not seeing land, (as I never had passed near the Canaries before without seeing them, even in thick weather or in the night.) I came to a determination to haul off to the N. W. by the wind at 10 P.M.. as I should then be by the log only thirty miles north of Cape Bajador. I concluded on this at nine, and thought my fears had never before so much prevailed over my judgment and my reckoning. I ordered the light sails to be handed, and the steering sail booms to be rigged in snug, which was done as fast as it could be by one watch, under the immediate direction of Mr. Savage.

We had just got the men stationed at the braces for hauling off, as the man at helm cried "ten o'clock." Our try-sail boom was on the starboard side, but ready for jibing; the helm was put to port, dreaming of no danger near. I had been on deck all the evening myself; the vessel was running at the rate of nine or ten knots, with a very strong breeze, and high sea, when the main boom was jibed over, and I at that instant heard a roaring; the yards were braced up—all hands were called. I imagined at first it was a squall, and was near ordering the sails to be lowered down; but I then discovered breakers foaming at a most dreadful rate under our lee. Hope for a moment flattered me that we could fetch off still, as there were no breakers in view ahead: the anchors were made ready; but these hopes vanished in an instant, as the vessel was carried by a current and a sea directly towards the breakers, and she struck! We let go the best bower anchor; all sails were taken in as fast as possible: surge after surge came thundering on, and drove her in spite of anchors, partly with her head on shore. She struck with such violence as to start every man from the deck. Knowing there was no possibility of saving her, and that she must very soon bilge and fill with water, I ordered all the provisions we could get at to be brought on deck, in hopes of saving some, and as much water to be drawn from the large casks as possible. We started several quarter casks of wine, and filled them with water. Every man worked as if his life depended upon his present exertions; all were obedient to every order I gave, and seemed perfectly calm;—The vessel was stout and high, as she was only in ballast trim;—The sea combed over her stern and swept her decks; but we managed to get the small boat in on deck, to sling her and keep her from staving. We cut away the bulwark on the larboard side so as to prevent the boast from staving when we should get them out; cleared away the long boat and hung her in tackles, the vessel continuing to strike very heavy, and filling fast. We however, had secured five or six barrels of water, and as many of wine,—three barrels of bread, and three or four salted provisions. I had as yet been so busily employed, that no pains had been taken to ascertain what distance we were from the land, nor had any of us yet seen it; and in the meantime all the clothing, chests, trunks, &c. were got up, and the books, charts, and sea instruments, were stowed in them, in the hope of their being useful to us in future.

The vessel being now nearly full of water, the surf making a fair breach over her, and fearing she would go to pieces, I prepared a rope, and put it in the small boat, having got a glimpse of the short, at no great distance, and taking Porter with me, we were lowered down on the larboard or lee side of the vessel, where she broke the violence of the sea, and made it comparatively smooth; we shoved off, but on clearing away from the bow of the vessel, the boat was overwhelmed with a surf, and we were plunged into the foaming surges: we were driven along by the current, aided by what seamen call the undertow, (or recoil of the sea) to the distance of three hundred yards to the westward, covered nearly all the time by the billows, which, following each other in quick succession, scarcely gave us time to catch a breath before we were again literally swallowed by them, till at length we were thrown, together with our boat, upon a sandy beach. After taking breath a little, and ridding our stomachs of the salt water that had forced its way into them, my first care was to turn the water out of the boat, and haul her up out of the reach of the surf. We found the rope that was made fast to her still remaining; this we carried up along the beach, directly to leeward of the wreck, where we fastened it to sticks about the thickness of handspikes, that had drifted on the shore from the vessel, and which we drove into the sand by the help of other pieces of wood. Before leaving the vessel, I had directed that all the chests, trunks, and everything that would float, should be hove overboard: this all hands were busied in doing. The vessel lay about one hundred fathoms from the beach, at high tide. In order to save the crew, a hawser was made fast to the rope we had on shore, one end of which we hauled to us, and made it fast to a number of sticks we had driven into the sand for the purpose. It was then tautened on board the wreck, and made fast. This being done, the long-boat (in order to save the provisions already in her) was lowered down, and two hands steadied her by ropes fastened to the rings in her stem and stern posts over the hawser, so as to slide, keeping her bow to the surf. In this manner they reached the beach, carried on the top of a heavy wave. The boat was stove by the violence of the shock against the beach; but by great exertions we saved the three barrels of bread in her before they were much damaged; and two barrels of salted provisions were also saved. We were now, four of us, on shore, and busied in picking up the clothing and other things which drifted from the vessel, and carrying them up out of the surf. It was by this time daylight, and high water; the vessel careened deep off shore, and I made signs to have the mast cut away, in the hope of easing her, that she might not go to pieces. They were accordingly cut away, and fell on her starboard side, making a better lee for a boat alongside the wreck, as they projected considerably beyond her bows. The masts and rigging being gone, the sea breaking very high over the wreck, and nothing left to hold on by, the mates and six men still on board, though secured, as well as they could be, on the bowsprit and in the larboard fore-channels, were yet in imminent danger of being washed off by every surge. The long-boat was stove, and it being impossible for the small one to live, my great object was now to save the lives of the crew by means of the hawser. I therefore made signs to them to come, one by one, on the hawser, which had been stretched taut for that purpose. John Hogan ventured first, and having pulled off his jacket, took to the hawser, and made for the shore. When he had got clear of the immediate lee of the wreck, every surf buried him, combing many feet above his head; but he still held fast to the rope with a death-like grasp, and as soon as the surf was passed, proceeded on towards the shore, until another surf, more powerful than the former, unclenched his hands, and threw him within our reach; when we laid hold of him and dragged him to the beach; we then rolled him on the sand, until he discharged the salt water from his stomach, and revived. I kept in the water up to my chin, steadying myself by the hawser, while the surf passed over me, to catch the others as they approached, and thus, with the assistance of those already on shore, was enabled to save all the rest from a watery grave.

The Wreck of the *Golden Mary*

CHARLES DICKENS

(with Wilkie Collins)

The Wreck

I was apprenticed to the Sea when I was twelve years old, and I have encountered a great deal of rough weather, both literal and metaphorical. It has always been my opinion since I first possessed such a thing as an opinion, that the man who knows only one subject is next tiresome to the man who knows no subject. Therefore, in the course of my life I have taught myself whatever I could, and although I am not an educated man, I am able, I am thankful to say, to have an intelligent interest in most things.

A person might suppose, from reading the above, that I am in the habit of holding forth about number one. That is not the case. Just as if I was to come into a room among strangers, and must either be introduced or introduce myself, so I have taken the liberty of passing these few remarks, simply and plainly that it may be known who and what I am. I will add no more of the sort than that my name is William George Ravender, that I was born at Penrith half a year after my own father was drowned, and that I am on the second day of this present blessed Christmas week of one thousand eight hundred and fifty-six, fifty-six years of age.

When the rumour first went flying up and down that there was gold in California—which, as most people know, was before it was discovered in the British colony of Australia—I was in the West Indies, trading among the Islands. Being in command and likewise part-owner of a smart schooner, I had my work cut out for me, and I was doing it. Consequently, gold in California was no business of mine.

But, by the time when I came home to England again, the thing was as clear as your hand held up before you at noonday. There was Californian gold in the museums and in the goldsmiths' shops, and the very first time I went upon 'Change, I met a friend of mine (a seafaring man like myself), with a Californian nugget hanging to his watch-chain. I handled it. It was as like a peeled walnut with bits unevenly broken off here and there, and then electrotyped all over, as ever I saw anything in my life.

I am a single man (she was too good for this world and for me, and she died six weeks before our marriage-day), so when I am ashore, I live in my house at Poplar. My house at Poplar is taken care of and kept ship-shape by an old lady who was my mother's maid before I was born. She is as handsome and as upright as any old lady in the world. She is as fond of me as if she had ever had an only son, and I was he. Well do I know wherever I sail that she never lays down her head at night without having said, "Merciful Lord! bless and preserve William George Ravender, and send him safe home, through Christ our Saviour!" I have thought of it in many a dangerous moment, when it has done me no harm, I am sure.

In my house at Poplar, along with this old lady, I lived quiet for best part of a year: having had a long spell of it among the Islands, and having (which was very uncommon in me) taken the fever rather badly. At last, being strong and hearty, and having read every book I could lay hold of, right out, I was walking down Leadenhall Street in the City of London, thinking of turning-to again, when I met what I call Smithick and Watersby of Liverpool. I chanced to lift up my eyes from looking in at a ship's chronometer in a window, and I saw him bearing down upon me, head on.

It is, personally, neither Smithick, nor Watersby, that I here mention, nor was I ever acquainted with any man of either of those names, nor do I think that there has been any one of either of those names in that Liverpool House for years back. But, it is in reality the House itself that I refer to; and a wiser merchant or a truer gentleman never stepped.

"My dear Captain Ravender," says he. "Of all the men on earth, I wanted to see you most. I was on my way to you."

"Well!" says I. "That looks as if you *were* to see me, don't it?" With that I put my arm in his, and we walked on towards the Royal Exchange, and when we got there, walked up and down at the back of it where the Clock-Tower is. We walked an hour and more, for he had much to say to me. He had a scheme for chartering a new ship of their own to take out cargo to the diggers and emigrants in California, and to buy and bring back gold. Into the particulars of that scheme I will not enter, and I have no right to enter. All I say of it is, that it was a very original one, a very fine one, a very sound one, and a very lucrative one beyond doubt.

He imparted it to me as freely as if I had been a part of himself. After doing so, he made me the handsomest sharing offer that ever was made to me, boy or man—or I believe to any other captain in the Merchant Navy—and he took this round turn to finish with:

"Ravender, you are well aware that the lawlessness of that coast and country at present, is as special as the circumstances in which it is placed. Crews of vessels outward-bound, desert as soon as they make the land; crews of vessels homewardbound, ship at enormous wages, with the express intention of murdering the captain and seizing the gold freight; no man can trust another, and the devil seems let loose. Now," says he, "you know my opinion of you, and you know I am only expressing it, and with no singularity, when I tell you that you are almost the only man on whose integrity, discretion, and energy—" &c. &c. For, I don't want to repeat what he said, though I was and am sensible of it.

Notwithstanding my being, as I have mentioned, quite ready for a voyage, still I had some doubts of this voyage. Of course I knew, without being told, that there were peculiar difficulties and dangers in it, a long way over and above those which attend all voyages. It must not be supposed that I was afraid to face them; but, in my opinion a man has no manly motive or sustainment in his own breast for facing dangers, unless he has well considered what they are, and is able quietly to say to himself, "None of these perils can now take me by surprise; I shall know what to do for the best in any of them; all the rest lies in the higher and greater hands to which I humbly commit myself." On this principle I have so attentively considered (regarding it as my duty) all the hazards I have ever been able to think of, in the ordinary way of storm, shipwreck, and fire at sea, that I hope I should be prepared to do, in any of those cases, whatever could be done, to save the lives intrusted to my charge.

As I was thoughtful, my good friend proposed that he should leave me to walk there as long as I liked, and that I should dine with him by-and-by at his club in Pall Mall. I accepted the invitation and I walked up and down there, quarter-deck fashion, a matter of a couple of hours; now and then looking up at the weathercock as I might have looked up aloft; and now and then taking a look into Cornhill, as I might have taken a look over the side.

All dinner-time, and all after dinner-time, we talked it over again. I gave him my views of his plan, and he very much approved of the same. I told him I had nearly decided, but not quite. "Well, well," says he, "come down to Liverpool to-morrow with me, and see the Golden Mary." I liked the name (her name was Mary, and she was golden, if golden stands for good), so I began to feel that it was almost done when I said I would go to Liverpool. On the next morning but one we were on board the Golden Mary. I might have known, from his asking me to come down and see her, what she was. I declare her to have been the completest and most exquisite Beauty that ever I set my eyes upon.

We had inspected every timber in her, and had come back to the gangway to go ashore from the dock-basin, when I put out my hand to my friend. "Touch upon it," says I, "and touch heartily. I take command of this ship, and I am hers and yours, if I can get John Steadiman for my chief mate."

John Steadiman had sailed with me four voyages. The first voyage John was third mate out to China, and came home second. The other three voyages he was my first officer. At this time of chartering the Golden Mary, he was aged thirty-two. A brisk, bright, blue-eyed fellow, a very neat figure and rather under the middle size, never out of the way and never in it, a face that pleased everybody and that all children took to, a habit of going about singing as cheerily as a blackbird, and a perfect sailor.

We were in one of those Liverpool hackney-coaches in less than a minute, and we cruised about in her upwards of three hours, looking for John. John had come home from Van Diemen's Land barely a month before, and I had heard of him as taking a frisk in Liverpool. We asked after him, among many other places, at the two boarding-houses he was fondest of, and we found he had had a week's spell at each of them; but, he had gone here and gone there, and had set off "to lay out on the main-to'-gallant-yard of the highest Welsh mountain" (so he had told the people of the house), and where he might be then, or when he might come back, nobody could tell us. But it was surprising, to be sure, to see how every face brightened the moment there was mention made of the name of Mr. Steadiman.

We were taken aback at meeting with no better luck, and we had wore ship and put her head for my friends, when as we were jogging through the streets, I clap my eyes on John himself coming out of a toyshop! He was carrying a little boy, and conducting two uncommon pretty women to their coach, and he told me afterwards that he had never in his life seen one of the three before, but that he was so taken with them on looking in at the toyshop while they were buying the child a cranky Noah's Ark, very much down by the head, that he had gone in and asked the ladies' permission to treat him to a tolerably correct Cutter there was in the window, in order that such a handsome boy might not grow up with a lubberly idea of naval architecture.

We stood off and on until the ladies' coachman began to give way, and then we hailed John. On his coming aboard of us, I told him, very gravely, what I had said to my friend. It struck him, as he said himself, amidships. He was quite shaken by it. "Captain Ravender," were John Steadiman's words, "such an opinion from you is true commendation, and I'll sail round the world with you for twenty years if you hoist the signal, and stand by you for ever!" And now indeed I felt that it was done, and that the Golden Mary was afloat.

Grass never grew yet under the feet of Smithick and Watersby. The riggers were out of that ship in a fortnight's time, and we had begun taking in cargo. John was always aboard, seeing everything stowed with his own eyes; and whenever I went aboard myself early or late, whether he was below in the hold, or on deck at the hatchway, or overhauling his cabin, nailing up pictures in it of the Blush Roses of England, the Blue Bells of Scotland, and the female Shamrock of Ireland: of a certainty I heard John singing like a blackbird.

We had room for twenty passengers. Our sailing advertisement was no sooner out, than we might have taken these twenty times over. In entering our men, I and John (both together) picked them, and we entered none but good hands—as good as were to be found in that port. And so, in a good ship of the best build, well owned, well arranged, well officered, well manned, well found in all respects, we parted with our pilot at a quarter past four o'clock in the afternoon of the seventh of March, one thousand eight hundred and fifty-one, and stood with a fair wind out to sea.

It may be easily believed that up to that time I had had no leisure to be intimate with my passengers. The most of them were then in their berths sea-sick; however, in going among them, telling them what was good for them, persuading them not to be there, but to come up on deck and feel the breeze, and in rousing them with a joke, or a comfortable word, I made acquaintance with them, perhaps, in a more friendly and confidential way from the first, than I might have done at the cabin table.

Of my passengers, I need only particularise, just at present, a bright-eyed blooming young wife who was going out to join her husband in California, taking with her their only child, a little girl of three years old, whom he had never seen; a sedate young woman in black, some five years older (about thirty as I should say), who was going out to join a brother; and an old gentleman, a good deal like a hawk if his eyes had been better and not so red, who was always talking, morning, noon, and night, about the gold discovery. But, whether he was making the voyage, thinking his old arms could dig for gold, or whether his speculation was to buy it, or to barter for it, or to cheat for it, or to snatch it anyhow from other people, was his secret. He kept his secret.

These three and the child were the soonest well. The child was a most engaging child, to be sure, and very fond of me: though I am bound to admit that John Steadiman and I were borne on her pretty little books in reverse order, and that he was captain there, and I was mate. It was beautiful to watch her with John, and it was beautiful to watch John with her. Few would have thought it possible, to see John playing at bo-peep round the mast, that he was the man who had caught up an iron bar and struck a Malay and a Maltese dead, as they were gliding with their knives down the cabin stair aboard the barque Old England, when the captain lay ill in his cot, off Saugar Point. But he was; and give him his back against a bulwark, he would have done the same by half-a-dozen of them. The name of the young mother was Mrs. Atherfield, the name of the young lady in black was Miss Coleshaw, and the name of the old gentleman was Mr. Rarx.

As the child had a quantity of shining fair hair, clustering in curls all about her face, and as her name was Lucy, Steadiman gave her the name of the Golden Lucy. So, we had the Golden Lucy and the Golden Mary; and John kept up the idea to that extent as he and the child went playing about the decks, that I believe she used to think the ship was alive somehow—a sister or companion, going to the same place as herself. She liked to be by the wheel, and in fine weather, I have often stood by the man whose trick it was at the wheel, only to hear her, sitting near my feet, talking to the ship. Never had a child such a doll before, I suppose; but she made a doll of the Golden Mary, and used to dress her up by tying ribbons and little bits of finery to the belaying-pins; and nobody ever moved them, unless it was to save them from being blown away.

Of course I took charge of the two young women, and I called them "my dear," and they never minded, knowing that whatever I said was said in a fatherly and protecting spirit. I gave them their places on each side of me at dinner; Mrs. Atherfield on my right and Miss Coleshaw on my left; and I directed the unmarried lady to serve out the breakfast, and the married lady to serve out the tea. Likewise I said to my black steward in their presence, "Tom Snow, these two ladies are equally the mistresses of this house, and do you obey their orders equally;" at which Tom laughed, and they all laughed.

Old Mr. Rarx was not a pleasant man to look at, nor yet to talk to, or to be with, for no one could help seeing that he was a sordid and selfish character, and that he had warped further and further out of the straight with time. Not but what he was on his best behaviour with us, as everybody was; for we had no bickering among us, for'ard or aft. I only mean to say, he was not the man one would have chosen for a messmate. If choice there had been, one might even have gone a few points out of one's course, to say, "No! Not him!" But, there was one curious inconsistency in Mr. Rarx. That was, that he took an astonishing interest in the child. He looked, and I may add, he was, one of the last of men to care at all for a child, or to care much for any human creature. Still, he went so far as to be habitually uneasy, if the child was long on deck, out of his sight. He was always afraid of her falling overboard, or falling down a hatchway, or of a block or what not coming down upon her from the rigging in the working of the ship, or of her getting some hurt or other. He used to look at her and touch her, as if she was something precious to him. He was always solicitous about her not injuring her health, and constantly entreated her mother to be careful of it. This was so much the more curious, because the child did not like him, but used to shrink away from him, and would not even put out her hand to him without coaxing from others. I believe that every soul on board frequently noticed this, and not one of us understood it. However, it was such a plain fact, that John Steadiman said more than once when old Mr. Rarx was not within earshot, that if the Golden Mary felt a tenderness for the dear old gentleman she carried in her lap, she must be bitterly jealous of the Golden Lucy.

Before I go any further with this narrative, I will state that our ship was a barque of three hundred tons, carrying a crew of eighteen men, a second mate in addition to John, a carpenter, an armourer or smith, and two apprentices (one a Scotch boy, poor little fellow). We had three boats;

the Long-boat, capable of carrying twenty-five men; the Cutter, capable of carrying fifteen; and the Surf-boat, capable of carrying ten. I put down the capacity of these boats according to the numbers they were really meant to hold.

We had tastes of bad weather and head-winds, of course; but, on the whole we had as fine a run as any reasonable man could expect, for sixty days. I then began to enter two remarks in the ship's Log and in my Journal; first, that there was an unusual and amazing quantity of ice; second, that the nights were most wonderfully dark, in spite of the ice.

For five days and a half, it seemed quite useless and hopeless to alter the ship's course so as to stand out of the way of this ice. I made what southing I could; but, all that time, we were beset by it. Mrs. Atherfield after standing by me on deck once, looking for some time in an awed manner at the great bergs that surrounded us, said in a whisper, "O! Captain Ravender, it looks as if the whole solid earth had changed into ice, and broken up!" I said to her, laughing, "I don't wonder that it does, to your inexperienced eyes, my dear." But I had never seen a twentieth part of the quantity, and, in reality, I was pretty much of her opinion.

However, at two P.M. on the afternoon of the sixth day, that is to say, when we were sixty-six days out, John Steadiman who had gone aloft, sang out from the top, that the sea was clear ahead. Before four P.M. a strong breeze springing up right astern, we were in open water at sunset. The breeze then freshening into half a gale of wind, and the Golden Mary being a very fast sailer, we went before the wind merrily, all night.

I had thought it impossible that it could be darker than it had been, until the sun, moon, and stars should fall out of the Heavens, and Time should be destroyed; but, it had been next to light, in comparison with what it was now. The darkness was so profound, that looking into it was painful and oppressive—like looking, without a ray of light, into a dense black bandage put as close before the eyes as it could be, without touching them. I doubled the look-out, and John and I stood in the bow side-by-side, never leaving it all night. Yet I should no more have known that he was near me when he was silent, without putting out my arm and touching him, than I should if he had turned in and been fast asleep below. We were not so much looking out, all of us, as listening to the utmost, both with our eyes and ears.

Next day, I found that the mercury in the barometer, which had risen steadily since we cleared the ice, remained steady. I had had very good observations, with now and then the interruption of a day or so, since our departure. I got the sun at noon, and found that we were in Lat. 58° S., Long. 60° W., off New South Shetland; in the neighbourhood of Cape Horn. We were sixty-seven days out, that day. The ship's reckoning was accurately worked and made up. The ship did her duty admirably, all on board were well, and all hands were as smart, efficient, and contented, as it was possible to be.

When the night came on again as dark as before, it was the eighth night I had been on deck. Nor had I taken more than a very little sleep in the daytime, my station being always near the helm, and often at it, while we were among the ice. Few but those who have tried it can imagine the difficulty and pain of only keeping the eyes open—physically open—under such circumstances, in such darkness. They get struck by the darkness, and blinded by the darkness. They make patterns in it, and they flash in it, as if they had gone out of your head to look at you. On the turn of midnight, John Steadiman, who was alert and fresh (for I had always made him turn in by day), said to me, "Captain Ravender, I entreat of you to go below. I am sure you can hardly stand, and your voice is getting weak, Sir. Go below, and take a little rest. I'll call you if a block chafes." I said to John in answer, "Well, well, John! Let us wait till the turn of one o'clock, before we talk about that." I had just had one of the ship's lanterns held up, that I might see how the night went by my watch, and it was then twenty minutes after twelve.

At five minutes before one, John sang out to the boy to bring the lantern again, and when I told him once more what the time was, entreated and prayed of me to go below. "Captain Ravender," says he, "all's well; we can't afford to have you laid up for a single hour; and I respectfully and earnestly beg of you to go below." The end of it was, that I agreed to do so, on the understanding that if I failed to come up of my own accord within three hours, I was to be punctually called. Having settled that, I left John in charge. But I called him to me once afterwards, to ask him a question. I had been to look at the barometer, and had seen the mercury still perfectly steady, and had come up the companion again to take a last look about me—if I can use such a word in reference to such darkness—when I thought that the waves, as the Golden Mary parted them and shook them off, had a hollow sound in them; something that I fancied was a rather unusual reverberation. I was standing by the quarter-deck rail on the starboard side, when I called John aft to me, and bade him listen. He did so with the greatest attention. Turning to me he then said, "Rely upon it, Captain Ravender, you have been without rest too long, and the novelty is only in the state of your sense of hearing." I thought so too by that time, and I think so now, though I can never kow for absolute certain in this world, whether it was or not.

When I left John Steadiman in charge, the ship was still going at a great rate through the water. The wind still blew right, astern. Though she was making great way, she was under shortened sail, and had no more than she could easily carry. All was snug, and nothing complained. There was a pretty sea running, but not a very high sea neither, nor at all a confused one.

I turned in, as we seamen say, all standing. The meaning of that is, I did not pull my clothes off—no, not even so much as my coat: though I did my shoes, for my feet were badly swelled with the deck. There was a little swing-lamp alight in my cabin. I thought, as I looked at it before shutting my eyes, that I was so tired of darkness, and troubled by darkness, that I could have gone to sleep best in the midst of a million of flaming gas-lights. That was the last thought I had before I went off, except the prevailing thought that I should not be able to get to sleep at all.

I dreamed that I was back at Penrith again, and was trying to get round the church, which had altered its shape very much since I last saw it, and was cloven all down the middle of the steeple in a most singular manner. Why I wanted to get round the church I don't know; but I was as anxious to do it as if my life depended upon it. Indeed, I believe it did in the dream. For all that, I could not get round the church. I was still trying, when I came against it with a violent shock, and was flung out of my cot against the ship's side. Shrieks and a terrific outcry struck me far harder than the bruising timbers, and amidst sounds of grinding and crashing, and a heavy rushing and breaking of water—sounds I understood too well—I made my way on deck. It was not an easy thing to do, for the ship heeled over frightfully, and was beating in a furious manner.

I could not see the men as I went forward, but I could hear that they were hauling in sail, in disorder. I had my trumpet in my hand, and, after directing and encouraging them in this till it was done, I hailed first John Steadiman, and then my second mate, Mr. William Rames. Both answered clearly and steadily. Now, I had practised them and all my crew, as I have ever made it a custom to practise all who sail with me, to take certain stations and wait my orders, in case of any unexpected crisis. When my voice was heard hailing, and their voices were heard answering, I was aware, through all the noises of the ship and sea, and all the crying of the passengers below, that there was a pause. "Are you ready, Rames?"—"Ay, ay, Sir!"—"Then light up, for God's sake!" In a moment he and another were burning blue-lights, and the ship and all on board seemed to be enclosed in a mist of light, under a great black dome.

The light shone up so high that I could see the huge Iceberg upon which we had struck, cloven at the top and down the middle, exactly like Penrith Church in my dream. At the same moment I could see the watch last relieved, crowding up and down on deck; I could see Mrs. Atherfield and Miss Coleshaw thrown about on the top of the companion as they struggled to bring the child up from below; I could see that the masts were going with the shock and the beating of the ship; I could see the frightful breach stove in on the starboard side, half the length of the vessel, and the sheathing and timbers spirting up; I could see that the Cutter was disabled, in a wreck of broken fragments; and I could see every eye turned upon me. It is my belief that if there had been ten thousand eyes there, I should have seen them all, with their different looks. And all this in a moment. But you must consider what a moment.

I saw the men, as they looked at me, fall towards their appointed stations, like good men and true. If she had not righted, they could have done very little there or anywhere but die—not that it is little for a man to die at his post—I mean they could have done nothing to save the passengers and themselves. Happily, however, the violence of the shock with which we had so determinedly borne down direct on that fatal Iceberg, as if it had been our destination instead of our destruction, had so smashed and pounded the ship that she got off in this same instant and righted. I did not want the carpenter to tell me she was filling and going down; I could see and hear that. I gave Rames the word to lower the Long-boat and the Surf-boat, and I myself told off the men for each duty. Not one hung back, or came before the other. I now whispered to John Steadiman, "John, I stand at the gangway here, to see every soul on board safe over the side. You shall have the next post of honour, and shall be the last but one to leave the ship. Bring up the passengers, and range them behind me; and put what provision and water you can get at, in the boats. Cast your eye for'ard, John, and you'll see you have not a moment to lose."

My noble fellows got the boats over the side as orderly as I ever saw boats lowered with any sea running, and, when they were launched, two or three of the nearest men in them as they held on, rising and falling with the swell, called out, looking up at me, "Captain Ravender, if anything goes wrong with us, and you are saved, remember we stood by you!"—"We'll all stand by one another ashore, yet, please God, my lads!" says I. "Hold on bravely, and be tender with the women."

The women were an example to us. They trembled very much, but they were quiet and perfectly collected. "Kiss me, Captain Ravender," says Mrs. Atherfield, "and God in heaven bless you, you good man!" "My dear," says I, "those words are better for me than a lifeboat." I held her child in my arms till she was in the boat, and then kissed the child and handed her safe down. I now said to the people in her, "You have got your freight, my lads, all but me, and I am not coming yet awhile. Pull away from the ship, and keep off!"

That was the Long-boat. Old Mr. Rarx was one of her complement, and he was the only passenger who had greatly misbehaved since the ship struck. Others had been a little wild, which was not to be wondered at, and not very blamable; but, he had made a lamentation and uproar which it was dangerous for the people to hear, as there is always contagion in weakness and selfishness. His incessant cry had been that he must not be separated from the child, that he couldn't see the child, and that he and the child must go together. He had even tried to wrest the child out of my arms, that he might keep her in his. "Mr. Rarx," said I to him when it came to that, "I have a loaded pistol in my pocket; and if you don't stand out of the gangway, and keep perfectly quiet, I shall shoot you through the heart, if you have got one." Says he, "You won't do murder, Captain Ravender!" "No, Sir," says I, "I won't murder forty-four people to humour you, but I'll shoot you to save them." After that he was quiet, and stood shivering a little way off, until I named him to go over the side.

The Long-boat being cast off, the Surf-boat was soon filled. There only remained aboard the Golden Mary, John Mullion, the man who had kept on burning the blue-lights (and who had lighted every new one at every old one before it went out, as quietly as if he had been at an illumination); John Steadiman; and myself. I hurried those two into the Surf-boat, called to them to keep off, and waited with a grateful and relieved heart for the Long-boat to come and take me in, if she could. I looked at my watch, and it showed me, by the blue-light, ten minutes past two. They lost no time. As soon as she was near enough, I swung myself into her, and called to the men, "With a will, lads! She's reeling!" We were not an inch too far out of the inner vortex of her going down, when, by the blue-light which John Mullion still burnt in the bow of the Surf-boat, we saw her lurch, and plunge to the bottom head-foremost. The child cried, weeping wildly, "O the dear Golden Mary! O look at her! Save her! Save the poor Golden Mary!" And then the light burnt out, and the black dome seemed to come down upon us.

I suppose if we had all stood a-top of a mountain, and seen the whole remainder of the world sink away from under us, we could hardly have felt more shocked and solitary than we did when we knew we were alone on the wide ocean, and that the beautiful ship in which most of us had been securely asleep within half an hour was gone for ever. There was an awful silence in our boat, and such a kind of palsy on the rowers and the man at the rudder, that I felt they were scarcely keeping her before the sea. I spoke out then, and said, "Let every one here thank the Lord for our preservation!" All the voices answered (even the child's), "We thank the Lord!" I then said the Lord's Prayer, and all hands said it after me with a solemn murmuring. Then I gave the word "Cheerily, O men, Cheerily!" and I felt that they were handling the boat again as a boat ought to be handled.

The Surf-boat now burnt another blue-light to show us where they were, and we made for her, and laid ourselves as nearly alongside of her as we dared. I had always kept my boats with a coil or two of good stout stuff in each of them, so both boats had a rope at hand. We made a shift, with much labour and trouble, to get near enough to one another to divide the blue-lights (they were no use after that night, for the sea-water soon got at them), and to get a tow-rope out between us. All night long we kept together, sometimes obliged to cast off the rope, and sometimes getting it out again, and all of us wearying for the morning—which appeared so long in coming that old Mr. Rarx screamed out, in spite of his fears of me, "The world is drawing to an end, and the sun will never rise any more!"

When the day broke, I found that we were all huddled together in a miserable manner. We were deep in the water; being, as I found on mustering, thirty-one in number, or at least six too many. In the Surf-boat they were fourteen in number, being at least four too many. The first thing I did, was to get myself passed to the rudder—which I took from that time—and to get Mrs. Atherfield, her child, and Miss Coleshaw, passed on to sit next me. As to old Mr. Rarx, I put him in the bow, as far from us as I could. And I put some of the best men near us in order that if I should drop there might be a skilful hand ready to take the helm.

The sea moderating as the sun came up, though the sky was cloudy and wild, we spoke the other boat, to know what stores they had, and to overhaul what we had. I had a compass in my pocket, a small telescope, a double-barrelled pistol, a knife, and a fire-box and matches. Most of my men had knives, and some had a little tobacco: some, a pipe as well. We had a mug among us, and an iron spoon. As to provisions, there were in my boat two bags of biscuit, one piece of raw beef, one piece of raw pork, a bag of coffee, roasted but not ground (thrown in, I imagine, by mistake, for something else), two small casks of water, and about half-a-gallon of rum in a keg. The Surf-boat, having rather more rum than we, and fewer to drink it, gave us, as I estimated, another quart into our keg. In return, we gave them three double handfuls of coffee, tied up in a piece of a handkerchief; they reported that they had aboard besides, a bag of biscuit, a piece of beef, a small cask of water, a small box of lemons, and a Dutch cheese. It took a long time to make these exchanges, and they were not made without risk to both parties; the sea running quite high enough to make our approaching near to one another very hazardous. In the bundle with the coffee, I conveyed to John Steadiman (who had a ship's compass with him), a paper written in pencil, and torn from my pocket-book, containing the course I meant to steer, in the hope of making land, or being picked up by some vessel—I say in the hope, though I had little hope of either deliverance. I then sang out to him, so as all might hear, that if we two boats could live or die together, we would; but, that if we should be parted by the weather, and join company no more, they should have our prayers and blessings, and we asked for theirs. We then gave them three cheers, which they returned, and I saw the men's heads droop in both boats as they fell to their oars again.

These arrangements had occupied the general attention advantageously for all, though (as I expressed in the last sentence) they ended in a sorrowful feeling. I now said a few words to my fellow-voyagers on the subject of the small stock of food on which our lives depended if they were preserved from the great deep, and on the rigid necessity of our eking it out in the most frugal manner. One and all replied that whatever allowance I thought best to lay down should be strictly kept to. We made a pair of scales out of a thin strap of iron-plating and some twine, and I got together for weights such of the heaviest buttons among us as I calculated made up some fraction over two ounces. This was the allowance of solid food served out once a-day to each, from that time to the end; with the addition of a coffee-berry, or sometimes half a one, when the weather was very fair, for breakfast. We had nothing else whatever, but half a pint of water each per day, and sometimes, when we were coldest and weakest, a teaspoonful of rum each, served out as a dram. I know how learnedly it can be shown that rum is poison, but I also know that in this case, as in all similar cases I have ever read of—which are numerous—no words can express the comfort and support derived from it. Nor have I the least doubt that it saved the lives of far more than half our number. Having mentioned half a pint of water as our daily allowance, I ought to observe that sometimes we had less, and sometimes we had more; for much rain fell, and we caught it in a canvas stretched for the purpose.

Thus, at that tempestuous time of the year, and in that tempestuous part of the world, we ship-wrecked people rose and fell with the waves. It is not my intention to relate (if I can avoid it) such circumstances appertaining to our doleful condition as have been better told in many other narratives of the kind than I can be expected to tell them. I will only note, in so many passing words, that day after day and night after night we received the sea upon our backs to prevent it from swamping the boat; that one party was always kept baling, and that every hat and cap among us soon got worn out, though patched up fifty times, as the only vessels we had for that service; that another party lay down in the bottom of the boat, while a third rowed; and that we were soon all in boils and blisters and rags.

The other boat was a source of such anxious interest to all of us that I used to wonder whether, if we were saved, the time could ever come when the survivors in this boat of ours could be at all indifferent to the fortunes of the survivors in that. We got out a tow-rope whenever the weather permitted, but that did not often happen, and how we two parties kept within the same horizon, as we did, He, who mercifully permitted it to be so for our consolation, only knows. I never shall forget the looks with which, when the morning light came, we used to gaze about us over the stormy waters, for the other boat. We once parted company for seventy-two hours, and we believed them to have gone down, as they did us. The joy on both sides when we came within view of one another again, had something in a manner Divine in it; each was so forgetful of individual suffering, in tears of delight and sympathy for the people in the other boat.

I have been wanting to get round to the individual or personal part of my subject, as I call it, and the foregoing incident puts me in the right way. The patience and good disposition aboard of us, was wonderful. I was not surprised by it in the women; for all men born of women know what great qualities they will show when men will fail; but, I own I was a little surprised by it in some of the men. Among one-and-thirty people assembled at the best of times, there will usually, I should say, be two or three uncertain tempers. I knew that I had more than one rough temper with me among my own people, for I had chosen those for the Long-boat that I might have them under my eye. But, they softened under their misery, and were as considerate of the ladies, and as compassionate of the child, as the best among us, or among men—they could not have been more so. I heard scarcely any complaining. The party lying down would moan a good deal in their sleep, and I would often notice a man—not always the same man, it is to be understood, but nearly all of them at one time or other—sitting moaning at his oar, or in his place, as he looked mistily over the sea. When it happened to be long before I could catch his eye, he would go on moaning all the time in the dismallest manner; but, when our looks met, he would brighten and leave off. I almost always got the impression that he did not know what sound he had been making, but that he thought he had been humming a tune.

Our sufferings from cold and wet were far greater than our sufferings from hunger. We managed to keep the child warm; but, I doubt if any one else among us ever was warm for five minutes together; and the shivering, and the chattering of teeth, were sad to hear. The child cried a little at first for her lost playfellow, the Golden Mary; but hardly ever whimpered afterwards; and when the state of the weather made it possible, she used now and then to be held up in the arms of some of us, to look over the sea for John Steadiman's boat. I see the golden hair and the innocent face now, between me and the driving clouds, like an angel going to fly away.

It had happened on the second day, towards night, that Mrs. Atherfield, in getting Little Lucy to sleep, sang her a song. She had a soft, melodious voice, and, when she had finished it, our people up and begged for another. She sang them another, and after it had fallen dark ended with the Evening Hymn. From that time, whenever anything could be heard above the sea and wind, and while she had any voice left, nothing would serve the people but that she should sing at sunset. She always did, and always ended with the Evening Hymn. We mostly took up the last line, and shed tears when it was done, but not miserably. We had a prayer night and morning, also, when the weather allowed of it.

Twelve nights and eleven days we had been driving in the boat, when old Mr. Rarx began to be delirious, and to cry out to me to throw the gold overboard or it would sink us, and we should all be lost. For days past the child had been declining, and that was the great cause of his wildness. He had been over and over again shrieking out to me to give her all the remaining meat, to give her all the remaining rum, to save her at any cost, or we should all be ruined. At this time, she lay in her mother's arms at my feet. One of her little hands was almost always creeping about her mother's neck or chin. I had watched the wasting of the little hand, and I knew it was nearly over.

The old man's cries were so discordant with the mother's love and submission, that I called out to him in an angry voice, unless he held his peace on the instant, I would order him to be knocked on the head and thrown overboard. He was mute then, until the child died, very peacefully, an hour afterwards: which was known to all in the boat by the mother's breaking out into lamentations for the first time since the wreck—for, she had great fortitude and constancy, though she was a little gentle woman. Old Mr. Rarx then became quite ungovernable, tearing what rags he had on him, raging in imprecations, and calling to me that if I had thrown the gold overboard (always the gold with him!) I might have saved the child. "And now," says he, in a terrible voice, "we shall founder, and all go to the Devil, for our sins will sink us, when we have no innocent child to bear us up!" We so discovered with amazement, that this old wretch had only cared for the life of the pretty little creature dear to all of us, because of the influence he superstitiously hoped she might have in preserving him! Altogether it was too much for the smith or armourer, who was sitting next the old man, to bear. He took him by the throat and rolled him under the thwarts, where he lay still enough for hours afterwards.

All that thirteenth night, Miss Coleshaw, lying across my knees as I kept the helm, comforted and supported the poor mother. Her child, covered with a pea-jacket of mine, lay in her lap. It troubled me all night to think that there was no Prayer-Book among us, and that I could remember but very few of the exact words of the burial service. When I stood up at broad day, all knew what was going to be done, and I noticed that my poor fellows made the motion of uncovering their heads, though their heads had been stark bare to the sky and sea for many a weary hour. There was a long heavy swell on, but otherwise it was a fair morning, and there were broad fields of sunlight on the waves in the east. I said no more than this: "I am the Resurrection and the Life, saith the Lord. He raised the daughter of Jairus the ruler, and said she was not dead but slept. He raised the widow's son. He arose Himself, and was seen of many. He loved little children, saying, suffer them to come unto Me, and rebuke them not, for of such is the kingdom of heaven. In His name, my friends, and committed to His merciful goodness!" With those words I laid my rough face softly on the placid little forehed, and buried the Golden Lucy in the grave of the Golden Mary.

Having had it on my mind to relate the end of this dear little child, I have omitted something from its exact place, which I will supply here. It will come quite as well here as anywhere else.

Foreseeing that if the boat lived through the stormy weather, the time must come, and soon come, when we should have absolutely no morsel to eat, I had one momentous point often in my thoughts. Although I had, years before that, fully satisfied myself that the instances in which human beings in the last distress have fed upon each other, are exceedingly few, and have very seldom indeed (if ever) occurred when the people in distress, however dreadful their extremity, have been accustomed to moderate for bearance and restraint; I say, though I had long before quite satisfied my mind on this topic, I felt doubtful whether there might not have been in former cases some harm and danger from keeping it out of sight and pretending not to think of it. I felt doubtful whether some minds, growing weak with fasting and exposure and having such a terrific idea to dwell upon in secret, might not magnify it until it got to have an awful attraction about it. This was not a new thought of mine, for it had grown out of my reading. However, it came over me stronger than it had ever done before—as it had reason for doing—in the boat, and on the fourth day I decided that I would bring out into the light that unformed fear which must have been more or less darkly in every brain among us. Therefore, as a means of beguiling the time and inspiring hope, I gave them the best summary in my power of Bligh's voyage of more than three thousand miles, in an open boat, after the Mutiny of the Bounty, and of the wonderful preservation of that boat's crew. They listened throughout with great interest, and I concluded by telling them, that, in my opinion, the happiest circumstance in the whole narrative was, that Bligh, who was no delicate man either, had solemnly placed it on record therein that he was sure and certain that under no conceivable circumstances whatever would that emaciated party, who had gone through all the pains of famine, have preyed on one another. I cannot describe the visible relief which this spread through the boat, and how the tears stood in every eye. From that time I was as well convinced as Bligh himself that there was no danger, and that this phantom, at any rate, did not haunt us.

Now, it was a part of Bligh's experience that when the people in his boat were most cast down, nothing did them so much good as hearing a story told by one of their number. When I mentioned that, I saw that it struck the general attention as much as it did my own, for I had not thought of it until I came to it in my summary. This was on the day after Mrs. Atherfield first sang to us. I proposed that, whenever the weather would permit, we should have a story two hours after dinner (I always issued the allowance I have mentioned at one o'clock, and called it by that name), as well as our song at sunset. The proposal was received with a cheerful satisfaction that warmed my heart within me; and I do not say too much when I say that those two periods in the four-and-twenty hours were expected with positive pleasure, and were really enjoyed by all hands. Spectres as we soon were in our bodily wasting, our imaginations did not perish like the gross flesh upon our bones. Music and Adventure, two of the great gifts of Providence to mankind, could charm us long after that was lost.

The wind was almost always against us after the second day; and for many days together we could not nearly hold our own. We had all varieties of bad weather. We had rain, hail, snow, wind, mist, thunder and lightning. Still the boats lived through the heavy seas, and still we perishing people rose and fell with the great waves.

Sixteen nights and fifteen days, twenty nights and nineteen days, twenty-four nights and twenty-three days. So the time went on. Disheartening as I knew that our progress, or want of progress, must be, I never deceived them as to my calculations of it. In the first place, I felt that we were all too near eternity for deceit; in the second place, I knew that if I failed, or died, the man who followed me must have a knowledge of the true state of things to begin upon. When I told them at noon, what I reckoned we had made or lost, they generally received what I said in a tranquil and resigned manner, and always gratefully towards me. It was not unusual at any time of the day for some one to burst out weeping loudly without any new cause; and, when the burst was over, to calm down a little better than before. I had seen exactly the same thing in a house of mourning.

During the whole of this time, old Mr. Rarx had had his fits of calling out to me to throw the gold (always the gold!) overboard, and of heaping violent reproaches upon me for not having saved the child; but now, the food being all gone, and I having nothing left to serve out but a bit of coffee-berry now and then, he began to be too weak to do this, and consequently fell silent. Mrs. Atherfield and Miss Coleshaw generally lay, each with an arm across one of my knees, and her head upon it. They never complained at all. Up to the time of her child's death, Mrs. Atherfield had bound up her own beautiful hair every day; and I took particular notice that this was always before she sang her song at night, when every one looked at her. But she never did it after the loss of her darling; and it would have been now all tangled with dirt and wet, but that Miss Coleshaw was careful of it long after she was herself, and would sometimes smooth it down with her weak thin hands.

We were past mustering a story now; but one day, at about this period, I reverted to the superstition of old Mr. Rarx, concerning the Golden Lucy, and told them that nothing vanished from the eye of God, though much might pass away from the eyes of men. "We were all of us," says I, "children once;

and our baby feet have strolled in green woods ashore; and our baby hands have gathered flowers in gardens, where the birds were singing. The children that we were, are not lost to the great knowledge of our Creator. Those innocent creatures will appear with us before Him, and plead for us. What we were in the best time of our generous youth will arise and go with us too. The purest part of our lives will not desert us at the pass to which all of us here present are gliding. What we were then, will be as much in existence before Him, as what we are now." They were no less comforted by this consideration, than I was myself; and Miss Coleshaw, drawing my ear nearer to her lips, said, "Captain Ravender, I was on my way to marry a disgraced and broken man, whom I dearly loved when he was honourable and good. Your words seem to have come out of my own poor heart." She pressed my hand upon it, smiling.

Twenty-seven nights and twenty-six days. We were in no want of rainwater, but we had nothing else. And yet, even now, I never turned my eyes upon a waking face but it tried to brighten before mine. O, what a thing it is, in a time of danger and in the presence of death, the shining of a face upon a face! I have heard it broached that orders should be given in great new ships by electric telegraph. I admire machinery as much as any man, and am as thankful to it as any man can be for what it does for us. But it will never be a substitute for the face of a man, with his soul in it, encouraging another man to be brave and true. Never try it for that. It will break down like a straw.

I now began to remark certain changes in myself which I did not like. They caused me much disquiet. I often saw the Golden Lucy in the air above the boat. I often saw her I have spoken of before, sitting beside me. I saw the Golden Mary go down, as she really had gone down, twenty times in a day. And yet the sea was mostly, to my thinking, not sea neither, but moving country and extraordinary mountainous regions, the like of which have never been beheld. I felt it time to leave my last words regarding John Steadiman, in case any lips should last out to repeat them to any living ears. I said that John had told me (as he had on deck) that he had sung out "Breakers ahead!" the instant they were audible, and had tried to wear ship, but she struck before it could be done. (His cry, I dare say, had made my dream.) I said that the circumstances were altogether without warning, and out of any course that could have been guarded against; that the same loss would have happened if I had been in charge; and that John was not to blame, but from first to last had done his duty nobly, like the man he was. I tried to write it down in my pocket-book, but could make no words, though I knew what the words were that I wanted to make. When it had come to that, her hands—though she was dead so long—laid me down gently in the bottom of the boat, and she and the Golden Lucy swung me to sleep.

All that follows, was written by John Steadiman, Chief Mate:

On the twenty-sixth day, after the foundering of the Golden Mary at sea, I, John Steadiman, was sitting in my place in the stern-sheets of the Surfboat, with just sense enough left in me to steer—that is to say, with my eyes strained, wide-awake, over the bows of the boat, and my brains fast asleep and dreaming—when I was roused upon a sudden by our second mate, Mr. William Rames.

"Let me take a spell in your place," says he. "And look you out for the Long-boat astern. The last time she rose on the crest of a wave, I thought I made out a signal flying aboard her."

We shifted our places, clumsily and slowly enough, for we were both of us weak and dazed with wet, cold, and hunger. I waited some time, watching the heavy rollers astern, before the Long-boat rose a-top of one of them at the same time with us. At last, she was heaved up for a moment well in view, and there, sure enough, was the signal flying aboard of her—a strip of rag of some sort, rigged to an oar, and hoisted in her bows.

"What does it mean?" says Rames to me in a quavering, trembling sort of voice. "Do they signal a sail in sight?"

"Hush, for God's sake!" says I, clapping my hand over his mouth. "Don't let the people hear you. They'll all go mad together if we mislead them about that signal. Wait a bit, till I have another look at it."

I held on by him, for he had set me all of a tremble with his notion of a sail in sight, and watched for the Long-boat again. Up she rose on the top of another roller. I made out the signal clearly, that second time, and saw that it was rigged half-mast high.

"Rames," says I, "it's a signal of distress. Pass the word forward to keep her before the sea, and no more. We must get the Long-boat within hailing distance of us, as soon as possible."

I dropped down into my old place at the tiller without another word—for the thought went through me like a knife that something had happened to Captain Ravender. I should consider myself unworthy to write another line of this statement, if I had not made up my mind to speak the truth, the whole truth, and nothing but the truth—and I must, therefore, confess plainly that now, for the first time, my heart sank within me. This weakness on my part was produced in some degree, as I take it, by the exhausting effects of previous anxiety and grief.

Our provisions—if I may give that name to what we had left—were reduced to the rind of one lemon and about a couple of handsfull of coffee-berries. Besides these great distresses, caused by the death, the danger, and the suffering among my crew and passengers, I had had a little distress of my own to shake me still more, in the death of the child whom I had got to be very fond of on the voyage out—so fond that I was secretly a little jealous of her being taken in the Long-boat instead of mine when the ship foundered. It used to be a great comfort to me, and I think to those with me also, after we had seen the last of the Golden Mary, to see the Golden Lucy, held up by the men in the Long-boat, when the weather allowed it, as the best and brightest sight they had to show. She looked, at the distance we saw her from, almost like a little white bird in the air. To miss her for the first time, when the weather lulled a little again, and we all looked out for our white bird and looked in vain, was a sore disappointment. To see the men's heads bowed down and the captain's hand pointing into the sea when we hailed the Long-boat, a few day's after, gave me as heavy a shock and as sharp a pang of heartache to bear as ever I remember suffering in all my life. I only mention these things to show that if I did give way a little at first, under the dread that our captain was lost to us, it was not without having been a good deal shaken beforehand by more trials of one sort or another than often fall to one man's share.

I had got over the choking in my throat with the help of a drop of water, and had steadied my mind again so as to be prepared against the worst, when I heard the hail (Lord help the poor fellows, how weak it sounded!)—

"Surf-boat ahoy!"

I looked up, and there were our companions in misfortune tossing abreast of us; not so near that we could make out the features of any of them, but near enough, with some exertion for people in our condition, to make their voices heard in the intervals when the wind was weakest.

I answered the hail, and waited a bit, and heard nothing, and then sung out the captain's name. The voice that replied did not sound like his; the words that reached us were:

"Chief-mate wanted on board!"

Every man of my crew knew what that meant as well as I did. As second officer in command, there could be but one reason for wanting me on board the Long-boat. A groan went all round us, and my men looked darkly in each other's faces, and whispered under their breaths:

"The captain is dead!"

I commanded them to be silent, and not to make too sure of bad news, at such a pass as things had now come to with us. Then, hailing the Long-boat, I signified that I was ready to go on board when the weather would let me—stopped a bit to draw a good long breath—and then called out as loud as I could the dreadful question:

"Is the captain dead?"

The black figures of three or four men in the after-part of the Long-boat all stooped down together as my voice reached them. They were lost to view for about a minute; then appeared again—one man among them was held up on his feet by the rest, and he hailed back the blessed words (a very faint hope went a very long way with people in our desperate situation): "Not yet!"

The relief felt by me, and by all with me, when we knew that our captain, though unfitted for duty, was not lost to us, it is not in words—at least, not in such words as a man like me can command—to express. I did my best to cheer the men by telling them what a good sign it was that we were not as badly off yet as we had feared; and then communicated what instructions I had to give, to William Rames, who was to be left in command in my place when I took charge of the Long-boat. After that, there was nothing to be done, but to wait for the chance of the wind dropping at sunset, and the sea going down afterwards, so as to enable our weak crews to lay the two boats alongside each other, without undue risk—or, to put it plainer, without saddling ourselves with the necessity for any extraordinary exertion of strength or skill. Both the one and the other had now been starved out of us for days and days together.

At sunset the wind suddenly dropped, but the sea, which had been running high for so long a time past, took hours after that before it showed any signs of getting to rest. The moon was shining, the sky was wonderfully clear, and it could not have been, according to my calculations, far off midnight, when the long, slow, regular swell of the calming ocean fairly set in, and I took the responsibility of lessening the distance between the Long-boat and ourselves.

It was, I dare say, a delusion of mine; but I thought I had never seen the moon shine so white and ghastly anywhere, either at sea or on land, as she shone that night while we were approaching our companions in misery. When there was not much more than a boat's length between us, and the white light streamed cold and clear over all our faces, both crews rested on their oars with one great shudder, and stared over the gunwale of either boat, panic-stricken at the first sight of each other.

"Any lives lost among you?" I asked, in the midst of that frightful silence. The men in the Long-boat huddled together like sheep at the sound of my voice.

"None yet, but the child, thanks be to God!" answered one among them.

And at the sound of his voice, all my men shrank together like the men in the Long-boat. I was afraid to let the horror produced by our first meeting at close quarters after the dreadful changes that wet, cold, and famine had produced, last one moment longer than could be helped; so, without giving time for any more questions and answers, I commanded the men to lay the two boats close alongside of each other. When I rose up and committed the tiller to the hands of Rames, all my poor fellows raised their white faces imploringly to mine. "Don't leave us, Sir," they said, "don't leave us." "I leave you," says I, "under the command and the guidance of Mr. William Rames, as good a sailor as I am, and as trusty and kind a man as ever stepped. Do your duty by him, as you have done it by me; and remember to the last, that while there is life there is hope. God bless and help you all!" With those words I collected what strength I had left, and caught at two arms that were held out to me, and so got from the stern-sheets of one boat into the stern-sheets of the other.

"Mind where you step, Sir," whispered one of the men who had helped me into the Long-boat. I looked down as he spoke. Three figures were huddled up below me, with the moonshine falling on them in ragged streaks through the gaps between the men standing or sitting above them. The first face I made out was the face of Miss Coleshaw; her eyes were wide open and fixed on me. She seemed still to keep her senses, and, by the alternate parting and closing of her lips, to be trying to speak, but I could not hear that she uttered a single word. On her shoulder rested the head of Mrs. Atherfield. The mother of our poor little Golden Lucy must, I think, have been dreaming of the child she had lost; for there was a faint smile just ruffling the white stillness of her face, when I first saw it turned upward, with peaceful closed eyes towards the heavens. From her, I looked down a little, and there, with his head on her lap, and with one of her hands resting tenderly on his cheek—there lay the Captain, to whose help and guidance, up to this miserable time, we had never looked in vain,—there, worn out at last in our service, and for our sakes, lay the best and bravest man of all our company. I stole my hand in gently through his clothes and laid it on his heart, and felt a little feeble warmth over it, though my cold dulled touch could not detect even the faintest beating. The two men in the stern-sheets with me, noticing what I was doing—knowing I loved him like a brother—and seeing, I suppose, more distress in my face than I myself was conscious of its showing, lost command over themselves altogether, and burst into a piteous moaning, sobbing lamentation over him. One of the two drew aside a jacket from his feet, and showed me that they were bare, except where a wet, ragged strip of stocking still clung to one of them. When the ship struck the Iceberg, he had run on deck leaving his shoes in his cabin. All through the voyage in the boat his feet had been unprotected; and not a soul had discovered it until he dropped! As long as he could keep his eyes open, the very look of them had cheered the men, and comforted and upheld the women. Not one living creature in the boat, with any sense about him, but had felt the good influence of that brave man in one way or another. Not one but had heard him, over and over again, give the credit to others which was due only to himself; praising this man for patience, and thanking that man for help, when the patience and the help had really and truly, as to the best part of both, come only from him. All this, and much more, I heard pouring confusedly from the men's lips while they crouched down, sobbing and crying over their commander, and wrapping the jacket as warmly and tenderly as they could over his cold feet. It went to my heart to check them; but I knew that if this lamenting spirit spread any further, all chance of keeping alight any last sparks of hope and resolution among the boat's company would be lost for ever. Accordingly I sent them to their places, spoke a few encouraging words to the men forward, promising to serve out, when the morning came, as much as I dared, of any eatable thing left in the lockers; called to Rames, in my old boat, to keep as near us as he safely could; drew the garments and coverings of the two poor suffering women more closely about them; and, with a secret prayer to be directed for the best in bearing the awful responsibility now laid on my shoulders, took my Captain's vacant place at the helm of the Long-boat.

This, as well as I can tell it, is the full and true account of how I came to be placed in charge of the lost passengers and crew of the Golden Mary, on the morning of the twenty-seventh day after the ship struck the Iceberg, and foundered at sea.

Ice Again!

RICHARD HENRY DANA, JR.

In our first attempt to double the Cape, when we came up to the latitude of it, we were nearly seventeen hundred miles to the westward, but, in running for the straits of Magellan, we stood so far to the eastward, that we made our second attempt at a distance of not more than four or five hundred miles; and we had great hopes, by this means, to run clear of the ice; thinking that the easterly gales, which had prevailed for a long time, would have driven it to the westward. With the wind about two points free, the yards braced in a little, and two close-reefed topsails and a reefed foresail on the ship, we made great way toward the southward; and, almost every watch, when we came on deck, the air seemed to grow colder, and the sea to run higher. Still, we saw no ice, and had great hopes of going clear of it altogether, when, one afternoon, about three o'clock, while we were taking a *siesta* during our watch below, "All hands!" was called in a loud and fearful voice. "Tumble up here, men!—tumble up!—don't stop for your clothes—before we're upon it!" We sprang out of our berths and hurried upon deck. The loud, sharp voice of the captain was heard giving orders, as though for life or death, and we ran aft to the braces, not waiting to look ahead, for not a moment was to be lost. The helm was hard up, the after yards shaking, and the ship in the act of wearing. Slowly, with the stiff ropes and iced rigging, we swung the yards round, everything coming hard, and with a creaking and rending sound, like pulling up a plank which has been frozen into the ice. The ship wore round fairly, the yards were steadied, and we stood off on the other tack, leaving behind us, directly under our larboard quarter, a large ice island, peering out of the mist, and reaching high above our tops, while astern; and on either side of the island, large tracts of field-ice were dimly seen, heaving and rolling in the sea. We were now safe, and standing to the northward; but, in a few minutes more, had it not been for the sharp look-out of the watch, we should have been fairly upon the ice, and left our ship's old bones adrift in the Southern ocean. After standing to the northward a few hours, we wore ship, and, the wind having hauled, we stood to the southward and eastward. All night long, a bright look-out was kept from every part of the deck; and whenever ice was seen on the one bow or the other, the helm was shifted and the yards braced, and by quick working of the ship she was kept clear. The accustomed cry of "Ice ahead!"—"Ice on the lee bow!"—"Another island!" in the same tones, and with the same orders following them, seemed to bring us directly back to our old position of the week before. During our watch on deck, which was from twelve to four, the wind came out ahead, with a pelting storm of hail and sleet, and we lay hove-to, under a close-reefed main topsail, the whole watch. During the next watch it fell calm, with a drenching rain, until daybreak, when the wind came out to the westward, and the weather cleared up, and showed us the whole ocean, in the course which we should have steered, had it not been for the head wind and calm, completely blocked up with ice. Here then our progress was stopped, and we wore ship, and once more stood to the northward and eastward; not for the straits of Magellan, but to make another attempt to double the Cape, still farther to the eastward; for the captain was determined to get round if perseverance could do it; and the third time, he said, never failed.

With a fair wind we soon ran clear of the field-ice, and by noon had only the stray islands floating far and near upon the ocean. The sun was out bright, the sea of a deep blue, fringed with the white foam of the waves which ran high before a strong south-wester; our solitary ship tore on through the water, as though glad to be out of her confinement; and the ice islands lay scattered upon the ocean here and there, of various sizes and shapes, reflecting the bright rays of the sun, and drifting slowly northward before the gale. It was a contrast to much that we had lately seen, and a spectacle not only of beauty, but of life; for it required but little fancy to imagine these islands to be animate masses which had broken loose from the "thrilling regions of thick-ribbed ice," and were working their way, by wind and current, some alone, and some in fleets, to milder climes. No pencil has ever yet given anything like the true effect of an iceberg. In a picture, they are huge, uncouth masses, stuck in the sea, while their chief beauty and grandeur,—their slow, stately motion; the whirling of the snow about their summits, and the fearful groaning and cracking of their parts,—the picture cannot give. This is the large iceberg; while the small and distant islands, floating on the smooth sea, in the light of a clear day, look like little floating fairy isles of sapphire.

From a north-east course we gradually hauled to the eastward, and after sailing about two hundred miles, which brought us as near to the western coast of Terra del Fuego as was safe, and having lost sight of the ice altogether,—for the third time we put the ship's head to the southward, to try the passage of the Cape. The weather continued clear and cold, with a strong gale from the westward, and we were fast getting up with the latitude of the Cape, with a prospect of soon being round. One fine afternoon, a man who had gone into the fore-top to shift the rolling tackles, sung out, at the top of his voice, and with evident glee,—"Sail ho!" Neither land nor sail had we seen since leaving San Diego; and any one who has traversed the length of a whole ocean alone, can imagine what an excitement such an announcement produced on board. "Sail ho!" shouted the cook, jumping out of his galley; "Sail ho!" shouted a man, throwing back the slide of the scuttle, to the watch below, who were soon out of their berths and on deck; and "Sail ho!" shouted the captain down the companion-way to the passenger in the cabin. Beside the pleasure of seeing a ship and human beings in so desolate a place, it was important for us to speak a vessel, to learn whether there was ice to the eastward, and to ascertain the longitude; for we had no chronometer, and had been drifting about so long that we had nearly lost our reckoning, and opportunities for lunar observations are not frequent or sure in such a place as Cape Horn. For these various reasons, the excitement in our little community was running high, and conjectures were made, and everything thought of for which the captain would hail, when the man aloft sung out—"Another sail, large on the weather bow!" This was a little odd, but so much the better, and did not shake our faith in their being sails. At length the man in the top hailed, and said he believed it was land, after all. "Land in your eye!" said the mate, who was looking through the telescope; "they are ice islands, if I can see a hole through a ladder;" and a few moments showed the mate to be right; and all our expectations fled; and instead of what we most wished to see, we had what we most dreaded, and what we hoped we had seen the last of. We soon, however, left these astern, having passed within about two miles of them; and at sundown the horizon was clear in all directions.

Having a fine wind, we were soon up with and passed the latitude of the Cape, and having stood far enough to the southward to give it a wide berth, we began to stand to the eastward, with a good prospect of being round and steering to the northward on the other side, in a very few days. But ill luck seemed to have lighted upon us. Not four hours had we been standing on in this course, before it fell dead calm; and in half an hour it clouded up; a few straggling blasts, with spits of snow and sleet, came from the eastward; and in an hour more, we lay hove-to under a close-reefed main topsail, drifting bodily off to leeward before the fiercest storm that we had yet felt, blowing dead ahead, from the eastward. It seemed as though the genius of the place had been roused at finding that we had nearly slipped through his fingers, and had come down upon us with tenfold fury. The sailors said that every blast, as it shook the shrouds, and whistled through the rigging, said to the old ship, "No, you don't!"—"No, you don't!"

For eight days we lay drifting about in this manner. Sometimes,—generally towards noon,—it fell calm; once or twice a round copper ball showed itself for a few moments in the place where the sun ought to have been; and a puff or two came from the westward, giving some hope that a fair wind had come at last. During the first two days, we made sail for these puffs, shaking the reefs out of the topsails and boarding the tacks of the courses; but finding that it only made work for us when the gale set in again, it was soon given up, and we lay-to under our close-reefs. We had less snow and hail than when we were farther to the westward, but we had an abundance of what is worse to a sailor in cold weather—drenching rain. Snow is blinding, and very bad when coming upon a coast, but, for genuine discomfort, give me rain with freezing weather. A snow-storm is exciting, and it does not wet through the clothes (which is important to a sailor); but a constant rain there is no escaping from. It wets to the skin, and makes all protection vain. We had long ago run through all our dry clothes, and as sailors have no other way of drying them than by the sun, we had nothing to do but to put on those which were the least wet. At the end of each watch, when we came below, we took off our clothes and wrung them out; two taking hold of a pair of trowsers,—one at each end,—and jackets in the same way. Stockings, mittens, and all, were wrung out also and then hung up to drain and chafe dry against the bulkheads. Then, feeling of all our clothes, we picked out those which were the least wet, and put them on, so as to be ready for a call, and turned-in, covered ourselves up with blankets, and slept until three knocks on the scuttle and the dismal sound of "All starbowlines ahoy! Eight bells, there below! Do you hear the news?" drawled out from on deck, and the sulky answer of "Aye, aye!" from below, sent us up again.

On deck, all was as dark as a pocket, and either a dead calm, with the rain pouring steadily down, or, more generally, a violent gale dead ahead, with rain pelting horizontally, and occasional variations of hail and sleet;—decks afloat with water swashing from side to side, and constantly wet feet; for boots could not be wrung out like drawers, and no composition could stand the constant soaking. In fact, wet and cold feet are inevitable in such weather, and are not the least of those little items which go to make up the grand total of the discomforts of a winter passage round the Cape. Few words were spoken between the watches as they shifted, the wheel was relieved, the mate took his place on the quarter-deck, the lookouts in the bows; and each man had his narrow space to walk fore and aft in, or, rather, to swing himself forward and back in, from one belaying pin to another,—for the decks were too slippery with ice and water to allow of much walking. To make a walk, which is absolutely necessary to pass away the time, one of us hit upon the expedient of sanding the deck; and afterwards, whenever the rain was not so violent as to wash it off, the weatherside of the quarter-deck, and a part of the waist and forecastle were sprinkled with the sand which we had on board for holystoning; and thus we made a good promenade, where we walked fore and aft, two and two, hour after hour, in our long, dull, and comfortless watches. The bells seemed to be an hour or two apart, instead of half an hour, and an age to elapse before the welcome sound of eight bells. The sole object was to make the time pass on. Any change was sought for, which would break the monotony of the time; and even the two hours' trick at the wheel, which came round to each of us, in turn, once in every other watch, was looked upon as a relief. Even the never-failing resource of long yarns, which eke out many a watch, seemed to have failed us now; for we had been so long together that we had heard each other's stories told over and over again, till we had them by heart; each one knew the whole history of each of the others, and we were fairly and literally talked out. Singing and joking, we were in no humor for, and, in fact, any sound of mirth or laughter would have struck strangely upon our ears, and would not have been tolerated, any more than whistling, or a wind instrument. The last resort, that of speculating upon the future, seemed now to fail us, for our discouraging situation, and the danger we were really in, (as we expected every day to find ourselves drifted back among the ice) "clapped a stopper" upon all that. From saying—"*when* we get home"—we began insensibly to alter it to—"*if* we get home"—and at last the subject was dropped by a tacit consent.

In this state of things, a new light was struck out, and a new field opened, by a change in the watch. One of our watch was laid up for two or three days by a bad hand, (for in cold weather the least cut or bruise ripens into a sore,) and his place was supplied by the carpenter. This was a windfall, and there was quite a contest, who should have the carpenter to walk with him. As "Chips" was a man of some little education, and he and I had had a good deal of intercourse with each other, he fell in with me in my walk. He was a Fin, but spoke English very well, and gave me long accounts of his country;—the customs, the trade, the towns, what little he knew of the government, (I found he was no friend of Russia,) his voyages, his first arrival in America, his marriage and courtship;—he had married a countrywoman of his, a dress-maker, whom he met with in Boston. I had very little to tell him of my quiet, sedentary life at home; and, in spite of our best efforts, which had protracted these yarns through five or six watches, we fairly talked one another out, and I turned him over to another man in the watch, and put myself upon my own resources.

I commenced a deliberate system of time-killing, which united some profit with a cheering up of the heavy hours. As soon as I came on deck, and took my place and regular walk, I began with repeating over to myself a string of matters which I had in my memory, in regular order. First, the multiplication table and the tables of weights and measures; then the states of the Union, with their capitals; the counties of England, with their shire towns; the kings of England in their order; and a large part of the peerage, which I committed from an almanac that we had on board; and then the Kanaka numerals. This carried me through my facts, and, being repeated deliberately, with long intervals, often eked out the two first bells. Then came the ten commandments; the thirty-ninth chapter of Job, and a few other passages from Scripture. The next in the order, that I never varied from, came Cowper's Castaway, which was a great favorite with me; the solemn measure and gloomy character of which, as well as the incident that it was founded upon, made it well suited to a lonely watch at sea. Then his lines to Mary, his address to the jackdaw, and a short extract from Table Talk; (I abounded in Cowper, for I happened to have a volume of his poems in my chest;) "Ille et nefasto" from Horace, and Gœthe's Erl King. After I had got through these, I allowed myself a more general range among everything that I could remember, both in prose and verse. In this way, with an occasional break by relieving the wheel, heaving the log, and going to the scuttlebutt for a drink of water, the longest watch was passed away; and I was so regular in my silent recitations, that if there was no interruption by ship's duty, I could tell very nearly the number of bells by my progress.

Our watches below were no more varied than the watch on deck. All washing, sewing, and reading was given up; and we did nothing but eat, sleep, and stand our watch, leading what might be called a Cape Horn life. The forecastle was too uncomfortable to sit up in; and whenever we were below, we were in our berths. To prevent the rain, and the sea-water which broke over the bows, from washing down, we were obliged to keep the scuttle closed, so that the forecastle was nearly air-tight. In this little, wet, leaky hole, we were all quartered, in an atmosphere so bad that our lamp, which swung in the middle from the beams, sometimes actually burned blue, with a large circle of foul air about it. Still, I was never in better health than after three weeks of this life. I gained a great deal of flesh, and we all ate like horses. At every watch, when we came below, before turning-in, the bread barge and beef kid were overhauled. Each man drank his quart of hot tea night and morning; and glad enough we were to get it, for no nectar and ambrosia were sweeter to the lazy immortals, than was a pot of hot tea, a hard biscuit, and a slice of cold salt beef, to us after a watch on deck. To be sure, we were mere animals, and had this life lasted a year instead of a month, we should have been little better than the ropes in the ship. Not a razor, nor a brush, nor a drop of water, except the rain and the spray, had come near us all the time; for we were on an allowance of fresh water; and who would strip and wash himself in salt water on deck, in the snow and ice, with the thermometer at zero?

After about eight days of constant easterly gales, the wind hauled occasionally a little to the southward, and blew hard, which, as we were well to the southward, allowed us to brace in a little and stand on, under all the sail we could carry. These turns lasted but a short while, and sooner or later it set in again from the old quarter; yet at each time we made something, and were gradually edging along to the eastward. One night, after one of these shifts of the wind, and when all hands had been up a great part of the time, our watch was left on deck, with the mainsail hanging in the buntlines, ready to be set if necessary. It came on to blow worse and worse, with hail and snow beating like so many furies upon the ship, it being as dark and thick as night could make it. The mainsail was blowing and slatting with a noise like thunder, when the captain came on deck, and ordered it to be furled. The mate was about to call all hands, when the captain stopped him, and said that the men would be beaten out if they were called up so often; that as our watch must stay on deck, it might as well be doing that as anything else.

Accordingly, we went upon the yard; and never shall I forget that piece of work. Our watch had been so reduced by sickness, and by some having been left in California, that, with one man at the wheel, we had only the third mate and three beside myself to go aloft; so that, at most, we could only attempt to furl one yard-arm at a time. We manned the weather yard-arm, and set to work to make a furl of it. Our lower masts being short, and our yards very square, the sail had a head of nearly fifty feet, and a short leach, made still shorter by the deep reef which was in it, which brought the clue away out on the quarters of the yard, and made a bunt nearly as square as the mizen royal-yard. Beside this difficulty, the yard over which we lay was cased with ice, the gaskets and rope of the foot and leach of the sail as stiff and hard as a piece of suction-hose, and the sail itself about as pliable as though it had been made of sheets of sheathing copper. It blew a perfect hurricane, with alternate blasts of snow, hail, and rain. We had to *fist* the sail with bare hands. No one could trust himself to mittens, for if he slipped, he was a gone man. All the boats were hoisted in on deck, and there was nothing to be lowered for him. We had need of every finger God had given us. Several times we got the sail upon the yard, but it blew away again before we could secure it. It required men to lie over the yard to pass each turn of the gaskets, and when they were passed, it was almost impossible to knot them so that they would hold. Frequently we were obliged to leave off altogether and take to beating our hands upon the sail, to keep them from freezing. After some time,—which seemed forever,—we got the weather side stowed after a fashion, and went over to leeward for another trial. This was still worse, for the body of the sail had been blown over to leeward, and as the yard was a-cock-bill by the lying over of the vessel, we had to light it all up to windward. When the yard-arms were furled, the bunt was all adrift again, which made more work for us. We got all secure at last, but we had been nearly an hour and a half upon the yard, and it seemed an age. It had just struck five bells when we went up, and eight were struck soon after we came down. This may seem slow work, but considering the state of everything, and that we had only five men to a sail with just half as many square yards of canvas in it as the mainsail of the Independence, sixty-gun ship, which musters seven hundred men at her quarters, it is not wonderful that we were no quicker about it. We were glad enough to get on deck, and still more, to go below. The oldest sailor in the watch said, as he went down,—"I shall never forget that main yard;—it beats all my going a fishing. Fun is fun, but furling one yard-arm of a course, at a time, off Cape Horn, is no better than man-killing."

During the greater part of the next two days, the wind was pretty steady from the southward. We had evidently made great progress, and had good hope of being soon up with the Cape, if we were not there already. We could put but little confidence in our reckoning, as there had been no opportunities for an observation, and we had drifted too much to allow of our dead reckoning being anywhere near the mark. If it would clear off enough to give a chance for an observation, or if we could make land, we should know where we were; and upon these, and the chances of falling in with a sail from the eastward, we depended almost entirely.

Friday, July 22nd. This day we had a steady gale from the southward, and stood on under close sail, with the yards eased a little by the weather braces, the clouds lifting a little, and showing signs of breaking away. In the afternoon, I was below with Mr. H——, the third mate, and two others, filling the bread locker in the steerage from the casks, when a bright gleam of sunshine broke out and shone down the companion-way and through the sky-light, lighting up everything below, and sending a warm glow through the heart of every one. It was a sight we had not seen for weeks,—an omen, a God-send. Even the roughest and hardest face acknowledged its influence. Just at that moment we heard a loud shout from all parts of the deck, and the mate called out down the companion-way to the captain, who was sitting in the cabin. What he said, we could not distinguish, but the captain kicked over his chair, and was on deck at one jump. We could not tell what it was; and, anxious as we were to know, the discipline of the ship would not allow of our leaving our places. Yet, as we were not called, we knew there was no danger. We hurried to get through with our job, when, seeing the steward's black face peering out of the pantry, Mr. H— hailed him, to know what was the matter. "Lan' o, to be sure, sir! No you hear 'em sing out, 'Lan' o?' De cap'em say 'im Cape Horn!"

This gave us a new start, and we were soon through our work, and on deck; and there lay the land, fair upon the larboard beam, and slowly edging away upon the quarter. All hands were busy looking at it,—the captain and mates from the quarter-deck, the cook from his galley, and the sailors from the forecastle; and even Mr. N., the passenger, who had kept in his shell for nearly a month, and hardly been seen by anybody, and who we had almost forgotten was on board, came out like a butterfly, and was hopping round as bright as a bird.

The land was the island of Staten Land, just to the eastward of Cape Horn; and a more desolate-looking spot I never wish to set eyes upon;—bare, broken, and girt with rocks and ice, with here and there, between the rocks and broken hillocks, a little stunted vegetation of shrubs. It was a place well suited to stand at the junction of the two oceans, beyond the reach of human cultivation, and encounter the blasts and snows of a perpetual winter. Yet, dismal as it was, it was a pleasant sight to us; not only as being the first land we had seen, but because it told us that we had passed the Cape,—were in the Atlantic,—and that, with twenty-four hours of this breeze, might bid defiance to the Southern ocean. It told us, too, our latitude and longitude better than any observation; and the captain now knew where we were, as well as if we were off the end of Long wharf.

In the general joy, Mr. N. said he should like to go ashore upon the island and examine a spot which probably no human being had ever set foot upon; but the captain intimated that he would see the island—specimens and all,—in—another place, before he would get out a boat or delay the ship one moment for him.

We left the land gradually astern; and at sundown had the Atlantic ocean clear before us.

Excerpt from *Robinson Crusoe*

DANIEL DEFOE

It was my lot, first of all, to fall into pretty good company in London, which does not always happen to such loose and unguided young fellows as I then was, the devil generally not omitting to lay some snare for them, very early; but it was not so with me. I first fell acquainted with the master of a ship who had been on the coast of Guinea; and who, having had very good success there, was resolved to go again; and who, taking a fancy to my conversation, which was not at all disagreeable at that time, hearing me say I had a mind to see the world, told me, if I would go the voyage with him I should be at no expense— I should be his messmate and his companion; and, if I could carry anything with me, I should have all the advantage of it that the trade would admit; and, perhaps, I might meet with some encouragement.

I embraced the offer; and, entering into a strict friendship with this captain, who was an honest and plain-dealing man, I went the voyage with him, and carried a small adventure with me, which, by the disinterested honesty of my friend the captain, I increased very considerably; for I carried about forty pounds in such toys and trifles as the captain directed me to buy. This forty pounds I had mustered together by the assistance of some of my relations, whom I corresponded with, and who, I believe, got my father, or at least my mother, to contribute so much as that to my first adventure.

This was the only voyage which I may say was successful in all my adventures, and which I owe to the integrity and honesty of my friend the captain; under whom also I got a competent knowledge of the mathematics, and the rules of navigation—learned how to keep an account of the ship's course, take an observation, and, in short, to understand some things that were needful to be understood by a sailor; for, as he took delight to instruct me, I took delight to learn; and, in a word, this voyage made me both a sailor and a merchant; for I brought home five pounds nine ounces of gold dust for my adventure, which yielded me in London, at my return, almost three hundred pounds; and this filled me with those aspiring thoughts which have since so completed my ruin.

Yet, even in this voyage, I had my misfortunes, too; particularly that I was continually sick, being thrown into a violent calenture by the excessive heat of the climate—our principal trading being upon the coast, from the latitude of fifteen degrees north, even to the Line itself.

I was now set up for a Guinea trader; and my friend, to my great misfortune, dying soon after his arrival, I resolved to go the same voyage again; and I embarked in the same vessel with one who was his mate in the former voyage, and had now got the command of the ship. This was the unhappiest voyage that ever man made; for though I did not carry quite £100 of my new gained wealth, so that I had £200 left, and which I lodged with my friend's widow, who was very just to me, yet I fell into terrible misfortunes in this voyage; and the first was this—namely, our ship, making her course towards the Canary Islands, or rather between those islands and the African shore, was surprised, in the grey of the morning, by a Moorish rover of Sallee, who gave chase to us with all the sail she could make. We crowded also as much canvas as our yards would spread, or our masts carry, to have got clear; but finding the pirate gained upon us, and would certainly come up with us in a few hours, we prepared to fight; our ship having twelve guns, and the rover eighteen. About three in the afternoon he came up with us, and bringing to, by mistake, just athwart our quarter, instead of athwart our stern, as he intended, we brought eight of our guns to bear on that side, and poured in a broadside upon him, which made him sheer off again, after returning our fire, and pouring in also his small shot, from near two hundred men which he had on board. However, we had not a man touched, all our men keeping close. He prepared to attack us again, and we to defend ourselves; but laying us on board the next time upon our other quarter, he entered sixty men upon our decks, who immediately fell to cutting and hacking the decks and rigging. We plied them with small shot, half-pikes, powder-chests, and such like, and cleared our deck of them twice. However, to cut short this melancholy part of our story, our ship being disabled, and three of our men killed, and eight wounded, we were obliged to yield, and were carried all prisoners into Sallee, a port belonging to the Moors.

The usage I had there was not so dreadful as at first I apprehended: nor was I carried up the country to the emperor's court, as the rest of our men were, but was kept by the captain of the rover, as his proper prize, and made his slave, being young and nimble, and fit for his business. At this surprising change of my circumstances, from a merchant to a miserable slave, I was perfectly overwhelmed; and now I looked back upon my father's prophetic discourse to me, that I should be miserable, and have none to relieve me; which I thought was now so effectually brought to pass, that I could not be worse—that now the hand of Heaven had overtaken me, and I was undone without redemption. But, alas! this was but a taste of the misery I was to go through, as will appear in the sequel of this story.

As my new patron or master had taken me home to his house, so I was in hopes that he would take me with him when he went to sea again, believing that it would be some time or other his fate to be taken by a Spanish or Portugal man-of-war, and that then I should be set at liberty. But this hope of mine was soon taken away; for when he went to sea, he left me on shore to look after his little garden and do the common drudgery of slaves about his house; and when he came home again from his cruise, he ordered me to lie in the cabin, to look after the ship.

Here I meditated nothing but my escape, and what method I might take to effect it; but found no way that had the least probability in it. Nothing presented to make the supposition of it rational; for I had nobody to communicate it to that would embark with me—no fellow-slave, no Englishman, Irishman, or Scotsman there, but myself; so that for two years, though I often pleased myself with the imagination, yet I never had the least encouraging prospect of putting it in practice.

After about two years, an odd circumstance presented itself, which put the old thought of making some attempt for my liberty again in my head: my patron lying at home longer than usual, without fitting out his ship, which, as I heard, was for want of money, he used constantly, once or twice a week, sometimes oftener, if the weather was fair, to take the ship's pinnace, and go out into the road a-fishing; and as he always took me and a young Moresco with him to row the boat, we made him very merry, and I proved very dexterous in catching fish; insomuch that sometimes he would send me with a Moor, one of his kinsmen, and the youth, the Moresco, as they called him, to catch a dish of fish for him.

It happened one time that going a-fishing with him on a calm morning, a fog rose so thick that, though we were not half a league from the shore, we lost sight of it; and rowing we knew not whither, or which way, we laboured all day, and all the next night; and when the morning came, we found we had pulled off to sea, instead of pulling in for the shore, and that we were at least two leagues from the land: however, we got well in again, though with a great deal of labour, and some danger, for the wind began to blow pretty fresh in the morning; but, particularly, we were all very hungry.

But our patron, warned by this disaster, resolved to take more care of himself for the future; and having lying by him the long-boat of our English ship which he had taken, he resolved he would not go a-fishing any more without a compass and some provision; so he ordered the carpenter of his ship, who also was an English slave, to build a little state-room, or cabin, in the middle of the long-boat, like that of a barge, with a place to stand behind it to steer, and haul home the main-sheet; and room before for a hand or two to stand and work the sails. She sailed with what we call a shoulder-of-mutton sail; and the boom jibbed over the top of the cabin, which lay very snug and low, and had in it room for him to lie, with a slave or two, and a table to eat on, with some small lockers to put in some bottles of such liquor as he thought fit to drink, but particularly to hold his bread, rice, and coffee.

We were frequently out with this boat a-fishing; and as I was most dexterous to catch fish for him, he never went without me. It happened one day, that he had appointed to go out in this boat, either for pleasure or for fish, with two or three Moors of some distinction, and for whom he had provided extraordinary; and had therefore sent on board the boat over night a larger store of provisions than usual, and had ordered me to get ready three fusils with powder and shot, which were on board his ship; for that they designed some sport of fowling, as well as fishing.

I got all things ready as he had directed, and waited the next morning with the boat washed clean, her ancient and pendants out, and every thing to accommodate his guests; when by and by my patron came on board alone, and told me his guests had put off going, upon some business that fell out, and ordered me, with the man and boy, as usual, to go out with the boat, and catch them some fish, for that his friends were to sup at his house; he commanded me, too, that as soon as I had got some fish, I should bring it home to his house: all of which I prepared to do.

This moment my former notions of deliverance darted into my thoughts, for now I found I was like to have a little ship at my command; and my master being gone, I prepared to furnish myself, not for fishing business, but for a voyage, though I knew not, neither did I so much as consider, whither I would steer; for any where to get out of that place was my way.

My first contrivance was to make a pretence to speak to this Moor, to get something for our subsistence on board; for I told him we must not presume to eat of our patron's bread. He said, that was true; so he brought a large basket of rusk, or biscuit of their kind, and three jars with fresh water, into the boat. I knew where my patron's case of bottles stood, which it was evident by the make were taken out of, some English prize, and I conveyed them into the boat while the Moor was on shore, as if they had been there before for our master: I conveyed also a great lump of bees'-wax into the boat, which weighed above half a hundred weight, with a parcel of twine or thread, a hatchet, a saw, and a hammer, all which were of great use to us afterwards, especially the wax to make candles. Another trick I tried upon him, which he innocently came into also. His name was Ismael, whom they called Muly, or Moley; so I called to him: "Moley," said I, "our patron's guns are on board the boat; can you not get a little powder and shot? It may be we may kill some alcamies (a fowl like our curlews) for ourselves, for I know he keeps the gunner's stores in the ship." "Yes," says he, "I'll bring some;" and accordingly he brought a great leather pouch, which held about a pound and a half of powder, or rather more, and another with shot, that had five or six pounds, with some bullets, and put all into the boat; at the same time I had found some powder of my master's in the great cabin, with which I filled one of the large bottles in the case, which was almost empty, pouring what was in it into another; and thus furnished with everything needful, we sailed out of the port to fish. The castle, which is at the entrance of the port, knew who we were, and took no notice of us; and we were not above a mile out of the port before we hauled in our sail, and set us down to fish. The wind blew from the north-north-east, which was contrary to my desire; for had it blown southerly, I had been sure to have made the coast of Spain, and at least reached to the bay of Cadiz; but my resolutions were, blow which way it would, I would be gone from that horrid place where I was, and leave the rest to fate.

After we had fished some time, and catched nothing—for when I had fish on my hook I would not pull them up, that he might not see them—I said to the Moor, "This will not do—our master will not be thus served—we must stand farther off." He, thinking no harm, agreed, and being in the head of the boat, set the sails; and as I had the helm, I ran the boat out near a league farther, and then brought her to as if I would fish; when, giving the boy the helm, I stepped forward to where the Moor was, and making as if I stooped for something behind him, I took him by surprise with my arm under his twist, and tossed him clear overboard into the sea; he rose immediately, for he swam like a cork, and called to me, begged to be taken in, told me he would go all over the world with me. He swam so strong after the boat, that he would have reached me very quickly, there being but little wind; upon which I stepped into the cabin, and fetching one of the fowling-pieces, I presented it at him, and told him, I had done him no hurt, and if he would be quiet I would do him none—"But," said I, "you swim well enough to reach to the shore, and the sea is calm—make the best of your way to shore, and I will do you no harm; but if you come near the boat, I'll shoot you through the head, for I am resolved to have my liberty"—so he turned himself about, and swam for the shore, and I make no doubt but he reached it with ease, for he was an excellent swimmer.

I could have been content to have taken this Moor with me, and have drowned the boy, but there was no venturing to trust him. When he was gone, I turned to the boy, whom they called Xury, and said, "Xury, if you will be faithful to me, I'll make you a great man; but if you will not stroke your face to be true to me (that is, swear by Mahomet and his father's beard), I must throw you into the sea, too." The boy smiled in my face, and spoke so innocently, that I could not mistrust him; and swore to be faithful to me, and go all over the world with me.

While I was in view of the Moor that was swimming, I stood out directly to sea with the boat, rather stretching to windward, that they might think me gone towards the Straits' mouth, as indeed any one that had been in their wits must have been supposed to do; for who would have supposed we were sailed on the southward to the truly barbarian coast, where whole nations of negroes were sure to surround us with their canoes, and destroy us; where we could never once go on shore, but we should be devoured by savage beasts, or more merciless savages of human kind?

But as soon as it grew dusk in the evening, I changed my course, and steered directly south and by east, bending my course a little toward the east, that I might keep in with the shore; and having a fair, fresh gale of wind, and a smooth, quiet sea, I made such sail, that I believe by the next day at three o'clock in the afternoon, when I first made the land, I could not be less than one hundred and fifty miles south of Sallee, quite beyond the Emperor of Morocco's dominions, or, indeed, of any other king thereabouts, for we saw no people.

Yet such was the fright I had taken at the Moors, and the dreadful apprehensions I had of falling into their hands, that I would not stop, or go on shore, or come to an anchor, the wind continuing fair, till I had sailed in that manner five days; and then the wind shifting to the southward, I concluded also that if any of our vessels were in chase of me, they also would now give over; so I ventured to make to the coast, and come to an anchor in the mouth of a little river, I knew not what or where—neither what latitude, what country, what nation, nor what river: I neither saw, nor desired to see, any people—the principal thing I wanted was fresh water. We came into this creek in the evening, resolving to swim on shore as soon as it was dark, and discover the country; but as soon as it was quite dark, we heard such dreadful noises of the barking, roaring, and howling of wild creatures, of we knew not what kinds, that the poor boy was ready to die with fear, and begged of me not to go on shore till day. "Well, Xury," said I, "then I won't; but, it may be, we may see men by day, who will be as bad to us as those lions." "Then we give them the shoot gun," says Xury, laughing, "make them run 'way." Such English Xury spoke by conversing among us slaves. However, I was glad to see the boy so cheerful, and I gave him a dram out of our patron's case of bottles, to cheer him up. After all, Xury's advice was good, and I took it; we dropped our little anchor, and lay still all night—I say still, for we slept none—for in two or three hours we saw vast great creatures (we knew not what to call them) of many sorts, come down to the sea-shore, and run into the water, wallowing and washing themselves for the pleasure of cooling themselves; and they made such hideous howlings and yellings, that I never indeed heard the like.

Xury was dreadfully frighted, and indeed so was I, too; but we were both more frighted when we heard one of these mighty creatures come swimming towards our boat. We could not see him, but we might hear him by his blowing, to be a monstrous, huge, and furious beast; Xury said it was a lion, and it might be so for aught I know. Poor Xury cried to me to weigh the anchor, and row away. "No," says I, "Xury, we can slip our cable with a buoy to it, and go to sea; they cannot follow us far." I had no sooner said so, but I perceived the creature (whatever it was) within two oars' length, which something surprised me; however, I immediately stepped to the cabin door, and taking up my gun fired at him; upon which he immediately turned about, and swam to the shore again.

But it was not possible to describe the horrible noises and hideous cries and howlings, that were raised, as well upon the edge of the shore, as higher within the country, upon the noise or report of a gun; a thing I have some reason to believe those creatures had never heard before. This convinced me that there was no going on shore for us in the night upon that coast; and how to venture on shore in the day, was another question, too; for to have fallen into the hands of any of the savages, had been as bad as to have fallen into the paws of lions and tigers; at least, we were equally apprehensive of the danger of it.

Be that as it would, we were obliged to go on shore somewhere or other for water, for we had not a pint left in the boat; when or where to get it was the point. Xury said if I would let him go on shore with one of the jars he would find if there was any water, and bring some to me. I asked him why he would go, why I should not go, and he stay in the boat? The boy answered with so much affection, that made me love him ever after. Says he, "If wild mans come, they eat me, you go away." "Well, Xury," said I, "we will both go, and if the wild mans come, we will kill them; they shall eat neither of us." So I gave Xury a piece of rusk bread to eat, and a dram out of our patron's case of bottles, which I mentioned before; and we hauled the boat in as near the shore as we thought was proper, and waded on shore, carrying nothing but our arms, and two jars for water.

I did not care to go out of sight of the boat, fearing the coming of canoes with savages down the river: but the boy, seeing a low place about a mile up the country, rambled to it; and by and by I saw him come running towards me. I thought he was pursued by some savage, or frighted with some wild beast, and I ran forward towards him to help him; but when I came nearer to him, I saw something hanging over his shoulders, which was a creature that he had shot, like a hare, but different in colour, and longer legs: however, we were very glad of it, and it was very good meat; but the great joy that poor Xury came with, was to tell me he had found good water, and seen no wild mans.

But we found afterwards that we need not take such pains for water, for a little higher up the creek where we were, we found the water fresh when the tide was out, which flows but a little way up; so we filled our jars, and feasted on the hare we had killed, and prepared to go on our way, having seen no footsteps of any human creature in that part of the country.

As I had been one voyage to the coast before, I knew very well that the islands of the Canaries, and the Cape de Verde Islands also, lay not far off from the coast. But as I had no instruments to take an observation to know what latitude we were in, and did not exactly know, or at least not remember, what latitude they were in, I knew not where to look for them, or when to stand off to sea towards them; otherwise I might now easily have found some of these islands. But my hope was, that if I stood along this coast till I came to that part where the English traded, I should find some of their vessels upon their usual design of trade, that would relieve and take us in.

By the best of my calculation, that place where I now was must be that country, which, lying between the Emperor of Morocco's dominions and the negroes, lies waste and uninhabited, except by wild beasts; the negroes having abandoned it, and gone farther south for fear of the Moors; and the Moors not thinking it worth inhabiting, by reason of its barrenness—and, indeed, both forsaking it because of the prodigious numbers of tigers, lions, leopards, and other furious creatures, which harbour there; so that the Moors use it for their hunting only, where they go like an army, two or three thousand men at a time—and, indeed, for near an hundred miles together upon this coast, we saw nothing but a waste uninhabited country by day, and heard nothing but howlings and roaring of wild beasts by night.

Once or twice in the day-time I thought I saw the Pico of Teneriffe, being the high top of the mountain Teneriffe in the Canaries, and had a great mind to venture out, in hopes of reaching thither; but having tried twice, I was forced in again by contrary winds, the sea also going too high for my little vessel; so I resolved to pursue my first design, and keep along the shore.

Several times I was obliged to land for fresh water, after we had left this place; and once, in particular, being early in the morning, we came to an anchor under a little point of land which was pretty high; and the tide beginning to flow, we lay still to go farther in. Xury, whose eyes were more about him than it seems mine were, calls softly to me, and tells me, that we had best go farther off the shore: "For," says he, "look—yonder lies a dreadful monster, on the side of that hillock, fast asleep." I looked where he pointed, and saw a dreadful monster indeed, for it was a terrible great lion that lay on the side of the shore, under the shade of a piece of the hill that hung, as it were, a little over him. "Xury," says I, "you shall go on shore and kill him." Xury looked frighted, and said, "Me kill! he eat me at one mouth!"—one mouthful he meant; however, I said no more to the boy, but bade him lie still, and I took our biggest gun, which was almost musket-bore, and loaded it with a good charge of powder, and with two slugs, and laid it down; then I loaded another gun with two bullets; and the third—for we had three pieces—I loaded with five smaller bullets. I took the best aim I could with the first piece to have shot him into the head, but he lay so with his leg raised a little above his nose, that the slugs hit his leg about the knee and broke the bone. He started up, growling at first, but finding his leg broke, fell down again, and then got up upon three legs, and gave the most hideous roar that ever I heard. I was a little surprised that I had not hit him on the head; however, I took up the second piece immediately, and, though he began to move off, fired again, and shot him into the head, and had the pleasure to see him drop, and make but little noise, but lie struggling for life. Then Xury took heart, and would have me let him go on shore. "Well, go," said I; so the boy jumped into the water, and, taking a little gun in one hand, swam to shore with the other hand, and coming close to the creature, put the muzzle of the piece to his ear, and shot him into the head again, which despatched him quite.

This was game indeed to us, but this was no food; and I was very sorry to lose three charges of powder and shot upon a creature that was good for nothing to us. However, Xury said he would have some of him; so he comes on board, and asked me to give him the hatchet. "For what, Xury?"

said I. "Me cut off his head," said he. However, Xury could not cut off his head, but he cut off a foot, and brought it with him, and it was a monstrous great one.

I bethought myself, however, that perhaps the skin of him might, one way or other, be of some value to us; and I resolved to take off his skin if I could. So Xury and I went to work with him; but Xury was much the better workman at it, for I knew very ill how to do it. Indeed, it took us both up the whole day, but at last we got off the hide of him, and, spreading it on the top of our cabin, the sun effectually dried it in two days' time, and it afterwards served me to lie upon.

* * *

After this stop, we made on to the southward continually for ten or twelve days, living very sparingly on our provisions, which began to abate very much, and going no oftener into the shore than we were obliged to do for fresh water: my design in this was, to make the river Gambia or Senegal, that is to say, any where about the Cape de Verde, where I was in hopes to meet with some European ship; and if I did not, I knew not what course I had to take, but to seek for the islands, or perish there among the negroes. I knew that all the ships from Europe, which sailed either to the coast of Guinea, or to Brazil, or to the East Indies, made this Cape, or those islands; and, in a word, I put the whole of my fortune upon this single point, either that I must meet with some ship, or must perish.

When I had pursued this resolution about ten days longer, as I have said, I began to see that the land was inhabited; and in two or three places, as we sailed by, we saw people stand upon the shore to look at us: we could also perceive they were quite black, and stark naked. I was once inclined to go on shore to them; but Xury was my better counsellor, and said to me, "No go, no go." However, I hauled in nearer the shore that I might talk to them, and I found they ran along the shore by me a good way: I observed they had no weapons in their hands, except one, who had a long slender stick, which Xury said was a lance, and that they would throw them a great way with good aim; so I kept at a distance, but talked with them by signs as well as I could, and particularly made signs for something to eat; they beckoned to me to stop my boat, and they would fetch me some meat. Upon this, I lowered the top of my sail, and lay by, and two of them ran up into the country, and in less than half an hour came back, and brought with them two pieces of dry flesh and some corn, such as is the produce of their country; but we neither knew what the one nor the other was however, we were willing to accept it. But how to come at it was our next dispute, for I was not for venturing on shore to them, and they were as much afraid of us; but they took a safe way for us all, for they brought it to the shore and laid it down, and went and stood a great way off till we fetched it on board, and then came close to us again.

We made signs of thanks to them, for we had nothing to make them amends; but an opportunity offered that very instant to oblige them wonderfully; for while we were lying by the shore, came two mighty creatures, one pursuing the other (as we took it) with great fury from the mountains towards the sea: whether it was the male pursuing the female, or whether they were in sport or in rage, we could not tell, any more than we could tell whether it was usual or strange, but I believe it was the latter; because, in the first place, those ravenous creatures seldom appear but in the night; and, in the second place, we found the people terribly frighted, especially the women. The man that had the lance, or dart, did not fly from them, but the rest did: however, as the two creatures ran directly into the water, they did not seem to offer to fall upon any of the negroes, but plunged themselves into the sea, and swam about as if they had come for their diversion. At last one of them began to come nearer our boat than at first I expected; but I lay ready for him, for I had loaded my gun with all possible expedition, and bade Xury load both the others. As soon as he came fairly within my reach, I fired, and shot him directly into the head: immediately he sank down into the water, but rose instantly, and plunged up and down as if he was struggling for life, and so indeed he was: he immediately made to the shore; but between the wound, which was his mortal hurt, and the strangling of the water, he died just before he reached the shore.

It is impossible to express the astonishment of these poor creatures at the noise and the fire of my gun; some of them were even ready to die for fear, and fell down as dead with the very terror. But when they saw the creature dead, and sunk in the water, and that I made signs to them to come to the shore, they took heart, and came to the shore, and began to search for the creature. I found him by his blood staining the water, and by the help of a rope, which I slung round him, and gave the negroes to haul, they dragged him on shore, and found that it was a most curious leopard, spotted and fine to an admirable degree, and the negroes held up their hands with admiration to think what it was I had killed him with.

The other creature, frighted with the flash of fire and the noise of the gun, swam on shore, and ran up directly to the mountains from whence they came, nor could I at that distance know what it was. I found quickly the negroes were for eating the flesh of this creature, so I was willing to have them take it as a favour from me, which, when I made signs to them that they might take him, they were very thankful for. Immediately they fell to work with him, and though they had no knife, yet, with a sharpened piece of wood, they took off his skin as readily, and much more readily, than we could have done with a knife. They offered me some of the flesh, which I declined, making as if I would give it to them, but made signs for the skin, which they gave me very freely, and brought me a great deal more of their provision, which, though I did not understand, yet I accepted; then I made signs to them for some water, and held out one of my jars to them, turning it bottom upward, to show that it was empty, and that I wanted to have it filled. They called immediately to some of their friends, and there came two women, and brought a great vessel made of earth, and burned, as I suppose, in the sun; this they set down for me, as before, and I sent Xury on shore with my jars, and filled them all three. The women were as stark naked as the men.

I was now furnished with roots and corn, such as it was, and water; and, leaving my friendly negroes, I made forward for about eleven days more, without offering to go near the shore, till I saw the land run out a great length into the sea, at about the distance of four or five leagues before me;

and the sea being very calm, I kept a large offing to make this point: at length, doubling the point, at about two leagues from the land, I saw plainly land on the other side to sea-ward; then I concluded, as it was most certain indeed, that this was the Cape de Verde, and those the islands, called from thence Cape de Verde Islands. However, they were at a great distance, and I could not well tell what I had best to do; for, if I should be taken with a fresh of wind, I might neither reach one nor the other.

In this dilemma, as I was very pensive, I stepped into the cabin and sat me down, Xury having the helm, when, on a sudden, the boy cried out, "Master, master, a ship with a sail!" and the foolish boy was frighted out of his wits, thinking it must needs be some of his master's ships sent to pursue us, when I knew we were gotten far enough out of their reach. I jumped out of the cabin, and immediately saw, not only the ship, but what she was, namely, that it was a Portuguese ship, and, as I thought, was bound to the coast of Guinea for negroes. But when I observed the course she steered, I was soon convinced they were bound some other way, and did not design to come any nearer to the shore; upon which I stretched out to sea as much as I could, resolving to speak with them if possible.

With all the sail I could make, I found I should not be able to come in their way, but that they would be gone by before I could make any signal to them; but after I had crowded to the utmost, and began to despair, they, it seems, saw me by the help of their perspective glasses, and that it was some European boat, which, as they supposed, must belong to some ship that was lost; so they shortened sail to let me come up. I was encouraged with this; and as I had my patron's ancient on board, I made a waft of it to them for a signal of distress, and fired a gun, both which they saw, for they told me they saw the smoke, though they did not hear the gun. Upon these signals they very kindly brought to, and lay by for me, and, in about three hours' time, I came up with them.

They asked me what I was, in Portuguese, and in Spanish, and in French; but I understood none of them: but, at last, a Scots sailor, who was on board, called to me, and I answered him, and told him I was an Englishman—that I had made my escape out of slavery from the Moors at Sallee. They bade me come on board, and very kindly took me in, and all my goods.

It was an inexpressible joy to me, as any one would believe, that I was thus delivered, as I esteemed it, from such a miserable and almost hopeless condition as I was in, and immediately offered all I had to the captain of the ship, as a return for my deliverance; but he generously told me he would take nothing from me, but that all I had should be delivered safe to me when I came to the Brazils. "For," says he, "I have saved your life on no other terms than I would be glad to be saved myself; and it may one time or other be my lot to be taken up in the same condition: besides," said he, "when I carry you to the Brazils, so great a way from your own country, if I should take from you what you have, you will be starved there, and then I only take away that life I have given. No, no, Seignor Inglese," says he, "Mr. Englishman, I will carry you thither in charity, and those things will help you to buy your subsistence there, and your passage home again."

As he was charitable in his proposal, so he was just in the performance to a tittle; for he ordered the seamen, that none should offer to touch anything I had: then he took every thing into his own possession, and gave me back an exact inventory of them, that I might have them; even so much as my earthen jars.

As to my boat, it was a very good one, and that he saw, and told me he would buy it of me for the ship's use, and asked me what I would have for it? I told him he had been so generous in every thing, that I could not offer to make any price of the boat, but left it entirely to him; upon which he told me, he would give me a note of his hand to pay me eighty pieces of eight for it at Brazil; and when it came there, if any one offered to give more, he would make it up: he offered me also sixty pieces of eight more for my boy Xury, which I was loath to take; not that I was not willing to let the captain have him, but I was very loath to sell the poor boy's liberty, who had assisted me so faithfully in procuring my own. However, when I let him know my reason, he owned it to be just, and offered me this medium, that he would give the boy an obligation to set him free in ten years, if he turned Christian. Upon this, and Xury saying he was willing to go to him, I let the captain have him.

We had a very good voyage to the Brazils, and arrived in the Bay de Todos los Santos, or All Saints' Bay, in about twenty-two days after. And now I was once more delivered from the most miserable of all conditions of life; and what to do next with myself I was now to consider.

The generous treatment the captain gave me, I can never enough remember. He would take nothing of me for my passage—gave me twenty ducats for the leopard's skin, and forty for the lion's skin, which I had in my boat, and caused every thing I had in the ship to be punctually delivered me; and what I was willing to sell he bought, such as the case of bottles, two of my guns, and a piece of the lump of bees'-war, for I had made candles of the rest—in a word, I made about two hundred and twenty pieces of eight of all my cargo; and with this stock I went on shore in the Brazils.

I had not been long here, but being recommended to the house of a good honest man like himself, who had an *ingenio*, as they call it—that is, a plantation and a sugar-house—I lived with him some time, and acquainted myself by that means with the manner of their planting and making of sugar; and seeing how well the planters lived, and how they grew rich suddenly, I resolved, if I could get license to settle there, I would turn planter among them; resolving, in the meantime, to find out some way to get my money, which I had left in London, remitted to me. To this purpose, getting a kind of a letter of naturalization, I purchased as much land that was uncured as my money would reach, and formed a plan for my plantation and settlement, and such a one as might be suitable to the stock which I proposed to myself to receive from England.

I had a neighbour, a Portuguese of Lisbon, but born of English parents, whose name was Wells, and in much such circumstances as I was. I call him neighbour, because his plantation lay next to mine, and we went on very sociably together. My stock was but low, as well as his; and we rather planted for food, than any thing else, for about two years. However, we began to increase, and our land began to come into order; so that the third year we planted some tobacco, and made each of us a large piece of ground ready for planting canes in the year to come; but we both wanted help: and now I found, more than before, I had done wrong in parting with my boy Xury.

But, alas! for me to do wrong, that never did right, was no great wonder. I had no remedy but to go on—I was gotten into an employment quite remote to my genius, and directly contrary to the life I delighted in, and for which I forsook my father's house, and broke through all his good advice—nay, I was coming into the very middle station, or upper degree of low life, which my father advised me to before; and which, if I resolved to go on with, I might as well have staid at home, and never have fatigued myself in the world as I had done; and I used often to say to myself, I could have done this as well in England among my friends, as have gone five thousand miles off to do it among strangers and savages in a wilderness, and at such distance, as never to hear from any part of the world that had the least knowledge of me.

In this manner I used to look upon my condition with the utmost regret. I had nobody to converse with, but now and then this neighbour—no work to be done but by the labour of my hands; and I used to say, I lived just like a man cast away upon some desolate island, that had nobody there but himself. But how just has it been, and how should all men reflect, that, when they compare their present conditions with others that are worse, Heaven may oblige them to make the exchange, and be convinced of their former felicity by their experience—I say, how just has it been, that the truly solitary life I reflected on in an island of mere desolation should be my lot, who had so often unjustly compared it with the life which I then led, in which, had I continued, I had, in all probability, been exceeding prosperous and rich.

I was, in some degree, settled in my measures for carrying on the plantation, before my kind friend, the captain of the ship, that took me up at sea, went back; for the ship remained there, in providing his loading, and preparing for his voyage, near three months; when, telling him what little stock I had left behind me in London, he gave me this friendly and sincere advice: "Seignor Inglese," says he, for so he always called me, "if you will give me letters, and a procuration here in form to me, with orders to the person who has your money in London, to send your effects to Lisbon, to such persons as I shall direct, and in such goods as are proper for this country, I will bring you the produce of them, God willing, at my return; but, since human affairs are all subject to changes and disasters, I would have you give orders but for one hundred pounds sterling, which, you say, is half your stock, and let the hazard be run for the first; so that, if it come safe, you may order the rest the same way, and, if it miscarry, you may have the other half to have recourse to for your supply."

This was so wholesome advice, and looked so friendly, that I could not but be convinced it was the best course I could take; so I accordingly prepared letters to the gentlewoman with whom I had left my money, and a procuration to the Portuguese captain, as he desired.

I wrote the English captain's widow a full account of all my adventures, my slavery, escape, and how I had met with the Portugal captain at sea, the humanity of his behaviour, and what condition

I was now in, with all other necessary directions for my supply; and when this honest captain came to Lisbon, he found means, by some of the English merchants there, to send over, not the order only, but a full account of my story, to a merchant at London, who represented it effectually to her; whereupon, she not only delivered the money, but, out of her own pocket, sent the Portugal captain a very handsome present for his humanity and charity to me.

The merchant in London vesting this hundred pounds in English goods, such as the captain had writ for, sent them directly to him at Lisbon, and he brought them all safe to me to the Brazils; among which, without my direction (for I was too young in my business to think of them) he had taken care to have all sorts of tools, iron-work, and utensils necessary for my plantation, and which were of great use to me.

When this cargo arrived, I thought my fortune made, for I was surprised with joy of it; and my good steward, the captain, had laid out the five pounds, which my friend had sent him for a present for himself, to purchase, and bring me over a servant under bond for six years' service, and would not accept of any consideration except a little tobacco, which I would have him accept, being of my own produce.

Neither was this all; but my goods being all English manufactures, such as cloth, stuffs, baize, and things particularly valuable and desirable in the country, I found means to sell them to a very great advantage; so that I may say I had more than four times the value of my first cargo, and was now infinitely beyond my poor neighbour, I mean in the advancement of my plantation; for the first thing I did, I bought me a negro slave, and an European servant also—I mean another besides that one which the captain brought me from Lisbon.

But as abused prosperity is oftentimes made the means of our greatest adversity, so was it with me. I went on the next year with great success in my plantation: I raised fifty great rolls of tobacco on my own ground, more than I had disposed of for necessaries among my neighbors; and these fifty rolls being each of above a hundred weight, were well cured and laid by against the return of the fleet from Lisbon. And now, increasing in business and in wealth, my head began to be full of projects and undertakings beyond my reach; such as are, indeed, often the ruin of the best heads in business.

Had I continued in the station I was now in, I had room for all the happy things to have yet befallen me, for which my father so earnestly recommended a quiet retired life, and of which he had so sensibly described the middle station of life to be full; but other things attended me, and I was still to be the wilful agent of all my own miseries; and particularly to increase my fault and double the reflections upon myself, which in my future sorrows I should have leisure to make, all these miscarriages were procured by my apparent obstinate adhering to my foolish inclination of wandering abroad, and pursuing that inclination, in contradiction to the clearest views of doing myself good in a fair and plain pursuit of those prospects and those measures of life which nature and Providence concurred to present me with, and to make my duty.

As I had done thus in my breaking away from my parents, so I could not be content now, but I must go and leave the happy view I had of being a rich and thriving man in my new plantation, only to pursue a rash and immoderate desire of rising faster than the nature of the thing admitted; and thus I cast myself down again into the deepest gulf of human misery that ever man fell into, or perhaps could be consistent with life and a state of health in the world.

To come, then, by just degrees, to the particulars of this part of my story: you may suppose, that, having now lived almost four years in the Brazils, and beginning to thrive and prosper very well upon my plantation, I had not only learnt the language, but had contracted acquaintance and friendship among my fellow planters, as well as among the merchants at St. Salvador, which was our port; and that in my discourse among them, had frequently given them an account of my two voyages to the coast of Guinea, the manner of trading with the negroes there, and how easy it was to purchase upon the coast, for trifles—such as beads, toys, knives, scissors, hatchets, bits of glass, and the like—not only gold dust, Guinea grains, elephants' teeth, etc., but negroes for the service of the Brazils in great numbers.

They listened always very attentively to my discourses on these heads, but especially to that part which related to buying negroes, which was a trade at that time not only not far entered into, but, as far as it was, had been carried on by the *assientos*, or permission, of the kings of Spain and Portugal, and engrossed in the public, so that few negroes were bought, and those excessively dear.

It happened, being in company with some merchants and planters of my acquaintance, and talking of those things very earnestly, three of them came to me the next morning, and told me they had been musing very much upon what I had discoursed with them of the last night, and they came to make a secret proposal to me; and, after enjoining me to secrecy, told me that they had a mind to fit out a ship to go to Guinea; that they had all plantations as well as I, and were straitened for nothing so much as servants; that as it was a trade could not be carried on, because they could not publicly sell the negroes when they came home, so they desired to make but one voyage, to bring the negroes on shore privately, and divide them among their own plantations; and, in a word, the question was, whether I would go their supercargo in the ship, to manage the trading part upon the coast of Guinea? and they offered me, that I should have my equal share of the negroes, without providing any part of the stock.

This was a fair proposal, it must be confessed, had it been made to any one that had not had a settlement and plantation of his own to look after, which was in a fair way of coming to be very considerable, and with a good stock upon it. But for me, that was thus entered and established, and had nothing to do but go on as I had begun, for three or four years more, and to have sent for the other hundred pounds from England, and who, in that time and with that little addition, could scarce have failed of being worth three or four thousand pounds sterling, and that increasing, too—for me to think of such a voyage, was the most preposterous thing that ever man in such circumstances could be guilty of.

But I, that was born to be my own destroyer, could no more resist the offer than I could restrain my first rambling designs, when my father's good counsel was lost upon me. In a word, I told them I would go with all my heart, if they would undertake to look after my plantation in my absence, and would dispose of it to such as I should direct, if I miscarried. This they all engaged to do, and entered into writings, or covenants, to do so; and I made a formal will, disposing of my plantation and effects in case of my death, making the captain of the ship that had saved my life as before, my universal heir, but obliging him to dispose of my effects as I had directed in my will, one half of the produce being to himself, and the other to be shipped to England.

In short, I took all possible caution to preserve my effects, and keep up my plantation; had I used half as much prudence to have looked into my own interest, and have made a judgment of what I ought to have done, and not to have done, I had certainly never gone away from so prosperous an undertaking, leaving all the probable views of a thriving circumstance, and gone upon a voyage to sea, attended with all its common hazards; to say nothing of the reasons I had to expect particular misfortunes to myself.

But I was hurried on, and obeyed blindly the dictates of my fancy, rather than my reason: and accordingly, the ship being fitted out, and the cargo furnished, and all things done as by agreement by my partners in the voyage, I went on board in an evil hour again, the 1st of September 1659, being the same day eight years that I went from my father and mother at Hull, in order to act the rebel to their authority, and the fool to my own interest.

Our ship was about one hundred and twenty tons burden, carried six guns, and fourteen men, besides the master, his boy, and myself; we had on board no large cargo of goods, except of such toys as were fit for our trade with the negroes, such as beads, bits of glass, shells, and odd trifles, especially little looking-glasses, knives, scissors, hatchets, and the like.

The same day I went on board we set sail, standing away to the northward upon our own coast, with design to stretch over for the African coast, when they came about ten or twelve degrees of northern latitude, which it seems, was the manner of their course in those days. We had very good weather, only excessively hot, all the way upon our own coast, till we came to the height of Cape St. Augustino, from whence, keeping farther off at sea, we lost sight of land, and steered as if we were bound for the isle Fernando de Noronha, holding our course north-east by north, and leaving those isles on the east. In this course we passed the Line in about twelve days' time, and were, by our last observation, in seven degrees twenty-two minutes northern latitude, when a violent tornado, or hurricane, took us quite out of our knowledge: it began from the south-east, came about to the north-west, and then settled into the northeast; from whence it blew in such a terrible manner, that for twelve days together we could do nothing but drive, and, scudding away before it, let it carry us whither ever fate and the fury of the winds directed; and during those twelve days, I need not say that I expected every day to be swallowed up, nor, indeed, did any in the ship expect to save their lives.

In this distress, we had, besides the terror of the storm, one of our men dead of the calenture, and one man and the boy washed overboard. About the twelfth day, the weather abating a little, the master made an observation as well as he could, and found that he was in about eleven degrees north latitude, but that he was twenty-two degrees of longitude difference west from Cape St. Augustino; so that he found he was gotten upon the coast of Guinea, or the north part of Brazil, beyond the river Amazons, toward that of the river Oroonoque, commonly called the Great River, and began to consult with me what course he should take; for the ship was leaky, and very much disabled, and he was for going directly back to the coast of Brazil.

I was positively against that, and, looking over the charts of the sea-coasts of America with him, we concluded there was no inhabited country for us to have recourse to, till we came within the circle of the Caribbee Islands; and therefore resolved to stand away for Barbadoes, which, by keeping off at sea, to avoid the indraft of the bay or gulf of Mexico, we might easily perform, as we hoped, in about fifteen days' sail: whereas we could not possibly make our voyage to the coast of Africa, without some assistance, both to our ship and ourselves.

With this design we changed our course, and steered away north-west by west, in order to reach some of our English islands, where I hoped for relief: but our voyage was otherwise determined; for, being in the latitude of twelve degrees, eighteen minutes, a second storm came upon us, which carried us away with the same impetuosity westward, and drove us so out of the very way of all human commerce, that, had all our lives been saved as to the sea, we were rather in danger of being devoured by savages than ever returning to our own country.

In this distress, the wind still blowing very hard, one of our men, early in the morning, cried out, "Land!" and we had no sooner run out of the cabin to look out, in hopes of seeing whereabouts in the world we were, but the ship struck upon a sand, and, in a moment, her motion being so stopped, the sea broke over her in such a manner that we expected we should all have perished immediately; and we were immediately driven into our close quarters, to shelter us from the very foam and spray of the sea.

It is not easy for any one, who has not been in the like condition, to describe or conceive the consternation of men in such circumstances: we knew nothing where we were, or upon what land it was we were driven—whether an island or the main, whether inhabited or not inhabited; and as the rage of the wind was still great, though rather less than at first, we could not so much as hope to have the ship hold many minutes without breaking in pieces, unless the wind, by a kind of miracle, should turn immediately about. In a word, we sat looking one upon another, and expecting death every moment, and every man acting accordingly, as preparing for another world; for there was little or nothing more for us to do in, this: that which was our present comfort, and all the comfort we had, was, that, contrary to our expectation, the ship did not break yet, and that the master said the wind began to abate.

Now, though we thought that the wind did a little abate, yet, the ship having thus struck upon the sand, and sticking too fast for us to expect her getting off, we were in a dreadful condition indeed, and had nothing to do but to think of saving our lives as well as we could. We had a boat at our stern just before the storm; but she was first staved by dashing against the ship's rudder, and, in the next place, she broke away, and either sunk or was driven off to sea; so there was no hope from her. We had another boat on board, but how to get her off into the sea was a doubtful thing; however, there was no room to debate, for we fancied the ship would break in pieces every minute, and some told us she was actually broken already.

In this distress the mate of our vessel lays hold of the boat, and, with the help of the rest of the men, they got her slung over the ship's side, and getting all into her, let go, and committed ourselves, being eleven in number, to God's mercy and the wild sea; for though the storm was abated considerably, yet the sea went dreadfully high upon the shore, and might well be called *den wild zee*, as the Dutch call the sea in a storm.

And now our case was very dismal indeed; for we all saw plainly, that the sea went so high that the boat could not live, and that we should be inevitably drowned. As to making sail, we had none, nor, if we had, could we have done any thing with it; so we worked at the oar towards the land, though with heavy hearts, like men going to execution; for we all knew, that when the boat came nearer the shore, she would be dashed in a thousand pieces by the breach of the sea. However, we committed our souls to God in the most earnest manner; and the wind driving us towards the shore, we hastened our destruction with our own hands, pulling as well as we could towards land.

What the shore was, whether rock or sand, whether steep or shoal, we knew not; the only hope that could rationally give us the least shadow of expectation was if we might happen into some bay or gulf, or the mouth of some river, where, by great chance, we might have run our boat in, or got under the lee of the land, and perhaps made smooth water. But there was nothing of this appeared; but, as we made nearer and nearer the shore, the land looked more frightful than the sea.

After we had rowed, or rather driven, about a league and a half, as we reckoned it, a raging wave, mountain-like, came rolling astern of us, and plainly bade us expect a watery grave. In a word, it took us with such a fury, that it overset the boat at once; and, separating us as well from the boat as from one another, gave us not time hardly to say "Oh God!" for we were all swallowed up in a moment.

Nothing can describe the confusion of thought which I felt when I sank into the water; for though I swam very well, yet I could not deliver myself from the waves so as to draw breath, till that wave having driven me, or rather carried me, a vast way on towards the shore, and, having spent itself, went back, and left me upon the land almost dry, but half dead with the water I took in. I had so much presence of mind, as well as breath left, that, seeing myself nearer the mainland than I expected, I got upon my feet, and endeavoured to make on towards the land as fast as I could, before another wave should return and take me up again. But I soon found it was impossible to avoid it; for I saw the sea come after me as high as a great hill, and as furious as an enemy, which I had no means or strength to contend with—my business was to hold my breath, and raise myself upon the water, if I could; and so, by swimming, to preserve my breathing, and pilot myself towards the shore, if possible—my greatest concern now being, that the sea, as it would carry me a great way towards the shore when it came on, might not carry me back again with it when it gave back towards the sea.

The wave that came upon me again, buried me at once twenty or thirty feet deep in its own body; and I could feel myself carried with a mighty force and swiftness towards the shore a very great way; but I held my breath, and assisted myself to swim still forward with all my might. I was ready to burst with holding my breath, when, as I felt myself rising up, so, to my immediate relief, I found my head and hands shoot out above the surface of the water; and though it was not two seconds of time that I could keep myself so, yet it relieved me greatly, gave me breath, and new courage. I was covered again with water a good while, but not so long but I held it out, and, finding the water had spent itself, and began to return, I struck forward against the return of the waves, and felt ground again with my feet. I stood still a few moments to recover breath, and till the water went from me, and then took to my heels, and ran with what strength I had farther towards the shore. But neither would this deliver me from the fury of the sea, which came pouring in after me again; and twice more I was lifted up by the waves, and carried forwards as before, the shore being very flat.

The last time of these two had well near been fatal to me; for the sea, having hurried me along as before, landed me, or rather dashed me, against a piece of a rock, and that with such force as it left me senseless, and indeed helpless, as to my own deliverance; for the blow taking my side and breast, beat the breath, as it were, quite out of my body, and had it returned again immediately, I must have been strangled in the water; but I recovered a little before the return of the waves, and, seeing I should be covered again with the water, I resolved to hold fast by a piece of the rock, and so to hold my breath, if possible, till the wave went back. Now, as the waves were not so high as at first, being near land, I held my hold till the wave abated, and then fetched another run, which brought me so near the shore, that the next wave, though it went over me, yet did not so swallow me up as to carry me away; and the next run I took I got to the mainland, where, to my great comfort, I clambered up the clifts of the shore, and sat me down upon the grass, free from danger, and quite out of the reach of the water.

I was now landed, and safe on shore, and began to look up and thank God that my life was saved, in a case wherein there was, some minutes before, scarce any room to hope. I believe it is impossible to express to the life what the ecstasies and transports of the soul are when it is so saved, as I may say, out of the very grave; and I do not wonder, now, at that custom, namely, that when a malefactor, who has the halter about his neck, is tied up, and just going to be turned off, and has a reprieve brought to him—I say, I do not wonder that they bring a surgeon with it, to let him blood that very moment they tell him of it, that the surprise may not drive the animal spirits from the heart, and overwhelm him:

For Sudden Joys, Like Griefs, Confound at First.

I walked about on the shore, lifting up my hands, and my whole being, as I may say, wrapt up in the contemplation of my deliverance, making a thousand gestures and motions which I cannot describe—reflecting upon all my comrades that were drowned, and that there should not be one soul saved but myself—for, as for them, I never saw them afterwards, or any sign of them, except three of their hats, one cap, and two shoes that were not fellows.

I cast my eyes to the stranded vessel, when, the breach and froth of the sea being so big, I could hardly see it, it lay so far off, and considered, Lord! how was it possible I could get on shore?

After I had solaced my mind with the comfortable part of my condition, I began to look round me, to see what kind of place I was in, and what was next to be done; and I soon found my comforts abate, and that in a word, I had a dreadful deliverance: for I was wet, had no clothes to shift me, nor any thing either to eat or drink to comfort me; neither did I see any prospect before me but that of perishing with hunger, or being devoured by wild beasts; and that which was particularly afflicting to me was, that I had no weapon either to hunt and kill any creature for my sustenance, or to defend myself against any other creature that might desire to kill me for theirs—in a word, I had nothing about me but a knife, a tobacco-pipe, and a little tobacco in a box; this was all my provision, and this threw me into terrible agonies of mind, that, for a while, I ran about like a madman. Night coming upon me, I began, with a heavy heart, to consider what would be my lot if there were any ravenous beasts in that country, seeing at night they always come abroad for their prey.

All the remedy that offered to my thoughts at that time was, to get up into a thick bushy tree like a fir, but thorny, which grew near me, and where I resolved to sit all night, and consider the next day what death I should die, for as yet I saw no prospect of life. I walked about a furlong from the shore to see if I could find any fresh water to drink, which I did, to my great joy; and having drunk, and put a little tobacco in my mouth to prevent hunger, I went to the tree, and getting up into it, endeavoured to place myself so as that if I should sleep I might not fall; and having cut me a short stick, like a truncheon, for my defence, I took up my lodging; and, having been excessively fatigued, I fell fast asleep, and slept as comfortably as, I believe, few could have done in my condition, and found myself the most refreshed with it that I think I ever was on such an occasion.

The Open Boat

*A Tale Intended to be After the Fact. Being the Experience
of Four Men Sunk From the Steamer Commodore*

STEPHEN CRANE

I

None of them knew the color of the sky. Their eyes glanced level, and were fastened upon the waves that swept toward them. These waves were of the hue of slate, save for the tops, which were of foaming white, and all of the men knew the colors of the sea. The horizon narrowed and widened, and dipped and rose, and at all times its edge was jagged with waves that seemed thrust up in points like rocks.

Many a man ought to have a bath-tub larger than the boat which here rode upon the sea. These waves were most wrongfully and barbarously abrupt and tall, and each froth-top was a problem in small boat navigation.

The cook squatted in the bottom and looked with both eyes at the six inches of gunwale which separated him from the ocean. His sleeves were rolled over his fat forearms, and the two flaps of his unbuttoned vest dangled as he bent to bail out the boat. Often he said: "Gawd! That was a narrow clip." As he remarked it he invariably gazed eastward over the broken sea.

The oiler, steering with one of the two oars in the boat, sometimes raised himself suddenly to keep clear of water that swirled in over the stern. It was a thin little oar and it seemed often ready to snap.

The correspondent, pulling at the other oar, watched the waves and wondered why he was there.

The injured captain, lying in the bow, was at this time buried in that profound dejection and indifference which comes, temporarily at least, to even the bravest and most enduring when, willy nilly, the firm fails, the army loses, the ship goes down. The mind of the master of a vessel is rooted deep in the timbers of her, though he command for a day or a decade, and this captain had on him the stern impression of a scene in the grays of dawn of seven turned faces, and later a stump of a top-mast with a white ball on it that slashed to and fro at the waves, went low and lower, and down. Thereafter there was something strange in his voice. Although steady, it was deep with mourning, and of a quality beyond oration or tears.

"Keep 'er a little more south, Billie," said he.

" 'A little more south,' sir," said the oiler in the stern.

A seat in this boat was not unlike a seat upon a bucking broncho, and, by the same token, a broncho is not much smaller. The craft pranced and reared, and plunged like an animal. As each wave came, and she rose for it, she seemed like a horse making at a fence outrageously high. The manner of her scramble over these walls of water is a mystic thing, and, moreover, at the top of them were ordinarily these problems in white water, the foam racing down from the summit of each wave, requiring a new leap, and a leap from the air. Then, after scornfully bumping a crest, she would slide, and race, and splash down a long incline and arrive bobbing and nodding in front of the next menace.

A singular disadvantage of the sea lies in the fact that after successfully surmounting one wave you discover that there is another behind it just as important and just as nervously anxious to do something effective in the way of swamping boats. In a ten-foot dingey one can get an idea of the resources of the sea in the line of waves that is not probable to the average experience, which is never at sea in a dingey. As each slaty wall of water approached, it shut all else from the view of the men in the boat, and it was not difficult to imagine that this particular wave was the final outburst of the ocean, the last effort of the grim water.

There was a terrible grace in the move of the waves, and they came in silence, save for the snarling of the crests.

In the wan light, the faces of the men must have been gray. Their eyes must have glinted in strange ways as they gazed steadily astern. Viewed from a balcony, the whole thing would doubtlessly have been weirdly picturesque. But the men in the boat had no time to see it, and if they had had leisure there were other things to occupy their minds. The sun swung steadily up the sky, and they knew it was broad day because the color of the sea changed from slate to emerald-green, streaked with amber lights, and the foam was like tumbling snow. The process of the breaking day was unknown to them. They were aware only of this effect upon the color of the waves that rolled toward them.

In disjointed sentences the cook and the correspondent argued as to the difference between a life-saving station and a house of refuge. The cook had said: "There's a house of refuge just north of the Mosquito Inlet Light, and as soon as they see us, they'll come off in their boat and pick us up."

"As soon as who see us?" said the correspondent.

"The crew," said the cook.

"Houses of refuge don't have crews," said the correspondent. "As I understand them, they are only places where clothes and grub are stored for the benefit of shipwrecked people. They don't carry crews."

"Oh, yes, they do," said the cook.

"No, they don't," said the correspondent.

"Well, we're not there yet, anyhow," said the oiler, in the stern.

"Well," said the cook, "perhaps it's not a house of refuge that I'm thinking of as being near Mosquito Inlet Light. Perhaps it's a life-saving station."

"We're not there yet," said the oiler, in the stern.

II

As the boat bounced from the top of each wave, the wind tore through the hair of the hatless men, and as the craft plopped her stern down again the spray slashed past them. The crest of each of these waves was a hill, from the top of which the men surveyed, for a moment, a broad tumultuous expanse; shining and wind-riven. It was probably splendid. It was probably glorious, this play of the free sea, wild with lights of emerald and white and amber.

"Bully good thing it's an on-shore wind," said the cook. "If not, where would we be? Wouldn't have a show."

"That's right," said the correspondent.

The busy oiler nodded his assent.

Then the captain, in the bow, chuckled in a way that expressed humor, contempt, tragedy, all in one. "Do you think we've got much of a show, now, boys?" said he.

Whereupon the three were silent, save for a trifle of hemming and hawing. To express any particular optimism at this time they felt to be childish and stupid, but they all doubtless possessed this sense of the situation in their mind. A young man thinks doggedly at such times. On the other hand, the ethics of their condition was decidedly against any open suggestion of hopelessness. So they were silent.

"Oh, well," said the captain, soothing his children, "we'll get ashore all right."

But there was that in his tone which made them think, so the oiler quoth: "Yes! If this wind holds!"

The cook was bailing: "Yes! If we don't catch hell in the surf."

Canton flannel gulls flew near and far. Sometimes they sat down on the sea, near patches of brown sea-weed that rolled over the waves with a movement like carpets on line in a gale. The birds sat comfortably in groups, and they were envied by some in the dingey, for the wrath of the sea was no more to them than it was to a covey of prairie chickens a thousand miles inland. Often they came very close and stared at the men with black bead-like eyes. At these times they were uncanny and sinister in their unblinking scrutiny, and the men hooted angrily at them, telling them to be gone. One came, and evidently decided to alight on the top of the captain's head. The bird flew parallel to the boat and did not circle, but made short sidelong jumps in the air in chicken-fashion. His black eyes were wistfully fixed upon the captain's head. "Ugly brute," said the oiler to the bird. "You look as if you were made with a jack-knife." The cook and the correspondent swore darkly at the creature. The captain naturally wished to knock it away with the end of the heavy painter, but he did not dare do it, because anything resembling an emphatic gesture would have capsized this freighted boat, and so with his open hand, the captain gently and carefully waved the gull away. After it had been discouraged from the pursuit the captain breathed easier on account of his hair, and others breathed easier because the bird struck their minds at this time as being somehow grewsome and ominous.

In the meantime the oiler and the correspondent rowed. And also they rowed.

They sat together in the same seat, and each rowed an oar. Then the oiler took both oars; then the correspondent took both oars; then the oiler; then the correspondent. They rowed and they rowed. The very ticklish part of the business was when the time came for the reclining one in the stern to take his turn at the oars. By the very last star of truth, it is easier to steal eggs from under a hen than it was to change seats in the dingey. First the man in the stern slid his hand along the thwart and moved with care, as if he were of Sevres. Then the man in the rowing seat slid his hand along the other thwart. It was all done with the most extraordinary care. As the two sidled past each other, the whole party kept watchful eyes on the coming wave, and the captain cried: "Look out now! Steady there!"

The brown mats of sea-weed that appeared from time to time were like islands, bits of earth. They were travelling, apparently, neither one way nor the other. They were, to all intents stationary. They informed the men in the boat that it was making progress slowly toward the land.

The captain, rearing cautiously in the bow, after the dingey soared on a great swell, said that he had seen the lighthouse at Mosquito Inlet. Presently the cook remarked that he had seen it. The correspondent was at the oars, then, and for some reason he too wished to look at the lighthouse but his back was toward the far shore and the waves were important, and for some time he could not seize an opportunity to turn his head. But at last there came a wave more gentle than the others, and when at the crest of it he swiftly scoured the western horizon.

"See it?" said the captain.

"No," said the correspondent, slowly, "I didn't see anything."

"Look again," said the captain. He pointed. "It's exactly in that direction."

At the top of another wave, the correspondent did as he was bid, and this time his eyes chanced on a small still thing on the edge of the swaying horizon. It was precisely like the point of a pin. It took an anxious eye to find a lighthouse so tiny.

"Think we'll make it, captain?"

"If this wind holds and the boat don't swamp, we can't do much else," said the captain.

The little boat, lifted by each towering sea, and splashed viciously by the crests, made progress that in the absence of sea-weed was not apparent to those in her. She seemed just a wee thing wallowing, miraculously, top-up, at the mercy of five oceans. Occasionally, a great spread of water, like white flames, swarmed into her.

"Bail her, cook," said the captain, serenely.

"All right, captain," said the cheerful cook.

III

It would be difficult to describe the subtle brotherhood of men that was here established on the seas. No one said that it was so. No one mentioned it. But it dwelt in the boat, and each man felt it warm him. They were a captain, an oiler, a cook, and a correspondent, and they were friends, friends in a more curiously iron-bound degree than may be common. The hurt captain, lying against the water-jar in the bow, spoke always in a low voice and calmly, but he could never command a more ready and swiftly obedient crew than the motley three of the dingey. It was more than a mere recognition of what was best for the common safety. There was surely in it a quality that was personal and heartfelt. And after this devotion to the commander of the boat there was this comradeship that the correspondent, for instance, who had been taught to be cynical of men, knew even at the time was the best experience of his life. But no one said that it was so. No one mentioned it.

"I wish we had a sail," remarked the captain. "We might try my overcoat on the end of an oar and give you two boys a chance to rest." So the cook and the correspondent held the mast and spread wide the overcoat. The oiler steered, and the little boat made good way with her new rig. Sometimes the oiler had to scull sharply to keep a sea from breaking into the boat, but otherwise sailing was a success.

Meanwhile the light-house had been growing slowly larger. It had now almost assumed color, and appeared like a little gray shadow on the sky. The man at the oars could not be prevented from turning his head rather often to try for a glimpse of this little gray shadow.

At last, from the top of each wave the men in the tossing boat could see land. Even as the light-house was an upright shadow on the sky, this land seemed but a long black shadow on the sea. It certainly was thinner than paper. "We must be about opposite New Smyrna," said the cook, who had coasted this shore often in schooners. "Captain, by the way, I believe they abandoned that life-saving station there about a year ago."

"Did they?" said the captain.

The wind slowly died away. The cook and the correspondent were not now obliged to slave in order to hold high the oar. But the waves continued their old impetuous swooping at the dingey, and the little craft, no longer under way, struggled woundily over them. The oiler or the correspondent took the oars again.

Shipwrecks are apropos of nothing. If men could only train for them and have them occur when the men had reached pink condition, there would be less drowning at sea. Of the four in the dingey none had slept any time worth mentioning for two days and two nights previous to embarking in the dingey, and in the excitement of clambering about the deck of a foundering ship they had also forgotten to eat heartily.

For these reasons, and for others, neither the oiler nor the correspondent was fond of rowing at this time. The correspondent wondered ingenuously how in the name of all that was sane could there be people who thought it amusing to row a boat. It was not an amusement; it was a diabolical punishment, and even a genius of mental aberrations could never conclude that it was anything but a horror to the muscles and a crime against the back. He mentioned to the boat in general how the amusement of rowing struck him, and the weary-faced oiler smiled in full sympathy. Previously to the foundering, by the way, the oiler had worked double-watch in the engine-room of the ship.

"Take her easy, now, boys," said the captain. "Don't spend yourselves. If we have to run a surf you'll need all your strength, because we'll sure have to swim for it. Take your time."

Slowly the land arose from the sea. From a black line it became a line of black and a line of white, trees, and sand. Finally, the captain said that he could make out a house on the shore. "That's the house of refuge, sure," said the cook. "They'll see us before long, and come out after us."

The distant light-house reared high. "The keeper ought to be able to make us out now, if he's looking through a glass," said the captain. "He'll notify the life-saving people."

"None of those other boats could have got ashore to give word of the wreck," said the oiler, in a low voice. "Else the life-boat would be out hunting us."

Slowly and beautifully the land loomed out of the sea. The wind came again. It had veered from the northeast to the southeast. Finally, a new sound struck the ears of the men in the boat. It was the low thunder of the surf on the shore. "We'll never be able to make the light-house now," said the captain. "Swing her head a little more north, Billie," said the captain.

"'A little more north,' sir," said the oiler.

Whereupon the little boat turned her nose once more down the wind, and all but the oarsman watched the shore grow. Under the influence of this expansion doubt and direful apprehension was leaving the minds of the men. The management of the boat was still most absorbing, but it could not prevent a quiet cheerfulness. In an hour, perhaps, they would be ashore.

Their back-bones had become thoroughly used to balancing in the boat and they now rode this wild colt of a dingey like circus men. The correspondent thought that he had been drenched to the skin, but happening to feel in the top pocket of his coat, he found therein eight cigars. Four of them were soaked with sea-water; four were perfectly scatheless. After a search, somebody produced three dry matches, and thereupon the four waifs rode in their little boat, and with an assurance of an impending rescue shining in their eyes, puffed at the big cigars and judged well and ill of all men. Everybody took a drink of water.

IV

"Cook," remarked the captain, "there don't seem to be any signs of life about your house of refuge."

"No," replied the cook. "Funny they don't see us!"

A broad stretch of lowly coast lay before the eyes of the men. It was of low dunes topped with dark vegetation. The roar of the surf was plain, and sometimes they could see the white lip of a wave as it spun up the beach. A tiny house was blocked out black upon the sky. Southward, the slim light-house lifted its little gray length.

Tide, wind, and waves were swinging the dingey northward. "Funny they don't see us," said the men.

The surf's roar was here dulled, but its tone was, nevertheless, thunderous and mighty. As the boat swam over the great rollers, the men sat listening to this roar. "We'll swamp sure," said everybody.

It is fair to say here that there was not a life-saving station within twenty miles in either direction, but the men did not know this fact and in consequence they made dark and opprobrious remarks concerning the eyesight of the nation's life-savers. Four scowling men sat in the dingey and surpassed records in the invention of epithets.

"Funny they don't see us."

The light-heartedness of a former time had completely faded. To their sharpened minds it was easy to conjure pictures of all kinds of incompetency and blindness and indeed, cowardice. There was the shore of the populous land, and it was bitter and bitter to them that from it came no sign.

"Well," said the captain, ultimately, "I suppose we'll have to make a try for ourselves. If we stay out here too long, we'll none of us have strength left to swim after the boat swamps."

And so the oiler, who was at the oars, turned the boat straight for the shore. There was a sudden tightening of muscles. There was some thinking.

"If we don't all get ashore—" said the captain. "If we don't all get ashore, I suppose you fellows know where to send news of my finish?"

They then briefly exchanged some addresses and admonitions. As for the reflections of the men, there was a great deal of rage in them. Perchance they might be formulated thus: "If I am going to be drowned—if I am going to be drowned—if I am going to be drowned, why, in the name of the seven mad gods who rule the sea, was I allowed to come thus far and contemplate sand and trees? Was I brought here merely to have my nose dragged away as I was about to nibble the sacred cheese of life? It is preposterous. If this old ninny-woman, Fate, cannot do better than this, she should be deprived of the management of men's fortunes. She is an old hen who knows not her intention. If she has decided to drown me, why did she not do it in the beginning and save me all this trouble. The whole affair is absurd. . . . But, no, she cannot mean to drown me. She dare not drown me. She cannot drown me. Not after all this work." Afterward the man might have had an impulse to shake his fist at the clouds: "Just you drown me, now, and then hear what I call you!"

The billows that came at this time were more formidable. They seemed always just about to break and roll over the little boat in a turmoil of foam. There was a preparatory and long growl in the speech of them. No mind unused to the sea would have concluded that the dingey could ascend these sheer heights in time. The shore was still afar. The oiler was a wily surfman. "Boys," he said, swiftly, "she won't live three minutes more and we're too far out to swim. Shall I take her to sea again, captain?"

"Yes! Go ahead!" said the captain.

This oiler, by a series of quick miracles, and fast and steady oarsmanship, turned the boat in the middle of the surf and took her safely to sea again.

There was a considerable silence as the boat bumped over the furrowed sea to deeper water. Then somebody in gloom spoke. "Well, anyhow, they must have seen us from the shore by now."

The gulls went in slanting flight up the wind toward the gray desolate east. A squall, marked by dingy clouds, and clouds brick-red, like smoke from a burning building, appeared from the southeast.

"What do you think of those life-saving people? Ain't they peaches?"

"Funny they haven't seen us."

"Maybe they think we're out here for sport! Maybe they think we're fishin'. Maybe they think we're damned fools."

It was a long afternoon. A changed tide tried to force them southward, but wind and wave said northward. Far ahead, where coast-line, sea, and sky formed their mighty angle, there were little dots which seemed to indicate a city on the shore.

"St. Augustine?"

The captain shook his head. "Too near Mosquito Inlet."

And the oiler rowed, and then the correspondent rowed. Then the oiler rowed. It was a weary business. The human back can become the seat of more aches and pains than are registered in books for the composite anatomy of a regiment. It is a limited area, but it can become the theatre of innumerable muscular conflicts, tangles, wrenches, knots, and other comforts.

"Did you ever like to row, Billie?" asked the correspondent.

"No," said the oiler. "Hang it."

When one exchanged the rowing-seat for a place in the bottom of the boat, he suffered a bodily depression that caused him to be careless of everything save an obligation to wiggle one finger. There was cold sea-water swashing to and fro in the boat, and he lay in it. His head, pillowed on a thwart, was within an inch of the swirl of a wave crest, and sometimes a particularly obstreperous sea came in-board and drenched him once more. But these matters did not annoy him. It is almost certain that if the boat had capsized he would have tumbled comfortably out upon the ocean as if he felt sure it was a great soft mattress.

"Look! There's a man on the shore!"

"Where?"

"There! See 'im? See 'im?"

"Yes, sure! He's walking along."

"Now he's stopped. Look! He's facing us!"

"He's waving at us!"

"So he is! By thunder!"

"Ah, now, we're all right! Now we're all right! There'll be a boat out here for us in half an hour."

"He's going on. He's running. He's going up to that house there."

The remote beach seemed lower than the sea, and it required a searching glance to discern the little black figure. The captain saw a floating stick and they rowed to it. A bath-towel was by some weird chance in the boat, and, tying this on the stick, the captain waved it. The oarsman did not dare turn his head, so he was obliged to ask questions.

"What's he doing now?"

"He's standing still again. He's looking, I think. . . . There he goes again. Toward the house. . . . Now he's stopped again."

"Is he waving at us?"

"No, not now! he was, though."

"Look! There comes another man!"

"He's running."

"Look at him go, would you."

"Why, he's on a bicycle. Now he's met the other man. They're both waving at us. Look!"

"There comes something up the beach."

"What the devil is that thing?"

"Why, it looks like a boat."

"Why, certainly it's a boat."

"No, it's on wheels."

"Yes, so it is. Well, that must be the life-boat. They drag them along shore on a wagon."

"That's the life-boat, sure."

"No, by——, it's—it's an omnibus."

"I tell you it's a life-boat."

"It is not! It's an omnibus. I can see it plain. See? One of these big hotel omnibuses."

"By thunder, you're right. It's an omnibus, sure as fate. What do you suppose they are doing with an omnibus? Maybe they are going around collecting the life-crew, hey?"

"That's it, likely. Look! There's a fellow waving a little black flag. He's standing on the steps of the omnibus.

There come those other two fellows. Now they're all talking together. Look at the fellow with the flag. Maybe he ain't waving it."

"That ain't a flag, is it? That's his coat. Why, certainly, that's his coat."

"So it is. It's his coat. He's taken it off and is waving it around his head. But would you look at him swing it."

"Oh, say, there isn't any life-saving station there. That's just a winter resort hotel omnibus that has brought over some of the boarders to see us drown."

"What's that idiot with the coat mean? What's he signaling, anyhow?"

"It looks as if he were trying to tell us to go north. There must be a life-saving station up there."

"No! He thinks we're fishing. Just giving us a merry hand. See? Ah, there, Willie."

"Well, I wish I could make something out of those signals. What do you suppose he means?"

"He don't mean anything. He's just playing."

"Well, if he'd just signal us to try the surf again, or to go to sea and wait, or go north, or go south, or go to hell — there would be some reason in it. But look at him. He just stands there and keeps his coat revolving like a wheel. The ass!"

"There come more people."

"Now there's quite a mob. Look! Isn't that a boat?"

"Where? Oh, I see where you mean. No, that's no boat."

"That fellow is still waving his coat."

"He must think we like to see him do that. Why don't he quit it. It don't mean anything."

"I don't know. I think he is trying to make us go north. It must be that there's a life-saving station there somewhere."

"Say, he ain't tired yet. Look at 'im wave."

"Wonder how long he can keep that up. He's been revolving his coat ever since he caught sight of us. He's an idiot. Why aren't they getting men to bring a boat out. A fishing boat—one of those big yawls—could come out here all right. Why don't he do something?"

"Oh, it's all right, now."

"They'll have a boat out here for us in less than no time, now that they've seen us."

A faint yellow tone came into the sky over the low land. The shadows on the sea slowly deepened. The wind bore coldness with it, and the men began to shiver.

"Holy smoke!" said one, allowing his voice to express his impious mood, "if we keep on monkeying out here! If we've got to flounder out here all night!"

"Oh, we'll never have to stay here all night! Don't you worry. They've seen us now, and it won't be long before they'll come chasing out after us."

The shore grew dusky. The man waving a coat blended gradually into this gloom, and it swallowed in the same manner the omnibus and the group of people. The spray, when it dashed uproariously over the side, made the voyagers shrink and swear like men who were being branded.

"I'd like to catch the chump who waved the coat. I feel like soaking him one, just for luck."

"Why? What did he do?"

"Oh, nothing, but then he seemed so damned cheerful."

In the meantime the oiler rowed, and then the correspondent rowed, and then the oiler rowed. Gray-faced and bowed forward, they mechanically, turn by turn, plied the leaden oars. The form of the light-house had vanished from the southern horizon, but finally a pale star appeared, just lifting from the sea. The streaked saffron in the west passed before the all-merging darkness, and the sea to the east was black. The land had vanished, and was expressed only by the low and drear thunder of the surf.

"If I am going to be drowned—if I am going to be drowned—if I am going to be drowned, why, in the name of the seven mad gods, who rule the sea, was I allowed to come thus far and contemplate sand and trees? Was I brought here merely to have my nose dragged away as I was about to nibble the sacred cheese of life?"

The patient captain, drooped over the water-jar, was sometimes obliged to speak to the oarsman.

"Keep her head up! Keep her head up!"

" 'Keep her head up,' sir." The voices were weary and low.

This was surely a quiet evening. All save the oarsman lay heavily and listlessly in the boat's bottom. As for him, his eyes were just capable of noting the tall black waves that swept forward in a most sinister silence, save for an occasional subdued growl of a crest.

The cook's head was on a thwart, and he looked without interest at the water under his nose. He was deep in other scenes. Finally he spoke. "Billie," he murmured, dreamfully, "what kind of pie do you like best?"

V

"Pie," said the oiler and the correspondent, agitatedly. "Don't talk about those things, blast you!"

"Well," said the cook, "I was just thinking about ham sandwiches, and—"

A night on the sea in an open boat is a long night. As darkness settled finally, the shine of the light, lifting from the sea in the south, changed to full gold. On the northern horizon a new light appeared, a small bluish gleam on the edge of the waters. These two lights were the furniture of the world. Otherwise there was nothing but waves.

Two men huddled in the stern, and distances were so magnificent in the dingey that the rower was enabled to keep his feet partly warmed by thrusting them under his companions. Their legs indeed extended far under the rowing-seat until they touched the feet of the captain forward. Sometimes, despite the efforts of the tired oarsman, a wave came piling into the boat, an icy wave of the night, and the chilling water soaked them anew. They would twist their bodies for a moment and groan, and sleep the dead sleep once more, while the water in the boat gurgled about them as the craft rocked.

The plan of the oiler and the correspondent was for one to row until he lost the ability, and then arouse the other from his sea-water couch in the bottom of the boat.

The oiler plied the oars until his head drooped forward, and the overpowering sleep blinded him. And he rowed yet afterward. Then he touched a man in the bottom of the boat, and called his name. "Will you spell me for a little while?" he said, meekly.

"Sure, Billie," said the correspondent, awakening and dragging himself to a sitting position. They exchanged places carefully, and the oiler, cuddling down to the sea-water at the cook's side, seemed to go to sleep instantly.

The particular violence of the sea had ceased. The waves came without snarling. The obligation of the man at the oars was to keep the boat headed so that the tilt of the rollers would not capsize her, and to preserve her from filling when the crests rushed past. The black waves were silent and hard to be seen in the darkness. Often one was almost upon the boat before the oarsman was aware.

In a low voice the correspondent addressed the captain. He was not sure that the captain was awake, although this iron man seemed to be always awake. "Captain, shall I keep her making for that light north, sir?"

The same steady voice answered him. "Yes. Keep it about two points off the port bow."

The cook had tied a life-belt around himself in order to get even the warmth which this clumsy cork contrivance could donate, and he seemed almost stove-like when a rower, whose teeth invariably chattered wildly as soon as he ceased his labor, dropped down to sleep.

The correspondent, as he rowed, looked down at the two men sleeping under foot. The cook's arm was around the oiler's shoulders, and, with their fragmentary clothing and haggard faces, they were the babes of the sea, a grotesque rendering of the old babes in the wood.

Later he must have grown stupid at his work, for suddenly there was a growling of water, and a crest came with a roar and a swash into the boat, and it was a wonder that it did not set the cook afloat in his life-belt. The cook continued to sleep, but the oiler sat up, blinking his eyes and shaking with the new cold.

"Oh, I'm awful sorry, Billie," said the correspondent, contritely.

"That's all right, old boy," said the oiler, and lay down again and was asleep.

Presently it seemed that even the captain dozed, and the correspondent thought that he was the one man afloat on all the oceans. The wind had a voice as it came over the waves, and it was sadder than the end.

There was a long, loud swishing astern of the boat, and a gleaming trail of phosphorescence, like blue flame, was furrowed on the black waters. It might have been made by a monstrous knife.

Then there came a stillness, while the correspondent breathed with the open mouth and looked at the sea.

Suddenly there was another swish and another long flash of bluish light, and this time it was alongside the boat, and might almost have been reached with an oar. The correspondent saw an enormous fin speed like a shadow through the water, hurling the crystalline spray and leaving the long glowing trail.

The correspondent looked over his shoulder at the captain. His face was hidden, and he seemed to be asleep. He looked at the babes of the sea. They certainly were asleep. So, being bereft of sympathy, he leaned a little way to one side and swore softly into the sea.

But the thing did not then leave the vicinity of the boat. Ahead or astern, on one side or the other, at intervals long or short, fled the long sparkling streak, and there was to be heard the whiroo of the dark fin. The speed and power of the thing was greatly to be admired. It cut the water like a gigantic and keen projectile.

The presence of this biding thing did not affect the man with the same horror that it would if he had been a picnicker. He simply looked at the sea dully and swore in an undertone.

Nevertheless, it is true that he did not wish to be alone with the thing. He wished one of his companions to awaken by chance and keep him company with it. But the captain hung motionless over the water-jar and the oiler and the cook in the bottom of the boat were plunged in slumber.

VI

"If I am going to be drowned—if I am going to be drowned—if I am going to be drowned, why, in the name of the seven mad gods, who rule the sea, was I allowed to come thus far and contemplate sand and trees?"

During this dismal night, it may be remarked that a man would conclude that it was really the intention of the seven mad gods to drown him, despite the abominable injustice of it. For it was certainly an abominable injustice to drown a man who had worked so hard, so hard. The man felt it would be a crime most unnatural. Other people had drowned at sea since galleys swarmed with painted sails, but still—

When it occurs to a man that nature does not regard him as important, and that she feels she would not maim the universe by disposing of him, he at first wishes to throw bricks at the temple, and he hates deeply the fact that there are no bricks and no temples. Any visible expression of nature would surely be pelleted with his jeers.

Then, if there be no tangible thing to hoot he feels, perhaps, the desire to confront a personification and indulge in pleas, bowed to one knee, and with hands supplicant, saying: "Yes, but I love myself."

A high cold star on a winter's night is the word he feels that she says to him. Thereafter he knows the pathos of his situation.

The men in the dingey had not discussed these matters, but each had, no doubt, reflected upon them in silence and according to his mind. There was seldom any expression upon their faces save the general one of complete weariness. Speech was devoted to the business of the boat.

To chime the notes of his emotion, a verse mysteriously entered the correspondent's head. He had even forgotten that he had forgotten this verse, but it suddenly was in his mind.

A soldier of the Legion lay dying in Algiers,
There was lack of woman's nursing, there was dearth of woman's tears;
But a comrade stood beside him, and he took that comrade's hand
And he said: "I shall never see my own, my native land."

In his childhood, the correspondent had been made acquainted with the fact that a soldier of the Legion lay dying in Algiers, but he had never regarded the fact as important. Myriads of his school-fellows had informed him of the soldier's plight, but the dinning had naturally ended by making him perfectly indifferent. He had never considered it his affair that a soldier of the Legion lay dying in Algiers, nor had it appeared to him as a matter for sorrow. It was less to him than breaking of a pencil's point.

Now, however, it quaintly came to him as a human, living thing. It was no longer merely a picture of a few throes in the breast of a poet, meanwhile drinking tea and warming his feet at the grate; it was an actuality—stern, mournful, and fine.

The correspondent plainly saw the soldier. He lay on the sand with his feet out straight and still. While his pale left hand was upon his chest in an attempt to thwart the going of his life, the blood came between his fingers. In the far Algerian distance, a city of low square forms was set against a sky that was faint with the last sunset hues. The correspondent, plying the oars and dreaming of the slow and slower movements of the lips of the soldier, was moved by a profound and perfectly impersonal comprehension. He was sorry for the soldier of the Legion who lay dying in Algiers.

The thing which had followed the boat and waited had evidently grown bored at the delay. There was no longer to be heard the slash of the cut-water, and there was no longer the flame of the long trail. The light in the north still glimmered, but it was apparently no nearer to the boat. Sometimes the boom of the surf rang in the correspondent's ears, and he turned the craft seaward then and rowed harder. Southward, someone had evidently built a watch-fire on the beach. It was too low and too far to be seen, but it made a shimmering, roseate reflection upon the bluff back of it, and this could be discerned from the boat. The wind came stronger, and sometimes a wave suddenly raged out like a mountain-cat and there was to be seen the sheen and sparkle of a broken crest.

The captain, in the bow, moved on his water-jar and sat erect. "Pretty long night," he observed to the correspondent. He looked at the shore. "Those life-saving people take their time."

"Did you see that shark playing around?"

"Yes, I saw him. He was a big fellow, all right."

"Wish I had known you were awake."

Later the correspondent spoke into the bottom of the boat.

"Billie!" There was a slow and gradual disentanglement. "Billie, will you spell me?"

"Sure," said the oiler.

As soon as the correspondent touched the cold comfortable sea-water in the bottom of the boat, and had huddled close to the cook's life-belt he was deep in sleep, despite the fact that his teeth played all the popular airs. This sleep was so good to him that it was but a moment before he heard a voice call his name in a tone that demonstrated the last stages of exhaustion. "Will you spell me?"

"Sure, Billie."

The light in the north had mysteriously vanished, but the correspondent took his course from the wide-awake captain.

Later in the night they took the boat farther out to sea, and the captain directed the cook to take one oar at the stern and keep the boat facing the seas. He was to call out if he should hear the thunder of the surf. This plan enabled the oiler and the correspondent to get respite together. "We'll give those boys a chance to get into shape again," said the captain. They curled down and, after a few preliminary chatterings and trembles, slept once more the dead sleep. Neither knew they had bequeathed to the cook the company of another shark, or perhaps the same shark.

As the boat caroused on the waves, spray occasionally bumped over the side and gave them a fresh soaking, but this had no power to break their repose. The ominous slash of the wind and the water affected them as it would have affected mummies.

"Boys," said the cook, with the notes of every reluctance in his voice, "she's drifted in pretty close. I guess one of you had better take her to sea again." The correspondent, aroused, heard the crash of the toppled crests.

As he was rowing, the captain gave him some whiskey and water, and this steadied the chills out of him. "If I ever get ashore and anybody shows me even a photograph of an oar—"

At last there was a short conversation.

"Billie. . . . Billie, will you spell me?"

"Sure," said the oiler.

VII

When the correspondent again opened his eyes, the sea and the sky were each of the gray hue of the dawning. Later, carmine and gold was painted upon the waters. The morning appeared finally, in its splendor with a sky of pure blue, and the sunlight flamed on the tips of the waves.

On the distant dunes were set many little black cottages, and a tall white wind-mill reared above them. No man, nor dog, nor bicycle appeared on the beach. The cottages might have formed a deserted village.

The voyagers scanned the shore. A conference was held in the boat. "Well," said the captain, "if no help is coming, we might better try a run through the surf right away. If we stay out here much longer we will be too weak to do anything for ourselves at all." The others silently acquiesced in this reasoning. The boat was headed for the beach. The correspondent wondered if none ever ascended the tall wind-tower, and if then they never looked seaward. This tower was a giant, standing with its back to the plight of the ants. It represented in a degree, to the correspondent, the serenity of nature amid the struggles of the individual—nature in the wind, and nature in the vision of men. She did not seem cruel to him, nor beneficent, nor treacherous, nor wise. But she was indifferent, flatly indifferent. It is, perhaps, plausible that a man in this situation, impressed with the unconcern of the universe, should see the innumerable flaws of his life and have them taste wickedly in his mind and wish for another chance. A distinction between right and wrong seems absurdly clear to him, then, in this new ignorance of the grave-edge, and he understands that if he were given another opportunity he would mend his conduct and his words, and be better and brighter during an introduction, or at a tea.

"Now, boys," said the captain, "she is going to swamp sure. All we can do is to work her in as far as possible, and then when she swamps, pile out and scramble for the beach. Keep cool now and don't jump until she swamps sure."

The oiler took the oars. Over his shoulders he scanned the surf. "Captain," he said, "I think I'd better bring her about, and keep her head-on to the seas and back her in."

"All right, Billie," said the captain. "Back her in." The oiler swung the boat then and, seated in the stern, the cook and the correspondent were obliged to look over their shoulders to contemplate the lonely and indifferent shore.

The monstrous inshore rollers heaved the boat high until the men were again enabled to see the white sheets of water scudding up the slanted beach. "We won't get in very close," said the captain. Each time a man could wrest his attention from the rollers, he turned his glance toward the shore, and in the expression of the eyes during this contemplation there was a singular quality. The correspondent, observing the others, knew that they were not afraid, but the full meaning of their glances was shrouded.

As for himself, he was too tired to grapple fundamentally with the fact. He tried to coerce his mind into thinking of it, but the mind was dominated at this time by the muscles, and the muscles said they did not care. It merely occurred to him that if he should drown it would be a shame.

There were no hurried words, no pallor, no plain agitation. The men simply looked at the shore. "Now, remember to get well clear of the boat when you jump," said the captain.

Seaward the crest of a roller suddenly fell with a thunderous crash, and the long white comber came roaring down upon the boat.

"Steady now," said the captain. The men were silent. They turned their eyes from the shore to the comber and waited. The boat slid up the incline, leaped at the furious top, bounced over it, and swung down the long back of the waves. Some water had been shipped and the cook bailed it out.

But the next crest crashed also. The tumbling boiling flood of white water caught the boat and whirled it almost perpendicular. Water swarmed in from all sides. The correspondent had his hands on the gunwale at this time, and when the water entered at that place he swiftly withdrew his fingers, as if he objected to wetting them.

The little boat, drunken with this weight of water, reeled and snuggled deeper into the sea.

"Bail her out, cook! Bail her out," said the captain.

"All right, captain," said the cook.

"Now, boys, the next one will do for us, sure," said the oiler. "Mind to jump clear of the boat."

The third wave moved forward, huge, furious, implacable. It fairly swallowed the dingey, and almost simultaneously the men tumbled into the sea. A piece of life-belt had lain in the bottom of the boat, and as the correspondent went overboard he held this to his chest with his left hand.

The January water was icy, and he reflected immediately that it was colder than he had expected to find it off the coast of Florida. This appeared to his dazed mind as a fact important enough to be noted at the time. The coldness of the water was sad; it was tragic. This fact was somehow mixed and confused with his opinion of his own situation that it seemed almost a proper reason for tears. The water was cold.

When he came to the surface he was conscious of little but the noisy water. Afterward he saw his companions in the sea. The oiler was ahead in the race. He was swimming strongly and rapidly. Off to the correspondent's left, the cook's great white and corked back bulged out of the water, and in the rear the captain was hanging with his one good hand to the keel of the overturned dingey.

There is a certain immovable quality to a shore, and the correspondent wondered at it amid the confusion of the sea.

It seemed also very attractive, but the correspondent knew that it was a long journey, and he paddled leisurely. The piece of life-preserver lay under him, and sometimes he whirled down the incline of a wave as if he were on a hand-sled.

But finally he arrived at a place in the sea where travel was beset with difficulty. He did not pause swimming to inquire what manner of current had caught him, but there his progress ceased. The shore was set before him like a bit of scenery on a stage, and he looked at it and understood with his eyes each detail of it.

As the cook passed, much farther to the left, the captain was calling to him, "Turn over on your back, cook! Turn over on your back and use the oar."

"All right, sir!" The cook turned on his back, and, paddling with an oar, went ahead as if he were a canoe.

Presently the boat also passed to the left of the correspondent with the captain clinging with one hand to the keel. He would have appeared like a man raising himself to look over a board fence, if it were not for the extraordinary gymnastics of the boat. The correspondent marvelled that the captain could still hold to it.

They passed on, nearer to shore—the oiler, the cook, the captain—and following them went the water-jar, bouncing gayly over the seas.

The correspondent remained in the grip of this strange new enemy—a current. The shore, with its white slope of sand and its green bluff, topped with little silent cottages, was spread like a picture before him. It was very near to him then, but he was impressed as one who in a gallery looks at a scene from Brittany or Algiers.

He thought: "I am going to drown? Can it be possible? Can it be possible? Can it be possible?" Perhaps an individual must consider his own death to be the final phenomenon of nature.

But later a wave perhaps whirled him out of this small deadly current, for he found suddenly that he could again make progress toward the shore. Later still, he was aware that the captain, clinging with one hand to the keel of the dingey, had his face turned away from the shore and toward him, and was calling his name. "Come to the boat! Come to the boat!"

In his struggle to reach the captain and the boat, he reflected that when one gets properly wearied, drowning must really be a comfortable arrangement, a cessation of hostilities accompanied by a large degree of relief, and he was glad of it, for the main thing in his mind for some moments had been horror of the temporary agony. He did not wish to be hurt.

Presently he saw a man running along the shore. He was undressing with most remarkable speed. Coat, trousers, shirt, everything flew magically off him.

"Come to the boat," called the captain.

"All right, captain." As the correspondent paddled, he saw the captain let himself down to bottom and leave the boat. Then the correspondent performed his one little marvel of the voyage. A large wave caught him and flung him with ease and supreme speed completely over the boat and far beyond it. It struck him even then as an event in gymnastics, and a true miracle of the sea. An overturned boat in the surf is not a plaything to a swimming man.

The correspondent arrived in water that reached only to his waist, but his condition did not enable him to stand for more than a moment. Each wave knocked him into a heap, and the under-tow pulled at him.

Then he saw the man who had been running and undressing, and undressing and running, come bounding into the water. He dragged ashore the cook, and then waded toward the captain, but the captain waved him away, and sent him to the correspondent. He was naked, naked as a tree in winter, but a halo was about his head, and he shone like a saint. He gave a strong pull, and a long drag, and a bully heave at the correspondent's hand. The correspondent, schooled in the minor formulae, said: "Thanks, old man." But suddenly the man cried: "What's that?" He pointed a swift finger. The correspondent said: "Go."

In the shallows, face downward, lay the oiler. His forehead touched sand that was periodically, between each wave, clear of the sea.

The correspondent did not know all that transpired afterward. When he achieved safe ground he fell, striking the sand with each particular part of his body. It was as if he had dropped from a roof, but the thud was grateful to him.

It seems that instantly the beach was populated with men with blankets, clothes, and flasks, and women with coffee-pots and all the remedies sacred to their minds. The welcome of the land to the men from the sea was warm and generous, but a still and dripping shape was carried slowly up the beach, and the land's welcome for it could only be the different and sinister hospitality of the grave.

When it came night, the white waves paced to and fro in the moonlight, and the wind brought the sound of the great sea's voice to the men on shore, and they felt that they could then be interpreters.

PART IV

Shipboard Lore

New Ship and Shipmates—My Watchmate

RICHARD HENRY DANA, JR.

Tuesday, Sept. 8th. This was my first day's duty on board the ship; and though a sailor's life is a sailor's life wherever it may be, yet I found everything very different here from the customs of the brig Pilgrim. After all hands were called, at daybreak, three minutes and a half were allowed for every man to dress and come on deck, and if any were longer than that, they were sure to be overhauled by the mate, who was always on deck, and making himself heard all over the ship. The head-pump was then rigged, and the decks washed down by the second and third mates; the chief mate walking the quarter-deck and keeping a general supervision, but not deigning to touch a bucket or a brush. Inside and out, fore and aft, upper deck and between decks, steerage and forecastle, rail, bulwarks, and water-ways, were washed, scrubbed and scraped with brooms and canvas, and the decks were wet and sanded all over, and then holystoned. The holystone is a large, soft stone, smooth on the bottom, with long ropes attached to each end, by which the crew keep it sliding fore and aft, over the wet, sanded decks. Smaller hand-stones, which the sailors call "prayer-books," are used to scrub in among the crevices and narrow places, where the large holystone will not go. An hour or two, we were kept at this work, when the head-pump was manned, and all the sand washed off the decks and sides. Then came swabs and squilgees; and after the decks were dry, each one went to his particular morning job. There were five boats belonging to the ship,—launch, pinnace, jolly-boat, larboard quarter-boat, and gig,—each of which had a coxswain, who had charge of it, and was answerable for the order and cleanness of it. The rest of the cleaning was divided among the crew; one having the brass and composition work about the capstan; another the bell, which was of brass, and kept as bright as a gilt button; a third, the harness-cask; another, the man-rope stanchions; others, the steps of the forecastle and hatchways, which were hauled up and holystoned. Each of these jobs must be finished before breakfast; and, in the meantime, the rest of the crew filled the scuttle-butt, and the cook scraped his kids (wooden tubs out of which the sailors eat) and polished the hoops, and placed them before the galley, to await inspection. When the decks were dry, the lord paramount made his appearance on the quarter-deck, and took a few turns, when eight bells were struck, and all hands went to breakfast. Half an hour was allowed for breakfast, when all hands were called again; the kids, pots, bread-bags, etc., stowed away; and, this morning, preparations were made for getting under weigh. We paid out on the chain by which we swung; hove in on the other; catted the anchor; and hove short on the first. This work was done in shorter time than was usual on board the brig; for though everything was more than twice as large and heavy, the cat-block being as much as a man could lift, and the chain as large as three of the Pilgrim's, yet there was a plenty of room to move about in, more discipline and system, more men, and more good will. Every one seemed ambitious to do his best: officers and men knew their duty, and all went well. As soon as she was hove short, the mate, on the forecastle, gave the order to loose the sails, and, in an instant, every one sprung into the rigging, up the shrouds, and out on the yards, scrambling by one another,—the first up the best fellow,—cast off the yard-arm gaskets and bunt gaskets, and one man remained on each yard, holding the bunt jigger with a turn round the tye, all ready to let go, while the rest laid down to man the sheets and halyards. The mate then hailed the yards—"All ready forward?"—"All ready the cross-jack yards?" etc., etc., and "Aye, aye, sir!" being returned from each, the word was given to let go; and in the twinkling of an eye, the ship, which had shown nothing but her bare yards, was covered with her loose canvas, from the royal-mast-heads to the decks. Every one then laid down, except one man in each top, to overhaul the rigging, and the topsails were hoisted and sheeted home; all three yards going to the mast-head at once, the larboard watch hoisting the fore, the starboard watch the main, and five light hands, (of whom I was one,) picked from the two watches, the mizen. The yards were then trimmed, the anchor weighed, the cat-block hooked on, the fall stretched out, manned by "all hands and the cook," and the anchor brought to the head with "cheerily men!" in full chorus. The ship being now under weigh, the light sails were set, one after another, and she was under full sail, before she had passed the sandy point. The fore royal, which fell to my lot, (being in the mate's watch,) was more than twice as large as that of the Pilgrim, and, though I could handle the brig's easily, I found my hands full, with this, especially as there were no jacks to the ship; everything being for neatness, and nothing left for Jack to hold on by, but his eyelids.

As soon as we were beyond the point, and all sail out, the order was given, "Go below the watch!" and the crew said that, ever since they had been on the coast, they had had "watch and watch," while going from port to port; and, in fact, everything showed that, though strict discipline was kept, and the utmost was required of every man, in the way of his duty, yet, on the whole, there was very good usage on board. Each one knew that he must be a man, and show himself smart when at his duty, yet every one was satisfied with the usage; and a contented crew, agreeing with one another, and finding no fault, was a contrast indeed with the small, hard-used, dissatisfied, grumbling, desponding crew of the Pilgrim.

It being the turn of our watch to go below, the men went to work, mending their clothes, and doing other little things for themselves; and I, having got my wardrobe in complete order at San Diego, had nothing to do but to read. I accordingly overhauled the chests of the crew, but found nothing that suited me exactly, until one of the men said he had a book which "told all about a great highwayman," at the bottom of his chest, and producing it, I found, to my surprise and joy, that it was nothing else than Bulwer's Paul Clifford. This, I seized immediately, and going to my hammock, lay there, swinging and reading, until the watch was out. The between-decks were clear, the hatchways open, and a cool breeze blowing through them, the ship under easy way, and everything comfortable. I had just got well into the story, when eight bells were struck, and we were all ordered to dinner. After dinner came our watch on deck for four hours, and, at four o'clock, I went below again, turned into my hammock, and read until the dog watch. As no lights were allowed after eight o'clock, there was no reading in the night watch. Having light winds and calms, we were three days on the passage, and each watch below, during the daytime, I spent in the same manner, until I had finished my book. I shall never forget the enjoyment I derived from it. To come across anything with the slightest claims to literary merit, was so unusual, that this was a perfect feast to me. The brilliancy of the book, the succession of capital hits, lively and characteristic sketches, kept me in a constant state of pleasing sensations. It was far too good for a sailor. I could not expect such fine times to last long.

While on deck, the regular work of the ship went on. The sailmaker and carpenter worked between decks, and the crew had their work to do upon the rigging, drawing yarns, making spun-yarn, etc., as usual in merchantmen. The night watches were much more pleasant than on board the Pilgrim. There, there were so few in a watch, that, one being at the wheel, and another on the look-out, there was no one left to talk with; but here, we had seven in a watch, so that we had long yarns, in abundance. After two or three night watches, I became quite well acquainted with all the larboard watch. The sailmaker was the head man of the watch, and was generally considered the most experienced seaman on board. He was a thoroughbred old man-of-war-man, had been to sea twenty-two years, in all kinds of vessels—men-of-war, privateers, slavers, and merchantmen;—everything except whalers, which a thorough sailor despises, and will always steer clear of, if he can. He had, of course, been in all parts of the world, and was remarkable for drawing a long bow. His yarns frequently stretched through a watch, and kept all hands awake. They were always amusing from their improbability, and, indeed, he never expected to be believed, but spun them merely for amusement; and as he had some humor and a good supply of man-of-war slang and sailor's salt phrases, he always made fun. Next to him in age and experience, and, of course, in standing in the watch, was an Englishman, named Harris, of whom I shall have more to say hereafter. Then, came two or three Americans, who had been the common run of European and South American voyages, and one who had been in a "spouter," and, of course, had all the whaling stories to himself. Last of all, was a broad-backed, thick-headed boy from Cape Cod, who had been in mackerel schooners, and was making his first voyage in a square-rigged vessel. He was born in Hingham, and of course was called "Bucket-maker." The other watch was composed of about the same number. A tall, fine-looking Frenchman, with coal-black whiskers and curly hair, a first-rate seaman, and named John, (one name is enough for a sailor,) was the head man of the watch. Then came two Americans (one of whom had been a dissipated young man of property and family, and was reduced to duck trowsers and monthly wages,) a German, an English lad, named Ben, who belonged on the mizen topsail yard with me, and was a good sailor for his years, and two Boston boys just from the public schools. The carpenter sometimes mustered in the starboard watch, and was an old sea-dog, a Swede by birth, and accounted the best helmsman in the ship. This was our ship's company, beside cook and steward, who were blacks, three mates, and the captain.

The second day out, the wind drew ahead, and we had to beat up the coast; so that, in tacking ship, I could see the regulations of the vessel. Instead of going wherever was most convenient, and running from place to place, wherever work was to be done, each man had his station. A regular tacking and wearing bill was made out. The chief mate commanded on the forecastle, and had charge of the head sails and the forward part of the ship. Two of the best men in the ship—the sailmaker from our watch, and John, the Frenchman, from the other, worked the forecastle. The third mate commanded in the waist, and, with the carpenter and one man, worked the main tack and bowline; the cook, *ex-officio*, the fore sheet, and the steward the main. The second mate had charge of the after yards, and let go the lee fore and main braces. I was stationed at the weather cross-jack braces; three other light hands at the lee; one boy at the spanker-sheet and guy; a man and a boy at the main topsail, top-gallant, and royal braces; and all the rest of the crew—men and boys—tallied on to the main brace. Every one here knew his station, must be there when all hands were called to put the ship about, and was answerable for every rope committed to him. Each man's rope must be let go and hauled in at the order, properly made fast, and neatly coiled away when the ship was about. As soon as all hands are at their stations, the captain, who stands on the weather side of the quarter-deck, makes a sign to the man at the wheel to put it down, and calls out "Helm's a lee'!" "Helm's a lee'!" answers the mate on the forecastle, and the head sheets are let go. "Raise tacks and sheets!" says the captain; "tacks and sheets!" is passed forward, and the fore tack and main sheet are let go. The next thing is to haul taught for a swing. The weather cross-jack braces and the lee main braces are each belayed together upon two pins, and ready to be let go; and the opposite braces hauled taught. "Main topsail haul!" shouts the captain; the braces are let go; and if he has taken his time well, the yards swing round like a top; but if he is too late, or too soon, it is like drawing teeth. The after yards are then braced up and belayed, the main sheet hauled aft, the spanker eased over to leeward, and the men from the braces stand by the head yards. "Let go and haul!" says the captain; the second mate lets go the weather fore braces, and the men haul in to leeward. The mate, on the forecastle, looks out for the head yards. "Well, the fore topsail yard!" "Topgallant yard's well!" "Royal yard too much! Haul into windward! So! well *that!*" "Well *all!*" Then the starboard watch board the main tack, and the larboard watch lay forward and board the fore tack and haul down the jib sheet, clapping a tackle upon it, if it blows very fresh. The after yards are then trimmed, the captain generally looking out for them himself. "Well the cross-jack yard!" "Small pull the main top-gallant yard!" "Well *that!*" "Well the mizen topsail yard!" "Cross-jack yards all *well!*" "Well all aft!" "Haul taught to windward!" Everything being now trimmed and in order, each man coils up the rigging at his own station, and the order is given—"Go below the watch!"

During the last twenty-four hours of the passage, we beat off and on the land, making a tack about once in four hours, so that I had a sufficient opportunity to observe the working of the ship; and certainly, it took no more men to brace about this ship's lower yards, which were more than fifty feet square, than it did those of the Pilgrim, which were not much more than half the size; so much depends upon the manner in which the braces run, and the state of the blocks; and Captain Wilson, of the Ayacucho, who was afterwards a passenger with us, upon a trip to windward, said he had no doubt that our ship worked two men lighter than his brig.

FRIDAY, SEPT. 11. This morning, at four o'clock, went below, San Pedro point being about two leagues ahead, and the ship going on under studding-sails. In about an hour we were waked up by the hauling of the chain about decks, and in a few minutes "All hands ahoy!" was called; and we were all at work, hauling in and making up the studding-sails, overhauling the chain forward, and getting the anchors ready. "The Pilgrim is there at anchor," said some one, as we were running about decks; and taking a moment's look over the rail, I saw my old friend, deeply laden, lying at anchor inside of the kelp. In coming to anchor, as well as in tacking, each one had his station and duty. The light sails were clewed up and furled, the courses hauled up, and the jibs down; then came the topsails in the buntlines, and the anchor let go. As soon as she was well at anchor, all hands lay aloft to furl the topsails; and this, I soon found, was a great matter on board this ship; for every sailor knows that a vessel is judged of, a good deal, by the furl of her sails. The third mate, sailmaker, and the larboard watch went upon the fore topsail yard; the second mate, carpenter, and the starboard watch upon the main; and myself and the English lad, and the two Boston boys, and the young Cape-Cod man, furled the mizen topsail. This sail belonged to us altogether, to reef and to furl, and not a man was allowed to come upon our yard. The mate took us under his special care, frequently making us furl the sail over, three or four times, until we got the bunt up to a perfect cone, and the whole sail without a wrinkle. As soon as each sail was hauled up and the bunt made, the jigger was bent on to the slack of the buntlines, and the bunt triced up, on deck. The mate then took his place between the knight-heads to "twig" the fore, on the windlass to twig the main, and at the foot of the mainmast, for the mizen; and if anything was wrong,—too much bunt on one side, clues too taught or too slack, or any sail abaft the yard,—the whole must be dropped again. When all was right, the bunts were triced well up, the yard-arm gaskets passed, so as not to leave a wrinkle forward of the yard—short gaskets with turns close together.

From the moment of letting go the anchor, when the captain ceases his care of things, the chief mate is the great man. With a voice like a young lion, he was hallooing and bawling, in all directions, making everything fly, and, at the same time, doing everything well. He was quite a contrast to the worthy, quiet, unobtrusive mate of the Pilgrim: not so estimable a man, perhaps, but a far better mate of a vessel; and the entire change in Captain T—'s conduct, since he took command of the ship, was owing, no doubt, in a great measure, to this fact. If the chief officer wants force, discipline slackens, everything gets out of joint, the captain interferes continually; that makes a difficulty between them, which encourages the crew, and the whole ends in a three-sided quarrel. But Mr. Brown (the mate of the Alert) wanted no help from anybody; took everything into his own hands; and was more likely to encroach upon the authority of the master, than to need any spurring. Captain T—gave his directions to the mate in private, and, except in coming to anchor, getting under weigh, tacking, reefing topsails, and other "all-hands-work," seldom appeared in person. This is the proper state of things, and while this lasts, and there is a good understanding aft, everything will go on well.

Having furled all the sails, the royal yards were next to be sent down. The English lad and myself sent down the main, which was larger than the Pilgrim's main top-gallant yard; two more light hands, the fore; and one boy, the mizen. This order, we always kept while on the coast; sending them up and down every time we came in and went out of port. They were all tripped and lowered together, the main on the starboard side, and the fore and mizen, to port. No sooner was she all snug, than tackles were got up on the yards and stays, and the long-boat and pinnace hove out. The swinging booms were then guyed out, and the boats made fast by geswarps, and everything in harbor style. After breakfast, the hatches were taken off, and all got ready to receive hides from the Pilgrim. All day, boats were passing and repassing, until we had taken her hides from her, and left her in ballast trim. These hides made but little show in our hold, though they had loaded the Pilgrim down to the water's edge. This changing of the hides settled the question of the destination of the two vessels, which had been one of some speculation to us. We were to remain in the leeward ports, while the Pilgrim was to sail, the next morning, for San Francisco. After we had knocked off work, and cleared up decks for the night, my friend S—came on board, and spent an hour with me in our berth between decks. The Pilgrim's crew envied me my place on board the ship, and seemed to think that I had got a little to windward of them; especially in the matter of going home first. S—was determined to go home in the Alert, by begging or buying; if Captain T—would not let him come on other terms, he would purchase an exchange with some one of the crew. The prospect of another year after the Alert should sail, was rather "too much of the monkey." About seven o'clock, the mate came down into the steerage, in fine trim for fun, roused the boys out of the berth, turned up the carpenter with his fiddle, sent the steward with lights to put in the between-decks, and set all hands to dancing. The between-decks were high enough to allow of jumping; and being clear, and white, from holystoning, made a fine dancing-hall. Some of the Pilgrim's crew were in the forecastle, and we all turned-to and had a regular sailor's shuffle, till eight bells. The Cape-Cod boy could dance the true fisherman's jig, barefooted, knocking with his heels, and slapping the decks with his bare feet, in time with the music. This was a favorite amusement of the mate's, who always stood at the steerage door, looking on, and if the boys would not dance, he hazed them round with a rope's end, much to the amusement of the men.

The next morning, according to the orders of the agent, the Pilgrim set sail for the windward, to be gone three or four months. She got under weigh with very little fuss, and came so near us as to throw a letter on board, Captain Faucon standing at the tiller himself, and steering her as he would a mackerel smack. When Captain T—was in command of the Pilgrim, there was as much preparation and ceremony as there would be in getting a seventy-four under weigh. Captain Faucon was a sailor, every inch of him; he knew what a ship was, and was as much at home in one, as a cobbler in his stall. I wanted no better proof of this than the opinion of the ship's crew, for they had been six months under his command, and knew what he was; and if sailors allow their captain to be a good seaman, you may be sure he is one, for that is a thing they are not always ready to say.

After the Pilgrim left us, we lay three weeks at San Pedro, from the 11th of September until the 2nd of October, engaged in the usual port duties of landing cargo, taking off hides, etc., etc. These duties were much easier, and went on much more agreeably, than on board the Pilgrim. "The more, the merrier," is the sailor's maxim; and a boat's crew of a dozen could take off all the hides brought down in a day, without much trouble, by division of labor; and on shore, as well as on board, a good will, and no discontent or grumbling, make everything go well. The officer, too, who usually went with us, the third mate, was a fine young fellow, and made no unnecessary trouble; so that we generally had quite a sociable time, and were glad to be relieved from the restraint of the ship. While here, I often thought of the miserable, gloomy weeks we had spent in this dull place, in the brig; discontent and hard usage on board, and four hands to do all the work on shore. Give me a big ship. There is more room, more hands, better outfit, better regulation, more life, and more company. Another thing was better arranged here: we had a regular gig's crew. A light whale-boat, handsomely painted, and fitted out with stern seats, yoke, tiller-ropes, etc., hung on the starboard quarter, and was used as the gig. The youngest lad in the ship, a Boston boy about thirteen years old, was coxswain of this boat, and had the entire charge of her, to keep her clean, and have her in readiness to go and come at any hour. Four light hands, of about the same size and age, of whom I was one, formed the crew. Each had his oar and seat numbered, and we were obliged to be in our places, have our oars scraped white, our tho-lepins in, and the fenders over the side. The bow-man had charge of the boat-hook and painter, and the coxswain of the rudder, yoke, and stern-sheets. Our duty was to carry the captain and agent about, and passengers off and on; which last was no trifling duty, as the people on shore have no boats, and every purchaser, from the boy who buys his pair of shoes, to the trader who buys his casks and bales, were to be taken off and on, in our boat. Some days, when people were coming and going fast, we were in the boat, pulling off and on, all day long, with hardly time for our meals; making, as we lay nearly three miles from shore, from forty to fifty miles' rowing in a day. Still, we thought it the best berth in the ship; for when the gig was employed, we had nothing to do with the cargo, except small bundles which the passengers carried with them, and no hides to carry, besides the opportunity of seeing everybody, making acquaintances, hearing the news, etc. Unless the captain or agent were in the boat, we had no officer with us, and often had fine times with the passengers, who were always willing to talk and joke with us. Frequently, too, we were obliged to wait several hours on shore; when we would haul the boat up on the beach, and leaving one to watch her, go up to the nearest house, or spend the time in strolling about the beach, picking up shells, or playing hop-scotch, and other games, on the hard sand. The rest of the crew never left the ship, except for bringing heavy goods and taking off hides; and though we were always in the water, the surf hardly leaving us a dry thread from morning till night, yet we were young, and the climate was good, and we thought it much better than the quiet, hum-drum drag and pull on board ship. We made the acquaintance of nearly half of California; for, besides carrying everybody in our boat,—men, women, and children,—all the messages, letters, and light packages went by us, and being known by our dress, we found a ready reception everywhere.

At San Pedro, we had none of this amusement, for, there being but one house in the place, we, of course, had but little company. All the variety that I had, was riding, once a week, to the nearest rancho, to order a bullock down for the ship.

The brig Catalina came in from San Diego, and being bound up to windward, we both got under weigh at the same time, for a trial of speed up to Santa Barbara, a distance of about eighty miles. We hove up and got under sail about eleven o'clock at night, with a light land-breeze, which died away toward morning, leaving us becalmed only a few miles from our anchoring-place. The Catalina, being a small vessel, of less than half our size, put out sweeps and got a boat ahead, and pulled out to sea, during the night, so that she had the sea-breeze earlier and stronger than we did, and we had the mortification of seeing her standing up the coast, with a fine breeze, the sea all ruffled about her, while we were becalmed, in-shore. When the sea-breeze died away, she was nearly out of sight; and, toward the latter part of the afternoon, the regular northwest wind set in fresh, we braced sharp upon it, took a pull at every sheet, tack, and halyard, and stood after her, in fine style, our ship being very good upon a taughtened bowline. We had nearly five hours of fine sailing, beating up to windward, by long stretches in and off shore, and evidently gaining upon the Catalina, at every tack. When this breeze left us, we were so near as to count the painted ports on her side. Fortunately, the wind died away when we were on our inward tack, and she on her outward, so we were in-shore, and caught the land-breeze first, which came off upon our quarter, about the middle of the first watch. All hands were turned up, and we set all sail, to the skysails and the royal studding-sails; and with these, we glided quietly through the water, leaving the Catalina, which could not spread so much canvas as we, gradually astern, and, by daylight, were off St. Buenaventura, and our antagonist nearly out of sight. The sea-breeze, however, favored her again, while we were becalmed under the headland, and laboring slowly along, she was abreast of us by noon. Thus we continued, ahead, astern, and abreast of one another, alternately; now, far out at sea, and again, close in under the shore. On the third morning, we came into the great bay of Santa Barbara, two hours behind the brig, and thus lost the bet; though, if the race had been to the point, we should have beaten her by five or six hours. This, however, settled the relative sailing of the vessels, for it was admitted that although she, being small and light, could gain upon us in very light winds, yet whenever there was breeze enough to set us agoing, we walked away from her like hauling in a line; and in beating to windward, which is the best trial of a vessel, we had much the advantage of her.

SUNDAY, OCT. 4th. This was the day of our arrival; and somehow or other, our captain always managed not only to sail, but to come into port, on a Sunday. The main reason for sailing on the Sabbath is not, as many people suppose, because Sunday is thought a lucky day, but because it is a leisure day. During the six days, the crew are employed upon the cargo and other ship's works, and the Sabbath, being their only day of rest, whatever additional work can be thrown into Sunday, is so much gain to the owners. This is the reason of our coasters, packets, etc., sailing on the Sabbath. They get six good days' work out of the crew, and then throw all the labor of sailing into the Sabbath. Thus it was with us, nearly all the time we were on the coast, and many of our Sabbaths were lost entirely to us. The

Catholics on shore have no trading and make no journeys on Sunday, but the American has no national religion, and likes to show his independence of priest-craft by doing as he chooses on the Lord's day.

Santa Barbara looked very much as it did when I left it five months before: the long sand beach, with the heavy rollers, breaking upon it in a continual roar, and the little town, imbedded on the plain, girt by its amphitheatre of mountains. Day after day, the sun shone clear and bright upon the wide bay and the red roofs of the houses; everything being as still as death, the people really hardly seeming to earn their sunlight. Daylight actually seemed thrown away upon them. We had a few visitors, and collected about a hundred hides, and every night, at sundown, the gig was sent ashore, to wait for the captain, who spent his evenings in the town. We always took our monkey-jackets with us, and flint and steel, and made a fire on the beach with the driftwood and the bushes we pulled from the neighboring thickets, and lay down by it, on the sand. Sometimes we would stray up to the town, if the captain was likely to stay late, and pass the time at some of the houses, in which we were almost always well received by the inhabitants. Sometimes earlier and sometimes later, the captain came down; when, after good drenching in the surf, we went aboard, changed our clothes, and turned in for the night—yet not for all the night, for there was the anchor watch to stand.

This leads me to speak of my watchmate for nine months—and, taking him all in all, the most remarkable man I have ever seen—Tom Harris. An hour, every night, while lying in port, Harris and myself had the deck to ourselves, and walking fore and aft, night after night, for months, I learned his whole character and history, and more about foreign nations, the habits of different people, and especially the secrets of sailors' lives and hardships, and also of practical seamanship, (in which he was abundantly capable of instructing me,) than I could ever have learned elsewhere. But the most remarkable thing about him, was the power of his mind. His memory was perfect; seeming to form a regular chain, reaching from his earliest childhood up to the time I knew him, without one link wanting. His power of calculation, too, was remarkable. I called myself pretty quick at figures, and had been through a course of mathematical studies; but, working by my head, I was unable to keep within sight of this man, who had never been beyond his arithmetic: so rapid was his calculation. He carried in his head not only a log-book of the whole voyage, in which everything was complete and accurate, and from which no one ever thought of appealing, but also an accurate registry of all the cargo; knowing, precisely, where each thing was, and how many hides we took in at every port.

One night, he made a rough calculation of the number of hides that could be stowed in the lower hold, between the fore and main mast, taking the depth of hold and breadth of beam, (for he always knew the dimension of every part of the ship, before he had been a month on board,) and the average area and thickness of a hide; he came surprisingly near the number, as it afterwards turned out. The mate frequently came to him to know the capacity of different parts of the vessel, and he could tell the sailmaker very nearly the amount of canvas he would want for each sail in the ship; for he knew the hoist of every mast, and spread of every sail, on the head and foot, in feet and inches. When we were at sea, he kept a running account, in his head, of the ship's way—the number of knots and the courses; and if the courses did not vary much during the twenty-four hours, by taking the whole progress, and allowing so many eighths southing or northing, to so many easting or westing; he would make up his reckoning just before the captain took the sun at noon, and often came wonderfully near the mark. Calculation of all kinds was his delight. He had, in his chest, several volumes giving accounts of inventions in mechanics, which he read with great pleasure, and made himself master of. I doubt if he ever forgot anything that he read. The only thing in the way of poetry that he ever read was Falconer's Shipwreck, which he was delighted with, and whole pages of which he could repeat. He knew the name of every sailor that had ever been his shipmate, and also, of every vessel, captain, and officer, and the principal dates of each voyage; and a sailor whom we afterwards fell in with, who had been in a ship with Harris nearly twelve years before, was very much surprised at having Harris tell him things about himself which he had entirely forgotten. His facts, whether dates or events, no one thought of disputing; and his opinions, few of the sailors dared to oppose; for, right or wrong, he always had the best of the argument with them. His reasoning powers were remarkable. I have had harder work maintaining an argument with him in a watch, even when I knew myself to be right, and he was only doubting, than I ever had before; not from his obstinacy, but from his acuteness. Give him only a little knowledge of his subject, and, certainly among all the young men of my acquaintance and standing at college, there was not one whom I had not rather meet, than this man. I never answered a question from him, or advanced an opinion to him, without thinking more than once. With an iron memory, he seemed to have your whole past conversation at command, and if you said a thing now which ill agreed with something said months before, he was sure to have you on the hip. In fact, I always felt, when with him, that I was with no common man. I had a positive respect for his powers of mind, and felt often that if half the pains had been spent upon his education which are thrown away, yearly, in our colleges, he would have been a man of great weight in society. Like most self-taught men, he over-estimated the value of an education; and this, I often told him, though I profited by it myself; for he always treated me with respect, and often unnecessarily gave way to me, from an over-estimate of my knowledge. For the capacities of all the rest of the crew, captain and all, he had the most sovereign contempt. He was a far better sailor, and probably a better navigator, than the captain, and had more brains than all the after part of the ship put together. The sailors said, "Tom's got a head as long as the bowsprit," and if any one got into an argument with him, they would call out—"Ah, Jack! you'd better drop that, as you would a hot potato, for Tom will turn you inside out before you know it."

I recollect his posing me once on the subject of the Corn Laws. I was called to stand my watch, and, coming on deck, found him there before me; and we began, as usual, to walk fore and aft, in the waist. He talked about the corn laws; asked me my opinion about them, which I gave him; and my reasons; my small stock of which I set forth to the best advantage, supposing his knowledge on the subject must be less than mine, if, indeed, he had any at all. When I had got through, he took the liberty of differing from me, and, to my surprise, brought arguments and facts connected with the subject which were new to me, and to which I was entirely unable to reply. I confessed that I knew almost nothing of the subject, and expressed my surprise at the extent of his information. He said that, a number of years before, while at a boardinghouse in Liverpool, he had fallen in with a pamphlet on the subject, and, as it contained calculations, had read it very carefully, and had ever since wished to find some one who could add to his stock of knowledge on the question. Although it was many years since he had seen the book, and it was a subject with which he had no previous acquaintance, yet he had the chain of reasoning, founded upon principles of political economy, perfect in his memory; and his facts, so far as I could judge, were correct; at least, he stated them with great precision. The principles of the steam engine, too, he was very familiar with, having been several months on board of a steamboat, and made himself master of its secrets. He knew every lunar star in both hemispheres, and was a perfect master of his quadrant and sextant. Such was the man, who, at forty, was still a dog before the mast, at twelve dollars a month. The reason of this was to be found in his whole past life, as I had it, at different times, from himself.

He was an Englishman, by birth, a native of Ilfracomb, in Cornwall. His father was skipper of a small coaster, from Bristol, and dying, left him, when quite young, to the care of his mother, by whose exertions he received a common-school education, passing his winters at school and his summers in the coasting trade, until his seventeenth year, when he left home to go upon foreign voyages. Of this mother, he often spoke with the greatest respect, and said that she was a strong-minded woman, and had the best system of education he had ever known; a system which had made respectable men of his three brothers, and failed only in him, from his own indomitable obstinacy. One thing he often mentioned, in which he said his mother differed from all other mothers that he had ever seen disciplining their children; that was, that when he was out of humor and refused to eat, instead of putting his plate away, as most mothers would, and saying that his hunger would bring him to it, in time, she would stand over him and oblige him to eat it—every mouthful of it. It was no fault of her's that he was what I saw him; and so great was his sense of gratitude for her efforts, though unsuccessful, that he determined, at the close of the voyage, to embark for home with all the wages he should get, to spend with and for his mother, if perchance he should find her alive.

After leaving home, he had spent nearly twenty years, sailing upon all sorts of voyages, generally out of the ports of New York and Boston. Twenty years of vice! Every sin that a sailor knows, he had gone to the bottom of. Several times he had been hauled up in the hospitals, and as often, the great strength of his constitution had brought him out again in health. Several times, too, from his known capacity, he had been promoted to the office of chief mate, and as often, his conduct when in port, especially his drunkenness, which neither fear nor ambition could induce him to abandon, put him back into the forecastle. One night, when giving me an account of his life, and lamenting the years of manhood he had thrown away, he said that there, in the forecastle, at the foot of the steps—a chest of old clothes—was the result of twenty-two years of hard labor and exposure—worked like a horse, and treated like a dog. As he grew older, he began to feel the necessity of some provision for his later years, and came gradually to the conviction that rum had been his worst enemy. One night, in Havana, a young shipmate of his was brought aboard drunk, with a dangerous gash in his head, and his money and new clothes stripped from him. Harris had seen and been in hundreds of such scenes as these, but in his then state of mind, it fixed his determination, and he resolved never to taste another drop of strong drink, of any kind. He signed no pledge, and made no vow, but relied on his own strength of purpose. The first thing with him was a reason, and then a resolution, and the thing was done. The date of his resolution he knew, of course, to the very hour. It was three years before I knew him, and during all that time, nothing stronger than cider or coffee had passed his lips. The sailors never thought of enticing Tom to take a glass, any more than they would of talking to the ship's compass. He was now a temperate man for life, and capable of filling any berth in a ship, and many a high station there is on shore which is held by a meaner man.

He understood the management of a ship upon scientific principles, and could give the reason for hauling every rope; and a long experience, added to careful observation at the time, and a perfect memory, gave him a knowledge of the expedients and resorts in times of hazard, which was remarkable, and for which I became much indebted to him, as he took the greatest pleasure in opening his stores of information to me, in return for what I was enabled to do for him. Stories of tyranny and hardship which had driven men to piracy;—of the incredible ignorance of masters and mates, and of horrid brutality to the sick, dead, and dying; as well as of the secret knavery and impositions practised upon seamen by connivance of the owners, landlords, and officers; all these he had, and I could not but believe them; for men who had known him for fifteen years had never taken him even in an exaggeration, and, as I have said, his statements were never disputed. I remember, among other things, his speaking of, a captain whom I had known by report, who never handed a thing to a sailor, but put it on deck and kicked it to him; and of another, who was of the best connections in Boston, who absolutely murdered a lad from Boston that went out with him before the mast to Sumatra, by keeping him hard at work while ill of the coast fever, and obliging him to sleep in the close steerage. (The same captain has since died of the same fever on the same coast.)

In fact, taking together all that I learned from him of seamanship, of the history of sailors' lives, of practical wisdom, and of human nature under new circumstances,—a great history from which many are shut out,—I would not part with the hours I spent in the watch with that man for any given hours of my life past in study and social intercourse.

Being Ashore

JOHN MASEFIELD

In the nights, in the winter nights, in the nights of storm when the wind howls, it is then that I feel the sweet of it, Aha, I say, you howling catamount, I say, you may blow. wind, and crack your cheeks, for all I care. Then I listen to the noise of the elm trees and to the creak in the old floorings, and, aha, I say, you whining rantipoles, you may crack and you may creak, but here I shall lie till daylight.

There is a solid comfort in a roaring storm ashore here. But on a calm day, when it is raining, when it is muddy underfoot, when the world is the colour of a drowned rat, one calls to mind more boisterous days, the days of effort and adventure; and wasn't I a fool, I say, to come ashore to a life like this life. And I surely was daft, I keep saying, to think the sea as bad as I always thought it. And if I were in a ship now, I say, I wouldn't be doing what I'm trying to do. And, ah! I say, if I'd but stuck to the sea I'd have been a third in the Cunard, or perhaps a second in a P.S.N. coaster. I wouldn't be hunched at a desk, I say, but I'd be up on a bridge—up on a bridge with a helmsman, feeling her do her fifteen knots.

It is at such times that I remember the good days, the exciting days, the days of vehement and spirited living. One day stands out, above nearly all my days, as a day of joy.

We were at sea off the River Plate, running south like a stag. The wind had been slowly freshening for twenty-four hours, and for one whole day we had whitened the sea like a battleship. Our run for the day had been 271 knots, which we thought a wonderful run, though it has, of course, been exceeded by many ships. For this ship it was an exceptional run. The wind was on the quarter, her best point of sailing, and there was enough wind for a glutton. Our captain had the reputation of being a "cracker-on," and on this one occasion he drove her till she groaned. For that one wonderful day we staggered and swooped, and bounded in wild leaps, and burrowed down and shivered, and anon rose up shaking. The wind roared up aloft and boomed in the shrouds, and the sails bellied out as stiff as iron. We tore through the seas in great jumps—there is no other word for it. She seemed to leap clear from one green roaring ridge to come smashing down upon the next. I have been in a fast steamer—a very fast turbine steamer—doing more than twenty knots, but she gave me no sense of great speed. In this old sailing ship the joy of the hurry was such that we laughed and cried aloud. The noise of the wind booming, and the clack, clack, clack of the sheet-blocks, and the ridged seas roaring past us, and the groaning and whining of every block and plank, were like tunes for a dance. We seemed to be tearing through it at ninety miles an hour. Our wake whitened and broadened, and rushed away aft in a creamy fury. We were running here, and hurrying there, taking a small pull of this, and getting another inch of that, till we were weary. But as we hauled we sang and shouted. We were possessed of the spirits of the wind. We could have danced and killed each other. We were in an ecstasy. We were possessed. We half believed that the ship would leap from the waters and hurl herself into the heavens, like a winged god. Over her bows came the spray in showers of sparkles. Her foresail was wet to the yard. Her scuppers were brooks. Her swing-ports spouted like cataracts. Recollect, too, that it was a day to make your heart glad. It was a clear day, a sunny day, a day of brightness and splendour. The sun was glorious in the sky. The sky was of a blue unspeakable. We were tearing along across a splendour of sea that made you sing. Far as one could see there was the water shining and shaking. Blue it was, and green it was, and of a dazzling brilliance in the sun. It rose up in hills and in ridges. It smashed into foam and roared. It towered up again and toppled. It mounted and shook in a rhythm, in a tune, in a music. One could have flung one's body to it as a sacrifice. One longed to be in it, to be a part of it, to be beaten and banged by it. It was a wonder and a glory and a terror. It was a triumph, it was royal, to see that beauty.

And later, after a day of it, as we sat below, we felt our mad ship taking yet wilder leaps, bounding over yet more boisterous hollows, and shivering and exulting in every inch of her. She seemed filled with a fiery, unquiet life. She seemed inhuman, glorious, spiritual. One forgot that she was man's work. We forgot that we were men. She was alive, immortal, furious. We were her minions and servants. We were the star-dust whirled in the train of the comet. We banged our plates with the joy we had in her. We sang and shouted, and called her the glory of the seas.

There is an end to human glory. "Greatness a period hath, no sta-ti-on." The end to our glory came when, as we sat at dinner, the door swung back from its hooks and a mate in oilskins bade us come on deck "without stopping for our clothes." It was time. She was carrying no longer; she was dragging. To windward the sea was blotted in a squall. The line of the horizon was masked in a grey film. The glory of the sea had given place to greyness and grimness. Her beauty had become savage. The music of the wind had changed to a howl as of hounds.

And then we began to "take it off her," to snug her down, to check her in her stride. We went to the clew-lines and clewed the royals up. Then it was, "Up there, you boys, and make the royals fast." My royal was the mizzen-royal, a rag of a sail among the clouds, a great grey rag, which was leaping and slatting a hundred and sixty feet above me. The wind beat me down against the shrouds, it banged me and beat me, and blew the tears from my eyes. It seemed to lift me up the futtocks into the top, and up the topmast rigging to the cross-trees. In the cross-trees I learned what wind was.

It came roaring past with a fervour and a fury which struck me breathless. I could only look aloft to the yard I was bound for and heave my panting body up the rigging. And there was the mizzen-royal. There was the sail I had come to furl. And a wonder of a sight it was. It was blowing and bellying in the wind, and leaping around "like a drunken colt," and flying over the yard, thrashing and flogging. It was roaring like a bull with its slatting and thrashing. The royal mast was bending to the strain of it. To my eyes it was buckling like a piece of whalebone. I lay out on the yard, and the sail hit me in the face and knocked my cap away. It beat me and banged me, and blew from my hands. The wind pinned me flat against the yard, and seemed to be blowing all my clothes to shreds. I felt like a king, like an emperor. I shouted aloud with the joy of that "rastle" with the sail. Forward of me was the main mast, with another lad fighting another royal; and beyond him was yet another, whose sail seemed tied in knots. Below me was the ship, a leaping mad thing, with little silly figures, all heads and shoulders, pulling silly strings along the deck. There was the sea, sheer under me, and it looked grey and grim, and streaked with the white of our smother.

Then, with a lashing swish, the rain squall caught us. It beat down the sea. It blotted out the view. I could see nothing more but grey, driving rain, grey spouts of rain, grey clouds which burst rain, grey heavens which opened and poured rain, Cold rain. Icy-cold rain. Rain which drove the dye out of my shirt till I left blue tracks where I walked. For the next two hours I was clewing up, and furling, and snugging her down. By nightfall we were under our three lower topsails and a reefed fore-course. The next day we were hove-to under a weather cloth.

There are varieties of happiness; and, to most of us, that variety called excitement is the most attractive. On a grey day such as this, with the grass rotting in the mud, the image and memory of that variety are a joy to the heart. They are a joy for this, if for no other reason. They teach us that a little thing, a very little thing, a capful of wind even, is enough to make us exalt in, and be proud of, our parts in the pageant of life.

The Mate's Story

ANONYMOUS

The sealing steamer *Greenland*, when berthed in Glasgow harbour, became a vessel of more than usual interest. The terrible disaster which befell her crew in March, 1898 when, of some 150 men who were sent out on the ice to "pan" seals, almost a third lost their lives, excited a great deal of attention.

The reports which appeared in the newspapers gave but a faint idea of the real nature of the disaster. It felt very different when one went down to the dock and looked at the blackened, battered, yet hardy-looking sealer, and talked to the second mate, who shared in the dangers of the memorable trip, and told so vividly of the storm and the search for his comrades on the ocean of ice.

The *Greenland*, a wood screw barque, was an ideal sealer. There was no new-fangled nonsense about her. A steamer, but with sails enough to make her independent of steam when on the fishing ground, one reminded one of the vessels described in the stories of adventure in which we revelled in our schoolboy days.

Ambrose Critch, the second mate, by birth a Newfoundlander, was the ideal of a sealing fisherman, and gave the impression, which is no doubt true, that he was more at home on the deck, or even on ice, than on a city's streets. Bronzed and weather-beaten, yet hardy and earnest, he spoke seriously, but without restraint, of the terrible three weeks spent on and among the ice off the coast of Newfoundland.

"You want to hear about the disaster?" he said to a visitor who boarded the *Greenland*. "I am not sure that I can tell the story very well. It is too terrible a story.

"We left St. John's on the 10th of March: a Thursday, it was. There were, I think, 207 of us on board altogether. Steering N.N.E., we made the Funks' the following day. About 60 miles, maybe, N.E. of the island, we struck seals—on the 12th, I think—it was the Saturday, anyhow. We kept getting seals from then-till the 20th—that was a Sunday, and, as perhaps you may know, we don't seal on Sundays.

"At three o'clock on Monday morning, Captain Barbour sent a watch out on the ice to kill and pan seals. At five he sent two other watches."

(Here Captain Vine, then in command of the *Greenland*, interposed to dispel the notetaker's puzzled look, by explaining that a watch generally consisted of from forty to fifty men, and that to "pan" seals was to gather them into heaps on the ice floes, so that they could be taken to the ship more conveniently.)

"The men were on the ice all day," the mate continued. "About five o'clock at night the storm came on—snow and drift. We could hardly see across the ship. It was like that from five on Monday till three on Tuesday afternoon, and we knew nothing of the poor men who were blindly wandering—perhaps frozen—among the ice and water. We knew the storm had made an opening that they could not get across. The ship was thrown on her beam ends by the wind, and the coal and provisions and seals had to be shifted to right her.

"At three on Tuesday the weather was better, and at five three men were seen on the ice, trying to make for the ship. Those on board were sent to search for the rest. Boats were provisioned and sent out, and before night we had found about eighty of the men. They were frostbitten, all of them, and some so badly injured that they had to be led on board. You see it was smooth ice, not the humpy, loose kind, on which the men could have built huts and sheltered themselves. So they could only stand or lie all the time. They were a mile or so from the ship—"

"A mile from the ship, and on ice?"

"A mile!" the sailor repeated, and he smiled a smile of pity at the ignorance of the man who had never been seal fishing. "Man, we are sometimes a dozen miles from the ship. Ay, a mile!"

Interruptions were few afterwards.

"The men were in extremity, and could not have lasted much longer. We got no bodies on the Tuesday. On Wednesday the drift had cleared, and more searchers were sent out, and on that day many of the dead men were found. Captain Barbour had hoisted flags at half-mast and men from the *Diana* and the *Iceland,* two other sealers, were sent to help us. The *Diana's* men found six bodies, and the *Iceland's* men four. The bodies were found scattered all over the ice, in ones and twos and threes. Many of the men seemed to have been crawling. They would know of the open water that was between them and the ship, and in the blinding drift they would be afraid to walk. One man, who was found alive, was creeping away from the ship. He had lost his mittens, and he had no feeling in his hands.

"The searchers got out the small boats, and hauled them over the ice with ropes. When they found bodies, they put them into the boat and hauled them back to our ship. Our own men did not use boats; they made 'drays'—things like lorries, but without wheels—and hauled them over the ice. We found twenty-four bodies in all."

"Was that the total number lost?"

"Over twenty-four. They must have suffered terribly. I never saw such a storm. It was a wonder how men could have lived at all on the pans. Some of them that the survivors told of actually went mad, and thought the ship was near, and ran into the open water to reach her, and were drowned. There was water all around them, you know.

"There were two boys saved, who had spent fifty-two hours on the ice, in the storm. We found them on the Wednesday, when the storm was over. They had been alone for a while, but they were joined by one of the men, and the three kept together.

"One curious thing there was. It was not the big, hardy-looking men who lived through the storm on the ice. They died, and those who survived were the slight and weak-looking kind.

"The last body we got was found on the Friday, about two miles from the ship. We cruised about for a while, but gave up the search on Saturday, and made for Bay de Verde. The twenty-four bodies were on board here, and I made a pound—a big box, you know—along by this stanchion, and put them all in. I iced them—you have seen salmon iced, a row of fish and a fold of ice—to keep them till we should reach port. We left Bay de Verde on Sunday morning, and after an uneventful voyage, we got to St. John's the same afternoon."

"And the bodies?"

"We saw them buried, of course. I had to take them out of the ice. When I put them in I had put tickets on them, so that we would know them again. No one of us knew them all, but among us we managed to find all their names. It was terrible work taking them out of the ice. The pound was one solid mass. I had to cut each body out in a square piece.

"It was an awful day in St. John's when we arrived. Not many of the lost and dead men belonged there, but there were other ships out, and the folks were frightened. They knew of the disaster, because our captain had telegraphed from Bay de Verde. The Governor did all he could, and the members of council all took part in the work of providing for the suffering, and disposing of the dead. We buried them in the cemeteries of their different churches.

"A relief fund was started, and the Glasgow owners of the ship, as well as the agent in St. John's, contributed handsomely. The crew all belonged to Newfoundland; most of them to Bonavista Bay.

"About the seals? The voyage was abandoned when the disaster happened. It lasted three weeks. We had 14,500 seals on board, and we left as many on the ice as would have loaded the ship. We landed the seals on Tuesday at Harbour Grace, after the bodies were buried and the ship stayed there until we took on board a cargo of oil and skins for Glasgow.

"You don't often have a sealer in your harbour, I daresay. No, I thought not. We had to come here because the vessel needed a new boiler. No, I don't think I can tell you much more about the disaster. There is plenty more to tell, but somehow I can't tell it. It was terrible."

It was.

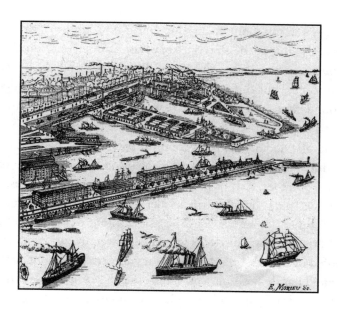

About All Kinds of Ships

MARK TWAIN

The Modern Steamer and the Obsolete Steamer

We are victims of one common superstition—the superstition that we realize the changes that are daily taking place in the world because we read about them and know what they are. I should not have supposed that the modern ship could be a surprise to me, but it is. It seems to be as much of a surprise to me as it could have been if I had never read anything about it. I walk about this great vessel, the *Havel*, as she plows her way through the Atlantic, and every detail that comes under my eye brings up the miniature counterpart of it as it existed in the little ships I crossed the ocean in fourteen, seventeen, eighteen, and twenty years ago.

In the *Havel* one can be in several respects more comfortable than he can be in the best hotels on the continent of Europe. For instance, she has several bathrooms, and they are as convenient and as nicely equipped as the bathrooms in a fine private house in America; whereas in the hotels of the continent one bathroom is considered sufficient, and it is generally shabby and located in some out-of-the-way corner of the house; moreover, you need to give notice so long beforehand that you get over wanting a bath by the time you get it. In the hotels there are a good many different kinds of noises, and they spoil sleep; in my room in the ship I hear no sounds. In the hotels they usually shut off the electric light at midnight; in the ship one may burn it in one's room all night.

In the steamer *Batavia*, twenty years ago, one candle, set in the bulkhead between two staterooms, was there to light both rooms, but did not light either of them. It was extinguished at 11 at night, and so were all the saloon lamps except one or two, which were left burning to help the passenger see how to break his neck trying to get around in the dark. The passengers sat at table on long benches made of the hardest kind of wood; in the *Havel* one sits on a swivel chair with a cushioned back to it. In those old times the dinner bill of fare was always the same: a pint of some simple, homely soup or other, boiled codfish and potatoes, slab of boiled beef, stewed prunes for dessert—on Sundays "dog in a blanket," on Thursdays "plum duff." In the modern ship the *menu* is choice and elaborate, and is changed daily. In the old times dinner was a sad occasion; in our day a concealed orchestra enlivens it with charming music. In the old days the decks were always wet; in our day they are usually dry, for the promenade-deck is roofed over, and a sea seldom comes aboard. In a moderately disturbed sea, in the old days, a landsman could hardly keep his legs, but in such a sea in our day the decks are as level as a table. In the old days the inside of a ship was the plainest and barrenest thing, and the most dismal and uncomfortable that ingenuity could devise; the modern ship is a marvel of rich and costly decoration and sumptuous appointment, and is equipped with every comfort and convenience that money can buy. The old ships had no place of assembly but the dining-room, the new ones have several spacious and beautiful drawing-rooms. The old ships offered the passenger no chance to smoke except in the place that was called the "fiddle." It was a repulsive den made of rough boards (full of cracks) and its office was to protect the main hatch. It was grimy and dirty; there were no seats; the only light was a lamp of the rancid-oil-and-rag kind; the place was very cold, and never dry, for the seas broke in through the cracks every little while and drenched the cavern thoroughly. In the modern ship there are three or four large smoking-rooms, and they have card tables and cushioned sofas, and are heated by steam and lighted by electricity. There are few European hotels with such smoking-rooms.

The former ships were built of wood, and had two or three water-tight compartments in the hold with doors in them which were often left open, particularly when the ship was going to hit a rock. The modern leviathan is built of steel, and the water-tight bulkheads have no doors in them; they divide the ship into nine or ten water-tight compartments and endow her with as many lives as a cat. Their complete efficiency was established by the happy results following the memorable accident to the *City of Paris* a year or two ago.

One curious thing which is at once noticeable in the great modern ship is the absence of hubbub, clatter, rush of feet, roaring of orders. That is all gone by. The elaborate maneuvers necessary in working the vessel into her dock are conducted without sound; one sees nothing of the processes, hears no commands. A Sabbath stillness and solemnity reign, in place of the turmoil and racket of the earlier days. The modern ship has a spacious bridge fenced chin-high with sailcloth, and floored with wooden gratings; and this bridge, with its fenced fore-and-aft annexes, could accommodate a seated audience of a hundred and fifty men. There are three steering equipments, each competent if the others should break. From the bridge the ship is steered, and also handled. The handling is not done by shout or whistle, but by signalling with patent automatic gongs. There are three tell-tales, with plainly lettered dials—for steering, handling the engines, and for communicating orders to the invisible mates who are conducting the landing of the ship or casting off. The officer who is astern is out of sight and too far away to hear trumpet calls; but the gongs near him tell him to haul in, pay out, make fast, let go, and so on; he hears, but the passengers do not, and so the ship seems to land herself without human help.

This great bridge is thirty or forty feet above the water, but the sea climbs up there sometimes; so there is another bridge twelve or fifteen feet higher still, for use in these emergencies. The force of water is a strange thing. It slips between one's fingers like air, but upon occasion it acts like a solid body and will bend a thin iron rod. In the *Havel* it has splintered a heavy oaken rail into broom-straws instead of merely breaking it in two, as would have been the seemingly natural thing for it to do. At the time of the awful Johnstown disaster, according to the testimony of several witnesses, rocks were carried some distance on the surface of the stupendous torrent; and at St. Helena, many years ago, a vast sea wave carried a battery of cannon forty feet up a steep slope and deposited the guns there in a row. But the water has done a still stranger thing, and it is one which is credibly vouched for. A marlinspike is an implement about a foot long which tapers from its butt to the other extremity and ends in a sharp point. It is made of iron and is heavy. A wave came aboard a ship in a storm and raged aft, breast high, carrying a marlinspike point first with it, and with such lightning-like swiftness and force as to drive it three or four inches into a sailor's body and kill him.

In all ways the ocean greyhound of to-day is imposing and impressive to one who carries in his head no ship pictures of a recent date. In bulk she comes near to rivaling the Ark; yet this monstrous mass of steel is driven five hundred miles through the waves in twenty-four hours. I remember the brag run of a steamer which I traveled in once on the Pacific—it was two hundred and nine miles in twenty-four hours; a year or so later I was a passenger in the excursion tub *Quaker City*, and on one occasion in a level and glassy sea, it was claimed that she reeled off two hundred and eleven miles between noon and noon, but it was probably a campaign lie. That little steamer had seventy passengers, and a crew of forty men, and seemed a good deal of a beehive. But in this present ship we are living in a sort of solitude, these soft summer days, with sometimes a hundred passengers scattered about the spacious distances, and sometimes nobody in sight at all; yet, hidden somewhere in the vessel's bulk, there are (including crew) near eleven hundred people.

The stateliest lines in the literature of the sea are these:

> "Britannia needs no bulwarks, no towers along the steep—
> Her march is o'er the mountain waves, her home is on the deep!"

There it is. In those old times the little ships climbed over the waves and wallowed down into the trough on the other side; the giant ship of our day does not climb over the waves, but crushes her way through them. Her formidable weight and mass and impetus give her mastery over any but extraordinary storm waves.

The ingenuity of man! I mean in this passing generation. To-day I found in the chart-room a frame of removable wooden slats on the wall, and on the slats was painted uninforming information like this:

Trim-Tank,	Empty
Double-Bottom No. 1,	Full
Double-Bottom No. 2,	Full
Double-Bottom No. 3,	Full
Double-Bottom No. 4,	Full

While I was trying to think out what kind of a game this might be and how a stranger might best go to work to beat it, a sailor came in and pulled out the "Empty" end of the first slat and put it back with its reverse side to the front, marked "Full." He made some other change, I did not notice what. The slat-frame was soon explained. Its function was to indicate how the ballast in the ship was distributed. The striking thing was that the ballast was water. I did not know that a ship had ever been ballasted with water. I had merely read, some time or other, that such an experiment was to be tried. But that is the modern way; between the experimental trial of a new thing and its adoption, there is no wasted time, if the trial proves its value.

On the wall, near the slat-frame, there was an outline drawing of the ship, and this betrayed the fact that this vessel has twenty-two considerable lakes of water in her. These lakes are in her bottom; they are imprisoned between her real bottom and a false bottom. They are separated from each other, thwartships, by water-tight bulkheads, and separated down the middle by a bulkhead running from the bow four-fifths of the way to the stern. It is a chain of lakes four hundred feet long and from five to seven feet deep. Fourteen of the lakes contain fresh water brought from shore, and the aggregate weight of it is four hundred tons. The rest of the lakes contain salt water—six hundred and eighteen tons. Upwards of a thousand tons of water, altogether.

Think how handy this ballast is. The ship leaves port with the lakes all full. As she lightens forward through consumption of coal, she loses trim—her head rises, her stern sinks down. Then they spill one of the sternward lakes into the sea, and the trim is restored. This can be repeated right along as occasion may require. Also, a lake at one end of the ship can be moved to the other end by pipes and steam pumps. When the sailor changed the slat-frame to-day, he was posting a transference of that kind. The seas had been increasing, and the vessel's head needed more weighting, to keep it from rising on the waves instead of plowing through them; therefore, twenty-five tons of water had been transferred to the bow from a lake situated well towards the stern.

A water compartment is kept either full or empty. The body of water must be compact, so that it cannot slosh around. A shifting ballast would not do, of course.

The modern ship is full of beautiful ingenuities, but it seems to me that this one is the king. I would rather be the originator of that idea than of any of the others. Perhaps the trim of a ship was never perfectly ordered and preserved until now. A vessel out of trim will not steer, her speed is maimed, she strains and labors in the seas. Poor creature, for six thousand years she has had no comfort until these latest days. For six thousand years she swam through the best and cheapest ballast in the world, the only perfect ballast, but she couldn't tell her master and he had not the wit to find it out for himself. It is odd to reflect that there is nearly as much water inside of this ship as there is outside, and yet there is no danger.

Noah's Ark

The progress made in the great art of ship-building since Noah's time is quite noticeable. Also, the looseness of the navigation laws in the time of Noah is in quite striking contrast with the strictness of the navigation laws of our time. It would not be possible for Noah to do in our day what he was permitted to do in his own. Experience has taught us the necessity of being more particular, more conservative, more careful of human life. Noah would not be allowed to sail from Bremen in our day. The inspectors would come and examine the Ark, and make all sorts of objections. A person who knows Germany can imagine the scene and the conversation without difficulty and without missing a detail. The inspector would be in a beautiful military uniform; he would be respectful, dignified, kindly, the perfect gentleman, but steady as the north star to the last requirement of his duty. He would make Noah tell him where he was born, and how old he was, and what religious sect he belonged to, and the amount of his income, and the grade and position he claimed socially, and the name and style of his occupation, and how many wives and children he had, and how many servants, and the name, sex, and age of the whole of them; and if he hadn't a passport he would be courteously required to get one right away. Then he would take up the matter of the Ark:

"What is her length?"

"Six hundred feet."

"Depth?"

"Sixty-five."

"Beam?"

"Fifty or sixty."

"Built of—"

"Wood."

"What kind?"

"Shittim and gopher."

"Interior and exterior decorations?"

"Pitched within and without."

"Passengers?"

"Eight."

"Sex?"

"Half male, the others female."

"Ages?"

"From a hundred years up."

"Up to where?"

"Six hundred."

"Ah—going to Chicago; good idea, too. Surgeon's name?"

"We have no surgeon."

"Must provide a surgeon. Also an undertaker—particularly the undertaker. These people must not be left without the necessities of life at their age. Crew?"

"The same eight."

"The same eight?"

"The same eight."

"And half of them women?"

"Yes, sir."

"Have they ever served as seamen?"

"No, sir."

"Have the men?"

"No, sir."

"Have any of you ever been to sea?"

"No, sir."

"Where were you reared?"

"On a farm—all of us."

"This vessel requires a crew of eight hundred men, she not being a steamer. You must provide them. She must have four mates and nine cooks. Who is captain?"

"I am, sir."

"You must get a captain. Also a chambermaid. Also sick nurses for the old people. Who designed this vessel?"

"I did, sir."

"Is it your first attempt?"

"Yes, sir."

"I partly suspected it. Cargo?"

"Animals."

"Kinds?"

"All kinds."

"Wild, or tame?"

"Mainly wild."

"Foreign or domestic?"

"Mainly foreign."

"Principal wild ones?"

"Megatherium, elephant, rhinoceros, lion, tiger, wolf, snakes—all the wild things of all climes—two of each."

"Securely caged?"

"No, not caged."

"They must have iron cages. Who feeds and waters the menagerie?"

"We do."

"The old people?"

"Yes, sir."

"It is dangerous—for both. The animals must be cared for by a competent force. How many animals are there?"

"Big ones, seven thousand; big and little together, ninety-eight thousand."

"You must provide twelve hundred keepers. How is the vessel lighted?"

"By two windows."

"Where are they?"

"Up under the eaves."

"Two windows for a tunnel six hundred feet long and sixty-five feet deep? You must put in the electric light—a few arc lights and fifteen hundred incandescents. What do you do in case of leaks? How many pumps have you?"

"None, sir."

"You must provide pumps. How do you get water for the passengers and the animals?"

"We let down the buckets from the windows."

"It is inadequate. What is your motive power?"

"What is my which?"

"Motive power. What power do you use in driving the ship?"

"None."

"You must provide sails or steam. What is the nature of your steering apparatus?"

"We haven't any."

"Haven't you a rudder?"

"No, sir."

"How do you steer the vessel?"

"We don't."

"You must provide a rudder, and properly equip it. How many anchors have you?"

"None."

"You must provide six. One is not permitted to sail a vessel like this without that protection. How many life-boats have you?"

"None, sir."

"Provide twenty-five. How many life-preservers?"

"None."

"You will provide two thousand. How long are you expecting your voyage to last?"

"Eleven or twelve months."

"Eleven or twelve months. Pretty slow—but you will be in time for the Exposition. What is your ship sheathed with—copper?"

"Her hull is bare—not sheathed at all."

"Dear man, the wood-boring creatures of the sea would riddle her like a sieve and send her to the bottom in three months. She *cannot* be allowed to go away in this condition; she must be sheathed. Just a word more: Have you reflected that Chicago is an inland city and not reachable with a vessel like this?"

"Shecargo? What is Shecargo? I am not going to Shecargo."

"Indeed? Then may I ask what the animals are for?"

"Just to breed others from."

"Others? Is it possible that you haven't enough?"

"For the present needs of civilization, yes; but the rest are going to be drowned in a flood, and these are to renew the supply."

"A flood?"

"Yes, sir."

"Are you sure of that?"

"Perfectly sure. It is going to rain forty days and forty nights."

"Give yourself no concern about that, dear sir, it often does that here."

"Not this kind of rain. This is going to cover the mountain tops, and the earth will pass from sight."

"Privately—but of course not officially—I am sorry you revealed this, for it compels me to withdraw the option I gave you as to sails or steam. I must require you to use steam. Your ship cannot carry the hundredth part of an eleven-months water supply for the animals. You will have to have condensed water."

"But I tell you I am going to dip water from outside with buckets."

"It will not answer. Before the flood reaches the mountain tops the fresh waters will have joined the salt seas, and it will all be salt. You must put in steam and condense your water. I will now bid you good day, sir. Did I understand you to say that this was your very first attempt at ship building?"

"My very first, sir, I give you the honest truth. I built this Ark without having ever had the slightest training or experience or instruction in marine architecture."

"It is a remarkable work, sir, a most remarkable work. I consider that it contains more features that are new—absolutely new and unhackneyed—than are to be found in any other vessel that swims the seas."

"This compliment does me infinite honor, dear sir, infinite; and I shall cherish the memory of it while life shall last. Sir, I offer my duty and most grateful thanks. Adieu."

No, the German inspector would be limitlessly courteous to Noah, and would make him feel that he was among friends, but he wouldn't let him go to sea with that Ark.

Columbus's Craft

Between Noah's time and the time of Columbus naval architecture underwent some changes, and from being unspeakably bad was improved to a point which may be described as less unspeakably bad. I have read somewhere, some time or other, that one of Columbus's ships was a ninety-ton vessel. By comparing that ship with the ocean greyhounds of our time one is able to get down to a comprehension of how small that Spanish bark was, and how little fitted she would be to run opposition in the Atlantic passenger trade to-day. It would take seventy-four of her to match the tonnage of the *Havel* and carry the *Havel*'s trip. If I remember rightly, it took her ten weeks to make the passage. With our ideas this would now be considered an objectionable gait. She probably had a captain, a mate, and a crew consisting of four seamen and a boy. The crew of a modern greyhound numbers two hundred and fifty persons.

Columbus's ship being small and very old, we know that we may draw from these two facts several absolute certainties in the way of minor details which history has left unrecorded. For instance, being small, we know that she rolled and pitched and tumbled in any ordinary sea, and stood on her head or her tail, or lay down with her ear in the water, when storm seas ran high; also, that she was used to having billows plunge aboard and wash her decks from stem to stern; also, that the storm racks were on the table all the way over, and that nevertheless a man's soup was oftener landed in his lap than in his stomach; also, that the dining-saloon was about ten feet by seven, dark, airless, and suffocating with oil-stench; also, that there was only about one stateroom, the size of a grave, with a tier of two or three berths in it of the dimensions and comfortableness of coffins, and that when the light was out the darkness in there was so thick and real that you could bite into it and chew it like gum; also, that the only promenade was on the lofty poop-deck astern (for the ship was shaped like a high-quarter shoe)—a streak sixteen feet long by three feet wide, all the rest of the vessel being littered with ropes and flooded by the seas.

We know all these things to be true, from the mere fact that we know the vessel was small. As the vessel was old, certain other truths follow, as matters of course. For instance: she was full of rats; she was full of cockroaches; the heavy seas made her seams open and shut like your fingers, and she leaked like a basket; where leakage is, there also, of necessity, is bilgewater; and where bilgewater is, only the dead can enjoy life. This is on account of the smell. In the presence of bilgewater, Limburger cheese becomes odorless and ashamed.

From these absolutely sure data we can competently picture the daily life of the great discoverer. In the early morning he paid his devotions at the shrine of the Virgin. At eight bells he appeared on the poop-deck promenade. If the weather was chilly he came up clad from plumed helmet to spurred heel in magnificent plate armor inlaid with arabesques of gold, having previously warmed it at the galley fire. If the weather was warm he came up in the ordinary sailor toggery of the time—great slouch hat of blue velvet with a flowing brush of snowy ostrich plumes, fastened on with a flashing cluster of diamonds and emeralds; gold-embroidered doublet of green velvet with slashed sleeves exposing under-sleeves of crimson satin; deep collar and cuff ruffles of rich limp lace; trunk hose of pink velvet, with big knee-knots of brocaded yellow ribbon; pearl-tinted silk stockings, clocked and daintily embroidered; lemon-colored buskins of unborn kid, funnel-topped, and drooping low to expose the pretty stockings; deep gauntlets of finest white heretic skin, from the factory of the Holy Inquisition, formerly part of the person of a lady of rank; rapier with sheath crusted with jewels, and hanging from a broad baldric upholstered with rubies and sapphires.

He walked the promenade thoughtfully, he noted the aspects of the sky and the course of the wind; he kept an eye out for drifting vegetation and other signs of land; he jawed the man at the wheel for pastime; he got out an imitation egg and kept himself in practice on his old trick of making it stand on its end; now and then he hove a life-line below and fished up a sailor who was drowning on the quarter-deck; the rest of his watch he gaped and yawned and stretched, and said he wouldn't make the trip again to discover six Americas. For that was the kind of natural human person Columbus was when not posing for posterity.

At noon he took the sun and ascertained that the good ship had made three hundred yards in twenty-four hours, and this enabled him to win the pool. Anybody can win the pool when nobody but himself has the privilege of straightening out the ship's run and getting it right.

The Admiral has breakfasted alone, in state: bacon, beans, and gin; at noon he dines alone, in state: bacon, beans, and gin; at six he sups alone, in state: bacon, beans, and gin; at eleven P.M. he takes a night relish alone, in state: bacon, beans, and gin. At none of these orgies is there any music; the ship orchestra is modern. After his final meal he returned thanks for his many blessings, a little overrating their value, perhaps, and then he laid off his silken splendors or his gilded hardware, and turned in, in his little coffin-bunk, and blew out his flickering stencher and began to refresh his lungs with inverted sighs freighted with the rich odors of rancid oil and bilgewater. The sighs returned as snores, and then the rats and the cockroaches swarmed out in brigades and divisions and army corps and had a circus all over him. Such was the daily life of the great discoverer in his marine basket during several historic weeks; and the difference between his ship and his comforts and ours is visible almost at a glance.

When he returned, the King of Spain, marveling, said—as history records:

"This ship seems to be leaky. Did she leak badly?"

"You shall judge for yourself, sire. I pumped the Atlantic Ocean through her sixteen times on the passage."

This is General Horace Porter's account. Other authorities say fifteen.

It can be shown that the differences between that ship and the one I am writing these historical contributions in are in several respects remarkable. Take the matter of decoration, for instance. I have been looking around again, yesterday and to-day, and have noted several details which I conceive to have been absent from Columbus' ship, or at least slurred over and not elaborated and perfected. I observe stateroom doors three inches thick, of solid oak and polished. I note companion-way vestibules with walls, doors, and ceilings paneled in polished hardwoods, some light, some dark, all dainty and delicate joiner-work, and yet every joint compact and tight; with beautiful pictures inserted, composed of blue tiles—some of the pictures containing as many as sixty tiles—and the joinings of those tiles perfect. These are daring experiments. One would have said that the first time the ship went straining and laboring through a storm-tumbled sea those tiles would gape apart and drop out. That they have not done so is evidence that the joiner's art has advanced a good deal since the days when ships were so shackly that when a giant sea gave them a wrench the doors came unbolted. I find the walls of the dining-saloon upholstered with mellow pictures wrought in tapestry and the ceiling aglow with pictures done in oil. In other places of assembly I find great panels filled with embossed Spanish leather, the figures rich with gilding and bronze. Everywhere I find sumptuous masses of color—color, color, color—color all about, color of every shade and tint and variety; and, as a result, the ship is bright and cheery to the eye, and this cheeriness invades one's spirit and contents it. To fully appreciate the force and spiritual value of this radiant and opulent dream of color, one must stand outside at night in the pitch dark and the rain, and look in through a port, and observe it in the lavish splendor of the electric lights. The old-time ships were dull, plain, graceless, gloomy, and horribly depressing. They compelled the blues; one could not escape the blues in them. The modern idea is right: to surround the passenger with conveniences, luxuries, and abundance of inspiriting color. As a result, the ship is the pleasantest place one can be in, except, perhaps, one's home.

A Vanished Sentiment

One thing is gone, to return no more forever—the romance of the sea. Soft sentimentality about the sea has retired from the activities of this life, and is but a memory of the past, already remote and much faded. But within the recollection of men still living, it was in the breast of every individual; and the further any individual lived from salt water the more of it he kept in stock. It was as pervasive, as universal, as the atmosphere itself. The mere mention of the sea, the romantic sea, would make any company of people sentimental and mawkish at once. The great majority of the songs that were sung by the young people of the back settlements had the melancholy wanderer for subject and his mouthings about the sea for refrain. Picnic parties paddling down a creek in a canoe when the twilight shadows were gathering always sang:

> Homeward bound, homeward bound
> From a foreign shore;

and this was also a favorite in the West with the passengers on sternwheel steamboats. There was another:

> My boat is by the shore
>   And my bark is on the sea,
> But before I go, Tom Moore,
>   Here's a double health to thee.

And this one, also:

> O pilot, 'tis a fearful night,
> There's danger on the deep.

And this:

> A life on the ocean wave
>   And a home on the rolling deep,

> Where the scattered waters rave
> And the winds their revels keep!

And this:

> A wet sheet and a flowing sea,
> And a wind that follows fair.

And this:

> My foot is on my gallant deck,
> Once more the rover is free!

And the "Larboard Watch"—the person referred to below is at the masthead, or somewhere up there:

> Oh, who can tell what joy he feels,
> As o'er the foam his vessel reels,
> And his tired eyelids slumb'ring fall,
> He rouses at the welcome call
> Of "Larboard watch—ahoy!"

Yes, and there was forever and always some jackass-voiced person braying out:

> Rocked in the cradle of the deep,
> I lay me down in peace to sleep!

Other favorites had these suggestive titles: "The Storm at Sea;" "The Bird at Sea;" "The Sailor Boy's Dream;" "The Captive Pirate's Lament;" "We are far from Home on the Stormy Main"—and so on, and so on, the list is endless. Everybody on a farm lived chiefly amid the dangers of the deep in those days, in fancy.

But all that is gone now. Not a vestige of it is left. The iron-clad, with her unsentimental aspect and frigid attention to business, banished romance from the war marine, and the unsentimental steamer has banished it from the commercial marine. The dangers and uncertainties which made sea life romantic have disappeared and carried the poetic element along with them. In our day the passengers never sing sea-songs on board a ship, and the band never plays them. Pathetic songs about the wanderer in strange lands far from home, once so popular and contributing such fire and color to the imagination by reason of the rarity of that kind of wanderer, have lost their charm and fallen silent, because everybody is a wanderer in the far lands now, and the interest in that detail is dead. Nobody is worried about the wanderer; there are no perils of the sea for him, there are no uncertainties. He is safer in the ship than he would probably be at home, for there he is always liable to have to attend some friend's funeral and stand over the grave in the sleet, bareheaded—and that means pneumonia for him, if he gets his deserts; and the uncertainties of his voyage are reduced to whether he will arrive on the other side in the appointed afternoon, or have to wait till morning.

The first ship I was ever in was a sailing vessel. She was twenty-eight days going from San Francisco to the Sandwich Islands. But the main reason for this particularly slow passage was, that she got becalmed and lay in one spot fourteen days in the center of the Pacific two thousand miles from land. I hear no sea-songs in this present vessel, but I heard the entire layout in that one. There were a dozen young people—they are pretty old now, I reckon—and they used to group themselves on the stern, in the starlight or the moonlight, every evening, and sing sea-songs till after midnight, in that hot, silent, motionless calm. They had no sense of humor, and they always sang "Homeward Bound," without reflecting that that was practically ridiculous, since they were standing still and not proceeding in any direction at all; and they often followed that song with " 'Are we almost there, are we almost there,' said the dying girl as she drew near home?"

It was a very pleasant company of young people, and I wonder where they are now. Gone, oh, none knows whither; and the bloom and grace and beauty of their youth, where is that? Among them was a liar; all tried to reform him, but none could do it. And so, gradually, he was left to himself; none of us would associate with him. Many a time since I have seen in fancy that forsaken figure, leaning forlorn against the taffrail, and have reflected that perhaps if we had tried harder, and been more patient, we might have won him from his fault and persuaded him to relinquish it. But it is hard to tell; with him the vice was extreme, and was probably incurable. I like to think—and, indeed, I do think—that I did the best that in me lay to lead him to higher and better ways.

There was a singular circumstance. The ship lay becalmed that entire fortnight in exactly the same spot. Then a handsome breeze came fanning over the sea, and we spread our white wings for flight. But the vessel did not budge. The sails bellied out, the gale strained at the ropes, but the vessel moved not a hair's breadth from her place. The captain was surprised. It was some hours before we found out what the cause of the detention was. It was barnacles. They collect very fast in that part of the Pacific. They had fastened themselves to the ship's bottom; then others had fastened themselves to the first bunch, others to these, and so on, down and down and down, and the last bunch had glued the column hard and fast to the bottom of the sea, which is five miles deep at that point. So the ship was simply become the handle of a walking cane five miles long—yes, and no more movable by wind and sail than a continent is. It was regarded by every one as remarkable.

Well, the next week—however, Sandy Hook is in sight.

The Pirate Crew Set Sail

MARK TWAIN

Tom's mind was made up now. He was gloomy and desperate. He was a forsaken, friendless boy, he said; nobody loved him; when they found out what they had driven him to, perhaps they would be sorry; he had tried to do right and get along, but they would not let him; since nothing would do them but to be rid of him, let it be so; and let them blame *him* for the consequences—why shouldn't they? What right had the friendless to complain? Yes, they had forced him to it at last: he would lead a life of crime. There was no choice.

By this time he was far down Meadow Lane, and the bell for school to "take up" tinkled faintly upon his ear. He sobbed, now, to think he should never, never hear that old familiar sound any more—it was very hard, but it was forced on him; since he was driven out into the cold world, he must submit—but he forgave them. Then the sobs came thick and fast.

Just at this point he met his soul's sworn comrade, Joe Harper—hard-eyed, and with evidently a great and dismal purpose in his heart. Plainly here were "two souls with but a single thought." Tom, wiping his eyes with his sleeve, began to blubber out something about a resolution to escape from hard usage and lack of sympathy at home by roaming abroad into the great world never to return; and ended by hoping that Joe would not forget him.

But it transpired that this was a request which Joe had just been going to make to Tom, and had come to hunt him up for that purpose. His mother had whipped him for drinking some cream which he had never tasted and knew nothing about; it was plain that she was tired of him and wished him to go; if she felt that way, there was nothing for him to do but succumb; he hoped she would be happy, and never regret having driven her poor boy out into the unfeeling world to suffer and die.

As the two boys walked sorrowing along, they made a new compact to stand by each other and be brothers and never separate till death relieved them of their troubles. Then they began to lay their plans. Joe was for being a hermit, and living on crusts in a remote cave, and dying, sometime, of cold and want and grief; but after listening to Tom, he conceded that there were some conspicuous advantages about a life of crime, and so he consented to be a pirate.

Three miles below St. Petersburg, at a point where the Mississippi River was a trifle over a mile wide, there was a long, narrow, wooded island, with a shallow bar at the head of it, and this offered well as a rendezvous. It was not inhabited; it lay far over toward the farther shore, abreast a dense and almost wholly unpeopled forest. So Jackson's Island was chosen. Who were to be the subjects of their piracies was a matter that did not occur to them. Then they hunted up Huckleberry Finn, and he joined them promptly, for all careers were one to him; he was indifferent. They presently separated to meet at a lonely spot on the riverbank two miles above the village at the favorite hour—which was midnight. There was a small log raft there which they meant to capture. Each would bring hooks and lines, and such provision as he could steal in the most dark and mysterious way—as became outlaws. And before the afternoon was done they had all managed to enjoy the sweet glory of spreading the fact that pretty soon the town would "hear something." All who got this vague hint were cautioned to "be mum and wait."

About midnight Tom arrived with a boiled ham and a few trifles, and stopped in a dense undergrowth on a small bluff overlooking the meeting place. It was starlight, and very still. The mighty river lay like an ocean at rest. Tom listened a moment, but no sound disturbed the quiet. Then he gave a low, distinct whistle. It was answered from under the bluff. Tom whistled twice more; these signals were answered in the same way. Then a guarded voice said:

"Who goes there?"

"Tom Sawyer, the Black Avenger of the Spanish Main. Name your names."

"Huck Finn the Red-Handed, and Joe Harper the Terror of the Seas." Tom had furnished these titles, from his favorite literature.

"'Tis well. Give the countersign."

Two hoarse whispers delivered the same awful word simultaneously to the brooding night: "Blood!"

Then Tom tumbled his ham over the bluff and let himself down after it, tearing both skin and clothes to some extent in the effort. There was an easy, comfortable path along the shore under the bluff, but it lacked the advantages of difficulty and danger so valued by a pirate.

The Terror of the Seas had brought a side of bacon, and had about worn himself out with getting it there. Finn the Red-Handed had stolen a skillet and a quantity of half-cured leaf tobacco, and had also brought a few corncobs to make pipes with. But none of the pirates smoked or "chewed" but himself. The Black Avenger of the Spanish Main said it would never do to start without some fire. That was a wise thought; matches were hardly known there in that day. They saw a fire smoldering upon a great raft a hundred yards above, and they went stealthily thither and helped themselves to a chunk. They made an imposing adventure of it, saying, "Hist!" every now and then, and suddenly halting with finger on lip; moving with hands on imaginary dagger hilts; and giving orders in dismal whispers that if "the foe" stirred to "let him have it to the hilt," because "dead men tell no tales." They knew well enough that the raftsmen were all down at the village laying in stores or having a spree, but still that was no excuse for their conducting this thing in an unpiratical way.

They shoved off, presently, Tom in command, Huck at the after oar and Joe at the forward. Tom stood amidships, gloomy browed, and with folded arms, and gave his orders in a low, stern whisper:

"Luff, and bring her to the wind!"

"Aye-aye, sir!"

"Steady, steady-y-y-y!"

"Steady it is, sir!"

"Let her go off a point!"

"Point it is, sir!"

As the boys steadily and monotonously drove the raft toward midstream it was no doubt understood that these orders were given only for "style," and were not intended to mean anything in particular.

"What sail's she carrying?"

"Courses, tops'ls, and flying jib, sir."

"Send the r'yals up! Lay out aloft, there, half a dozen of ye—foretopmaststuns'l! Lively, now!"

"Aye-aye, sir!"

"Shake out that maintogalans'l! Sheets and braces! *Now*, my hearties!"

"Aye-aye, sir!"

"Hellum-a-lee—hard aport! Stand by to meet her when she comes! Port, port! *Now*, men! With a will! Steady-y-y-y!"

"Steady it is, sir!"

The raft drew beyond the middle of the river; the boys pointed her head right, and then lay on their oars. The river was not high, so there was not more than a two- or three-mile current. Hardly a word was said during the next three-quarters of an hour. Now the raft was passing before the distant town. Two or three glimmering lights showed where it lay, peacefully sleeping, beyond the vague vast sweep of star-gemmed water, unconscious of the tremendous event that was happening. The Black Avenger stood still with folded arms, "looking his last" upon the scene of his former joys and his later sufferings, and wishing "she" could see him now, abroad on the wild sea, facing peril and death with dauntless heart, going to his doom with a grim smile on his lips. It was but a small strain on his imagination to remove Jackson's Island beyond eyeshot of the village, and so he "looked his last" with a broken and satisfied heart. The other pirates were looking their last, too; and they all looked so long that they came near letting the current drift them out of the range of the island. But they discovered the danger in time, and made shift to avert it. About two o'clock in the morning the raft grounded on the bar two hundred yards above the head of the island, and they waded back and forth until they had landed their freight. Part of the little raft's belongings consisted of an old sail, and this they spread over a nook in the bushes for a tent to shelter their provisions; but they themselves would sleep in the open air in good weather, as became outlaws.

They built a fire against the side of a great log twenty or thirty steps within the somber depths of the forest, and then cooked some bacon in the frying pan for supper, and used up half of the corn "pone" stock they had brought. It seemed glorious sport to be feasting in that wild free way in the virgin forest of an unexplored and uninhabited island, far from the haunts of men, and they said they never would return to civilization. The climbing fire lit up their faces and threw its ruddy glare upon the pillared tree trunks of their forest temple, and upon the varnished foliage and festooning vines.

When the last crisp slice of bacon was gone and the last allowance of corn pone devoured, the boys stretched themselves out on the grass, filled with contentment. They could have found a cooler place, but they would not deny themselves such a romantic feature as the roasting campfire.

"*Ain't* it gay?" said Joe.

"It's *nuts!*" said Tom. "What would the boys say if they could see us?"

"Say? Well, they'd just die to be here—hey, Hucky!"

"I reckon so," said Huckleberry; "anyways, *I'm* suited. I don't want nothing better'n this. I don't ever get enough to eat, gen'ally—and here they can't come and pick at a feller and bullyrag him so."

"It's just the life for me," said Tom. "You don't have to get up, mornings, and you don't have to go to school, and wash, and all that blame foolishness. You see a pirate don't have to do *anything*, Joe, when he's ashore, but a hermit *he* has to be praying considerable, and then he don't have any fun, anyway, all by himself that way."

"Oh, yes, that's so," said Joe, "but I hadn't thought much about it, you know. I'd a good deal rather be a pirate, now that I've tried it."

"You see," said Tom, "people don't go much on hermits, nowadays, like they used to in old times, but a pirate's always respected. And a hermit's got to sleep on the hardest place he can find, and put sackcloth and ashes on his head, and stand out in the rain, and—"

"What does he put sackcloth and ashes on his head for?" inquired Huck.

"*I* dono. But they've *got* to do it. Hermits always do. You'd have to do that if you was a hermit."

"Derned if I would," said Huck

"Well, what would you do?"

"I dunno. But I wouldn't do that."

"Why, Huck, you'd *have* to. How'd you get around it?"

"Why, I just wouldn't stand it. I'd run away."

"Run away! Well, you *would* be a nice old slouch of a hermit. You'd be a disgrace."

The Red-Handed made no response, being better employed. He had finished gouging out a cob, and now he fitted a weed stem to it, loaded it with tobacco, and was pressing a coal to the charge and blowing a cloud of fragrant smoke—he was in the full bloom of luxurious contentment. The other pirates envied him this majestic vice, and secretly resolved to acquire it shortly. Presently Huck said:

"What does pirates have to do?"

Tom said:

"Oh, they have just a bully time—take ships and burn them, and get the money and bury it in awful places in their island where there's ghosts and things to watch it, and kill everybody in the ships—make 'em walk a plank."

"And they carry the women to the island," said Joe; "they don't kill the women."

"No," assented Tom, "they don't kill the women—they're too noble. And the women's always beautiful, too."

"And don't they wear the bulliest clothes! Oh, no! All gold and silver and di'monds," said Joe, with enthusiasm.

"Who?" said Huck.

"Why, the pirates."

Huck scanned his own clothing forlornly.

"I reckon I ain't dressed fitten for a pirate," said he, with a regretful pathos in his voice; "but I ain't got none but these."

But the other boys told him the fine clothes would come fast enough, after they should have begun their adventures. They made him understand that his poor rags would do to begin with, though it was customary for wealthy pirates to start with a proper wardrobe.

Gradually their talk died out and drowsiness began to steal upon the eyelids of the little waifs. The pipe dropped from the fingers of the Red-Handed, and he slept the sleep of the conscious-free and the weary. The Terror of the Seas and the Black Avenger of the Spanish Main had more difficulty in getting to sleep. They said their prayers inwardly, and lying down, since there was nobody there with authority to make them kneel and recite aloud; in truth, they had a mind not to say them at all, but they were afraid to proceed to such lengths as that, lest they might call down a sudden and special thunderbolt from heaven. Then at once they reached and hovered upon the imminent verge of sleep—but an intruder came, now, that would not "down." It was conscience. They began to feel a vague fear that they had been doing wrong to run away; and next they thought of the stolen meat, and then the real torture came. They tried to argue it away by reminding conscience that they had purloined sweetmeats and apples scores of times; but conscience was not to be appeased by such thin plausibilities; it seemed to them, in the end, that there was no getting around the stubborn fact that taking sweetmeats was only "hooking," while taking bacon and hams and such valuables was plain simple *stealing*—and there was a command against that in the Bible. So they inwardly resolved that so long as they remained in the business, their piracies should not again be sullied with the crime of stealing. Then conscience granted a truce, and these curiously inconsistent pirates fell peacefully to sleep.

A Sailor's Glossary

ABACK: When a sailing ship is suddenly taken with the wind filling her sails from forward, pressing them back against the masts and spars. A very dangerous predicament, liable to dismast her. Usually caused by careless handling or lack of seamanship and happening with devastating suddenness. Hence the expression, "taken aback" - "taken flat aback" indicating one's being perilously surprised.

ABAFT: Towards the sternmost part of the ship from amidships. It is also used to indicate the bearing of some object from the vessel. "Ship three points abaft the starboard beam" indicates that it bears approximately 124 degrees from right ahead.

AFORE or FOR'ARD OF: The opposite of ABAFT.

AMIDSHIPS: In the centre, or the middle of the vessel.

ATHWART: Lying across—for instance, a boat that has drifted against a ship's anchor-cables as it lies moored is said to be "athwart her hawse."

AVAST: The command to stop. "Avast hauling" indicates to stop pulling at a rope.

BACKSTAYS: Ropes running from a mast-head, lower, top, or topgallant mast in a fore-and-aft direction, secured to the ship's sides, designed to stay the spar against longitudinal stresses and strains (see *Shrouds*) from aft. FORESTAYS do the same for stresses from forward.

BARE POLES (under): Indicates a ship driving before a storm with no canvas set. Only the bare poles of her yards or gaffs are showing.

BARQUE: A three- or four-masted ship square-rigged on all the masts except the aftermost one, which carries only fore-and-aft sail (see *Full-rigged Ship*).

BARQUENTINE: Three- or four-masted, with square rig on only her foremast, all the rest being fore-and-aft rigged (see *Schooner*).

BATTENS: Thin strips of wood or metal engaging in cleats around the hatch-coamings to hold down the tarpaulin coverings. They are secured by hammered-in wedges. Hence the term indicating everything is secured: "battened-down."

BEAMS: The strong cross-members running from side to side in the hull which support her ribs, knees and outer hull, and also her decks. Thus when a ship is said to be "over on her beam-ends" she is lying on her broadside in a state of complete capsize. But "the beam" also means a direction, at right angles from her fore-and-aft line. Thus "on the lee-beam" means something at right angles from the ship on the side sheltered from the wind: on the windward side at right angles, it would be "on the weather-beam."

BEND: To make fast a line or rope.

BIGHT: The loop or the doubled part of a rope when held. It also means a bay or an inlet. The Bight of Benin is perhaps the largest of these, as usually they indicate a small inlet or bend in a coastline.

BINNACLE: The case containing the compass by which the ship is steered. Originally it was a square, rough box, but later became a helmet-shaped brass container, fitted with a permanent lamp.

BLOCK: A pulley. A piece of wood with one or more sheaves, or wheels in it, through which ropes run, or are rove, to ease the labour involved in lifting heavy objects, or those under severe strains. Usually blocks are made to take a specified size of rope but SNATCH BLOCK is specially adapted, with a lifting slide, to accommodate several thicknesses at will.

BOBSTAY: The line holding the bowsprit down to the stem, preventing it being lifted or destroyed by the upward tugging of the jibs or headsails.

BOLTS: Large nails or bars of metal used to unite various parts of the ship. Bolts made of wood, used in ancient times more than nowadays, were TREE-NAILS. It is also a measure of canvas.

BOLT-ROPE: The rope surrounding a sail to which the canvas is sewn.

BOOM: A soar, rigged fore and aft when stretching a sail set in that direction. Also used in olden days for studding-sails, spread from the end of the yardarms when the wind was fair. Booms were also used to hold boats when at anchor out from the ship's side. TO BOOM OFF means to thrust something away with the aid of a pole or boom. BOOMs were also used as floating obstructions in harbour defence.

BRACES: Ropes at the yardarms by which the yards where swung, or "braced" to bring them to the correct angle to set the sail to the wind.

BRAILS: The ropes by which the lower corners of fore-and-aft sails are hauled up and so shortened.

BRIG: A two-masted sailing-ship carrying square-rig on both.

BRIGANTINE: Two-masted ship square-rigged on the foremast only.

BULKHEAD: Temporary or permanent partitions dividing a ship into separated compartments. Some are "watertight" and meant to act as dams in case of flooding.

BULWARK: The wood or metal solid protection around the outer and upper edging of the upper deck.

BUNT: The middle section, or belly, of a sail.

BUNTLINES: The ropes for hauling up the bunt.

CABLE: Until the 1820's these were almost invariably of thick hemp rope. Now normally of chain cable, securing the ship to her anchor. The cable is also a unit of measurement, but one that varies greatly, ranging from 120 fathoms or 720 feet in American ships to 200 fathoms in the Royal Navy of Nelson's time.

CAT-HEAD: A large, usually squared baulk of timber projecting from the side of the forecastle, or the fore-part, to which the anchor was hoisted and secured (catted) by its ring, the flukes being led further aft.

CHAFING-GEAR: Old rope-yarns and other material wrapped around the rigging or the spars at friction-points to minimise chafing.

CLEAT: A piece of timber secured to the deck or the bulwarks, fashioned with projecting arms from the centre, around which ropes could be turned-up, or belayed, to secure them.

CLEW: The after lower corner of a fore-and-aft sail and the lower corners of square ones.

CLOSE HAULED: A ship with her sails trimmed to creep as close to the wind's flow as possible. She is trying to make headway against an unfavourable breeze without losing ground by being drifted down to leeward.

COIL: Rope stowed away in a ring. The act of stowing it in this fashion.

CRINGLE: The rope that runs around a sail but varying from a *Bolt-rope* (q.v.).

CROSS-TREES: Small projecting timbers supported by the "trestle-trees" and "cheeks." supporting-timbers, at the mast-head to hold the "tops" at the head of the lower-mast and also at the top-mast head to spread more widely the topgallant rigging.

DAVITS: Timbers or metal cranes, with sheaves at their ends outboard, meant to support and hoist the ship's boats so they project clear of her sides to enable them to be lowered in safety.

DEAD RECKONING: A calculation of the ship's various courses and speeds, taken at fixed and frequent intervals, if possible with due note of tides, currents and winds, which can give some indication of her position. The method is very prone to inaccuracy, but was essential in olden times, when it was impossible, or very difficult, to fix the longitude, either because of the lack of a chronometer or inability to "shoot" the stars, moon or the sun.

DOG WATCHES: Half-watches of two hours instead of the normal four. They came between 16.00 and 20.00 each day. Their purpose was to vary the actual hours so that the same watch was not on duty from midnight until 04.00 every day of the voyage. The watches changed at each four-hour period after midnight, when eight bells were struck. Thereafter each half-hour added a stroke to the bell, thus at 15.00 six bells were struck; at 15.30 seven. The custom arose in the days when times at sea were measured in thirty-minute sand-glasses, the quartermaster striking a bell for the number of the glass just emptying itself; eight of the sand glasses were kept in the rack before him and reversed as needed. The term "dog watch" has the same connotation as the "dog" in "dog roses." "dog violet." etc., i.e. pseudo. Thus four bells were struck at 18.00, but only one at 18.30. But instead of four following the three at 19.30 the full eight were sounded at 20.00 to mark the ending of a watch. At midnight on December 31st/January 1st sixteen bells were struck — eight for the Old and eight for the New Year.

DOWN-HAUL: A rope to haul down jibs, staysails and other canvas such as studding-sails.

DROGUE: A canvas sleeve, or drag, towed astern to slow a ship. This was also often used by privateers or men-of-war under sail when they wanted to lure an enemy to destruction.

EARRING: The rope attached to the CRINGLE (q.v.) of a sail by which it is bent or netted. (A network of small lines by which sails and hammocks are lashed and stowed away).

EYE-BOLT: An iron bar with a loop or an eye at one end driven through the side or deck of a ship with the eye projecting to allow a hook to be affixed. If there is a ring through this eye it is called a RINGBOLT.

EYE-SPLICE: A rope with a permanent loop formed at one end by tucking individual strands in succession into the lay of the rope. A SHORT SPLICE is used to join two ends of a rope by interweaving the opposing strands. A LONG SPLICE is the same, but, by a system of halving the strands, the joined rope is no thicker than the original, so allowing it to be rove through a similar sheaved block. A BACK SPLICE is formed by tucking the strands back into the lay to prevent the end of the line being frayed by remaining loose.

FID: A wooden pin of various sizes employed to lift the lay of ropes while a strand is being tucked through to form one part of a splice. Also a fid can be a block of metal, usually of iron, or wood, which was thrust through the heel of a mast to support it. The metal counterpart of the fid used in splicing is a marline-spike.

FISH: To repair or strengthen a damaged spar or yard by passing cordage arund it. TO FISH AN ANCHOR entails raising its flukes upon the gunwale or bulwarks, the flukes being the point at each end of the bill, which is at the end of the upright shank, which is surmounted at right angles by the stock.

FOOT-ROPE: Formerly called the "horse." It is the looped rope slung beneath a yard on which the seamen stand while reefing, furling or doing any other work upon the sail.

FORECASTLE: The part of the deck, usually raised in sailing-ships, right in the bows forward of the foremast. It is the name used, as a rule, to designate the accommodation for the seamen, which was in this part of the vessel.

FOUNDERING: The act of sinking when a ship fills with water.

FURL: The rolling up of a sail and securing it.

GAFF: The spar to which the head of a fore-and-aft sail is bent. BOOM is the name for the lower spar.

GASKETS: The ropes securing a sail to a spar or a yard when it has been furled.

GRAPNEL: Small anchor with several flukes, or claws, usually found in boats and very small craft. Used for grappling.

GRATING: A wooden lattice-work used for covering open hatches in fine weather. In old men-of-war, the place where flogging was carried out.

GUNWALE: The uppermost part of the side of a boat or small ship.

GUY: A rope used for steadying a spar or mast, or to swing a derrick or spar either way when hoisting something from its upper end.

HALYARDS: Ropes and tackles employed in hoisting and lowering yards, sails and gaffs. Also thinner ones for hoisting flags, known as the SIGNAL HALYARDS.

HATCH OR HATCHWAY: Opening in the decks to allow passage to spaces beneath. The coverings of the holds are also called HATCHES.

HAWSE PIPE or HOLE: The holes in the bows through which the anchor-cables run.

HAWSER: A larger and much stronger rope used for towing, warping and other heavy 'duties where more slender ones would not suffice.

HAZE: Bullying a man.

HEAD SAILS: Used for all canvas setting forward of the fore-mast.

HEEL: The part of the keel nearest the rudder-post. TO HEEL means to list, or to lean over.

HELM: The complete mechanism by which a ship is steered.

HITCH: To secure; or a particular form of knots used for a special purpose.

HOLD: The interior, open part of a ship, where, for instance, her cargo or stores are stowed.

HOLY-STONE: A block of sandstone used for scrubbing and whitening wooden decks by abrasion. There were names for their various shapes and sizes, e.g. "Boston Bible." "Bristol Prayer-book." the ecclesiastical implication being appropriate because holystoning was a chore often performed kneeling on the deck.

IRONS: A ship was "in irons" when, after messing up an attempt to tack and come around on the opposite course, she failed to swing through the wind's eye and hung there unable to help herself and usually "caught flat a-back." a position of considerable danger in a strong breeze. TO PUT A MAN IN IRONS was to fetter him.

JACKSTAYS: Ropes stretched tautly along a yard, or elsewhere, to bend sails or other ropes on to.

JIB: A triangular head-sail set fore and aft. Set on a stay forward of the foremast.

JIB-BOOM: The spar or boom rigged out beyond the bowsprit to which the tack of the jib is lashed.

JOLLYBOAT: One of the smallest boats carried, usually lashed across the stern in merchantmen.

JURY RIG: Temporary repairs to masts and sails and spars executed at sea. Jury masts and other replacements were erected to replace those damaged, but vitally needed.

KEDGE: A small anchor with an iron stock used for warping a vessel out of a narrow channel or to gain an offing when required.

KEEL and KEELSON: The keel is the spine of a ship, the lowermost of her timbers, running her entire length, the backbone on which she rests. The keelson is a timber sheath over the keel.

KNEES: The crooked timbers, or ribs, of a ship used to connect the beams to the rest of her framework.

KNOT: The nautical unit of speed which means the time needed to cover one nautical mile in terms of the number made good in one hour. Its name comes from the knots formed at certain intervals in the log-line which was streamed astern to find the speed. By measuring the time taken, using a sand-glass, for a certain number of these knots to run out from the reel, the hourly speed at that moment could be calculated. It is as wrong to speak of distances as being so many knots as it is to say a ship travels at so many knots *an hour*. The knot is a combined time-distance unit of measurement.

LANYARDS: Ropes rove through the DEAD EYES to set up the rigging and hold it taut. DEAD EYES are round pieces of timber, usually pierced with three holes and used in pairs. By tautening the lanyard between the upper and lower lanyard, the proper tension needed to keep the SHROUDS (q.v.) can be maintained. In vessels with hemp rigging the shrouds and stays would be stretched while to windward and require tightening after the ship came on to the other tack.

LARBOARD: The old name for port, or the left side of a ship when one looks forward from aft.

LAUNCH: A large boat. Often the LONG-BOAT.

LAY: To come or go. To LAY-TO is to heave-to, bring the ship up to ride to wind and sea, seeking safety untill a storm abates.

LEAD: The hand-lead is a small version used for soundings in not more than 20 fathoms. It has a hollow at its lower end meant to be charged with a piece of tallow to recover a specimen of the sea-floor. The DEEP-SEA LEAD was much larger and could sound depths up to 100 fathoms. The LEAD-LINE attached to it was marked at intervals to indicate the depths attained.

LEE: The side opposite to the one from which the wind is blowing. That would be the WEATHER SIDE. LEEWAY is the distance lost by a ship's drift to leeward. In a small craft it may easily be calculated by the angle between the wake and the fore-and-aft line of the vessel. This shows how far she is being set down from the course she appears to be lying and can be corrected with ease, once known.

LIFE LINES: Ropes carried along yard, or decks, to help men to their footings.

LOG: The log-book is the official diary and record of all that happens aboard a ship. In merchantmen it is usually kept by the Second Officer nowadays, though in earlier times it was the Mate's sole responsibility. The LOG, however, is a piece of timber, thrown overboard and secured by a rope, by means of which the speed is calculated in knots (q.v.)

LUFF: To alter the helm so as to bring the ship's head closer to the direction of the wind. "To bring her up."

MARTINGALE: A short, perpendicular spar set under the end of the bowsprit and used for a guy for the head-sails to prevent the bowsprit and jib-boom from being sprung upwards by their pull.

MESS: Any number of men who eat together.

MIZEN or MIZZEN MAST: the aftermost of the three masts of a three-master. In ships with four, the after one is usually called the JIGGER, though there are variations. In a BRIG (q.v.) the after of the two masts is the MAINMAST and there is no mizzen.

PAINTER: The rope from the bow of a boat for the purpose of attaching her to a wharf, to a stake, or to her parent-ship.

QUARTER-DECK: That part of the upper deck abaft the mainmast, the second mast. The name stems from the sixteenth century, when ships had half- and quarter-decks as well as a poop. The HALF-DECK is now the name given to quarters of the apprentices or cadets.

RATLINES: The rope lying across the shrouds (q.v.), like the rungs of a ladder, used to help men get aloft.

ROYALS: Light sails for fine weather set above the top gallant sails.

SCHOONER: Fore-and-aft rigged ship without tops, but with two or more masts. There were variants, such as the TOPSAIL SCHOONER, which carried a pair of topsails on her foremast. One that was two-masted and had a pair of topsails on each of her masts was an HERMAPHRODITEBRIG.

SCUPPERS: Holes cut in the waterways to enable the decks to clear themselves.

SHEET: The rope used to set a sail by keeping the CLEW (q.v.) down to its place.

SHEET ANCHOR: The ship's largest anchor.

SHROUDS: The ropes from the mastheads of lower, top and topgallant masts secured to the ship's sides and intended to sustain all lateral strains and stresses, as opposed to STAYS, which take those longitudinally applied.

SKY-SAIL: A light sail setting above the royals.

SLOOP: A small, one-masted fore-and-aft rigged vessel. A KETCH had a tall foremast and a short mizzen, its difference from a YAWL being that the ketch's steering gear was placed forward of the mizzen-mast, while a yawl had hers abaft it. A CUTTER was also one-masted, but differed in several particulars from a SLOOP.

SPANKER: The aftermost sail, fore and aft, of any ship of size. It set with BOOM and GAFF.

STANCHIONS: Upright posts meant to support the BEAMS, or the bulwarks.

STANDING RIGGING: The parts of a ship's rigging intended to remain fast and immovable, as opposed to the RUNNING RIGGING used to manoeuvre her.

STAYSAIL: A triangular, fore-and-aft sail which sets upon a STAY (q.v.).

STEERAGE: The parts below decks just forward of the after cabin.

STEM: The cutwater; a piece of staunch timber from the forward end of the keel up to the bowsprit heel.

STERN POST: The aftermost timber of a ship or the after-end of the vessel.

STRAND: A number of yarns twisted together to form part of a rope.

STRIKE: To lower sails or colours.

STUDDING-SALES (often written STUNSAILS): Light sails set outside the ordinary sails on the yards, set from booms sliding along the yard themselves and used only in fair weather. Nelson carried his fleet into action at Trafalgar under studding-sails because of the light favourable S.W. wind.

TACK: To put the ship about by turning head to wind and so bringing it on to the other side. By turning stern to wind, one WEARED or WORE ship. The TACK is also one of the ropes used to control fore-and-aft sails.

TAFFRAIL: The rail running around a ship's rails astern.

TAUNT or ATAUNTO: Meaning high or tall, and usually applied to a ship's masts.

TAUT: Tight.

TILLER: The bar of wood or metal which moves the rudder by means of the TILLER ROPES, which lead from the tiller-head to the barrel of the steering wheel, from whence she is controlled by the helmsmen.

TOPMAST: The second mast above the deck, above the lower mast. Above is sometimes stepped the third or TOPGALLANT MAST.

TOPSAILS (lower and upper): Usually the second and third sails above the deck. Over them went the upper and lower topgallants in ships rigged after 1885. Above them again were some variants, such as royals and skysails. All were square sails.

TRANSOMS: The timbers crossing the stern-post to strengthen the hull.

TRAVELLER: An iron ring fitted to slide up and down a rope or along a bar.

TRESTLE TREES: Two strong pieces of timber placed horizontally and fore-and-aft on opposite sides of the lower masthead to support the cross-trees (q.v.) and tops. In ancient times seamen stricken with mortal injuries and dying on deck without a confessor or chaplain believed they could win remission of all the punishment due to sin and complete absolution by turning their eyes to the cross-trees and expressing their contrition.

TRYSAIL: Fore-and-aft sail, setting with boom and gaff.

UNBEND: To cast-off or untie a line.

WAIST: The part of the upper-deck between the quarter-deck and the forecastle.

WARE or WEAR: See TACK.

WEATHER GAUGE; TO WEATHER: A vessel which is to windward of another holds the weather gauge of her. To weather a cape or an obstruction means a ship can claw far enough up into the wind not to be driven on to the rocks. WEATHER HELM signified that an individual ship had a tendency to bring her head up into the wind and needed constant correction of the helm and much vigilance if she was not to be caught aback.

WEIGH: To raise anchor or to lift a mast or spar.

WINDLASS: The machine used, like capstan, to weigh the anchor.

WRING BOLTS: Bolts securing the planks to the timbers.

YAWING: The motion of a ship lurching off her course.

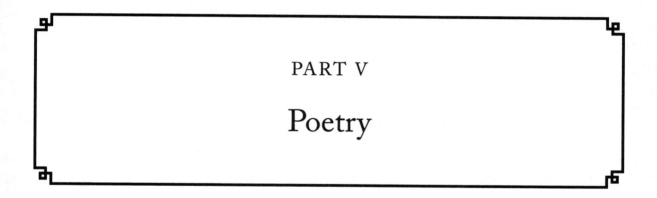

PART V

Poetry

The Demon-Ship

THOMAS HOOD

'Twas off the Wash—the sun went down—the sea look'd black and grim,
For stormy clouds, with murky fleece, were mustering at the brim:
Titanic shades! enormous gloom!—as if the solid night
Of Erebus rose suddenly to seize upon the light!
It was a time for mariners to bear a wary eye,
With such a dark conspiracy between the sea and sky!
Down went my helm—close reef'd—the tack held freely in my hand—
With ballast snug—I put about, and scudded for the land.
Loud hiss'd the sea beneath her lee—my little boat flew fast,
But faster still the rushing storm came borne upon the blast.
Lord! what a roaring hurricane beset the straining sail!
What furious sleet, with level drift, and fierce assaults of hail!
What darksome caverns yawn'd before! what jagged steeps behind!
Like battle-steeds, with foamy manes, wild tossing in the wind.
Each after each sank down astern, exhausted in the chase,
And where it sank another rose and gallop'd in its place;
As black as night—they turned to white, and cast against the cloud
A snowy sheet, as if each surge upturn'd a sailor's shroud:—
Still flew my boat; alas! alas! her course was nearly run!
Behold yon fatal billow rise—ten billows heap'd in one!

With fearful speed the dreary mass came rolling, rolling fast,
As if the scooping sea contain'd one only wave at last!
Still on it came, with horrid roar, a swift pursuing grave;
It seem'd as though some cloud had turned its hugeness to a wave!
Its briny sleet began to beat beforehand in my face—
I felt the rearward keel begin to climb its swelling base!
I saw its alpine hoary head impending over mine!
Another pulse—and down it rush'd—an avalanche of brine!
Brief pause had I, on God to cry, or think of wife and home;
The waters clos'd—and when I shriek'd, I shriek'd below the foam!
Beyond that rush I have no hint of any after deed—
For I was tossing on the waste, as senseless as a weed.

"Where am I?—in the breathing world or in the world of death?"
With sharp and sudden pang I drew another birth of breath;
My eyes drank in a doubtful light, my ears a doubtful sound—
And was that ship a *real* ship whose tackle seemed around?
A moon, as if the earthly moon, was shining up aloft;
But were those beams the very beams that I had seen so oft?
A face, that mock'd the human face, before me watched alone;
But were those eyes the eyes of man that looked against my own?

Oh, never may the moon again disclose me such a sight
As met my gaze, when first I look'd, on that accursèd night!
I've seen a thousand horrid shapes begot of fierce extremes
Of fever; and most frightful things have haunted in my dreams—
Hyenas—cats—blood-loving bats—and apes with hateful stare—
Pernicious snakes, and shaggy bulls—the lion, and she-bear—
Strong enemies with Judas looks, of treachery and spite—
Detested features, hardly dimm'd and banished by the light!

Pale-sheeted ghosts, with gory locks, upstarting from their tombs—
All phantasies and images that flit in midnight glooms—
Hags, goblins, demons, lemures, have made me all aghast,—
But nothing like that GRIMLY ONE who stood beside the mast!
His cheek was black—his brow was black—his eyes and hair as dark:

His hand was black, and where it touch'd, it left a sable mark;
His throat was black, his vest the same, and when I looked beneath,
His breast was black—all, all was black, except his grinning teeth.
His sooty crew were like in hue, as black as Afric slaves!
Oh, horror! e'en the ship was black that plough'd the inky waves!

"Alas!" I cried, "for love of truth and blessed mercy's sake!
Where am I? in what dreadful ship? upon what dreadful lake?
What shape is that, so very grim, and black as any coal?
It is Mahound, the Evil One, and he has gained my soul!
Oh, mother dear! my tender nurse! dear meadows that beguil'd
My happy days, when I was yet a little sinless child,
My mother dear—my native fields, I never more shall see:
I'm sailing in the Devil's Ship, upon the Devil's Sea!"
Loud laugh'd that SABLE MARINER, and loudly in return
His sooty crew sent forth a laugh that rang from stem to stern—
A dozen pair of grimly cheeks were crumpled on the nonce—
As many sets of grinning teeth came shining out at once:
A dozen gloomy shapes at once enjoy'd the merry fit,
With shriek and yell, and oaths as well, like Demons of the Pit.
They crow'd their fill, and then the Chief made answer for the whole:—
"Our skins," said he, "are black, ye see, because we carry coal;
You'll find your mother sure enough, and see your native fields—
For this here ship has pick'd you up—the *Mary Ann* of Shields!"

The Voyage

ALFRED TENNYSON

We left behind the painted buoy
    That tosses at the harbour-mouth;
And madly danced our hearts with joy,
    As fast we fleeted to the South:
How fresh was every sight and sound
    On open main or winding shore!
We knew the merry world was round,
    And we might sail for evermore.

O hundred shores of happy climes,
    How swiftly stream'd ye by the bark!
At times the whole sea burn'd, at times
    With wakes of fire we tore the dark;

At times a carven craft would shoot
From havens hid in fairy bowers,
With naked limbs and flowers and fruit,
But we nor paused for fruit nor flowers.

For one fair Vision ever fled
Down the waste waters day and night,
And still we follow'd where she led,
In hope to gain upon her flight.
Her face was evermore unseen,
And fixt upon the far sea-line;
But each man murmur'd, "O my Queen,
I follow till I make thee mine."

And now we lost her, now she gleam'd
Like Fancy made of golden air,
Now nearer to the prow she seem'd
Like Virtue firm, like Knowledge fair,
Now high on waves that idly burst
Like Heavenly Hope she crown'd the sea,
And now, the bloodless point reversed,
She bore the blade of Liberty.

And only one among us—him
We pleased not—he was seldom pleased;
He saw not far: his eyes were dim:
But ours he swore were all diseased.
"A ship of fools," he shriek'd in spite,
"A ship of fools," he sneer'd and wept.
And overboard one stormy night
He cast his body, and on we swept.

And never sail of ours was furl'd,
Nor anchor dropt at eve or morn;
We loved the glories of the world,
But laws of nature were our scorn.

For blasts would rise and rave and cease,
    But whence were those that drove the sail
Across the whirlwind's heart of peace,
    And to and thro' the counter-gale?

Again to colder climes we came,
    For still we follow'd where she led:
Now mate is blind and captain lame,
    And half the crew are sick or dead.
But, blind or lame or sick or sound,
    We follow that which flies before:
We know the merry world is round,
    And we may sail for evermore.

The Ship of Fools

ST. JOHN LUCAS

We are those fools who could not rest
In the dull earth we left behind,
But burned with passion for the West
And drank a frenzy from its wind;
The world where small men live at ease
Fades from our unregretful eyes,
And blind across uncharted seas
We stagger on our enterprise.

Starboard and port, the lean waves leap
Like white-fanged wolves about our prow,
Where Mary with her Christ asleep
Is carved to hear the wanderer's vow.
The thirsty decks have drunk our blood,
Our hands are tettered from the oar;
Wan ghosts upon a spectral flood
We drive towards a phantom shore.

And we have sailed in haunted seas
Dreadful with voices, where the mast
Gleamed blue with deathlights, and the breeze

Bore madness, and have gazed aghast
To see beyond our splintered spars,
That rattled in the shrill typhoon,
A heaven all strange with tawny stars
And monstrous with an alien moon.

Lean, naked, bruised, like famished slaves,
We shiver at the sweeps; each one
A jest for all the scornful waves,
And food for laughter to the sun.
But never voice, nor deathlight flare,
Nor moon shall stay us with their spell,
Whose eyes are calm as God, and stare
Confusion in the face of Hell.

The worn ship reels, but still unfurled
Our tattered ensign flouts the skies;
And doomed to watch a prudent world
Of little men grown mean and wise,
The old sea laughs for joy to find
One purple folly left to her,
When glimmers down the riotous wind
The flag of the adventurer!

O watchman leaning from the mast,
What of the night? The shadows flee;
The stars grow pale, the storm is past;
The blood-red sunrise stains the sea.
At length, at length, O steadfast wills,
Luck takes the tiller and foul tides turn;
Superb amid majestic hills
The domes of Eldorado burn.

Sailor's Consolation

CHARLES DIBDIN

Charles Dibdin, British musician, dramatist, novelist, actor and song writer, was born at Southampton, March 4, 1745. He turned early to music and established his reputation by the music to the play, "The Padlock." In addition to composing over fourteen hundred songs, he is the author of many poems that won for him the characterization of the "king of sea poets." He died in London on July 25, 1814, from paralysis.

One night came on a hurricane,
  The sea was mountains rolling,
When Barney Buntline turned his quid,
  And said to Billy Bowling:
"A strong nor-wester's blowing, Bill:
  Hark! Don't ye hear it roar now?
Lord help 'em! How I pities all
  Unhappy folks on shore now!

"Fool-hardy, chaps who live in towns,
  What danger they are all in,
And now lie quaking in their beds,
  For fear the roof should fall in;
Poor creatures! How they envies us,
  And wishes, I've a notion,
For our good luck, in such a storm
  To be upon the ocean!

"And as for them who're out all day
 On business from their houses,
And late at night are coming home,
 To cheer their babes and spouses;
While you and I, Bill, on the deck
 Are comfortably lying,
My eyes! What tiles and chimney-pots
 About their heads are flying!

"And very often have we heard
 How men are kill'd and undone,
By overturns of carriages,
 By thieves, and fires in London.
We know what risks all landsmen run,
 From noblemen to tailors;
Then, Bill, let us thank Providence
 That you and I are sailors!"

Excerpt from "The Rime of the Ancient Mariner"

SAMUEL TAYLOR COLERIDGE

Samuel Taylor Coleridge was born in Devonshire, England, October 21, 1772. In 1791 he was entered at Jesus College, Cambridge, but soon grew discontented with its limitations and went to London, where he sold his first poem for a guinea. He tried the army and the ministry, but liked neither. Of his finished poems two of his most famous are "The Ancient Mariner" and "Kubla Khan." He died in 1834.

And now the Storm-blast came, and he
Was tryannous and strong:
He struck with his o'ertaking wings,
And chased us south along.

With sloping masts and dipping prow,
As who pursued with yell and blow
Still treads the shadow of his foe,
And forward bends his head,
The ship drove fast, loud roared the blast.
And southward aye we fled.

And now there came both mist and snow,
And it grew wondrous cold:
And ice, mast-high, came floating by,
As green as emerald.

And through the drifts the snowy clifts
Did send a dismal sheen:
Nor shapes of men nor beasts we ken—
The ice was all between.

The ice was here, the ice was there,
The ice was all around:
It cracked and growled, and roared and howled,
Like noises in a swound!

The fair breeze blew, the white foam flew,
The furrow followed free;
We were the first that ever burst
Into that silent sea.

Down dropt the breeze, the sails dropt down,
'Twas sad as sad could be;
And we did speak only to break
The silence of the sea!

All in a hot and copper sky,
The bloody Sun, at noon,
Right up above the mast did stand,
No bigger than the Moon.

Day after day, day after day,
We stuck, nor breath nor motion;
As idle as a painted ship
Upon a painted ocean.

Water, water, everywhere,
And all the boards did shrink;

Water, water, everywhere,
Nor any drop to drink.

The very deep did rot: O Christ!
That ever this should be!
Yea, slimy things did crawl with legs
Upon the slimy sea.

About, about, in reel and rout
The death-fires danced at night;
The water, like a witch's oils,
Burnt green, and blue, and white.

And some in dreams assured were
Of the Spirit that plagued us so,
Nine fathom deep he had followed us
From the land of mist and snow.

And every tongue, through utter drought,
Was withered at the root;
We could not speak, no more than if
We had been choked with soot.

Psalm CVII, 23–30

They that go down to the sea in ships, that do business in great waters;

These see the works of the LORD, and his wonders in the deep.

For he commandeth, and raiseth the stormy wind, which lifteth up the waves thereof.

They mount up to the heaven, they go down again to the depths: their soul is melted because
    of trouble.

They reel to and fro, and stagger like a drunken man, and are at their wit's end.

Then they cry unto the LORD in their trouble, and he bringeth them out of their distresses.

He maketh the storm a calm, so that the waves thereof are still.

Then are they glad because they be quiet; so he bringeth them unto their desired haven.

A Passer-By

ROBERT BRIDGES

Whither, O splendid ship, thy white sails crowding,
　　Leaning across the bosom of the urgent West,
That fearest nor sea rising, nor sky clouding,
　　Whither away, fair rover, and what thy quest?
　　Ah! soon, when Winter has all our vales opprest,
When skies are cold and misty, and hail is hurling,
　　Wilt thou glide on the blue Pacific, or rest
In a summer haven asleep, thy white sails furling.

I there before thee, in the country that well thou knowest,
    Already arrived, am inhaling the odorous air:
I watch thee enter unerringly where thou goest,
    And anchor queen of the strange shipping there,
    Thy sails for awnings spread, thy masts bare:
Nor is augnt, from the foaming reef to the snow-capped grandest
    Peak that is over the feathery palms, more fair
Than thou, so upright, so stately and still thou standest.

And yet, O splendid ship, unhailed and nameless,
    I know not if, aiming a fancy, I rightly divine
That thou hast a purpose joyful, a courage blameless,
    Thy port assured in a happier land than mine.
    But for all I have given thee, beauty enough is thine,
As thou, aslant with trim tackle and shrouding,
    From the proud nostril curve of a prow's line
In the offing scatterest foam, thy, white sails crowding.

Where Lies the Land?

A. H. CLOUGH

Where lies the land to which the ship would go?
Far, far ahead, is all her seamen know.
And where the land she travels from? Away,
Far, far behind, is all that they can say.

On sunny noons upon the deck's smooth face,
Linked arm in arm, how pleasant here to pace;
Or, o'er the stern reclining, watch below
The foaming wake far widening as we go.

On stormy nights when wild north-westers rave,
How proud a thing to fight with wind and wave!
The dripping sailor on the reeling mast
Exults to bear, and scorns to wish it past.

Where lies the land to which the ship would go?
Far, far ahead, is all her seamen know.
And where the land she travels from? Away,
Far, far behind, is all that they can say.

Sea Fever

JOHN MASEFIELD

I must go down to the seas again, to the lonely sea and the sky,
And all I ask is a tall ship and a star to steer her by;
And the wheel's kick and the wind's song and the white sail's shaking,
And a grey mist on the sea's face and a grey dawn breaking.

I must go down to the seas again, for the call of the running tide
Is a wild call and a clear call that may not be denied;
And all I ask is a windy day with the white clouds flying,
And the flung spray and the blown spume, and the seagulls crying.

I must go down to the seas again, to the vagrant gipsy life,
To the gull's way and the whale's way where the wind's like a whetted knife;
And all I ask is a merry yarn from a laughing fellow-rover,
And quiet sleep and a sweet dream when the long trick's over.